A Handbook on
Historic Preservation Law

The Conservation Foundation
Board of Trustees

Ernest Brooks, Jr.
Chairman
William H. Whyte
Vice Chariman
T.F. Bradshaw
John A. Bross
Louise B. Cullman
Gaylord Donnelley
Maitland A. Edey
David M. Gates
Philip G. Hammer
Walter E. Hoadley
William F. Kieschnick
William T. Lake
Richard D. Lamm

Melvin B. Lane
David Hunter McAlpin
Ruth H. Neff
Eugene P. Odum
Richard B. Ogilvie
Walter Orr Roberts
James W. Rouse
Anne P. Sidamon-Eristoff
George H. Taber
Henry W. Taft
Pete Wilson
Rosemary M. Young

William K. Reilly
President

The National Center for Preservation Law
Board of Directors

Paul S. Byard, Esq.
Chairman
Tersh Boasberg, Esq.
President
Leopold Adler, II
David Bonderman, Esq.
Donald D. Etter, Esq.
Henry R. Lord, Esq.
Ralph C. Menapace, Esq.
Howard Moskof, Esq.

Whitney North Seymour, Esq.
David Sive, Esq.
Barbara Timken
Carl Westmorland
Frederick C. Williamson
Arthur T. Ziegler, Jr.

New York Project
Stephen L. Kass, Esq.

A Handbook on Historic Preservation Law

edited by
CHRISTOPHER J. DUERKSEN

with contributions from
DAVID BONDERMAN
CHRISTOPHER J. DUERKSEN
DONALD DWORSKY
MICHAEL MANTELL
VIRGINIA MCVARISH
KATE M. PERRY
SUSAN MEAD ROBINSON
RICHARD J. RODDEWIG
ANTONIO ROSSMANN

and
RECOMMENDED MODEL PROVISIONS FOR A PRESERVATION ORDINANCE, WITH ANNOTATIONS
prepared by
STEPHEN N. DENNIS
for
THE NATIONAL TRUST FOR HISTORIC PRESERVATION

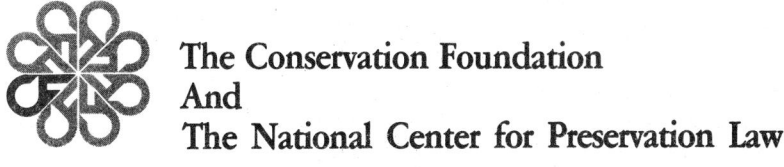

The Conservation Foundation
And
The National Center for Preservation Law

To Barbara Hoffstot and others like her for caring so deeply about what happens to our cities and towns, buildings, and landscapes, and even more for going out and doing something about it. Coming generations will revel in their handiwork.

A Handbook on Historic Preservation Law
©1983 by The Conservation Foundation and
The National Center for Preservation Law

All rights reserved. No part of this book may be reproduced in any form without permission of The Conservation Foundation and The National Center for Preservation Law.

Cover design by Sally A. Janin
Typography by Rings-Leighton, Ltd., Washington, D.C.
Printed by Urban Litho, Inc., Baltimore, Maryland

The preparation of this handbook has been financed in part with federal funds from the National Park Service, U.S. Department of the Interior, administered through the Bureau for Historic Preservation, Pennsylvania Historical and Museum Commission.

The Conservation Foundation
1717 Massachusetts Avenue, N.W.
Washington, D.C. 20036

Library of Congress Cataloging in Publication Data
Main entry under title:

A Handbook on historic preservation law.

   Bibliography: p.
   Includes index.
   1. Historic sites—Law and legislation—United States. 2. Historic buildings—Law and legislation—United States. I. Duerksen, Christopher J., 1948-   . II. Bonderman, David. III. Dennis, Stephen N. IV. National Trust for Historic Preservation in the United States.
KF4310.H36 1983   344.73'094   83-7699
ISBN 0-89164-074-6   347.30494
ISBN 0-89164-079-7 (pbk.)

Contents

Foreword by William K. Reilly and Tersh Boasberg   xvii

Preface by Christopher J. Duerksen   xxi

Chapter 1
Preservation Law:
Where It's Been, Where It's Going
by Christopher J. Duerksen and David Bonderman   1

PRESERVATION LAW, LOOKING BACK	1
The Early Days of Preservation	1
The Expansion of Regulatory Powers	3
The Infancy of Preservation Law: 1930-1955	5
Preservation Grows Up: 1956-1970	8
Preservation Law in The Environmental Decade: 1970-1980	11
The New York City Landmarks Law	13
Grand Central Terminal as a Landmark	14
The Penn Central Litigation in the Lower Courts	15
The Supreme Court Decision in Penn Central	16
Tax Incentives	18
PRESERVATION LAW: THE 1980s	20
The Defederalization of Preservation	20
Preservation Law: What Lies Ahead?	22
Preservation Law at the National Level	23
Preservation Law at the Local and State Levels	25

Chapter 2
Local Preservation Law
by Christopher J. Duerksen   29

PART 1: THE "COMPLEAT" PRESERVATION PROGRAM   32
WHY SHOULD A LOCAL GOVERNMENT HAVE A
  PRESERVATION PROGRAM?   32
WHAT MAKES A PRESERVATION PROGRAM
  "COMPREHENSIVE"?   37
The Survey and Study Element   38
Economic and Technical Assistance   41
The Coordination Element   43
  Why Coordinate?   43
  How to Coordinate   46
    Zoning   47
    Building Codes   53
    Subdivision Regulations   56
    Coordination with Other Laws and Ordinances 57

PART 2: DRAFTING AND ADMINISTERING THE
  ORDINANCE   58
THE FIRST STEPS IN DRAFTING   60
Recognition of Enabling Authority   60
Defining Local Goals and Capabilities   61
  Defining a Purpose   61
  Deciding What to Protect   61
  Deciding How to Protect What the Community Values 62
  Administering and Enforcing the Ordinance   62
DRAFTING THE KEY PROVISIONS OF A
  PRESERVATION ORDINANCE   63
The Purpose Clause   63
Creating a Review Body: Composition and Grant of Powers   67
  Composition   67
  Scope of Powers   70
  Final Review Authority   73
Owner Consent: The Property Owner's Role in Designation
  and Permit Reviews   75

Defining Key Terms	76
Standards, Procedures, Hearings	78
Standards for Designating Landmarks and Districts	80
Following Sound Survey Techniques	81
Drafting Acceptable Designation Standards	82
Deciding What to Designate	85
The Role of Economics	87
Procedures for Designating Landmarks and Districts	88
Reviewing Applications for Demolition, Alteration, or New Construction	90
Setting Review Standards	90
Narrowing Broad Review Standards	93
Standards Found in Background Documents	94
Procedural Safeguards	96
Applying Review Standards: The Role of Economics	98
Owner's Knowledge of Landmark Restriction	99
Current Economic Return	99
Owner's Bona Fide Attempt to Rent or Sell Property	100
Feasibility of Profitable Alternative Uses	100
Procedure for Reviewing Certificates of Appropriateness	101
Disclosure of Pecuniary and Personal Interests	103
Personal Knowledge as the Basis for a Decision	104
Economic Hardship and Safety Valve Provisions	104
Maintenance and Upkeep of Landmarks	107
Publicly Owned Property	113
Coordination with Other Municipal Laws and Actions	117
Emergency Demolition Bans and Development Moratoriums	117
Enforcement	120
Remedies to Ensure Compliance	121
Injunctive Relief and Compliance Orders	121
Receiverships/Entry onto Land to Correct Violation	122
Forcing Reconstruction	123
Fixing Responsibility: Against Whom and by Whom?	124
Administration	124
FURTHER READINGS	126

Chapter 3
State Preservation Law
by Michael Mantell   **129**

STATE ENABLING AUTHORITY FOR LOCAL
   GOVERNMENT PRESERVATION PROGRAMS   **131**
The Authority to Regulate   133
   Historic District and Landmark Preservation Enabling Acts   134
      Objectives   135
      Process for Designating and Administering Districts   135
      Grants of Power   138
      Improving Regulatory Enabling Laws   141
The Authority to Acquire   143
The Authority to Tax   145
STATE PRESERVATION RESPONSIBILITIES UNDER
   FEDERAL PROGRAMS   **147**
States and the NHPA   147
   Evolving State Responsibilities   148
   SHPO Duties   148
      Certification   149
      Section 106 Review   150
      Preservation Planning   151
      Working with Other Agencies and Individuals   151
      Grants and Preservation Funding   152
      Prospects   153
Federal Preservation Tax Benefits and the States   153
   National Register Properties   154
   Registered Historic District Properties   155
      Certifying Historic Districts   155
      Certifying Properties within Registered Districts   155
   Certifying the Rehabilitation   156
STATE PRESERVATION PROGRAMS   **157**
State Registers of Historic Places   159
   Improving State Registers   162
Making Preservation a Responsibility of All State Agencies   164
   Creating Comprehensive State Laws   167
State Tax Laws and Preservation   167

STATES AND ENVIRONMENTAL POLICY	168
State Environmental Policy Acts (SEPAs)	169
SEPA Policy	171
SEPA Process	172
Initial Determination	172
Draft EIS	174
Final EIS and the Agency's Decision	177
Courts and SEPAs	178
Coordinating SEPA with Other Preservation Regulatory Programs	180
Resolving Intergovernmental Disputes	181
State Constitutions and Environmental Policy	182
CONCLUSION	185
FURTHER READINGS	187

Chapter 4
Federal Law
by Donald Dworsky, Virginia McVarish, Kate M. Perry, and Susan Mead Robinson   191

AN OVERVIEW OF FEDERAL PRESERVATION LAW	193
THE DEVELOPMENT OF FEDERAL LAW	193
THE NATIONAL HISTORIC PRESERVATION ACT, AS AMENDED	195
Identification and Listing of Resources	197
Qualifications for Listing in the National Register	199
Nomination Procedures	200
Nomination by the SHPO	200
Nomination by Certified Local Governments	203
Nomination by Federal Agency	204
Owner Objection or Consent	205
Effects of Listing	207
Determination of Eligibility and Its Effect	209
The Advisory Council on Historic Preservation	210
Other Provisions of NHPA	212
Summary	214

THE NATIONAL ENVIRONMENTAL POLICY ACT	215
A NEPA Overview	216
OTHER IMPORTANT FEDERAL PRESERVATION AGENCIES, LAWS, AND PROGRAMS	220
The National Park Service	220
NPS Programs	224
Listings in the National Register of Historic Places	224
"Determinations of Eligibility" for Inclusion in the National Register	225
Designations of National Historic Landmarks	225
Tax Certification	225
National Historic Preservation Fund Grants-in-Aid	226
Transfer of Historic Surplus Federal Property	226
Technical Preservation Information and Assistance	227
Recording Historic Sites	227
Archaeological Protection	228
National Historic Landmarks Program	228
The Historic Sites Act of 1935	230
Archaeology	233
The Antiquities Act of 1906	235
The National Park Service and the Reservoir Salvage Act	236
Archaeological Resource Protection Act of 1979	238
Native American Religious Freedom Act	238
General Considerations	239
Department of Transportation Act and Other Transportation Legislation	239
Department of Transportation Act	239
Other Transportation Laws	241
Executive Order 11593	242
Federal Property Management	242
Land-Use Planning Laws	243
International Activities	244
ASSESSMENT OF FEDERAL PRESERVATION PROGRAMS	245
A LEGAL ANALYSIS OF NHPA AND NEPA PROJECT IMPACT REVIEW REQUIREMENTS	**246**
THE SECTION 106 PROCESS	246
Federal Actions Subject to Section 106	247

Continuing Federal Actions	252
Determination of Effect	255
Determination of Adverse Effect	255
Opportunity to Comment—Consultation Process	256
Memorandum of Agreement	257
Parties Subject to Section 106	260
Public Participation in the Section 106 Process	262
Citizen Enforcement of Section 106	263
Standing	263
Jurisdiction	265
Proper Compliance	265
Parties	266
Enforcement Actions	266
Remedies	268
Recovery of Attorneys' Fees	269
PROJECT REVIEW UNDER NEPA	**270**
Procedural Requirements	270
Major Federal Action	270
"Significantly Affecting the Quality of the Human Environment"	276
NEPA Procedures	281
Environmental Assessment	283
The Determination Not to Prepare an EIS	283
Updating the Analysis of Impacts	284
The EIS Process	286
Contents of the EIS	291
Environmental Consequences	293
Adequacy	294
Other Compliance Provisions of NEPA	296
Agency Decision Making	297
Mitigation	298
Judicial Review under NEPA	299
Remedies	301
Summary	305
NHPA/NEPA COORDINATION	305
HOUSING AND COMMUNITY DEVELOPMENT PROGRAMS: A NEGLECTED RESOURCE	**309**
TYPES OF PROGRAMS	312

Mortgage Insurance and Loan Guarantees	312
Federal Credit Institutions	315
Low-Rent Public Housing	318
Housing Assistance Programs	318
Community Development Programs	319
Urban Development Action Grants	324
Comprehensive Planning Grants	326
Rehabilitation Loans	327
Neighborhood Self-Help Development Grants	327
Urban Homesteading	327
Other Programs	328
CONCLUSION	**328**
FURTHER READINGS	**329**
APPENDIXES	**331**

Chapter 5
Constitutional Law
by David Bonderman   343

PROCEDURAL DUE PROCESS ISSUES	**344**
Right to a Hearing	345
Notice	346
Timing	346
Nature of Hearing	347
Decision	348
Criteria and Standards	348
THE "TAKING" ISSUE	**350**
What Is a "Taking"?	350
What Is Taken?	356
Who Can Claim a "Taking"?	358
When Can a "Taking" Be Claimed?	360
Ripeness	360
Moratorium	361
What Is the Remedy for a "Taking"?	362
Constitutional Remedies	362
Section 1983	364
Practical Suggestions for Avoiding "Takings"	366

Evidence of Study and Forethought	367
Spreading Benefits and Burdens	367
Multiple Public Goals	367
Formal Administrative Review Process	368
FIRST AMENDMENT ISSUES	**369**
Sign Ordinances	369
Church Properties	371
FURTHER READINGS	**373**

Chapter 6
Administrative and Judicial Litigation
by Antonio Rossmann — 375

LITIGATION STRATEGY: THE FIRST STEPS	**377**
Identify Relevant Agencies	377
Ascertaining Appropriate Standards of Judicial Review	378
Assessing the Chances of Success	379
THE ADMINISTRATIVE PROCESS	**380**
Building the Preservation Case	380
Getting Help from Other Agencies and Institutions	384
Acting Early	386
Buying Time	386
Building a Rational Decision	387
Preparing for Judicial Relief	388
THE JUDICIAL PROCESS: PETITIONERS FOR JUDICIAL RELIEF	**389**
Pleadings on the Merits	390
Verified Petition for Relief	390
Memorandum of Law in Support of the Petition	390
Proposed Order to Show Cause or Notice of Motion for Hearing on the Merits	391
Pleadings to Obtain Injunctive Relief	391
The Record for Injunctive Relief	391
The Pleadings Generally	393
Application for Injunctive Relief	394
Memorandum of Law	395

    Proposed Temporary Stay or Restraining Order   395
    Proposed Order to Show Cause   396
Framing the Petition for Relief: The Essential Elements of the Case   396
    Court: State or Federal   396
    Venue   398
    Party Petitioner: Establishing Standing   399
    Party Defendant or Respondent   401
    Real Party in Interest   402
    Statement of Proceedings Below   403
    Causes of Action   404
    Prayer for Relief   405
    Verification   406
Discovery: A Strategic Decision   406
    Reasons for Securing Discovery   406
    Reasons for Not Pursuing Discovery   407
Evidence and Experts   408
    Situations Requiring Experts   410
        Designating Landmarks   410
        Establishing Alternatives   410
        Defeating a "Takings" Claim   411
        Applying Standards to a Threatened Structure   411
        Crucial Nonpreservation Issues   411
    Guidelines For Selecting and Using Experts   412
        Choosing Experts with Care and Caution   412
        Selecting and Using Experts at the Very Beginning of the Preservation Effort   412
        Using Experts to Identify Gaps in the Opponents' Case   412
        Using Experts as a Source of Information   412
Hearings   413
    Temporary Stay Order   413
    Preliminary Stay, or Injunction, Pending Determination of the Merits   414
    Hearing on the Merits   415
Post-Trial Findings and Judgment   416
Post-Trial Injunctive Relief   417
Appeal on the Merits   418
PRESERVATIONISTS AS RESPONDENTS IN COURT   **420**
The Government Agency   420

The Private Preservation Society or Citizen	421
Acting as an Intervenor	421
Acting as Amicus Curiae	422
Defending Claims for Injunctive Relief	423
Defending on the Merits	424
Expanding the Record	424
CONCLUSIONS: LITIGATION CANNOT BECOME A WAY OF LIFE	425
FURTHER READINGS	426

Chapter 7
Preservation Law and Economics: Government Incentives to Encourage For-Profit Preservation
by Richard J. Roddewig — 427

DETERMINING THE FEASIBILITY OF RENOVATION	432
The Income and Expense Analysis	434
Financing Considerations	437
After-Tax Income Considerations	442
REAL PROPERTY TAXES	446
The Importance of Property Taxes	446
A Survey of Existing Property Tax Incentives	448
Property Tax Exemptions, Abatements, and Assessment Freezes	449
Exemption or Abatement for Renovation Projects	453
Property Tax Credits for Renovation	454
Current-Use Assessment	454
Directions for Reform	457
FEDERAL INCOME TAXES	460
Past Legislation	461
The Tax Reform Act of 1976	461
The Revenue Act of 1978 and the Investment Tax Credit	464
The Economic Recovery Tax Act of 1981	467
The Act in Practice	471
The 25 Percent versus the 20 Percent Investment Tax Credit: Is Certification Worth the Cost?	479

CONSERVATION EASEMENTS	485
Valuation of Easements: The Crucial Inquiry	486
PACKAGING INCENTIVES	499
The Unity Example: A Proper Feasibility Analysis	500
Land Cost Write-Down	508
Reduced Construction Loan Interest Rate	510
Reduced Property Taxes	510
Reduced Mortgage Interest Rates	511
The Effect of a 25 Percent Investment Tax Credit	513
CONCLUSION: THE CASE FOR PROPERTY TAX, FINANCING, AND INCOME TAX INCENTIVES	519
FURTHER READINGS	522

Appendix A
Recommended Model Provisions for a Preservation Ordinance, with Annotations
by Stephen N. Dennis — A1

Appendix B
Overview: Economic Recovery Tax Act of 1981
by Thomas A. Coughlin III — B1

Appendix C
Easements: Introductory Materials
by Thomas A. Coughlin III — C1

Table of Cases

Index

Authors' Biographies

Foreword

In 1971 a young lawyer on the staff of the President's Council on Environmental Quality (CEQ) was asked to address himself to legal issues in historic preservation before a conference for lawyers sponsored by the National Trust for Historic Preservation. He chose to speak about a series of exciting, pathbreaking judicial decisions that broadened courts' willingness to allow those without a direct economic interest to contest a public development decision affecting the environment. These new, more expansive interpretations of what is necessary to establish legal standing had been won principally by environmental groups seeking to protect natural areas against development. The CEQ lawyer did a workmanlike job of developing the case law and the implications for future conflicts and then concluded, feeling good about having brought some highly useful information to people who could soon put it to use. The first question from the audience signaled the dimensions of the speech's failure. "It's all well and good," said a lawyer near the front, "that environmentalists have won these standing cases, but what's the relevance to historic preservation?"

Today that question would not be asked. Historic preservationists have caught up with and possibly surpassed environmentalists in achieving access to the courts and in winning recognition for preservation. But environmentalists and historic preservationists still constitute two communities and fail to exploit a shared identity of values and concerns for the nation's cultural heritage, which includes its natural endowment. At a time when economic conditions and government cutbacks threaten a variety of conservation and preservation programs, those who speak for cultural, noneconomic interests would do well to unite whenever possible. In that spirit The Conservation Foundation and the National Center for Preservation Law undertook to cooperate in producing this book.

In 1975, The Conservation Foundation began its work in urban conservation by cosponsoring the first major national conference on neighborhood preservation. The conference's premise was that, unless the nation matched its effort to conserve natural resources and the countryside with efforts to conserve cities and towns, people would increasingly choose to leave them. Such a movement would, of course, have serious impacts on the countryside—loss of prime agricultural lands and critical natural resources like wetlands are only two examples.

The Foundation soon found that the nascent historic preservation movement was playing a major role in shaping cities and towns across the country, making them more livable places. Although the preservation movement was hardly a new one (the National Trust for Historic Preservation dates back to the 1940s), only recently has it begun to assert itself much the way environmentalists did in the late 1960s. New laws and regulations have been enacted at all levels of government to ensure that significant buildings and historic areas are not ignored in city planning and development. Tax laws have been changed so that rehabilitation could better compete with new construction. But much of this growth in what would come to be called "historic preservation law" has been uncoordinated and certainly nowhere near as comprehensive as national environmental legislation like the Clean Air and Water Acts.

The National Center for Preservation Law was formed in 1977 in response to the need for lawyers to take a more active role in the historic preservation movement. It sought to provide intellectual leadership for the legal community and better access to interested attorneys for local preservation groups and public officials. Around the same time, The Conservation Foundation brought an attorney with experience in preservation law and policy, Chris Duerksen, on staff. In 1978, Duerksen began a series of occasional discussions with the leadership of the National Center about the state of preservation law and the need for a primer that would summarize the field and review important laws, regulations, and court decisions.

With the generous support of Barbara Hoffstot, the Beverly Glen (California) Environmental Protection Association, and the Pennsylvania State Historic Preservation Office, the Foundation and Center embarked on a joint project under Duerksen's direction to produce this practical handbook on historic preservation law.

We believe this handbook helps to fill a major gap in preservation legal literature. It is designed to provide a comprehensive overview of historic preservation law at all levels of government. Perhaps more importantly, it offers practical advice to anyone involved in the preservation process—attorneys, developers, city officials, and preservationists—

on how to protect the historic and architectural resources that add so much to our towns and cities, and how to do so in a fair and progressive fashion.

The historic preservation movement has come of age far beyond its early days. It is a movement led by concerned individuals and citizen organizations—not the government. It reflects a new awareness within America that bigger and newer is not always better; that our man-made resources, like their natural counterparts, have finite limits; and that the private citizen has the ultimate responsibility for shaping the contours of his own workplace and neighborhood.

With the growth and maturity of the preservation movement comes its inevitable clash with competing interests in our pluralistic society. Attempts to save older downtown buildings will conflict with equally vociferous claims for new convention centers. Neighborhood revitalization will raise cries of low-income displacement.

Indeed, as de Tocqueville has observed about America, "In a modern democracy, social problems become translated into legal problems—if the democracy coheres." This is why lawyers need to become more involved in the historic preservation movement as it gains in numbers and enlarges its objectives. Now, more than ever, there is a need to ensure that the country's laws and legal institutions keep pace with the great expectations many have for preservation in fostering economic growth, revitalizing our work places, and improving the general quality of our lives. This handbook will, we hope, play a valuable supporting role in accomplishing that goal.

William K. Reilly
President
The Conservation Foundation

Tersh Boasberg
President
National Center for Preservation Law

Preface

In 1957 a New Orleans attorney named Jacob Morrison published a book entitled *Historic Preservation Law*, the first primer on the subject. When Morrison updated his pioneer work in 1965, he was able to cover all federal, state, and local preservation laws and court cases in only 54 pages. There were then so few local preservation ordinances that he could include a comprehensive review of each one in a single appendix. Today there are over 1,000 local preservation ordinances; every state has at least some preservation-related laws; and there are more than a dozen federal statutes and literally hundreds of pages in the Code of Federal Regulations pertaining to preservation programs. This handbook's length—which cannot be attributed solely to the prolixity of lawyers—tells the story better than words: preservation law has emerged dramatically as a new and complex legal field.

The exponential growth of preservation law in the last 25 years reflects, of course, the growing concern in the United States about the loss of older buildings and historic areas to urban renewal, highways, and other developmental pressures. It shows that people in cities, small towns, and rural areas alike care deeply about the size and scale of their immediate surroundings and that they are willing to do something to shape them in a more humane, more livable fashion. And, increasingly, it means that preservation makes good economic sense.

Just what is "preservation law"? It is a collage, cutting across and drawing from several other established areas of law: land use and zoning, real property, taxation, local government, constitutional, and administrative. In many ways preservation law, particularly at the local level, is closest to land use and zoning; the rules are very similar. For example, the standards that dictate governmental behavior in enacting and administering zoning ordinances are virtually identical to those applicable to local landmark and historic district laws, and the constitutional doctrines governing regulation of private property are similar.

But preservation law has outgrown its local law origins and now has its own distinctive provisions—pertinent state and federal administrative procedures, an indigenous regulatory scheme, and special tax laws to name only a few. As a result, the days when preservationists had only to know how to run the local historical museum are gone. Today they must know local zoning and land-use law, how the federal income tax code works, what the state enabling law provides, and what the U.S. Supreme Court thinks about preservation ordinances and private property. The same holds for developers, municipal attorneys, and anyone else involved with historic landmarks and districts. The stakes in the preservation arena are great—not only in terms of dollars and cents but also in terms of the quality of life for ourselves and our children.

That is where this handbook fits in. Several years ago an energetic landmarks commissioner from a Florida town wrote me at The Conservation Foundation describing in graphic detail the trials and tribulations she and her fellow preservationists were experiencing in enacting and implementing a landmark protection ordinance. Property owners were in an uproar, and their attorneys were threatening suit. Her letter ended with a plaintive, "We need help and quick!" Unfortunately there was no practical guide to preservation law that could be sent by Express Mail to help her. By the same token, municipal attorneys and lawyers representing developers often found that there was no quick reference available when a preservation-related question arose in their practice.

This handbook is designed to fill that gap. Its primary purpose is to set out in easily accessible fashion current preservation law. The introductory chapter is devoted to an overview of preservation law—of where it has been and where it is going. The remaining chapters are more detailed, each focusing on a specific area of preservation law—local, state, and federal law, litigation, and economics—setting forth the basic legal principles, laws, and cases plus practical tips and advice.

The book can be divided into three sections. Part One tells how preservation programs work at the three levels of government. It starts with the community level, where the major responsibility and substantial power to preserve historic resources rests, focusing on how to design a comprehensive and equitable local program and how to draft and administer a local ordinance. The chapter on state law describes the increasingly important role of state preservation offices, surveys a wide variety of state preservation laws, and suggests some new directions for state programs. The federal law chapter describes the ample body of federal preservation law, explaining how federal preservation programs are organized and focusing on laws with regulatory elements, like the National Historic Preservation Act and the National Environmental Policy Act. Tax provisions are dealt with in a later chapter.

Part Two, covering preservation litigation and constitutional law, might be subtitled "the practicing lawyer's guide." While written in highly readable fashion, these chapters will be of most immediate interest to lawyers or those engaged in litigation. However, both chapters offer practical advice to preservationists and public officials on how to stay out of court and avoid legal problems.

The final section on preservation law and economics breaks new ground in a field of growing importance. While it describes what the law is—for example, it contains a detailed discussion of recently enacted federal tax incentives for preservation—it is not a comprehensive tax or investment guide. It focuses more on how developers, local governments, and preservationists can analyze the economics of preservation projects and how the results of that analysis can result in efficient development incentives. Clearly the future of preservation lies not only in laws controlling demolition, but equally in making revitalization of landmark buildings and historic districts an economically sound proposition. This chapter helps provide a blueprint for action.

Many people have contributed a great deal of time and effort to this project. The greatest credit goes to the authors who worked and reworked their chapters, usually cheerfully, going far beyond the call of duty in donating their time. They received valuable assistance from a succession of interns at the Foundation, including Lisa Cristal, Bill Heinemann-Ethier, Fred Meyerson, Edward Rappaport, and William MacRostie (who, drawing on his experience with the preservation programs at the National Park Service, also wrote a short section of the federal law chapter). All have vowed never to check another legal citation.

Each chapter was reviewed by several experts in the particular field of law. Our deepest thanks go to Brenda Barrett, Fred Bosselman, Peter Brink, David Callies, Gaylon Greer, Foster Knight, Wendy Larsen, Rodney Little, Dorothy Miner, Howard Moskoff, and R. Marlin Smith for their labors. We absolve them of any blame for shortcomings herein.

We received special assistance from John Fowler and Thomas King at the Advisory Council on Historic Preservation in writing and reviewing the federal law chapter. Harrison Wetherill, Stephen Dennis, Thomas Coughlin, and the legal staff at the National Trust for Historic Preservation were also particularly helpful and contributed important appendixes to the handbook. Nicholas Robinson of Pace University Law School provided valuable advice in the early phases of planning the book.

Multiauthor volumes are not the most painless of publications, and this one has undergone an extended birth. John H. Noble, vice-president at the Foundation, left his usual fingerprints throughout the manuscript; Robert McCoy supervised editing and production of this mammoth volume; and Laura O'Sullivan oversaw typing, cite checking, and many other odds and ends throughout. Among those who assisted them were Jenny Billet, Ira Brodsky, Bethany Brown, Tony Brown, Beth Davis, and Nancy Heneson. All have retired from the law book business. Through it all, William K. Reilly, president of The Conservation Foundation, and Tersh Boasberg, founder and president of the National Center for Preservation Law, stood by us, never once letting us think it would never get done, although that thought surely crossed their minds.

We hope that the reader will find this handbook helpful in dealing with a wide range of preservation law questions, and that, if it does not have all the answers (something lawyers never admit), at least it will serve as a starting point for further inquiry.

Christopher J. Duerksen
June 1983

Chapter 1
Preservation Law: Where It's Been, Where It's Going

CHRISTOPHER J. DUERKSEN AND DAVID BONDERMAN

PRESERVATION LAW: LOOKING BACK*

The Early Days of Preservation

The historic preservation movement, according to its chronicler Charles Hosmer, was underway in earnest by the mid-1800s.[1] Most early efforts were concerned with the buildings in which famous people had lived or great events had taken place, not with preservation of architectural gems or community character. Landmark regulations and ordinances were unheard of; threatened structures were protected, if at all, by preservationists purchasing them with private funds.

The long struggle to save Mount Vernon was typical of 19th-century preservation. The owner had placed such a high price on the mansion and grounds—$200,000—that neither the federal government nor the state of Virginia was in any mood to buy it. Mount Vernon began falling into disrepair, and by the early 1850s, rumors had it being sold as a hotel and tourist attraction or for industrial development. Salvation appeared in the form of Miss Pamela Sue Cunningham of Virginia, who shamed her countrymen into opening their pocketbooks to save George Washington's

---

* Some of the material in this chapter first appeared in David Bonderman, "The Grand Central Terminal Litigation and the Development of Preservation Law," in *Grand Central Terminal: City Within a City* (New York: Municipal Art Society of New York, 1982), pp. 129-34.

1. This discussion of early preservation efforts draws heavily on Charles B. Hosmer's standard work *Presence of the Past* (New York: G. P. Putnam's & Sons, 1965). Another excellent reference is Walter Whitehill's essay "Promoted to Glory . . . The Origin of Preservation in the United States," in *With Heritage So Rich* (New York: Random House, 1966).

home. Miss Cunningham's efforts, writes Hosmer, served as a blueprint for preservation organizations for many years. Thus, the early preservation movement was focused at the local level and in individual towns and cities, usually rallied in response to the threatened destruction of a single building. There was no national movement.

State and local governments only occasionally, and after much cajoling, became involved in preservation disputes by appropriating funds to purchase threatened buildings. In 1816 the city of Philadelphia appropriated $70,000 to save the old state capitol and its environs, which the state of Pennsylvania proposed to sell off for building lots. The state of New York rescued Hasbrouck House in Newburgh (the building had close associations with George Washington) by paying off a mortgage and turning the structure into a hotel.

The U.S. Congress entered the preservation picture some years later when it began buying Civil War battlefield sites as memorials. This action gave rise to the first significant preservation-related litigation, *United States v. Gettysburg Electric Railway Co.*[2] Decided by the Supreme Court in 1896, this case involved the condemnation of private property for the creation of a national battlefield memorial at Gettysburg. At the time, the idea that the federal government might, even by purchase, be legitimately involved in the preservation of historic sites was novel. The railway claimed that the condemnation was not for a valid "public purpose" as that principle was understood in constitutional law and, accordingly, was beyond the power of the federal government. The Court rejected that narrow view, concluding that the preservation of an important monument to the country's past was indeed a proper purpose. It reasoned that the history the battle represented "is rendered plainer and more durable by the fact that the Government of the United States, through its representatives in Congress assembled, appreciates and endeavors to perpetuate it by this most suitable recognition."[3]

Here then, for the first time, the Supreme Court recognized that preservation of a historic site was within the government's power, at least when the purchase of property was at issue. The Court did not consider, of course, whether government might achieve a similar result by regulation or justify its actions on aesthetic grounds alone without relying on historical associa-

---

2. 160 U.S. 668 (1896). Other early cases involving the taking of private property for public preservation or beautification purposes include *Woodstock v. Gallup*, 28 Vt. 587 (1856); *Shoemaker v. United States*, 147 U.S. 282 (1893); *In Re Clinton Ave.*, 68 N.Y. 196 (1901); *Roe v. Kansas ex rel. Smith*, 278 U.S. 191 (1929).

3. 160 U.S. 682 (1896).

tions. These two questions would be on center stage in the next phase of preservation law.

The Expansion of Regulatory Powers[4]

As America became more urban and as new architectural and building techniques allowed the construction of ever more massive structures, cities and towns showed increasing concern about retaining their character. Drawing on European precedents, particularly from Germany, local governments began to experiment on a broad scale with land-use controls and zoning. The proposition that government regulatory powers were sufficient to control certain noxious uses—such as slaughterhouses, tanneries, gunpowder manufacturers, and the like—had, of course, been accepted in the common law since medieval times. But it was not clear whether government regulation could be extended to limit uses and structures that were not inherently obnoxious and even less clear whether regulations could be used to restrict the height of buildings or forbid their demolition, particularly where compensation was not paid to an owner.

This uncertainty did not, however, restrain local governments from attempting such regulation. In 1904 the city of Baltimore adopted a 70-foot maximum height regulation to maintain the character of its neighborhoods and commercial areas. The same year, the city of Boston, which had grown sensitive to preservation when, in the late 1800s, many historic buildings were destroyed, enacted similar legislation that prescribed a lower height for buildings constructed in residential, rather than commercial, areas. The Baltimore regulation was upheld in 1908 by Maryland's highest court on the ground that it was designed to lessen fire hazards in addition to advancing aesthetic goals.[5] The Boston ordinance was challenged in a case entitled *Welch v. Swasey*,[6] which eventually made its way to the U.S. Supreme Court. The Supreme Court upheld the restrictions on the ground that they were reasonably related to the public health and safety, notably fire prevention. But while upholding the regulation, the Court sidestepped

---

4. Jacob H. Morrison recounts this early regulatory period in some detail in *Historic Preservation Law* (Washington, D.C.: The National Trust for Historic Preservation, 1974 ed.), pp. 20-24.
5. *Cochran v. Preston*, 108 Md. 220, 70 A. 113 (1908).
6. 214 U.S. 91 (1909). In an earlier case, *Williams v. Parker*, 188 U.S. 491 (1903), the Court had upheld a height limit on buildings around historic Copley Square in Boston, but the ordinance provided for compensation. Importantly, the Court did not even question the legitimacy of the law, only its impact.

the issue of whether government could regulate on the basis of aesthetics alone.

Although these cases represented an extension of the state's police power beyond hard-core health and safety issues, they did not authorize regulation for aesthetic purposes alone. Thus, preservationists were never entirely sure if landmark controls would survive until the issue was settled once and for all. They had to wait another 50 years until *Penn Central Transportation Co. v. New York City*.[7]

The other primary issue raised in early zoning and preservation cases was, in essence, an economic one. How stringent could a regulation be before it overburdened a landowner, thereby amounting to what lawyers call an unconstitutional "taking" of property? The Fifth Amendment to the Constitution, which applies to the federal government directly and to state and local governments through the Fourteenth Amendment, provides that property shall not be "taken" by the government without the payment of "just compensation." In practical terms, this means that if the government elects to build a highway through your house, it may use its power of eminent domain to do so, but it must pay you the fair market value of the property. While the authors of the Constitution apparently understood this "taking" clause to refer to eminent domain proceedings only, in the latter part of the 19th century and early part of the 20th century, the courts began to apply the "taking" clause to government regulation, particularly but not exclusively to land-use regulation. As Supreme Court Justice Oliver Wendell Holmes said in a famous 1922 decision involving a state regulation of coal mining, *Pennsylvania Coal v. Mahon*: "The general rule at least is that while property may be regulated to a certain extent, if regulation goes too far, it will be recognized as a taking."[8]

What Holmes apparently meant was that the government was free to regulate property for appropriate reasons without making payment: but if the economic burden imposed on a landowner was too great (whatever that might mean in a particular case), then the regulation would either be struck down or payment would be required.

In 1926 the Supreme Court faced the "taking" issue in a zoning context. All across the country, communities were enacting newfangled zoning laws prompted in part by the U.S. Department of Commerce, which, under the direction of Herbert Hoover, was actively promoting a widely copied standard zoning enabling act. But property owners were upset

---

7. 438 U.S. 104 (1978).
8. *Pennsylvania Coal Co. v. Mahon*, 260 U.S. 393, 415 (1922).

because these new controls sometimes diminished the value of their property, and some courts viewed them skeptically. By 1926 over half the state courts that had considered zoning regulations found that, as applied, zoning was an unconstitutional interference with private property. This set the stage for *Village of Euclid v. Ambler Realty Co.*[9] The essence of this dispute was whether a zoning ordinance adopted by the Cleveland suburb of Euclid, which precluded the realty company from using its property for commercial development as planned and as a result lowered its value by nearly 90 percent, amounted to an unconstitutional "taking." The Court answered no. It found that the effect of the ordinance was not too severe. The Court reached this result because it decided that the so-called mutuality of benefits and burdens imposed by these ordinances made them fair to the owners. Put simply, the Court held that the burden imposed on a property owner by limiting the use of his property was permissible without compensation because the same burden was imposed on all other nearby property owners and because the benefits—better light, less noise, and so forth—of the use limitation also applied to all property owners. Thus, the burden was considered to be nondiscriminatory and reasonable.

While the Court upheld land-use regulations in *Euclid*, it also made clear that in some instances a land-use regulation might go "too far." Indeed, just two years later the Supreme Court struck down another zoning ordinance as unconstitutional.[10] Thus, it was clear that land-use controls would not be immune from invalidation. Moreover, the zoning regulations the Court had approved of applied to many properties, not to individual parcels. This left unanswered whether an ordinance that applied to single landmarks, rather than to entire districts, might somehow be discriminatory.

This was the background for the development of local land-use laws during the late 1920s and 1930s.

The Infancy of Preservation Law: 1930-1955[11]

Unlike zoning and other land-use controls that caught on quickly in many areas of the country after *Euclid*, few preservation laws were enacted. Local governments were proceeding cautiously, and the federal government was

---
9. 272 U.S. 365 (1926).
10. *Nectow v. City of Cambridge*, 277 U.S. 183 (1928).
11. For excellent discussions of these early laws, see John Codman, *Preservation of Historic Districts by Architectural Controls* (Chicago: American Society of Planning Officials, 1956); Charles B. Hosmer, *Preservation Comes of Age*, (Charlottesville: University Press of Virginia, 1981).

taking its first halting steps beyond preserving battlefields and other national monuments.

New Orleans created a preservation commission in 1925, based on special state constitutional provisions enacted in 1921, but the law was not effective. In 1936 the state of Louisiana amended the state constitutional provisions, extending the district's boundaries and giving the local commission greater power. New Orleans responded by adopting a new local ordinance that, with minor amendments, remains in effect today. In 1931 Charleston, South Carolina, enacted the first effective comprehensive preservation law, which covered the antebellum section of the city. San Antonio passed a preservation law a few years later, in 1939.

World War II slowed local preservation efforts dramatically, and when the American Society of Planning Officials (now the American Planning Association) surveyed local preservation laws in 1956, it found that only an additional handful of cities had enacted laws: Alexandria, Virginia (1946); Williamsburg, Virginia (1947); Winston-Salem, North Carolina (1948); Georgetown in Washington, D.C. (1950); Natchez, Mississippi (1951); Annapolis, Maryland (1951); Beacon Hill in Boston and Nantucket, Massachusetts (1955); and Salem, Massachusetts (1956). These laws had several features in common with the three pioneer ordinances of the 1930s.

First, probably because of the decisions of the Supreme Court (discussed earlier) and judicial hesitancy to approve aesthetic regulation, the common stated rationale for the ordinances was economic, usually to encourage and preserve the local tourist industry. Although many of the statutes and ordinances referred to historic and architectural considerations, these factors were rarely used as the primary legal basis for the legislation.

Second, each of the statutes functioned in a fashion similar to the zoning ordinances that had previously been approved by the Supreme Court. That is, they applied, not to a single structure, but to an entire area, and thus they were consistent with the notion of mutuality of burden and benefit.

Third, most of these ordinances represented a major advance in the sense that they imposed architectural controls and in some instances either required owners to maintain their properties. adequately or prohibited demolition or alteration without approval or both.

These early preservation controls proved very controversial. The 1956 survey noted previously found that compliance was generally voluntary and based on negotiation. Some respondents to the survey even thought that a law without controls might work better because it "helps avoid criticism by those injured." Others recommended establishing revolving funds to buy properties from owners who opposed the controls and were willing to sell.

Despite owner opposition, virtually every challenge to local historic district ordinances during this period was rejected. For example, the highest courts of Louisiana and Massachusetts both upheld preservation ordinances.[12] However, state courts were still striking down land-use controls if they were based solely on aesthetic considerations. Then, in what ironically would prove to be a major spur to a new wave of local preservation laws, the U.S. Supreme Court used language in *Berman v. Parker*, a 1954 decision involving condemnation for an urban renewal project, that gave strong support for government action based on aesthetic considerations:

> The concept of the public welfare is broad and inclusive. . . . The values it represents are spiritual as well as physical, aesthetic as well as monetary. It is within the power of the legislature to determine that the community should be beautiful as well as healthy, spacious as well as clean, well-balanced as well as carefully patrolled. In the present case, the Congress and its authorized agencies have made determinations that take into account a wide variety of values. It is not for us to reappraise them. If those who govern the District of Columbia decide that the Nation's Capital should be beautiful as well as sanitary, there is nothing in the Fifth Amendment that stands in the way.[13]

This language, coupled with favorable state court reviews of historic preservation ordinances, persuaded a growing number of communities that action was imperative in the face of continuing destruction of landmarks by highway, urban renewal, and other projects. Local preservation law was ready to enter its next stage.

While local preservation efforts expanded slowly during the period 1930-1955, state governments were virtually dormant. Several established state historical commissions or agencies, but these were generally museum oriented. The most significant state activity was the enactment of enabling legislation allowing local governments to adopt local preservation ordinances. The federal government was somewhat more ambitious, concentrating on protecting historic sites on land it already owned and on

---

12. See *City of New Orleans v. Impastato*, 198 La. 206, 3 So.2d 559 (1941) (upholding the New Orleans Vieux Carre Ordinance); *Opinion of the Justices*, 128 N.E.2d 557 (Mass. 1955) (upholding state legislation creating local historic district commissions in Boston and Nantucket).

13. 348 U.S. 26, 33 (1954).

surveying the nation's stock of landmark structures.[14]

In 1906 Congress had passed the Antiquities Act,[15] which allowed the president to designate national monuments. The act was valuable in protecting major archaeological sites and did bring the executive branch more actively into preservation, but, as before, the act focused largely on sites already owned by the federal government. Not until 1935 did Congress take a broader view. In the Historic Sites Act,[16] it embraced for the first time the notion of historic preservation as national policy and called upon federal agencies to consider preservation in their programs and plans. Perhaps even more importantly, it authorized the Department of the Interior to begin surveying and identifying historic sites throughout the United States. Thirty years later, this survey program would serve as the groundwork for the National Register of Historic Places. The federal government also entered the business of helping to protect *private* landmarks through a National Historic Landmarks Program. While voluntary and without any controls or important incentives, that program also helped to lay the groundwork for the present National Register.

Preservation Grows Up: 1956-1970

An extraordinary period of activity in preservation law began in 1956. Local governments forged ahead with preservation ordinances, sometimes without waiting for specific state enabling legislation. And states suddenly began playing a more active role. A 1964 report entitled *Planning For Preservation*,[17] published jointly by the National Trust for Historic Preservation and the American Society of Planning Officials, reported that of 47 states responding to a survey conducted by the Kentucky Attorney General's Office, 42 said they had state preservation programs. The survey found a broad range of state initiatives including enabling legislation, easement laws, and coordination mechanisms.

The federal government, increasingly the culprit behind wholesale destruction of historic areas and buildings through urban renewal and

---

14. Chapter 4 also discusses the development of federal efforts. The best journal article on federal preservation law, though somewhat dated, remains John Fowler's *Federal Historic Preservation Law: National Historic Preservation Act, Executive Order 11593, and Other Recent Developments in Federal Law*, 12 Wake Forest L. Rev. 31 (1976).

15. 16 U.S.C. § 431 *et seq.* (1974 & Supp. 1982).

16. 16 U.S.C. § 461 *et seq.* (1974 & Supp. 1982).

17. Robert L. Montague and Tony P. Wrenn, *Planning for Preservation* (Chicago: American Society of Planning Officials, 1964).

highway projects, was goaded into action by an influential 1965 report sponsored by the U.S. Conference of Mayors and entitled *With Heritage So Rich*.[18] The report, citing the fact that over half of the structures identified by the federal Historic American Buildings Survey had been demolished, made a series of disturbing findings:

> Out of the turbulence of building, tearing down and rebuilding the face of America, more and more Americans have come to realize that as the future replaces the past, it destroys much of the physical evidence of the past. The current pace of preservation effort is not enough. It is as though the preservation movement were trying to travel up a down escalator. The time has come for bold, new measures and a national plan of action to insure that we, our children, and future generations may have a genuine opportunity to appreciate and to enjoy our rich heritage. . . . If the preservation movement is to be successful, it must go beyond saving bricks and mortar. It must go beyond saving occasional historic houses and opening museums. It must be more than a cult of antiquarians. It must do more than revere a few precious national shrines. It must attempt to give a sense of orientation to our society, using structures and objects of the past to establish values of time and place.[19]

The report recommended a series of detailed actions, many of which were enacted over the next 15 years to form the backbone of the current national preservation program. It urged, among other things, that Congress establish an Advisory Council on Historic Preservation to advise the president and Congress on historic preservation matters and to develop policies and guidelines to review and resolve conflicts between various federal and federally aided programs affecting historic preservation. A second major recommendation asked Congress to establish a National Register of Historic Places and a preservation program within the Department of the Interior to administer it. The report was perhaps at its most prescient in suggesting that federal preservation policy go beyond regulations and project review to consider economics: "If the effort to preserve historic and architecturally significant areas as well as individual buildings is to succeed, intensive thought and study must be given to economic conditions and tax policies which will affect our efforts to preserve such areas as living parts of the community."[20] Accordingly, the report advised Congress to make several changes in the Internal Revenue Code to foster

---

18. This report gives an excellent snapshot view of the state of preservation in the United States as of the early 1960s. The special committee responsible for this landmark work included Albert Rains, Edmund Muskie, William Widnall, Philip Hoff, Raymond Tucker, Gordon Gray, and Laurance Henderson. (New York: Random House, 1966).

19. *Id.* at 204, 207.

20. *Id.*, at 208.

preservation.

The very next year the recommendations regarding an advisory council and a National Register were enacted into law as the National Historic Preservation Act of 1966 (NHPA), which, with subsequent amendments, remains the basic federal statute regarding preservation.[21] Several of the tax code changes were made, but the more far-reaching recommendations, such as tax deductions for private rehabilitation, would have to wait another decade before becoming law. Congress also took notice of the bulldozer mentality of highway officials and included a special provision in the Transportation Act of 1966[22] that required the secretary of transportation to avoid damaging or demolishing structures listed in the National Register of Historic Places unless there was "no prudent and feasible alternative." Similarly, the 1966 Model Cities Act[23] also required the Department of Housing and Urban Development to recognize preservation in urban renewal plans and to authorize preservation activities as an eligible project cost.

In addition to recommending changes in federal law, *With Heritage So Rich* contained thoughtful advice for state and local governments, but its suggestions were generally overlooked in the excitement over the new program Congress had passed to control federal government actions. The report urged states, for example, to establish preservation agencies and an organizational structure to provide leadership for local governments. Local governments were urged, not only to enact protective ordinances, but to relate and incorporate preservation policies into official general plans and community renewal programs. Like the tax code changes, this wise advice would not take hold until the following decade.

Despite the advances in preservation and the accompanying legislative initiatives, preservation law showed no signs of emerging as a distinct field. The American Society of Planning Officials and the National Trust, rather than the legal community, provided much of the basic thinking and research in the preservation law field in the late 1950s and early 1960s, and even that was scant.[24] There was little innovative thinking about tax policies or implementation of historic district ordinances. The enactment of the National Historic Preservation Act in 1966 planted the seeds for

---

21. 16 U.S.C. § 470 *et seq.* (1974 & Supp. 1982).
22. Department of Transportation Act, Pub. L. 89-670 § 4, 80 Stat. 931-935 (1966).
23. Demonstration Cities and Metropolitan Development Act of 1966, Pub. L. 89-754, §§ 601-706, 80 Stat. 1255, 1278-1281 (1966).
24. The American Bar Association's Section on Real Property, Probate and Trust Law did address historic preservation issues at some of its meetings. See American Bar Associa-

a preservation bar, but still by 1970 there was, at best, a handful of lawyers in the country who could be called specialists in preservation law.

Preservation Law in the Environmental Decade: 1970-1980

The 1970s have been termed the Environmental Decade. During this 10-year period more national environmental legislation was enacted than during the preceding 200 years. The new field of environmental law sprang up with all the usual accoutrements, such as national legal conferences, bar association committees, and legal treatises. Attorneys began specializing in environmental law because it was good business. Industries had to know what was required of them or face serious penalties, and plants often could not be built without government approval. Environmentalists pushed the government and industry to comply with the new laws and regulations.

But in the 1960s and early 1970s preservation law had languished. The organized bar's interest was sporadic. The National Trust acted mainly as a clearinghouse for legally related preservation material; it did not lobby or litigate, although occasionally it did file "friend of the court" briefs.[25] Thus there was no national preservation organization equivalent to the Sierra Club or Natural Resources Defense Council to provide leadership for a public interest preservation bar. And because federal preservation law was really no more than a consultative process triggered when a federally initiated or approved project affected historic resources, it did not have the relevance to most private commercial or industrial interests that environmental law did. There were no preservation equivalent of the Clean Air Act, for example, and no direct federal controls over demolition of structures at the local level.

As has been so often the case in preservation, it took the loss of several important landmarks to bring about change. In Lexington, Kentucky, the razing of seven historic buildings in 1969 by the city renewal authority led to formation of a neighborhood association that sued then-HUD Secretary George Romney for allowing destruction of National Register

---

tion, *Proc. of the A.B.A. Sec. Real Prop. Prob. and Tr. L.* (Chicago: Aug. 11-13, 1963). However, this activity was sporadic. Similarly, few useful legal articles appeared during the period. One of the best was a well-researched student note in the *Columbia Law Review*. Note, *The Police Power, Eminent Domain and the Preservation of Historic Property*. 63 Colum. L. Rev. 708 (1963). For a comprehensive bibliography of early publications, see 12 *Wake Forest L. Rev.* 275 (1976).

25. The Trust's early efforts in preservation law are described by Elizabeth D. Mulloy in *The History of the National Trust for Historic Preservation 1963-1973* (Washington, D.C.: Preservation Press, 1976), pp. 26, 41, 42, 72-73.

properties. The same year preservationists in Memphis, Tennessee, began a long legal battle against the Department of Transportation to stop a federally aided highway that would bisect a city park. The Memphis case, *Citizens to Preserve Overton Park v. Volpe*,[26] eventually turned out favorably, but preservationists' claims in the Lexington case, *South Hill Neighborhood Association v. Romney*,[27] were ultimately rejected on procedural grounds. About the same time in Chicago, preservationists found that their highly touted local ordinance was pathetically weak in the face of a determined developer. In February 1970, the Chicago Commission on Historical and Architectural Landmarks was notified that Louis Sullivan's landmark Stock Exchange Building would be demolished to make way for a new high rise. Preservationists took two years to organize and learn the legal ropes; by that time the Stock Exchange was no more.

Clearly something was wrong. Despite the federal laws and an increasing number of local ordinances, landmarks were being lost as rapidly as ever. Part of the problem was that the laws were too weak to be of much use in most instances, a shortcoming exacerbated by the lack of even a small contingent of knowledgeable preservation lawyers. Each time a crisis arose, it seemed that preservationists had to learn the law again from scratch.

This state of affairs led Robert Stipe, a University of North Carolina professor of public law and government, to issue a plea in the July 1970 issue of *Preservation News* (the National Trust's monthly newsletter). "Preservation Lawyers—Unite!" he urged.[28] Stipe believed it was high time lawyers organized themselves as had other professionals in the preservation field. He listed several key needs: an annotated bibliography of legal publications, dissemination of legal advice through a special lawyers advisory body, and a loose-leaf reporter for new cases and legislation.[29] This call to organize was, in effect, the beginning of a preservation law bar in the United States. The National Trust responded in 1971 by scheduling the first national conference on preservation legal techniques ranging from local historic district ordinances and use of easements to federal tax policy.[30]

Two developments stand out as the most important legal events of the remainder of the 1970s. The first concerned a preservation suit involving New York City's Grand Central Terminal. This case would ultimately be

---

26. 401 U.S. 402 (1971).
27. 421 F.2d 454 (1969), *cert. denied*, 397 U.S. 1025 (1970).
28. 10:7 *Preservation News* 5 (July 1970).
29. *Id.* at 190-91.
30. Several papers from the conference were published in 36 *Law and Contemp. Probs.* 308-444 (Duke University Law School 1971), which was devoted to historic preservation.

PRESERVATION LAW: INTRODUCTION   13

decided by the U.S. Supreme Court. The second was the enactment by Congress of a series of economic and tax incentives aimed at fostering rehabilitation of landmark structures and areas.

Even though more and more cities and towns were enacting local preservation ordinances, there were still gnawing doubts about whether the U.S. Supreme Court would uphold preservation restrictions. Most experts predicted that the Court would uphold the restrictions given its past pronouncements in land-use cases[31] and the fact that practically every state court that had heard a preservation case upheld local controls.[32] But still, the U.S. Supreme Court had not spoken. And thus, when the Court decided to review a New York Court of Appeals' decision upholding New York City's landmarks law, the preservation world held its breath. Because of its position at the center of preservation law, that case—*Penn Central Transportation Co. v. New York City*—bears a close review.

The New York City landmarks law. The same growth of historical awareness that led to the pressure for national battlefield monuments and the protection of historic districts in cities like Charleston and New Orleans led ultimately to heightened national consciousness about the importance of individual buildings and structures of great merit. Some of the historic buildings initially considered as worthy of preservation were in the hands of the federal, state, or local governments, but the great majority, of which Grand Central Terminal is a leading example, were privately owned. In 1956 New York became the first state to authorize its municipalities to enact "landmark" ordinances designed to protect individual buildings, as opposed to historic districts. And in 1965 New York City became the first major city to pass a landmarks ordinance with any significant protection for designated individual buildings.

Accordingly, the city established a statutory plan pursuant to which a

---

31. See *Berman v. Parker*, 348 U.S. 26, 33 (1954) "It is within the power of the legislature to determine that the community should be beautiful as well as healthy, spacious as well as clean, well-balanced as well as carefully patrolled"; *City of New Orleans v. Dukes*, 427 U.S. 297 (1976) upholding exclusion of a hot dog vendor from the Vieux Carre on the ground that the historic area was of great importance to the city's economy thus justifying strong police power regulations to protect it; *Young v. American Mini-Theatres, Inc.*, 427 U.S. 50 (1976), in approving an "innovative land use regulation" requiring dispersal of "adult uses," the Court points out that cities have broad latitude to make land-use classifications to further legitimate local goals.

32. See *Santa Fe v. Gamble-Skogmo, Inc.*, 73 N.M. 410, 389 P.2d 13 (1964); *Bohannan v. City of San Diego*, 30 Cal. App. 3d 416, 106 Cal.Rptr. 333 (1973); *Figarsky v. Historic District Commission of City of Norwich*, 171 Conn. 198, 368 A.2d 163 (Conn. 1976).

landmarks preservation commission was created and empowered to designate qualifying structures of significant historic or aesthetic merit as landmarks and regulate their restoration, alteration, and demolition. (The commission also was authorized to designate and regulate qualifying areas and neighborhoods as historic districts.) A proposed modification of a designated property was not to be allowed unless the commission found that it would have no effect on the protected architectural features, was otherwise consistent with the purposes of the landmarks law, or was required to avoid economic hardship to the owners.[33]

Grand Central Terminal as a landmark. Acting pursuant to the landmarks law, the New York City Landmarks Preservation Commission has designated nearly 600 individual buildings and structures as landmarks, along with 41 historic districts, 25 interior landmarks, and 8 scenic landmarks. One of the first landmark designations, and one of the most important, was Grand Central Terminal. The owner of the terminal, the Penn Central Transportation Company, opposed the designation but did not appeal the city's action. Accordingly, the designation became final, and the Grand Central Terminal was subject to the protections of the New York landmarks law.

In 1968 Penn Central and some of its subsidiaries entered into a lease with UGP Properties, Inc., a subsidiary of a British company. UGP proposed to construct a 55-story office building atop the terminal. To carry out this scheme, UGP and Penn Central hired the internationally known architect Marcel Breuer, who proposed two alternate plans, which became known as Breuer I and Breuer II Revised. Both schemes would have placed a tower approximately 500 feet high on the top of the terminal and required the destruction of a portion of the interior concourse. The Breuer II Revised plan would have also required the demolition of the terminal's 42nd Street facade. Under either plan, Grand Central Terminal and its Park Avenue environs would have been radically altered.

In accordance with the New York landmarks law, Penn Central and UGP filed applications with the Landmarks Preservation Commission requesting a certificate either that the proposed construction and demolition would

---

33. In addition, a section of the New York zoning resolutions (which has the force of law) allows a property owner to "transfer" (under certain restrictions) unused "development rights"—called TDRs—from a landmark to other nearby property. (New York City Zoning Resolutions Sections 74-79/793). New York City is virtually alone in adopting TDRs for presrvation purposes; Denver adopted a TDR ordinance in 1982, but only a few transfers have taken place.

have no effect on the protected architectural features of the terminal's exterior or that any effect produced would be "appropriate." On August 26, 1969, the commission denied the Penn Central/UGP applications on the ground that the proposed tower and demolitions would "affect and change the exterior architectural features" and that those changes would be highly inappropriate.[34] According to the commission,

> ... To balance a 55-story office tower above a flamboyant Beaux-Arts facade seems nothing more than an aesthetic joke.... The "addition" would be four times as high as the existing structure and would reduce the landmark itself to the status of a curiosity.[35]

The Landmarks Preservation Commission thus rejected both of the Penn Central/Breuer proposals, setting the stage for protracted litigation.

The Penn Central *litigation in the lower courts.* On October 7, 1969, shortly after receiving the decision of the landmarks commission, Penn Central filed a lawsuit against the city, but at the heart of its lawsuit were two claims. The first was that the effect of the commission's denial of the building permit was so burdensome as to amount to a "taking" of Penn Central's property without just compensation. The second was that the effect of the landmarks ordinance was to unconstitutionally discriminate against Penn Central: by designating the terminal a landmark, the city of New York had required Penn Central to bear burdens not required of other nearby landowners. In other words, Penn Central was claiming that there was no mutuality of benefits and burdens.

During the trial, Penn Central's major effort was directed to the "taking" issue. Accordingly, the company introduced evidence attempting to show that it had been operating Grand Central Terminal at a loss of nearly $2 million a year for some years and that it could not earn a reasonable return on its property in the current circumstances. The company also introduced its agreement with UGP Properties pursuant to which Penn Central was to receive $1 million rent per year during construction of the proposed tower and $3 million a year for 50 years thereafter. Thus, according to Penn Central, denial of the certificate to construct the Breuer tower effectively precluded it from earning large sums and prevented it from operating its property at a profit.

The trial judge, who was apparently not a fan of the terminal ("It leaves no reaction here other than of long neglected faded beauty"), found that Penn Central had shown sufficient economic hardship to establish that

---

34. New York Landmarks Preservation Commission Decision Nos. LPC 69005, 69006.
35. *Id.* at 10.

the landmark restrictions were an unconstitutional "taking" of its property.[36] He issued an order striking down as unconstitutional the designation of the terminal and the subsequent restrictions. This order, if upheld, would have allowed Penn Central to build either of the Breuer schemes or, for that matter, to demolish the terminal entirely. Preservationists were shocked. If the trial judge was correct, then not only would the Grand Central Terminal be gone, but the message to other cities and towns would be clear: profitable demolition would be stopped with great difficulty or not at all.

The city appealed the trial judge's decision and won a three-to-two reversal, thereby upholding the decision of the landmarks preservation commission.[37] On the all-important "taking" question, the court concluded that the relevant issue was whether the restrictions imposed by the landmarks commission deprived Penn Central of "all reasonable use" of its property. The majority held that Penn Central had not met that burden because it could and did operate the terminal as a railway station. The state's highest court later unanimously upheld the intermediate court's decision.[38]

Penn Central then sought and obtained review by the Supreme Court of the United States. Such review, discretionary with the Supreme Court, is granted in less than 1 percent of the cases brought to it; many viewed the Court's action as an ominous sign. Why else would it take a case that had been decided unanimously by New York's highest court if it did not intend to reverse? Thus, the Grand Central Terminal dispute became one of the very few land-use regulation cases of any sort to reach the Court since *Euclid* in 1926 and the first, and to date only, such case to consider the merits of landmark preservation. Preservationists and land-use attorneys watched the case closely.

The Supreme Court decision in Penn Central. In the Supreme Court, Penn Central made arguments that, although refined in certain respects, were quite like those it made in the lower courts. The company's major claim was that rejecting the permit to build the Breuer tower atop Grand Central was an unconstitutional "taking" of its property because the rejection completely denied it the use of the "air rights" over the terminal. Penn Central also claimed that the landmark designation was unconstitu-

---

36. The lower court decision does not appear in the official legal reports.
37. The Appellate Division decision appears at 50 A.D.2d 265, 377 N.Y.S.2d 20 (1975).
38. The Court of Appeals decision is reported at 42 N.Y.2d 324, 397 N.Y.S.2d 914, 366 N.E.2d 1271 (1977).

tionally discriminatory in that it singled out one property for special unfavorable treatment.

In view of the importance of the case, briefs were filed, not only by the parties, but by a variety of other governmental units and private groups whose interests might have been affected by the Court's decision. Thus, for example, the Pacific Legal Foundation—an organization whose conservative philosophy resembles that of now-Secretary of the Interior James Watt's Mountain States Legal Foundation—and the New York Real Estate Board filed briefs in support of Penn Central. On the other hand, the solicitor general of the United States, several states and cities, the National Trust for Historic Preservation, and several other conservation and preservation groups filed briefs in support of New York City.

The Supreme Court's 1978 opinion[39] was a major victory for the future of Grand Central Terminal and significantly strengthened the hand of preservationists. Justice Brennan, writing for a six-justice majority, upheld the action of the New York City Landmarks Preservation Commission. First, the Court laid to rest the notion that aesthetic considerations alone are not a proper basis for the use of the government's police power, explicitly noting "that states and cities may enact land use restrictions or controls to enhance the quality of life by preserving the character and desirable aesthetic features of a city. . . ."[40] Second, in rejecting the Penn Central "taking" claim, the Court made clear that when it comes to economic impact, local historic preservation controls are nothing more or less than another form of land-use regulation as far as the law is concerned. Justice Brennan's decision accomplished this by applying the same concepts that have been used in the zoning cases starting at the turn of the century, as described earlier. As a result, although the Court did not entirely resolve the economic issue, based on a series of subsequent lower court decisions, it is now reasonable to conclude that to successfully show a "taking" in a preservation case, a landowner will have to demonstrate that retaining the historic structure will deny him *all reasonable economic use* of the property, not just that there has been a diminution in value

---

39. *Penn Central Transportation Co. v. New York City*, 438 U.S. 104 (1978).
40. Id at 129. In *City of New Orleans v Dukes*, 427 U.S. 297, 304 (1976), which upheld a New Orleans ordinance barring most pushcart vendors from the historic French Quarter, the Court intimated that aesthetic considerations were a valid basis for police power regulation but did not explicitly so hold. The *Penn Central* holding has now been followed by most states.

due to landmark restrictions.[41]

Perhaps the most significant new factor to emerge from the *Penn Central* case is that it is now plain that protection can be given to individual landmarks as well as to historic districts. The Court explicitly rejected the claim that designating individual landmarks is discriminatory and therefore improper, at least where a city has designated a substantial number of landmarks.

Even though *Penn Central* did not settle every major preservation issue permanently—in theory, Penn Central could come back at a later time with evidence that it could not make reasonable use of the terminal—it did provide a major impetus to adoption of stronger state and local landmark restrictions. Now it was clear that cities and towns could say no to demolition, and unless an owner could prove he had no reasonable use remaining, such action was constitutionally valid.

Tax incentives. While the *Penn Central* case was winding its way to the U.S. Supreme Court, preservationists began to see that strong legal controls on demolition, even if upheld, were not the complete answer. Something had to be done to get at the strong economic motivations behind demolitions. Preservationists therefore focused on what some perceived to be a substantial bias in the federal Internal Revenue Code in favor of new construction at the expense of existing structures. In what was clearly the most important national legislative victory for preservation in the 1970s, Congress enacted the Tax Reform Act of 1976,[42] which contained a series of far-reaching changes designed to encourage the renovation of historic buildings. The act offered owners of structures listed in the National Register of Historic Places (or which were part of registered districts) very favorable depreciation rates for approved rehabilitation expenditures. Another incentive was the allowance of a charitable deduction if an owner donated a preservation easement (such as an easement promising not to alter or demolish a landmark) to a nonprofit entity or government. The act also attempted to create a deterrent to demolition of registered landmarks by denying deduction of demolition expenses and use of accelerated depreciation for replacement structures.

---

41. For example, *Maher v. City of New Orleans*, 516 F.2d 1051 (5th Cir. 1975); *William C. Haas & Co. v. City and County of San Francisco*, 605 F.2d 1117 (9th Cir. 1979); *900 G Street Associates v. Department of Housing and Community Development*, 430 A.2d 1387 (D.C. App. 1981).

42. 26 U.S.C. 191 (The tax benefits of the 1976 act were subsequently improved by the Economic Tax Recovery Act of 1981, Pub. L. 97-34, 95 Stat. 172 (1981), for a good overview, see chapter 7 on economics and the law.

While experts would later debate the relative advantages of these new incentives and disincentives, there is little doubt that they spurred a great deal of renovation and, more importantly, tremendous interest in preservation by developers who had heretofore been oriented strictly toward new construction. By 1981 the Department of the Interior estimated that these provisions had helped spur $1.8 billion in rehabilitation work.[43] Thanks in part to the lobbying efforts of the National Trust and the newly organized grass-roots lobbying group, Preservation Action, these preservation benefits were made substantially more favorable in some respects by the Economic Recovery Tax Act of 1981.[44]

The *Penn Central* decision and the changes in the tax laws ensured preservation law a substantial new following. *Penn Central* made clear that localities could forbid demolition or stop new construction for preservation purposes. Thus, a landowner who did not understand local preservation law could face serious economic consequences. Similarly, developers who failed to consider federal tax benefits might unnecessarily forego significant benefits. Suddenly, as never before, preservation law had become worth studying and practicing, just as environmental law had almost a decade earlier.

By 1980 the American Bar Association had several subcommittees devoted solely to preservation law, each with dozens of members, and preservation legal conferences were now an annual fixture. Shortly after the *Penn Central* decision, a group of preservation-minded attorneys incorporated a new public interest organization, the National Center for Preservation Law, whose primary purpose was to function as an advocate for preservation in the courtroom. And the National Trust legal department became more active, publishing a landmarks commission newsletter in 1975, as well as filing an increasing number of *amicus curiae* briefs in preservation-related cases. In 1981 it began publication of a full-fledged preservation law reporter covering recent legal developments in the area. The very existence of that reporter, which has been widely subscribed to, stands as strong testimony to preservation law's emergence as a distinct and legitimate legal field.

Given the sudden prominence of preservation, it was probably inevitable that the laws, regulations, and procedures established in the 1970s, which

---

43. Statement by Ward Jandl, Chief, Branch of Preservation Projects, Technical Preservation Service, National Park Service, at a conference on preservation tax incentives in Washington, D.C., May 17, 1982.

44. Pub. L. 97-34, 95 Stat. 172 (1981); chapter 7 discusses the act in detail.

helped elevate preservation to new heights, would be subject to increasing scrutiny. Thus, it is not surprising that the 1970s era of expansion would be followed by a period of retrenchment and refinement in the 1980s. The first signs of the new period were first seen on the federal level.

PRESERVATION LAW: THE 1980s

The Defederalization of Preservation

Emboldened by their success with tax and economic incentives, preservationists attempted in late 1980 to persuade Congress to enact a very ambitious preservation agenda. They pressed for stronger controls over federal agency actions that might affect National Register properties; they lobbied for the creation of a federal preservation agency that would be independent of the Department of the Interior; they urged Congress to adopt legislation aimed at effecting stronger state preservation controls. In the end, they got none of these, and while they did secure some important gains, overall they saw the beginning of what appeared to some to be an actual erosion in federal preservation programs. Like some of their environmental brethren, preservationists had seriously misread the mood in Congress and across the country, particularly toward new forms of regulation and federal government initiatives.

At the center of this erosion of the corpus of national preservation law was the National Register. From merely honoring historic properties, the Register had increasingly become a device for triggering reviews, benefits, and penalties. Broadened application, coupled with a growing body of regulations, focused attention on the Register and tested the relatively informal and imprecise nomination and designation procedures that had drawn little fire as long as Register designation was largely honorary.

Increasingly, agencies and officials affected by the Register took action to avoid or weaken its impact. One example is HUD's Urban Development Action Grant (UDAG) program, created by Congress in 1977 to draw private investment into distressed cities quickly and with a minimum of red tape. UDAG administrators adopted the position—upheld by several federal courts—that localities, and not the federal government, had the primary responsibility to review the impacts of proposed UDAG properties on the community's historic resources even though large amounts of federal money might be involved.

Local officials reacted, too. The mayor of St. Louis lobbied hard in 1980 to change National Register procedures. He took strong exception to the nomination of nearly all his city's 360-acre central business core as a historic district, a nomination for which consultation with the mayor or any city official was not required. The mayor feared that constraints imposed by a Register listing—such as the tax disincentives and federal reviews and delays—could stifle needed economic development in downtown St. Louis.

Thus, notwithstanding current wisdom that it was the election of Ronald Reagan that spelled the contraction of federal preservation initiatives, even before the 1980 election, the nation had begun a process of localization of historic preservation. Late in 1980, Congress amended the National Historic Preservation Act, and while preservationists did secure some important gains, overall the results were far different than they had envisioned.[45] Local governments were given a new role in the Section 106 review process under the NHPA and the power to veto a listing on the Register if both the local mayor and landmarks commission objected to a nomination.

More startling was an ill-considered provision providing that no property could be added to the Register if an owner objected. Despite an owner's objections, federal protections would still apply if a property was "eligible for" the Register. The precedent such a provision set for local preservation ordinances, however, was an extremely poor one.

Then President Reagan took office in 1981 and immediately slashed preservation funding to the bone. Both the Advisory Council on Historic Preservation, which oversees implementation of the NHPA, and the National Trust took substantial budget cuts. Funding for state preservation programs also was reduced dramatically even though the administration said it expected states to assume more of the burden of administering the National Register process. While there were some bright spots, like the generous tax credit provisions in the 1981 Economic Recovery Tax Act for rehabilitating Register landmarks,[46] and even though a Democratically controlled House did not go along with all the cuts, the handwriting on the wall seemed clear: preservation would be defederalized, and while the federal government would still play an important role, now more than ever if preservation was to be effective it would be done locally.

Thus, when the Reagan administration proposed massive budget cuts and made clear its intent to rely more on state and local governments in dealing with many public issues, as far as preservation was concerned these

---

45. Chapter 4 contains a detailed discussion of these changes.

46. Chapter 7 discusses these provisions at greater length. The fascinating lobbying and behind-the-scenes maneuvering that preceded their enactment is recounted in Steve Weinberg, *Lobbying Congress—The Inside Story*, 34 Historic Preservation 16 (1982).

actions simply reinforced a preexisting trend. In the wake of the *Penn Central* decision, local governments and preservationists had already been quietly working to strengthen local ordinances. They realized that most direct threats to landmarks come from private, not public, actions. Moreover, they recognized that existing federal protections, like the project review procedures established in the NHPA, were delaying and mitigating mechanisms at best, not anti-demolition guarantees. There was also an increasing recognition that the most effective preservation planning, both to forestall demolition and to encourage renovation, comes about when public agencies and interest groups understand the dynamics of the *local* real estate market and make preservation an integral part of local development and growth policies.

Richard Miller, an attorney who founded the Chicago Landmarks Preservation Council (now the Landmarks Preservation Council of Illinois) after demolition of the Chicago Stock Exchange in the early 1970s, exemplifies the changing mood at the local level. Miller has been a firm advocate of regulation, authoring an Illinois preservation law which protects landmarks listed on a state register of historic places. While he still recognizes the need for controls, now he sees things somewhat differently. "Preservation is a complex exercise in real estate economics and urban function. Buildings have to work. They have to generate cash flow; the bills needed to operate and maintain them have to be paid. If financing for a building comes from investors, then investors must have a return on their investment. You can't just pass a law somewhere or make a decision in a body somewhere saying that a certain building shall be preserved for all time. It just doesn't work that way."[47]

Of course, Miller would probably agree that preservationists can hardly rely on market forces alone since preserving a historic structure is often not as profitable for a developer as ripping it down and building a new office tower. The last hundred years have shown that in the absence of strong statutory controls on demolition, preservation is not guaranteed. But Miller's comments do show the growing awareness among preservationists that controls alone may not achieve their goals.

Preservation Law: What Lies Ahead?

There is compelling evidence that the preservation movement has come of age and along with it, preservation law. Overall, laws designed to foster

---

47. Quoted in Richard Cahan, *Rescuing our Architectural Heritage*, Barrister, 6:4 (1979): 46, 52.

preservation have succeeded far beyond what anyone might have predicted in 1970. The solid legal basis established in the *Penn Central* case and the widespread use of preservation tax incentives have created the climate for even greater advances in the years ahead. Of course, now that preservation laws, regulations, and incentives really mean something and are in common use, we can expect demands for more sophisticated and careful attention to every phase of the development regulatory process—designations, permit reviews, and so forth—and in the formulation and implementation of economic incentives. Thus, the immediate future of preservation law will most likely be one of refinement and consolidation: how to make controls more effective *and* fair; how to draft regulations more precisely and define standards more clearly; how to fine tune tax incentives to foster preservation without handing out windfalls.

Emerging forces and trends—continuing huge federal budget deficits, a growing reluctance to increase regulatory burdens, fiscal constraints at the state and local levels, and demographic data showing a major population migration to rural areas and to the West and South—will have an impact on preservation and the body of law that surrounds it. How will governments react? What do these changes mean for preservation organizations? How will the preservation bar adapt? These are the questions for the coming years.

Preservation Law at the National Level

Even though preservationists will look less often to Washington for help in the foreseeable future, federal influence on the built environment will remain substantial. Congress will continue to tinker with the tax code, and these changes will have an important role in the development and renovation equation. The current tax credits for rehabilitation are an obvious example, but other less visible tax code amendments may be of equal importance. For example, lowering the marginal maximum tax rate from 70 percent to 50 percent may make real estate in general a less attractive investment. Tax breaks for development in so-called enterprise zones may have both positive and negative effects. And despite budget cutbacks, the federal government will continue to spend large sums on or provide subsidies to major development projects that will affect landmarks. Notwithstanding some doubts within the Reagan administration, the Urban Development Action Grant program, which has helped spur the renovation of some buildings while at the same time generating intense controversy in other instances where it funded demolition (the Portman Hotel battle in New York is one recent example), looks like a candidate for survival. Subsidies for energy and minerals development in the West will continue, albeit at reduced levels, thus affecting directly archaeological sites and indirectly small historic towns that will bear the brunt of population surges.

Preservationists at the national level will have to be much more sophisticated in approaching these issues than was necessary when the focus was on regulation. The main challenge will be to retain a sound framework of federal laws that will enable preservation to advance at the local level. To date, preservation lobbyists have produced impressive results in shaping the Internal Revenue Code, but it will be essential to go further and analyze a broader array of programs, such as mortgage subsidies, energy policy, and the like, to be really effective.

To maintain past gains, and to obtain new ones, preservationists also will be forced to better justify the value of their own programs and subsidies. As one preservation lobbyist put it, "I feel like the proverbial emperor without his clothes when I go before Congress. I don't have a lot of hard evidence about preservation's worth." And new alliances will be essential to success in lobbying Congress. For example, preservationists have already teamed up with developers to argue successfully for rehabilitation tax benefits. Closer links with environmentalists more concerned with natural resources may also prove productive in some instances. For example, if Congress is considering subsidies for energy development in the West or highway interchanges that could spur outlying commercial development at the expense of central business districts and natural areas, a team approach might help ensure that both natural and cultural resources are protected.

Preservation attorneys will also need to keep a close watch on federal agency projects that might have an adverse impact on landmark buildings or areas. In the current administration, some agencies believe they can downplay the importance of historic resources in planning and executing projects or issuing permits and licenses. Unfortunately, the only national organization whose compliance efforts were backed by the threat of litigation, the National Center for Preservation Law, has withdrawn from this role. However, the 1980 amendments to the National Historic Preservation Act provide for attorneys' fees for prevailing plaintiffs in suits to enforce the act's provisions, and this provision may help convince local preservation attorneys and their clients to enforce the law.[48] Moreover, the National Trust has recently indicated its intention to become directly involved

---

48. 16 U.S.C. § 470w-4 (1974 & Supp. 1982).

in litigation and has added an experienced attorney to its staff for that purpose.

Preservation Law at the Local and State Levels

As at the federal level, much of the focus at the state and local levels will be on refining existing laws to make them work better. Similarly, the challenge will be to take advantage of the great opportunities created by advances made during the 1970s, particularly in the face of national trends affecting preservation that are mirrored locally: budget cuts, a slowing of new regulatory efforts, and renewed support for economic growth. Add to these some powerful demographic trends, such as the movement of people to rural areas and the South and West, which will increase development pressures on landmark buildings, and the challenges at the local and state levels are indeed formidable, as are the opportunities.

As noted earlier, economics will play a significant role in preservation efforts. Preservationists will likely be called upon to help design local incentives—property tax breaks and the like—that are effective and efficient. In the current budgetary crunch, such incentives will be placed under increasing scrutiny. There also will be increased interest in regulations that, not only ensure protection against demolition (and there is no mistaking that such regulations will be as vital in the future as now), but that seek to rely on market forces to accomplish their objectives. Regulatory incentives, such as development bonuses and marketable development rights for owners who preserve their landmark buildings, may attract greater interest.

Preservation attorneys also will be more deeply involved in what might be called preventive maintenance. Instead of being called in for a court battle over a demolition, lawyers more frequently will be asked to render advice on how to avoid the courthouse. Responsible developers will rely more on lawyers who are mediators capable of working with preservationists and local officials to seek common ground. Preservationists will seek advice on how they can coordinate preservation laws with community development policies.

But though the marketplace will play a more important role in preservation, the lynchpin of an effective local preservation program will remain an effective ordinance that controls demolition and alteration. All the fine words about public/private partnerships and the importance of economics should not breed a false sense of security among preservationists. Compromise and reason will not always carry the day, and sometimes local governments will need to say no to a new project, asserting the public good over private interests. A strong local preservation ordinance is therefore a must. The challenge in the 1980s for preservation attorneys will be to fine tune existing laws and to prepare for increasingly sophisticated attempts to weaken or overturn them.

Likewise, while courts have shown a strong deference to local landmarks commissions in establishing and applying designation and review standards, we can expect increasing scrutiny now that landmark ordinances have real teeth and, as a result, serious economic consequences when applied in individual cases. No doubt there will be an increasing number of challenges based on claims that designation or permit review standards are unconstitutionally vague or that review procedures and hearings are inadequate.[49] Communities may find it necessary to be more precise in defining what is worthy of protection, particularly if the preservation movement continues to emphasize architecture and aesthetics while placing less emphasis on the historic.[50] Likewise, broad review standards may need fine tuning and narrowing in some instances, and more formal hearings may be required to protect affected interests.

Intergovernmental preservation conflicts—for instance, where a state- or county-operated hospital proposes to tear down a designated landmark against the wishes of a city preservation commission—are also likely to become more prevalent as more structures and districts are designated. These cases are particularly knotty and will require thoughtful balancing between the important societal interests that are often involved.

Small towns and rural areas will face some unique challenges. Recent census data confirm that Americans are, for a variety of reasons, moving to such locales in numbers never before witnessed. This movement has been a source of vitality in many communities as newcomers renovated old houses and injected funds into dying downtowns, but there is also a downside. Most rural jurisdictions and small town governments have neither the resources nor legal expertise to enact and implement a comprehensive preservation program that can deal effectively with new development pressures. And even those that do pass landmark ordinances sometimes find they lack needed legal, architectural, and other advice when time comes to make a decision. State governments will have a role in fill-

---

49. Standards and procedures are discussed more fully in chapters 2 and 5.
50. Architect John Wiebenson explores this phenomenon in an essay about the fate of the Rhodes Tavern in Washington, D.C. John Wiebenson, *The Rhodes Tavern Case: Are We Ignoring History?"* 34 Historic Preservation 12 (1982).

ing this gap as will statewide and national preservation groups and bar associations.

*   *   *

This handbook cannot, of course, predict the future or respond now to arguments that well may seem obvious a few years down the road. But it can, and we hope it does in the succeeding chapters, take a hard look at preservation law today and provide the reader with detailed suggestions regarding current preservation issues.

Chapter 2
Local Preservation Law

CHRISTOPHER J. DUERKSEN

During the 1970s, there was a flurry of preservation activity at the federal and state levels. Congress passed laws to strengthen protections for properties listed on the National Register of Historic Places and provided an increasing number of economic incentives for preservation. The states and their historic preservation offices emerged as important forces with the establishment of statewide preservation programs, often supplemented by state laws to protect landmarks and historic districts.[1]

But smart local preservationists were not lulled to sleep. They knew that the real responsibility and legal power to protect landmarks rested at home, at the local level. Listing a structure on the National Register was helpful but not an ironclad guarantee against demolition. True, such designation did lend prestige to the structure, could trigger helpful federal financial and tax provisions, and was useful when a federal action threatened a landmark. But preservationists recognized that, when the crunch came and an owner wanted to demolish, National Register status often would only delay things a bit. State landmark laws have not had much more success. Few states have done more than authorize local action; of those that have gone further, most require only the filing of an environmental impact statement or provide for a waiting period between an owner's filing a notice to demolish a building listed on a state landmark register and the actual deed.[2]

As the country enters the 1980s, it is not clear what role federal and state governments will play in preservation. Both levels of government

---

1. Throughout this chapter, the terms "landmark" and "historic district" are used interchangeably unless otherwise indicated. Generally, it is not of overriding legal significance whether a structure is designated individually as a landmark or is part of a larger historic district.
2. Chapter 3 discusses this issue more fully.

are going through a period of retrenchment due to fiscal belt-tightening. There also appears to be a conservative mood bent on less federal activism. Already Congress has enacted legislation allowing private landmark owners to veto the listing of their structures on the National Register, a step that may seriously erode the most important protections the Register now offers.

This is not to play down the vital role of the federal and state governments in historic preservation, particularly in building a positive framework for local programs and providing financial assistance, or to suggest that they will completely abandon the field. It is only to point out that landmark protection today is very much a local responsibility. Of course, none of this is news to experienced local landmarks commissioners, preservationists, or anyone who actually has tried to save a building or establish a historic district.

Many cities and towns already have adopted strong and imaginative preservation programs that not only protect their landmarks and districts and strengthen their localities' economic base but also ensure, through financial assistance and procedural safeguards, that property owners are treated in a fair and equitable fashion. It is not enough, however, simply to replicate these plans throughout the country—what's good for New York City may not play in Peoria. Each jurisdiction must carefully tailor its preservation program according to a host of variables.

From a strictly legal perspective, local preservation controls—the heart of any preservation program—are on firm ground. Just as the U.S. Supreme Court placed its imprimatur on zoning in the 1920s, so has it now spoken in favor of zoning's sibling, preservation controls, in the celebrated case involving New York City's Grand Central Terminal, *Penn Central Transportation Co. v. New York City*.[3] No longer can it be argued that the U.S. Constitution forbids local governments from enacting controls to protect landmark buildings and districts.

But that does not mean, of course, that preservationists can ignore the legal end of things. Far from it. Just as judges clarified the details of land-use controls in the years after the Supreme Court's pronouncements on zoning, so are modern-day jurists grappling with the details of local preservation controls—the standards and procedures, the economic issues, the practicalities of enforcement. Thus far, preservationists have an impressive record in the relatively few reported preser-

---

3. 438 U.S. 104 (1978).

vation cases—and they are few indeed when compared to the thousands of zoning cases in law reports—but the history of zoning cautions against declaring victory. Only two years after upholding zoning controls in *Euclid v. Ambler*,[4] the Supreme Court struck down a zoning ordinance in *Nectow v. Cambridge*.[5] By drafting preservation ordinances and administering and enforcing local regulations with care, preservationists can avoid a repeat performance.

Because of increasing judicial scrutiny, the local preservation ordinance and regulatory apparatus must be set up in accordance with state enabling legislation unless that state has adopted "home rule," which allows local governments greater flexibility. State court decisions also must be reviewed carefully; landmark controls that might pass legal muster in Maryland may have a very difficult time in more conservative jurisdictions.

From a practical point of view, preservation can succeed only if its goals become part of local growth and economic development policies. By exercising its police power through preservation ordinances and programs for landmarks and historic districts,[6] a locality can work affirmatively for conservation of the built environment, can control adverse alterations and demolitions, and can ensure compatible development around landmark buildings.

The type and number of landmarks to be protected will differ greatly from city to city and town to town, as will the pressures that threaten them. Local attitudes toward property rights and government regulation will dictate what is politically feasible, not just what is legally acceptable. This is what local preservation law is all about—a finely spun fabric of straightforward legal considerations similar to those found in local zoning, interwoven with practical economic and political notions.

Because of the variations and differences in state law, local politics, and the like, local preservation law cannot be capsulized with a few rules. Thus, the suggestions, advice, and examples that follow are just that. They are meant only as guidelines to aid communities in constructing a comprehensive program that will help protect their landmark structures and give them leverage in dealing with federal and state agencies; there is not an instant preservation ordinance to be found here.

---

4. 272 U.S. 365 (1926).
5. 277 U.S. 183 (1928).
6. "Police power" refers to a local government's general authority to enact laws to protect the public health, safety, and welfare.

Thus, this chapter is designed to help local preservationists think comprehensively when devising a positive local program to foster preservation of landmarks and their surroundings. Of equal importance is the advice it offers on how local governments can avoid the courthouse by establishing clear standards for designating landmarks and fair and efficient procedures for reviewing developments that might adversely affect them. It also aims to assist local governments in drafting plans that are legally defensible should a court challenge materialize.

Part 1 of the chapter focuses on why a local government should have something more than just a local landmarks ordinance and discusses how to put together a community preservation program. Part 2 turns its attention to the details of drafting a sound local ordinance, administering and enforcing it in a legally acceptable fashion, and defending that ordinance should it be challenged in court.

Part 1
The "Compleat" Preservation Program

WHY SHOULD A LOCAL GOVERNMENT HAVE A PRESERVATION PROGRAM?

To many people, a local government preservation program means a landmarks ordinance, administered by an official commission, that controls demolition and alteration of designated buildings. There is no denying that such ordinances are the heart of any preservation program, but just as Izaak Walton argued in the *Compleat Angler* that fishing is more than just casting a gob of worms and hoisting fish into a bucket, so too is the "compleat" preservation program more; it is based on a sound survey, it provides economic and technical assistance, and it is coordinated with other community policies and ordinances such as zoning.

There are a number of compelling reasons, both legal and practical, for a local government to adopt a preservation program that goes further than just an ordinance controlling demolition of landmarks. From a legal perspective, if a local government can demonstrate that it has made preservation part of its overall effort to foster and promote the general welfare and well-being of the community as a whole, the local landmarks law stands a better chance of surviving judicial scrutiny. The practical benefits are even more important. An effective preservation program will not only give local government access to federal and state funding and greater leverage over federal projects that affect historic properties and areas. It also can inject an element of certainty into the local development regulatory process, thereby fostering needed and compatible economic development.

The legal motive for adopting a community landmarks program is evidenced in the landmark U.S. Supreme Court decision *Penn Central Transportation Co. v. New York City*.[7] In that case, several justices were troubled by the apparent unfairness of treating a landmark owner differently from neighboring property owners. Grand Central Station had been designated as a landmark while many nearby buildings had not been. As a result, the Penn Central Company alleged it was being forced to preserve Grand Central Station in the public interest while surrounding property owners had wide latitude to redevelop their land in a very lucrative manner. Lower courts that heard the case expressed the same concerns. In fact, the New York Court of Appeals, while upholding New York's landmarks law and preventing alteration of the station, ventured that the "burden" of landmark designation "is borne by a single owner" and thus resembles "discriminatory" zoning restrictions that have been properly condemned over the past 50 years, since the Supreme Court approved the use of such controls by local governments.

This notion of fair and equal treatment in the application of land-use controls comes from both the Fifth and Fourteenth Amendments to the U.S. Constitution. The Fifth Amendment states, in part, that no person shall be deprived of property without due process of law. This injunction has been interpreted "to bar Government from forcing some people alone to bear public burdens which, in all fairness and justice, should be borne by the public as a whole."[8] Similarly, the Fourteenth Amendment forbids any state from denying "to any person within its jurisdiction the equal protection of the laws."

In theory, at least, these pronouncements have meant that all property owners in a designated area should be treated in a similar fashion and bear equally any land-use regulatory burden. If I cannot tear my home down to build a fast-food restaurant, at least I am assured my neighbor is similarly restrained. Any regulatory burden on one property owner is offset to a certain degree by the value of similar restric-

---

7. 438 U.S. 104 (1978).
8. Armstrong v. United States, 364 U.S. 40, 49 (1960).

tions on the use of neighboring land, what Justice Holmes once called "an average reciprocity of advantage." Equal treatment provides assurances against discriminatory government action.

One way state legislatures and courts in several jurisdictions have sought to protect further against discrimination in zoning is by requiring that all restrictions be based on an overall, comprehensive community master plan that indicates the general policies and guiding principles a community intends to follow in its development and growth.[9] The theory behind this approach was explained by a New York court:

> ... the comprehensive plan is the essence of zoning. Without it there can be no rational allocation of land use. It is the assurance that the public welfare is being served and that zoning does not become nothing more than just a Gallup poll.[10]

But where was this reciprocity of advantage in the *Penn Central* case? Where was the comprehensive plan? Penn Central argued that its neighbors who could build profitable high-rise office buildings had the advantage of a beautiful, not-so-profitable terminal nearby while Penn Central got nothing in return but a white elephant.

Three justices embraced this superficially appealing argument, but the majority disagreed, reasoning that, even though a landmarks law may affect some owners more than others, this fact does not render the law constitutionally invalid: "Legislation designed to promote the general welfare commonly burdens some landowners more than others."[11] The Court also stressed that the charge of discrimination was factually untrue because New York City had designated over 400 individual landmarks and 31 historic districts, a number of them in the vicinity of the Grand Central Terminal. Thus New York in effect did have a comprehensive landmarks plan that benefited all property owners, including the owners of the terminal:

> In contrast to discriminatory zoning, which is the antithesis of land use control as part of some comprehensive plan, the New York City law embodies a *comprehensive* plan to preserve structures of historic or aesthetic interest wherever they may be found in the city.[12] (Emphasis added.)

---

9. Comprehensive master plans typically set forth broad policies relating to land use, transportation, community facilities, housing, and so forth.
10. *Udell v. Haas*, 21 N.Y.2d 463, 469, 288 N.Y.S.2d 888, 893-94 (1968).
11. *Penn Central Transportation Co. v. New York City*, 438 U.S. 104, 133 (1978).
12. *Id.* at 132.

In essence, the Supreme Court was saying that the "comprehensive" landmarks plan could be found by looking at the local landmarks law and the buildings designated thereunder. Yet no one can go to city hall in New York and purchase a copy of a "comprehensive" landmarks plan the way he can purchase the New York City master plan on which zoning controls are based. The Court was forced to create a fiction, one that worked well because New York had been very active in designating landmarks and had coordinated its preservation activities with land use and zoning in the community in general. The Court apparently was borrowing its reasoning from early zoning cases in which zoning judges were forced to adopt a similar fiction. Most state enabling laws required that local zoning be "in accordance with a comprehensive plan." Many local governments, however, adopted zoning ordinances without first producing a document labeled "comprehensive plan." To avoid invalidating such ordinances, courts often held that the comprehensive plan was embodied in the zoning ordinances, regulations, and zoning maps.[13]

But what of the small town that has comparatively few significant structures? Or a big city like Chicago that has, compared to New York City, used its preservation ordinance sparingly? Would their landmarks laws stand up in court to a claim of discrimination? Based on the Supreme Court's language in *Penn Central*, it appears certain that they would. The fact that the burden of landmark protection falls generally more heavily on some owners than on others is of no constitutional import.[14] But in a close case in which a landmarks regulation is particularly onerous as applied to an individual property owner, a local government can strengthen its position substantially if that regulation is part of an overall landmarks program.

An overall community landmarks program is even more important from a practical, nonlegal standpoint. By reconciling and coordinating

---

13. The classic work on the role of the comprehensive plan in zoning is by Harvard professor Charles Harr, *In Accordance with a Comprehensive Plan*, 68 Harv. L. Rev. 1154 (1955). Professor Norman Williams also has written a useful analysis. Norman Williams, *American Land Planning Law* (Chicago: Callaghan, 1974), § 23.01 *et seq*. Charles Siemon and Wendy Larsen analyze recent cases in "In Accordance with a Comprehensive Plan—The Myth Revisited," in *Institute on Planning, Zoning, and Eminent Domain* (New York: Matthew Bender for Southwest Legal Foundation, 1979), p. 105.

14. See chapter 5 for a more thorough discussion of this point.

historic preservation policies with other local policies, such as housing, economic development, and transportation, historic preservation goals can be advanced in the broader context of community development. Administrators of these other programs are thereby given guidance on how to bring preservation into their efforts in a positive fashion rather than fighting it as a drag on economic development and growth. Another benefit is that last-minute battles to save landmarks, which have damaged the credibility of preservationists and developers alike, often can be avoided. Comprehensive landmark planning injects an element of certainty into the preservation regulatory system. Owners or potential developers know more precisely what they can and cannot do with landmark buildings, thus making ownership less burdensome and development plans less risky.

Federal legislation also puts a premium on local governments enacting effective preservation programs. In the past, local governments have had very little legal authority over the listing of local properties on the National Register of Historic Places, even though such a listing could slow and sometimes stop local development and revitalization plans. In the 1970s, a number of federally assisted local revitalization projects, particularly in central business districts, were thwarted or greatly delayed because of their impact on listed buildings—the ferocious battles in Charleston, Louisville, and Burlington, Vermont, are well known to most preservationists. Now, under the National Historic Preservation Act Amendments of 1980, local governments are given significant power over Register nominations if their local historic preservation programs meet certain minimum standards. Having a certified local program also opens the door for federal and state preservation funding programs.[15]

---

15. Pub. L. No. 96-515, 94 Stat. 2987, 16 U.S.C. § 470 (1980). Section 101(c)(1) of the act provides for state certification of local programs if the local government:

(a) enforces appropriate state or local legislation for the designation and protection of historic properties;
(b) has established an adequate and qualified historic preservation review commission by state or local legislation;
(c) maintains a system for the survey and inventory of properties . . . ;
(d) provides for adequate public participation in the local historic preservation program, including the process of recommending properties for nomination to the National Register;
(e) satisfactorily performs the responsibilities delegated to it under this Act.

Pursuant to Section 101(c)(3), only local programs that are certified or are in the process of certification are eligible for direct federal preservation grants to support

A comprehensive preservation program also gives local government greater leverage over federally funded or approved projects that adversely affect local historic areas. Under the National Environmental Policy Act, project proponents must take local land-use plans into account in evaluating the impact of a proposed development.[16]

But how can a local government best devise a community landmarks program? The following section addresses this crucial question.

WHAT MAKES A PRESERVATION PROGRAM "COMPREHENSIVE"?

Some people reacted to the *Penn Central* decision by recommending that local governments make haste to designate every potential landmark in sight—creating an instant "comprehensive" landmarks plan. But designating landmarks without adequate forethought is the antithesis of sound preservation planning. If we are to ask a relatively few property owners to preserve their landmarks, preservationists must ensure that the landmarks planning process is a rational one with careful surveys, adequate opportunity for hearings and comments on designation, and technical and economic assistance when appropriate. This does not mean that small towns must adopt a complex landmarks program akin to New York City's, with all its wondrous preservation devices administered by a professional landmarks commission and staff. A three-house historic district overseen by a volunteer landmarks body can pass the test if local preservationists do their homework.

Good landmarks programs will vary from jurisdiction to jurisdiction; there are, however, three elements that should be common to all. Each plan should contain a survey and study element that establishes the basis for designation and regulation. Technical and economic assistance, while not mandatory, can be useful. The landmarks program should also, to the extent feasible, be synchronized with the jurisdiction's comprehensive master plan, if one exists, and with the local zoning ordinance and other local regulatory programs, such as the building code. If all these elements can be reflected or referenced in a single document entitled "Comprehensive Preservation Program," so much the better, although, more

---

local programs as provided in Section 103(c). As of late 1982 it is not clear how much money, if any, will be available to certified local governments over the next few years, although if funds become available in the future, certified local governments will have first call on them.

16. See chapter 4 for a discussion of this point.

realistically, such a preservation program will likely be an amalgam of policies set forth in various policy statements, ordinances, and regulations. The important factor is that the local government consciously construct a preservation program, one that it can demonstrate existed prior to any legal challenge.

The Survey and Study Element

Several cities and towns across the country, emboldened by the *Penn Central* decision, already have responded by enacting strict preservation ordinances that forbid demolition of landmarks and by designating a wave of new landmarks. Undoubtedly, preservation commissions will, with increasing frequency, deny development that threatens a landmark. We can be equally certain that more landowners will challenge designations and permit denials and that courts will scrutinize even more carefully the actions of preservation commissions. This is not to say that local governments stand to lose every designation challenge. To the contrary, courts show an extraordinary deference to local designations in most instances in which the locality has made an honest effort based on the information before it. Indeed, designations probably will withstand judicial scrutiny even if credible supporting evidence and documentation are produced *after* the fact at trial. The local government's determination carries with it a "presumption of validity";[17] preservationists must take care that this presumption is not squandered.

There are, however, from a few courts, some rumblings of discontent about eleventh-hour attempts by local governments and preservationists to designate a landmark, thereby thwarting demolition or alteration permitted under the then-existing law. The case of *Texas Antiquities Committee v. Dallas Community College District*,[18] stands as a sober warning. There, the Texas Supreme Court, heavily influenced by what it perceived as a less-than-good-faith effort by preservationists who rushed through an application for National Register status without giving notice to the owner, permitted buildings of admittedly landmark quality to

---

17. See *Bohannan v. City of San Diego*, 30 Cal. App. 3d 416, 106 Cal. Rptr. 333, 336 (1973), upholding local determination of district boundaries; with regard to designation of individual landmarks, see *Manhattan Club v. New York City Landmarks Preservation Commission*, 273 N.Y.S.2d 848, 851(1966); *Society for Ethical Culture v. Spatt*, 68 App. Div. 2d 112, 416 N.Y.S.2d 246 (1979). The second part of this chapter explores this point more fully.

18. 554 S.W.2d 924 (Tex. 1977).

be demolished. Similarly, in *Life of the Land, Inc. v. City of Honolulu*,[19] the Supreme Court of Hawaii held that a developer who already had spent money on planning and design for a new high-rise could not be denied a building permit pursuant to a subsequently enacted preservation ordinance.[20]

This last-minute brand of planning can give preservation a bad name. At a conference in 1980, sponsored jointly by the National Trust for Historic Preservation and the Urban Land Institute, a think tank representing development interests, participants agreed unanimously that the most glaring weakness in the existing system was the lack of adequate inventories of landmark structures. Potential landmarks should be surveyed and the architectural or historical significance of individual landmarks and districts documented *before* designation takes place.

In the *Penn Central* case, the Supreme Court pointed out the importance of the survey and study element: the "function . . . of identifying properties and areas" of historical and architectural importance is "critical to any landmark preservation effort."[21] Historic building surveys are a key element in making city preservation planning and development goals complementary. Such surveys help in evaluating the impact of new development; they enable planning decisions to be made against a preservation background; they are useful in developing special planning tools and incentives; and, by making information available early in the project planning process, such surveys help the review process to operate more efficiently. The 1980 amendments to the National Historic Preservation Act also put a premium on surveys and inventories. Under Section 202(a) of the amendments, local governments must maintain surveys to be eligible for National Register nomination and funding programs.[22]

Ideally, such surveys will be conducted by experienced professionals, but there are no reported cases in which preservation ordinances have been struck down on the ground that a survey was inadequate or the surveyor unqualified. In smaller communities, volunteer efforts should

---

19. 606 P.2d 866 (Hawaii 1980).

20. Another case echoing the reasoning of these two decisions is *Committee to Save the Fox Building v. Birmingham Branch of the Federal Reserve Bank of Atlanta*, 497 F. Supp. 504 (N.D. Ala., Sept. 1980).

21. 438 U.S. 104, 110 (1978).

22. Pub. L. No. 96-515 (1980). The act also requires states to maintain a statewide inventory (Section 201(a)) and allows the secretary of the interior to make 70 percent grants for state and local surveys (Section 202(a)).

suffice, particularly when they draw on the extensive expertise available through state historic preservation offices, the federal government, universities, and preservation organizations such as the National Trust.[23] The key is to maintain high standards in documentation.

Using the survey as a guide, the community then should choose carefully those structures or areas it believes worth preserving. Attention to detail at this point will pay dividends later on, as cases from Colorado and North Carolina indicate. In *South of Second Associates v. Georgetown, Colorado*,[24] the Colorado Supreme Court struck down a preservation ordinance that designated the entire city as a historic district on the ground that, in practice, the local commission treated areas within the district differently, thus indicating that district boundaries should have been drawn with greater precision.[25] Similarly, in *A-S-P Associates v. City of Raleigh*,[26] a North Carolina appellate court questioned the inclusion of the plaintiff's property in a restrictive historic district zone around the governor's mansion when neighboring buildings had been specifically exempted:

> The record on appeal does not indicate that the defendant offered any explanation for its exclusion of the remainder of the properties of the State Medical

---

23. One good source is Harleyn McKee, *Recording Historic Buildings* (Washington, D.C.: U.S. Dept. of the Interior, 1970), which outlines the standards and techniques used by the Department of the Interior Historic American Buildings Survey (HABS). The National Trust also has a number of useful publications, such as *A Guide to Delineating Edges of Historic Districts* (Washington, D.C.: Preservation Press, 1976). Many state historic preservation offices have published useful survey guides. *College Hill: A Demonstration Study of Historic Area Renewal* (Providence, R.I.: City Plan Commission, 1959), with its thorough and detailed approach, has long been considered a model historic survey document. This study contains a detailed discussion of survey methodology. The New York City Landmarks Preservation Commission employs the most sophisticated survey techniques in the United States today, using a detailed computerized evaluation form. Information on New York's Urban Cultural Resources Survey can be obtained from the commission. For a discussion of the legal aspects of surveying, see the second part of this chapter.

24. 580 P.2d 807 (Colo. 1978).

25. The importance of careful surveys is also discussed in *Southern National Bank v. City of Austin*, 582 S.W.2d 229 (Tex. Civ. App. 1979); *Maher v. City of New Orleans*, 516 F.2d 1051, 1063 (5th Cir. 1975); and *Bohannan v. City of San Diego*, 30 Cal. App. 3d 416, 106 Cal. Rptr. 333 (Cal. App. 1973). A National Trust publication, *Delineating Edges of Historic Districts*, contains a good discussion of the factors to consider in establishing district boundaries.

26. 38 N.C. App. 271, 247 S.E.2d 800 (1978), *rev'd*, 258 S.E.2d 444 (N.C. 1979).

Society or other properties in nearby blocks from the requirements of the Oakwood Ordinance, while including the plaintiff's lot.

While this decision was subsequently reversed on appeal, the message is clear.

Surveys and studies cannot be done overnight. It takes time to gather essential documentation and to complete necessary fieldwork. When owners of potential landmarks catch wind of such activity, some will react by rushing to city hall for a demolition permit. The answer may be for the local government to enact a development or demolition moratorium during the study period. Zoning moratoriums ranging from six months to two years are routinely upheld by courts, which see them as preferable alternatives to hastily conceived permanent development bans.[27] Moratoriums likewise have been upheld in the landmark preservation context. In *City of Dallas v. Crownrich*,[28] the city successfully argued that a 60-day development moratorium was essential to protect landmarks while the city was formulating a preservation plan.[29]

Once a community has completed its initial survey and designated landmarks and districts, it should ensure that the survey is periodically reviewed and updated. Buildings that were overlooked the first time around may be discovered, or some that were consciously omitted may assume a new significance. What a community considers unworthy of protection may change over the course of only a few years.

Economic and Technical Assistance

Most local historic preservation plans focus on control—telling an owner or developer what can and cannot be done with the designated building. The U.S. Supreme Court condoned that approach in the *Penn Central* case, holding that the New York City ordinance had not deprived the railroad terminal owner of property rights by prohibiting construction of a high-rise above the station. In other words, the city regulation was not invalid simply because it prevented Penn Central from developing

---

27. Professor Norman Williams's treatise on planning law contains a general discussion of zoning moratorium cases and factors to consider in drafting and adopting moratoriums. Norman Williams, *American Land Planning Law*, 1980 Supp. (Chicago: Callaghan, 1980), § 30.01. The use of moratoriums in a preservation context is discussed in greater detail in the second part of this chapter.

28. 506 S.W.2d 654 (Tex. Civ. App. 1974).

29. See also *Don't Tear It Down, Inc. v. Washington*, 399 F. Supp. 153 (D.D.C. 1975).

its property for a more lucrative use. But it is also clear from the *Penn Central* decision that the Court was impressed by the fact that New York City had established a scheme to mitigate any financial burden on landmark owners, in this case, by adopting a system of transferable development rights (TDRs) that, in effect, allowed owners to sell the air rights over their buildings to developers of other parcels:

> . . . the New York courts here supportably found that, at least in the case of the terminal, the rights afforded are valuable. While these rights may well not have constituted "just compensation" if a "taking" had occurred, the rights nevertheless undoubtedly mitigate whatever financial burdens the law has imposed on appellants and for that reason, are to be taken into account in considering the impact of regulation.[30]

Thus while the U.S. Constitution did not require New York City to provide economic assistance in the form of TDRs, the city strengthened its hand by doing so.

This aspect of the *Penn Central* case teaches an important lesson: courts will view historic preservation regulations with greater favor if municipalities have made some form of economic assistance available to a landmark owner, particularly when a structure stands alone and is not in a historic district. In fact, such aid can help avoid litigation, particularly if a landmark owner faces economic hardship.

But does providing economic assistance mean that each city or town should offer TDRs, which are quite complicated to administer, as New York City does? Not necessarily—there are many other options available. As discussed in greater detail in chapter 7, many jurisdictions across the country are providing property tax breaks for landmark owners. Others have established direct grant programs or revolving funds for rehabilitation. Still others have passed laws enabling owners to donate facade easements to the local government or private organizations, thereby making the owner eligible for special federal income tax deductions. And money is not the only tool here. Several cities have initiated programs to help landmark owners obtain private financing for rehabilitation or locate prospective buyers. The possibilities are limitless. A city might adopt a policy to house government offices in designated buildings or establish a listing service to attract potential tenants to a landmark. These approaches have one thing in common; they will help defuse the economic issues surrounding landmark designation.

---

30. 438 U.S. 104, 137 (1978).

Not every community, particularly the smaller ones, will be able to offer the various forms of economic assistance noted above—nor does the law require that they do so. Fortunately, the economic development stakes are not as great in those places as they are in big cities in which millions of dollars may be involved in a single development.

In addition to economic assistance, cities and towns should recognize the importance of technical assistance for landmark owners. As Kent Barwick, chairman of the New York Landmarks Commission, has written: "Ignorance is still the greatest enemy of preservation. Much more technical assistance must be provided through publications and workshops."[31] Notwithstanding the publicity often given demolition battles, they are not the norm. Several cities, such as Seattle and Cincinnati, have set up special offices to advise owners and developers about their rehabilitation plans. Baltimore has gone another step. It runs a "salvage depot" that collects and sells hard-to-get furnishings—like oak doors, brass doorknobs, and similar items—for historic buildings.[32]

Again, the idea is to make preservation easy for landmark owners. Technical and economic assistance not only may help preserve buildings but also may help keep a difficult case out of court. And if litigation does arise, such aids may make the difference to a court that would like to uphold restrictions but is troubled by a seemingly severe economic impact on the owner.[33]

The Coordination Element

Why Coordinate?

Historic preservationists are beginning to realize that a local landmarks protection ordinance, standing alone, is only a first step. That ordinance and the goals it exemplifies must be coordinated with overall municipal planning and development goals to relate preservation to other elements, such as transportation, housing, economic development, zoning, and the like. Coordination is particularly important in medium-sized towns and larger cities. Too often, preservationists have struggled to enact an

---

31. Kent Barwick, *Landmarks Commission Should Stick to Basics*, 32 Historic Preservation 27 (July/August 1980).
32. For a description of this and other similar programs, see Vivian Martin, *Let the Salvage Buyer Beware*, 33 Historic Preservation 32 (March/April 1981).
33. See *Dempsey v. Boys' Club of the City of St. Louis*, 558 S.W.2d 262 (1977).

ordinance to control design details or forbid demolition by private developers in a historic neighborhood, only to discover that the real threat in the area is a city zoning policy encouraging high-rise development. In short, preservationists have focused on design issues and on saving threatened buildings when the key issue is more often how landmarks and their surrounding areas will be developed according to local zoning classifications and redevelopment programs.

To the extent possible, historic preservation goals should be made part of the local government's comprehensive master plan. For example, preservation and conservation might be made an integral element of a city's housing plan so that rehabilitation becomes an accepted alternative to redevelopment. Coordination might extend to smaller matters: placement and design of lighting and traffic signs or street widenings in historic districts might be made subject to review by the local landmarks commission.

In addition to these practical advantages, there are compelling legal reasons for coordination. A small but growing number of states require by law that local comprehensive plans include a preservation element.[34] Moreover, coordination strengthens the preservationists' position if the landmarks ordinance is challenged in court. In a recent case, the North Carolina Supreme Court upheld a historic district ordinance enacted by the city of Raleigh because, among other reasons, the city had adopted a comprehensive plan that included a preservation element:

> ... the evidence showed that before the City adopted the Oakwood Ordinance, planning studies of the area proposed to be included in the Historic District were conducted, which gave careful and comprehensive consideration to the potential effect on other ways in which the City is attempting to protect and promote the general welfare through the exercise of its zoning powers.[35]

The forethought shown by the city in considering the relationship between its comprehensive plan and its historic district ordinance helped

---

34. Such requirements vary greatly from state to state. Compare Oregon Land Conservation and Development Commission, *Statewide Planning Goals and Guidelines* (Salem, Or., 1980), p.7, Group 5, with the role of the state under Vermont's state land-use law as interpreted in *Committee to Save the Bishop's House, Inc. v. Medical Center Hospital of Vermont, Inc.*, 400 A.2d 1015 (Vt. 1979), for examples of state laws requiring a preservation element. Historic preservation is also a mandatory element of coastal plans under the federal Coastal Zone Management Act, 16 U.S.C. §§ 1451-64 (1977). For a more extensive discussion of the role of states in this area, see chapter 3.

35. *A-S-P Associates v. City of Raleigh*, 258 S.E.2d 444, 458 (N.C. 1979).

convince the court that the challenged restrictions were not arbitrary and unreasonable.

But coordination does not benefit preservationists alone. Developers recently have come to realize that the lack of coordination between local government development policy and preservation policy adds up to uncertainty—the bane of builders. A paper on historic preservation and development conflict published in 1980 by the Urban Land Institute stressed this point:

> Frequently it seems the responsibility for preservation plans and policies and development plans and policies is split between different local agencies and the respective policies and plans are pursued somewhat independently of one another. The conflicts are not exposed until a development project is announced which does not accord with preservation policy. The developer may have expended considerable time and money in formulating a project which he thought met local policy requirements, while the preservation agency was unaware of the project until late in the process.[36]

Coordination thus provides advantages for both preservationists and developers. By ignoring the need to coordinate or, more likely, putting it off until they solve the 101 day-to-day problems confronting them, preservationists are missing a real opportunity to work positively with the very interests they so often find sitting on the opposite side of the table.

Coordination also can provide practical bonuses for city governments. Increasingly bitter battles over federally funded local redevelopment projects that adversely affect landmark buildings are worrying federal officials who make those grants. If a city can demonstrate it has done its preservation homework, the money will flow more quickly. Local governments should be able to secure federal funding from discretionary programs, such as the Urban Development Action Grants (UDAG), much more expeditiously if their preservation program is in order. Coordination also can strengthen the position of a municipality when it is bargaining with the federal government over a federally funded or approved development project that the city opposes. For example, if a city has designated its downtown a historic district as part of a revitalization plan, the federal government will think twice about funding a state-supported highway project to widen the main street in the locality.

---

36. E. D. Baker and J. T. Black, "Historic Preservation and Development Conflict," a background paper prepared for the ULI-NTHP Symposium on Preservation and Development Accommodation (May 22, 1980), p. 8.

The arguments in favor of synchronization are compelling. This is not to say, however, that a municipality's preservation ordinance is legally defective without explicit coordination. The Supreme Court has held to the contrary. Furthermore, in small towns with only a few landmarks, the need to synchronize preservation policy with other ordinances is less urgent. As a practical matter, coordination will probably occur because municipal officials automatically will consider the impact of their actions on the one local historic district or prominent town landmark. Coordination is far more important in medium-sized towns and larger cities in which development pressures are more intense and conflicting municipal goals more common. But even there, a conscious coordination policy is not a legal requisite—it simply makes good sense.

How to Coordinate[37]

A municipality can coordinate in many ways. Including historic preservation goals in housing policy already has been mentioned as one example. City building codes might be amended so that archaic regulations do not frustrate rehabilitation of historic properties. Subdivision regulations might be rewritten to make parceling landmark properties, particularly large estates, less attractive.

The legal considerations and restrictions in coordinating preservation policy with other local programs are important but not overwhelming. The first step is to show the powers that be that coordination makes good sense, a task that, despite the logic behind coordination, is not always easy. Consider this example from Washington, D.C., a city that has one of the strongest preservation ordinances in the country.

In an area called Dupont Circle, one mile northwest of the White House, local preservationists have worked hard to protect a series of low-rise 1880s buildings, whose mansard roofs, scrolled gables, and chimneys give the neighborhood a distinctly European flavor. This neighborhood has attracted many professionals who want to live in a pleasant, diverse area close to where they work. But it has also brought developers who want to cash in on the surging demand for office and commercial space. The problem is that, while most existing buildings are no more than 50 feet tall, the zoning allows 90 foot structures. It is not hard to guess

---

37. A publication available from the State of California Office of Planning and Research, *Historic Preservation Element Guidelines* (Sacramento, 1976), contains an excellent practical discussion of how a community can ensure that other municipal programs complement historic preservation goals.

that there are plans to raze some of the historic buildings for more lucrative office blocks. Preservationists petitioned to have the height limit reduced from 90 to 50 feet, but the zoning commission was not sympathetic. Several commissioners concluded that "like it or not, there is another body charged with historic fabric—the law does not give us that responsibility." Not only is this position misguided as a matter of law—the D.C. courts have held that preservation is a proper concern in zoning decisions—but it is an incredibly narrow view of sound community planning that zoning and preservation must be pigeonholed and kept apart. Preservationists may face such insular attitudes in their campaign to coordinate.

While zoning probably will be the most important area that should be coordinated with preservation efforts, there are several other prime candidates: building codes, subdivision regulations, and the like.

Zoning. For most local governments, the first and most important step is to coordinate landmarks policy and regulations with the local zoning ordinance. This does not mean that preservation controls must be made part of the local zoning ordinance. In fact, in most states it is not legally mandatory that historic preservation policies and regulations be coordinated with the local zoning ordinance, and a few cities have pursued effective preservation policies without close coordination. As already noted, however, there are significant advantages in bringing historic preservation and zoning together.

Synchronizing historic preservation policy with the local zoning ordinance can ease pressure for altering or demolishing landmarks. Too often, historic preservation controls are enacted in a vacuum, becoming, in effect, another layer of regulation on top of existing zoning restrictions. Thus, a preservation ordinance may forbid alteration or demolition of a particular landmark while the applicable zoning classification provides an incentive to tear it down by favoring a more lucrative use.

Chicago's landmarks ordinance illustrates this point. The Chicago Landmarks Commission may, for example, recommend designation of an architecturally significant early 19th-century skyscraper in the Loop central business district. But, even if the city council approves that recommendation, the underlying zoning, which promotes redevelopment of the site with a much bigger and more profitable (both for the developer and city) new high-rise office building, typically remains unchanged. It is little wonder then that developers, with dollar signs dancing in their heads, submit plans to tear the landmarks down, and the city council regularly approves them. Recently, however, the council recognized that the zoning/preservation relationship is fundamental. To relieve development pressure in a historic area just north of the central business district, it enacted a general "downzoning" that decreased the size of buildings that could be built. That action was upheld against a claim that it violated the owners' property rights.[38]

A similar scene is played out on a different scale in many other towns. Old residential areas are often rezoned to a commercial status by city councils that hope to attract business to an area. In the meantime, the neighborhood is suddenly "rediscovered" by citizens who push for landmark designation. The underlying zoning remains the same, however, and almost inevitably, someone submits an application to tear down a landmark to make way for a fast-food restaurant or perhaps a hotel in order to cash in on the neighborhood's newly found affluence. These conflicts can be avoided if the zoning ordinance is changed to reflect historic preservation goals. Historic preservation should move beyond design and into the realm of zoning—density of development, types of permitted uses, and the like.

In their thoughtful book on the role of zoning in fostering city revitalization, zoning experts Clifford Weaver and Richard Babcock describe how the city of Seattle coordinated preservation efforts with zoning controls in an attempt to preserve the gains made by designating Pioneer Square as a historic district in the face of new development in an adjacent area:

> . . . there is a real threat to the vitality of Pioneer Square, and, as is often the case, it arises from an equally legitimate public decision, namely, to locate an enclosed 50,000-seat stadium near to the historic district. The potential threat to Pioneer Square was apparent. The stadium was an invitation to a proliferation of parking lots and fast-food franchises. Two steps were taken to mitigate any adverse impact. First, in another bold refusal to accommodate the motor vehicle, Kingdome was designed with only 1,800 public parking spaces. The ticket holder just does not have much choice: a shuttle bus system from downtown is heavily used when there is an event at the stadium. Second, because the historic district ordinance was concerned with architectural design, not use, an overlay ordinance creating a special review district was superimposed to control use and to limit the market that otherwise would have been stimulated by the stadium.[39]

---

38. *Amdur v. City of Chicago*, 638 F.2d 37 (7th Cir. 1980).
39. Clifford L. Weaver and Richard F. Babcock, *City Zoning: The Once and Future Frontier* (Chicago: Planners Press, 1979), p. 122.

Coordinating historic preservation policy with zoning also helps satisfy concerns about "comprehensiveness" expressed by the U.S. Supreme Court in *Penn Central*. Most towns and cities will not be able to meet that concern as New York City did by designating hundreds of landmarks and districts. In fact, many towns will have only a few landmarks or one historic district. The solution? That a single historic district can be made an integral part of the jurisdiction's zoning plan and given a preservation classification, just as an area with townhouses is classified multifamily residential.[40] An added benefit is that innovative zoning devices, such as development bonuses, planned unit developments, and special districts, can be used to foster historic preservation, thereby letting zoning work for preservation rather than against it, as is so often the case.[41] For example, a developer who saves a landmark as part of a major redevelopment plan might be given a bonus in the form of an increased density allowance for the rest of the project.

The link with zoning can be particularly important in cases in which large historic homes can no longer be feasibly used as single-family dwellings. This problem promises to be one of the most difficult preservation issues of the 1980s. If the zoning ordinance is not flexible enough to allow multifamily or nonresidential use, the only alternative may be demolition.

Denver has taken a common-sense approach to this problem, inserting a special-use variance in its local zoning ordinance that permits nonresidential use of landmarks in residential zones when the owner can demonstrate economic hardship. By limiting this type of relief, the variance provision avoids opening the door to widespread conversion of homes in residential areas to offices.[42]

---

40. American Law Institute, *A Model Land Development Code: Complete Text & Reporters' Commentary* (St. Paul, Minn., 1976). In this excellent source for anyone concerned with preservation law, the reporters recommend such an integrated approach. See § 2-209.

41. See Weaver and Babcock, *City Zoning*, p. 119. For an example of how one town integrated its preservation and zoning ordinances, see *Natale v. Kennebunkport Board of Zoning Appeals*, 363 A.2d 1372, 1374 (Me. 1976).

42. See Denver, Colo., Rev. Municipal Code § 611.6-4(3)(9) (1979). For a more detailed discussion of the legal aspects, see the section of this chapter entitled "Economic Hardship and Safety Valve Provisions." Courts generally have been quite liberal in allowing variations of zoning laws for preservation purposes. See *Coliseum Square Association v. Board of Zoning Adjustment of City of New Orleans*, 374 So.2d 177 (La. App. 1977), upholding the grant of a variance from local parking requirements

Links between preservation and zoning can be particularly crucial in a rural setting where protecting landscapes around landmarks is as important as protecting the structures themselves. A landmarks ordinance might designate individual buildings, while the local zoning ordinance ensures that incompatible development does not take place on surrounding property. Another approach, used in Loudoun County, Virginia, is to overlay historic district regulations on existing zoning controls so that any applications to construct, demolish, or alter a building in the district must have approval from the landmarks commission in addition to complying with zoning controls.[43]

From a legal point of view, perhaps the most significant reason for coordinating historic preservation with zoning has to do with how judges handle challenges to landmarks controls. While local and state court judges in many jurisdictions are familiar with the language of preservation and how preservation ordinances work, to some judges, such ordinances are still something different—newfangled devices that look suspiciously like sometimes-condemned aesthetic controls. While a majority of jurisdictions regularly uphold controls based solely on aesthetics, a few state and local courts still view them with a jaundiced eye.[44]

On the other hand, courts are more at ease with zoning and its well-established ground rules and language—zoning was approved by the U.S. Supreme Court over 50 years ago—and the validity of a zoning

---

to avoid demolition of part of a historic building. Preservationists should exercise a great deal of care, however, in drafting variance provisions and should keep an eye out for attempts to subvert the purposes they were enacted for. For example, in Denver, preservationists are concerned that while the office variance provision is a good one in theory, the local landmarks commission is undercutting historic areas by being too free with landmark designations that are a prerequisite to relief. As a result, owners of single-family structures that are designated as landmarks but are not of landmark quality are able to convert to more lucrative uses, much to the chagrin of their neighbors.

43. An excellent summary of the Loudoun County program is contained in *The Development of Rural Conservation Programs: A Case Study of Loudoun County, Virginia*, National Trust for Historic Preservation Information Sheet No. 29 (Washington, D.C., 1981). Most rural historic district ordinances do not cover buildings used primarily for agricultural purposes, although some ordinances do apply when the change would have clear and substantial detrimental impact on the district's character.

44. See *Board of Supervisors of James City County v. Rowe*, 216 Va. 128, 216 S.E.2d 199 (1975), *Euclid v. Fitzthum*, 48 Ohio App. 297, 357 N.E.2d 402 (1976), and similar cases discussed in *Aesthetic Zoning: The Creation of a New Standard*, 48 J. Urb. L. 740 (1971) and Williams, *American Land Planning Law*, 1980 Supp., § 1.243.

ordinance is assumed until proved otherwise. The U.S. Supreme Court in *Penn Central* recognized the similarities between historic preservation controls and zoning:

> When a property owner challenges the application of a zoning ordinance to his property, the judicial inquiry focuses upon whether the challenged restrictions can reasonably be deemed to promote the objectives of the community land-use plan, and will include consideration of the treatment of similar parcels. When a property owner challenges a landmark designation or restriction as arbitrary or discriminatory, a similar inquiry presumably will occur.[45]

The case of *Lafayette Park Baptist Church v. Scott*[46] illustrates the point from a practical perspective. There the court was faced with the first challenge ever in Missouri to a preservation law. The court found comfort in favorable preservation decisions from other jurisdictions but emphasized the fact that "such an ordinance is essentially a zoning ordinance and Missouri courts have frequently determined the validity and scope of those."[47] The court proceeded to approve of historic preservation ordinances because they met the test of validity applied in zoning cases—whether the restrictions bore a substantial relation to the public health, safety, or general welfare. "The ordinance," the court said, "is clearly in the best interests of the general welfare of the City of St. Louis."[48] Thus, in many instances, it will be desirable to offer preservation ordinances to the judiciary as land-use controls that differ little in principle from everyday zoning restrictions.

---

45. 438 U.S. 104 133 n.29 (1978).
46. 553 S.W.2d 856 (Mo. App. 1977).
47. *Id.* at 861.
48. *Id.* at 561. Also, in a case involving the Abe Lincoln Historic District in Springfield, Illinois, the Illinois Supreme Court put historic preservation ordinances and zoning within the same box. There, an irate landowner who claimed he had the right to build a drive-in restaurant near Lincoln's home challenged Springfield's refusal to allow any commercial uses in the district. The trial court ruled for the property owner, and the city took a special appeal to the Illinois Supreme Court. But that court refused to give special attention to the case, noting that it was "no different than a typical zoning dispute" and that no unusual constitutional arguments had been presented below. The case was thus transferred to a lower appellate court, which also viewed the action as nothing more than a garden-variety zoning case with the burden of proof on the landowner. It reversed the lower court decision and upheld the city's action. *Rebman v. City of Springfield*, 111 Ill. App. 2d 444, 250 N.E.2d 282 (1969). Similar language can be found in a number of other preservation cases, such as *Maher v. City of New Orleans*, 516 F.2d 1051, 1066 (5th Cir. 1975), and *Lutheran Church in America v. New York City*, 25 N.Y.2d 121, 359 N.Y.S. 200, 207, 217 (1974).

Once the decision is made to coordinate a municipality's preservation ordinance with its zoning plan, the question is how to do it. The options are many, ranging from full integration of the preservation controls to coordination through interagency agreements. The choice depends in part on practical considerations—the political power of preservation interests—and the statutory authority a city or town has. In some jurisdictions, such as Illinois, state law specifically allows the use of zoning for preservation purposes.[49] Those cases are the least difficult from a legal viewpoint. Historic areas can be placed in preservation zones with their own rules and regulations, or a historic district classification might be "overlaid" on existing zones, adding new regulations to current ones. Thus, preservation is made part and parcel of the local zoning law instead of the two working against each other.

Although full integration has much to recommend it, not every community will choose to pursue this approach. Practical considerations may dictate otherwise. Some state zoning enabling acts and local zoning ordinances require that final decisions on zoning regulations be made by a city council, zoning board, or planning commmission, which may not be sympathetic to preservation goals.[50] In these cases, final say over applications to demolish or requests for variances in a historic district may be taken out of the hands of the landmarks commission. Preservationists in each community will have to assess the advantages of full integration in the context of these considerations.

There are, of course, options available short of making preservation restrictions part of the zoning ordinance. If a city's preservation and zoning ordinances are to operate independently, then there should be a proviso in each that states, in the event of a conflict, the preservation ordinance and decisions made under it take precedence.[51] But while this type of provision is adequate for cases in which, for example, a zoning ordinance permits commercial development of a site occupied

---

49. Ill. Rev. Stat. ch. 24, § 11-13-1 (Supp. 1979). Home rule powers, which give municipalities greater authority to deal with local affairs, might be used where state enabling legislation is absent or restrictive.

50. See *Hayes v. Smith*, 167 A.2d 546 (R.I. 1961), for an example of a zoning board overruling a landmarks commission decision that rejected plans for an addition to a designated landmark. Similarly, in *Heritage Hill Association v. City of Grand Rapids*, 211 N.W.2d 77 (Mich. 1973), the town board granted a zoning variance to permit demolition of a church within a historic district.

51. See Rochester, N.Y., Code § 115-37(o)(2) (1980).

by a landmark residential structure, it may not be adequate when a proposed variance will have a deleterious impact on a landmark or district or when adverse developments are proposed in surrounding zones.

At a minimum, the landmarks commission should have an opportunity to comment on such change or development. Preferably, a provision would be inserted in the zoning ordinance stating that there is a presumption against developments, rezonings, and variances that adversely affect landmarks or historic districts (assuming that this is allowable under state enabling law). The landmarks commission might even be given veto power in certain circumstances. On the other hand, such provisions need not have only a negative orientation. The zoning ordinance might allow variances and special permits that otherwise would be rejected in historic areas *if* the modification would foster preservation and is supported by the landmarks commission. New York City, Denver, and a number of other communities across the country have already adopted this approach.

There are, of course, less legalistic means of coordination. For example, a zoning commission might enter into an informal agreement with the landmarks commission to notify it of all proposed developments in and around historic areas as well as information about proposed variances, special permits, and the like, that might affect designated landmarks. Similarly, the landmarks commission might be given a chance to participate in hearings on major areawide rezonings. While such arrangements may not be as satisfactory as a statutory requirement, they are much better than no coordination at all.

Thus, there are a variety of methods that can be used to coordinate. Differences in legal and institutional arrangements mean there is no right or wrong way to coordinate, a situation that presents opportunities for creative approaches.

Building Codes. Synchronization of local preservation and zoning ordinances is only a first step, albeit an important one. Preservationists also need to focus on the relationship between building codes and landmarks policies.[52] Architects involved in preservation rehabilitation projects can tell frustrating tales of projects delayed or thwarted because of a door that opened inward instead of outward or because of a stairway that was two inches too narrow—all in violation of a building code

---

52. This section focuses on building codes, but the discussion is equally applicable to other ordinances designed to protect the public health and safety, such as fire, health, and housing codes.

written for new ranch-style houses or modern shoe-box high-rises.

The basic conflict is that building officials look first at the safety of a building as defined by a city code and only secondarily at its landmark qualities and the desirability of retaining the structure. As one code official explained, the burden of proof rests with preservationists when an old landmark building is being renovated for a new use: "The structure should be considered as having characteristics that are a potential threat until a thorough investigation has either vindicated it or confirmed the presence of provable dangers."[53] Building code officials are not natural enemies of preservation; they simply march to the tune of a different drummer—hence the "show me" attitude.

Great strides have been made over the last decade to reconcile preservation goals with building code requirements; the National Trust for Historic Preservation, the American Institute of Architects, and the Building Officials and Code Administrators International (BOCA) have led the way. A 1976 survey of 47 states disclosed that 16 had adopted special provisions or administrative regulations applicable to the renovation of historic or architecturally significant buildings; 15 of 24 cities surveyed followed a similar course.[54] Perhaps most significantly, BOCA amended its Basic Building Code, which serves as a model for many communities, to make special provision for rehabilitation of landmark buildings:

> The provisions of this code relating to the construction, repair, alteration, enlargement, restoration and moving of buildings or structures shall not be mandatory for existing buildings or structures identified and classified by the state and/or local government authority as historic buildings, subject to the approval of the board of appeals when such buildings are judged by the Building Official to be safe and in the public's interest of health, safety and welfare regarding any proposed construction, alteration, repair, enlargement, relocation, and location within the fire limits. All such approvals must be based on the applicant's complete submission of professional architectural and engineering plans and specifications bearing the professional seal of the designer.[55]

The BOCA approach represents a balanced effort to reconcile safety considerations with preservation goals.

---

53. Robert Bannon, "Historic Buildings and the Uniform Building Code," in *Preservation and Building Codes* (Washington, D.C.: National Trust for Historic Preservation, 1975), p. 61.

54. Green and Cooke, *Survey of Building Code Provisions for Historic Structures*, Technical Report No. 918 (Washington, D.C.: National Bureau of Standards, 1976).

55. Building Officials & Code Administrators International, Inc., Basic Building Code, § 516.1 (Homewood, Ill. 1981).

The local preservationists' role is to ensure that their city's or town's building officials follow the BOCA example. In states that have uniform building codes applicable to all municipalities, the first step is to check state law to determine if it has a BOCA-type clause. If it does, the local building code official should be made aware of it. If not, some legislative work is in order. If, however, municipalities in a state are free to adopt their own building codes, then preservationists should review the local code to see if the BOCA approach, in one form or another, has been adopted. There is nothing sacred about the BOCA language—flexibility is the key.

If an amendment to the local code is necessary, building officials should be approached in the spirit of cooperation. Most can be persuaded that changes are in order if preservationists (1) present a thoughtful case—for example, by presenting problems already being encountered in the community because of an inflexible code; (2) make clear that the change being proposed is nothing radical by listing other communities that already have taken such a step; and (3) facilitate efforts by having amendatory language based on the BOCA model code already drafted. Building code officials can be great allies of preservation if approached in a positive fashion.

Preservationists also must keep an eye on amendments to state and local building codes to make certain that the codes do not inadvertently hinder rehabilitation. For example, many jurisdictions are considering energy-saving code provisions that may be difficult for old buildings to meet if they are renovated. Energy conservation goals should not be pursued with blinders on. Special provisions for energy efficiency in landmark buildings may be necessary; but, at a minimum, codes should retain flexibility so that preservation efforts are not thwarted. Historic structures should not be turned into altars to the gods of solar energy, leaving their exteriors a tangle of angled glass panels, copper tubing, and black paint. By the same token, landmark controls should be drafted with some flexibility to allow use of energy-saving devices, such as solar panels, that are sensitively designed and located.[56]

In addition to the substantive provisions of building codes, preservationists should pay attention to the procedure for granting building permits. In the past, there have been instances in which building per-

---

56. For a discussion of a Connecticut report recommending standards for reviewing solar energy systems, see 6 Landmark and Historic District Commissions 2 (April 1980), p. 1.

mits (or demolition permits) have been issued by the city building department despite the fact that the landmarks commission had not approved the projects. Preservationists should make certain that the local law clearly states that no building permits should be issued, even if the local code is met, unless approval for the development or change has been issued by the landmarks commission.

Subdivision Regulations. Ask most preservationists how their community's subdivision regulations affect historic preservation and you are apt to get blank looks from them. Local governments are generally authorized or required by state law to adopt regulations controlling the design and improvement of land subdivisions before land is developed. Regulations setting minimum lot size, street widths, and other improvement standards are normally associated with new suburban residential developments. Some states allow local governments to exact land or money from developers for parks, schools, and sewers in return for subdivision approval. Given these characteristics, the link between subdivision regulation and preservation of older structures is not readily apparent.

But note this example of how a developer can thwart preservation restrictions through subdivision of a lot. The owner of a landmark midrise apartment building surrounded by a large, private park-like garden decides to make more money on his investment. The owner cannot tear down the apartment building and construct something bigger, but nothing stops him from subdividing his parcel and selling off the garden to a developer who will build the high-rise. And once the garden is sold, it is very difficult from a legal standpoint to stop the new development.[57] Sound far-fetched? With only minor variations, just such a case was decided in the developer's favor in *Fred R. French Investing Co. v. New York City*.[58]

The problem of subdivision regulations also arises in the context of large estates that have been designated as landmarks. Several years ago, preservationists in the suburbs of a midwestern city discovered that a

---

57. In the *Penn Central* case, the U.S. Supreme Court rejected Penn Central's argument that the city had "taken" its air rights over the terminal by refusing to allow the railroad to build a high-rise above it, noting that for purposes of constitutional analysis a parcel could not be divided into discrete elements. However, if Penn Central had sold the air rights and the purchaser could not have developed them, the outcome might have been different.

58. 39 N.Y.2d 587, 385 N.Y.S.2d 5 (1976).

mansion they thought was safe would soon be surrounded by new homes on the estate grounds. They had forgotten to specify anything about new construction in their preservation ordinance and had overlooked the fact that local subdivision regulations allowed the surrounding grounds to be cut up into small parcels without considering preservation measures.

Only in a few cities and towns have preservationists made certain that subdivision regulations do not work against preservation. The District of Columbia has been a leader, enacting the following language:

> (a) Before the Mayor may admit to the record any subdivision of an Historic Landmark or of a property in an Historic District, the Mayor shall review the application for admission to record in accordance with this section. . . . (e) No subdivision subject to this act shall be admitted to the record unless the Mayor finds that admission to the record is necessary in the public interest or that a failure to do so will result in unreasonable economic hardship to the owner.[59]

Preservationists should examine their local situations to determine if subdivision problems might arise. If so, the District of Columbia ordinance offers a model to follow.[60]

Coordination with Other Laws and Ordinances. In addition to zoning ordinances, building codes, and subdivision regulations, local governments have a host of other laws that affect preservation efforts. Many cities have sign controls, others have open space ordinances, and an increasing number have environmental protection laws. These laws should be coordinated with a locality's preservation law to make sure they do not work against protection of landmark structures and districts. For example, many coastal communities have prepared plans, pursuant to the federal Coastal Zone Management Act,[61] for the conservation and development of the coastal zone within their respective jurisdictions. Federal regulations require that these plans have a historic resource element. Preservationists should make sure that the coastal plans do, in fact, adequately address landmark protection. Similarly, a number of communities, such as Rochester, New York, have environmental impact laws that require an assessment of the environmental impacts of municipal projects or actions. However, these laws do not always clear-

---

59. The Historic Landmark and Historic District Protection Act of 1978, D.C. Law 2-144 §§ 7(a) and 7(e).

60. As usual, a caveat is in order. Enabling authority, either state or local, must exist to control subdivision for preservation purposes.

61. 16 U.S.C. § 1451 (1977).

ly apply to decisions affecting the built environment or historic resources.[62] Preservationists should work to ensure that such laws do apply.

Perhaps one of the most innovative approaches to coordinating preservation with other local programs can be found in Seattle and Cincinnati. These cities have created the post of an urban conservator, who not only serves the local landmarks commission but also works with the city planning and other departments to ensure that preservation goals are considered in their programs.

These are only a few examples. The message here is that preservationists should stop thinking of their mission and the means to accomplish it in narrow terms. By making preservation part of the fabric of local government development and conservation policies, preservationists can better achieve their ambitious agenda.

Part 2
Drafting and Administering the Ordinance

It is important for preservationists and local governments to do their homework and outline a comprehensive approach to preservation before drafting a law or ordinance to control demolition of landmarks. But the local preservation ordinance will undoubtedly be the centerpiece of any local effort, the heart of its preservation plan. It may create a powerful landmarks commission with the authority to deny any application to demolish a designated landmark, or it may establish a board with little power to do anything more than advise the local legislative body on preservation matters. Just as each community is unique, so will each preservation ordinance be unique. Ordinances across the country

---

62. See *Hoboken Environment Committee, Inc. v. German Seaman's Mission of New York*, 161 N.J. Super. 256, 391 A.2d 577 (1978), holding that the granting of a demolition permit is not a municipal or state action subject to review under state environmental rights law. Contrast this case to the decisions holding that the National Environmental Policy Act (NEPA) requires the preparation of an environmental impact statement assessing the impact of federal or federally funded projects on the built environment. See *Hanly v. Kleindienst*, 471 F.2d 823 (2d Cir. 1972); *City of Rochester v. United States Postal Service*, 541 F.2d 967 (2d Cir. 1976).

are becoming more dissimilar all the time, as communities adopt new laws or rewrite old ones to fit their particular needs. Officials at the Department of the Interior report there is a remarkable and growing diversity among the local ordinances they review for federal tax certification purposes. As Richard Roddewig, a land-use and preservation attorney from Illinois, advises localities considering entering the landmarks field:

> Local historic preservation ordinances are like old buildings. No two are alike. Nor should they be. It took skilled craftsmen to hew the grey stone in the fine old mansions of Chicago's Astor Street, to carve the Italianate bracketing in the river mansions of Galena, and to assemble the marble mosaics of the State Capitol. It takes some old-fashioned craftsmanship and 20th-century ingenuity to create a local preservation ordinance that fits the needs and aspirations of a particular Illinois community.[63]

For these reasons, an ordinance cannot spring forth from a legal form book or by copying another locality's law. While drafting aids can be very useful (an excellent compilation of model provisions prepared by the National Trust is included as appendix A), each ordinance must be tailored to meet local needs, state enabling authority, and applicable judicial guidelines.

This section is designed, first, to help communities ask the right questions when they reach the ordinance-drafting stage. Does state law prescribe a particular form for organizing a local preservation commission? What powers should the local commission have? What is the best way to review proposals to designate landmarks? How should restrictions on local landmarks be enforced?

The section also suggests the basic components of an effective preservation ordinance, ranging from the purpose clause to enforcement provisions, and offers advice on drafting and administering these components so they are effective and legally defensible. And for those communities that already have preservation commissions and ordinances—by last tally, they numbered over 900—this section suggests revisions to ensure that those ordinances will work efficiently and will survive the increasing judicial scrutiny that is sure to come in the 1980s, especially in the area of designation standards and procedures. As one preservation attorney quipped, "A preservation ordinance, like a historic

---

63. Richard J. Roddewig, "Components of a Good Historic Preservation Ordinance," a speech delivered to a Historic Preservation Commissions conference in Springfield, Illinois (April 28, 1979).

building, may need restoration or renovation occasionally."

THE FIRST STEPS IN DRAFTING

Recognition of Enabling Authority

A fair number of landmarks ordinances have their beginnings around a kitchen table on a Sunday afternoon. With laws from other cities and towns in hand, preservationists gather to start the drafting process. A prerequisite to these kitchen klatches is a thorough understanding of the degree of local government authority available in adopting a preservation ordinance. In some jurisdictions, where local communities can exercise only those powers specifically granted to them by the state, state legislation enabling preservation must be followed very closely. Thus, although a town in Virginia may desire to adopt a landmarks ordinance that would allow a local commission to forbid demolition of any designated building, that state's preservation enabling legislation has narrowly defined and limited the powers that a locality may exercise. In fact, some localities (for example, counties in Ohio) have no power whatsoever to adopt preservation laws.

In contrast, local governments in other states have several options. In Illinois, for example, communities might rely on the state preservation enabling law or on their general zoning power (which state law allows to be used for preservation purposes) or, depending on their population, on inherent home rule powers granted by the Illinois Constitution.

In many instances, the state enabling legislation will grant local governments adequate power to adopt effective ordinances. However, when enabling legislation is absent or found wanting, communities might invoke their zoning powers to supplement or replace this basic authority. Many state zoning enabling acts (in California and Illinois, for example) specifically allow municipalities to use their zoning authority for preservation purposes. Similarly, a majority of states grant some form of home rule authority to local governments, either by statute or constitutional provision.[64] While the scope of home rule authority varies widely from state to state, such power, if available, may offer local govern-

---

64. McQuillan, *Municipal Corporations*, 3d ed. (Chicago: Callaghan, 1971). Some municipalities operate under charters that also grant them wide latitude in dealing with issues of local concern.

ments the opportunity to tailor a local preservation law to fit the unique needs of the community. The key here is to undertake some basic legal research to determine what authority is available; because there may be a variety of sources on which to base the local landmarks law, it should cite specifically its source of legitimacy.[65]

Anyone drafting a preservation ordinance also will have to pay close attention to local ordinance review guidelines applied by the U.S. Department of the Interior. If these guidelines are not met, local properties will not be eligible for federal tax benefits for rehabilitation of landmarks nor will the local government be able to participate in National Register nomination and funding programs.[66]

Defining Local Goals and Capabilities

Once the applicable statutory authority is ascertained, the community will need to ask a number of questions before beginning to draft the ordinance. The answer to these questions will help shape the community's preservation ordinance. Following are suggestions of some key issues to be addressed.

Defining a Purpose. Asking the question "Why preserve?" is a crucial step in determining the form and scope of any preservation ordinance. What is the reason for preservation in the community? Is it important from an economic standpoint, or is the interest mainly architectural or historical? Can preservation be linked with neighborhood conservation?

Deciding What to Protect. Does the community have only a few scattered buildings worth saving, or should the focus be broader—on districts and neighborhoods? Has a survey already been conducted, or must this information still be developed?

---

65. See *People ex rel. Marbro Corp. v. Ramsey*, 28 Ill. App. 2d 252, 171 N.E.2d 246 (1960), in which a city exceeded its statutory authority in delaying a demolition permit. Note, however, that state enabling authority may be altered from time to time, either substantively or merely by renumbering provisions in the state statute book. Preservationists should review state enabling acts periodically to make certain any reference in their local ordinance is current.

66. These guidelines can be found in the Code of Federal Regulations (36 C.F.R. 67) and in the National Historic Preservation Act Amendments of 1980, Pub. L. No. 96-515, § 101(c)(1), 94 Stat. 2988, 16 U.S.C. § 470 (1980). In general, they require that the local law establish a review body with adequate powers to protect designated landmarks and districts and to review applications for alteration or demolition. The Department of the Interior is now in the process of writing new regulations pursuant to Pub. L. No. 96-515.

What features of historic buildings are important and worth preserving? Should the focus be on exterior facades or on interior features, on open space associated with historic resources or new construction in historic areas?

What is the current state of repair of historic resources in the community? Are they in need of renovation, and if so, is it realistic to expect rehabilitation to occur? Is maintenance of existing structures a concern?

Deciding How to Protect What the Community Values. After determining enabling authority, preservationists need to consider the best way to protect landmarks and historic areas. What is the primary use of existing historic structures? Residential, commercial, industrial, or a mix? Who owns the key structures—homeowners, businesses, charitable organizations, the government?

Is there a general understanding of and sympathy toward preservation? How is this reflected in the community, by business, or within the local government? Do citizens see a need for action to preserve landmarks?

Is a strong preservation ordinance liable to be attacked? If so, would the local government be willing and able to defend it, or would that task fall to local preservationists?

Have state courts rendered any relevant decisions in historic preservation cases? Are there decisions in allied fields, such as land-use, zoning, or administrative law, that should be considered?

Do preservationists have confidence in existing community zoning and land-use planning mechanisms? Will the local zoning board and planning commission be knowledgeable and sensitive to preservation goals? Should one of those bodies wear the official preservation mantle?

Are there currently any threats to a particular landmark or historic area calling for immediate action? What about future development threats?

Administering and Enforcing the Ordinance. The ordinance should be drafted to meet the goals of effectiveness, administrative efficiency, and fairness to parties involved in the process. What kind of preservation-oriented talent is available in the community? Are there enough knowledgeable people to run yet another volunteer commission or advisory group? Can the local government supply staff to support a new landmarks body?

Are the important historic or architectural features of buildings in the community of one style or type? Are they easily identifiable? Can clear and understandable standards and criteria for designation and permit review be devised?

How will the ordinance be enforced? Does the local government have the capability to monitor developments in the community, or will that task fall to preservationists?

Only after these questions have been considered should the drafting of a new ordinance (or the redrafting of an existing one) begin. The answers to such questions, combined with the community's legal authority, will help shape the most appropriate local ordinance. Perhaps the most important thing to keep in mind is that each community is unique, and those drafting the ordinance should not feel constrained by what other cities and towns have done.

DRAFTING THE KEY PROVISIONS OF A PRESERVATION ORDINANCE

While no two preservation ordinances will or should be identical, all will have basic provisions setting forth fundamental purposes, creating a review body and granting powers to it, establishing review procedures, and so forth. Within these provisions, there is likely to be wide variation from community to community. Thus, rather than suggesting specific model language that can be adapted in all cases, this section raises various issues that should be considered in drafting the key sections of any ordinance.

For example, when defining what powers and duties might be given to a landmarks commission, preservationists should focus on the crucial issues of controlling adverse alterations, demolitions, and new construction rather than on less critical points, such as granting the landmarks body power to receive funding from outside sources or to employ staff. For more detailed language and examples of what other communities have done, the reader should refer to appendix A, the National Trust model preservation ordinance.

The Purpose Clause

The purpose clause sets forth the local government's reasons for enacting the preservation law. These reasons generally fall into four categories:

Economic. Preservation can be very important to the community's economy, usually through business and jobs generated by renovation activities and tourism. Stabilization and improvement of property values are also relevant.

Educational/Cultural. Preserving landmarks and architecturally significant structures contributes to the community's sense and understanding of its history and ensures that its cultural and historic heritage will be imparted to present and future generations.

Social. Preservation can contribute to urban and neighborhood conservation or to the character of a town and thus to the "quality of life" and social fabric of the community.

Aesthetic. Preservation contributes to the beauty and livability of the community.

There are compelling practical reasons for invoking a variety of positive purposes to support a preservation ordinance. In mustering political support for a landmarks law, preservationists often will find it necessary to build a broad-based coalition of community interests. Support from the local historical society will not usually be enough, particularly in larger towns and cities. Business people must be persuaded that the preservation law will not stifle growth. If a link between preservation and tourism can be established, so much the better, but often a more subtle argument will have to be constructed, one that links the strength of neighborhoods to the community's economic well-being. The promise of neighborhood conservation also can attract activists intent on maintaining the strength of their local communities. Appeals to civic pride, for example, by preserving the work of a particularly well known local architect or the home of a local luminary, are also important. By thinking through carefully the many and diverse reasons for enacting a landmarks ordinance, preservationists can begin to mold the political support they will need to pass a local landmarks law.

A purpose clause also can be useful administratively as a guide to later landmarks commissioners and others who must implement the preservation law. Similarly, the purpose clause can be important from a legal perspective, although an ordinance will rarely, if ever, fail based only on an inadequate purpose clause. In fact, there are no reported cases of any jurisdiction striking down a preservation ordinance solely because of a faulty statement of purpose. In the early years of preservation, ordinances were often grounded in their importance to the community's economy, but in the *Penn Central* decision, the U.S. Supreme Court recognized that preservation ordinances enacted solely for aesthetic reasons—as opposed to economic ones—are valid under the U.S.

Constitution:

> ... this Court has recognized, in a number of settings, that states and cities may enact land-use restrictions or controls to enhance the quality of life by preserving the character and desirable aesthetic features of a city. . . . New York City's objective of preserving structures and areas with special historic, architectural, or cultural significance is an entirely permissible governmental goal.[67]

That is not to say, however, that the purpose clause does not demand attention. From a legal viewpoint, the purpose clause can serve an important function. While the general trend is clearly toward a view that land-use ordinances can be based on aesthetic purposes alone, some local and state court judges are uneasy with laws based solely on aesthetic goals, which are, to a certain extent, inevitably subjective. A few courts still hold that, under *state* constitutional principles or statutory authority, aesthetic considerations alone are inadequate.[68] These same judges, however, may accept goals such as promoting the local economy, fostering neighborhood conservation, or educating the citizenry. There are many cases from the formative years of preservation law in which the local ordinance was upheld because controls were linked with the economy of the community, particularly through tourism. A case involving historic Nantucket, Massachusetts, is a good example. There, the Supreme Judicial Court of Massachusetts upheld the state legislation designed to protect a historic area on Nantucket:

> We may also take judicial notice . . . that the sedate and quaint appearance of the old island town has to a large extent still remained unspoiled and in all probability constitutes a substantial part of the appeal which has enabled it to build up its summer vacation business to take the place of its former means of livelihood. . . . It is not difficult to imagine how the erection of a few wholly incongruous structures might destroy one of the principal assets of the town. . . .[69]

---

67. 438 U.S. 104, 129 (1978).

68. See *Board of Supervisors of James City County v. Rowe*, 216 Va. 128, 216 S.E.2d 199 (1975), where the Virginia Supreme Court expressed its uneasiness with regulations based solely on aesthetics. Similar cases are compiled in *Annot.* 21 A.L.R. 3d 1222 (1968). Recently, courts in Tennessee and North Carolina have accepted the proposition that zoning and other police power regulations may be founded primarily on aesthetics and goals. *State v. Smith*, 618 S.W.2d 474 (Tenn. 1981); *State v. Jones*, 281 S.E.2d 91 (N.C. App. 1981).

69. *Opinion of the Justices to the Senate*, 128 N.E.2d 557, 562 (Mass. 1955). Similar language can be found in *Maher v. City of New Orleans*, 516 F.2d 1051 (5th Cir. 1975), *cert. denied*, 426 U.S. 905 (1976); *City of New Orleans v. Impastato*, 198 La. 206, 3 So.2d 559 (1941); *Lafayette Park Baptist Church v. Scott*, 553 S.W.2d

The approach to dealing with the bias of some judges against aesthetically-based enactments is obvious. The purpose clause should invoke a range of reasons for enacting the ordinance—aesthetic, cultural, social, and economic. Future challenges to preservation ordinances will, in many situations, attempt to frame the case as an aesthetic one on the theory that, the more a landmarks law looks like a subjective aesthetic control, the greater its chance of failure. While it can be argued that adverse precedents from aesthetic zoning cases are inapplicable to historic preservation,[70] already a number of communities have adopted the approach of invoking a variety of purposes, and their ordinances have won judicial approval. A case from North Carolina, upholding the city of Raleigh's preservation law, illustrates the increasingly sophisticated judicial view of preservation:

> The preservation of historically significant residential and commercial districts protects and promotes the general welfare in distinct yet intricately related ways. It provides a visual, educational medium by which an understanding of our country's historic and cultural heritage may be imparted to present and future generations. That understanding provides in turn a unique and valuable perspective on the social, cultural, and economic mores of past generations of Americans, which remain operative to varying degrees today. Historic preservation moreover serves as a stimulus to protection and promotion of the general welfare in related, more tangible respects. It can stimulate revitalization of deteriorating residential and commercial districts in urban areas, thus contributing to their economic and social stability. It tends to foster architectural creativity by preserving physical examples of outstanding architectural techniques of the past. It also has the potential, documented in numerous instances, e.g., in the Vieux Carre section of New Orleans, of generating substantial tourism revenues. Although it is also recognized that historic preservation legislation, particularly historic district ordinances, may adversely affect the welfare of certain segments of society and infringe on individual liberty, the wisdom of such legislation is "fairly

---

856 (Mo. App. 1977); *City of Santa Fe v. Gamble-Skogmo, Inc.*, 73 N.M. 410, 389 S.W.2d 13 (1964).

70. As the New Mexico Supreme Court explained in upholding Santa Fe's preservation law, "The cases relied upon by defendants deal with purely aesthetic regulations having no connection with preservation of an historical area or an historical style of architecture, and are, accordingly, either distinguishable upon their facts or are not persuasive under the facts of the instant case." *City of Santa Fe v. Gamble-Skogmo, Inc.*, 389 S.W.2d 13, 17 (N.M. 1964). The North Carolina Supreme Court agreed in *A-S-P Associates v. City of Raleigh*, 258 S.E.2d 444, 450 (N.C. 1979). Courts have recognized that landmarks controls are typically administered by an expert body applying standards and criteria based on a distinctive architectural style.

debatable," precluding substitution of our judgment for that of the General Assembly.[71]

In addition to helping meet concerns about aesthetic regulation, the purpose clause will help establish the rationality of a commission's action in reviewing a demolition or other permit application. For example, in *Groch v. City of Berkeley*,[72] the plaintiffs argued that a local preservation law was vague because it gave no guidance to the Board of Adjustment in reviewing demolition permit applications. The court rejected this argument on the ground that the purpose clause gave clear and explicit guidance that the board had to consider in granting or denying a permit.

Creating a Review Body: Composition and Grant of Powers

The composition of a review body created by a landmarks ordinance and the powers granted to it are two of the most crucial drafting considerations. The possible variations are virtually endless, limited mainly by state enabling legislation, relevant judicial decisions, and practical political and staffing considerations.

Composition

The composition of a landmarks commission is important from both a legal and a practical standpoint. A broadly based membership can protect the ordinance and its administration from a claim of arbitrariness and can help distinguish preservation restrictions from other aesthetic controls that are sometimes invalidated by courts.

Some state enabling laws and many local preservation ordinances do specify the composition or prescribe certain professions—an architect, lawyer, historian, urban planner, or real estate expert—to be represented on a local landmarks commission.[73] Similarly, the National Historic Preservation Act Amendments require that certain disciplines and interests be included on local preservation review commissions as a pre-

---

71. *A-S-P Associates v. City of Raleigh*, 298 N.C. 207, 258 S.E.2d 444, 450 (1979) (references omitted).

72. 173 Cal. Rptr. 534 (1981).

73. See, for example, North Carolina law (G.C. 160A-396) as discussed in *A-S-P Associates v. City of Raleigh*, 298 N.C. 207, 258 S.E.2d 444, 453-54 (1979), which requires that a majority of the local commission have a demonstrated special interest, experience, or education in history or architecture.

requisite to federal certification of local preservation programs.[74]

Even in jurisdictions in which state law is not specific, most local landmarks ordinances require that the commission be broadly based both in terms of expertise and interests represented, thus avoiding any problem of balance.[75] The Cincinnati historic conservation legislation, for example, contains the following language:

> At least one member shall be a professional historic preservationist, one an historian, one an architect, one an urban designer, one an attorney, and one a person engaged in the real estate or development business. At least two members of the board must be registered architects and at least three members shall be community representatives.[76]

---

74. Pub. L. No. 96-515, § 301(13) (1980) defines a local commission to include: "(A) professionals in the disciplines of architecture, history, architectural history, planning, archaeology, or related disciplines, to the extent such professionals are available in the community concerned, and (B) such other persons as have demonstrated special interest, experience or knowledge in history, architecture or related disciplines and as will provide for an adequate and qualified commission." The legislative history of the act notes that "the local preservation commission is, moreover, expected to include individuals experienced and knowledgeable in the field of historic preservation who are able to make objective evaluations concerning the property's historic significance." H.R. Rep. No. 96-1457, 96th Cong., 2d Sess. 26 (1980).

75. There has been some confusion over the propriety of appointing a committed preservationist to a landmarks commission. The governor of one midwestern state questioned whether it was proper to appoint a person with strong preservation credentials to a state landmarks board, even though the state legislation specifically reserved one seat for preservation interests, on the ground that such a person might be biased in favor of strong controls. That position is without legal merit. As one Supreme Court justice has observed, the law does not require ". . . an amorphous dummy unspotted by human emotions . . . ." *Berger v. United States*, 255 U.S. 22, 43 (1921). Bias in the sense of a preconceived point of view about issues of law or policy is no ground for disqualification. *NLRB v. Donnelly Garment Co.*, 330 U.S. 219 (1947); *Laird v. Tatum*, 409 U.S. 824 (1972); Kenneth C. Davis, *Administrative Law in the Seventies* (Rochester, N.Y.: Rochester Lawyers Cooperative, 1976), § 12.01. If it were, the Federal Energy Regulatory Commission could not draw on the experienced businessman for its membership nor could the U.S. Environmental Protection Agency have a knowledgeable environmentalist from the Sierra Club in a policy-making position. Clearly, such a rule would seriously deplete the ranks of available talent for government positions. What is crucial is that a commission member not be biased in the sense of partiality or personal prejudice regarding the facts of a particular case.

76. Cincinnati, Ohio, Historic Conservation Legislation, Ordinance No. 189-1980 (June 1980).

Some courts, while not holding that the composition of a commission is dispositive when an ordinance is challenged, note that having a range of disciplines and interests represented helps refute any claims that the actions of the review body are arbitrary. In *Maher v. City of New Orleans*,[77] the court noted that the Vieux Carre ordinance "curbed the possibility for abuse by the Commission . . . by specifying the composition of that body and its manner of selection." The Colorado Supreme Court, in its opinion in *South of Second Associates v. Georgetown, Colorado*,[78] addressed the relative strengths of a landmarks ordinance that specified a broadly based commission membership and one that did not:

> Under Ordinance No. 205, the seven-member [Historic Preservation] Commission had to include an architect, the chairman of the City Planning Commission, and the chairman of the Board of Adjustment. These membership requirements were abolished by Ordinance No. 206 after which Commission members were required only to be residents and property owners within the town of Georgetown. . . . [We] note that the membership requirements under Ordinance No. 206 ensured that applications for certificates of appropriateness would be considered by a commission partially composed of persons familiar with architectural styles and zoning provisions in general. Such factors . . . may weigh heavily in a[n] action concerned with an alleged arbitrary enforcement of an otherwise valid ordinance.[79]

These cases indicate that careful wording can strengthen the legal case for an ordinance by specifying a knowledgeable, representative membership for a local landmarks commission.[80]

Settling on the composition of a local commission is sometimes a difficult undertaking in small communities that simply do not have a cadre of professionals to draw on. There may be only one or two architects in the area, and they may be hesitant to serve if volunteering means foregoing preservation projects that might come before the commission. The solution is not an easy one. State historic preservation offices can

---

77. 516 F.2d 1051, 1062 (5th Cir. 1975).
78. 580 P.2d 807 (Colo. 1978).
79. *Id.* at 808-9 n.1.
80. While the issue of commission membership was not raised in the *Penn Central* case, the U.S. Supreme Court specifically noted that the "primary responsibility for administering the law is vested in the Landmarks Preservation Commission, a broad-based, 11-member agency . . ." and recognized what the commission's former chairman called its "prudent tradition" of including one or two lawyers. 438 U.S. 104, 110 (1978).

be of great assistance by making available an architect to "ride circuit," rendering expert advice to key members of small preservation commissions. State preservation enabling legislation also might be altered to recognize the peculiar needs of smaller communities, perhaps exempting them from strict membership requirements if practitioners of certain disciplines are not available.

There are a host of other, less crucial, considerations in appointing a commission: how many members should the commission have; how long should they serve; should they be paid? These points, which may be covered by state law, are discussed more fully in the National Trust model ordinance (appendix A).

Scope of Powers

One of the most significant facets of any local ordinance will be the scope of powers granted to the review body. Again, these powers may be specified by state law, or a local government may have wide latitude under home rule powers. The following is a noninclusive list of possible powers that may be granted to a commission:
- to survey and identify historically and architecturally significant structures and areas;
- to designate and protect landmarks and their surroundings and landmark districts;
- to review applications for alteration, construction, or demolition of landmark buildings and all structures within a historic district;
- to require affirmative maintenance of historic structures;
- to make recommendations regarding zoning amendments and comments on the local comprehensive plan;
- to undertake educational programs and activities;
- to establish standards and procedures for designation and development review;
- to accept funds from federal, state, and private sources;
- to buy, sell, or accept donations of property;
- to exercise the power of eminent domain;
- to accept easements and other less-than-fee interests in property.

The most important powers that can be vested in a landmarks commission have all been held valid under the U.S. Constitution by various courts: the power to deny an application to demolish or alter landmarks (upheld by the Supreme Court in the *Penn Central* case); to regulate new construction or development in the vicinity of a landmark or district (approved in *A-S-P Associates v. City of Raleigh*[81]); and to impose affirmative maintenance requirements on landmark owners (upheld in *Maher v. City of New Orleans*[82]). Of course, courts retain the authority to review how such powers are exercised in individual cases, but, in legal parlance, such provisions are valid on their face.

Thus, ordinance draftsmen have latitude in granting powers to a landmarks commission, keeping in mind appropriate state constitutional and statutory requirements. Draftsmen also should pay attention to the aforementioned federal requirements promulgated by the Department of the Interior regarding qualification of local ordinances for tax purposes, which require the establishment of local commissions with power to designate districts and review proposals for alteration and demolition and to protect significant structures in them.[83]

As is true with other provisions of a landmarks ordinance, practical considerations will shape the scope of powers granted to a commission as much as legal requirements. If a community is concerned primarily with exterior facades of landmarks, then it makes little sense to add to the administrative burden by directing control of interior changes. Similarly, in a small town with a volunteer landmarks commission that will be able to meet only once a month, the commission may be overwhelmed if it must review every application for a building permit within a historic area. In such instances, it may be advisable to exempt certain changes or allow the local building permit official or city manager to handle applications for minor alterations as defined by the commission. On the other hand, in places like the Vieux Carre district in New Orleans, where any exterior alteration may be detrimental, the commission may need to control not only all external alterations to landmarks (even in the rear of a building) but also alterations to neighboring structures that

---

81. 298 N.C. 207, 258 S.E.2d 444 (1979).
82. 516 F.2d 1051 (5th Cir. 1975).
83. National Historic Preservation Act Amendments of 1980, Pub. L. No. 96-515, § 101(c)(1), 16 U.S.C. § 470 (1980). See also 36 C.F.R. § 67 ("Historic Preservation Certifications Pursuant to the Tax Reform Act of 1976 and the Revenue Act of 1978"). While the National Park Service within the Department of the Interior has been flexible in administering the tax certification provisions, several local ordinances have been denied certification. One ordinance did not provide for a body empowered to review alterations, demolitions, and new construction within historic districts, and others were rejected because the local commission only had authority over selected landmarks. In another instance, certification was denied because local districts could be created only if all owners in the area consented.

are not of landmark quality.

The key point is that the review body be given adequate power to protect landmarks, and this will almost certainly require that it have the power to forbid demolition or alteration, not just delay it, even though such power may be exercised infrequently. Experience throughout the country shows that landmarks commissions without ultimate authority to say "no" are not as effective as those that have such power.

Another secondary issue that should be given some attention is whether a preservation review body should be granted discretion in turning down a designation despite the fact that the proposed landmark or district meets all applicable ordinance criteria. And further, how much latitude should it have in granting permits for demolition, alteration, or new construction despite an established adverse effect on a landmark or district? In one case involving a National Register nomination in California, *Young v. Mellon*,[84] a state court initially upheld a state historic preservation officer's refusal to forward a National Register nomination to the Department of the Interior despite a favorable recommendation by the State Historical Resources Commission. (The opinion was later withdrawn and thus cannot be cited as precedent in California.) The court reasoned that the applicable legislation and regulations gave the officer considerable discretion:

> These statements of the fundamental purposes for historic preservation make it clear that determinations of SHPO's [state historic preservation officer] should not be made in a vacuum. The architectural and historical characteristics of a building must be weighed against its societal functions and the significance of its preservation in human terms.[85]

The important point here is not whether the local review body should be given discretion to consider factors other than architectural or historical criteria in reviewing designations or permit applications. That is for the community to decide. Once the decision is made, however, the operative factors should be spelled out with some precision to avoid confusion or challenge at a later time. As will be discussed in the following sections of this chapter, most preservation ordinances do contain special provisions giving local review bodies discretion in dealing with hardship cases.

---

84. No. 739026 (Calif.) Super. Ct. (June 8, 1978), *aff'd*, 93 Cal. App. 3d 1001, reporter of decisions directed not to publish this opinion in official reports.

85. *Young v. Mellon*, 156 Cal. Rptr. at 169.

Final Review Authority

Another important issue closely related to the scope of a reviewing body's power is the question of on whom final authority should rest for designating structures and reviewing applications for demolition or for new construction. Should final authority be vested with a newly created, appointive landmarks commission or with an existing body, such as a city planning commission or the community's elective governing body?

Statutory requirements may prescribe which body will exercise final authority, but if the draftsman has leeway, the choice may be a difficult one. One approach, perhaps the least attractive to preservationists, is to have the local law grant the landmarks commission advisory authority only regarding designations and vest no absolute power to deny demolition permits in either the landmarks commission or the legislative body. Chicago, Illinois, is a prime example of this approach, which, while providing for close political control over preservation and limiting restrictions on owners who may want to demolish their landmarks, is fraught with problems from a preservation standpoint.[86]

A second approach, exemplified by the New Orleans, Louisiana, preservation law, places greater authority with both the landmarks commission and the local legislative body. While the landmarks commission still does not have final say over designations and permit applications, its decisions can only be overridden by appealing to the local elected council. Even more important, the council has power to deny absolutely an application to demolish when the circumstances warrant. The Washington, D.C., ordinance also fits in this mold, although there the mayor, rather than the council, has the final say. This model, more acceptable to preservationists because of the balance it strikes among conservation goals, property rights, and political control, is common throughout the country and has been upheld regularly by the courts.[87]

In a third category are ordinances that vest final review power over designations and demolition permit reviews with the local landmarks

---

86. Ironically, although the state of Illinois enacted detailed enabling legislation to allow the city of Chicago to use the well-publicized "Costonis" plan for preservation (which involves transfer of development rights), Chicago has never adopted that approach.

87. *City of New Orleans v. Pergament*, 198 La. 852, 5 So.2d 129 (1941); *Maher v. City of New Orleans*, 516 F.2d 1051 (5th Cir. 1975); *900 G Street Associates v. D.C. Department of Housing and Community Development*, 430 A.2d 1387 (D.C. App. 1981).

commission. From a preservation point of view, this approach is most attractive because, to a certain extent, it removes preservation from the political arena and allows local commissions to forbid demolition according to prescribed standards and procedures as authorized in the Supreme Court's *Penn Central* decision. Rochester, New York, and New York City have adopted this approach. Courts also have upheld uniformly this type of ordinance, as witnessed by the *Penn Central* decision.

If strong preservation controls are to be exercised by the review body, then local elected officials almost inevitably will want final review authority over designations and permit applications to rest with the local legislative body, the mayor, or with a planning commission or similar body that has a broader view of community development. Preservationists may have to choose between having stronger controls exercised by a less sympathetic body or weaker controls vested in a friendly landmarks commission. There are pros and cons to either approach. If the local planning commission or zoning board is put in charge of making final decisions, then preservationists may find that it is more difficult to get landmarks listed or that the review body occasionally allows demolition or adverse developments that a more preservation-oriented body might reject.[88] Yet that risk may be worthwhile if the alternative is vesting limited powers—perhaps authority only to delay demolitions rather than veto them—in a preservation commission.

In most instances, a good case can be made for establishing a separate landmarks commission with specific expertise and the time to devote to special preservation programs. Moreover, as discussed earlier, for a local government to qualify for certain federal historic preservation programs and funding and to assert authority over local National Register nominations, the community must establish a separate landmarks commission with adequate authority to designate historic districts, review proposals for alteration within a district, and protect significant structures.

There are practical aspects to keep in mind as well. Is there sufficient expertise, or are there enough willing citizens available in the community to establish yet another volunteer commission, particularly in smaller

---

88. For examples of review bodies making rulings adverse to local preservation interests, see *Tucker v. City Council for the City of New Orleans*, 343 So.2d 396 (La. App. 1977), city council allowed church to demolish 100-year-old residence in historic district to make room for a parking lot; *Heritage Hill Association, Inc. v. City of Grand Rapids*, 211 N.W.2d 77 (Mich. App. 1973), town board granted a variance to demolish

towns? If an existing body, such as the planning commission, is given authority over landmarks, will these added duties overburden it? Who will do staff work for the review body? Would staff from a planning or zoning commission be sympathetic to preservation goals? Should the review body concern itself only with major alterations or demolitions, or is greater control warranted?

There are a host of other important, but less controversial, powers every preservation review body should have—the power to accept easements, administer a revolving fund, and so forth—powers that raise fewer difficult legal questions. They are discussed more fully in appendix A.

Owner Consent: The Property Owner's Role in Designations and Permit Reviews

The role of affected property owners in the designation process is an issue that promises to grow in importance. The challenge here is to balance preservation goals and the needs of the community as a whole with the need to bring landowners into the preservation process in a positive fashion. Too often, landmark owners, particularly those in historic districts, feel that the local landmarks commission—a nonelective body sitting in a building downtown making decisions that can have an enormous impact on them—is out-of-touch with their needs. In some communities, the response has been to allow affected owners to veto designations of landmarks or districts—often termed "owner consent" provisions. For an ordinance intended to provide effective protection, these provisions make little sense; landmarks are landmarks no matter what an owner might think and should be designated and protected accordingly. It would be considered odd indeed if individual landowners could veto any zoning restrictions placed on their properties. In some communities, it may be impossible to enact any form of preservation law absent an "owner consent" provision, but if at all possible. such a limitation should be avoided. Designation of landmarks should not become a Gallup poll among those who often have narrow economic

---

a church in a historic district; and *Hayes v. Smith*, 167 A.2d 546 (R.I. 1961), zoning board overruled the local historic district commission's rejection of a proposed addition to a church. However, in some cases, landmarks commission rulings allowing demolitions or alterations have been overturned by legislative bodies. See *Maher v. City of New Orleans*, 516 F.2d 1051 (5th Cir. 1975).

self-interests any more than zoning or other community land-use laws are.[89]

This is not to say that local property owners should be denied a say when designation is being considered or that they should be denied a role in the continuing management of the district they are a part of. But the designation process should take the interests of the entire community into account and pay heed to the architectural and historical merits of each proposal. A number of communities have addressed the question of owner participation by establishing neighborhood advisory groups to consult with, and act as a liaison between, the local commission and owners in a designated district.

Defining Key Terms

The preservation ordinance, in granting a commission power to control alterations, demolitions, and new developments, should be very careful in defining those terms. The necessity for precision is demonstrated in the case of *Commissioner of District of Columbia v. Benenson*,[90] in which the court held that an ordinance requiring local review of "alterations" (but not demolitions) did not apply to a developer who wanted to gut completely the historic Willard Hotel, leaving only the facade standing. Fortunately, the Willard Hotel survived this strange piece of judicial logic, but the point is clear. A trial court case from Ohio teaches a similar lesson. Pursuant to its preservation ordinance, the city of Miamisburg attempted to control the posting of outdoor signs in a historic district. The court held that the city had no such power because the preservation law, by its language, applied only to buildings and structures, not signs.[91]

---

89. The Department of the Interior has denied federal tax certification of one local ordinance that required the consent of all owners before designation could take place on the ground that such a provision might impede proper identification of historical resources. The legislative history of the National Historic Preservation Act Amendments of 1980, which do allow owners to veto *federal* National Register listings, has this to say about owner consent provisions: "The Committee does not intend, by adopting the so-called 'owner consent' provisions, to affect state or local laws nor to encourage such owner consent provisions at the state or local level. Indeed, it is at the state and local levels of government, which have the police powers of zoning and other related regulatory tools, where more protective controls are appropriate." H.R. Rep. No. 96-1457, 96th Cong., 2d Sess. 27 (1980).

90. 329 A.2d 437 (D.C. App. 1974).

91. *City of Miamisburg v. Hannah*, No. 80-8-CRB12, Miamisburg, Ohio, Mun. Ct. (1981).

While it probably is not possible to draft definitions that will cover every conceivable development activity related to preservation, the major issues can be anticipated. The Cincinnati landmarks ordinance contains good definitions for the operative terms "alteration," "demolition," and "environmental change":

> "Alteration" means any material change in the external architectural features of any historic structure or structure within an historic site or district, or in [the] interior of any such structure when and to the extent that its interior features are specifically included in the designation relevant to it;
>
> "Demolition" means the substantial deterioration or complete or substantial removal or destruction of any historic structure or any structure which is located within an historic district or site;
>
> "Environmental change" means any material alteration, removal, construction or addition of private or public improvement to an historic structure or within an historic site or district, if subject to public view, subject to the provisions of this chapter. "Environmental change" shall include any new construction.[92]

The American Law Institute's *Model Land Development Code*[93] takes a different approach, defining the term "development" in a broad fashion that encompasses alteration, demolition, and other material change in the use or appearance of a structure or land. The following are relevant parts of the definition that may be useful in drafting a preservation ordinance:

> (1) Except where the context otherwise requires, and in the absence of a more limiting provision in an ordinance, "development" means the performance of any building or mining operation, the making of any material change in the use or appearance of any structure or land, the division of land into two or more parcels, and the creation or termination of right of access or riparian rights.
> (2) The following activities or uses shall be taken for the purposes of this Code to involve development as defined in this Section unless expressly excluded by ordinance or rule: . . .
>   (b) a reconstruction, alteration of the size, or material change in the external appearance, of a structure or land;

---

92. Cincinnati, Ohio, Municipal Code ch. 741, §§ 741-A, 741-D, 741-E, Ordinance 190-1980 (1980).

93. American Law Institute, *A Model Land Development Code*, § 1-202. The *Code* is an excellent overall aid to anyone drafting a preservation ordinance. Another useful source is Harvey S. Moskowitz and Carl G. Lindbloom, *The Illustrated Book of Development Definitions* (Piscataway, N.J.: Rutgers Center for Urban Policy Research, 1981).

(c) a material increase in the intensity of use of land, such as an increase in the number of businesses, manufacturing establishments, offices or dwelling units in a structure or on land; . . .
(e) demolition of a structure or removal of trees; . . .
(k) departure from the normal use for which development permission has been granted, or failure to comply with the conditions of an ordinance, rule or order granting the development permission under which the development was commenced or is continued.
(3) The following operations or uses do not constitute development for purposes of this Code: . . .
(c) work for the maintenance, renewal, improvement, or alteration of any structure, if the work affects only the interior or the color of the structure or decoration of the exterior of the structure but does not otherwise materially affect the external appearance of the structure; . . .
(i) the creation or termination of easements, covenants concerning development of land, or other rights in land not otherwise involving development.

Standards, Procedures, Hearings

In the wake of the *Penn Central* decision, the majority of challenges to local preservation laws have focused on ordinance standards and procedures for designating landmarks and reviewing applications for demolition, alteration, or new construction. How much leeway does a commission have in designating one structure but not a neighboring one? What standard should be used in reviewing an application to alter a designated landmark? Can landmarks commissioners rely on personal knowledge in making decisions? What procedures should be followed in permit reviews? Preservationists and landmarks commissions need to consider questions like these in anticipation of the judicial scrutiny to which their actions will at some point be subjected. The following points out some crucial considerations and offers suggestions to immunize local action against legal challenge.

The Fifth Amendment to the U.S. Constitution states that a person shall not be deprived of property without due process of law. The due process clause has been interpreted as requiring that regulations and standards be understandable by those subject to them[94] and that the local police power—the source of local authority to regulate landmarks—be exercised pursuant to procedures that ensure affected persons will

---

94. *Connally v. General Construction Co.*, 269 U.S. 385 (1926); *Rose v. Locke*, 423 U.S. 48 (1975); *Washington Mobilization Committee v. Cullinane*, 566 F.2d 107 (D.C. Cir. 1977).

be given adequate notice of contemplated government action and an opportunity to be heard.[95]

The issue of adequate notice and hearing is an important one but should not cause any particular difficulties in a preservation context, since virtually all local ordinances require hearings prior to designation and when an application is filed to demolish or alter a landmark or for new construction in a historic district. As discussed in chapter 5, the key issues concern when the hearing must be held and what type of hearing it should be. More than anything else, the local review body must be careful to follow the procedures that govern its actions. If the local ordinance requires that the owner of a landmark proposed for designation be given notice by registered mail 60 days prior to any hearing, 30 days prior notice by regular mail is simply not acceptable. Seemingly mundane details like this must be attended to.

Some courts find the issue of adequate review standards to be more difficult than those involving procedures. Preservation standards, by their very nature, involve an element of taste or unquantifiable aesthetic judgment that is somewhat difficult to reduce to written standards. But courts like to rely on preestablished standards as a benchmark in reviewing actions of local governments. Standards are a safeguard against unbridled and arbitrary discretion. But, is a standard that says a commission should reject any new construction "incongruous" with the existing character of a historic district specific enough? Does it give an applicant fair notice of what is required? Can it be used to judge the rationality of the review commission's action in the case?

Although decisions vary from jurisdiction to jurisdiction, in the vast majority of landmark cases, courts have shown a remarkable deference to local landmarks review bodies in establishing and applying standards for designating landmarks and districts and reviewing applications, particularly when the locality has completed an adequate survey. The Supreme Court itself rejected out-of-hand the contention that regulation of landmarks is inevitably arbitrary because it is a matter of taste:

> There is no basis whatsoever for a conclusion that courts will have any greater difficulty in identifying arbitrary or discriminatory action in the context of landmark regulation than in the context of zoning or any other context.[96]

There are a handful of preservation standards cases in which ordinances or actions were struck down, but they are all examples of egregious situa-

---

95. *Fuentes v. Shevin*, 407 U.S. 67 (1972).
96. *Penn Central Transportation Co. v. New York City*, 438 U.S. 104, 133 (1978).

tions in which there were virtually no standards to restrain governmental discretion. By and large, courts have demonstrated their support of local preservation bodies that have made an honest attempt to articulate designation and review standards.

Standards for Designating Landmarks and Districts

The reasons for designating a landmark or district are many—architectural, cultural, historical, social, archaeological, and geographical, among others—and designations by preservation commissions have been uniformly upheld by the courts. The *Penn Central* decision, upholding New York City's ordinance against a claim that it violated the plaintiff's constitutionally protected property rights, has persuaded many attorneys representing developers and owners to probe for new chinks in the preservation armor. A number of recent cases have refocused attention on designation of landmarks and districts. In several, plaintiffs have questioned survey techniques: are designations based on an automobile windshield survey (where the surveyors make their judgments from the front seat of a car while driving slowly through a proposed district) sound? In other cases, plaintiffs have questioned why a commission designated one building and not the building next door or whether the designation standards in the ordinance are clear enough to give adequate guidance to the commission making designations.

Few such challenges have met with success, because courts have given local governments great latitude in designating both landmarks and districts. And well they should when reasonably clear standards are articulated prior to government action and then applied by an expert body or by a legislative body on the advice of a qualified landmarks commission. An early preservation case from New York exemplifies the deference courts show in landmark designations. In *Manhattan Club v. New York City Landmarks Preservation Commission*,[97] the plaintiff, a social club, wanted to tear down its building to make way for a lucrative high-rise development in New York City. When a demolition permit was denied, its first line of attack was that the structure was not of landmark quality. That contention was given short shrift by the court:

> There is no merit to the petitioner's contention that the determination is unsupported by substantial evidence. A hearing was held and the issues thoroughly aired. The architectural, historical and aesthetic value of the improvement was fully established, and the court may not substitute its judgment for that of

---

97. 51 Misc. 556, 273 N.Y.S.2d 848 (1966).

an administrative agency. . . .[98]

The same leeway is given to local governments in drawing historic district boundaries. In upholding the city of San Diego's preservation ordinance, a California appellate court rejected the plaintiff's argument that the boundaries of the local historic district were too extensive:

> The city council is authorized to determine boundaries of the area subject to control, and the court should not interfere with its determination absent a clear showing of abuse of its authority.[99]

Even in the leading case in which a boundary determination was struck down, *South of Second Associates v. Georgetown, Colorado*,[100] the issue was not whether the area designated was indeed historic. Instead, the court invalidated the local ordinance that designated the entire small mountain town of Georgetown, Colorado, as one district because the evidence showed that the local commission treated areas within the district differently in practice. Thus, the court was not saying that the standards for designation were arbitrary or that local structures were not of historic or architectural significance but that perhaps there should have been two or three districts in the town instead of just one.

Local governments and preservationists can keep their winning string intact and guard against even these rare instances of invalidation by taking several precautionary steps.

Following Sound Survey Techniques

In a pending Florida case[101] involving Palm Beach's preservation ordinance, the plaintiff has focused on the methods used to identify buildings that were later designated for protection by the local preservation commission, arguing that there was no rational basis for the designation. Several hundred potential landmarks were identified in an automobile windshield survey conducted by the town's leading preservationist, who was assisted by a volunteer graduate architectural stu-

---

98. *Id.*, 273 N.Y.S.2d at 851. Similar language can be found in *Society for Ethical Culture v. Spatt*, 68 App. Div. 2d 112, 416 N.Y.S.2d 246 (1979).

99. *Bohannan v. City of San Diego*, 30 Cal. App. 3d 416, 106 Cal. Rptr. 333, 336 (1973). Accord, *A-S-P Associates v. City of Raleigh*, 258 S.E.2d 444, 457 (N.C. 1979), "legislative bodies may make rational distinctions with less than mathematical exactitude"; *New Orleans v. Duke*, 427 U.S. 297 (1976).

100. 580 P.2d 807 (Colo. 1978).

101. *De Mendoza v. Town of Palm Beach*, No. 80-2437, 15th Jud. Cir. Ct. (filed May 16, 1980).

dent. Both were intimately familiar with the architectural style of the area and its history, and they followed criteria used for National Register nominations. The court must now decide if their survey technique and qualifications were adequate or whether a community must spend more money and hire a professional to identify landmarks prior to designation.

While it may be best to conduct professional surveys before designation, they are clearly not a legal requisite. In fact, there is no constitutional requirement that a survey be done prior to designation if the local government can prove at trial that the designated structure or district is of architectural or historic significance as defined in the local ordinance. Thus, any sort of survey, amateur or professional, buttresses the local government's position that its action has a rational basis. What is important is that the local review body study the survey to see if its members agree with the survey's conclusions and to ensure that the members follow designation criteria in the ordinance.

Drafting Acceptable Designation Standards

A second common-sense action already undertaken by most local governments involved in preservation is to articulate designation standards *before* actually designating a landmark or district. These standards can be set forth in the preservation ordinance itself, or, when state law and judicial decisions allow, the ordinance may delegate the duty to establish standards to the local review body. In most states, either course is generally acceptable,[102] as long as there is an attempt to articulate standards that will give the landmark owner a fair indication of what criteria the

---

102. Many state preservation enabling laws delineate the reasons that can be invoked for designation; in those instances, local ordinances often repeat the state standards. In other instances, the local ordinance may set forth broad standards (for example, historical associations, architectural quality), and the local commission is directed to develop more detailed guidelines. See Kenneth C. Davis, *Administrative Law Treatise*, 2d ed. (Davis, Cal.: University of San Diego Press, 1978), §§ 13.1-13.15; *Bohannan v. City of San Diego*, 30 Cal. App. 3d 416, 106 Cal. Rptr. 333 (1973). The correct approach will depend to a certain extent on the willingness of state courts to permit state and local legislative bodies to delegate the function of setting standards to an administrative body such as a landmarks commission. Ordinance draftsmen should research state law if there is any question on this point. Several jurisdictions, notably Florida and Texas, still take a restrictive view of what is commonly known as the delegation doctrine. See *Askew v. Cross Key Waterways*, 372 So.2d 1913 (Fla. 1978); *Texas Antiquities Commission v. Dallas County Community College District*, 554 S.W.2d 924 (Tex. 1977).

landmarks body will use in reviewing a proposed designation and what criteria can be used by the courts to determine whether an action by the review body has been arbitrary or discriminatory.[103]

The ordinances included in appendix A all set forth clear standards that should satisfy judicial scrutiny. Notice they do more than just state that the local preservation review body can designate structures of historical, cultural, architectural, geographic, or archaeological importance. The ordinances give meaning to these terms. For example, the Seattle, Washington, ordinance described in the National Trust model provisions defines the standard of "historical and cultural importance" like this:

Historical, Cultural Importance
(1) has significant character, interest or value, as part of the development, heritage or cultural characteristics of the City, State or Nation; or is associated with the life of a person significant in the past; or
(2) is the site of an historic event with a significant effect on society; or
(3) exemplifies the cultural, political, economic, social or historic heritage of the community.

New York City has a similar standard—the proposed landmark must possess "a special character or special historical or aesthetic interest or value as part of the development, heritage, or cultural characteristics of the city, state, or nation"—that has been upheld in several cases.[104]

Neither the New York City nor the Seattle standard is elaborate, but each is one that owners and judges can understand. Some ordinances are not so specific as Seattle's; in those instances, the local landmarks commission might consider adopting its own guidelines to augment and explain the ordinance standard.

Contrast these standards with two cases in which courts invalidated designations because the designation criteria were vague or absent entirely. In *Texas Antiquities Commission v. Dallas County Community College District*,[105] the Texas Supreme Court was asked to stop demolition of several state-owned structures under a state law that automatically designated and protected all state-owned buildings of "historical in-

---

103. For a further discussion of this point, see chapter 5 and the following authorities: Davis, *Administrative Law Treatise*, §§ 13.1-13.15; *Environmental Defense Fund v. Ruckelshaus*, 439 F.2d 584 (D.C. Cir. 1971).
104. See *Society for Ethical Culture v. Spatt*, 416 N.Y.S.2d 246, 250 (1979), *aff'd*, 415 N.E.2d 922 (N.Y. 1980).
105. 554 S.W.2d 924 (Tex. 1977).

terest" as state archaeological landmarks. The court, troubled by the state antiquities commission's failure to define what "historical interest" meant, even though it had such power under the state statute, struck down the ordinance on the ground that such language was overly broad and vague:

> ... "historical" includes all of the past; "interest" ranges broadly from public to private concerns and embraces fads and ephemeral fascinations. All unrestorable structures ordinarily hold some nostalgic tug upon someone and may qualify as "buildings . . . of historical . . . interest" upon the basis of the statute now before us. We are unconvinced that we should renounce the settled law of Texas that the legislature may not delegate its powers without providing some criteria or safeguards. . . .[106]

An even more egregious example of the need for standards is exemplified in a case involving the federal government and the national landmarks program. In *Historic Green Springs, Inc. v. Bergland*,[107] the plaintiffs alleged that the proposed 14,000-acre district had no historic value of national significance and challenged as arbitrary the secretary of the interior's decision to designate it as a National Historic Landmark (to be distinguished from National Register properties) pursuant to the Historic Sites Act of 1935.[108] The court noted that it was required to uphold the secretary's decision "unless there has been a clear error of judgment" but pointed out that the "absence of any . . . clear formal standards concerning national historic significance hinders the court in ensuring that relevant factors were accurately considered."[109] The Department of the Interior admitted there were no formal standards but argued adequate standards could be found in the language of two pamphlets it published, which explained the national landmarks program. But the court was not satisfied because the secretary had not mentioned the standards in making his decision, and there was no evidence that he had followed the criteria set out in the pamphlets. Thus, the court concluded:

> . . . without published rules of procedure and substantive criteria for qualification as a landmark, the plaintiffs have been denied any meaningful opportunity for informal response to the proposed action and the Court has been precluded from meaningful review of the Secretary's decision.[110]

---

106. *Id.* at 927.
107. 497 F. Supp. 839 (E.D. Va. 1980).
108. 16 U.S.C. § 46 *et seq.*
109. 497 F. Supp. 839, 850-51 (E.D. Va. 1980).
110. *Id.* at 854.

In both of these cases, it is clear that the courts recognized the historic and aesthetic merits of the buildings or area in question but felt constrained by the lack of standards. There is simply no excuse for putting a court in a position in which it has no basis to formulate a decision favorable to preservation.

Deciding What to Designate

A third important issue focuses on what is being designated. Should a commission designate only structures of extraordinary landmark quality, or should it also protect lesser structures, the grounds that surround a landmark, or buildings in a historic district that do not qualify as landmarks? There is ample legal authority to support each of these actions, and, in practice, a preservation commission may find itself impotent to stop adverse development if its authority does not extend beyond protecting extraordinary landmark structures.

Generally, designation standards should not be hard to draft. There are several subsidiary points, however, that an ordinance draftsman should consider. First, some commissions tend to define "historic" in terms of how old a building is. This is an inflexible approach that has little to recommend it. There is nothing wrong with making age one factor among others in determining "historic" status, but some ordinances do not allow designation unless a building is a predetermined age, typically over 50 years old. Not only does such a standard run the risk of eliminating a number of worthy landmarks from protection (some of Frank Lloyd Wright's best buildings are not 50 years old), but it effectively prevents federal certification of the local ordinance for federal tax and other benefits. In three cases, the federal government has denied certification when selection was predetermined by a qualifying age requirement greater than 50 years on the ground that the effects of alteration or demolition can best be evaluated on a case-by-case basis independent of age.

It is clear that buildings do not have to be of extraordinary significance to be protected. In *Society for Ethical Culture v. Spatt*,[111] the Society argued that there was "no evidence to suggest that the Meeting House is of extraordinary architectural distinction or that it was ever the scene of any noted historical event or the residence of any noted personage," but its pleas fell on deaf ears:

---

111. 68 App. Div. 2d 112, 416 N.Y.S.2d 246 (1979), *aff'd*, 415 N.E.2d 922 (N.Y. 1980).

While relevant, this is not determinative. If the preservation of landmarks were limited to only that which has extraordinary distinction or enjoys popular appeal, much of what is precious in our architectural and historical heritage would soon disappear. It is the function of the Landmarks Preservation Commission to ensure the continued existence of those landmarks which lack the widespread appeal to preserve themselves.[112]

Courts also have recognized the need to regulate nonlandmark buildings that serve as a setting or act as a buffer for more special structures. In *A-S-P Associates v. City of Raleigh*,[113] the North Carolina Supreme Court explicitly rejected the notion that protection could be extended only to landmarks:

> It is widely recognized that preservation of the historic aspects of a district requires more than simply the preservation of those buildings of historical and architectural significance within the district. In rejecting a similar challenge, the District Court in *Maher v. City of New Orleans*, 371 F. Supp. 653, 663 (E.D. La. 1974), observed: "just as important is the preservation and protection of the setting and scene in which structures of architectural and historical significance are situated."[114]

The Maryland Court of Appeals has also taken a dim view of the argument that local commissions are powerless to regulate development around landmarks:

> ... the whole concept of historic zoning "would be about as futile as shoveling smoke" if, e.g., ... because a building being demolished had no architectural significance a historic district commission was powerless to prevent its demolition and the construction in its stead of a modernistic drive-in restaurant immediately adjacent to the State House in Annapolis.[115]

This same reasoning is applicable to grounds or gardens that might surround and complement a landmark. If surrounding grounds or gardens are not designated, then an owner may subdivide a landmark site and attempt to sell off or build on the undeveloped part. This may present difficult problems even in a historic district where the preservation review body has power to control new construction, but it may completely hamstring a commission in dealing with a free-standing landmark. An owner may be able to subdivide the site and claim a "taking"

---

112. *Id.*, 416 N.Y.S.2d at 250.
113. *A-S-P Associates v. City of Raleigh*, 258 S.E.2d 444, 451 (N.C. 1979).
114. *Id.* Similar reasoning was employed in *City of New Orleans v. Pergament*, 198 La. 852, 5 So.2d 129 (1941), and *Figarsky v. Historic District Commission of City of Norwich*, 368 A.2d 163 (Conn. 1976).
115. *Faulkner v. Town of Chestertown*, 428 A.2d 879 (Md. 1981).

of his property under the U.S. Constitution if development is not allowed on the former grounds or garden. By coordinating its designation powers with the local subdivision ordinance, the landmarks commission can avoid this knotty situation.[116]

The Role of Economics

Another question concerns the role economics should play in designation. Most ordinances do not require economic issues to be considered when designating a landmark, under the theory that issues of reasonable use and economic hardship should be considered only in the context of an actual proposal to alter or demolish a structure. Designation should be made on the basis of the structure's or area's architectural, historical, or similar significance, not on the economic impact such action might have on an owner.

From a legal viewpoint, that position is fully justified. The simple act of identifying and designating landmarks will not give rise to an economic deprivation of constitutional dimensions. In *Virginia Historic Landmarks Commission v. Board of Supervisors of Louisa County*,[117] for example, a Virginia court held that identification of the Historic Green Springs area by the state landmarks commission was merely a hortatory act and did not deprive the affected owners of any property rights despite an incidental effect on values.[118]

In practice, however, excluding consideration of economics is often difficult and will become increasingly so as landmarks controls become stronger and as preservation is integrated into a community's overall comprehensive plan. It will be very difficult to persuade a city council that it should not consider the economic impact of designating its central business area as a landmark district subject to controls that may make large-scale redevelopment difficult. But if economic factors are to be considered in the designation process, they should be only one element

---

116. The subject of coordination is discussed in greater detail in Part 1 of this chapter.

117. 21 Va. 468, 230 S.E.2d 449 (1976).

118. Designation of an area as a National Historic Landmark was held not to amount to a "taking" under the U.S. Constitution in the *Historic Green Springs* case, 497 F. Supp. 839, 848-50 (E.D. Va. 1980); in *Agins v. City of Tiburon*, 100 S. Ct. 2138 (1980), the Supreme Court held that the mere fact that an ordinance subjected the plaintiff's land to regulation (one residential unit per five acres allowed as of right) did not give rise to a "taking" in the absence of an application to develop the property. See also *Faulkner v. Town of Chestertown*, 428 A.2d 879 (Md. 1981).

and not necessarily an overriding one, and the inquiry should be made into the economic impact on the community, not on an individual owner. If an owner finds that designation causes economic hardship, provisions should be available to petition for relief, but that relief should only be granted if it is supported by actual experience, not just speculation over hypothetical deprivation.[119]

Procedures for Designating Landmarks and Districts

Procedural aspects of landmarks designation are likely to become increasingly important in the next few years as those opposing designation probe for weak points that will persuade courts to invalidate local action. Recent cases have raised the following procedural issues. Did the landmarks commission follow designation procedures as set forth in state or local law? Did the owner receive legal notice of the proposed designation? Was the owner given an adequate opportunity to challenge the designation?

As discussed in chapter 5, the requirements of the U.S. Constitution regarding procedure are not particularly onerous: the landmark owner must be given notice of the proposed designation and an opportunity for a hearing.[120] From a constitutional perspective, the hearing should be held prior to designation (except in emergencies), but it need not be a formal trial-type affair with cross-examination of witnesses and a verbatim record.[121] In many cases, however, notice and hearing requirements will be controlled by state enabling legislation or administrative procedure acts. Generally, written notice to interested parties and an opportunity to present relevant facts at an informal hearing are all that are required when designating a structure or district, something less than may be necessary when an application to alter, demolish, or construct, with its concomitant economic issues, is involved.

Most landmarks commissions operating today not only meet but exceed constitutional and statutory notice and hearing requirements. There are several pitfalls, however, that review bodies should avoid. In some communities, listing of landmarks and districts on the National Register of Historic Places has preceded local landmarks designation. While cur-

---

119. The following section suggests administrative procedures to determine the actual economic impact of a regulation on an owner.

120. *Ewing v. Mytinger & Casselberry, Inc.*, 339 U.S. 594 (1950); *Board of Regents v. Roth*, 408 U.S. 564 (1972).

121. The important issues of timing and type of hearing are also addressed in chapter 5.

rent federal regulations require that the owner of a prospective National Register landmark be given notice and an opportunity to be heard, in the past a hearing was not always held simply because National Register listing had little real impact on the owner's rights. In a few instances, such listing has been the basis for local designations, which may take place without a new hearing, even though controls imposed pursuant to the local ordinance might be more far-reaching than those imposed under National Register listing. In those cases, the owner should be given notice and an opportunity to be heard to avoid a possible challenge on due process grounds. If a community is considering local designation at the time of the National Register listing, then it might utilize concurrent notice and hearings.

Another important point in making a designation is for the local review body to give reasons for its decision based on the evidence before it. Findings for designations need not be as elaborate as those for applications to alter or demolish or for new construction (see discussion in following section). A summary of the evidence presented, a recitation of standards applied, and a brief statement of the reasons why the commission took the action it did are more than sufficient. In upholding a designation of a landmark by the New York City landmarks commission, the lower court in *Society for Ethical Culture v. Spatt* wrote approvingly of this approach:

> In making this finding the Commission relied on the history of the Society, which was founded in 1876; the architecture of the building itself, and the account in *Architecture* magazine, which referred to the building as "certainly quite the best piece of Art Nouveau architecture yet designed in this country." Thus there was a rational basis for the finding.[122]

This does not mean, however, that a commission can simply parrot the language of the local ordinance in making findings and giving reasons. As observed in the commentary to the *Model Land Development Code*, "The courts are no longer willing to tolerate a decision on a mimeographed form containing findings and conclusions good for any occasion."[123]

---

122. 116 N.Y.S. 246, 250 (1979).
123. American Law Institute, *A Model Land Development Code*, §§ 2-301, 304. See also *Historic Green Springs, Inc. v. Bergland*, 497 F. Supp. 839 (E.D. Va. 1980).

Reviewing Applications for Demolition, Alteration, or New Construction

Perhaps the most visible, and often most controversial, of powers exercised by preservation commissions is reviewing applications to demolish or alter a landmark or for new construction in a historic area, often referred to collectively as applications for certificates of appropriateness. Applications to demolish a landmark often will engender heated arguments, bringing commissions face-to-face with the difficult task of juggling and balancing preservation goals with economic and political pressures. Dealing with alteration proposals—often less controversial than demolitions but far more frequent—will be no less difficult. The challenge here will be to encourage upgrading and continued maintenance of existing landmarks and to guide the process of change so that it is sympathetic to the existing character of the historic area. In all but a few historic areas, freezing things in time will be neither feasible nor desirable.

The process of setting standards to govern this review process and establishing sound administrative procedures to apply them is crucial not only from a legal standpoint but also as a way for preservationists to evaluate where their preservation program is leading. What kind of development, if any, do they really want in the local historic area? How do they intend to evaluate proposed changes? What is the most efficient and fair method of administering review standards? The following subsections discuss these key questions and emphasize those points in the process at which commissioners should pay close attention to standards and procedures.

Setting Review Standards

Setting standards for reviewing such applications is normally a trickier task than setting standards for making designations. Preservationists are concerned that a demolition "not have an adverse effect on the fabric of the district" or that new construction not be "incongruous," but "in harmony," with the "character," "significant features," or "atmosphere" of the area. Each of these terms is to a degree subjective and needs to be defined and limited in some fashion to give applicants reasonable notice of what is expected of them and to allow courts to judge the validity of the local decision.

In his treatise on land-use planning law, Professor Norman Williams lists various considerations that might be used by a local commission in determining whether a proposed demolition or change is compat-

ible with the landmark or district:
- mass—the height of a building, its bulk, and the nature of roof line;
- the proportions between the height of a building and its width (is its appearance predominantly horizontal or predominantly vertical?);
- the nature of the open spaces around buildings, including the extent of setbacks, the existence of any side yards (with an occasional view to the rear) and their size, and the continuity of such spaces along the street;
- the existence of trees and other landscaping, and the extent of paving;
- the nature of the openings in the facade, primarily doors and windows—their location, size, and proportions;
- the type of roof—flat, gabled, hip, gambrel, mansard, etc.;
- the nature of projections from the buildings, particularly porches;
- the nature of the architectural details—and, in a broader sense, the predominant architectural style;
- the nature of the materials
- color;
- texture;
- the details of ornamentation;
- signs.[124]

Not all these considerations will necessarily be relevant to every landmark or district, but the list does suggest how broad review standards can be narrowed.

Promulgating adequate review standards is much less difficult in historic areas that have a distinctive style or character. No one would object strenuously if a landmarks commission rejected a proposal to add a redwood railing around a second floor porch in the Vieux Carre district in New Orleans; everyone knows that iron railings are de rigueur. In places like New Orleans, Old Santa Fe, Old Town Alexandria, and Nantucket, the problem virtually solves itself. Thus, in a number of challenges to preservation restrictions, judges had little trouble upholding

---

124. Williams, *American Land Planning Law*, 3.31 § A.07. A good discussion of preservation criteria can be found in Weming Lu, "Preservation Criteria: Defining and Protecting Design Relationships," in *Old and New Architecture: Design Relationships* (Washington, D.C.: Preservation Press, 1980), p. 180. As Lu notes, some local ordinances use sketches to illustrate standards. These sketches are typically contained in documents incorporated by reference into the ordinance.

the action of the local review body because of the district's distinctive style. The legal rationale for those decisions is best explained in an early preservation case, *Town of Deering v. Tibbetts*:

> While determination of what is compatible with the atmosphere of the town may on first impression be thought to be a matter of arbitrary and subjective judgment, under consideration it proves not to be. . . . [T]he language "takes clear meaning from the observable character of the district to which it applies."[125]

Similar reasoning was employed in *A-S-P Associates v. City of Raleigh*[126] to uphold a very broad review standard, even though the local district encompassed several architectural styles. The Raleigh preservation ordinance required the local landmarks commission to prevent activity "which would be incongruous with the historic aspects of the Historic District." The owner of a vacant lot within the city's Oakwood Historic District claimed this "incongruity" standard was so vague that it amounted to an unconstitutional delegation of legislative authority by the city council to the historic district commission. The Supreme Court of North Carolina, in one of the better-reasoned preservation decisions to date, found that the "incongruity" standard sufficiently limited the commission's discretion:

> The general policy and standard of "incongruity," adopted by both the General Assembly and the Raleigh City Council, in this instance is best denominated as "a contextual standard." A contextual standard is one which derives its meaning from the objectively determinable, interrelated conditions and characteristics of the subject to which the standard is to be applied. In this instance the standard of "incongruity" must derive its meaning, if any, from the total physical environment of the Historic District. That is to say, the conditions and characteristics of the Historic District's physical environment must be sufficiently distinctive and identifiable to provide reasonable guidance to the Historic District Commission in applying the "incongruity" standard.
>
> Although the neighborhood encompassed by the Historic District is to a considerable extent an architectural melange, the heterogeneity of architectural style is not such as to render the standard of "incongruity" meaningless. The predominant architectural style found in the area is Victorian, the characteristics of which are readily identifiable. City of Raleigh, Planning Department, A Proposal to Designate Oakwood as a Historic District, p. 1 (1975); N.C. Department of Cultural Resources. National Register Nomination Form, Oakwood Historic District (1974).
>
> . . . It is therefore sufficient that a general, yet meaningful contextual standard has been set forth to limit the discretion of the Historic District Commission. Strikingly similar standards for administration of historic district ordinances

---

125. 105 N.H. 481, 202 A.2d 232 (1964).
126. 258 S.E.2d 444 (1979).

have long been approved by courts of other jurisdictions.[127]

The application of permit review standards to landmarks or districts that do not exhibit a single, distinctive style has been more troublesome to some legal commentators, but, as the cases that follow demonstrate, even when a district lacks a distinct style, courts have almost universally upheld the local commission's decision. In some instances in which an ordinance contained relatively vague review standards, the court attached great importance to other criteria in the local law or regulations that narrowed commission discretion. In others, courts have looked to background studies and surveys that were incorporated by reference into the law. Courts also have relied on procedural protections to uphold broad standards. In still other instances, courts have held that appointing people with special expertise to a commission helps limit what might otherwise have been excessive discretion.

Narrowing Broad Review Standards. The typical preservation ordinance sets forth broad review standards for demolition or development permits—often directing the commission to "maintain the character of the district"—and then recites criteria relating to, for example, height, texture of materials, and architectural style to further define that broad standard. Courts have uniformly approved the broad review standard in such cases. The Georgetown, Colorado, case is the best example.

The plaintiff developer alleged, among other things, that the standard the local commission was to apply in reviewing its application to construct new townhouses—what effect the proposed construction might have upon "the general historical and/or architectural character of the structure or area"—was unconstitutionally vague. The Colorado Supreme Court disagreed. It noted that the phrase "historical and/or architectural significance" was defined in the ordinance, and, more importantly, the ordinance set forth "six specific criteria which focus the attention of the commission and of potential applicants for certificates of appropriateness on objective and discernible factors."[128] The court attached

---

127. A number of other courts are in agreement with this reasoning. See *City of Sante Fe v. Gamble-Skogmo, Inc.*, 389 S.W. 2d 13 (N.M. 1964); *Maher v. City of New Orleans*, 516 F.2d 1051 (5th Cir. 1975); *Groch v. City of Berkeley*, 173 Cal. Rptr. 534 (1981).

128. 580 P.2d 807, 810 (Colo. 1978). The six criteria to be considered were:
1. The effect of the proposed change on the general historical and/or architectural character of the structure or area.
2. The architectural style, arrangement, texture, and materials used on existing and proposed structures, and their relation to other structures in the area.

particular relevance to one criterion that directed the commission to consider the "architectural style, arrangement, texture and materials used on existing and proposed structures, and their relation to other structures in the area," reasoning that "these objective and easily discernible factors give substance to the ordinance's historical and/or architectural character" language.[129] The court cited several decisions from other jurisdictions that upheld similar standards and concluded that the ordinance "contains sufficient standards to advise ordinary and reasonable men as to the type of construction permitted, permits reasonable application by the commission, and limits the commission's discretionary powers."[130]

If a local ordinance does not contain such narrowing criteria, the preservation commission would be well-advised to adopt them by way of regulation or informal review guidelines (assuming the commission has power to do so).

Standards Found in Background Documents. The best example of a court approving a local action based on criteria found in documents outside the preservation ordinance is *Maher v. City of New Orleans*.[131] In this case, the court upheld the New Orleans preservation ordinance even though the city admitted it had not articulated any review standards:

> . . . other fertile sources are readily available to promote a reasoned exercise of the professional and scholarly judgment of the Commission. It may be difficult to capture the atmosphere of a region through a set of regulations. However, it would seem that old city plans and historic documents, as well as photographs and contemporary writings, may provide an abundant and accurate compilation of data to guide the Commission. And as the district court observed, "In this case, the meaning of a mandate to preserve the character of the Vieux Carre takes clear meaning from the observable character of the district to which it applies."

---

3. The effects of the proposed work in creating, changing, destroying, or affecting otherwise, the exterior architectural features of the structure upon which such work is done.
4. The effects of the proposed work upon the protection, enhancement, perpetuation, and use of the structure or area.
5. The use to which the structure or area will be put.
6. The condition of existing improvements and whether or not they are a hazard to public health or safety. *Id.* at 809-10.

129. *Id.* at 810.
130. *Id.* at 811. Also see *Faulkner v. Town of Chestertown*, 428 A.2d 879 (Md. 1981).
131. 516 F.2d 1051, 1063 (5th Cir. 1975).

Aside from such contemporary indicia of the nature and appearance of the French Quarter at earlier times, the Commission has the advantage at present of a recent impartial architectural and historical study of the structures in the area. The Vieux Carre Survey Advisory Committee conducted its analysis under a grant to Tulane University from the Edward G. Schleider Foundation. Building by building, the Committee assessed the merit of each structure with respect to several factors. For example, regarding the Maher cottage at issue here, the Louisiana Supreme Court noted that the Survey Committee "was of the opinion that this cottage was worthy of preservation as part of the overall scene." While the Schleider survey in no way binds the Commission, it does furnish an independent and objective judgment respecting the edifices in the area. The existence of the survey and other historical source material assist in mooring the Commission's discretion firmly to the legislative purpose.[132]

The favorable decision in *A-S-P Associates v. City of Raleigh* was grounded, in part, on similar reasoning. The court, influenced by the existence of guidelines and standards in a city document that had proposed designation of the local district, held:

> The architectural guidelines and design standards incorporated into the Oakwood ordinance (described in note 4, *supra*) provide an analysis of the structural elements of the different styles and provide additional support for our conclusion that the contextual standard of "incongruity" is a sufficient limitation on the Historic District Commission's discretion.[133]

The incorporated guidelines and standards the court referred to were quite specific:

> There are three major divisions to the architectural guidelines and design standards: those which apply to proposed changes to existing structures; those which apply to new construction; and those which apply to landscaping. Those which apply to existing structures of the Victorian style are further subdivided into nine categories, each of which focuses on a different structural element, e.g., materials, colors, and fenestration patterns. A description of the different Victorian styles as they relate to a particular structural element is given. Specific and general prohibitions of designs, materials and styles that are incongruous with the existing elements of particular Victorian styles are also set forth. Similar, although less developed, consideration is given to the other architectural styles of historical interest found in the Historic District.
>
> Those guidelines which apply to new construction are similarly subdivided with crossreferences to the structural element categories of existing structures. In addition, this section of the guidelines sets forth limitations on such things as spacing, lot coverage, and height, which are flexibly related to the same characteristics of existing structures in proximity to a proposed new structure.

---

132. *Id.* at 1063.
133. 258 S.E.2d 444, 454 (N.C. 1979).

Consideration is also given to characteristics such as spacing, orientation, scale, and proportions of new structures in a third part of this section.[134]

A number of other courts also have relied on incorporated standards to uphold local ordinances.[135]

Employing a variation on this approach, the court in *Figarsky v. Historic District Commission of City of Norwich*[136] pointed out that the local ordinance incorporated by reference the state enabling act that set forth specific review criteria, and that the local commission had sought expert outside opinion in deciding whether a building should be retained because it contributed to the overall importance of Norwichtown Green as a landmark.

Procedural Safeguards. Although these safeguards may not be dispositive of the review standards issue, the fact that there are procedural protections or that a landmarks commission, because of the expertise of individual members, is uniquely qualified to determine whether a demolition or new development might damage the character of a historic area has heavily and favorably influenced a number of courts. In at least two instances, procedural protections have received approving judicial reviews. In the *A-S-P* case, the court felt that they helped to ensure against arbitrary action:

> The procedural safeguards provided will serve as an additional check on potential abuse of the Historic District Commission's discretion. Provisions for appeal to the Board of Adjustment from an adverse decision of the Historic District Commission will afford an affected property owner the opportunity to offer expert evidence, cross-examine witnesses, inspect documents, and offer rebuttal evidence. Similar protection is afforded to a property owner by the right to appeal from a decision of the Board of Adjustment to the Superior Court of Wake County.[137]

The aforementioned *Maher* decision contains parallel language:

> The elaborate decision-making and appeal process set forth in the ordinance creates another structural check on any potential for arbitrariness that might exist. Decisions of the Commission may be reviewed ultimately by the City Council itself. Indeed, that is the procedure that was followed in the present case.[138]

---

134. *Id.* at 453 n.4.
135. See *Lafayette Park Baptist Church v. Scott*, 553 S.W.2d 856, 862 (Mo. App. 1977).
136. 368 A.2d 163 (Conn. 1976).
137. 258 S.E.2d 444, 455 (N.C. 1979).
138. 516 F.2d 1051, 1062-63 (5th Cir. 1975).

The court also observed that the Vieux Carre ordinance "curbed the possibility for abuse . . . by specifying the composition of that body and its manner of selection."[139]

Similarly, in a footnote to its decision interpreting the Georgetown, Colorado, preservation ordinance, the Colorado Supreme Court acknowledged the importance of a commission's expertise as a safeguard against arbitrary action:

> Although the composition of the Commission is a matter exclusively within the municipality's legislative discretion, we note that the membership requirements under Ordinance No. 205 ensured that applications for certificates of appropriateness would be considered by a commission partially composed of persons familiar with architectural styles and zoning provisions in general. Such factors, while not important in the context of the present proceeding, may weigh heavily in a Rule 106 action concerned with an alleged arbitrary enforcement of an otherwise valid ordinance.[140]

The existence of comprehensive background studies, the obvious character of most historic areas, and the application of standards by a uniquely qualified body all serve to distinguish historic preservation cases from those involving architectural review boards and aesthetic controls in less distinct areas. To a large extent these differences help to explain why courts look so favorably on historic preservation controls but sometimes view other aesthetic regulations with a dubious eye. Contrast the historic preservation cases just discussed with an aesthetic regulation case from New Jersey. In *Morristown Road Associates v. Bernardsville*,[141] the court held that review standards such as "displeasing" and "harmonious" as applied to new construction in a nonhistoric neighborhood were unconstitutionally vague. Several courts have specifically recognized that cases like *Morristown* are not applicable to preservation disputes:

> While most aesthetic ordinances are concerned with good taste and beauty . . . a historic district zoning ordinance . . . is not primarily concerned with whether the subject of regulation is beautiful or tasteful, but rather with preserving it as it is, representative of what it was, for such educational, cultural, or economic values as it may have. Cases dealing with purely aesthetic regulations are distinguishable from those dealing with preservation of a historical area of a historical style of architecture.[142]

---

139. *Id.* at 1062.
140. 580 P.2d 808-9 n.1 (Colo. 1978).
141. 103 N.J. Super. 58, 394 A.2d 157 (1978).
142. *A-S-P Associates v. City of Raleigh*, 258 S.E.2d 444, 450 (N.C. 1979). Quoting

Applying Review Standards: The Role of Economics

Once a commission has established an adequate set of standards to review applications, it must apply those standards carefully. As more and more courts reject frontal challenges to landmarks ordinances and review standards, commissions should expect that litigation will focus on economic and procedural matters—such as whether the owner is earning a reasonable return on the property, or whether commission members have improperly taken into account evidence that was not in the record before them, or if they had a pecuniary or other interest that might have biased the outcome.

While economics plays no major role in designating landmarks, it will inevitably play a central role in reviewing applications for certificates of appropriateness. As discussed in chapter 5, the Fifth Amendment to the U.S. Constitution requires that a landmark owner not be denied all reasonable use of his property by a landmarks regulation, and the Supreme Court has indicated this determination must be made on a case-by-case basis. While most local preservation review bodies do consider the economic impact of the landmarks regulation on the applicant, many do it somewhat haphazardly. Others, like New York City's landmarks commission, apply a fixed statutory definition of what constitutes a reasonable return (6 percent under the New York landmarks law).

The first approach is not only an invitation for a court challenge but also may fail to give the local commission all the information it needs to make a reasoned decision. In many instances, the real economic facts of a case may support preservation rather than demolition. The second approach may work well if the commission has resources to make a very sophisticated analysis of reasonable return. In most jurisdictions, however, a far better answer is to establish an administrative procedure to bring out certain facts that courts have held important in determining whether a land-use regulation is overly burdensome. By ascertaining these facts early in the process, the locality can help defuse a prospective suit; if a suit is brought, there will be ample economic evidence to support the reasonableness of the reviewing body's decision.[143]

Arden Rathkopf, *The Law of Zoning and Planning*, 4th ed. (New York: Clark Boardman, Co., Ltd., 1975), § 15.01, p. 15-4. See also *City of Sante Fe v. Gamble-Skogmo, Inc.*, 380 P.2d 13, 17 (N.M. 1964).

143. For an example of how lack of adequate economic evidence can undermine

Thus, the local ordinance (or the local commission, through regulation or informal procedure) should require an applicant to submit evidence relevant to the following issues, and the reviewing body should examine these factors in making a decision. (If the owner can show that there is economic hardship, then the commission might consider special relief, as discussed later in this chapter.)

Owner's Knowledge of Landmark Restriction. Many land-use cases hold that an owner who purchases a landmark with knowledge of preservation restrictions is in a weak position to claim a "taking" under the U.S. Constitution.[144] In one preservation case, *900 G Street Associates v. Department of Community Housing and Development*,[145] the court found that the owner had prior knowledge of the preservation restrictions being challenged and held that because of such knowledge the claim of economic deprivation carried little weight, since the price paid for the property should have reflected the restrictions on its development.

Current Economic Return. A key inquiry in determining whether a preservation regulation is onerous centers on the current economic return on the property in light of the amount originally invested, taxes, and other considerations, including caliber of management. As the Supreme Court noted in *Penn Central Transportation Co. v. New York City*,[146] courts will examine whether a landmark owner can earn a "reasonable return" and whether the landmark is "economically viable" in its present use or form.

The reviewing body should therefore require an applicant for a certificate of appropriateness to produce information regarding the price originally paid for the property, potential rental or lease income, the level of taxes, and the net profit derived from the landmark, if any, over the past several years. Opponents of the proposed application might be given an opportunity to show there are feasible alternatives to demolition or that the landmark could earn a reasonable return if properly managed. As Judge Breitel observed in his well-written New York Court of Appeals decision in the Grand Central case, *Penn Central Transportation Co. v. New York City*,[147] a landowner cannot mismanage the

---

the preservationist position, see *Broadview Apartments Co. v. Commission for Historical and Architectural Preservation*, 433 A.2d 1214, 49 Md. App. 538 (1981).

144. See *C.F. Lytle Co. v. Clark*, 491 F.2d 834, 838 (10th Cir. 1978); *Lafayette Park Baptist Church v. Scott*, 553 S.W.2d 856, 859 (Mo. App. 1977).

145. 430 A.2d 1387 (D.C. App. 1981).

146. 438 U.S. 104, 136, 138 (1978).

147. 366 N.E.2d 1271, 1276 (N.Y. 1977).

property or fail to use his best efforts to obtain a reasonable return and then claim that the regulation is confiscatory.

The Washington, D.C., landmarks ordinance demonstrates just how effective this approach can be. It establishes an administrative procedure whereby anyone seeking to demolish or alter a landmark must produce evidence that a denial of a permit would cause serious economic deprivation. Relevant information can be found in sections 5-1001 through 5-1015. Since the ordinance was enacted, these provisions have been instrumental in court cases upholding the D.C. ordinance.[148]

Owner's Bona Fide Attempt to Rent or Sell Property. Several courts have held that an important factor in determining whether an owner has been deprived of all economic use of his property is whether there has been any bona fide effort to rent or sell the property. If an owner is holding the property off the market in anticipation of being able to demolish it, then any claim that the regulations prevent all reasonable use rings hollow. As explained in *First Presbyterian Church of York v. City Council of York*:[149]

> . . . the Church, having failed to show that a sale of the property was impracticable, that commercial rental could not provide a reasonable return or that other potential uses of the property were foreclosed, had not carried its burden of proving a taking without just compensation.[150]

Thus, a landmarks commission should delve into this issue. Has the property been offered for sale through a real estate broker? Has the property been advertised in any newspapers? How was the selling price established and is it reasonable? Some local ordinances require that the local reviewing body make a specific finding that the owner has made a bona fide attempt to sell the landmark before it may grant a certificate of appropriateness.

Feasibility of Profitable Alternative Uses. The landmark owner should be required to show that the existing use is not profitable and that it would not be feasible to renovate the property or undertake an alter-

---

148. See *900 G Street Associates v. D.C. Department of Community Housing and Development*, 430 A.2d 1387 (D.C. App. 1981).

149. 360 A.2d 257, 261 (Pa. Commw. 1976).

150. A number of other courts have recognized the importance of attempts to rent or sell. *Maher v. City of New Orleans*, 516 F.2d 1051, 1066 (5th Cir. 1975); *Lafayette Park Baptist Church v. Scott*, 553 S.W.2d 856, 863-64 (Mo. App. 1977); *Dempsey v. Boys' Club of City of St. Louis*, 558 S.W.2d 262, 268 (1977); *900 G Street Associates v. D.C. Department of Housing and Community Development*, 430 A.2d 1387 (D.C. App. 1981).

native development compatible with preservation concerns.

Evidence regarding a profitable alternative use of the existing structure or development sensitive to preservation concerns is relevant to the issue of reasonable use. As required by the court in *Lafayette Park Baptist Church v. Board of Adjustment of City of St. Louis*,[151] a landowner could be asked to make a case that alternatives to demolition are impracticable:

> In order for the landowner to raise the question of unconstitutional application as to his property, he must prove that it is impractical to rehabilitate, and as we have stated, this contemplates not only infeasibility because of physical condition but also a negative answer to the question as to whether the property can be turned to use or account profitably. Economic profitability contemplates restoration, and if not then the question arises: Can it be sold profitably? If the owner is unable to restore from an economic standpoint he must then establish it is impractical to sell or lease the property or that no market exists for it at a reasonable price. Only then is he entitled to a demolition permit. And only then are his constitutional rights denied.[152]

Of course, lack of any evidence regarding the feasibility of renovation can be damaging to the preservation case.[153] Another option is to give preservationists and other interest groups an opportunity to present alternative plans. In several cases, courts have ruled that alternative plans presented by those opposed to a project are important in determining the reasonableness of the regulations in question.[154]

Procedure for Reviewing Certificates of Appropriateness

From a legal standpoint, the procedural considerations in reviewing applications for certificates of appropriateness are quite similar to those for designating landmarks or districts. Basically, the landmark owner must be given an opportunity to be heard, to present his case, and to rebut the opposing case.[155] State law often will prescribe the minimum

---

151. 599 S.W.2d 61 (Mo. 1980).
152. *Id.* at 66.
153. See *Broadview Apartments Co. v. Commission for Historical and Architectural Preservation*, 433 A.2d 1214, 49 Md. App. 538 (1981).
154. *First Presbyterian Church of York v. City Council of York*, 360 A.2d 257, 261 (Pa. Commw. 1976); *Maher v. City of New Orleans*, 516 F.2d 1051, 1066 (5th Cir. 1975). There are a number of zoning cases directly on point. *American National Bank and Trust Co. v. City of Chicago*, 195 N.E.2d 627 (Ill. 1964); *Pillman v. Village of Northbrook*, 382 N.E.2d 399 (Ill. App. 1978).
155. For a full discussion of the constitutional requirements relating to procedure, see chapter 5.

procedures for reviewing applications for certificates of appropriateness. Commissions can help ensure fair, orderly hearings by making clear beforehand the rules that will govern their deliberations.

It is particularly important to many judges that the reviewing body give reasons for its decision. Again, state law may require these findings, but, even if it does not, a local review body is well advised to do so.

In commenting on the favorable opinion in the important case of *Figarsky v. Historic District of the City of Norwich*,[156] preservation attorney Russell Brenneman stressed that the case was won on appeal because the local landmarks commission compiled an extensive record and gave specific reasons for its decision.[157] Without a statement of findings, courts feel they have no benchmark from which to evaluate the local action. In the *Historic Green Springs* case, involving designation of 14,000 acres of Virginia countryside as a National Historic Landmark, the court rebuked the secretary of the interior for failing to give reasons for his decision, because:

> . . . without them [statement of reasons] the conclusory findings of national historic importance and of acceptability of the easements provide little insight into whether the Secretary's discretion was properly exercised.[158]

Aside from making judges happy, giving reasons for a decision is a useful, practical exercise for any reviewing body, helping to ensure that it has taken action based on permissible standards set forth in the ordinance. In several cases, local commissions have had their decisions overturned because they were based on impermissible considerations or because a required finding was omitted.

For example, in *Gumley v. Board of Selectmen of Nantucket*,[159] a decision of the local landmarks commission disapproving a new development was overturned because it was based on open space considerations rather than on "external architectural features" as specified in the ordinance. A local commission's decision to allow demolition of a struc-

---

156. 368 A.2d 163 (Conn. 1976).

157. The nature of review proceedings and scope of judicial review are usually established by state law. In many instances, the proceedings will be administrative or quasi-judicial in nature, and thus the reviewing court will look only at the record and evidence produced before the preservation review body. In some jurisdictions, however, such actions may be characterized as legislative so that judicial review is *de novo* and not limited by the record below. New evidence can thus be introduced at trial.

158. 497 F. Supp. 839, 851 (E.D. Va. 1980).

159. 358 N.E.2d 1011 (Mass. 1977).

ture in a historic area was likewise invalidated in *Dempsey v. Boys' Club of the City of St. Louis*[160] on the ground that the commission did not have sufficient evidence before it to make a finding required by the local ordinance regarding the practicability of rehabilitation.

Disclosure of Pecuniary and Personal Interests

People are often appointed to preservation commissions because they have some special expertise—architectural training, real estate experience, legal knowledge—that should be helpful to the commission in making decisions on certificates of appropriateness. But the use of this expertise and the past affiliations that are often part of it raise several interesting legal issues that commissioners should be sensitive to.

What if a commissioner has a direct pecuniary interest in a case, perhaps through a partnership with the developer applying for a demolition permit? Clearly, the commissioner should disqualify himself in such situations.[161] But that is the easy case. What of cases in which the interest is only indirect—for example, when a commissioner owns nearby property that might appreciate in value if a big, new high-rise office building is allowed in a historic area? That question is a difficult one. In several zoning cases, courts have invalidated zoning decisions because of the possibility of a conflict of interest.[162] Commissioners should be very careful to disclose any potential direct or indirect gain or loss that could flow from a commission decision.[163]

What if a commissioner, because of a past affiliation—say, the presidency of a local private landmarks pressure group—is perceived to have an inherent bias against, or for, a particular proposal? Should that

---

160. 558 S.W.2d 262 (Mo. 1977).
161. See *Crall v. Leonminster*, 284 N.E.2d 610 (Mass. 1972); *Olley Valley Estates, Inc. v. Fussell*, 208 S.E.2d 801 (Ga. 1974).
162. For an extreme example, see *Tuxedo Conservation and Taxpayers Association v. Town Board of the Town of Tuxedo*, 418 N.Y.S.2d 638 (App. Div. 1979), where the court threw out a local zoning decision because the deciding vote was cast by a town board member who was an executive in a large advertising agency that stood to obtain business from the project. The court thought that the vote might have been swayed by "jingling the guinea" rather than sound planning grounds. "Like Caesar's wife," the court said, "a public official must be above suspicion."
163. See also *Buell v. City of Bremerton*, 495 P.2d 1358 (Wash. 1972), striking down a local zoning decision because the chairman's property might increase in value as a result of the zoning. For a general discussion of the bias issue, see Davis, *Administrative Law in the Seventies*, § 12.03.

person be disqualified? Generally not, *unless* the commissioner cannot keep an open mind and is not willing to consider evidence supporting a contrary position and to make a finding on the record presented.[164]

Personal Knowledge as the Basis for a Decision

Another disclosure issue that landmarks commissions are facing with increasing frequency is whether commissioners can base decisions on personal knowledge or expertise. For example, if an architect knows from long years of study and personal experience that a proposed development in a historic district is not compatible with the character of the district and that alternative designs are possible, can such knowledge form the basis for a negative decision? Similarly, can a commissioner make a personal visit to a landmark that an owner wants to demolish and base his decision on impressions from that visit?

Generally, the answer to both of these questions is "yes." A decision can be based on personal knowledge and expertise, provided that knowledge is noted in the record.[165]

Economic Hardship and Safety Valve Provisions

To keep the administration of a preservation ordinance running smoothly and to deal with cases of hardship, every ordinance should have what might be termed "safety valves." Generally, landmarks commissions will need flexibility in dealing with two situations: first, when an owner faces economic hardship because there is no reasonable economic use for the landmark and, second, when there is an economic use, but legal restrictions, such as zoning regulations or building codes, preclude necessary renovations. If an owner can satisfy the reviewing body that applicable landmark restrictions are causing a unique and serious economic hardship, that body might grant relief (in the form of a permit to allow an alteration or new construction) that not only saves the landmark but also helps to avoid a costly legal battle. Or if the local

---

164. For a discussion of this point, see note 75 *supra*. See also Davis, *Administrative Law in the Seventies*, § 12.01; *Lead Industries Association v. Environmental Protection Agency*, 647 F.2d 1130 (D.C. Cir. 1980), *cert. denied*, 101 S. Ct. 621 (1980).

165. See *Ohio Bell Telephone Co. v. Public Utilities Commission*, 301 U.S. 292 (1937); *Russo v. Stevens*, 7 App. Div. 2d 575, 184 N.Y.S.2d 981 (1959); Kenneth C. Davis, *Administrative Law*, 3d ed. (St. Paul, Minn.: West, 1972), chap. 19.

landmarks or zoning ordinance contains provisions that are needlessly thwarting a feasible use of the existing structure, the reviewing body might approve the change in use and perhaps avoid demolition by neglect.

The economic questions may be the leading preservation issue of the 1980s. Already landmarks commissions across the country are agonizing over what to do about white elephant mansions with huge grounds that are no longer feasible for single-family use. In Palm Beach, Florida, the town is considering allowing conversion of large landmark single-family homes to multifamily condominiums, but it worries that such a move may weaken the town's ability to maintain the single-family status for surrounding properties. As one commissioner wrote in a letter to the author, "Something has to be done about these large landmark houses, yet the residents are up in arms about more and more people crowding in . . . . Help! We need relief." In other cities—Washington, D.C., and Brookline, Massachusetts, for example—old mansions have been saved by conversion to multifamily use and the addition of architecturally compatible townhouses on the surrounding estate grounds. The design and layout of the developments were restricted severely to satisfy abutting owners.

While it is easy to sympathize with a landmark owner who is having a difficult time making ends meet because of high taxes, energy costs, and the like, the simple fact that a property is located in a historic district should never be, in and of itself, a reason to allow a variance from local preservation and land-use controls or to grant a demolition permit. Nor should the owner's desire to increase the property's economic return be adequate ground for relief. Such claims were rightly rejected in a case from New Orleans in which the landmark owner wanted to construct, in violation of the local ordinance, another building on a lot on which a landmark was situated:

> . . . in the absence of a showing that approval of . . . nonviolative construction could not have been obtained from the Vieux Carre Commission, we cannot hold appellant suffered financial loss in being denied an opportunity to obtain an increased return from its property. Even if financial loss had been shown, such loss is only a factor to be considered in determining hardship and will not, standing alone, constitute a hardship sufficient to justify a variance. And here the hardship referred to, the requirement of conformity to two separate and sometimes conflicting standards of construction, is neither "unusual" nor "particular" to Mercier. It is common to all property owners in the zoning district in which Mercier's lot is located and therefore is not a hardship which justifies the granting of a variance. To hold otherwise would have the effect

of destroying the zoning district.[166]

To the extent that local preservation controls are made part of the local zoning ordinance, state law may control situations in which relief due to economic hardship can be granted. The state preservation enabling legislation also may define economic hardship for purposes of variances. When the local government has latitude, however, the best approach is to establish an administrative procedure whereby an owner who seeks relief bears the burden of showing that the landmark cannot be put to some reasonable economic use in its present state. The Washington, D.C., ordinance contains the following provision:

> No permit shall be issued unless the Mayor finds that such issuance is necessary in the public interest or that a failure to issue a permit will result in unreasonable economic hardship to the owner.[167]

The ordinance defines unreasonable economic hardship in terms of reasonable use. Unless the owner can show that the existing use is economically unfeasible and that sale, rental, or rehabilitation of the property is not possible, then demolition, alteration, or subdivision is not allowed. Moreover, the term "public interest" is defined to allow construction of special projects of special merit "having significant benefits to the District of Columbia or to the community by virtue of exemplary architecture, specific features of land planning, or social or other benefits having a high priority for community services." (Exercise of this "special merit" clause was upheld in *Citizens Committee to Save Historic Rhodes Tavern v. District of Columbia Department of Housing and Community Development*.[168] As a result, a developer was given permission to demolish or move the historic Rhodes Tavern to make way for a new development of "special merit" that incorporated the facades of two architecturally significant structures.)

As mentioned in the first part of this chapter, Denver has taken a similar approach, inserting a special-use variance in its local zoning ordinance that permits nonresidential use of landmarks, such as profes-

---

166. *Phillips v. Board of Zoning Adjustments of City of New Orleans*, 197 So.2d 916, 919-20 (La. 1967).

167. Historic Landmark and Historic District Protection Act, D.C. Law 2-144 § 5(e) (1978).

168. *Citizens Committee to Save Historic Rhodes Tavern v. District of Columbia Department of Housing and Community Development*, 432 A.2d 710 (D.C. App. 1981).

sional offices, in residential zones where the owner can demonstrate economic hardship. Such relief is limited to designated landmarks, thereby avoiding the problem of widespread conversion of homes to commercial uses in residential areas.

The procedures discussed earlier relating to the role of economics in reviewing certificates of appropriateness are particularly relevant in the case of hardship relief. In considering whether to grant relief, the reviewing body might require the owner to produce evidence regarding prior knowledge of the landmark restriction, current economic return on the property, attempts to rent or sell the property, and the feasibility of profitable alternative uses.[169]

Maintenance and Upkeep of Landmarks

The issue of maintaining landmarks in a reasonable state of repair has three key facets. First, communities must be sensitive to the possibility

---

169. The issues of hardship and reasonable return may present themselves in a slightly different fashion when a charitable, nonprofit organization, such as a church, owns the landmark property. In these cases, it obviously makes little sense to talk in terms of reasonable return because charitable organizations are not generally in the business of making a profit. A church can hardly argue that it must be allowed to demolish its meeting house because it is not earning a 6 percent return; yet there are instances in which landmark controls may cause a charitable organization serious problems. Perhaps a church desires to expand to accommodate a burgeoning membership, or a home for indigents will cease operation unless it can redevelop its property with lucrative commercial office space. How should a landmarks commission handle these cases? Do First Amendment freedom of religion considerations dictate special treatment for churches?

Courts generally have upheld restrictions that place reasonable conditions on the use or development of church property. In fact, the general trend across the country is to cut down on the previously favored position of churches in land-use disputes, the general rule being that local governments may place reasonable restrictions on uses of church property. See generally Williams, *American Land Planning Law,* 1980 Supp., chap. 77; *Corporation of Presiding Bishop of Church of Jesus Christ of Latter Day Saints v. City of Portersville,* 203 P.2d 823 (1949), *appeal dismissed,* 338 U.S. 805 (1949), upholding exclusion of church from residential area; *Kurman v. Zoning Board of Adjustment of City of Philadelphia,* 351 Pa. 247, 40 A.2d 381 (1945), approving stricter yard requirements for religious use; *Board of Zoning Appeals of Decatur v. Decatur, Indiana Company of Jehovah's Witnesses,* 233 Ind. 83, 117 N.E.2d 115 (1954), upholding setback restrictions on church; *Society for Ethical Culture v. Spatt,* 416 N.Y.S.2d 246, *aff'd,* 415 N.E.2d 922 (N.Y. 1980), upholding designation of meeting house. For a more detailed discussion, see chapter 5.

that complex and time-consuming procedures associated with landmark controls may persuade some owners to forego needed repairs simply to avoid the bureaucratic hassle. Second, there may be situations that call for the imposition of affirmative maintenance requirements where landmarks are being demolished de facto by neglect. Finally, preservationists should be aware that most local municipal building and health codes allow landmarks to be torn down despite opposition from the local preservation review body on the ground that the buildings have fallen into such disrepair that they are a threat to public safety. This section examines these three issues and suggests ways to deal with them.

Earlier sections of this chapter contained caveats about overly strict building codes that might hinder rehabilitation and cautioned against subjecting every minor change or alteration of a landmark structure to review by the local preservation commission, particularly in smaller communities.[170] That advice was practical in nature, a warning that maintenance of landmarks may be hindered unintentionally. Scrutiny by a landmarks commission of every minor alteration or change has another downside. If owners are forced to obtain a permit for every minor repair to their buildings, the results will probably be either that the repairs are not made or are made without a permit. Moreover, burdensome procedures will win the preservation review process no friends politically. The answer to this problem is to insert an exclusion in the ordinance for ordinary maintenance or minor alterations. The precise language will vary from community to community based in part on established local procedures for granting building permits. The ordinance might give the local building code official some leeway in deciding what constitutes a major change that must be reviewed by the landmarks commission, or it might exempt improvements below a specified dollar amount unless the impact on the landmark is significant. As with other operative terms in a preservation ordinance, "ordinary maintenance" should be defined carefully. The model ordinance of the National Trust for Historic Preservation contains some suggested language (see appendix A).

Another important aspect of maintaining landmarks, one that has received a good deal of judicial attention, is that of affirmative or

---

170. The section on enforcement of preservation ordinances, which appears later in this chapter, deals with legal problems that can arise if a local review body does not enforce maintenance requirements uniformly.

minimum maintenance. Many local preservation ordinances require that landmarks be maintained in accordance with local building and housing codes. Others, notably the New Orleans preservation law, go further, specifying a list of structural defects or faults that must be repaired by an owner on a continuing basis.

Minimum maintenance standards are not particularly controversial from a legal standpoint. The leading case is *Maher v. City of New Orleans*,[171] in which the court rejected an argument that the local ordinance's maintenance provision was unconstitutional:

> Once it has been determined that the purpose of the Vieux Carre legislation is a proper one, upkeep of buildings appears reasonably necessary to the accomplishment of the goals of the ordinance. . . . The fact that an owner may incidentally be required to make out-of-pocket expenditures in order to remain in compliance with an ordinance does not per se render that ordinance a taking. In the interest of safety, it would seem that an ordinance might reasonably require buildings to have fire sprinklers or to provide emergency facilities for exits and light. In pursuit of health, provisions for plumbing or sewage disposal might be demanded. Compliance could well require owners to spend money. Yet, if the purpose be legitimate and the means reasonably consistent with the objective, the ordinance can withstand a *frontal* attack of invalidity.[172] (Emphasis added.)

Many other cases from across the country uphold minimum maintenance requirements contained in local building codes. However, that is not the end of the legal inquiry. Notice that the *Maher* court said the regulations could withstand a *frontal* attack. That was legal shorthand for the proposition that if an owner can show affirmative maintenance requirements are overly burdensome *as applied*, then they may be invalid. That is the general rule for virtually all building code requirements. A law that obligates owners of new apartment buildings to install expensive smoke detectors, fire and other prevention equipment may be valid on its face, but a court might strike it down as applied retroactively to a small, 50-year-old apartment building on which the rental return is very low. Although courts have almost uniformly upheld tough code provisions despite relatively large expenditures, for the most part, courts apply a reasonableness test in assessing the constitutionality of building code provisions—the importance of the public

---

171. 516 F.2d 1051 (5th Cir. 1975).
172. *Id.* at 1066-67.

interest at stake versus the economic burden on the owner.[173] Local review bodies thus should be prepared to defend affirmative maintenance requirements with adequate proof of public need and evidence that rehabilitation is economically feasible or include relief provisions in the local ordinance to deal with the more difficult cases.[174]

Affirmative maintenance requirements raise another important legal issue related to property inspections. Compliance with most preservation restrictions, notably those relating to demolition or alteration, can be policed with relative ease because violations are obvious and usually can be discovered from a public street without entering onto the property itself. But what about cracks in the foundation that threaten a landmark building or a leaky roof that might eventually cause serious structural problems? To detect such problems, landmark commissions might be forced to undertake a program of periodic inspections. Such inspections, often called administrative searches, raise constitutional questions.[175]

Prior to 1967 such administrative searches of private property were held by the court to be outside the scope of the Fourth Amendment protection against unreasonable searches and seizures, so that no search warrant was necessary to conduct periodic inspections. Then, in *Camara v. Municipal Court*[176] and *See v. City of Seattle*,[177] the U.S. Supreme Court ruled that the Fourth Amendment did apply to administrative searches and that a warrant was required before an inspection could occur. This meant that a building inspector could no longer knock on a homeowner's door and demand entry if the homeowner objected.

---

173. See, e.g., *Kaukus v. City of Chicago*, 27 Ill. 2d 197, 188 N.E.2d 694 (1963), *appeal dismissed*, 375 U.S. 8 (1963); *City of Chicago v. Kutil*, 43 Ill. App. 3d 826, 357 N.E.2d 200 (1976); *State v. Larsen Transfer and Storage, Inc.*, 246 N.W.2d 176 (Minn. 1976).

174. See *State ex rel. Powderly v. Erickson*, 301 N.W.2d 324 (Minn. 1981), for case in which one court erroneously shifted the burden of proof regarding feasibility of renovation from the owner to the municipality.

175. Administrative searches generally are defined as inspections, such as building and fire code inspections, that are conducted pursuant to an administrative plan *without* probable cause to believe that any violation exists in a particular structure. If the inspecting agency has received a complaint or has actual knowledge of a violation, then based on probable cause, it may secure a warrant to inspect.

176. 387 U.S. 523 (1967).

177. *Id.* at 541.

Now, the Court said, the inspector would have to get a warrant based on "administrative probable cause."

Unfortunately, the Court failed to give much guidance on what constitutes "administrative probable cause." It did explain that there is sufficient probable cause to issue a warrant

> ... if reasonable legislative or administrative standards for conducting an area inspection are satisfied with respect to a particular dwelling. Such standards ... may be based on the passage of time, the nature of the building (e.g., a multifamily apartment house), or the condition of the entire area, but they will not necessarily depend upon specific knowledge of the condition of the particular dwelling. If a valid public interest justifies the intrusion contemplated, then there is probable cause to issue a suitably restricted search warrant.[178]

This principle was extended in *See v. City of Seattle*.[179]

The *Camara* decision unleashed much commentary, with civil libertarians believing that the possible gross misuse of warrantless inspections had been curbed and building code administrators predicting that the decision would halt effective code enforcement. However, a post-*Camara* survey revealed that the decision has had little real effect.[180] Most of the cities polled in the study replied that their practice both pre-1960 and post-1960 was that, if a citizen strongly objected to an inspection, that home was simply omitted from the list. The authors of the survey also point out that few citizens realize they have a right to refuse entry to an inspector. It is interesting that in the cities studied, covering 35 million people, not more than 150 warrants were obtained in 1971-1972 for some 1.5 million annual inspections.

Thus, a periodic inspection program may run into fewer Fourth Amendment objections in practice than in theory. Still, it is important that such a program be governed by predetermined standards as suggested in *Camara* to dispel any claim that the program does not meet the dictates of that case.[181]

---

178. *Camara v. Municipal Court of the City and County of San Francisco, id.* at 523, 538-39.

179. *Id.* at 541.

180. Fuerst and Bielawas, *Is the Right of Entry of Building Officials Unlimited?* The Building Official and Code Administrator 26 (May 1975).

181. For a discussion of legal developments in this area since *Camara*, see Note, Ga. L. Rev. vol. 15:233 (1978); *Burkart Randall v. Marshall*, 625 F.2d 1313 (7th Cir. 1980); *Marshall v. Barlow's, Inc.*, 436 U.S. 307 (1978); *Hanna v. Drobnick*, 514 F.2d 393 (6th Cir. 1975).

Another subsidiary legal issue in the context of affirmative maintenance is who exactly should be made responsible for maintenance requirements. In most cases, the owner of a structure will be primarily responsible, but in some instances, a lessee or renter will have actual effective control. If a historic area has many apartment buildings, or if the significant structures are leased for commercial use, then the local ordinance may put some responsibility on other parties in addition to an owner.[182]

In either case, local commissions will find it very useful if they have the authority to protect a property that is being demolished by neglect. A number of communities have enacted laws that permit a specified local agency (often public works) to take necessary steps to secure a derelict landmark against vandalism. Others go even further, granting the agency power to make repairs and bill the owner for them to avoid what is often called demolition by neglect. The validity of these more far-reaching laws will generally depend on the economic impact on an owner. Courts are less likely to make an owner pay if the chances of earning a reasonable return on the property are slim.

A final important issue regarding maintenance revolves around what is commonly known as the public safety exclusion. Many local preservation ordinances contain provisions whereby a landmark declared to be a public hazard can be altered, repaired, or, as is more likely the case, demolished without the local preservation review body having any say whatsoever. On their face, public safety exclusions appear reasonable—if a building is about to tumble down on pedestrians below, surely something must be done quickly—but in practice, they are sometimes used by a local government or owner to circumvent local review procedures or to avoid facing up to hard choices between a proposed redevelopment scheme and preservation of an important landmark.[183]

At a minimum, local preservation ordinances should attempt to strike a balance between concerns about public safety and preservation, perhaps allowing the landmarks review body to comment on the proposed demo-

---

182. Some property owners have attempted to escape any responsibility for code maintenance by shifting the burden to lessees. These attempts generally are not successful. See *City of Chicago v. Atwood*, 289 Ill. 624, 110 N.E. 127 (1915); *Housing and Development Administration v. Johan Realty Co.*, 403 N.Y.S.2d 835 (1978).

183. For an example of a local preservation commission's denial of a demolition permit being overridden on public safety grounds, see *Wolk v. Reisem*, 413 N.Y.2d 60 (N.Y. App. 1979).

lition unless the legislative body specifically finds there is an immediate and serious threat to the public safety that cannot be addressed through less drastic measures. At least one city, Washington, D.C., has taken another step. Its local preservation ordinance provides that the local Board of Condemnation cannot issue permits for demolition of private landmarks except in accordance with the procedures and standards set forth in the preservation law.[184]

Publicly Owned Property

Some of the most bitter and unfortunate preservation disputes involve municipal landmarks commissions facing off against other public institutions, such as state colleges, county hospitals, and even other municipal agencies. When the government becomes a developer, it often attempts to ignore the rules that govern private enterprise. If it is politically feasible to do so, a local preservation ordinance should include a provision subjecting all owners of landmark buildings, public or private, to its review procedures. If that is not realistic, the preservationists should push for allowing the local review body to comment on development plans for government agencies.

From a legal perspective, dealing with other local agencies is the easiest matter. If the local legislative body duly passes a landmarks law requiring all local agencies under its jurisdiction to comply with landmarks review procedures, there is little question they must do so. But what about county or state institutions following the requirements of a municipal landmarks law? Judicial decisions from around the country are split on this point. If the opposing public entity—a county hospital or township council—is another local government, or branch thereof, then courts generally tend to require that the local landmarks law be observed. A case from Maryland, *Mayor of Annapolis v. Anne Arundel County*,[185] illustrates the point. There, the county government sought to tear down a church, which had been designated as a landmark by the Annapolis preservation commission, to make way for a parking lot to serve the county courthouse. The court rejected the county's argument that it was not subject to the local law, noting that, if the state general assembly had desired to exempt the county, it could easily have

---

184. Historic Landmark and Historic District Protection Act, D.C. Law 2-144 § 12 (1978).
185. 271 Md. 265, 316 A.2d 807 (1974).

done so by inserting a provision in the state preservation enabling law.[186]

If the public institution involved in the dispute is not coequal but rather a state agency, the problem is more difficult. A majority of courts would hold it immune from local regulation, the rationale being that state agencies operate under a higher authority than do local governments, and, if the local law interferes with their legislative mandate, they need not comply unless the state legislature specifically has subjected them to it. That reasoning, which has come under increasing fire from legal commentators, is exemplified in *State of Washington v. City of Seattle*.[187] There, the University of Washington Board of Regents successfully fought application of Seattle's preservation law. While the court refused to grant the university blanket immunity from all local laws, it found that this particular local law conflicted with state law granting the Board of Regents full control of university property and was thus invalid.[188]

The problem with these cases is twofold. The blanket immunity rule is inflexible and does not attempt to reconcile the often-conflicting public goals at stake. It forecloses discussion of possible alternatives to demolition and ignores local land-use goals. Furthermore, even when courts refuse to grant blanket immunity and look to state legislative intent, the result, given the entrenched legal attitudes of state supremacy over local governments, is that the state agency need not comply. The flaw here is that judges who lean toward state power can conjure up a legislative intent to fit the desired result because the intent of the state legislature is rarely clear. In fact, in all probability, the state legislature never gave any thought at all to possible conflicts between a state university's building plans and local landmark restrictions. And, because few states maintain legislative histories of state laws, it is virtually impossible to determine legislative intent in any realistic fashion. The University of Washington case is a prime example of the difficulty in discerning what the state legislature really intended. The dissent in that case pointed

---

186. A county was also held subject to a local preservation law in *City of Ithaca v. County of Tompkins*, 355 N.Y.S.2d 275 (1974).

187. 615 P.2d 461 (Wash. 1980).

188. A similar result was reached in *Texas Antiquities Commission v. Dallas County Community College District*, 554 S.W.2d 924 (Tex. 1977), where the Texas Supreme Court held that to subject the college to a state preservation law would be an unconstitutional diversion of funds from educational purposes. See also *City of Santa Fe v. Armijo*, 634 P.2d 685 (N.M. 1981).

out that the Washington state legislature had declared its support for historic preservation by enacting a number of laws, such as a state environmental policy act, strongly supporting historic preservation as a state goal, *after* the university's enabling legislation had been passed. Wasn't that an expression of intent to subject state agencies to local landmarks laws? the dissenting judge asked.

Courts in several jurisdictions are edging away from the immunity/legislative intent approach.[189] A number of recent zoning cases illustrate the trend. In *City of Temple Terrace v. Hillsborough Association for Retarded Citizens, Inc.*,[190] a nonprofit association, under state contract, attempted to establish a day-care facility for retarded persons in a residential neighborhood in violation of the city zoning ordinance. The trial court held that the association, acting on behalf of a state agency, was immune from local control. The appellate court reversed, rejecting the old immunity test in favor of one that balanced the public interests involved:

> The adoption of the balancing of interests test will compel government agencies to make more responsible land-use decisions by forcing them to consider the feasibility of other sites for the facility as well as alternative methods of making the use of the proposed site less detrimental to the local zoning scheme.[191]

The balancing of interests test by no means indicates the local preservation commission will always prevail. There may be cases in which, for example, a state hospital for retarded children is severely overcrowded and has no option but to expand, even though it is located in a historic district. If there are no alternative sites available or if a lack of funds precludes a new structure elsewhere, then the local preservation body may have to agree to the addition of a new wing. But that addition should be in keeping with the architectural character of the main structure and the surrounding area. The great value of the balancing of public interests test is that it compels the project proponent to sit down with

---

189. For an excellent discussion of recent trends in this area, see Barbara Ross, *Intergovernmental Zoning Disputes: A Continuing Problem*, 7 Land Use & Zoning Digest 6 (1980).

190. 322 So.2d 571 (Fla. App. 1975), *aff'd*, 332 So.2d 610 (Fla. 1976).

191. 322 So.2d 571, 578-79 (Fla. App. 1975). Cases employing similar reasoning include *City of Fargo v. Harwood Township*, 256 N.W.2d 694 (N.D. 1977); *Lincoln County v. Johnson*, 257 N.W.2d 453 (S.D. 1977); *Brown v. Kansas Forestry, Fish & Game Commission*, 576 P.2d 230 (Kan. App. 1978); *Rutgers v. Piluso*, 286 A.2d 697 (N.J. 1972).

the local preservation commission and explore feasible alternatives.

But what of jurisdictions where courts still apply the immunity doctrine? In those situations, the local commission should look to state preservation enabling legislation for expressions of support for protecting landmarks. Also, as discussed further in chapter 3, many jurisdictions have state environmental protection acts that require state and local agencies to consider the impact of their actions on historic resources. While such laws may not force state agencies to comply with local laws, these laws often require consideration of feasible, less environmentally damaging alternatives to the project proposed.

Although the picture for controlling adverse developments by state and local agencies shows some signs of improving, the situation with federal agencies remains a difficult one. Under the Supremacy Clause of the U.S. Constitution, the federal government is generally immune from local land-use regulations.[192] However, Congress has enacted several laws directing federal agencies to examine and avoid where possible the adverse environmental impacts of their actions or undertakings. These protections apply to historic structures, particularly those listed on the National Register of Historic Places.[193] In dealing with federal agencies, local preservationists should not overlook laws such as the federal Coastal Zone Management Act (CZMA), which applies to the most highly developed and densely populated areas of the nation. That act, which directs state and local land-use plans to include a preservation element, requires that federal developments on private land in coastal areas covered by an approved plan be consistent with state and local land-use enactments to the extent feasible.[194] While neither CZMA nor environmental impact laws will stop a committed project proponent, they are useful in giving the local preservation review body some leverage in dealing with federal agencies.

---

192. U.S. Constitution, art. VI, cl. 2; *Maun v. United States* 347 F.2d 970 (9th Cir. 1965); *Demetriadis v. United States Postal Service*, 465 F. Supp. 597 (E.D.N.Y. 1979).

193. Chapter 4 discusses these provisions in detail.

194. The Coastal Zone Management Act, 16 U.S.C. §§ 1451-64 (1977). The organic legislation of federal agencies often contains similar consistency requirements. See, for example, the Federal Land Policy and Management Act, Pub. L. No. 94-579, 90 Stat. 2743 (1976).

Coordination with Other Municipal Laws and Actions

Ensuring that the local preservation ordinance meshes with other local laws is just as important as securing compliance by federal and state agencies. This chapter already has discussed methods to coordinate the preservation ordinance with the local zoning law, building code, and subdivision provisions, among others, and addressed the potential problems with public safety exclusions contained in many preservation ordinances.

The main point to keep in mind here is that coordination does not mean that preservation considerations must take precedence over other local goals as expressed in zoning ordinances or building codes. The aim of preservationists should be to ensure, however, that preservation considerations are not ignored or relegated to secondary status, as is so often the case. For example, some preservation laws contain a provision stating that in case of a conflict with local zoning requirements, the zoning requirements, even if less restrictive, prevail. This is backwards. The better approach is to require that the more strict provisions be met, unless a case for hardship relief can be made.

Preservationists also should pay attention to the internal policies of other municipal agencies. Some of the most adverse impacts on historic districts originate within city traffic or street departments. Street widenings and proliferating traffic signs are only two examples of local department actions that can detract seriously from the value of a historic area. Some cities have addressed this problem by giving the local preservation review body the power to comment on and reject actions by other city agencies that adversely affect historic districts.

Emergency Demolition Bans and Development Moratoriums

Because many local governments lack a comprehensive survey of landmark structures, situations continue to arise in which an owner secures, unbeknownst to preservationists, a permit to demolish a building of clear landmark quality. When the preservationists learn of the plans, a bloody 11th-hour battle to protect the structure often ensues. In other instances, a landmarks commission may announce its intent to study a neighborhood for possible designation. Some owners, in an attempt to circumvent future restrictions, may rush to city hall to secure demolition permits. What can a local government do under these circumstances to protect threatened landmarks without violating the legal rights of developers?

In the best of worlds, local preservation commissions would be armed with comprehensive landmarks inventories, making 11th-hour rescue attempts a thing of the past. Unfortunately, such is not the case now nor is it likely to be for years to come. Surveys take time and can be expensive, and, even when a survey has been completed, it may be several years before identification is translated into designation. What, then, should a local commission do when a building of landmark quality that enjoys no official protection is threatened with demolition? Assuming state law allows,[195] the local government or commission should enact a temporary ban or moratorium that would revoke an already-issued building permit or stop demolition. Courts generally have upheld such emergency provisions, realizing that surveys, studies, and ordinance drafting cannot be done overnight.

Invoking emergency demolition bans will raise two major legal issues involving procedural due process and "vested rights." While the constitutional guarantee of due process generally requires that affected persons be given notice and an opportunity to be heard before adoption and application of a restrictive ordinance, it is well established that a governmental body may take temporary emergency action without prior notice or hearing if affected persons are afforded an opportunity to be heard before such action becomes final. As Justice Douglas explained in *Ewing v. Mytinger & Casselberry, Inc.*,[196] a case involving seizure of drugs without a hearing by the Food and Drug Administration: "It is sufficient, where only property rights are concerned, that there is at some stage an opportunity for a hearing and a judicial determination."[197] Therefore, a local government can *enact* a temporary emergency prohibition if the developer is subsequently given an opportunity to be

---

195. Because the authority and procedures for adopting moratoriums will vary from state to state, city officials should determine the extent of their power before proceeding. Some courts have held that the power to zone generally or to control demolition of landmarks necessarily carries with it the power to enact a moratorium to maintain the status quo until a final ordinance is adopted. Other courts, however, require that the state zoning or preservation enabling legislation must be followed, particularly with respect to providing notice and an opportunity to be heard before any restrictions take effect. R.M. Anderson, ed., *American Law of Zoning*, 2d ed. (Rochester, N.Y.: Rochester Lawyers Cooperative, 1976), § 5.15; *State ex rel. Christian v. Miller*, 545 P.2d 660 (Mont. 1976).

196. 339 U.S. 594 (1950).

197. *Id.* at 599.

heard.[198] As soon as possible after enacting a demolition ban, the local government should afford the owner or developer an opportunity to be heard and contest designation or revocation of a building permit. As with most recommendations made in this chapter, a caveat is in order. Such a provision may be adopted only after the ordinance draftsman has checked to make certain that the ability to enact emergency restrictions is not limited by state enabling legislation or state court decisions.

Assuming that the local government has satisfied procedural due process dictates, it must still face the so-called "vested rights" issue. This arises, for example, when a developer, relying on existing law, spends money in anticipation of demolishing a building of landmark quality. Although there is no such thing as a "vested right" under the U.S. Constitution, most state courts recognize it in some form.[199] If a developer has done nothing more than obtain a demolition or building permit, he probably cannot claim a vested right to proceed. If, however, the developer has signed a contract with a demolition company and has spent funds to plan for a new development on the site prior to enactment of the ban, the question is a more difficult one. And, if the developer actually has started constructing the project, the chances of stopping a development are even slimmer. Vested rights law varies from state to state. A majority of jurisdictions hold that, until actual construction of a project has begun, developers have no vested right to continue despite the fact that they have all necessary permits and have spent money in reliance thereon. Other states are more liberal in the developer's favor.

The vested rights issue can be defused by establishing an administrative proceeding that places the burden on developers to produce evidence that they should be allowed to proceed. In this way, the local government can determine if the facts support its decision to forbid demolition.

While valuable and often essential to preservation, moratoriums have serious ramifications and thus require forethought. Of equal importance, they should not be used as an excuse to do nothing. The ordinance

---

198. The Supreme Court has reaffirmed this rule in *New Motor Vehicle Board v. Orrin W. Fox Co.*, 434 U.S. 1345 (1977). Chapter 5 discusses this point in greater detail.

199. Constitutional aspects of vested rights law are discussed in chapter 5. For a discussion of vested rights and zoning at the state level, see Charles Siemon and Wendy Larsen with Douglas Porter, *Vested Rights* (Washington, D.C.: The Urban Land Institute 1982).

establishing the moratorium[200] should state the reasons for its invocation, set forth a specific expiration date,[201] and contain a safety valve to allow the landmarks commission to deal with hardship cases. From a practical perspective, the types of development or alteration to be prohibited or made subject to review should be carefully delineated. More than one landmarks commission has found itself swamped with work after enacting a moratorium requiring its review of all applications for building permits in prospective historic districts. In many instances, commissions will need to worry only about demolitions or major exterior alterations.

Enforcement

Preservationists tend to give little thought to enforcement of landmarks laws, a seemingly mundane section of a local ordinance. But ignoring the details of enforcement is a trap for the unwary. As the *Model Land Development Code* explains in its introductory commentary on enforcement:

> Enforcement of land use laws has been a problem since such laws were first devised. Beginning in 1580 Queen Elizabeth and her Stuart successors endeavored to reduce the pressure of London's urban growth by a series of proclamations and laws severely restricting new construction of housing in the London area. But enforcement of these restrictions proved difficult, and the use of Star Chamber proceedings to prosecute landlords in the early 17th century became one of the grievances that led to the downfall of the Stuart kings.[202]

---

200. Courts can be expected to react more favorably to invocation of an emergency restriction if the invoking body had statutory authority to do so prior to the particular emergency before the court, although this is not a strict legal requirement. Thus, landmarks ordinances should contain a provision allowing the local legislative body or preservation commission to prohibit demolitions on an emergency basis if a structure would likely qualify under normal circumstances as a landmark under criteria set forth in the ordinance for designation.

201. Courts routinely have upheld zoning moratoriums for "reasonable" periods of time. Generally, six months to two years is considered a reasonable duration. Williams, *American Land Planning Law*, 1980 Supp., § 1:30.01. But see *Southern National Bank of Houston v. City of Austin*, 582 S.W.2d 229 (Tex. Civ. App. 1979), invalidating an open-ended ban on demolition during designation hearings. Moratoriums have likewise been upheld in a landmarks preservation context. In *City of Dallas v. Crownrich*, 506 S.W.2d 654 (Tex. Civ. App. 1974), the city successfully argued that a six-month moratorium was essential to protecting landmarks while the city was formulating a preservation plan. See also *Don't Tear It Down, Inc. v. Washington*, 399 F. Supp. 153 (D.D.C. 1975).

202. American Law Institute, *A Model Land Development Code*, p. 444.

While a landmarks commission may not be sentenced to the Tower of London for overlooking enforcement issues, recent experience across the country demonstrates the necessity of careful drafting. In Chicago, for example, Rincker House, the second-oldest structure in the city and a designated landmark, was torn down without official approval by a developer who apparently found that the prospective profits from redeveloping the site far outweighed the puny penalties contained in the local landmarks ordinance. In other towns, landmarks commissions are finding that the enforcement of local controls, particularly in large districts, is causing some serious administrative headaches—it is simply too expensive and time-consuming to keep an eye on designated landmarks to make sure the local law is being observed by owners.

Thus, in drafting enforcement provisions of an ordinance, one should keep in mind two major issues: remedies for noncompliance and administration.

Remedies to Ensure Compliance

As more and more landmarks are designated and the scope of preservation controls is broadened to control everything from demolition of exterior features to day-to-day upkeep, the issue of remedies for noncompliance is certain to become more crucial. The challenge in drafting enforcement provisions will be to craft remedies strong enough to deter violations and induce compliance but not so draconian that courts shy away from imposing them. The experience with building and housing codes regulations is instructive. If monetary fines are set at a low level (as fines for ignoring landmarks law often are), owners do a little arithmetic and conclude that, even if they are caught violating a building code provision, the economic consequences are insignificant, in effect, just another cost of doing business. On the other hand, experience also demonstrates that heavy reliance on criminal penalties is misplaced. Judges in most jurisdictions simply do not put people into jail for this sort of offense.

There are, however, middle-ground options that can be more effective, particularly when used in combination with one another.[203]

Injunctive Relief and Compliance Orders. The primary goal of an enforcement provision should be to secure compliance with the local landmarks law and to protect landmarks, not to punish the offenders.

---

203. The usual caveat about checking applicable state enabling legislation and other local laws (for example, building code enforcement regulations) is in order here.

Thus, while fines may be a necessary measure to deter future violations, the landmarks ordinance should vest the local government with power to seek injunctive relief, for example, to put an immediate stop to an illegal demolition. In more minor, everyday cases—say, when an owner has altered a landmark without permission—administrative compliance orders issued by the landmarks commission may be useful in securing voluntary compliance as well as establishing a firm ground for court action if necessary.

Receiverships/Entry onto Land to Correct Violation. If a landmark owner ignores an administrative compliance order and refuses to redo an illegal alteration or to comply with affirmative maintenance requirements, a court-ordered receivership, which a court can usually establish under its power authorizing injunctive relief, can be very effective. The procedure works like this. The local commission first secures a court order requiring that an illegal alteration be redone or that the owner undertake repairs as necessary, but the owner refuses to comply. Of course, the owner might be fined or held in contempt of court, but neither of these remedies necessarily ensures the landmark is protected. The commission could then ask that the court establish a receivership overseen by a third party who would collect rents, make repairs, and manage the property until compliance is achieved.

A variation on this approach is to give the local government the power, upon securing a judicial decree, to enter onto the owner's property, make necessary repairs or alterations, and then place a lien on the property. Then, before the property can be sold, the local government must be reimbursed.[204]

Money Fines. Money fines are the most widely used method of enforcing building and housing codes. A local government generally has statutory authority to issue a notice of violation (not unlike a traffic ticket) and then go to court and collect a fine, if it can prove its case. The major problem with fines in a preservation context is that they are generally not high enough to deter violators. A fine of $500 for an illegal demolition is simply inadequate to deter anyone, but particularly

---

204. Neither of these remedies is foolproof. Use of a receivership assumes that the landmark is earning a reasonable return, but that may not be the case if it is located in a deteriorated area. The use of a lien to recoup government-incurred rehabilitation costs also has shortcomings. It may be some time before the government gets its money, and in some cases, the lien may be subordinated to a mortgage or other liens so that the local government never collects its expenditures.

commercial developers who stand to gain much by clearing a site for lucrative new construction.

The answer, of course, is to increase the level of fines provided for in the ordinance.[205] A sliding scale might be used to cover a variety of situations: a nominal fine for a first offender who out of ignorance fails to, for example, secure a necessary alteration permit and who agrees to rectify the error; a larger fine, perhaps $500, plus a further fine of several hundred dollars for each day the violation continues, for second offenders or where a violator is recalcitrant; a significant fine, measured by the amount of the pecuniary gain derived from the offense,[206] for a persistent offender or one who acted willfully to demolish a building.

When used in tandem with other remedies, such as injunctive relief, fines can be a key method of deterring future violations as well as depriving an owner from ill-gotten economic gain.

Forcing Reconstruction. There will be times when preservationists feel that reconstruction is the only adequate remedy in a case when a landmark (or at least part of it) has been destroyed. While it may be useful to include such a provision in the local ordinance as an option in egregious cases, experience in analagous zoning cases tells us that courts can be expected to enforce such a penalty only under the most exceptional circumstances. In zoning cases, the analogous situation is in reverse: an owner builds a structure in violation of the zoning ordinance, and the court forces it to be demolished. But this is only done in the rarest of cases. Courts are just as unlikely to force reconstruction, particularly

---

205. Constitutionally speaking, a fine may not be set to be wholly disproportionate to the offense and obviously unreasonable. The dollar amount of the penalty must bear some relationship to the type of conduct intended to be deterred. See *St. Louis, Iron Mountain and Southern Railway Co. v. Williams*, 251 U.S. 63 (1919). In practice, courts rarely strike down fine provisions as unreasonable.

206. American Law Institute, *A Model Land Development Code*, p. 116, adopts this approach. See § 10-204 with accompanying commentary. The *Code* provides that a judge may impose a fine "not to exceed an amount equal to double the pecuniary gain derived from the offense by the offender." In a recent case involving Chicago's historic Rincker House, which was illegally demolished without a permit, the city of Chicago has sued, seeking $500,000 in punitive damages and a creation of a constructive trust that would require the owner to use any future profits and gains from the property for preservation purposes. The city council also responded by adding a new provision to the local preservation ordinance, imposing a heavy penalty—no building permit for the site can be issued for five years and then only after review by the landmarks commission—on owners who willfully or through gross negligence cause all or part of any landmark to be demolished or altered without city approval.

given the impracticability of rebuilding a landmark from foundation up. More likely, forced reconstruction will be imposed in cases of partial demolition, where the building can be repaired to its original state without starting from scratch.

Fixing Responsibility: Against Whom and by Whom?

A subsidiary compliance issue is who should be liable for the fines or duty to repair. Most land-use ordinances provide that the property owner or person controlling the property, particularly a lessee, can be held liable for violations. In a preservation context, the ordinance draftsmen should consider allowing actions against entities such as construction firms or demolition companies responsible for illegal demolition or alterations.

Another issue is who should be able to enforce local preservation regulations—the local government, private citizens, or both. Many environmental and land-use laws allow citizens to bring suits to enforce preservation provisions, particularly when the relevant government body has refused or failed to act. The *Model Land Development Code* allows citizen suits but only by a select group, including nearby property owners and certain neighborhood organizations.[207]

Who can be responsible for enforcement will depend largely on local considerations. Does the local government have adequate resources to enforce the law? Is a citizen suit provision politically feasible? Is it likely that citizens or neighborhood groups would use such a power?

Administration

Elaborate controls on alterations, strong affirmative maintenance requirements, and tough enforcement provisions may look good on paper but be unworkable in practice because the local government lacks the work force to enforce the law.

From a practical aspect, local commissions should establish procedures to ensure uniform and efficient enforcement of the operative provisions of the preservation law. The city of New Orleans, which has been in the preservation business as long as anyone, offers some tips to reduce the administrative burden. The New Orleans landmarks commission not only exercises control over demolition and alterations but also requires affirmative maintenance of hundreds of landmarks. How does

---

207. American Law Institute, *A Model Land Development Code*, p. 116 (§§ 10-102 and 9-103).

it keep track of the condition of all those structures with a relatively small enforcement staff? One key is that it maintains a portfolio of photographs for each landmark. If an owner illegally alters a structure, the change will usually show up clearly in photographs. These photos also are very useful evidence in court enforcement proceedings.[208]

What other information should be in the files maintained on each property? Do not overlook the simple fact of who owns the property. This information may be crucial if emergency action is necessary to stop an illegal demolition or alteration, because usually before a court will act, notice must be given to the property owner. The file also should include a history of the property from an enforcement perspective—past violations, inspection results, and so forth.

All this information will be crucial if a case goes to court. Typically, enforcement cases will be handled by a municipal attorney who is completely unfamiliar with the case and who has little time to brush up on the facts before trial. Thus, whether a case is lost or won often will depend on whether the landmarks commission enforcement staff has put together a good case. The property file can supply essential evidence, particularly photographs and inspection records. A chronology summarizing the case for the attorney—notices of violation, attempts at voluntary compliance, and the like—also can be very helpful.

A sound enforcement program may become particularly critical in the future, especially in those jurisdictions that have designated many landmarks and exercise restrictive control over alterations and upkeep. If a landmark owner who has been taken to court for making alterations without necessary permits can show that the local landmarks commission has not prosecuted other violators, the owner may be able to escape liability on the ground of illegal discrimination.

---

208. Of course, photographs will not be of any value unless periodic inspections are made. Preservation commissions in larger cities may be able to cooperate with local building departments in this regard, but, in smaller communities, private preservation groups often act as the enforcement eyes, relaying information about possible violations to the commission for action. The issues of administrative inspections and constitutional limitations on warrantless searches are discussed in the preceding section on affirmative maintenance. Because most violations of preservation regulations will be readily apparent without a search of the premises—for example, a major alteration of a facade usually will be visible from the street—institutional questions regarding warrantless administrative inspections will not generally be an issue in preservation enforcement cases except for those involving affirmative maintenance or protection of interior features.

While the general rule is that a claim of illegal discrimination under the equal protection clause of the Fourteenth Amendment to the U.S. Constitution will not succeed unless the discrimination is shown to be intentional, purposeful, or systematic in nature,[209] the fact that many violators of a preservation ordinance go unprosecuted is likely to leave a bad taste in a judge's mouth. The case of *City of New Orleans v. Levy*[210] is a good lesson. There, the city sought to compel removal of a plastic covering over a courtyard in the French Quarter. The defendant, Levy, whose restaurant business might have been doomed if the plastic were removed, conceded the addition did not conform to applicable rules but argued that the injunction should not be granted because the city did not enforce the restrictions uniformly. The Louisiana Supreme Court recognized that there was no valid claim under the Fourteenth Amendment because the discrimination was not "clear and intentional," yet it was obviously bothered by evidence that the city overlooked equally serious violations and ruled that notions of fairness prevented it from granting the injunction.

Clearly, municipalities should attempt to enforce landmarks restrictions as even-handedly as possible. Failure to do so may not lead to a wholesale invalidation of such restrictions, but in close cases in which compliance would create a serious economic hardship, the courts may be hesitant to enforce the local law.

FURTHER READINGS

Legal literature on local preservation law is somewhat sparse although there are a growing number of books, articles, and publications that are helpful. Some of the most useful references are works on local land-use regulation, in which preservation controls are a subset.

The classic preservation law reference, though now dated, is Jacob Morrison's *Historic Preservation Law* (Washington, D.C.: The National Trust for Historic Preservation, 1965). When read with Wrenn's and Montague's 1964 report on local preservation programs—Robert L. Montague and Tony

---

209. *Snowden v. Hughes*, 321 U.S. 1 (1943); for a general discussion of housing code enforcement, see Dan Mandelker, Barry Gibb, and Annette Kolis, *Differential Enforcement of Housing Codes—The Constitutional Dimension*, 55 J. Urb. L. 517 (1978).

210. 233 La. 844, 98 So.2d 210 (1957).

P. Wrenn, *Planning For Preservation* (Chicago: American Society of Planning Officials, 1964)—it gives a good summary of the field in the early years. The National Trust for Historic Preservation has also published a series of case digests that summarizes early preservation cases.

The best contemporary references for local preservation law are Daniel R. Mandelker's *Land Use Law* (Charlottesville, Va.: Michie Co., 1982) and Norman Williams's *American Land Planning Law* (Chicago: Callaghan, 1974). Both contain excellent chapters on local historic preservation law and planning. A number of law reviews carry useful articles on local preservation law. The *Urban Law Annual* and the *Urban Lawyer* have paid particular attention to legal issues involved in local preservation regulation. The best source of current developments in the field of preservation law is the National Trust's *Preservation Law Reporter*, a bimonthly looseleaf service that summarizes recent cases and laws and presents articles on preservation law issues.

For those interested in constitutional questions involved in local land-use regulation there are many excellent sources. David Godschalk et al., *Constitutional Issues of Growth Management*, 2d ed. (Chicago: APA Planners Press, 1979) examines the key legal issues facing local governments in regulating land use. Fred Bosselman, David Callies, and John Banta, *The Taking Issue* (Washington, D.C.: GPO, 1973), while a decade old, remains an authoritative source on the limits of regulations as they affect property rights. The American Planning Association publishes monthly its excellent *Land Use Law and Zoning Digest*, which summarizes the most recent cases from across the United States as well as articles on topics of current concern.

Planning aspects of local preservation programs are dealt with in several publications by the National Trust for Historic Preservation, including *A Guide to Delineating Edges of Historic Districts* (Washington, D.C.: Preservation Press, 1976). Arthur Ziegler's two books on local preservation planning and strategies, *Historic Preservation in Inner City Areas* (Pittsburgh: Allegheny Press, 1971) and, with Walter Kennedy, *Historic Preservation in Small Towns* (Nashville: American Association for State and Local History, 1980), are helpful manuals of practice. The American Planning Association's *Planning* magazine and the Urban Land Institute's *Urban Land* carry from time to time articles and case studies on historic preservation at the local level.

For a highly readable account of local zoning practices and procedures that preservationists should be familiar with, see Richard Babcock's acclaimed book *The Zoning Game* (Madison, Wis.: University of Wisconsin Press, 1966). His excellent contemporary account, with Clifford Weaver, *City Zoning* (Chicago: American Planning Association, 1979) is also highly recommended.

Chapter 3
State Preservation Law

MICHAEL MANTELL

In the late 1950s and early 1960s, states were leaders in government preservation activities, particularly in authorizing local government actions.[1] By the late 1960s, with the passage of the National Historic Preservation Act (NHPA), creation of the National Register of Historic Places, and increasing federal spending and presence, state activities expanded and diversified but were largely relegated to a supporting role. States were given a central part in the federal preservation program, but they initiated very few preservation activities on their own. Indeed, until very recently, states came to be thought of as minor, were sometimes ignored, and, in some cases, were unwilling participants in historic preservation programs.

Some of the most familiar forms of state involvement do result from federal laws and requirements. Each state has its own historic preservation office—often created in response to the NHPA of 1966 and now required by it—that performs several functions to ensure state and local compliance with the act. Grants for preservation projects, certification of properties for tax benefits, and review of federal activities that affect properties listed on the National Register are a few of the ways federal laws have made states an important partner in the national historic preservation program. The 1980 amendments to the NHPA increased state responsibility under the federal program.

But changes and potential cutbacks in federal preservation programs

---

1. A 1964 report published by the National Trust for Historic Preservation and the American Society of Planning Officials included the results of a survey on state preservation activities conducted by the Kentucky attorney general's office. Of the 47 states that participated in the survey, 42 reported that they had state preservation programs, which included a wide variety of state initiatives. Robert Montague and Tony Wrenn, *Planning for Preservation* (Chicago: American Society of Planning Officials, 1964).

may alter the role of states. At first glance it may seem that any federal retrenchment would drastically curtail state involvement in preservation activities; in particular, reduced funding may restrict state activities. Defederalization and other changes, however, are providing tremendous opportunities for states to innovate and assume significant responsibilities for preservation. And regardless of what happens to state responsibilities under federal law, preservation requirements under state laws will remain. Indeed, they have been growing.

Virtually every state now plays a significant role in initiating and encouraging preservation efforts and preventing destruction of historic resources. States have gone beyond merely authorizing preservation actions by local governments and implementing federal requirements and are now an affirmative, independent participant in preservation efforts. State preservation programs are marked by diversity and responsiveness to the needs of individual states. In nearly every state, however, the basic components of state involvement include providing a link between federal and local programs, authorizing and initiating local activities, planning and developing acquisition and regulatory programs, and performing educational and enforcement functions.

More specifically, states have involved themselves in historic preservation through the following types of laws:

- First, states have granted powers to local governments to preserve historic resources through zoning, establishing historic districts and commissions, and through planning, acquiring, and utilizing other preservation mechanisms.
- Second, all states have enacted laws creating state agencies with preservation responsibilities and, in some cases, a state register of historic places.
- Third, a majority of states have environmental policy acts, which generally require that the adverse effects of government actions on historic resources be considered and mitigated.
- Finally, preservation of the built environment has been included as a goal in a few state constitutions.

Thus every participant in preservation activity should ask: What can the state do for me? How can the state help? Can the state prevent demolition? Can it provide aid and technical assistance? Can it enforce preservation laws? Can it promote compatible development?

These are some of the questions this chapter addresses. States are important catalysts and partners in preservation efforts; the first two parts of this chapter examine these roles. First, the chapter looks at state laws authorizing local government action. Learning more about the types of preservation powers delegated by states and the processes required to exercise them can help preservationists and local officials to better structure local programs. Examples of methods for strengthening and improving existing laws are included. Next, the chapter describes briefly the state partnership in federal preservation programs, notably the procedures involved in placing properties on the National Register of Historic Places, certifying them for federal tax benefits, securing grants, and minimizing the adverse effects of federal agency actions on National Register properties.

The chapter then turns to the direct protections many states afford historic resources. State preservation programs are examined, focusing on what can be done if a state agency or local government attempts to demolish historic resources or ignore state preservation policy. State environmental policy can often be another important avenue for protection, and the chapter next looks at how state environmental policy acts and constitutional provisions can be used to further the objectives of preservation. The chapter concludes with a few observations on the state role in preservation and areas for future state involvement. Of course, because of the variety of state laws and programs, each reader must assess the applicability of a specific point to his or her particular situation.

STATE ENABLING AUTHORITY FOR LOCAL GOVERNMENT PRESERVATION PROGRAMS

Regulation, acquisition, and taxation are the principal means state governments have to protect historic resources. In most instances, states have delegated these powers in various degrees to local governments—counties, cities, villages, townships, and the like.

Many localities have only those powers that are delegated to them by state enabling legislation. Others have been granted home rule status by state statute or by a state constitution, in which case the local government drafts its own charter and defines its power in accord with general state requirements. These are generally referred to as home rule or charter cities.

Regardless of the type of locality, the authority for it to act is crucial. The source of local powers, whether state enabling legislation or home rule charter, determines what the locality has the power to do. Does it allow the locality to give tax incentives for preserving buildings and districts? To regulate alteration or demolition? To acquire sites? To accept easements or enter into preservation-related contracts? Is a local preservation commission authorized? If so, what are its duties and what procedures are required?

State enabling legislation is diverse, making it difficult to categorize. Some state laws allow localities to exercise only certain powers—regulatory, acquisition—reserving others, like tax incentives, to the state. Others prescribe detailed procedures that must be followed, while a few simply grant preservation-related powers but leave the process for exercising them up to the individual local government, subject to judicial review.

Because state enabling legislation prescribes permitted powers and, in some cases, processes for exercising them, the scope of the legislation may be critical when local actions are challenged in court. In some cases, plaintiffs will call upon courts to examine enabling legislation to determine whether it authorizes the local activity in question. In most reported cases, local preservation action has been found by the courts to be within the scope of authority granted by the enabling legislation. The key for those concerned with preservation is to understand the powers delegated, the duties imposed under them, and, in those localities with weak or only partial authority, what is necessary to strengthen them. For these reasons, citizens and local officials must be familiar with the scope of their locality's enabling authority to ensure that the preservation ordinances they pass, the taxes they levy, the properties they acquire, and the manner in which they take these actions are legally permissible.

State enabling legislation and home rule charters—whether for regulating, acquiring, or taxing—should also be examined to ensure that they are comprehensive enough to meet today's local needs. Preservationists in localities with strong commitments to preservation should seek enabling authority sufficient to allow a broad spectrum of preservation activity. Preservationists in localities with ambivalent or weak interest in preservation might want to seek more forceful and specific direction from their states to require greater local involvement. In every case, preservation objectives, processes, and powers delegated by the state will influence the effectiveness of local action. This section looks at how states have generally delegated these authorities to localities, the kinds of ordinances and commissions they require, and what should be done if the enabling legislation is inadequate.

The Authority to Regulate

State enabling legislation provides localities with the authority to enact and implement police power regulations—those designed to protect and promote the public's health, safety, and general welfare. Local preservation ordinances that regulate land uses, such as ones designating and protecting historic sites and districts, must be within the scope of the regulatory authority delegated by the state.

There are various types of regulatory enabling authority. One recent survey found that at least 40 states authorize some form of local historic district zoning, while 20 states specifically allow local designation of individual landmarks or sites.[2] In addition, every state has delegated to some (if not all) of its local governments the general authority to enact land-use regulations, such as zoning. Most states list historic preservation as a permissible objective of general zoning and other regulatory controls on land use.[3] Thus, general zoning power can often be used to protect historic areas by establishing historic zones and requiring special standards and review procedures for actions proposed within these areas. Even in the few states that do not specifically mention preservation in land-use enabling laws, the power to regulate in ways that further the general welfare may be sufficient by itself to enable localities to zone for the purpose of historic preservation.

Regulations designating landmarks and establishing historic districts and zones with the intent to foster tourism, economic stability, historic, cultural, and architectural appreciation, and, in some states, aesthetics, have been upheld by courts as part of a locality's authority to promote the general welfare.[4] Such regulations have been held constitutionally valid by the U.S. Supreme Court—in *Penn Central Transportation Co. v. New York City*[5]—and in numerous state court cases.[6]

---

2. James P. Beckwith, Jr., *Preservation Law 1976-1980: Faction, Property Rights, and Ideology*, 11 N.C. Cent. L.J. 276, 278, 280 (1980). An appendix to this article contains a complete listing of preservation-related state laws.

3. See, for example, N.Y. Gen. Mun. Law § 96-a (McKinney 1977); N.M. Stat. Ann. § 3-22-2 (1978); Va. Code § 15.1-489 (1981).

4. In the past, some state courts have not permitted local land-use regulations based solely on aesthetics (for example, see *Board of Supervisors v. Rowe*, 216 S.E.2d 199 (Va. 1975)), although it is unclear whether these holdings are still valid under more recent rulings like *Penn Central Transportation Co. v. City of New York*, 438 U.S. 104 (1978); *Agins v. City of Tiburon*, 100 S. Ct. 2138 (1980); and *A-S-P Associates v. City of Raleigh*, 258 S.E.2d 444 (N.C. 1979).

5. *Penn Central Transportation Co. v. City of New York*, supra note 4, at 104, 108.

6. See, for example, *City of Santa Fe v. Gamble-Skogmo, Inc.*, 389 P.2d 13 (N.M.

In addition to delegating power to local governments, some states have created individual historic districts under special legislation. Florida, for example, has established a board of trustees for certain localities, including St. Augustine, Pensacola, Tallahassee, and Key West, to preserve historic sites within their jurisdictions.[7] The boards operate within the Florida Department of State, and members are appointed by the governor. Louisiana's constitution has designated specific areas, notably the Vieux Carre section of New Orleans, for preservation.[8] In Maryland, special enabling legislation provides for regulatory controls within certain areas, such as St. Mary's City and Montgomery County.[9]

For the most part, states have provided various combinations of these different types of authority to their localities. Zoning power is generally sufficient to authorize regulatory actions, but it may not be comprehensive enough to address the complex problems historic resources face. Individual districts and specific provisions for them can be tailored to the special needs of certain areas, but creating this authority requires the state legislature to spend time and effort that might better be allocated to more generic preservation concerns.

Historic District and Landmark Preservation Enabling Acts

Because historic district and landmark preservation enabling acts are the most widely used, they are worth examining in greater detail.[10] Their specificity and clear grants of power also provide the strongest basis of

---

1964); *Bohannan v. City of San Diego*, 106 Cal. Rptr. 333 (1973); *Rebman v. City of Springfield*, 250 N.E.2d 282 (Ill. 1969); *City of New Orleans v. Impastato*, 3 So.2d 559 (La. 1941).

7. Fla. Stat. Ann. § 266.01-.07 (West 1975) (St. Augustine); *id.* at § 266.101-.108 (Pensacola); *id.* at § 266.110-.117 (Tallahassee); *id.* at § 266.201-.208 (Key West). State-established historic districts, such as Charleston, South Carolina; Nantucket, Massachusetts; and the Vieux Carre in New Orleans, were among the earliest approaches adopted by states to preserve historic resources.

8. La. Const. of 1921 art. 14, § 22A; see also *id.* at art. 6, § 17. In addition to historic district designation, Indiana provides for an Indianapolis street's preservation. Ind. Code Ann. § 14-3-3.3-1 to -14 (Burns 1981).

9. Md. Ann. Code art. 41, § 365-74A (1978 Supp. 1981); *id.* at art. 66D, § 8-101 (c) (1978). This authority was upheld in *Montgomery County v. Woodward & Lothrop, Inc.*, 376 A.2d 483 (Md. 1977).

10. This section describes briefly various approaches states have taken. Chapter 2 on local preservation law examines in more detail how these laws have been and should

support if local preservation actions are challenged in court. As with most state laws, tremendous diversity exists among these acts. All, however, delegate to localities the specific authority to designate and regulate historic districts or specific sites. Their stated objectives, the processes established, and the powers granted constitute their most significant features and, at the same time, their most noteworthy differences.

Objectives. The stated purposes of these acts often vary, but, almost without exception, their rationales have proved sufficient to withstand court challenges alleging that they are not valid police power enactments. Some, such as Pennsylvania's, emphasize the importance of preserving some distinctive architectural or historical heritage, while others, such as Georgia's, go further, expressly seeking to "stimulate the revitalization of central business districts" and enhance tourist attractions that will also benefit local businesses.[11] The objective of Arkansas's enabling act is to promote education and the cultural, economic, and general welfare by preserving and protecting historic districts and buildings.[12] The declaration of policy in Illinois's enabling legislation notes that "the movements and shifts of population and the changes in residential areas, . . . buildings, . . . and other objects having special historical, community or aesthetic interest" require that preservation policies be instituted to ensure sound community planning and promote the general welfare.[13] More recent enactments, such as New York's, seek to "clarify and amplify" previous enabling acts, which have already been found acceptable by the courts.[14]

Process for Designating and Administering Districts. The processes required for designating and administering historic district and landmark ordinances differ from state to state, but the majority contain some common features. A more or less "typical" historic district or landmark enabling act requires the governing authority to appoint a commission or board to conduct a study of the area or site and make recommenda-

---

be implemented.

11. Pa. Stat. Ann. tit. 53, § 8002 (Purdon Supp. 1982); Ga. Code Ann. § 23-2602a (Supp. 1980).
12. Ark. Stat. Ann. § 19-5002 (1980).
13. Ill. Rev. Stat. ch. 24, § 11-48.2-1 (Supp. 1982).
14. N.Y. Gen. Mun. Law § 119-aa (McKinney Supp. 1981). See also National Center for Preservation Law, *A Primer on Preservation Law in the State of New York* (New York, 1981).

tions for its preservation. (A preexisting administrative agency, such as the planning commission, can also serve this function.) A hearing on the study and its recommendations may be required by the enabling legislation before going to the local governing body for formal approval. If a commission is specially created, the recommendations may have to be reviewed and commented on by the local planning authority before reaching the governing body. This body—the board of supervisors, city council, or the like—can then take any number of actions: adopt the recommendations, which most likely will include enacting an ordinance; send them back with specific instructions; adopt some and call for further study on others; or reject them all outright and provide for additional review.[15] In almost all cases, a public hearing will be held; it is required when an ordinance is being considered. Once a designation ordinance has been adopted, most enabling acts authorize the governing body to appoint a new historic district or landmarks commission to implement and administer the actions it has taken.

Membership in the local historic commission—the number of appointees and who selects them, required qualifications, and terms of office—along with its powers and duties, is frequently spelled out in state enabling statutes. In some states, for example, Louisiana and Michigan, the size of the commission authorized varies with the size of the locality.

Most often the commission is given jurisdiction over exterior alterations, new construction, and demolition of all landmarks and structures within the area to ensure compliance with the ordinance. Generally this power is exercised through issuing permits or "certificates of appropriateness," as they are called, which a property owner or developer must get before beginning construction on the site. Broad permitting standards are included in the enabling act. Also, in some states, construction on nearby property that would affect the historic area or site is also subject to commission review.[16] In some states, certificates from the historic commission must be coordinated with other required building permits. Appeal procedures are generally provided for in these acts.

Some important procedural variations, however, do exist. A grow-

---

15. Iowa allows creation of a historic district not only by the local governing body but also by a majority of voters if 10 percent of the residents petition to get the measure on the ballot. Iowa Code Ann. § 303.21-.25 (West Supp. 1982).

16. See the discussion in *Bohannan v. City of San Diego, supra* note 6, upholding this authority.

ing number of states prescribe in detail the procedures localities must follow in implementing historic district and landmark preservation enabling legislation. For example, Indiana sets forth the membership requirements, terms, and duties of local preservation commissions and the time periods for hearings and decisions of the commissions.[17] Similarly, Arkansas, Georgia, Louisiana, and Michigan, to name a few other states with enabling acts worth reviewing, include detailed procedures for administering historic commissions and establishing districts. They even specify when hearings must take place, the type of notice required, and the time period allowed for decision making on both designating districts and ruling on applications for proposed alteration, construction, and demolition.[18]

Other state enabling acts also contain elaborate specifications for the composition, terms, qualifications, and duties of local commissions but allow more local discretion on other things, such as the hearing process and decision-making schedules. In North Carolina, a hearing is not required by statute (although judicially it may be), and each commission must establish its own rules to ensure fairness.[19] Maryland and Pennsylvania also provide for local flexibility within state-required processes for some aspects of commission procedures.

Other states provide few requirements or little guidance to localities in their historic district or landmark enabling legislation. For example, Alaska, Mississippi, and Nebraska allow the establishment of local preservation commissions and districts but leave procedural details and implementation almost entirely up to individual local governments.[20] In New Mexico, the state preservation agency is authorized but not required to prescribe by regulations the procedures that local governments must follow. Virginia's enabling law allows for local discretion in setting up preservation commissions and districts and landmarks but specifies the

---

17. Ind. Code Ann. § 36-7-11-1 to -18 (Burns 1981 & Supp. 1982); *id.* at § 36-7-11.1-1 to -14 (Burns Supp. 1982).
18. Ark. Stat. Ann. § 19-5001 to -5011 (1980); Ga. Code Ann. § 23-2601a to -2612a (Supp. 1980); La. Const. art. 6, § 17; La. Rev. Stat. Ann. § 25:731-:767 (West 1975 1982 Supp.); *id.* at § 33:4571-:4573 (West 1982 Supp.); Mich. Comp. Laws Ann. § 5.3407(1)-(12) (1975 Supp. 1982).
19. N.C. Gen. Stat. § 160A-397, 399.5(1) (1981).
20. Alaska Stat. § 29.48.108-.110 (Supp. 1981); Miss. Code Ann. § 39-13-3 (Supp. 1981); Neb. Rev. Stat. § 14-2001 to -2002 (1977). The exercise of these powers is generally subject to requirements set forth by other laws, such as a state administrative procedures act, and various judicial rulings.

procedure for appeals and the standard of review for courts to use in determining whether the commissions acted correctly.[21]

State involvement in the local preservation commission and ordinance process also varies. In Pennsylvania, the state preservation agency must certify the historic significance of each local district before the ordinance designating it can take effect.[22] Arkansas, Georgia, and North Carolina require state review of the districts and landmarks that localities intend to designate under their ordinances.[23] New York similarly authorizes a local report and survey on historic areas and actions recommended by the locality, subject to state guidelines and review.[24] Virginia's enabling legislation allows the state preservation agency to step in and establish local districts if the local governing body has failed to designate any such areas.[25]

Grants of Power. The regulatory powers delegated to local bodies by state enabling legislation generally include designating districts or sites, ensuring compatible exterior alterations and construction, and participating in other local decisions that may affect applicable historic resources.[26] On the whole, however, the powers given vary among the states and even within a state, with some enabling acts delegating strong, far-reaching authority in one section and weaker authority in others.

Statutes in some states go beyond the designation and review powers typically authorized by state enabling acts. For example, Indiana provides that an approved historic district plan will become part of the locality's comprehensive plan, giving it perhaps more strength than if it stood by itself, particularly against charges that certain landowners are being unfairly singled out to bear the burdens of the entire community.[27] Moreover, where the historic district ordinance conflicts with general

---

21. Va. Code § 15.1-503.2(c) (1981).
22. Pa. Stat. Ann. tit. 53, § 8002 (Purdon Supp. 1982).
23. Ark. Stat. Ann. § 19-5003A (1980); Ga. Code Ann. § 23-2606a(b)(1) (Supp. 1980); N.C. Gen. Stat. § 160A-395, 399.5(2)(1981).
24. N.Y. Gen. Mun. Law § 119-cc (McKinney Supp. 1981).
25. Va. Code § 10-141 (1978).
26. These powers are in addition to others frequently granted, such as acquiring, maintaining, and taxing historic resources, which are discussed later in this section.
27. Ind. Code Ann. § 36-7-11.1-6(h) (Burns Supp. 1982). The legal importance of comprehensive plans is discussed in Daniel R. Mandelker and Edith Netter, *A New Role for the Comprehensive Plan*, 33 Land Use Law Zoning Digest 5 (September 1981). The issue of landowners claiming they have been unfairly discriminated against by preservation regulations amounting to a denial of equal protection is examined in chapter 5, which deals with constitutional law.

zoning laws, the more restrictive of the two applies in Indiana.[28] Indiana also requires a detailed survey, inventory, and report, conforming to specific requirements set forth in the state legislation. In Michigan, the denial of a certificate from the local commission is expressly binding on all other local authorities; a proposed exterior alteration or demolition of affected property cannot go forward through any other local building or permitting department without the commission's approval.[29] Arkansas requires applicants to get a certificate from the local commission, even if no other local building permit is required. An innovative provision in the District of Columbia ordinance authorizes the power to require parties that demolish property in violation of a preservation ordinance to rebuild it as it existed prior to demolition.[30]

The Illinois enabling act authorizes a variety of sophisticated tools, including transfer of development rights and a development rights bank to accommodate the needs of preservation to the needs of development.[31] Such tools have yet to be used by any Illinois municipality. The Illinois act also requires just compensation if a denial of a permit results in a "taking" of private property.[32] However, the statute sets out a standard to be used in determining whether a permit denial is a "taking"— namely, if it deprives the owner of all reasonable use of the property—that is difficult to meet.[33]

To alleviate "takings" problems, most enabling statutes allow local commissions to grant variances to specific properties where the application of an ordinance or permitting requirement would result in severe economic hardship to the property owner. For example, local commissions in Michigan must issue a permit for demolition if "retention of the structure would cause undue financial hardship to the owner."[34] If the denial by a local preservation board of a certificate of ap-

---

28. Ind. Code Ann. § 36-7-11-3 (Burns 1981). In the past, provisions such as these have been added as boilerplate by some states, but they are increasingly important given the conflicts in local plans and local development projects.

29. Mich. Comp. Laws Ann. § 5.3407(9) (1976).

30. D.C. Code Ann. § 5-1010(b) (1981).

31. Ill. Ann. Stat. ch. 24, § 11-48.2-2 (Smith-Hurd Supp. 1982).

32. *Id.* at §11-48.2-5. For a complete discussion of the "takings" clause and what it means, see chapter 5.

33. *Id.*

34. Mich. Comp. Laws Ann. § 5.3407(5C) (Supp. 1982). Some state laws, such as Pennsylvania's, do not contain variance provisions; instead, courts and local preservation bodies are left to structure appropriate relief.

propriateness to alter or demolish will render a building "incapable of earning an economic return," Indiana law provides that demolitions may be permitted.[35] However, before demolition is approved, the local board can arrange to have the building acquired or preserved in some other manner; the enabling act gives the board at least 60 days and up to one year to notify the public and find alternative means of preservation.[36]

Virginia's enabling act contains an unusual provision that has been criticized by some preservationists because it does not allow local governments to prevent demolition. It provides that an owner of a historic structure has the "right" to demolish it once there has been an application to the local governing body and a good faith attempt, for a time specified in the statute, to sell the property to the locality and other interested parties.[37] The specified period is related to the price of the building; for example, buildings with a price tag of less than $25,000 have three months; buildings worth from $50,000 to $75,000 have six months; buildings worth more than $90,000 have one year.[38] Since the historic value of a property may not be completely reflected in its market value, setting grace periods in this fashion may not adequately protect significant structures. Moreover, in a depressed real estate market, historic properties have little chance of being purchased and preserved by this mechanism. Virginia's statutory time periods, however, may give an incentive to property owners to offer their buildings at a lower price to gain advantage of the shorter time requirements.

On the other hand, North Carolina, which has a detailed enabling act providing strong regulatory powers to localities, does not allow denial of a certificate of appropriateness authorizing demolition. Instead, a local commission has up to 180 days to negotiate with the owner and other parties to find alternative ways of preserving the structure. If no alternative has been found by the time the period ends, demolition must be authorized.[39]

Some state enabling acts exempt particular agencies or localities from compliance. Affected local governments and preservationists have found these exemptions troublesome. Georgia's enabling law exempts the

---

35. Ind. Code Ann. § 36-7-11-14(b) (Burns 1981).
36. *Id.*
37. Va. Code § 15.1-503.2(c) (1981).
38. *Id.*
39. N.C. Gen. Stat. § 160A-399 (Supp. 1981).

state's Department of Transportation—a key agency—and contractors and local governments performing work funded by it from the requirements of the act, including having to seek certificates of appropriateness. The local preservation commission must be notified and given at least 45 days to review the proposed activity of the Department of Transportation and provide written comments on how to minimize its adverse effect.[40] It has no power, though, to prevent the action. Other acts exempt localities of a certain size, home rule areas, or even counties from their requirements.[41]

Variance and other provisions that allow for waiver of restrictions in cases of genuine economic hardship are important because they recognize the need for flexibility to handle special situations. Similarly, exempting certain agencies or localities from these laws may remove burdens on already overtaxed institutions. State enabling acts should be reviewed, however, to ensure that these relaxations and exemptions do not excessively weaken local powers.

Improving Regulatory Enabling Laws. Many state regulatory enabling laws need revision in light of recent experience and today's needs. For example, important local jurisdictions, such as counties, may be excluded and provisions requiring that certain professionals, such as architects, be included among commission members may be difficult for small communities to meet. Recent steps taken by some states indicate ways in which these laws can be made more effective.

Increasingly, states are delegating more detailed and sophisticated preservation powers, often as part of revised preservation acts that revamp state preservation responsibilities as well. Arkansas, Georgia, New York, and North Carolina are among the states that have broadened local enabling authority to respond to growing preservation needs within the context of a strengthened state preservation program.

Some states have revamped procedural and regulatory requirements for local actions. These measures have provided more uniformity while still allowing for local discretion. By outlining in some detail local procedures and powers, states help localities satisfy the procedural rights of various parties and defend against legal challenges on these and other grounds. Moreover, this uniformity gives developers some notion of what

---

40. Ga. Code Ann. § 23-2607a(b) (Supp. 1980).

41. For example, see *id.*; Pa. Stat. Ann. Tit. 53, § 8001 (Purdon Supp. 1982); National Center for Preservation Law, *A Primer on Historic Preservation Law in Pennsylvania* (Washington, D.C., 1982), p. 21.

to expect from locality to locality, allowing them to anticipate, and participate in, review processes and preservation planning more effectively. Local flexibility remains crucial, but it is flexibility within a more tightly defined, predictable framework.

A few states have moved one step farther and begun authorizing and even requiring that historic preservation goals be incorporated into local land planning. In California, preservation of historic and cultural resources is optional as a separate element of local land-use plans required by state law, but it must be addressed as part of the open-space and conservation elements, which are mandatory.[42] Local ordinances must be consistent with these planning elements. Oregon's statewide law on land planning requires local planning jurisdictions to inventory historic and cultural resources and to manage them so as to preserve their original character. Conflicting uses of inventoried resources must be identified and local programs developed in response to state requirements.[43] On the local level, more states are requiring preservation plans and actions to be coordinated more closely with other land-use responsibilities.[44] Protecting historic resources and requiring local land-use and preservation plans to be coordinated may not be enough to save a specific property. However, these efforts do provide additional impetus for local action.

Building code enabling authority can also strengthen local powers. State and local building code standards often conflict with the objectives of preservation by requiring historic properties to modernize. A few states have adopted measures to lessen this tension. California's state historic building code authorizes localities, as well as state agencies, to adopt alternative building standards and regulations for qualified historic

---

42. Cal. Gov't Code § 65302, 65303 (West Supp. 1982).

43. Oregon Land Conservation and Development Commission, *Statewide Planning Goals and Guidelines* (Salem, Or., 1980), p.7, Group 5. Or. Admin. R. ch. 660, § 10 (1977). Interviews with Edward Sullivan, Esq., O'Donnell, Rhoades, Gerber, Sullivan & Rames, and Robert Stacey, Esq., One Thousand Friends of Oregon, Portland, Oregon (August 1981). In Vermont, the state's role in reviewing local land-use (preservation) decisions to ensure compliance with Act 250, the state's land-use law, was limited in a decision on a demolition permit for a house within a historic district. *Committee to Save the Bishop's House v. Medical Center, Inc.*, 400 A.2d 1015 (Vt. 1979).

44. Mich. Comp. Laws Ann. § 5-3407(8) (1975); Ind. Code Ann. at § 36-7-11.1-5(b) (Burns Supp. 1982); *id.* at § 36-7-11.1-6(e)-(h); Ga. Code Ann. § 23-2606a(a)(1) (Supp. 1980). The importance of coordinating and integrating historic preservation and land-use planning activities is discussed in chapter 2.

structures.[45] A special state board acts in this capacity as an advisory, support, and review body.[46] Similarly, Hawaii authorizes localities to modify building codes to protect and enhance use of historic structures.[47] Both South Dakota and Idaho allow local governing bodies to exempt historic sites from those building code provisions that could otherwise work to undermine their preservation.[48] These and similar measures adopted in other states, such as Connecticut and Massachusetts, are important elements of local preservation enabling authority.

The Authority to Acquire

As previously mentioned, most states authorize local preservation commissions and governing bodies to acquire historic sites.[49]

In many of these states, there is power to acquire not only in full fee (complete ownership of the property) but also in less-than-fee arrangements, such as preservation easements.[50] Enabling authority also generally includes the power of eminent domain, which results in condemning property for a public use and paying "just compensation" for it. In most of the states authorizing acquisition, localities are also delegated responsibility to raise and appropriate money to foster preservation as well as to maintain and preserve the properties they own.[51]

The authority for traditional full-fee acquisition is contained in most

---

45. Cal. Health & Safety Code § 18958 (West Supp. 1982).
46. *Id.* at § 18960.
47. Hawaii Rev. Stat. § 6E-15 (1976).
48. S.D. Codified Laws Ann. § 1-19B-54 (1980); Idaho Code § 67-4618 (1980). The major building codes, such as the Building Officials and Code Administrators International, Inc. (BOCA), American Insurance Association, and Southern Building Code Conference, have sections allowing discretionary treatment of historic structures. These codes have been the basis of revised statewide and local codes. See the discussion on building codes in chapter 2.
49. James P. Beckwith, Jr., *Developments in the Law of Historic Preservation and a Reflection on Liberty*, 12 Wake Forest L. Rev. 93, 115 (1976).
50. As discussed in chapter 7, a preservation easement is a formal agreement between the owner of a historic structure and a government agency or preservation organization giving the latter the right to review and approve changes to the building before they are undertaken. In exchange for giving the preservation organization or government entity a legally enforceable right to protect the historic character of the site that amounts to a property interest, the building's owner may receive tax or some other economic benefits.
51. See, for example, Mich. Comp. Laws Ann. § 5.3395 (1975 & Supp. 1982); *id.* at § 5.3407(5)(2); N.Y. Gen. Mun. Law § 119-aa to 119-dd (McKinney Supp. 1981).

state preservation enabling acts, although the expense of acquisition, coupled with the fact that it takes property off local tax rolls, has limited its use. Michigan's enabling act is among the most restrictive, authorizing acquisition by local governing bodies only after the historic district commission concludes that all other preservation efforts have failed or that public ownership is most suitable and recommends purchase.[52]

Acquisition powers may be granted to local preservation boards as well as to local elected bodies. For example, Indiana delegates acquisition authority directly to the local preservation commission.[53] Virginia, like many other states, provides authority for the acquisition of historic resources not only in the preservation commission enabling act but in its general local enabling provisions as well.[54]

In addition to authorizing local governments to acquire property in full fee, some states have expressly delegated to them the authority to accept preservation easements, enter into and enforce partial acquisition contracts and convenants, and exchange property—in effect, engage in a full range of alternatives to full-fee acquisition. These alternatives are less costly in most cases than outright acquisition but offer many of the same protective benefits.

In some states, preservation enabling acts expressly authorize the use of less-than-fee acquisition techniques by localities. North Carolina's preservation enabling act authorizes local historic property commissions to "acquire by any lawful means the fee or any lesser included interest" in designated historic buildings.[55] In Illinois, the preservation enabling authority grants similar powers.[56] A general grant of more traditional acquisition power might be sufficient in some states to allow localities to acquire easements and engage in other less-than-fee acquisitions. The enabling authority is implied, but use of these tools is arguably part of broad acquisition authority.[57]

Both North Carolina and Illinois, as well as a few other states, also have additional, more explicit statutory authority for preservation easements, covenants, and the like. These acts typically apply to natural and scenic resources as well as to historic ones. The Illinois Conserva-

---

52. Mich. Comp. Laws Ann. § 5.3407(7) (1975).
53. Ind. Code Ann. § 36-7-11.1-6(10) (Burns Supp. 1982).
54. Va. Code § 15.1-18.1 (1981); *id.* at § 15.1-503.2(d).
55. N.C. Gen. Stat. § 160-A-399.3(3) (Supp. 1981).
56. Ill. Rev. Stat. ch. 24, § 11-48.2-2 (Supp. 1982).
57. Paul E. Wilson and H. James Winkler III, *The Response of State Legislation to Historic Preservation*, 36 Law & Contemp. Probs. 329, 340 (1971).

tion Rights Act, for example, promotes and allows conveyances of conservation rights or scenic easements to localities.[58] There are several important advantages to specific state legislation on conservation easements. It makes clear the powers possessed by local governments to accept easements and by whom the easements can be enforced. It also addresses the question of whether future owners of the property are bound by the restrictions, thereby ensuring that landowners who donate easements will be eligible for federal tax benefits.[59]

The stated purposes and procedures contained in these acts will determine in large part the scope of local powers.[60] The acts generally allow both local governments and charitable preservation organizations to convey and enforce the property interests involved, although North Carolina also allows enforcement by any business.[61] California authorizes local governing bodies to contract with owners of historic property within designated historic zones to restrict alteration and retain a property's historical characteristics. Each contract must be for a minimum of 20 years, and, if it is breached and canceled for noncompliance prior to its expiration, the property owner must pay a fee equal to 12.5 percent of the full value of the property.[62]

Whether to preserve significant property facing certain demolition, spur preservation activity in a newly rediscovered area, or provide incentives for continued preservation, acquisition by any of these methods can often be the difference between success and failure. The biggest drawback, of course, is the expense. Even alternatives to full-fee acquisition have administrative and other costs, and, in some cases, lost tax revenues must also be taken into account. But authority from the state for less-than-fee approaches should be sought by localities and those interested in furthering the productive use of historic property. Such authority may qualify landowners for tax benefits and can be an incentive for private actions that preserve historic resources.

The Authority to Tax

Many states have enacted tax laws to promote preservation. Some delegate

---

58. Ill. Ann. Stat. ch. 30, § 401 (Smith-Hurd Supp. 1982). See also Landmarks Preservation Council of Illinois, *Preservation Easements in Illinois* (Chicago, 1981).

59. These tax benefits are discussed in chapter 7.

60. See Russell L. Brenneman, *Historic Preservation Restrictions: A Sampling of State Statutes*, 8 Conn. L. Rev. 231 (1975-76).

61. N.C. Gen. Stat. § 121-35(2) (1981).

62. Cal. Gov't Code § 50280-50290 (West Supp. 1982).

to localities specific power to reduce tax burdens on historic property, thereby providing incentives for preservation. Tax incentives for preservation have been an effective tool but have been more successfully used by the federal government than by local entities. With increasing fiscal demands on them, localities may become more reluctant to use fully their delegated taxing authority for the benefit of preservation.

Different approaches are authorized, but all have a common goal. Maryland authorizes localities to award tax credits up to a specified percent for property owners who rehabilitate, restore, or even construct architecturally compatible new structures within historic districts.[63] New Mexico also permits local tax credits but with a few key differences. The property must be on the state register, and, unlike Maryland, the tax credit only applies to actual restoration and preservation expenses, not compatible new development. Moreover, no statutory limit is set on the amount of credit provided, allowing registered property to be exempt from local property taxes for the full costs of renovation.[64]

Other states have set stricter criteria for localities to follow in granting tax relief. Connecticut localities are permitted by state law to abate, either partially or fully, property taxes on buildings of historical or architectural merit. Responsibility for determining merit rests with the locality, which may delegate it to a local preservation or architectural organization. Before becoming eligible, however, the property owner must show that the current taxes levied are a material factor threatening preservation of the structure. The state may provide financial assistance to the locality to the extent revenues are foregone. If the taxes are abated by the locality and the structure is subsequently destroyed or remodeled in an incompatible manner, the owner must repay the taxes saved.[65] Pennsylvania authorizes localities to abate property taxes on commercial, business, and residential property for improvements, including rehabilitation. The property must be in a deteriorated or blighted area, and abatement schedules applying to residential structures differ from those applying to commercial or business property.[66] In an unusual delegation of tax power, New York's general enabling law for preservation allows localities to satisfy awards for damages in

---

63. Md. Ann. Code art. 81, § 12G (1975).
64. N.M. Stat. Ann. § 18-6-13 (1980).
65. Wilson and Winkler, *supra* note 57, at 341-42.
66. Pa. Stat. Ann. tit. 72, § 4722-27 (Purdon Supp. 1982). *Id.* at § 4711-101 *et seq.* See also National Center for Preservation Law, *supra* note 41.

preservation "takings" cases by limiting or remitting taxes.[67]

The track record of local property tax initiatives is mixed at best. Local governments have been reluctant to enact laws for a variety of reasons: some enabling laws are poorly designed, and, in many cases, local governments fear losing tax revenues. A complete discussion of these laws and recommendations for improving them are contained in chapter 7, which deals with economics and preservation law.

STATE PRESERVATION RESPONSIBILITIES UNDER FEDERAL PROGRAMS

In addition to providing enabling authority for local governments, states fulfill a central role in the federal preservation program. In response to federal requirements, most states have created state preservation agencies, and all have a program headed by a state historic preservation officer (SHPO) to implement the National Historic Preservation Act (NHPA) and applicable state laws.[68]

SHPOs and the state preservation agencies they generally run are the focal point of state preservation efforts. SHPOs have key responsibilities for implementing federal requirements, such as statewide preservation surveys and studies, the National Register nomination process, the Section 106 process that seeks to minimize the adverse effects of federal undertakings on historic sites, tax certification, and preservation grants. This part of the chapter examines state responsibilities under federal preservation laws. First, the state role in implementing the NHPA is discussed, followed by a review of state involvement with property owners receiving federal tax benefits.

States and the NHPA

States are key in many respects to the workings of the NHPA and its 1980 amendments. (The NHPA is discussed in detail in chapter 4, which looks at federal preservation law.) If state programs are approved under the act, they hold the purse strings to federal money for themselves and the local governments they certify.

---

67. N.Y. Gen. Mun. Law § 96-a (McKinney 1977).
68. Interview with Peter King, Executive Director, National Conference of State Historic Preservation Officers, Washington, D.C. (May 1980).

Evolving State Responsibilities

The National Historic Preservation Act of 1966 established a matching (50-50) grant program for the states. The grants were to be used for, among other things, creating and administering a state historic preservation office, conducting surveys and preparing statewide, comprehensive historic preservation plans, and rehabilitating historic properties to standards set by the Department of the Interior.

The act and the grants provided under it stimulated state involvement. Over the next decade or so, every state created a preservation office, designated a SHPO, and began to assume more responsibilities, largely to meet requirements attached to the receipt of federal dollars. For example, as a condition for receiving federal grants, the Department of the Interior required SHPOs to assist the federal Advisory Council on Historic Preservation and nominate properties to the National Register of Historic Places. New federal tax incentives to stimulate historic restoration brought additional duties to states receiving federal grants.

These and other SHPO responsibilities were formally recognized by the 1980 NHPA amendments. These amendments attempt to structure and solidify the preservation partnership of federal and state governments envisioned by the drafters of the 1966 act. The House of Representatives' report on the amendments specifically noted that "[d]espite the increased responsibilities placed on them, and despite the growth in their professional capabilities and experience, the States have not been treated as the full 'partner' in the Federal program, envisioned by the Congress in the 1966 Act."[69] All of the state programs have been approved by the secretary of the interior[70] and thus receive federal funding, although the secretary is required to review and evaluate them at least every four years to ensure compliance with federal requirements.

SHPO Duties

Regarding the responsibilities of SHPOs, the 1980 amendments largely codify what had previously been in regulations.[71] Besides administering

---

69. H.R. Rep. No. 95-1457, 96th Congress, 2d Sess. 23 (1980).

70. Approval requires the state appointment of an SHPO, employment of a qualified staff, designation of a qualified review board, and adequate public participation in the program.

71. The 1966 NHPA, § 101(a), described the duties of the SHPO within the context of the powers authorized to the secretary of the interior. The SHPO's responsibilities were not outlined in the statute but in 36 C.F.R. § 61.2 and 800.5 (1981).

federal assistance, the SHPO must generally engage in short- and long-term preservation planning and aid federal agencies and local governments in carrying out their preservation duties by performing a variety of tasks. More specifically, the act requires the SHPO to:
1. Compile and maintain a statewide survey and inventory of historic properties;
2. Implement a statewide historic preservation plan;
3. Administer federal assistance to the state grants-in-aid program;
4. Aid federal, state, and local governments in carrying out their historic preservation duties;
5. Identify, nominate, and process eligible properties for listing on the National Register;
6. Work with the secretary of the interior, the Advisory Council on Historic Preservation, and federal and state agencies to ensure that historic properties are considered throughout planning and development;
7. Serve as an information, education, training, and technical source for federal and state historic preservation programs; and
8. Help develop local programs for certification pursuant to qualification criteria contained in the act.[72]

Certification. Certification of local governments is the chief new responsibility imposed on the SHPO by the 1980 amendments. To be certified by the state, local governments must enforce a state or local program for designating and protecting historic properties; establish a qualified historic preservation review commission; maintain a system for survey and inventory of historic properties; provide for public participation in the local historic preservation program, including the National Register nomination process; and satisfactorily perform responsibilities designated to them under the NHPA. Any local government that has been certified or is "making efforts to become so certified" is eligible to receive a minimum of 10 percent of the federal historic preservation funds allocated to the state for its preservation programs and projects.[73] All funds pass through the SHPO, who determines the specific allotments. The NHPA also provides for participation of certified local governments in the National Register nomination process.[74]

---

72. The state may contract to have these responsibilities carried out by a qualified nonprofit organization or educational institution.
73. 16 U.S.C.A. § 470a(c)(3) (West Supp. 1982).
74. *Id.* at § 470a(c)(1).

(Because no implementing regulations have been issued by the Department of the Interior, no local governments have as yet been certified.) Thus, in addition to authorizing certification power, the act expands the SHPO's control of federal funds in the state by authorizing a pass-through of funds to certified local governments. However, only a few states have established a formal pass-through program.

While a step in the right direction, these certification requirements by no means guarantee a strong state or even local program. For example, the state or local designation and protection program that localities must enforce to become certified does not necessarily include strong powers that, say, prevent demolition. Similarly, simply establishing a qualified review commission on historic preservation is no guarantee that the local governing body will in fact pay attention to it, let alone follow its recommendations. States and localities must take the well-crafted but loosely designed foundation provided by the NHPA and build a strong structure on it.

Secton 106 Review. As explained in detail in the chapter on federal law (chapter 4), the SHPO's participation is an integral part of the Section 106 review process. This process attempts to minimize the adverse effects of federal agency actions on properties listed or eligible for listing on the National Register. It requires federal agencies to consider the effects of their actions and give the federal Advisory Council on Historic Preservation an opportunity to comment on them.

The 106 process often begins with the SHPO. The SHPO will generally learn about the proposed action through an A-95 clearinghouse review meeting and take the initial step by advising the federal agency of the potential impacts of its proposed action.[75] The SHPO will then work with the federal agency and the advisory council, attempting to minimize the project's adverse effects.

The process only applies to federal agencies and cannot force them

---

75. The A-95 review process, which developed from the Office of Management and Budget Circular A-95 and the Intergovernmental Cooperation Act of 1968, provides an early opportunity for statewide and areawide agencies to review and comment on applications for federal assistance to development projects that will affect them. Conflicts between federal assistance and state and local plans and needs are to be identified and, to the extent possible, resolved at this stage before the project proceeds further in the regulatory process. As this book went to press, the A-95 process was revoked by the Reagan administration; it was replaced by Executive Order 12372, which requires federal agencies to simply provide opportunities for state and local government consultation on federal projects. It also requires that when a state has established a review

to take protective actions. Generally, strong public support is needed. Some states, including Massachusetts, have used portions of their federal funds under the NHPA to publish useful books on SHPO duties, how their Section 106 process works, and other NHPA activities, thereby informing the public and allowing them to participate more effectively.[76]

Preservation Planning. The role of SHPOs in preservation surveying and planning is often neglected, particularly as attention tends to focus on more immediate and site-specific concerns. But the SHPO is required to develop and implement a system of resource management for comprehensive statewide historic preservation planning.[77]

The plan establishes the objectives and priorities for the state preservation program. Statewide surveying and planning of historic resources are basic components and probably necessary first steps in a coordinated preservation program.[78] Here information is gathered and priorities set that not only become the keystone of a successful program but also may provide valuable evidence for a case to be made to protect a specific property or district. Preservationists should, therefore, become involved in this process—encouraging SHPOs to take it seriously—to ensure that relevant information is gathered and considered.

Regulations under the NHPA also require that SHPOs integrate historic preservation planning into all levels of state planning.[79] Like federal agencies, state agencies can often present major obstacles to the goals of preservation. A number of states have instituted various measures to get state agencies to incorporate preservation considerations into their planning and development activities. Regulations under the NHPA are one force behind this effort. Others are discussed later in this chapter.

Working with Other Agencies and Individuals. The SHPO's role is further defined by NHPA amendments requiring SHPO participation with other parties under certain circumstances. Before a property within a certified local government's jurisdiction may be considered for nomination to the National Register, the job of notifying the owner, the chief local elected official, and the local preservation commission falls on the

---

process, federal agencies must cooperate with it. It is not clear whether state or regional councils of government will continue the process voluntarily.

76. See, for example, Massachusetts Historical Commission, *Public Planning and Environmental Review: Archeology and Historic Preservation* (Boston, April 1979).
77. 36 C.F.R. § 61.2 (1981).
78. Wilson and Winkler, *supra* note 57, at 333.
79. 36 C.F.R. § 61.2 (1981).

SHPO.[80] Direct grants and insured private lender loans for preservation of properties listed on the Register can be made by the secretary of the interior only after consultation with the SHPO.[81] Each federal agency must cooperate with the SHPO in order to locate, inventory, and nominate all agency-controlled properties qualified for inclusion on the Register.[82]

While provisions under the act may serve to get a building designated, actually save it, or get other government agencies to cooperate with preservation objectives, legally they often are insufficient by themselves to bring about a desired result. Preserving historic resources generally has to be done on a political or administrative level—through letter writing, hearings, elections, and the like—and one of the act's greatest contributions is in the preservation institution building it encourages and the political support that can follow. In states with an effective, determined SHPO, the act can be used to strengthen the preservation agency's position, educate and build constituencies, and assist local governments and other state agencies. These actions will in turn help lessen noncompliance with the act's substantive provisions. But with a weaker, more reluctant SHPO, serious deficiencies in the act are revealed; there is no mechanism to force the SHPO to become stronger or actually require compliance with its objectives by other government agencies or property owners. In this situation, the best asset can be a strong constituency at the local level.

Grants and Preservation Funding. Grants are among the NHPA's most important contributions to state and local preservation efforts. The grants allow the planning, institution building, education, and assistance so vital to the state's role in preservation. Under the 1980 amendments, the federal government (secretary of the interior) must provide 50 percent of the aggregate costs to states carrying out the program. The government also provides 70 percent of the aggregate costs of state or local historical surveys or inventories in any one fiscal year.[83] To receive federal funding, state programs must provide a mechanism for the SHPO to certify local governments to carry out the purposes of the NHPA and receive a portion of federal funds allocated to the states. A minimum of 10 percent of the annual federal grant to the state must be trans-

---

80. 16 U.S.C.A. § 470a(c)(1) (West Supp. 1982). A description of the National Register process and the SHPO's role in it is in chapter 4.
81. *Id.* at § 470a(d)(3)(A), (B).
82. *Id.* at § 470h-2.
83. *Id.* at § 470i.

ferred by the SHPO to certified local governments.

Grants are equally important (surprising as it may seem) to federal cost-saving efforts. State support under the 50 percent matching grant has been a relatively cost-effective way for the federal government to pay for preservation work, since the state conducts so much work for, and at the direction of, the federal government. Should federal financial support for state preservation offices and programs end (as has been proposed) and states be either unable or unwilling to replace the funds, the federal government would be faced with assuming total administration and 100 percent of the costs of the program rather than the 50 percent currently paid to the states.[84]

Prospects. While SHPO duties under the NHPA have grown and are now codified, they are no less difficult to enforce given the vagueness of mandatory duties in the law and prior court decisions under it. It remains to be seen whether a lessening of federal funds and support, among other factors, will prevent states from participating as the partners envisioned by the 1980 amendments. Recent appropriation battles in Congress over continuing support for state preservation programs have demonstrated the commitment many states have to assuming the responsibilities delegated to them under the NHPA. But federal funding is precarious at best: the 1982 federal appropriation excluded the required 10 percent set aside for local governments, and budget proposals of the Reagan administration have attempted to eliminate the bulk of the grants to state historic preservation offices.

Federal Preservation Tax Benefits and the States

The involvement of state historic preservation officers in federal preservation tax incentives began with the Tax Reform Act of 1976 and has

---

84. A recent survey by the National Conference of State Historic Preservation Officers (NCSHPO) showed that out of an average state preservation office of almost 20 employees, nearly 12 of them work virtually fulltime on duties required by the federal government. Moreover, Maryland's historic preservation office estimated that it reviews about 15,000 federal actions yearly in working with federal agencies to minimize adverse effects under the Section 106 process. Of these, roughly 5 actions cannot be resolved and are referred to the Advisory Council. If Maryland could not assume this responsibility, the Advisory Council and other federal agencies would have been legally required to review all 15,000 actions. Memorandum from J. Rodney Little, Maryland SHPO, to NCSHPO, April 15, 1981; see also Don Dworsky, National Center for Preservation Law, *The Proposed Elimination of Federal Grants to States for Historic Preservation Rests on Faulty Assumptions and Flawed Analyses* (Washington, D.C.: National Center for Preservation Law, April 27, 1981).

been greatly expanded under the Economic Recovery Tax Act (ERTA) of 1981.[85] The SHPO now plays a critical part in ensuring that qualified historic properties receive federal tax benefits under ERTA. This section briefly summarizes the process involved and the SHPO's role in it. The broader implications of these benefits for preservation projects are discussed in chapter 7; appendix B provides detailed citations to the act and applicable regulations.

In terms of preservation, ERTA provides a 25 percent tax credit on taxpayer expenditures incurred in rehabilitating "Certified Historic Structures."[86] The historic character of the structure must be certified as well as the quality of the rehabilitation work. A certified structure is any building subject to depreciation under the Internal Revenue Code that is either listed individually in the National Register or located in a registered historic district and certified by the secretary of the interior as contributing to the historic significance of the district. The rehabilitation must also be certified by the secretary of the interior as being consistent with the historic character of the structure or the historic district in which it is located. To secure the tax benefits, property owners must complete a two-part Historic Preservation Certification Application and receive certification from the secretary of the interior, who relies heavily on the SHPO's review. This process can take many months. In each case, the SHPO receives and reviews applications and recommends actions before they go to the secretary for final action.

National Register Properties

All individually listed National Register properties are automatically considered certified historic structures (if subject to depreciation under the Internal Revenue Code). Part 1 of the Historic Preservation Certification Application does not have to be completed by owners of these properties, although they must get the proposed rehabilitation certified (as discussed below) by completing part 2 of the application. If doubt exists about whether a property is individually listed in the National Register, the SHPO should be consulted. Getting listed in the National

---

85. I.R.C. § 46 (a)(2)(F) (Supp. 1982).

86. Eligible structures do not include taxpayer residences, in most instances; they must be depreciable commercial, industrial, or rental residential properties. ERTA also provides credits for older nonhistoric buildings: those 40 years or older that are being rehabilitated are eligible for a 20 percent investment tax credit, while a 15 percent credit is available to those 30 to 39 years old.

Register can be time consuming, but the tax benefits can be taken on a conditional basis, and at the taxpayer's risk, before the process is completed. Actual listing must be secured within 30 months of when the first deduction is taken.[87]

Registered Historic District Properties

If a property is not listed in the National Register, it can qualify for federal preservation tax benefits if it is located in a registered historic district and certified as being of historic significance to the district. A registered historic district is one either listed in the National Register or designated as a historic district under an approved state statute or local ordinance. If the district is designated by a state or local government, the statute or ordinance creating it must be certified by the secretary of the interior and the district itself must be certified as substantially meeting National Register criteria.

Certifying Historic Districts. To be eligible, state statutes and local ordinances must contain criteria that will "substantially achieve the purpose of preserving and rehabilitating buildings of historic significance to the district."[88] The statute or ordinance must generally contain procedures establishing a board or commission with powers to review proposed alterations to buildings within designated districts. Requests for certification of statutes and state or local districts established under them must be made to the SHPO by an authorized representative of the governmental body that enacted the law.

A number of documents are required as part of the application for certification of registered districts. Copies of the ordinance and applicable state enabling legislation must be submitted. Applications must include a description of a district's appearance, a statement of significance, a map illustrating boundaries, an indication of buildings that do not contribute to the district's significance, and representative photographs.

Certifying Properties within Registered Districts. Whether listed on the National Register or as part of a certified state or local district, a district property seeking preservation tax credits must be certified as contributing to the historic significance of the district. Applications are submitted to the SHPO, who reviews the historic significance of the building

---

87. Brenda Barrett, "Certification of Historic Significance," in *Federal Tax Incentives for Historic Preservation* (Harrisburg, Pa.: Pa. Bar Institute, 1982), p. 44.

88. National Park Service, U.S. Dept. of the Interior, *Tax Incentives for Rehabilitating Historic Buildings*, Program Leaflet 6 (Washington, D.C.: GPO, 1982).

and forwards the application, along with a recommendation, to the applicable regional office of the National Park Service for final evaluation. The significance of structures within historic districts is evaluated by the SHPO and the National Park Service in accordance with the secretary of the interior's "Standards for Evaluating Structures within Registered Historic Districts."[89] Generally the structure's location, design, setting, materials, workmanship, feeling, and association are examined to see if they add to the district's sense of time, place, and historical development.

Certifying the Rehabilitation

Once the structure is certified, the rehabilitation work itself must also be reviewed and certified. Although demolition is unlikely to qualify as rehabilitation and receive federal tax benefits, new in-fill construction as part of a larger project can, if it harmonizes with existing surrounding structures. The property owner must complete and submit part 2 of the Historic Preservation Certification Application to the SHPO and, ultimately, the appropriate office of the National Park Service. In reviewing the rehabilitation, the SHPO will follow the secretary of the interior's "Standards for Rehabilitation and Guidelines for Rehabilitating Historic Buildings" in determining whether it is consistent with the historical character of the structure.[90]

The process for certifying rehabilitation can be initiated at any time during the course of rehabilitation work, although it should be reviewed by the SHPO at the earliest practicable time to avoid unnecessary expenditures, design changes, and other problems that could jeopardize certification. In fact, a number of common, though avoidable, problems have arisen in processing rehabilitation applications, often causing delays in approval and requiring negotiations between SHPOs and project sponsors.

One type of problem frequently encountered by SHPOs is incomplete documentation. Common problems with documentation involve photographs, descriptions of structures, and reasons for planned alterations. Often the documentation provided does not meet the following requirements:

---

89. See 36 C.F.R. § 67.5 (1981).
90. See *id.* at § 67.7. Within 30 days of receiving the National Park Service's regional office decision, an appeal can be filed with the director of the National Park Service. *Id.* at § 67.10.

1. Photographs must be of a sufficient quality and number to indicate all interior and exterior areas that are to be rehabilitated and the conditions prior to rehabilitation.
2. Descriptions of conditions and features prior to rehabilitation and the proposed or completed work must be completed. Detailed specifications or technical descriptions have to be supplied, particularly for masonry repair, repointing, and replacing mortar formulations.
3. Significant changes have to be justified adequately.[91]

Problems have also developed with certain proposed treatments. For example:
1. Inappropriate or incorrect masonry treatments, such as sandblasting, are not permitted.
2. Complete window replacements are generally difficult to get approved unless documentation shows severe deterioration and the proposed windows duplicate the originals.
3. Similarly, alterations designed to make a building appear to belong to an older period or not based on accurate evidence of the period intended to be depicted are difficult to justify in the application.[92]

Developers and preservationists need to work closely with the SHPO to ensure that all relevant documentation is provided and that a timely and defensible recommendation can be made. Hence, the earlier the SHPO is consulted, the better for those seeking federal tax benefits.

STATE PRESERVATION PROGRAMS

Aside from participating in federal programs, many states have established state-level preservation laws that provide direct protection for significant buildings. These laws range from simply establishing a state preservation commission to creating a comprehensive statewide program for historic preservation with regulatory powers. In most states these laws impose a host of varied duties on the SHPO, such as administering state registers and tax incentive programs, acquiring and managing sites, providing assistance (technical, educational, financial, and regulatory) to support local activities, and promoting and enforcing state preservation policy among other state agencies. While some are stronger than others,

---

91. Donna Williams, "Recurring Rehabilitation Issues in the Historic Preservation Certification Process," in *Federal Tax Incentives for Historic Preservation* (Harrisburg, Pa.: Pa. Bar Institute, 1982), p. 221.

92. *Id.*

these laws generally form the heart of the state preservation program and provide a legal basis for state preservation activities that often go beyond those required under federal law.

While there is variation among state preservation laws, some common features do emerge. Generally a state preservation commission is created, and then appointed by the governor, with membership, qualifications, and terms of office specified. The head of the commission is designated the SHPO, and frequently a board is also established to advise the commission, scrutinize some of the actions it takes, and project future state preservation needs. These bodies typically have the power to implement the requirements of the National Historic Preservation Act, acquire property, establish standards for the care of registered property, work with state agencies and local governments to minimize adverse effects of their actions on historic properties, and review a host of public and private activities to encourage and assure the furthering of preservation objectives.

State preservation commissions are not necessarily organized along similar lines, or even located within the same department or agency, from state to state. For example, some state preservation departments are connected with state park agencies (Arizona); others function in the state archives (North Carolina and Nebraska); others are within state agencies like the Department of Transportation (Oregon). A recent survey found that the number of state public agencies having complete responsibility over preservation has increased by at least 12 since 1975.[93] The vast majority of state preservation agencies are public bodies funded by state revenues; a few are quasi-public organizations chartered and funded in part by the states.

While many states have preservation offices with legislatively established programs to implement,[94] some states simply provide, by statute, for participation in federal programs such as the NHPA—disbursing funds, nominating National Register properties, and so on. Examples include Alaska, Indiana, Kentucky, and Utah.[95] Participation in the federal preservation program is mentioned in a number of other state laws, including those of New Hampshire, North Carolina, and Penn-

---

93. Beckwith, *supra* note 2, at 285, 286.

94. See, for example, Cal. Pub. Res. Code § 5020-5026 (West Supp. 1982); N.Y. Parks & Rec. Law § 14.01-14.09 (McKinney 1980); N.C. Gen. Stat. § 121-1 to -13 (1981).

95. Alaska Stat. § 41.35.180 (1977); Ind. Code Ann. § 14-3-3.3-3(a) (Burns 1981); Ky. Rev. Stat. § 171.382 (1980); Utah Code Ann. § 63-18-38 (1978).

sylvania.[96] Some of these states, such as Alaska, also authorize the state agency to assist local governments in creating historic districts, to disburse funds for local use, and to review the effects of proposed projects on significant local historic resources.[97] Virtually every state has laws to protect archaeological resources.[98]

The number of states with comprehensive legislative programs to preserve historic resources is increasing. Many of these programs apply to actions of state and even local government agencies and thus go beyond the protections afforded by the NHPA. In fact, state and local government projects, and in some cases private actions authorized by them, that affect historic resources have come under increasing scrutiny and regulation by state preservation offices. Roughly one-half of the states have laws authorizing or requiring SHPO or preservation agency review of proposed nonfederal projects that threaten archaeological or historic sites. Two of the more prominent tools states have used are laws that create state registers or lists of historic properties and ones that impose preservation duties on other state agencies and, in a few cases, local government bodies. These aspects of state programs are examined below.[99]

State Registers of Historic Places

What if a state agency approves or helps fund a private development project that proposes to demolish or significantly alter a 60-year-old, architecturally distinct structure? Can anything be done to stop the project or minimize its adverse effects? Several states, such as California, Hawaii, Illinois, Kansas, and New York, have state registers or lists of historic places that can afford varying degrees of protection in situations like this. If the site is on, or eligible for listing on, the state register, the state agency involved will generally have to consult with the SHPO, comply with various regulations, and, in some instances, either demonstrate that a feasible alternative does not exist or mitigate the project's adverse effects.

While National Register protection extends only to federally financed

---

96. N.H. Rev. Stat. Ann. § 227-C:1-9 (1977 & Supp. 1981); N.C. Gen. Stat § 121-1 to -13 (1981); Pa. Stat Ann. tit. 71, § 1047.1 (Purdon Supp. 1980).

97. Alaska Stat. § 41.35.180(5) (1977).

98. Beckwith, *supra* note 49, at 117.

99. A third legal constraint on state and local government actions that affect historic resources—state environmental policy acts—is discussed later in this chapter.

or licensed projects, historic sites on, or eligible for, state registers can be protected to some extent from projects financed or licensed by state agencies. Moreover, local government-approved projects are subject to state register requirements and SHPO regulations in a handful of states. Because the criteria for listing on a state register may be less stringent than National Register requirements and because the registration process may not be as time consuming, state registers may incorporate a wider variety of historic structures than the National Register. And in almost every case, if a state has a register, it automatically incorporates those sites listed on the National Register.

One of the most significant features of state registers is that when a listed resource is threatened by destruction or alteration, state registers allow added time for SHPOs to work with the involved parties in an attempt to find a way to preserve it. If a property is listed on Hawaii's register, for example, a landowner must notify the Department of Land and Natural Resources, which houses the Historic Places Review Board, of any proposed construction. The landowner cannot begin or continue construction until the department has had 90 days to either approve the project, initiate condemnation proceedings to acquire it, or undertake salvage operations to preserve the structure.[100] A fine of $1,000 per violation per day can be levied against noncomplying landowners.

Illinois, whose state preservation law resembles the NHPA, provides a longer grace period and more options than Hawaii for its preservation agency to minimize the adverse effects of development on state register property.[101] When a site is designated on the Illinois state register by the SHPO, it includes a description of "critical historic features" that cannot be significantly altered or demolished without a permit (called a certificate of compliance) from the SHPO.[102] In essence, the statute allows up to a 210-day "cooling off period" for the SHPO to negotiate with the owner and other interested parties on either preserving the structure and its critical features or at least minimizing the adverse impacts of the proposed project. A permit can be issued within 120 days if the SHPO is convinced that negotiations have been conducted in good faith and that continuing them would be useless, that the effect of the proposed action is not serious enough to justify more

---

100. Hawaii Rev. Stat. § 6E-8 to -10 (1976). See David Callies, *A Survey of State Legislation*, Historic Hawaii News, January 1981, pp. 4-5.
101. Ill. Ann. Stat. ch. 127, § 133d1 to d14 (Smith-Hurd 1981).
102. *Id.* at § 133d7.

time, or that recommended modifications in construction have been accepted. On the other hand, the SHPO can use an additional 90 days to require further negotiations. A permit must be issued after this period, if requested by the applicant.

Projects in Illinois funded in whole or in part by the state face even more stringent regulations if they will affect sites on the state register. With projects financed by state funds, protection is accorded to the entire site, not just critical historical features. Moreover, if the project will have an adverse effect, a permit can be denied completely unless the SHPO determines that the project will significantly benefit the public and that its adverse effect is minimized to the greatest extent feasible.[103] As of August 1982, 16 sites had been listed on the Illinois register.[104]

Kansas legislation contains one of the strongest statutory protections for sites listed on its state register. The state register presently contains 371 sites, including 25 that are not listed on the National Register.[105] A state historical society serves as the state preservation agency and is empowered to conduct surveys, prepare and maintain a statewide preservation plan and state register, work with federal and local officials on preservation issues, get and disburse funds, and provide educational and technical assistance, among other responsibilities.[106] The state historical sites board of review, composed of members appointed by the governor and the SHPO, approves nominations to state and national registers, reviews the state preservation survey and plan, and recommends listings to the state register and removes listings (when appropriate). A statutory provision patterned after Section 4(f) of the federal Department of Transportation Act requires that any state or local government work that threatens to encroach upon, damage, or destroy register property or its "environs" may not proceed until the governor (if a state agency project) or the local governing body (if a local agency project) finds "there is no feasible and prudent alternative to the proposal and that it includes all possible planning to minimize harm."[107] Notice of the project and an opportunity to comment on it must be given to the

---

103. *Id.* at § 133d9.

104. Interview with Michael Ward, Assistant National Register Coordinator, Illinois Department of Conservation, Division of Historic Sites, August 1982.

105. Interview with Nora Pat Small, Architectural Historian, Kansas State Historical Society, August 1982.

106. Kansas Stat. Ann. § 75-2715 to -2724 (1977 & Supp. 1982).

107. *Id.* at § 75-2724 (Supp. 1982). This Department of Transportation Act provision is discussed in chapter 4.

SHPO, who must initiate an investigation of the project within 30 days. If the SHPO fails to do so, the project will be considered approved and not subject to further review.[108] Appeals of the decisions by either the governor or local governing body go to the district court, which will review the evidence *de novo* (as if there were no previous decision).

Other state laws contain noteworthy processes for projects that could adversely affect properties on, or determined to be eligible for, the state register. New York's recently enacted preservation law requires the SHPO and involved state agencies to explore all feasible and prudent alternatives to avoid or mitigate alteration or demolition.[109] It attempts to avoid duplicating the NHPA Section 106 process: if the affected property is listed on, or eligible for, both the national and state registers, the Section 106 NHPA process is to be followed to the fullest extent possible in satisfying the state register requirements. In another attempt to streamline the process and avoid duplication, it requires that reviews of these projects be conducted concurrently with state environmental reviews.[110] New Mexico provides for an emergency classification of property by temporarily listing it on its state register for up to one year. During this time, the SHPO is to study the property and determine its eligibility while it receives the protections of the register.[111] In California, before a state agency can alter, transfer, or demolish a listed historical resource, the agency must give the SHPO 30 days to review and comment on the proposed action. "Prudent and feasible" measures to eliminate or mitigate any adverse effects must be agreed upon by the SHPO and the involved agency. If no agreement is reached, the SHPO and the affected state agency must submit to mediation by the state's Office of Planning and Research, located within the governor's office.[112]

Improving State Registers

These and other state register requirements can provide important protection to historic resources, particularly against actions by other state agencies and local governments. To be effective, however, they need

---

108. *Id.*
109. N.Y. Parks & Rec. Law § 14.01-14.09 (McKinney 1981).
110. These acts, which generally require an environmental impact statement, are discussed later in this chapter.
111. N.M. Stat. Ann. § 18-6-12 (1978). See also James P. Bieg, *The Power to Preserve: New Mexico Historic Preservation Laws and Techniques* (Santa Fe: New Mexico Municipal League, 1980).
112. Cal. Pub. Res. Code § 5024.5 (West Supp. 1982).

to be made enforceable, broadly applicable to a wide range of activities, and administratively workable within the state government apparatus. A number of questions should be asked in devising a state register or determining its effectiveness:

- Does the state register actually have the potential to bring about greater protection to listed or eligible resources? Hawaii's register allows a 90-day waiting period but does not require the party to engage in mitigation measures or to search for alternatives to alteration. A New Jersey court recently held that under that state's register law, granting a demolition permit was not an "undertaking" of a project that triggered protection.[113] On the other hand, Illinois authorizes the SHPO to explore a variety of mitigation measures within a sufficiently flexible time frame, while Kansas actually requires mitigation. Yet the Illinois register process, which seeks to provide strong protection, has been used only sparingly, hampered by disputes over how the criteria for designation should be applied and the lack of legislative history to guide determinations over which types of property the legislature actually intended to be registered.
- What is the register's scope? Are private as well as state and local government actions that affect register sites subject to review? Does the process apply to eligible sites or only those already listed? The reach of register protection to private projects and properties eligible to be listed can be crucial to preserving historic resources.
- Is the process for listing and reviewing proposed alteration or demolition fair, efficient, and realistic? It should not be so cumbersome that it discourages listing (particularly where owner consent is required, as in Massachusetts) or unnecessarily burdens other state agencies or local governments. Consolidating various reviews (as in New York) is an important ingredient. California's requirement of mediation before a neutral body, when the SHPO and applicable state agency cannot agree on mitigation measures, attempts to balance the needs of preservation with the need to run state government smoothly.

Register legislation must be reviewed or enacted with these types of questions in mind. SHPOs are not all-powerful and must be able to work with localities and state agencies on a variety of preservation issues. State register and preservation laws that contain firm duties and sup-

---

113. *Hoboken Environment Committee, Inc. v. German Seaman's Mission of New York*, 391 A.2d 577 (N.J. Super. Ct. Ch. Div. 1978).

portable criteria make the SHPO's tasks easier. State registers, and projects that affect properties on them, can be controversial and are often subject to intense political pressure. Therefore, protecting state register properties and, for that matter, preservation in general should become a concern of all state agencies.

Making Preservation a Responsibility of All State Agencies

State register requirements are not the only way that preservation touches state agencies. A growing number of states require all state agencies to assume a variety of preservation duties. Some laws are more legally enforceable than others, but all take an important step in bringing about greater state sensitivity to the objectives of preservation. One cannot expect various state agencies with clear, primary missions and strong constituencies immediately to become strong advocates of preservation. Nevertheless, these laws do represent a beginning, an attempt to weave preservation objectives more tightly into the fabric of state policies.

Preservation responsibilities of state agencies have increased in some states—a result of recent comprehensive state laws. Arizona, along with California, New York, and Oregon, has put a premium on the reuse of state-owned historic buildings: all state agencies must give first priority to reusing historic buildings under state control rather than leasing, buying, or constructing other ones.[114] The SHPO in each of these states is to maintain a listing of all historic buildings available for state agency use. Each state agency must assist in compiling the list, and buildings generally do not have to be on the state register to qualify. For example, California requires the inventory to include all buildings over 50 years old, regardless of whether they are on the register.[115] New York further provides that any register-listed or eligible property that a state agency intends to sell or transfer should be protected by a preservation restriction such as an easement.[116] Similarly, Pennsylvania requires all

---

114. See Arizona Historic Preservation Act § 41-861 to -862 (April 19, 1982). Changes in Arizona's preservation law were the result of recommendations made by a state task force on historic preservation appointed by the governor. Several states have recently formed task forces to make recommendations to the governor and legislature on improving state preservation laws. These have frequently included state, local, and private preservation interests. Nancy Shanahan, *State Legislative Task Forces in the West*, 1 Preservation L. Rptr. 2061 (1982).

115. Cal. Pub. Res. Code § 5024 (West Supp. 1982).

116. N.Y. Pub. Bldgs. Law § 63 (McKinney 1981).

state agencies to submit proposals to transfer or alter state property to the SHPO for review and, where appropriate, to execute "covenants, deed restrictions, or other contractual arrangements" to preserve the historic resource.[117]

In addition to ensuring that steps are taken to preserve state property, states are placing increased emphasis on coordinating agency actions and bringing consistency to state preservation policy. For example, New York requires every state agency and municipality to designate a preservation officer, who will serve as a liaison to the SHPO, coordinate preservation policy for the particular agency or unit of government, and oversee compliance with state preservation laws.[118] By executive order, Maryland directs all state agencies to guide physical and economic development into existing developed areas in a manner that not only protects historic resources but encourages their reuse.[119] The newly formed state development council, composed of various state agencies and the SHPO, targets areas for development compatible with historic preservation.[120] Pennsylvania's law requires each state agency to initiate procedures for considering historic resources in administering its own programs.[121] In Arizona, the SHPO must submit an annual report to the governor that comments on the preservation performance of each state agency.[122]

Coordination of, and stronger action on, preservation activities can also arise from the implementation of other state laws. New York's integration of preservation and environmental quality reviews, in some situations, attempts to get state agencies to consider and minimize the adverse effects of their actions on various resources.

Coastal zone plans are another avenue for improving coordination of state policy. At least 31 states and territories have adopted coastal zone plans that have been approved under the federal Coastal Zone Management Act.[123] Protecting cultural and historical resources is a mandatory element of each. In Hawaii's coastal plan, for example, counties can deny a permit for any development that threatens a "significant"

---

117. Pa. Stat. Ann. tit. 71, § 1047.1k (Purdon Supp. 1980).
118. N.Y. Parks & Rec. Law § 14.05 (McKinney 1981).
119. Interview with Rodney Little, SHPO, Maryland Historic Trust, June 1982.
120. *Id.*
121. Pa. Stat. Ann. tit. 71, § 1047.1a -.1n (Purdon Supp. 1980).
122. Arizona Historic Preservation Act § 41-1352 (April 19, 1982).
123. See Council on Environmental Quality, *Environmental Quality—1979* (Washington, D.C.: GPO, 1979), p. 901.

coastal resource, which is defined to include any property listed on the state register.[124] State agencies must also comply with the plan, thereby giving stronger protection to register resources than the state's preservation law would allow.

These laws do not necessarily guarantee that all actions by state agencies will be compatible with preservation goals, nor do they necessarily allow courts to require compliance with them. In fact, Maryland's executive order expressly prohibits enforcement of the state's development policy by third parties. And Arizona's policy of having state agencies take the lead in preservation, and marking the way for individuals and other levels of government to follow, does not seem to create any specifically enforceable duty.

A sound working relationship between state agencies and local government is increasingly important to the achievement of many preservation objectives. Some state agencies effectively assist, support, and cooperate with local preservation efforts; others do not. Conflicts between state and local agencies often arise over proposed state agency actions on state-controlled property, which is generally outside the jurisdiction of local preservation laws. For example, in *State of Washington v. City of Seattle*, the Washington Supreme Court ruled that the local preservation regulation yielded to state law that allowed state agencies to control their buildings and land.[125] In *City of Santa Fe v. Armijo*, the New Mexico Supreme Court also found that the city's preservation ordinance did not allow it to regulate a structure placed by the state commissioner of public lands on premises of the state land office building.[126] Although it did not rule whether cities in New Mexico could have the power to regulate state land, the court held that the city would, at a minimum, have to reenact its ordinance with a specific reference to the preservation enabling legislation in order for the local preservation commission to have the possible power to regulate state properties. Increasingly diverse and demanding responsibilities under various federal as well as state laws, coupled with the prospects of reduced federal support, place added emphasis on the need for state agencies to work more closely with local governments and their preservation bodies.

Some laws that attempt to make preservation a responsibility of all

---

124. Callies, *supra* note 100, at 5.
125. 615 P.2d 461 (Wash. 1980).
126. 634 P.2d 685 (N.M. 1981).

state agencies should make it easier for state preservation offices to prevent these agencies from undermining local preservation policies. Some provisions in these laws do seem to establish mandatory duties, particularly with regard to state-owned property. Compiling a list of state-owned or -controlled historic property is clearly required, and demonstrating that it is not feasible to use one of these properties is a prerequisite, under some of these laws, to constructing a new state building. These are significant duties—states do utilize extensive office space—and should be emulated and improved upon in other jurisdictions.

Creating Comprehensive State Laws

State preservation laws should be comprehensive enough to articulate a strong state policy and to implement it through creation of a state preservation office or delegation of responsibilities, including planning and coordination, to a state agency. An effective state register should be created. Preservation responsibilities for sites listed on it, other state-controlled buildings, and other programs should be vested in all state agencies, with the SHPO having authority to ensure that state preservation policies are being implemented. Of course, the successful working of these laws depends to a large extent on the continued availability of funds for preservation programs.

State Tax Laws and Preservation

Several states have enacted tax incentives to encourage the preservation and restoration of historic structures. These programs differ in both the types of benefits provided and their effectiveness. In Oregon, the taxed value of a property listed on the National Register can be frozen for 15 years, which lets the owner make improvements to the property without being taxed on the value of those improvements. Certification of the property for tax benefits must come from the SHPO.[127] Over 500 property owners are receiving this benefit. Other states have not been as successful, largely because the programs are too complicated or inadequately tailored to the needs of property owners. Maryland allows owners of "certified nondepreciable historic structures" (as defined in the Internal Revenue Code) to deduct amounts expended for rehabilitation from state income taxes over a 60-month period.[128] North Carolina

---

127. Or. Rev. Stat. § 358.475-.565 (1981).
128. Md. Ann. Code art. 81, § 281A (1978).

permits a 50 percent tax deferral on historic property for as long as the property remains historic.[129]

In other states, localities have sometimes attempted to limit the applicability of state preservation tax benefits. For example, in Texas, the city of San Antonio challenged a local conservation society's claim of state tax exemptions for preserving the home of a notable state figure. The Texas Supreme Court ruled that the state statute exempting historic buildings from taxation did not violate a state constitutional provision limiting exemptions. While the conservation society was not a public body, the court found it entitled to the statute's benefits since it had assumed an obligation that otherwise would have been undertaken by the state or locality.[130]

Like state statutes authorizing localities to grant preservation tax benefits, these programs on the whole have not been widely used. To be more effective, state tax programs should recognize the real needs of property owners and developers as well as the goals of preservation. For a complete discussion of how this can be done and of the various state tax policies that attempt to promote preservation, see chapter 7 on preservation law and economics.

STATES AND ENVIRONMENTAL POLICY

Over the last decade, the development of state preservation laws and processes has taken place alongside significant advances in state environmental policy and law. In some cases, the constituency for each has been the same and has shown similar concerns for aesthetics and the quality of life, among other issues. And as processes have been devised to ensure that preservation policies are considered by government decision makers, so, too, have processes been devised to protect environmental interests. Indeed, as noted in chapter 4 on federal preservation law and elsewhere in this handbook, environmental laws can often support and even strengthen preservation objectives.

These laws, particularly state environmental policy acts, have often been overlooked as preservation tools, but they can be used to make a critical difference in preservation disputes. They apply to many situations where other preservation laws may not; they can prompt negotia-

---

129. N.C. Gen. Stat. § 105-277(f) (1979).
130. *San Antonio Conservation Society v. City of San Antonio*, 455 S.W.2d 743 (Tex. 1970).

tions or provide the time needed for negotiations to be successful; and in a few cases, they can help effect preservation-oriented decisions.

This section looks at two types of state environmental involvement—environmental policy acts and constitutions that contain environmental quality provisions—and how they can best be used in a preservation context.

State Environmental Policy Acts (SEPAs)

Several states have laws or programs embodied in state environmental policy acts (SEPAs) that require comprehensive environmental review of the actions they plan to take. Most of these SEPAs are modeled closely after the National Environmental Policy Act (NEPA). In fact, a few are almost verbatim versions of the federal legislation.[131] Like the NEPA, they generally use the same action-forcing process—the environmental impact statement (EIS)—to require that state agencies, and in some cases local governments, consider and when possible minimize the adverse environmental impacts of projects they fund, approve, license, or permit. Also, like the NEPA, the state acts grew out of the concern to provide decision makers and the public with useful information about the environmental effects of government actions so that decision making could be improved, citizen access to it increased, and accountability provided for.

A SEPA is generally triggered and some sort of environmental review required when a major state or local agency action, such as financing or licensing a development project, may have a significant effect on the quality of the environment. How do SEPAs involve historic preservation? In nearly every SEPA, historic properties and resources are included within the definition of the environment. For example, regulations implementing New York's SEPA define environment to include "objects of historic or aesthetic significance . . . and existing community or neighborhood character," and California's SEPA defines the term

---

131. A kind of reverse federalism exists between the NEPA and SEPAs; as one commentator has observed, ". . . in the instance of the National Environmental Policy Act of 1969 . . . the federal government has served as an experimental laboratory for the various states." Nicholas C. Yost, *NEPA's Progeny: State Environmental Policy Acts*, 3 Envtl. L. Rep. (Envtl. L. Inst.) 50090 (1974). The NEPA is discussed in chapter 4; many of the cases decided under it are applicable to SEPAs. These decisions should be used to support SEPA claims. See Neil Orloff, *SEQRA: New York's Reformation of NEPA*, 46 Albany L. Rev. 1128 (1982).

similarly.[132] Thus, the granting of a permit to demolish a registered historic property would undoubtedly come under most SEPAs, particularly those that apply to decisions of local governments, as that action would have an effect on the quality of the environment. The same is probably true for demolition permits for structures eligible but not yet listed, as well as for a nonhistoric building within a historic district when the building is important to the district's existing character or when the project will adversely affect the district's character. SEPAs may even apply to government-approved or -funded actions on buildings outside historic districts when they might significantly affect the district.

SEPAs are often involved in the same projects that bring the NEPA, the National Historic Preservation Act (NHPA), or state registers into play, but the most important contribution of SEPAs may be in government activities that are generally outside the scope of these other laws. States and localities are generally much more involved than the federal government in day-to-day land-use activities and permitting, giving SEPAs greater applicability to the many different types of projects that affect historic resources. Even state registers, which apply to state and sometimes local government activities, are limited to listed or eligible sites, instead of to the environment in general as are SEPAs. Thus SEPAs can force consideration of historic resources into several kinds of projects that primarily involve nonhistoric places or structures. Moreover, in some states, SEPAs have the potential to inject historic preservation concerns far deeper into state and local agency decision making than any of the more strictly preservation-related state laws. By imposing a duty on agencies to pursue less damaging alternatives where possible or at least to institute measures to reduce adverse effects when approving a project, SEPAs have the potential to force more preservation-oriented decisions than many of the state registers.

If followed properly, SEPAs can act as a cooperative device at the design stage of a project to identify adverse effects on historic resources and resolve them before large expenditures of time and money have been made. If ignored or not fully complied with, they can cause significant project delays and, in some cases, be the basis for permit or funding denials, even though no other preservation law may apply.

SEPAs and their EIS requirements have been established through legislation, executive order, or administrative action in about half the

---

132. N.Y. Admin. Code tit. 6, § 617.2(j) (1978). See National Center for Preservation Law, *supra* note 14, at p. 17; Cal. Pub. Res. Code § 21060.5 (West 1977).

states.[133] While these acts closely resemble the policies, goals, and processes of the NEPA, important variations among SEPAs exist, both in their substance and their interpretation. What follows is a brief discussion of the types of actions SEPAs address, what they require of state and local governments, and how they can be used to further preservation objectives.

SEPA Policy

Environmental policy is generally contained in the first part of SEPAs. These provisions attempt to make protection of the environment (and historic resources) a concern of all government agencies. The NEPA is followed very closely in SEPA policy statements. For example, Washington's SEPA closely parallels NEPA policy and is similar to many other states:

> [I]t is the continuing responsibility of the state of Washington and all agencies of the state to use all practicable means, consistent with other essential considerations of state policy, to improve and coordinate plans, functions, programs, and resources to the end that the state and its citizens may:
> (a) Fulfill the responsibilities of each generation as trustee of the environment for succeeding generations;
> (b) Assure for all people of Washington, safe, healthful, productive, and esthetically and culturally pleasing surroundings;
> (c) Attain the widest range of beneficial uses of the environment without degradation, risk to health or safety, or other undesirable and unintended consequences;
> (d) Preserve important historic, cultural, and natural aspects of our national heritage;
> (e) Maintain, wherever possible, an environment which supports diversity and variety of individual choice;
> (f) Achieve a balance between population and resource use which will permit high standards of living and a wide sharing of life's amenities; and
> (g) Enhance the quality of renewable resources and approach the maximum attainable recycling of depletable resources.[134]

The problem lies in translating this statement of policy into effective action, particularly when it conflicts with the interpretation of other state goals, such as economic development and employment. By themselves, SEPA policy statements do not automatically result in en-

---

133. Council on Environmental Quality, *supra* note 123, at 595-602. See Nicholas A. Robinson, *SEQRA's Siblings: Precedents from Little NEPA's in Sister States*, 46 Albany L. Rev. 1155 (1982).

134. Wash. Rev. Code Ann. § 43.21C (Supp. 1982).

vironmentally sound decisions. The SEPA process is intended to bring about implementation of the policy. The process requires the principal or lead agency supporting or permitting a project to go through a series of internal and external steps that are intended to lead to more informed decisions and greater public and agency access to them.

SEPA Process

The SEPA process is very much like the NEPA process. It involves government actions that could have a significant effect on the environment. The mechanism is primarily the EIS, which includes four stages—the initial determination, draft EIS, final EIS, and the agency decision—all of which provide for public access and an opportunity to challenge agency decisions.

Initial Determination. First, an initial determination must be made of whether SEPA applies and, if so, what it requires. Before the SEPA process can be applicable, several questions must be answered. Is the agency authorizing or funding the action subject to the SEPA? A handful of SEPAs, such as Wisconsin's, do not apply to county or other local government actions, only to state agencies.[135] Given that many decisions on preservation occur at the local level, this can be a significant drawback. In some cases, certain state agencies also may be outside of SEPA authority.

Another important question is whether the action itself is subject to the SEPA. Many SEPAs exempt certain types of actions or agency decisions from their requirements. For example, California and New York SEPAs apply only to discretionary decisions, not ministerial ones. (Ministerial decisions are those that do not require subjective judgments but merely the application of fixed standards or objective measurements.) A California court recently held that where localities have adopted a preservation ordinance that gives a preservation commission authority to designate sites and review projects affecting the sites, the issuance of a demolition permit by the building department is a discretionary act, subject to the SEPA.[136] Other categories of actions may be exempted if they clearly do not significantly affect the environment. California

---

135. *Robinson v. Kunach*, 251 N.W.2d 449 (Wis. 1977).

136. *San Diego Trust Savings Bank v. Friends of Gill*, 174 Cal. Rptr. 784 (Cal. Ct. App. 1981). For another view on this issue, see *Environmental Law Fund, Inc. v. City of Watsonville*, 177 Cal. Rptr. 542 (Ct. App. 1981), which involved the demolition of a building for a parking lot as part of the city's redevelopment plan.

categorically exempts a number of actions applicable to existing facilities, such as repair, maintenance, or minor alteration, which involve negligible or no expansion of use.[137] Most SEPAs also contain exemptions for emergency projects necessary to prevent or mitigate an impending emergency or to recover from a disaster.

When the SEPA process does apply, the significance of the potential effects on the environment of the agency's proposed action must be determined. If the effects are determined to be insignificant, then an assessment giving the grounds for that determination must be issued. If they could be significant, then a full-blown EIS is required.

Basically the SEPA process requires that before an agency decides to fund, approve, or take any other "major" action on an activity that may have a significant adverse effect on historic resources, it must make an initial determination of how significant and adverse those effects might be. This determination can generally only be made after some sort of preliminary review of the proposed project's effects. If the effects are found to be quite minor, such as those resulting from a small improvement to a structure's facade, the agency will most likely issue a short environmental assessment that documents the effects and provides the basis for determining that they are insignificant. This is often called a "negative declaration." On the other hand, if the effects appear to be significant and adverse, like those of demolishing a historic structure, the agency generally must prepare a draft EIS. The effects may not always be this clear-cut, but the agency will have to undertake some sort of initial review before it decides to go any further.

This initial determination is an important step: it provides the public and various agencies an early opportunity to become involved in a project and to comment on its possible effects, and ensures that the principal or lead agency is examining them closely before going forward. It is also the first stage in the SEPA process at which an agency decision can be challenged in court.

Key concerns at this point in the SEPA process include when the process should be started, who must do it, and what constitutes a significant effect on the environment. The agency must begin the SEPA process as soon as it starts considering whether to fund, license, or engage in any activity that could have an effect on historic resources. The timing is crucial; the SEPA/EIS process should not be used to justify decisions already made. It must be an integral part of the decision-making

---

137. Cal. Admin. Code tit. 14, § 15101 (1980), State EIR Guidelines.

process, and most states demand that SEPA inquiries be initiated at the earliest practicable time.

The lead agency, which has the principal responsibility for carrying out or approving a project, generally must initiate and follow the SEPA process through.[138] In addition to the lead agency, other agencies responsible for carrying out or approving specific parts of the project also may review the EIS. The lead agency can generally contract out the responsibility for the EIS and may in some cases base a few of its findings on an independent analysis of the information provided by the project's sponsor. For example, Neiman-Marcus supplied much of the information contained in the environmental impact report (California's EIS) for its proposal to demolish the City of Paris building in San Francisco. The court allowed this since it found that the lead agency conducted an independent review of the information it received and reacted to public comments.[139]

No short and easy rules exist for determining what is a significant effect on the environment. The case law in each jurisdiction should be examined to see how this clause has been interpreted and applied. As California has indicated, for an effect to be significant there should be evidence of "a substantial, or potentially substantial, adverse change in any of the physical conditions of the area affected by the activity including land . . . and objects of historic or aesthetic significance."[140] An approval to build a large, outlying shopping center that would draw business away from the downtown historic district would most likely be considered a significant effect. Similarly, demolition of a Register property or a substantial alteration of a site within a historic district would also have a significant effect.

Is there a possibility of significant effects? Are the effects disputed, or is a controversy over the project likely? If the answer to any of these is yes, or if there are any doubts, then an EIS should be prepared.

Generally, the effect must be adverse, in addition to significant. Thus, a decision to designate a site as historic or to certify it for tax benefits would not be subject to the SEPA process.

Draft EIS. The draft EIS generally describes and analyzes the impacts of a proposed action, particularly those impacts that cannot be avoided

---

138. *Id.* at § 15030.
139. *Foundation for San Francisco's Architectural Heritage v. City and County of San Francisco*, 165 Cal. Rptr. 401 (Cal. Ct. App. 1980) [hereinafter cited as *Foundation*].
140. Cal. Pub. Res. Code § 21060.5, 21068 (West 1977).

if the proposal is implemented, and discusses alternatives to the proposed action and measures to mitigate adverse environmental impacts.

While the impacts an EIS must consider are similar to those considered under the NEPA, some states expressly require that additional ones, which can be particularly relevant to preservation concerns, also be addressed. For example, secondary and growth-inducing environmental impacts of proposed actions must be considered in several states, including Connecticut, Indiana, Massachusetts, California, Montana, New York, and Washington.[141] For example, if a proposal were made to demolish an eligible property in a historic district and to put in its place a large office and retail complex, the draft EIS in these states would have to examine not only the immediate impacts of the project but its effects on transportation, on infrastructure, such as roads and sewers, on neighborhood character, on future development in the area, and so on. Similarly, if a historic site or district could be directly or indirectly affected by a project at another location, those impacts must also be evaluated. Under Washington's SEPA, an EIS on a proposal to construct a 13-story building disclosed that the building would create numerous adverse impacts. It would have obstructed views, dwarfed neighborhood structures, produced adverse shadows, induced secondary growth, and increased traffic and noise. The significance of these impacts led the city's superintendent of buildings to deny the project a permit, which action was upheld by the Washington Supreme Court.[142]

SEPAs in states such as Connecticut require lead agencies to examine a project's impact on energy use and conservation, an important factor in ensuring that preservation concerns are addressed.[143] Some states also require a weighing of environmental costs and benefits, which similarly would help demonstrate the feasibility of preservation in some situations.

The alternatives considered in the EIS will also be crucial. Like the NEPA, a SEPA environmental impact statement must generally look at alternatives that could achieve or nearly approximate the project's objectives, at alternatives that reduce the environmental impacts even

---

141. Kenneth Pearlman, *State Environmental Policy Acts: Local Decision Making and Land Use Planning*, 43 Journal of the American Institute of Planners 42, 45 (1977).

142. *Polygon Corp. v. City of Seattle*, 578 P.2d 1309 (Wash. 1978).

143. Conn. Gen. Stat. Ann. § 22a-1 to -1h (West 1975 & Supp. 1982). See Marc A. Pridgeon, Jerald P. Anderson, and James P. Delphey, *State Environmental Policy Acts: A Survey of Recent Developments*, 2 Harv. Environmental L. Rev. 419, 445 (1977) [hereinafter cited as Pridgeon].

if they cost more and do not achieve or nearly approximate the project, and at the "no project" alternative.[144] Preservationists should propose feasible alternatives that would reduce the damage to historic resources and ensure that these alternatives are evaluated in the EIS.

Some SEPAs require agencies to mitigate adverse effects or implement less damaging alternatives when feasible.[145] In the suit to prevent demolition of San Francisco's City of Paris building, preservationists claimed that an offer made to buy the structure should have been addressed by the EIS in its consideration of alternatives to demolition. The court ruled, however, that the offer was infeasible and obviously unacceptable to the building's owner and thus not required to be considered.[146] Nonetheless, this is the type of information preservationists must present to a lead agency and bring to a court's attention. While the alternatives presented need not be exhaustive, those who are concerned about a project's effects on preservation should ensure that all reasonable alternative courses are brought before the lead agency and considered by it in the EIS.

Measures that can be taken to mitigate the adverse effects of the proposed activity must also be described. These can often permit a project to be approved but modified so that its significant environmental effects are reduced.

After the draft EIS is completed, regulations implementing SEPAs generally require agencies to hold hearings and seek comments—from the agencies involved and the public—on the draft EIS. Moreover, New York's SEPA specifically provides that a public hearing may be required any time a project authorized by a state or government agency directly or indirectly affects a landmark.[147] Public participation is central to the SEPA process and what it is intended to do: full disclosure and citizen involvement in decision making are among the chief reasons for requiring an EIS. The final EIS should explicitly respond to the public comments received on the draft.

---

144. Pridgeon, *supra* note 143, at 436. For an illustration of the types of impacts and alternatives an EIS over a proposed shopping center should address, see *Barrie v. Kitsap County*, 613 P.2d 1148 (Wash. 1980).

145. See Cal. Pub. Res. Code § 21002 (West 1977).

146. *Foundation*, *supra* note 139, at 411. According to the court, the offer was made three weeks after the final EIS was certified by the lead agency.

147. Comment, *Cultural Ecology: The Urban Landmark as an Environmental Resource*, 11 U.S.F.L. Rev. 720, 814 (1977). See National Center for Preservation Law, *supra* note 14, at 16.

Final EIS and the Agency's Decision. What effect will the EIS process and the SEPA's policy statements have on an agency's decision to fund or approve a project? Can the SEPA policies and process combine to produce an agency decsion favorable to preservation? The short answer to these questions: it depends. It depends on the severity of the impacts disclosed, the feasible alternatives available, the public's interest in the project, the agency making the decision, and the particular SEPA involved. Where the impacts are severe or the threatened resource especially valued, where a specific, practical alternative exists, the public's involvement is intense, and the lead agency is not committed from the start to a particular result, it is more likely that the SEPA will have a substantive effect. Actually, any one of these factors, if particularly strong, can be decisive.

The record on what substantive effect SEPAs have on final agency decisions is mixed. Some state and local agencies have become quite adept at simply ignoring SEPA policies and jumping through its procedural hoops before making the decision they intended to all along. In other situations, SEPA policies and the EIS have been part of the agency decision-making process and have actually been the basis for reaching a preservation-oriented result. In still other cases and in some states in particular, a vigilant public and the courts have been instrumental in putting substance into the SEPA. For example, in a Minnesota SEPA case, *State of Minnesota by Powderly v. Erickson*, the court ruled that a developer could not demolish historic row houses unless he could prove that the alternatives discussed in the EIS were not feasible.[148] It went on to hold that:

> [The] protection of [historical] resources is to be given paramount consideration, and those resources should not be . . . destroyed unless there are truly unusual factors present in the case or the cost of community disruption from the alternatives reaches an extraordinary magnitude.[149]

The government was enjoined from issuing a demolition permit.

The case returned to the Minnesota Supreme Court about a year and a half later, however, when the developer sought demolition again on the ground that he had not been able to sell, renovate, or have the government purchase the houses. This time the court ruled that it had a duty to enjoin destruction until all the parties interested in preserving the structures had a reasonable opportunity to protect them. Yet

---

148. 285 N.W.2d 84 (Minn. 1979), *modified*, 301 N.W.2d 324 (Minn. 1981).
149. *State of Minnesota by Powderly v. Erickson*, 285 N.W.2d 84, 89 (Minn. 1979).

the court noted that once a reasonable time had expired and if no means of preservation had become apparent, the owner had an absolute right to destroy the buildings;[150] the SEPA cannot prevent demolition forever.

This case illustrates at least one major preservation advantage of SEPAs. These acts can provide willing parties with valuable time to negotiate and perhaps find alternative solutions to destroying or injuring historic resources. State register provisions can have a similar effect, but they may not allow sufficient time, apply to as many situations, or be as forceful as SEPAs.

Of course, not every SEPA has been interpreted in the same manner, nor does every situation allow the SEPA decisive influence on an agency's actions. California's SEPA provides that "[e]ach public agency shall mitigate or avoid the significant effects on the environment of projects it approves or carries out whenever it is feasible to do so."[151] In one case, a California appellate court ruled that the state's SEPA does not require the agency to choose the environmentally best feasible project if mitigation measures can be imposed to reduce the environmental impacts to an acceptable level.[152] The substantive effect of other SEPAs, such as ones in Maryland, Indiana, and Wisconsin, has been weakened by narrow interpretations of concepts such as "significant effect on the environment" or by limiting the scope of the SEPA to only certain state agencies.[153]

Courts and SEPAs

An agency can be taken to court for violating the SEPA at any of the stages of the SEPA process: making an initial determination, drafting an EIS, issuing a final EIS, and making its decision. A time limit or statute of limitations is often applicable when challenging agency SEPA actions and decisions.[154]

Two types of challenges can be brought under SEPAs: substantive and procedural. Substantive enforcement of the SEPA seeks to prohibit

---

150. *Id.*; 301 N.W.2d 324 (Minn. 1981).

151. Cal. Pub. Res. Code § 21002.1(b) (West Supp. 1982).

152. *Laurel Hills Homeowners Association v. City Council*, 147 Cal. Rptr. 842 (Cal. Ct. App. 1978). For comparison with New York's SEPA, see Philip H. Gitlen, *The Substantive Impact of SEQRA*, 46 Albany L. Rev. 1241 (1982).

153. See Pridgeon, *supra* note 143, at 419; *Pitman v. Washington Suburban Sanitary Commission*, 368 A.2d 473 (Md. 1977).

154. William H. Rodgers, Jr., *Handbook on Environmental Law* (St. Paul, Minn.: West Publishing Co., 1977), p. 820.

an agency from approving a proposed project. In contrast, procedural enforcement gets a court to order the agency to reconsider the matter because it did not comply with the SEPA properly the first time in examining the environmental impacts of a project or alternatives to it.[155]

The scope of judicial review varies; courts have used different standards to review agency actions under SEPAs. Most determine whether the agency action is supported by substantial evidence.[156] Was there enough evidence in the record for the agency to rule the way it did? A few courts, especially when reviewing procedural issues, look to see if the agency acted reasonably under the circumstances. Others attach greater weight to agency decisions by requiring only that they not be "arbitrary and capricious" or "clearly erroneous."[157] Has a mistake been made, some procedure not complied with, or some important fact overlooked? Under these tests, the court is basically reviewing the administrative record to see if it supports the agency's decision, with a view toward upholding the decision if it can. The burden of proof is generally placed by these types of tests on the side challenging the agency's SEPA decision, making it difficult to prove agency noncompliance and thus to overturn its action.

At the other extreme, one or two courts will conduct *de novo* review of the proposed project, giving no weight to the agency's contested decision in looking at how the SEPA process should be applied.[158] In effect, the agency and those supporting it must prove that they acted properly.

Because courts examine agency actions according to different standards of review and place the burden of proof on different sides, some of these acts have been interpreted as being stronger than others. In most cases, however, it is far easier to get a court to require an agency to comply procedurally with a SEPA than it is to get substantive enforcement. In terms of substantive effect, preservationists are far more successful in court when defending a favorable agency decision under SEPA, such as denying a building permit because the proposed structure would adversely affect historic resources, than when seeking to overturn a decision that goes against their interests. The key is getting the agency to comply with the SEPA and to rule in favor of protection,

155. Comment, *Substantive Enforcement of the California Environmental Quality Act*, 69 Calif. L. Rev. 112, 114-15 (1981).
156. See Rodgers, *supra* note 154.
157. See Pridgeon, *supra* note 143, at 443.
158. See Comment, *supra* note 155, at 112, 173.

not waiting for the court to require the agency to undo its decision and give the relief sought.

Coordinating SEPA with Other Preservation Regulatory Programs

Some situations require compliance with the SEPA as well as with provisions under state register acts and federal laws, such as the NHPA and NEPA. If the processes are not carefully designed, overlapping requirements can create unnecessary administrative burdens. The relationship between these laws needs to be understood and accounted for in agency procedures.

All these acts will generally apply in cases involving federal and state permitting (or funding) of a project that affects property listed on, or eligible for, both federal and state registers. Some effort has been made to minimize duplicative agency procedures. Where there is federal action by virtue of federal grants to states, federal agency EIS requirements under the NEPA can be satisfied by a state agency's compliance with the SEPA.[159] Similarly, many states allow federal agency actions under the NEPA to serve as the basis for state agency SEPA review. Where differences exist between the requirements of the two acts, the distinguishing features must be complied with individually, and, even if differences do not exist, every affected government agency must still independently review the EIS, comment on it, and hold hearings where applicable. Similar attempts to streamline the process but still allow for effective review have been made with the NHPA and state registers. As noted, New York and other states allow their state register law to be satisfied by compliance with the federal Section 106 process when both apply. In addition, the Section 106 and state register processes may be expedited if activities under the NEPA and SEPA are integrated.

The needs for government efficiency and cost effectiveness are real and are receiving greater attention. Placing SEPA requirements and procedures on top of other preservation laws can result in increased protection, but, if duplicative or unnecessarily burdensome, they may end up spreading government preservation efforts too thin or even alienating fiscally strapped localities or agencies. Yet efforts to cut costs by eliminating or reducing compliance may be short-sighted and undermine the intent of SEPAs. For example, exempting localities from complying with SEPAs may reduce administrative burdens, but it also significantly lessens a SEPA's effectiveness. On the other hand, provi-

---

159. 42 U.S.C.A. § 4332 (D) (1977).

sions that allow some of the costs of complying with SEPAs to be passed on to private developers may be a more effective way to achieve compliance.[160]

Resolving Intergovernmental Disputes

SEPAs can also help identify and resolve preservation disputes between state and local agencies.[161] In many cases, local governments cannot restrict state agency activities or projects. SEPAs can provide localities with the means to get state agencies to consider, and perhaps comply with, their local preservation needs. In *Citizens for Saving the Historic Thurston County Courthouse v. Department of General Services Administration (GSA)*,[162] the state GSA sought to demolish a courthouse, located in the city of Olympia in Washington, that had been recommended for designation on the state's register by the state's Advisory Council on Historic Preservation but rejected by the SHPO. While the state GSA determined that the project had no significant effect on the environment under the SEPA, the city determined that it did. But GSA agreed to assist Olympia in preparing an EIS, under which it would seek a demolition permit. The city assumed lead agency status under the SEPA, prepared an EIS, and denied the permit because of the environmental effects discovered in the EIS. But in a memorandum agreeing to the EIS and seeking a demolition permit, GSA had reserved its legal position of freedom from compliance with either. This allowed GSA to assert these positions if the agency went to court over the issue, and, not surprisingly, that is where the matter wound up.

The court enjoined GSA from demolishing the courthouse until GSA complied with the city permit conditions pertaining to the SEPA. Thus, the SEPA provided the tool for a locality to get a state agency to heed its wishes.[163] It also provided time: while the SEPA suit was pending, a new state administration took office and recommended National Register designation while ordering a rehabilitation study for the court-

---

160. See Cal. Pub. Res. Code § 21089 (West 1977). See also Pridgeon, *supra* note 143, at 446.
161. State agency compliance with local preservation laws is also discussed in chapter 2.
162. No. 79 2 0120 3 (Wash. Super. Ct. July 10, 1980).
163. The ruling did not provide a complete SEPA victory for preservation and state compliance with local needs since the site was on state capitol grounds and the court ruled that the city did not have constitutional authority to deny permits on the basis of SEPA. The state's constitution was interpreted to authorize local permit denials in these situations only when it found noncompliance with the state building code.

house. The building stands today, listed in the National Register and with an approved rehabilitation plan.[164] This case illustrates the important effect a SEPA can have when other preservation laws do not apply.

The SEPA may also provide preservationists with an opportunity to ensure that the EIS mitigation measures required by an agency's decision are complied with when a project is completed. If a decision under the SEPA is conditioned upon preserving certain features or structures and those conditions are not adhered to, the offending agency can be sued, and, in some states, reconstruction (where feasible) or damages can be ordered.[165] This can be used not only to remedy adverse effects of a project but also to deter agencies from seeking to run around SEPAs in the future.

State Constitutions and Environmental Policy

During the late 1960s and early 1970s, several states amended their constitutions to include provisions protecting the environment. Previously, only a few state constitutions had mentioned historic preservation as one of the areas appropriate for state legislation and appropriations.[166] But more recent amendments have reflected the increased importance attached to environmental and historical values. For example, the Illinois constitution states that:

> The public policy of the state and the duty of each person is to provide and maintain a healthful environment for the benefit of this and future generations.[167]

A 1971 amendment to Pennsylvania's constitution provides that "[t]he people have a right to clean air, pure water, and to the preservation of the natural, scenic, historic, and esthetic value of the environment. . . ."[168] Do these provisions and others like them require protection of historic resources? Do they create any enforceable duties? What has been their effect thus far?

---

164. Interview with Richard J. Fink, plaintiff's attorney, September 1982.
165. See *Ogunquit Village Corp. v. Davis*, 553 F.2d 243 (1st Cir. 1977); Comment, *Enforcing the "Commitments" Made in Impact Statements: A Proposed Passage Through a Thicket of Case Law*, 10 Envtl. L. Rep. (Envtl. L. Inst.) 10153 (1980).
166. Howard, *State Constitutions and the Environment*, 58 Va. L. Rev. 193, 197, 200 (1972). See Mo. Const. art. 3, § 48.
167. Ill. Const. art. 11, § 1.
168. Pa. Const. art. 1, § 27.

Basically, three types of provisions in state constitutions focus on the environment and historic preservation: one proclaims a right to a decent environment; the second states that the development, maintenance, and preservation of a decent environment is a public policy; the third authorizes the use of preferential assessments to achieve it.[169] Pennsylvania's statement of the people's right to preserve the historic value of the environment is an example of the first, whereas the statement from the Illinois constitution exemplifies the second type of provision. Louisiana's constitution, like many others, allows taxes on historic properties to be based on their current-use value rather than their market value, thereby attempting to provide incentives for preservation.[170]

These provisions might be used in challenges very similar to suits under state registers or SEPAs. These could include actions against a state or local government agency for granting a permit to demolish a registered or eligible structure, adopting a master plan that disregards the preservation of historic resources to which people are given a constitutional right, or approving construction of a completely incompatible structure within a historic district. On the other hand, they might be used defensively by these same governments against claims that their preservation actions are unconstitutional.[171] Like SEPAs, they may be applicable to historic resources that are unprotected by state registers or, in fact, may help strengthen claims of a substantive violation of the SEPA.

Even though various state constitutions contain articles proclaiming the virtues of historic preservation, they have been the subject of very few reported cases. And in these few cases, they have received only minor attention from the courts. The strongest type of provision—that providing a right to a decent environment (found in at least five constitutions[172])—has not fared significantly better than the others. One notable exception has been Pennsylvania, where a court, in a case involving a street widening project that affected a historic site, set down a three-part inquiry to determine compliance with the constitution: Has there been compliance with all statutes and regulations applicable to protecting resources? Have reasonable efforts been made to reduce en-

---

169. Roland M. Frye, Jr., *Environmental Provisions in State Constitutions*, 5 Envtl. L. Rep. (Envtl. L. Inst.) 50028, 50029-30 (1975).

170. La. Const. art. 7, § 18C.

171. David R. Godschalk et al., *Constitutional Issues of Growth Management* (Washington, D.C.: American Planning Association, 1979), p. 107.

172. Frye, *supra* note 169, at 50030. The states are Illinois, Massachusetts, Pennsylvania, Rhode Island, and Texas.

vironmental harm? Does the threatened environmental harm clearly outweigh the potential benefits from the challenged action so that to proceed further would be an abuse of discretion?[173] The court found that the agency had complied with the test it proposed, enabling the project to go forward.

Important unresolved issues have kept these provisions, even the one in Pennsylvania, from achieving more success in preservation efforts. One recurring issue is whether these provisions are self-executing (immediately enforceable) or whether they require the state legislature to adopt implementing laws. The article in Pennsylvania's constitution has been found self-executing in a lower court decision on historic preservation, although the state's supreme court has not ruled directly on the issue.[174] Other provisions, particularly policy statements, are generally not considered to be self-executing, and, where the state legislature has not acted further, courts are generally reluctant to force them to do so. It is difficult to discern from the provisions themselves if they are self-executing or not; two Virginia circuit courts have ruled opposite ways on this issue in historic preservation cases before them.[175]

A second problem concerns which parties can sue and be sued under these articles. Courts in many of the states have not resolved whether the right to enforce these articles lies with citizens or just the state government and whether they apply to private actions that threaten to degrade the environment as well as to public ones.

A third issue concerns the scope of these articles. Declarations are generally vaguely worded—citizens have a right to clean air, to the preservation of historic sites, and so on—and the standards that should be used or how they should be reconciled with other important concerns has not been set forth.

In answering these questions, states have taken different approaches but have generally imposed a limited duty on public agencies to inquire into the environmental impacts of projects.[176] This duty is similar to requirements under SEPAs, without the formal EIS procedure, and has broader application than SEPAs since the provisions are not limited

---

173. *Payne v. Kassab*, 312 A.2d 86 (Pa. Commw. Ct. 1973), *aff'd*, 361 A.2d 263 (1976).

174. *Id.; Commonwealth v. National Gettysburg Battlefield Tower, Inc.*, 311 A.2d 588 (Pa. 1973). See National Center for Preservation Law, *supra* note 41, at 23.

175. K. Richard Temple, *Historic Preservation in Virginia: Current Problems, Future Needs*, 30 Va. Bar News 21 (April 1982).

176. Godschalk et al., *supra* note 171, at 108.

to "major actions significantly affecting the quality of the environment." The provisions apply in general to any action that threatens historic resources. Moreover, in states that do not have SEPAs, these provisions can function somewhat as surrogates.

So far, at least, courts and agencies give statutory duties under state registers and SEPAs more weight than constitutional provisions on the environment, but these articles should not be neglected in presenting the case for preservation. They are at least supplemental evidence of state policy and the state's commitment to protection. Preservationists should work with agencies and legislatures in developing procedures to implement these provisions. In light of the state's constitution, Pennsylvania's Department of Environmental Resources has developed SEPA-like procedures to identify and consider the environmental effects of proposed actions and to weigh the costs and benefits of alternatives to the projects.[177] This can presumably be duplicated under other similar state constitutions, especially in those states that do not have SEPAs.

CONCLUSION

States are important players in the preservation of historic resources. They have a role of their own that goes beyond implementing federal requirements and acting as catalysts for local action. State laws provide avenues for direct protection; well-administered state policies result in activities, such as surveying, planning, and funding, that give strength to preservation efforts. Varied state activity is crucial to realizing a wide range of preservation objectives.

How states will strengthen their involvement in preservation or whether they even will be able to maintain current levels in light of defederalization and growing fiscal constraints is uncertain. Nevertheless, there are some important implications of the current state role, as outlined in this chapter, that need to be addressed by those concerned with preservation.

One is the continual need to think about what states can do to improve preservation efforts. States help in a key way by assisting local governments. Given cutbacks in federal programs, the need for states to assist, support, and cooperate with local preservation efforts will become even greater. States cannot legitimately complain about the failure of federal agencies to treat states as partners under federal preser-

---

177. National Center for Preservation Law, *supra* note 41, at 24.

vation programs and then turn around and neglect or similarly treat local governments.

States also can aid preservation by developing and maintaining effective laws. While recent attention has turned to public/private development partnerships and other cooperative efforts, strong preservation laws and regulations often are central to providing the necessary incentive for negotiation. This chapter has suggested a variety of ways state preservation laws can be strengthened, from enabling legislation to state registers to environmental policy acts. All states can improve their laws in some fashion.[178] Enforcement is a key component of a law's effectiveness, and preservationists, as well as SHPOs, need to work more closely with state agencies, including state attorney generals, to ensure that preservation laws receive greater attention.[179]

Finally, even with strong laws and enforcement, there is an increasing need to improve the implementation of state preservation policy, that is, to exert effective executive and legislative leadership to implement preservation objectives. Strong laws by themselves are simply not enough. There are several things that state historic preservation officers can do. Since the effectiveness of state preservation programs is often determined by the political support SHPOs have, regularly informing the public of SHPO objectives and accomplishments and increasing their involvement in programs can strengthen support. Through informative pamphlets and publications, many SHPOs and state preservation offices (California, Massachusetts, New Hampshire, and New York, among others) now educate citizens about the values of preservation and how better to utilize state and local programs. In budget disputes, policy differences, or proposed state agency actions that threaten historic resources, public knowledge and support can make the crucial difference.

More effective attention to the needs of the private sector also may reduce opposition to preservation activities and help ease administrative burdens. As was observed over ten years ago:

> ... the most significant role of state legislation and the greatest opportunity for innovative policy-making probably lies in the area of providing such services, standards, controls, and incentives as will encourage the practice of preservation techniques by private owners and users of historic properties.[180]

---

178. For a look at how some states have recently done this through recommendations of a state task force on historic preservation, see Shanahan, *supra* note 114.

179. See Rufus L. Edmisten, *Marshaling Preservation Law Resources*, 12 The Urban Lawyer 42 (1980).

180. Wilson and Winkler, *supra* note 57, at 331.

Preservation requirements, protections, and incentives that consider realistic development or rehabilitation needs will not only make preservation programs more efficient, they also will create new allies. Encouraging private preservation groups and other support organizations to assist in monitoring compliance may help supplement the efforts of state preservation offices. Shifting more of the administrative costs of preservation programs to developers may also serve to eliminate some of the pressures on the public funds.

In addition to building support, preservation leadership at the state level is needed to minimize conflict among state policies. Greater SHPO involvement with state commerce, economic development, and tourism agencies, for example, may increase awareness of preservation options and the benefits of pursuing compatible actions. While some recent laws that attempt to make preservation a responsibility of all state agencies may help to coordinate state policy in development projects, preservation objectives should be elevated so that they are a factor in state agency planning and budgeting.

Federal involvement as a spur to state preservation action is not likely to increase in the next few years. Even if states continue to get sizable amounts of federal dollars, the development, implementation, and soundness of preservation programs will be largely up to them. States thus have a pivotal role in designing innovative responses to new problems and ensuring that workable processes exist to further the goals of preservation.

FURTHER READINGS

The diversity in state preservation laws is reflected in the literature. Concise summaries and analyses of the various approaches states have taken to preserve historic resources are virtually impossible to find.

Two compilations of state laws have appeared since 1976. They are a helpful starting point for anyone interested in reading the state laws that exist in this area, although with each passing year and resulting changes in the laws, they become slightly out of date. *A Guide to State Historic Preservation Programs* was published in 1976 by the National Trust for Historic Preservation. The second is an appendix to an article by James P. Beckwith, Jr., *Preservation Law 1976-1980: Faction, Property Rights, and Ideology*, 11 N.C. Cent. L.J. 276 (1980), which contains a listing of preservation-related state laws. The National Trust also published a helpful summary titled *Significant State Historic Preservation Statutes* (Information Sheet No. 21) in 1979.

The states themselves are one of the best sources of information on state preservation laws and programs. Most state historic preservation offices have published a variety of books and pamphlets explaining how that particular state's program works, what it is assigned to do, and how developers and citizens can best work with it. Examples include, Massachusetts Historical Commission, *Public Planning and Environmental Review: Archeology and Historic Preservation* (Boston, 1979); Division for Historic Preservation, Office of Parks and Recreation, New York, *Historic Resources Survey Manual* (Albany, 1974); Texas Historical Commission, *Historical Preservation in Texas* (Austin, 1973). Many of these have been published through the support of the U.S. Department of the Interior and contain advice on how to best utilize the state in securing the benefits of federal preservation programs.

In several states, task forces have recently examined the state's preservation program and issued a report containing recommendations for new policies. One such report, *Historic Preservation in the State of Washington*, was made by the Ad Hoc Committee on Historic Preservation of the Washington State Senate (Olympia, 1981). Other states, such as Arizona and Oregon, also had historic preservation task forces that completed their work within the last few years. A state legislative heritage task force in California began its work in January 1983 and will issue its report in 1984.

Legally oriented publications are another source of information about state preservation laws. The National Center for Preservation Law has prepared readable primers on the laws and programs of two states. They are *A Primer on Historic Preservation Law in Pennsylvania* (Washington, D.C., 1982) and *A Primer on Historic Preservation Law in New York* (New York, 1981). See also, Grady Gammage, Jr., Philip N. Jones, and Stephen L. Jones, *Historic Preservation in California* (Sanford, Calif.: Stanford Environmental Law Society and National Trust for Historic Preservation, 1975). The monthly journal *Land Use Law & Zoning Digest* (Chicago: American Planning Association) contains commentaries, descriptions of changes in state preservation laws, and summaries of opinions issued in preservation as well as other land-use cases.

Similarly, state environmental policy acts (SEPAs) are the topic of numerous legal articles and publications. William H. Rogers, Jr., *Handbook on Environmental Law* (St. Paul, Minn.: West Publishing Co., 1977) contains an overview of SEPAs. An analysis of California's SEPA is contained in Comment, *Substantive Enforcement of the California En-*

vironmental Quality Act, 69 Calif. L. Rev. 112 (1981) and Comment, *Cultural Ecology: The Urban Landmark as an Environmental Resource*, 11 U.S.F.L. Rev. 720 (1977). New York's SEPA was recently the subject of a comprehensive symposium in volume 46, number 4 of the *Albany Law Review* (Summer 1982), which includes an article that compares New York's SEPAs with SEPAs in other states. Pridgeon, Anderson, and Delphey, *State Environmental Policy Acts: A Survey of Recent Developments*, 2 Harv. Envtl. L. Rev. 419 (1977) looks at several SEPAs and the interpretations various state courts have given to them.

Chapter 4
Federal Law

DONALD DWORSKY, VIRGINIA MCVARISH,
KATE M. PERRY, AND SUSAN MEAD ROBINSON

This chapter focuses on federal preservation law, which includes programs to designate and protect so-called "cultural resources"—historic buildings, archaeological sites, and the like—to plan and review federal agency impacts on these resources, and to regulate and control investment in the built environment. Important federal tax benefits and the procedures to qualify for them are dealt with in separate chapters (see chapters 3 and 7).

Although the federal government has been in the preservation business since the late 1800s and federal programs have spurred state and local action and private rehabilitation development, federal preservation laws overall are weak sisters to federal environmental laws, which not only command the protection of natural resources but establish strong regulatory and enforcement programs to accomplish those goals. In contrast, the linchpin of federal preservation law, the National Historic Preservation Act (NHPA), contains no direct controls to guarantee protection of the built environment. It is in reality a consultation and mitigation mechanism, triggered only when the federal government is involved in an action that threatens designated or significant structures.

The National Environmental Policy Act (NEPA), another law being used increasingly for preservation purposes, functions in a similar fashion. Federal preservation law is complicated by the existence of numerous other acts that affect cultural resources directly or indirectly. For example, highway projects funded by the Department of Transportation are subject to special requirements that are designed to protect properties on the National Register of Historic Places, and some of the most important aspects of what might be called federal preservation policy are found in tax benefits and housing and community development programs, which have an indirect but often important impact on cultural resources.

This chapter provides a road map of federal laws and programs that preservationists and practitioners might have occasion to invoke or run up against. The first section is designed to acquaint the reader with federal preservation law by providing an overview of the major preservation acts and the agencies responsible for their implementation. This summary is followed by a detailed legal analysis of the impact review requirements of the two primary federal preservation statutes, NHPA and NEPA, which may be triggered when federal agency action affects a cultural resource. If a federal action is subjected to legal test, such a challenge will most likely be based on one of these statutes. These more detailed sections provide a comprehensive discussion of regulations and of court cases that have implemented and interpreted these two key laws and should be of particular interest to attorneys involved in projects that need federal permits or that rely on federal funds.

The final section reviews an array of federal housing, rehabilitation, and community development programs that, even though they have an important impact on cultural resources, have often been overlooked by preservationists. This last section is more policy-oriented and exploratory in nature, suggesting ways preservationists can use these broader programs and laws to accomplish their goals.

Overall, the message of this chapter is that while preservationists would be ill-advised to rely heavily on federal preservation laws (particularly those, such as NHPA, with regulatory elements) to protect landmarks and historic areas, they must be prepared to invoke the protections that do exist when faced with recalcitrant agencies and project proponents whose self-interests lie elsewhere. Just as important, they must begin to understand the impact of other federal programs on the built environment and how such programs can be utilized in a positive fashion.

An Overview of Federal Preservation Law

THE DEVELOPMENT OF FEDERAL LAW

As discussed in chapter 1, federal preservation law has steadily expanded in scope since its beginnings in the late 1800s.[1] Initial efforts commemorated nationally significant public figures and events in military history. Preservation of archaeological resources on public lands followed, accompanied by the creation of a government bureau—the National Park Service—that was authorized to operate technical assistance and record-keeping preservation programs as well as to administer recreational lands in a systematic attempt to categorize American history based on themes such as national battlefields. Other federal agencies received special directives to preserve cultural resources they might affect, and the land-management agencies were directed to preserve, or regulate the taking of, archaeological resources. By the early 1960s, federal preservation law rested on four bases:

1. study and designation of nationally significant sites;
2. regulation of the taking of archaeological resources;
3. acquisition and preservation of privately owned properties and the preservation of sites on federal lands; and
4. National Park Service assistance and specific legislative directives to several federal agencies with the power to adversely affect historic resources.

Despite these efforts, there was a sense that significant historic resources were being lost, particularly items of more regional than national significance.

In the 1966 National Historic Preservation Act (NHPA), the National Park Service was given authority to designate privately owned cultural resources as significant and to subsidize their rehabilitation through grants-in-aid. The act's authorization of federal grants to the states resulted in the creation of state preservation offices to work cooperatively with federal preservation efforts. Another federal agency—the Advisory Council on Historic Preservation (ACHP)—was created by the act to

---

1. For a detailed discussion of early federal preservation efforts, the best reference is the excellent two-volume standard work by Charles Hosmer, *Presence of the Past: A History of the Preservation Movement in the United States before Williamsburg* (New York: Putnam, 1965) and *Preservation Comes of Age: From Williamsburg to the National Trust, 1926-1949* (Charlottesville: University Press of Virginia, 1981).

consult with federal agencies regarding the possible effects of their actions (permits, grants, and so forth) on historic properties and to advise the Congress on preservation policy. Completing the expanding federal preservation picture was NHPA's broad definition of historic resources of federal interest. No longer were only nationally significant properties to be designated as historic. Instead, the act defined the national patrimony as resources of significance to Americans at the local and state as well as the national level. The NHPA immediately became the basic federal statute for historic preservation, and it remains so today.

In 1976, after a decade of experience under the act, the ACHP assessed the national program against criteria it developed for what a complete national program should include.[2] The council found that an effective program could only exist if there were first a comprehensive inventory of historic properties. The council's assessment found that no such inventory existed.[3] The ACHP also concluded that properties identified in a national inventory require evaluation to determine which properties should be protected.[4] The assessment of the council, however, found that since a national inventory of properties did not exist, comparative evaluations could not be made to determine which properties should be protected. The council noted that evaluations that were made did not guide later decisions affecting the evaluated properties.[5] Further, the council found that the evaluation criteria were not uniformly applied to properties that had been identified.[6]

The ACHP also concluded that identified properties that meet the evaluation criteria require protection.[7] However, the assessment of the council was that the government's choice of protective tactics was too limited. Only federal acquisition, preservation through the federal grant-in-aid program, and review and comment by the advisory council were available as tools. Private adverse effects on National Register properties were uncontrolled.[8] The council found that state and local preservation efforts did not complement the federal protective system.[9] Finally,

---

2. Senate Committee on Interior and Insular Affairs, *The National Historic Preservation Program Today*, Committee Print, 94th Cong., 2d Sess. (1976).
3. *Id.* at 11, 14.
4. *Id.* at 21.
5. *Id.* at 30.
6. *Id.* at 28.
7. *Id.* at 37.
8. *Id.* at 42.
9. *Id.* at 46.

the council noted that the limited protections were available for all National Register properties, regardless of the degree of significance (i.e., state, local, or national), and regardless of the nature of the listed property. An archaeological site held equal status and was treated the same as a historic area or a single building with significant architectural features.[10]

The study made several other telling criticisms of national policy, such as pointing out the bias in the Internal Revenue Code toward new construction. This analysis by the ACHP had an impact, and over the next four years, Congress made numerous changes in national policy to benefit preservation. The tax code was changed in 1976 and again in 1978 and 1981 to stimulate the reuse of older buildings (see discussion in chapter 7). The General Services Administration was directed to attempt to reuse historic properties,[11] and in 1980, major amendments to the NHPA of 1966 were enacted. Additionally, two other areas of law developed. The National Environmental Policy Act of 1969 rapidly became a much-used tool to protect the natural and the built environment. Federal community development programs, which would sometimes help preserve landmarks and at other times lead to their demolition, also were created. These laws and programs, as well as a number of other less visible ones, are discussed in greater detail in the following sections.

THE NATIONAL HISTORIC PRESERVATION ACT, AS AMENDED

The National Historic Preservation Act of 1966 (NHPA)[12] is the key federal law designed to encourage identification and preservation of America's cultural resources. The act commits federal agencies to a program of identification and protection of historic properties on land they own and establishes the National Register of Historic Places to designate public or privately owned resources and to encourage identification and planning for compatible use of the properties. Properties not listed on the Register because of owners' objections may be determined to be "eligible" for inclusion in the Register and are protected from federal actions just as listed properties are.

---

10. *Id.* at 44.
11. Public Buildings Cooperative Use Act, 40 U.S.C. §§ 490, 601(a), 606, 611, 612a (1976 & Supp. IV 1980).
12. 16 U.S.C. § 470 (1976 & Supp. IV 1980).

The act coordinates federal efforts with those of the other sectors in the preservation spectrum: state historic preservation officers (SHPOs) are statutorily integrated into all aspects of federal preservation activity, and local governments may be certified to carry out delegated responsibilities and apply for federal funds.[13]

Critical to the federal preservation effort is the Section 106 review requirement that agencies afford the Advisory Council on Historic Preservation (ACHP) an opportunity to comment on actions of the agencies that may affect properties included in, or eligible for inclusion in, the National Register. The agencies are required to "take into account" the comments of the council.

Nevertheless, preservation of historic and cultural resources remains merely an encouraged goal and not a required action. Federal involvement is required to trigger ACHP review; the act does not address private actions or state or local government actions potentially harmful to historic properties. Moreover, federal agencies ultimately have considerable discretion to undertake or approve projects that affect historic properties. The council's review mechanism requires only that an agency first follow the prescribed consultation procedure. The ACHP can suggest alternatives to proposed actions but cannot require agencies to protect cultural resources.

NHPA's preservation program is also dependent on a number of discretionary factors, such as appropriations to implement the act. The act's implementing regulations, to be issued by the Department of the Interior and the ACHP, can also be redrafted by each administration to reflect its own policies.

These limitations and political vulnerabilities, however, do not necessarily negate NHPA's preservation effectiveness. While NHPA is less stringent and far-reaching than some other environmental laws, such as the Clean Air and Water Acts, the 1980 amendments, which are still relatively unused, strengthened NHPA's enforcement potential. Furthermore, NHPA functions in tandem with many other laws; combined with Section 4(f) of the Department of Transportation Act or

---

13. All of the states and territories have enacted historic preservation laws. James P. Beckwith, Jr., *Appendix of State and Territorial Historic Preservation Statutes and Session Laws*, 11 N.C. Cent. L.J. 308-40 (1980). In addition, at least 832 historic district or landmark commissions had been created as of 1981. Stephen N. Dennis, ed., *Directory of American Preservation Commissions* (Washington, D.C.: National Trust for Historic Preservation, 1981), p. iii.

the National Environmental Policy Act and its interpretive case law, NHPA can serve as a formidable legal tool. Moreover, listing a property on the Register triggers significant benefits under federal income tax law, which can produce a strong incentive for preservation.

Identification and Listing of Resources

Section 101(a)(1)(a) of NHPA authorizes the secretary of the interior to "expand and maintain" a National Register of Historic Places, the official listing of the nation's historic properties and cultural resources found worthy of preservation.

Properties may be included in the National Register in one of four ways:[14]

1. nomination by the state historic preservation officer (SHPO), qualified local governments, or individuals in states where there is no Interior Department-approved state program;[15]
2. nomination by federal agency head;[16]
3. designation as a National Historic Landmark by the secretary of the interior;[17] and
4. addition to the National Park System by act of Congress, if the area is determined by Congress to be of historic significance.

The Register is to be composed of "districts, sites, buildings, structures, and objects significant in American history, architecture, archaeology, engineering and culture."[18] Properties listed in the Register may be of local, state, or national significance. The Register is administered by the Keeper of the National Register within the National Park Service of the Department of the Interior.[19] Although no accurate count

---

14. 46 Fed. Reg. 56,211 (1981) (proposed rule to be codified at 36 C.F.R. § 60.8) provides for nominations by persons or local governments in states without approved state historic preservation programs. All states have approved programs as of the date of this writing. Note that the interim rules, 46 Fed. Reg. 56,184 (1981), no longer allow SHPO nomination of properties under federal ownership or control. See 46 Fed. Reg. 56,191 (1981) (to be codified at 60.6(y)).

15. 16 U.S.C. § 470a-d (Supp. IV 1980).

16. Executive Order No. 11593 § 2(a), 36 Fed. Reg. 8,921 (1971), reprinted in 16 U.S.C. § 470h-2 (Supp. IV 1980).

17. 16 U.S.C. §§ 461-69 (1976).

18. *Id.* at § 470a(b)(2).

19. The Heritage Conservation and Recreation Service (HCRS) administered the federal historic preservation program between 1978 and 1981. Pursuant to Secretarial Order No. 3060, Amendment No. 1 (February 19, 1981), HCRS was abolished, and the National Park Service reassumed responsibility.

is kept of properties listed in the National Register, the National Park Service estimates that there are about 24,500 listings, of which roughly 2,450 are historic districts,[20] for a total of between 750,000 to 1 million buildings on the Register.

As defined in regulations, the types of properties that can be added to the National Register are:

> (a) Building. A building is a structure created to shelter any form of human activity, such as a house, barn, church, hotel, or similar structure. Building may refer to a historically related complex such as a courthouse and jail or a house and barn. Examples: Molly Brown House, Denver, Colorado; Meek Mansion and Carriage House, Hayward, California; Huron County Courthouse and Jail, Norwalk, Ohio; Fairntosh Plantation, Durham vicinity, North Carolina . . . .
>
> (d) District. A district is a geographically definable area, urban or rural, possessing a significant concentration, linkage, or continuity of sites, buildings, structures, or objects united by past events or aesthetically by plan or physical development. A district may also comprise individual elements separated geographically but linked by association or history. Examples: Georgetown Historic District, Washington, D.C.; Martin Luther King Historic District, Atlanta, Georgia; Durango-Silverton Narrow-Gauge Railroad, right-of-way between Durango and Silverton, Colorado . . . .
>
> (j) Object. An object is a material thing of functional, aesthetic, cultural, historical, or scientific value that may be, by nature or design, movable yet related to a specific setting or environment. Examples: Delta Queen Steamboat, Cincinnati, Ohio; Adams Memorial, Rock Creek Cemetery, Washington, D.C.; Sumpter Valley Gold Dredge, Sumpter, Oregon . . . .
>
> (l) Site. A site is the location of a significant event, a prehistoric or historic occupation or activity, or a building or structure, whether standing, ruined, or vanished, where the location itself maintains historical or archaeological value regardless of the value of any existing structure. Examples: Cabin Creek Battlefield, Pensacola vicinity, Oklahoma; Mound Cemetery Mound, Chester vicinity, Ohio; Mud Springs Pony Express Station Site, Dalton vicinity, Nebraska. . . .
>
> (p) Structure. A structure is a work made up of interdependent and interrelated parts in a definite pattern of organization. Constructed by humans, it is often an engineering project large in scale. Examples: Swanton Covered Railroad Bridge, Swanton vicinity, Vermont; Old Point Loma Lighthouse, San Diego, California; North Point Water Tower, Milwaukee, Wisconsin; Reber Radio Telescope, Green Bay vicinity, Wisconsin.[21]

---

20. Telephone call, Donald Dworsky to National Register staff member Beth Grosvenor, March 23, 1982.

21. 36 C.F.R. § 60.2 (1981).

Qualifications for Listing in the National Register

To qualify for inclusion in the National Register, properties must meet the evaluation criteria in the Code of Federal Regulations summarized below:

> *National Register criteria for evaluation.* The quality of significance in American history, architecture, archaeology, engineering, and culture is present in districts, sites, buildings, structures, and objects that possess integrity of location, design, setting, materials, workmanship, feeling, and association, and
>
> (a) that are associated with events that have made a significant contribution to the broad patterns of our history; or
>
> (b) that are associated with the lives of persons significant in our past; or
>
> (c) that embody the distinctive characteristics of a type, period, or method of construction, or that represent the work of a master, or that possess high artistic values, or that represent a significant and distinguishable entity whose components may lack individual distinction; or
>
> (d) that have yielded, or may be likely to yield, information important in prehistory or history.[22]

Cemeteries and graves, birthplaces, religious properties, reconstructions, commemorative properties, relocated buildings, and properties that have achieved significance within the past 50 years generally are not eligible for National Register listing except as part of a historic district.[23] However, the regulations allow broad exceptions to the general rule.

The criteria are general by necessity. A comparison of the national criteria with local or international evaluation criteria reveals few, if any, differences. Not only is the definition of "significance" subjective, but significance varies depending upon the quality of the resource and its location. Those initially developing the evaluation criteria tried to eliminate subjectivity by requiring the evaluating staff at the state level and in the National Park Service to possess professional qualifications, such as training in archaeology or architectural history.[24] A series of procedural checks was also established for processing the evaluations: development of documentation by a local, state, or federal official; review by a state review board; review again by the SHPO; and final review

---

22. *Id.* at § 60.6. The National Register regulations apply as "interim rules," pending a comment period.
23. *Id.* at § 60.6(d).
24. See, e.g., *id.* at § 61.4.

by the Interior Department.[25] Control over subjectivity is limited, however, since the SHPO can reject a proposed nomination that the review board has approved but cannot approve of a nomination if the review board has rejected it.[26] Further, there is no requirement that the evaluation criteria be applied in a written decision. This is a potential source of litigation.

Once properties have been listed in the Register, they may be removed only if a mistake in professional judgment as to eligibility is proved, if procedures for listing were not followed, if the property has been altered so that it no longer meets the National Register criteria, or if additional information shows that the property does not satisfy the criteria.[27] Section 101(a)(1)(B) of the 1980 NHPA amendments, however, legislatively recognized all properties listed on the Register or designated as national landmarks as of December 12, 1980. Only alterations subsequent to this date constitute grounds for removal from the Register.

Nomination Procedures

Nomination by the SHPO. Listing usually occurs through nomination by the SHPO.[28] The process begins with the preparation of an Interior Department-prescribed nomination form, usually by the staff of the SHPO or a consultant retained by that office, but it may also be submitted by the property owner, a local preservation organization, the municipality where the property is located, or another interested party.[29] Preparation and submission of nominations are to follow "statewide priorities" established by the SHPO, consistent with an approved state historic preservation plan. The *Historic Preservation Grant-in-Aid Manual*, issued annually to the states by the National Park Service, details the requirements states must meet.

---

25. 46 Fed. Reg. 56,190-91 (1981) (to be codified at 36 C.F.R. § 60.6(k)(1)).
26. *Id.* at 56,190 (to be codified at 36 C.F.R. § 60.6(e)).
27. 36 C.F.R. § 60.17 (1981).
28. 46 Fed. Reg. 56,209 (1981) (to be codified at 36 C.F.R. § 60.6).
29. Individuals may prepare nomination forms and request the SHPO or a federal agency official actually to nominate a property. Information on preparing National Register nominations may be found in *How to Complete National Register Forms*, published in 1977 and obtainable from the National Register Division, Office of Archaeology and Historic Preservation, National Park Service, U.S. Department of the Interior, Washington, D.C. In addition, a guide entitled *How to Apply National Register Criteria* is now being compiled by the Register staff. Further information and assistance are available from the state historic preservation offices.

Notice is provided to the property owner[30] and local and county authorities of the intent to nominate the property, and comments are solicited. In addition, since 1980, owners of private property are given an opportunity to concur in or object to listing on the Register (this requirement is discussed in detail below).

Completed nomination forms are submitted to a state review board,[31] which usually consists of five people designated by the SHPO.[32] A majority of the members must be professionals from the fields of history, archaeology, architectural history, and architecture. The board typically meets at least three times a year to review National Register nominations and appeals. The board determines whether nominated properties meet the criteria for evaluation.[33]

If the review board recommends that the SHPO approve of the nomination, the nomination is reviewed by the SHPO.[34] If the SHPO approves of the nomination, it is forwarded to the Keeper of the National Register[35] in Washington, D.C.[36] If the SHPO disagrees with the state review board's recommendation that a property should be nominated, the SHPO may submit the nomination and his opinions on the nomination, including whether it meets the evaluation criteria, to the Keeper together with the opinions of the board.[37] Alternatively, the review board or the chief elected local official of the governmental subdivision in which the property is located may request such a submission within 45 days of the review board meeting.[38] However, should

---

30. Ownership is determined by official land records, tax records, or an alternative source requested by a state.
31. At least one state, Connecticut, has a statute providing for submission of National Register nominations to advisory local review boards. Conn. Gen. Stat. Ann. § 10-321(q) (West Supp. 1982).
32. 46 Fed. Reg. 56,189 (1981) (to be codified at 36 C.F.R. § 60.3(o)).
33. *Id.* at 56,188 (to be codified at 36 C.F.R. § 60.6(j)).
34. *Id.* at 56,212 (to be codified at 36 C.F.R. § 60.11 (e)) requires the SHPO to notify an applicant if he decides not to submit a nomination and to explain the reasons for the decision.
35. "The Keeper of the National Register of Historic Places is the individual who has been delegated the authority by the National Park Service to list properties and determine their eligibility for the National Register." 46 Fed. Reg. 56,188 (1981) (to be codified at 36 C.F.R. § 60.3(f)).
36. *Id.* (to be codified at 36 C.F.R. § 60.6(k)).
37. *Id.* (to be codified at 36 C.F.R. § 60.6(l)).
38. *Id.*

the review board not approve the nomination, it is not forwarded to the SHPO, even if he might disagree with the board's findings.

In the past there has been some debate whether nomination by a SHPO was a ministerial duty mandatory upon a third party's initiation or an action over which the SHPO had final discretion.[39] Section 101(a)(5) of the 1980 NHPA amendments moots this issue by permitting any person or local government to appeal to the secretary of the interior a nomination or the failure or refusal to nominate a property to the National Register.[40]

Upon the Keeper's receipt of nominations from the SHPO, notice of consideration of the nominations for listing is published in the *Federal Register* for a 15-day comment period.[41] Nominations are reviewed by the Office of Archeology and Historic Preservation within the National Park Service for technical and professional sufficiency and conformance with National Register criteria and, on approval, are listed in the National Register. The interim regulations specify, however, that any person or organization may petition the Keeper during the nomination process either to accept or reject a nomination. The Keeper must then substantively review the nomination[42] but need not apply the evaluation criteria in writing. The Keeper usually affirms the information in the nomination submitted by the applicant. Although the regulations only require the Keeper to "respond" to a request for a determination of eligibility,[43] the Keeper usually makes a brief comment on qualities and important characteristics of properties determined eligible for inclusion in the Register. Application of the evaluation criteria is not explicitly required. The interim regulations authorize the Keeper to issue written opinions in certain cases that carry precedent value in later

---

39. See *Young v. Mellon*, 156 Cal. Rptr. 165 (Cal. App. 1979), holding the SHPO did have discretion whether to forward a nomination. The case was later ordered omitted from official publication and thus is not a citable precedent.

40. See 46 Fed. Reg. 56,212-13 (1981) (to be codified at 36 C.F.R. § 60.12) regarding the appeals process. At least two preservation cases have arisen out of the appeals authority. In *Battista v. Watt*, No. 81-65E (W.D.N.Y. filed August 7, 1981), plaintiff sought a declaratory judgment of his right to appeal under the 1980 amendments. In *Natural Resources Defense Council, Inc. v. City of New York*, 528 F. Supp. 1245 (S.D.N.Y. 1981), an appeal was granted in a stipulation with the Department of the Interior.

41. 36 C.F.R. § 60.13 (1981).

42. *Id.* at § 60.12(b).

43. Cf. *Environmental Defense Fund, Inc. v. Ruckelshaus*, 439 F.2d 584 (D.C. Cir. 1971).

reviews. However, the interim regulations do not direct that adjudicatory or rule-making procedures be followed. The lack of independent written findings by the Keeper as to how the evaluation criteria apply for each nomination may invite appeals and provide opportunities for legal challenge on procedural due process grounds.

Nomination forms that are technically or professionally inadequate are returned to the applicant for revision and resubmission. Nominations that are sufficient professionally and technically, and for property that meets the criteria for evaluation, are approved by the Keeper and added to the Register.[44] Once the property is listed, the SHPO, the appropriate congressional delegation, and the owner are notified.[45] The completed nomination forms are maintained by the National Park Service, and copies are kept by the SHPO.[46]

The staff of the National Register monitors properties on the Register to ensure that the listed properties maintain the qualifications and the integrity for which they were listed. Changes or revisions to the boundaries of the property and proposed relocations of the property must be reviewed and approved by the National Park Service if the property is to be kept in the Register. The views of the SHPO or the appropriate federal preservation officer on the change must also be submitted to the Department of the Interior.[47] Properties that have lost the qualities that caused them to be listed in the Register, which have been lost or destroyed, or for which there have been professional or procedural errors in the listing process may also be removed by the National Park Service, but such properties may also be submitted for relisting.[48]

Nomination by Certified Local Governments. The 1980 NHPA amendments provide for local government involvement in the National Register listing process. Until the 1980 amendments, local governments did not necessarily receive notification of local property nominations to the National Register. Section 101(a)(2)(F) requires the secretary of the interior to notify the owner of the property, the local government,

---

44. 36 C.F.R. § 60.15(b)(6) (1981).
45. 46 Fed. Reg. 56,190 (1981) (to be codified at 36 C.F.R. § 60.6(g)).
46. Additions to and changes in the National Register and properties included in or determined eligible for the Register are printed in the *Federal Register* each year. The last comprehensive cumulative listing of properties included in or determined eligible for the National Register was printed at 44 Fed. Reg. 7,415-649 (1979).
47. *Id.*; 46 Fed. Reg. 56,193-94 (1981) (to be codified at 3 6 C.F.R. § 60.14).
48. 46 Fed. Reg. 56,194-95 (1981) (to be codified at 36 C.F.R. § 60.15).

and the general public when a property is being considered for inclusion in the National Register. Section 101(a)(b) requires that the owner, the SHPO, the Advisory Council on Historic Preservation (ACHP), and local chief elected officials be informed of a determination-of-eligibility finding by the Interior Department. These provisions were a response to a growing dissatisfaction among local government officials who claimed they had no say in the nominations of properties in their jurisdictions.

Section 101(c)(1) now provides that local governments may be certified by the SHPO and the secretary of the interior to carry out the purposes of NHPA if criteria regarding local survey, inventory, designation, and protection of historic properties are met.[49] Once a local government is certified, it may nominate properties within its jurisdiction to the National Register after notice and opportunity for comment are given to the owner, the chief local elected official, and, if one exists, the local historic preservation commission. If both the local official and the commission recommend that a property nominated by a third party not be designated, the SHPO will pursue the nomination only if a timely appeal is filed under Section 101(a)(5).[50]

Nomination by Federal Agency. The 1980 NHPA amendments codified the requirements placed on federal agencies in Executive Order 11593 (see below) and thus required more of the federal agencies than the requirement of Section 106 that they consider the effects of their undertakings on National Register or Register-eligible properties. Section 110(a)(2) codified the directive in Executive Order 11593 that each federal agency establish a program to nominate to the Register all apparently eligible properties under that agency's ownership or control.[51] Aided by the secretary of the interior and the SHPO, each agency must establish a program to locate, inventory, and nominate such properties.[52] Section 110(c) requires agency designation of a "preservation officer" to coordinate all activity under the act.

---

49. The National Register interim rules reserve 36 C.F.R. §§ 60.6(i) and 60.7 for future publication of the regulations concerning local government certification. See 46 Fed. Reg. 56,185 (1981).

50. 16 U.S.C. § 470a-d (Supp. IV 1980).

51. According to National Register staff estimates, a total of 25 federal agencies submitted nominations between 1973 and mid-1981. Seven hundred and seventy-five listings resulted, almost half of which were initiated by the National Park Service. The next most active agencies were the Forest Service, General Services Administration, and Bureau of Land Management, averaging 75 successful nominations each.

52. The National Park Service's inventory, for example, includes roughly 10,000 major properties, most of which are eligible for Register listing if not in fact listed.

Nominations by the federal preservation officer are submitted to the appropriate SHPO for comment.[53] The chief elected county or municipal officials must also be notified and allowed 45 days in which to comment. The federal officer may choose to forward the nomination to the Keeper of the National Register for a final determination of whether to include the property in the National Register. The officer may submit the nomination form even if he does not believe that the property meets the criteria for being listed in the Register. In such a case, the officer is required to state his views as to whether the property meets the criteria for addition to the Register.

For a nomination he supports, the federal officer must also include an opinion of the property's qualifications as well as comments received on the nomination. The Keeper may approve or disapprove of the nomination following publication in the *Federal Register* for a 15-day comment period. During the nomination process any person or organization may petition the Keeper either to accept or to reject a nomination. The Keeper must then substantively review the nomination under the same procedure as if it were a nomination from the state.

The federal preservation officer and the SHPO are encouraged to cooperate on nominations, particularly when a portion of an area being nominated by the federal official is not on federal lands but is an integral part of the cultural resource being nominated.[54] However, the regulations do not authorize the SHPO unilaterally to nominate properties on federal lands. The SHPO may complete the nomination form but must then submit it to the federal preservation officer for review and comment. The federal official may approve of the nomination and transmit it to the Interior Department but is not required to do so.[55] If the federal officer refuses to submit the nomination to the Department of the Interior, the SHPO may encourage the federal official to at least seek a determination of eligibility. If the federal officer refuses, individuals may appeal the failure of a nominating authority under 36 C.F.R. § 60.12, "Proposed Rules." However, the regulations do not clearly cover this point, nor do they squarely address the issue of whether the state may nominate properties on federal lands.

Owner Objection or Consent. Until enactment of the 1980 NHPA amendments, inclusion of a property in the National Register did not

---

53. 46 Fed. Reg. 56,192 (1981) (to be codified at 36 C.F.R. § 60.9).
54. *Id.* at 56,192-93 (to be codified at 36 C.F.R. § 60.10).
55. *Id.* at 56,191-92 (to be codified at 36 C.F.R. § 60.6(y)).

require the owner's consent on the presumptions that: (a) the Register is a list of properties that meets an objective evaluation, which applies criteria and professional standards regardless of a current owner's opinion of the property; (b) the owner's opinion has no bearing on whether a property is historic; and (c) inclusion in the Register does not directly restrict a private owner's use of his property in any manner. Although the drafters of the 1980 amendments expressly recognized these facts, they argued that inclusion may affect how owners choose to use their properties. They maintained that enactment of the 1976 tax provisions encouraging historic preservation triggered tax disincentives, albeit minor, for demolition of certain properties covered by Section 2124 of the 1976 Tax Reform Act, 26 U.S.C. §§ 167(n) and 280(B).[56] Moreover, the review process of the ACHP that applied to National Register properties was perceived as a needless regulatory delay by the users of public lands and proponents of projects requiring federal approval. Some mayors also complained they had no say over inclusions that were an impediment to their urban development plans.

The proponents of owner consent carried the day politically, and Section 101(a)(6) of the 1980 amendments requires a form of owner consent for listing. It provides that before any property or district may be included in the National Register or designated a National Historic Landmark, the property owner or owners[57] must be given the opportunity to concur in or object to the designation. If there is an objection by the sole owner of a property, or by the majority of owners of a property or properties, the property may not be included in the Register or designated a National Historic Landmark.[58] When properties are nominated as part of a district, a majority vote of owners in the area is required to reject listing. Each owner is allowed one vote regardless

---

56. 26 U.S.C. § 167(n) (1976), *repealed by* Economic Recovery Tax Act of 1981, Pub. L. No. 97-34, § 212(d)(1), 95 Stat. 239. No individual has a vested right to deductions or benefits available under federal tax law. *Helvering v. United States Trust Co.*, 111 F.2d 576 (2d Cir. 1940), *cert. denied subnom. United States Trust Co. of New York v. Commissioner of Internal Revenue*, 311 U.S. 678 (1940). In fact, neither the tax consequences nor any other supposed effects of listing in the National Register constitutionally require owner consent. See *Historic Green Springs, Inc. v. Bergland*, 497 F. Supp. 839 (E.D. Va. 1980), holding that listing in the National Register is not a "taking of property in violation of the 5th Amendment to the United States Constitution."

57. The House report expressly anticipated problems of definition in cases of multiple and absentee ownership. See H. Rep. No. 1457, 96th Cong., 2d Sess. (1980).

58. See 46 Fed. Reg. 56,183 (1981) (to be codified at 36 C.F.R. § 60).

of how many properties, or what part of one property, each owner owns and regardless of whether the property contributes to the district's significance. If owners object, the secretary of the interior is obligated nonetheless to make a determination of whether the property is eligible for inclusion in the Register.[59] If determined eligible, the property would fall under the review of the ACHP, even without the owner's consent, and would probably meet the test for being certified to qualify for certain federal tax benefits. However, it would not be eligible to receive the grant-in-aid, which only can go to National Register properties.

Effects of Listing

Inclusion in the National Register or a determination of eligibility for inclusion plays three major roles. First, it creates an inventory of properties that can be used as a planning tool by government, private organizations, and persons to help identify cultural resources worthy of preservation. Second, it is a legal instrument that ensures that federal, federally assisted, or federally licensed undertakings affecting properties listed in or eligible for listing in the Register will undergo Section 106 review and comment. Third, it makes properties eligible for benefits such as the National Historic Preservation Fund grants and loans, if the programs are implemented by the Interior Department and if there are appropriations.

Section 106 of NHPA requires that federal agencies take into account the effect of their undertakings on included or eligible properties and that the ACHP be given the opportunity to comment on such undertakings.

Although Section 106 applies only to federal, federally funded, federally subsidized, or federally licensed undertakings, these activities often involve actions by private parties—for example, private contractors hired by a federal agency or recipients of federal funds or licenses. Consequently, injunctions for noncompliance with Section 106 may be issued against nonfederal parties and municipalities involved in federal actions.[60]

Section 106, however, is a procedural requirement that does not prohibit a proposed undertaking that has a negative effect on Register prop-

---

59. 16 U.S.C. § 470a-d (Supp. IV 1980).
60. See, e.g., *Biderman v. Morton*, 497 F.2d 1141, 1147 (2d Cir. 1974); *Jones v. Lynn*, 477 F.2d 885 (1st Cir. 1973); *Save the Courthouse Committee v. Lynn*, 408 F. Supp. 1323, 1344 (S.D.N.Y. 1975).

erties. A federal agency only can be made to consider the effects of its undertakings, including undertakings or effects identified by the ACHP, and to provide the council with an opportunity to comment. Having done so, the agency has complied with Section 106 and may proceed with its planned action, including demolition of Register buildings if desired. An agreement between the agency and the ACHP on how to treat historic properties, however, is enforceable as a contract. (Section 106 is discussed in more detail below.)

Register inclusion may also qualify properties for matching grants-in-aid through the National Historic Preservation Fund when such funds are appropriated by Congress.[61] In addition, property owners who rehabilitate their National Register properties in accordance with the secretary of the interior's "Standards for Rehabilitation and Guidelines for Rehabilitating Historic Buildings"[62] may qualify for a substantial investment tax credit. Other available tax advantages are discussed in chapter 7. The only tax disincentive denies deduction of costs when a Register property is demolished.[63] Thus, although National Register inclusion does not directly restrict private property owners, it may affect how owners choose to use their properties, particularly if federal action is somehow involved.

Some state and local laws also grant tax benefits to owners of properties listed in the National Register. For instance, a Norwalk, Connecticut, ordinance permits a 10-year phase-in period of property tax increases resulting from rehabilitation that conforms to Department of the Interior guidelines.[64]

Mere listing of a property on the Register will generally not give rise to an unconstitutional deprivation of property under the Fifth Amendment. Several courts have held that simply because designation triggers

---

61. Information on grants and tax benefits may be obtained from the state historic preservation office.

62. U.S. Department of the Interior, HCRS Pub. No. 7, *The Secretary of the Interior's Standards for Historic Preservation Projects with Guidelines for Applying the Standards* (Washington, D.C.: GPO, 1979).

63. These provisions are discussed in chapter 7.

64. Norwalk, Conn., Code 78-1; state enabling legislation is found in the Conn. Gen. Stat. Ann. § 12-65(c)-65(f) (West 1982). For other examples, see chapter 7.

federal statutes that discourage incompatible development, there is no interference sufficient to effect an unconstitutional "taking."[65]

Determination of Eligibility and Its Effect

Properties may be determined "eligible" for inclusion in the National Register for purposes of Section 106 of NHPA in either of two ways. First, a property nominated to the Register whose owner does not consent to inclusion may be declared eligible by the secretary of the interior acting through the Keeper; or second, the secretary of the interior may make a determination of eligibility if a federal agency requests such a determination pursuant to Sections 106 or 110 of the 1980 NHPA amendments. Eligible properties are protected by Section 106 review just as properties included in the Register are, but they do not qualify for the tax advantages afforded by federal tax law or for federal grants-in-aid, despite the fact that eligible properties must meet the same evaluation criteria as Register properties.

When a federal undertaking occurs, properties are identified by a designated agency official,[66] who is required to consult with the SHPO of the state where the undertaking will occur.[67] The SHPO provides information on properties known to be in the area and recommends whether a survey of the area's historic resources is needed. The agency official decides what further actions are necessary to identify area

---

65. *Historic Green Springs, Inc. v. Bergland*, 497 F. Supp. 839, 849 (E.D. Va. 1980). See also *Penn Central Transportation Co. v. City of New York*, 438 U.S. 104 (1978). The term "taking" properly refers to government exercise of the eminent domain power requiring just compensation under the Fifth Amendment. An unconstitutional "taking" occurs when the government has acquired private property without payment of compensation. Although literally incorrect, the term "taking" has also been used to refer to oppressive regulation under the police power. See, e.g., *Pamel Corp. v. Puerto Rico Highway Authority*, 621 F.2d 33, 35-36 (1st Cir. 1980). The latest U.S. Supreme Court pronouncement on "takings" and an interesting scholarly analysis can be found in *San Diego Gas and Electric v. City of San Diego*, 450 U.S. 621 (1981).

66. "Agency official" is defined to be "the head of the federal agency having responsibility for the undertaking or a designee authorized to act for the agency official." 36 C.F.R. § 800.2(i) (1981). The recipient of an urban development action grant is the legal delegatee under 24 C.F.R. § 570.45 4(b)(2) and § 570.458(c)(14)(vii) (1982).

67. 36 C.F.R. § 800.4(a) (1981). See *Commonwealth of Puerto Rico v. Muskie*, 507 F. Supp. 1035 (D.P.R. 1981), federal defendants violated NHPA when their outside consultant failed to consult with the SHPO regarding historic properties within area of potential impact prior to undertaking her archaeological survey.

resources; recommendations of the SHPO in this matter are to be followed.[68]

After area resources are identified, the agency official, in consultation with the SHPO, gives his opinion as to whether the National Register criteria are met for any of the historic, architectural, archaeological, or cultural resources found. A written application of the criteria is not required. If either the federal agency official or the SHPO finds that any property meets or may meet the criteria or if the two disagree, the federal agency official must request a "determination of eligibility" from the secretary of the interior.[69] However, the regulations require only that the Keeper of the National Register "respond" to a request for a determination;[70] a written application of the criteria is implied but not required. If the agency official and the SHPO agree that no identified property meets the National Register criteria and the keeper has not otherwise determined any property to be Register-eligible, this finding is documented by the agency and the undertaking may proceed.[71]

The two determination-of-eligibility processes are clearly inconsistent procedurally. Federal agency determination requires none of the procedural obligations—such as the notice and hearing requirements—that flows from nominations for which owners have objected to listing. These procedural differences reflect the difference in effects of the two determinations: only the formal nomination process raises the possibility that federal tax consequences will be triggered; an eligibility determination only triggers the Section 106 review.

The Advisory Council on Historic Preservation

The Advisory Council on Historic Preservation (ACHP) is a small (20-person staff; $1 million annual budget), independent federal agency created by NHPA to advise other federal agencies on the effects agency

---

68. See *Bayou St. John Improvement Association v. Sands*, No. 81-1358 (E.D. La. May 28, 1981) (injunction modified June 17, 1982), court found that NHPA requires an agency to "consult" with the SHPO and that, although compliance with the SHPO's recommendations is not mandatory, good cause must be shown for not complying.

69. The secretary of the interior has the authority to list under the statute (see *Stop H-3 Association v. Coleman*, 533 F.2d 434 (9th Cir. 1976)), but this authority has been delegated to the Keeper of the National Register (see *Central Oklahoma Preservation Alliance, Inc. v. Oklahoma City Urban Renewal Authority*, 471 F. Supp. 68 (W.D. Okla. 1979)). The Keeper may also make determinations of eligibility.

70. 36 C.F.R. § 800.4 (1981).

71. *Id.* at § 800.4(3).

actions may have on historic properties and to advise the president and Congress on preservation issues.[72] The council consists of 19 members: 6 federal agency heads, the architect of the capitol, 1 governor, 1 mayor, the president of the National Conference of State Historic Preservation Officers, the chairman of the National Trust for Historic Preservation, 4 preservation experts, and 4 members of the general public.[73]

The ACHP's advisory review regulations[74] provide a number of opportunities for the council's staff, or a team of council members, to complete the council's review. The procedures of the council, including the use of staff and delegated discretionary power to the executive director, have been challenged in only a few cases.

In *Natural Resources Defense Council v. City of New York*[75] and *National Center for Preservation Law v. Landrieu*,[76] plaintiffs attacked various council procedures and actions: expedited reviews by the ACHP; the use of staff and teams of council members to review projects; failure of the full council to comment on federal activities; delegation of council responsibilities to project proponents; behavior by council members and staff and the use of memorandums of agreement as arbitrary and capricious; political influence on the council; and agreements between the council and the agency that permit the demolition of properties. All of these claims were rejected.

The ACHP's effectiveness is limited by its makeup, funding, and legal authority, and thus it should not be perceived as the preservation equivalent of the U.S. Environmental Protection Agency. Because the council is a collegial body, some members of which are political appointees, proposals of the federal agencies may not always be criticized. This fundamentally weakens the protective role of the council. In addition, budgetary limitations have curtailed the number of times the full council actually meets. On the other hand, the council does raise preservation as a concern of federal agencies, holds agency actions af-

---

72. Although created by the 1966 NHPA, the ACHP became an independent agency through an amendment to the Land and Water Conservation Fund Act of 1965, 16 U.S.C. §§ 4601-4 (1976).

73. 16 U.S.C. § 470a-d (Supp. IV 1980). The required presidential appointments appear to violate the ruling in *Buckley v. Valeo*, 424 U.S. 1 (1976), but this has not been litigated.

74. 36 C.F.R. § 800 (1981).

75. 528 F. Supp. 1245 (S.D.N.Y. 1981).

76. 496 F. Supp. 716 (D.S.C. 1980), *aff'd*, 635 F.2d 324 (4th Cir. 1980).

fecting historic resources up to the public light, and often secures the preservation of cultural resources through its mediation efforts.

In addition to reviewing federal undertakings under NHPA, the council's duties include:
- advising the president and Congress on historic preservation;
- recommending ways to coordinate governmental and private preservation activities;
- advising on the dissemination of preservation information;
- encouraging public interest and participation in preservation;
- recommending studies regarding preservation legislation and the effects of tax policies;
- advising on drafting of state and local preservation legislation;
- encouraging training and education in preservation;
- reviewing agency policies and programs and recommending methods to improve their consistency with NHPA; and
- educating governmental and private entities about the council's activities.

The ACHP is also directed to submit an annual report to the president and Congress regarding its activities and studies, including its assessment of current preservation problems and the effectiveness of all preservation programs in implementing NHPA.[77] Most of these activities can also be performed by the Department of the Interior.

Other Provisions of NHPA

In addition to the major features outlined above, the NHPA contains a varied collection of preservation requirements and programs. The encouragement offered to the General Services Administration to reuse older buildings in the 1976 Public Buildings Cooperative Use Act (see below) is strengthened by Section 110(a), which requires that "each federal agency shall use, to the maximum extent feasible, historic properties available" to it before "acquiring, constructing, or leasing buildings." However, this mandate is being ignored by Congress and federal agencies and has not yet been tested in court. Section 110(e) requires that the secretary of the interior "review and approve the plans of transfer of surplus federally owned historic properties. . . ." This authority, too, has not yet been implemented or enforced through litigation.

---

77. 16 U.S.C. § 470j(b) (Supp. IV 1980).

In addition to the requirement of surveying properties on lands controlled by agencies and nominating such properties to the National Register, federal agencies are directed to:
- behave consistently with the act and undertake preservation of historic properties owned or controlled by the agencies, "consistent with . . . the mission of the agency. . . ."[78]
- exercise caution that properties that may be eligible to be listed are not inadvertently transferred, demolished, or allowed to deteriorate.[79]
- make and deposit records of historic properties altered or demolished by federal actions.[80]

Federal agencies are given discretionary power to pass on preservation costs to federal licensees and permittees and to include preservation costs as an eligible project cost.[81] They are also authorized to expend funds authorized for their programs in order to implement the NHPA.[82] Agencies may also lease historic properties to anyone, following compliance with Section 106, and may use the proceeds from leasing for preservation activities.[83]

The act establishes several new mechanisms and incentives for preservation.
- It authorizes an annual preservation award program for employees of federal, state, and certified local governments in recognition of preservation efforts.[84]
- It authorizes direct grants to restore National Historic Landmarks; the grants can be made directly by the Interior Department at 100 percent of the cost, as opposed to passing the money through the SHPO on a cost-sharing basis as is done for other preservation grants.[85] It directs the Interior Department to establish a loan in-

---

78. *Id.* at § 470h-2(a)(1).
79. *Id.* at § 470h-2(a)(2).
80. *Id.* at § 470h-2(b).
81. *Id.* at § 470h-2(g).
82. *Id.* at § 470w-1. This last provision permits federal agencies that are conducting archaeological salvage under the 1-percent-of-project-cost rule of the 1974 Reservoir Salvage Act amendments to pay for preservation costs in excess of 1 percent.
83. *Id.* at § 470h-3.
84. *Id.* at § 470h-2.
85. *Id.* at § 470c.

surance program for the preservation of properties on the National Register, but this remains unimplemented.[86]
- It contains several directives on how the annual federal preservation grants made available by Congress are to be used.[87] The states are required to name a SHPO in order to obtain the grants, and the state officer must perform a variety of specified functions.[88]
- It allows courts to award attorneys' fees in civil actions brought to enforce the act.[89]

Summary

The NHPA pulls together four basic activities that comprise the federal preservation program: (1) identification of historic and cultural resources; (2) evaluation and registration of resources that meet the evaluation criteria for determining significance; (3) protection of resources; and (4) encouragement of preservation activities at the state and local levels of government.

However, the act provides very limited protection from adverse private actions and only procedural safeguards for adverse federal effects on cultural and historic properties. Listed or eligible properties fall under the Section 106 review only if there is some federal involvement. Further, there must be an element of discretion in the federal undertaking if adverse effects are to be avoided. Properties not specifically listed in the National Register, included in a district listed in the Register, or eligible for listing receive no protection under the act.

The ACHP review process covers a broad range of federal actions from a single perspective. The make-up of the governing board of the council is unusual, and its comments and recommendations are advisory only. Perhaps, the most significant protection offered by the Section 106 process lies in the light of day that the council's review process can shed on proposed federal activities. The procedures of the council are flexible and provide no rigorous standard of review that all agencies must meet. Moreover, the ACHP staff has been given great discretion in handling individual cases without full council participation. Preservationists have attempted to challenge the procedures used by the council and its failure

---

86. *Id.* at § 470d.
87. *Id.* at § 470b, c, h.
88. *Id.* at § 470a(b)(1).
89. Attorneys' fees and costs were awarded under Section 305 in a ruling subsequent to the decision in *WATCH v. Harris*, 535 F. Supp. 9 (D. Conn. 1981).

to ensure the preservation of all properties affected by the projects brought before it, but they have not as yet prevailed. Nevertheless, the staff and council's review generally compels agencies to consider effects of their actions on historic resources. The mandatory nature of the review can provide a preservation attorney with a useful procedural tool. Other important provisions of the NHPA that could be enforced by the public have not yet been implemented.

THE NATIONAL ENVIRONMENTAL POLICY ACT

The National Environmental Policy Act (NEPA)[90] requires that federal agencies evaluate the environmental impacts of their proposed actions and consider alternatives to proposed actions. This evaluation is to provide federal decision makers with information on the potential environmental effects of their decisions, to disclose to the public these potential effects, and to improve the quality of decisions by ensuring consideration of their impact.

As developed by the courts, NEPA is one of the principal procedural federal environmental statutes. It applies to major federal actions significantly affecting the quality of the human environment. Although NEPA has been used most frequently to protect natural resources, it also offers procedural protection from federal action for the historic and cultural resources of the human environment. In fact, with the prospect that the National Historic Preservation Act (NHPA) and other preservation laws may be weakened, NEPA could play an increasingly important role in preservation.

NEPA applies to historic resources even if they have not been found eligible for listing in, or have not been listed in, the National Register. On the other hand, NHPA can be easier to apply as it requires only a federal "undertaking" to trigger the Section 106 process, not the "major federal action" required under NEPA. Also, NHPA applies to all "effects" of an agency's action and is not limited by NEPA's definition of impacts "significantly affecting the quality of the human environment."

NEPA shares many of the limitations of the NHPA:
- Both apply only to federal actions.
- Private actions or those involving only local and state governments are not subject to either law.

---

90. 42 U.S.C. §§ 4321-61 (1976).

- Both laws only require agencies to evaluate their effects on the built environment and historic resources.
- Neither requires or prohibits federal action to preserve cultural resources.

Through a large number of court cases, however, a rather extensive and complex body of law interpreting NEPA has developed, presenting numerous opportunities for the preservation attorney to make use of NEPA to protect historic resources. The following section briefly describes both the uses and the limitations of NEPA. A later section examines NEPA regulations and case law in much greater detail.

A NEPA Overview

Title I of NEPA establishes policies and sets goals for protection of our country's environment (Section 101) and provides mechanisms, primarily the environmental impact statement (EIS), for carrying them out (Section 102).

Section 101 of NEPA states that:

> [I]t is the continuing responsibility of the Federal Government to use all practicable means, consistent with other essential considerations of national policy, to . . . (2) assure for all Americans safe, healthful, productive, and *esthetically and culturally pleasing surroundings*; . . . (4) *preserve important historic, cultural* and natural *aspects of our national heritage*, and maintain, wherever possible, an environment which supports diversity and variety of individual choice; . . . (6) enhance the quality of renewable resources and *approach the maximum attainable recycling of depletable resources.* (Emphasis added.)

This language is a clear statement of congressional intent to include preservation of the built environment within NEPA's purview. However, its legal implications are unclear. Most courts view Section 101 as no more than a statement of national environmental policy goals that does not create a substantive right to a healthful environment.[91] As stated by the U.S. Supreme Court in *Strycker's Bay Neighborhood Council, Inc. v. Karlen*:

> NEPA, while establishing "significant" substantive goals for the Nation; imposes upon agencies duties that are "essentially procedural" . . . . [O]nce an agency has made a decision subject to NEPA's procedural requirements, the only role for the court is to insure that the agency has considered the environmen-

---

91. See, e.g., *Environmental Defense Fund, Inc. v. Corps of Engineers*, 325 F. Supp. 749, 755 (E.D. Ark. 1971); *Tanner v. Armco Steel Corp.*, 340 F. Supp. 532, 538 (S.D. Tex. 1972).

tal consequences; it cannot interject itself within the area of discretion of the executive as to the choice of the action to be taken.[92]

Of course, a court could interject itself if the agency action is arbitrary or capricious.

Section 102 of NEPA establishes procedural requirements for federal agencies, such as using systematic, interdisciplinary approaches to planning and decision making,[93] developing ways to ensure that environmental amenities and values are considered in decision making,[94] and developing alternatives to recommended courses of action.[95] Chief among the requirements is that agencies must:

> Include in every recommendation or report on proposals for legislation and other major Federal actions significantly affecting the quality of the human environment, a detailed statement by the responsible official on—
> (i) The environmental impact of the proposed action,
> (ii) Any adverse environmental effects which cannot be avoided should the proposal be implemented,
> (iii) Alternatives to the proposed action,
> (iv) The relationship between local short-term use of man's environment and the maintenance and enhancement of long-term productivity, and
> (v) Any irreversible and irretrievable commitments of resources which would be involved in the proposed action should it be implemented.[96]

Section 102(2)(C) also requires that, before preparing the EIS, the responsible federal agency official must consult with and obtain comments of other federal agencies regarding the proposed action. Copies of the statement and comments of appropriate federal, state, and local agencies must be made available to the president, the Council on Environmental Quality (CEQ), and the public and must accompany the proposal through the agency's existing review process.

Although the EIS process does not prohibit environmentally damaging actions, it does provide public input to agency decision-making data and helps to ensure that federal officials involved in planning and decision making consider environmental factors. It also limits agency action while proposals are being evaluated. During this time, those opposing environmentally damaging projects may sometimes be able to develop and convince the agency to adopt a preferable alternative.

---

92. 444 U.S. 223, 227 (1980), quoting *Kleppe v. Sierra Club*, 427 U.S. 390, 410 n.21 (1976).
93. 42 U.S.C. § 4332(2)(A) (1976).
94. *Id.* at § 4332(2)(B).
95. *Id.* at § 4332(2)(E).
96. *Id.* at § 4332(2)(C).

218   A HANDBOOK ON HISTORIC PRESERVATION LAW

Subchapter II establishes the Council on Environmental Quality. CEQ regulations implementing NEPA went into effect in 1979.[97] The regulations, which replaced nonbinding guidelines adopted by the CEQ in 1971, are generally regarded as having the force of law.[98] Executive Order 11991,[99] which called for their promulgation, ordered compliance with CEQ regulations by all federal agencies, and the U.S. Supreme Court, in dictum, in *Andrus v. Sierra Club*,[100] stated that compliance by federal agencies operating pursuant to NEPA is mandatory.

The regulations describe how the federal agencies are to comply with the EIS process. The definition of impacts that agencies must consider specifically includes "aesthetic, historic, [and] cultural" impacts, "whether direct, indirect, or cumulative."[101] "Indirect effects may include growth inducing effects . . . related to induced changes in the pattern of land use, population density or growth rate. . . ."[102] The regulations define "human environment" to "be interpreted comprehensively to include the natural and physical environment and the relationship of people with that environment."[103] The regulations also specifically note that impact statements shall be prepared "concurrently with and integrated with environmental impact analyses and related surveys and studies required by the . . . National Historic Preservation Act. . . ."[104] Finally, the regulations specify that the determination of significance of effect must consider unique features of a locale, such as historic or cultural resources, and "the degree to which the action may affect districts, sites, highways, structures, or objects listed in or

---

97. 40 C.F.R. §§ 1500-1517.7 (1981).

98. The guidelines were always considered nondiscretionary standards for agency decision making by the CEQ, but several courts had found them to be only advisory. Still, most courts had accorded them great weight. Compare *Hiram Clarke Civic Club, Inc. v. Lynn*, 476 F.2d 421; 423-24 (5th Cir. 1973); and *Andrus v. Sierra Club*, 442 U.S. 347, 358 (1979), with *Greene County Planning Board v. Federal Power Commission*, 455 F.2d 412, 421 (2d Cir. 1972), *cert. denied*, 409 U.S. 849 (1972); *Natural Resources Defense Council, Inc. v. Callaway*, 524 F.2d 79, 86 n.8 (2d Cir. 1975); and *Sierra Club v. Morton*, 514 F.2d 856, 873 (D.C. Cir. 1975), *cert. dismissed*, 424 U.S. 901 (1976).

99. 40 C.F.R. § 459 (1982).

100. 442 U.S. 347, 358 (1979). See also *National Indian Youth Council v. Andrus*, 501 F. Supp. 649 (D.N.M. 1980); *Warm Springs Dam Task Force v. Gribble*, 621 F.2d 1017 (9th Cir. 1980).

101. 40 C.F.R. § 1508.08(b) (1981).

102. *Id*.

103. *Id*. at § 1508.14.

104. *Id*. at § 1502.25(a).

eligible for listing in the National Register of Historic Places or may cause loss or destruction of significant . . . cultural or historic resources."[105]

The federal agencies are required to adopt implementing procedures for complying with NEPA.[106] Most, if not all, of the implementing procedures specify that historic and cultural resources are to be routinely considered within the analysis of environmental effects. The counterpart regulations of the Department of Housing and Urban Development (HUD) define human environment as including social, cultural, and aesthetic factors.[107] Examples provided in the regulations are cultural resources, urban design, and quality of the built environment.[108] The regulations of the Department of Agriculture (USDA), entitled "Cultural and Environmental Quality," require that direct and indirect effects on cultural resources be considered.[109] The counterpart regulations of the U.S. Environmental Protection Agency (EPA) specify that archaeological and historic resources be considered in evaluating effects.[110]

The regulations do not apply to any draft EIS filed before the effective date of the regulations (July 30, 1979).[111] However, they are applicable to the fullest extent practicable to federal agency activities and environmental documents begun before the effective date.[112] Thus, if an urban renewal project was begun, for instance, in the early 1970s without compliance with NEPA and compliance is now ordered, the agency must conform to the 1979 regulations.

With very few exceptions, courts have applied NEPA to issues concerning the built environment and historic and cultural resources. *Ely v. Velde*[113] stated that "NEPA expresses a strong federal policy in favor of preserving the natural environment, including our 'historic and

---

105. *Id.* at § 1508.27(b)(3), (8).
106. For a listing of agencies whose final NEPA compliance procedures have been published in the *Federal Register*, see 46 Fed. Reg. 25,5025 (1981).
107. 24 C.F.R. § 50.3 (1982).
108. *Id.* at 50.21(j).
109. 7 C.F.R. § 3100.45(e) (1981).
110. 40 C.F.R. § 6.203(c) (1981).
111. See *National Center for Preservation Law v. Landrieu*, 496 F. Supp. 716 (D.S.C. 1980), *aff'd*, 635 F.2d 324 (4th Cir. 1980).
112. 40 C.F.R. § 1506.12(a) (1981), cited in *National Indian Youth Council v. Andrus*, 501 F. Supp. 649, 654-55 (D.N.M. 1980).
113. 451 F.2d 1130, 1132 n.4 (4th Cir. 1971).

cultural heritage.' " *Stop H-3 v. Brinegar*[114] held that the "EIS . . . should describe the significant impacts on historic sites, landmarks, cultural or scenic resources of national, state, or local significance. . . ." In *Save the Courthouse v. Lynn*,[115] the court stated that "[t]he National Environmental Policy Act extends its procedural protections both to natural and cultural resources." *Aluli v. Brown*[116] held that "an EIS must consider the possible effects of major federal actions upon historic and cultural resources."

As noted, section 2 of this chapter covers the legal requirements of NEPA in much greater detail.

OTHER IMPORTANT FEDERAL PRESERVATION AGENCIES, LAWS, AND PROGRAMS

In addition to the provisions of the National Historic Preservation Act (NHPA), the current federal preservation program consists of the operations of the National Park Service (NPS), the National Historic Landmarks program, the Archaeological Resources and Protection Act of 1979, and a number of other laws that direct federal agencies to consider or support historic preservation.

The National Park Service

The NPS contains two broad categories of programs connected with historic preservation: (1) those dealing with historic sites and structures within the National Park System and (2) those associated with historic sites and structures located on other federal lands and in the private domain. Because properties located inside the parks have limited impact on the legal and commercial activities of the general public, this overview of NPS preservation programs focuses on the latter category.[117]

Most of the programs described here are carried out regionally. Policy and planning functions—including the promulgation of regulations—are

---

114. 389 F. Supp. 1102, 1110 (D. Hawaii 1974).
115. 408 F. Supp. 1323, 1340 (S.D.N.Y. 1975).
116. 437 F. Supp. 602, 608 (D. Hawaii 1977), *rev'd on other grounds*, 602 F.2d 876 (9th Cir. 1979).
117. Inquiries may be addressed to the appropriate division or office, in care of the National Park Service, U.S. Department of the Interior, Washington, D.C. 20240; or to the appropriate regional office. The National Park Service has a total of 10 regional offices to assist the individual park sites. However, only 5 of the 10 offices have specially trained staff to respond to inquiries on historic preservation activities outside the parks. These offices are listed below, accompanied by a list of the states they serve.

carried out in Washington, D.C., while program implementation is performed, for the most part, in regional offices located around the country.[118]

National Historic Preservation Programs

Western Regional Office National Park Service 450 Golden Gate Avenue Box 36063 San Francisco, CA 94102	Arizona, California, Hawaii, Idaho, Nevada, Oregon, Washington, American Samoa, and Guam
Division of Cultural Resources Rocky Mountain Regional Office National Park Service 655 Parfet Street P.O. Box 25287 Denver, CO 80225	Colorado, Illinois, Iowa, Kansas, Minnesota, Missouri, Montana, Nebraska, New Mexico, North Dakota, Oklahoma, South Dakota, Texas, Utah, Wisconsin, and Wyoming
Office of Cultural Programs Mid-Atlantic Regional Office National Park Service 143 S. Third Street Philadelphia, PA 19106	Connecticut, Delaware, District of Columbia, Indiana, Maine, Maryland, Massachusetts, Michigan, New Hampshire, New Jersey, New York, Ohio, Pennsylvania, Rhode Island, Vermont, Virginia, and West Virginia
Preservation Services Division Southeast Regional Office National Park Service 75 Spring Street S.W., Room 1140 Atlanta, GA 30303	Alabama, Arkansas, Florida, Georgia, Kentucky, Louisiana, Mississippi, North Carolina, South Carolina, Tennessee, Puerto Rico, and the Virgin Islands
Cultural Resources Division Alaska Regional Office National Park Service 540 W. 5th Avenue Anchorage, AK 99501	Alaska

More detailed information on a given program may be obtained by writing the appropriate office listed above.

118. Although the NPS has 10 regional offices nationwide, effective October 1, 1982, the cultural programs began operating in 5 regions (see note 117).

222 A HANDBOOK ON HISTORIC PRESERVATION LAW

NATIONAL PARK SERVICE
CULTURAL RESOURCES PROGRAMS

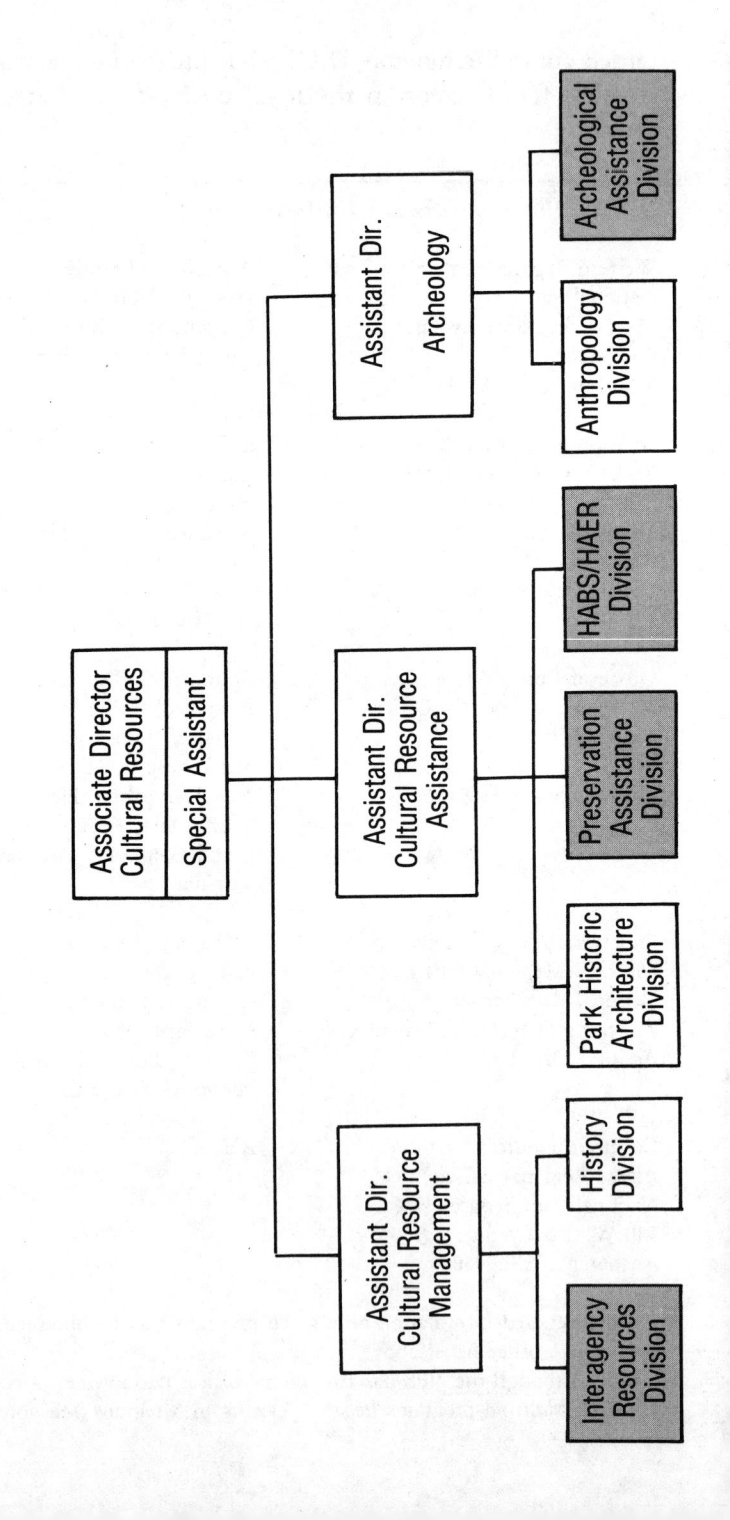

```
                        Associate Director
                        Cultural Resources
                        Special Assistant
                               │
        ┌──────────────────────┼──────────────────────┐
        │                      │                      │
  Assistant Dir.         Assistant Dir.         Assistant Dir.
  Cultural Resource      Cultural Resource          Archeology
    Management              Assistance
        │                      │                      │
   ┌────┴────┐         ┌───────┼───────┐         ┌────┴────┐
   │         │         │       │       │         │         │
 History  Interagency  Park   Preservation HABS/HAER  Anthropology Archeological
 Division Resources   Historic Assistance  Division   Division    Assistance
          Division   Architecture Division                         Division
                     Division
```

FEDERAL LAW 223

Planning	Historic Landmarks	Architecture Preservation Programs	Preservation Services	American Buildings Survey	Anthropology Programs	Consulting Archeologist Activities
*National Register of Historic Places	*Historic Research	*Registrar of Park Historic Properties	*Curatorial Services	*Historic American Engineering Record		*Technical Assistance
*Natural Landmarks	*Bureau History	*Acid Rain Research Coordination	*HPF Grants Administration			

Note: The March 1983 reorganization merged the "internal" (park preservation) programs and the "external" historic preservation programs under one Associate Director.

■ Formerly identified as "external," "National Register Programs," and "Archeology and Historic Preservation."

Source: Office of Cultural Resource Programs, National Park Service, Washington, D.C.

Program policy and guidance are the tasks of four Washington, D.C., divisions, the chiefs of which report to the three assistant directors who, in turn, report to the associate director, Cultural Resources.[119] This associate director reports to the agency's deputy director, who reports to the director. (See organizational chart.)

Program implementation in the five regional offices is carried out by program managers with various titles, all of whom report to their respective regional directors. The regional directors, in turn, report to the director of the agency.

NPS Programs

Listings in the National Register of Historic Places.[120] While most NPS preservation programs have been regionalized, the National Register continues to be maintained in Washington, D.C., and made available to the public by the Interagency Resource Management Division (IRM). As discussed earlier, properties are nominated to the National Register by state historic preservation officers (SHPOs), federal agencies, and, in certain cases, local governments and citizens. Nominations are evaluated according to criteria contained in Interior Department regulations.[121] Among many other functions, IRM provides policy and

---

119. The NPS "external" cultural programs (i.e., those relating to programs operating outside the parks) were reorganized in March 1983, merging with the "internal" programs under one Associate Director for Cultural Resources. Three assistant directors—one for cultural resources management, one for cultural resource assistance, and one for archaeology—report to the associate director. The "external" divisions supervised by this associate director and the three assistant directors are: (1) the Interagency Resources Division, which is responsible for maintaining the National Register, certifying historic properties for tax benefits, administering the National Landmarks Program, providing standards and guidelines for developing comprehensive plans to protect historic resources, and implementing the survey and planning activities of the grants-in-aid program; (2) the Preservation Assistance Division, which is responsible for developing preservation standards for preserving, restoring, and maintaining historic properties and providing program direction for certifying rehabilitation work for tax benefits and for Historic Preservation Fund (HPF) development projects; (3) the Historic American Building Survey (HABS) and Historic American Engineering Record (HAER) Division, which remains unchanged; and (4) the Archeological Assistance Division, which contains Departmental Consulting Archeologist Activities and Technical Assistance.

120. The Register was created by the National Historic Preservation Act of 1966, Pub. L. No. 59-665, 80 Stat. 915 (codified as amended in 16 U.S.C. § 470-470n (1976 & Supp. V 1981).

121. 36 C.F.R. § 60.6 (1981).

regulations that give property owners the opportunity to concur in or object to listing. Owners also may appeal state or local decisions for or against listing their properties on the basis of historic significance.

"Determinations of Eligibility" for Inclusion in the National Register.[122] "Determinations of eligibility," like National Register listings, are a program function carried out by IRM in the nation's capital. Requests for determinations of eligibility are made by federal agencies, or by individual persons, to meet the compliance requirements in Section 106 of the NHPA of 1966.

Designations of National Historic Landmarks.[123] National Historic Landmarks (NHL) are designated by the secretary of the interior. The major responsibility for selecting and studying properties for recommendation to the interior secretary rests with the History Division.[124] Because many NHL designations were made over the years without drawing clearly defined boundaries, another element of the NHL program involves setting specific boundaries for these previously designated properties. The regional offices carry out this task with policy guidance and coordination from IRM in Washington, D.C. The Preservation Assistance Division (PAD) in the nation's capital prepares annual reports to Congress on endangered NHLs. A known or anticipated threat to an NHL's integrity warrants its inclusion in this report.

Tax Certification.[125] Policy guidance and oversight in the two-step program for property owners to become eligible for rehabilitation tax incentives (discussed more fully in chapter 7) are provided jointly by IRM and PAD in Washington, D.C. IRM sets policy and maintains regulations[126] for certifications and decertifications of historic significance as well as certifications of state and local statutes. PAD provides the

---

122. Authorized by the National Historic Preservation Act of 1966, Pub. L. No. 59-665, 80 Stat. 915 (codified as amended in 16 U.S.C. § 470-470n (1976 & Supp. V 1981).

123. Created by the Historic Sites Act of 1935, Pub. L. No. 74-292 (codified as amended in 16 U.S.C. §§ 461-67).

124. Unusual among National Park Service preservation programs, the NHL program is run primarily by a division whose main responsibilities lie within the parks. The major responsibilities of the History Division are directed toward the National Park System.

125. Tax Reform Act of 1976, Pub. L. No. 94-455, 90 Stat. 1519, as amended by the Revenue Act of 1978, Pub. L. No. 95-600, 92 Stat. 2828, as amended by the Economic Recovery Tax Act of 1981, 26 U.S.C. § 1167 (Supp. 1982); Pub. L. No. 97-34, 95 Stat. 239.

126. 36 C.F.R. § 67.1 (1981).

same function for rehabilitation certifications. The regional offices, taking into account the advice of the SHPOs, carry out application reviews and make decisions on both significance and rehabilitation certification, based upon standards contained in the regulations.[127] Denials of significance certification and of rehabilitation certification, along with decertification, may be appealed to the associate director, Cultural Resources. Decisions on appeal are the property owner's final administrative remedy.

National Historic Preservation Fund Grants-in-Aid.[128] The National Historic Preservation Fund provides matching grants to the states and, in certain cases, to local governments for historic preservation surveying, planning, acquisition, and development. Because of the current limited appropriations to the fund, few, if any, states are making grants as they have in the past for National Register site acquisition and project development. Most states continue, however, to use grant funds to carry out their primary preservation goals (e.g., making National Register nominations, performing tax certification review, developing technical preservation information). PAD and IRM cooperate in providing policy guidance to and oversight of the regional offices in the program. The regions, in turn, work directly with SHPOs in monitoring the latter's use of grant funds.

Transfer of Historic Surplus Federal Property.[129] In order for the transfer of a "historic monument" surplus federal property (i.e., one listed in or eligible for inclusion in the National Register) to be made by the General Services Administration (GSA), the grantee must develop a preservation plan to ensure the property's historic and financial integrity. The Preservation Assistance Division provides policy guidance to the regional offices in reviewing and approving these plans. The regional offices make final recommendations to GSA for approval of the transfer and conduct follow-up property inspections and financial statement reviews.

---

127. *Id.* at § 67.3.
128. Authorized by the National Historic Preservation Act of 1966, 16 U.S.C. § 470 (1976).
129. Federal Property and Administrative Services Act of 1949, ch. 288, 63 Stat. 377 (codified as amended at 40 U.S.C. § 304a-2); Executive Order No. 11593, 36 Fed. Reg. 8,921 (1971), reprinted in 16 U.S.C. § 470h-2 (1976 & Supp. V 1981).

Technical Preservation Information and Assistance.[130] PAD develops and disseminates information on technical preservation issues relating to building materials, rehabilitation, design, and development economics. PAD also evaluates and disseminates, if appropriate, technical information produced outside the agency. The regional offices perform, on a more limited basis, the same information production and evaluation functions and act as distribution centers for their own information as well as that emanating from Washington, D.C. In addition to disseminating information, PAD provides site-specific advice to other federal agencies on technical preservation issues.

Recording Historic Sites.[131] Under the policy guidance and direction of the Historic American Building Survey/Historic American Engineering Record (HABS/HAER) Division in Washington, D.C., significant historic structures, as well as engineering and industrial sites (e.g., bridges and factories), are recorded, and such records are then placed in the Library of Congress. These recording projects typically produce written histories, photographs, and high-quality architectural drawings. While a small number of nationally significant sites are recorded by both the HABS/HAER staff, most projects are done by student summer teams and other practitioners outside of the agency. A major objective of the program shared by the HABS/HAER Division and the regional offices is the development of funding sources outside the agency for projects that lead to donation of documents to NPS. Federal agencies are frequently required to record historic sites under the terms of a memorandum of agreement with the Advisory Council on Historic Preservation (ACHP) (pursuant to Section 106 of the NHPA of 1966). Regional offices accept, review, and transmit to the Library of Congress documentation received under these circumstances.

---

130. National Historic Preservation Act of 1966, Pub. L. No. 59-665, 80 Stat. 915 (codified as amended in 16 U.S.C. § 470-470n); Executive Order No. 11593, 36 Fed. Reg. 8,920 (1971), reprinted in 16 U.S.C. § 470h-2 (1976 & Supp. V 1981).

131. Historic Sites Act of 1935, Pub. L. No. 74-292 (codified as amended in 16 U.S.C. §§ 461-67 (1976 & Supp. V 1981)); National Historic Preservation Act of 1966, Pub. L. No. 59-665, 80 Stat. 915 (codified as amended in 16 U.S.C. § 470-470n (1976 & Supp. V 1981)); Executive Order No. 11593, 36 Fed. Reg. 8,921 (1971), reprinted in 16 U.S.C. § 470h-2 (1976 & Supp. V 1981).

Archaeological Protection.[132] Policy guidance, coordination, and oversight in NPS archaeological programs are carried out by the departmental consulting archaeologist, with program implementation in Washington, D.C., emanating from IRM. With review and recommendations made by the regional offices, IRM issues permits for the investigation and removal of antiquities from federal lands. IRM also prepares annual reports to Congress on the status of national archaeology programs and on archaeological and paleontological investigations on public and Indian lands. The regional offices, on a limited basis, conduct themselves, or contract for data recovery, work involving archaeological resources threatened by federal, federally assisted, or federally licensed projects. In this compliance role, however, regional offices more commonly act as liaisons between private contracting archaeologists and federal agencies.

National Historic Landmarks Program[133]

National Historic Landmarks (NHLs) are properties determined to be of national historic significance by the NPS.[134] In 1966 the list of NHLS was folded into the National Register of Historic Places, which was created that year pursuant to the Historic Preservation Act. The NHL program was later codified as part of the National Historic Preservation Act of 1980.

Potential landmarks are identified through studies conducted by the NHL Program in the NPS and by nominations made by state officials and other interested parties. When a property is to be studied, notice and information on the program are provided to the owner, municipality or county, SHPO, and congressional representatives of the district and state in which the property is located. In addition, general notice through

---

132. A discussion of federal archaeological programs and laws appears later in this section. See Archaeological and Historic Preservation Act of 1974, Pub. L. No. 93-291, 88 Stat. 174; Historic Sites Act of 1935, 16 U.S.C. §§ 461-69 (1976); Reservoir Salvage Act of 1960, Pub. L. No. 86-523, 74 Stat. 220; National Historic Preservation Act amendments of 1980, Pub. L. No. 96-515, 94 Stat. 2987; Antiquities Act of 1906, Pub. L. No. 59-209, 34 Stat. 225; Archaeological Resources Protection Act of 1979, Pub. L. No. 96-545, 93 Stat. 721; and Executive Order No. 11593, 36 Fed. Reg. 8,921 (1971), reprinted in 16 U.S.C. § 470h-2 (1976 & Supp. V 1981).

133. 16 U.S.C. § 462(b) (1976).

134. Examples of National Historic Landmarks are Mount Vernon, Virginia (home of George Washington); Luther Burbank House and Garden, California; Winslow Homer Studio, Maine; the Alamo, Texas; Room 405, George Herbert Jones Laboratory, University of Chicago (site of first man-made plutonium element).

the local newspaper is used for districts with more than 50 property owners. An NHL program researcher visits the property and may hold a public information meeting.

The designation process must then follow the procedures set forth in federal regulations (36 C.F.R. Part 65), except in emergencies when a potential NHL is threatened with damage or destruction. In those cases, the secretary of the interior may invoke accelerated procedures.

Under normal circumstances, if the NPS concludes the property qualifies as an NHL, it then presents its evaluation and recommendation to the National Park System Advisory Board, which is appointed by the secretary of the interior, for evaluation of the property's significance, integrity, and boundaries. If the NPS opposes designation, that decision can be appealed to the NPS director.

Once the National Park Service has recommended designation, the advisory board encourages comments by interested parties. The board then recommends to the secretary of the interior those properties appearing to meet the NHL criteria found at 36 C.F.R. Part 65. Although the criteria are similar to those for National Register inclusion, NHL properties must be of significance to the nation as a whole and thus the number of NHLs is far smaller than the total number of Register properties.

The secretary of the interior receives the recommendation of the board and decides on the NHL designation, subject to owner consent. A property that receives designation is automatically listed in the National Register unless the owner has objections. Notice of the designation is provided, as explained above, and, in some cases, notice is extended to other interested authorities, persons, or organizations.

Once the property is designated, the owner receives a plaque if he agrees to display the plaque "publicly and appropriately." The NPS is also directed by regulation to maintain a continuing relationship with owners, making periodic site visits and offering technical advice. This is not routinely done for other National Register properties.[135] As with National Register listing, the NHL owner relinquishes no property rights.

Pursuant to Section 110(f) of the National Historic Preservation Act, landmarks receive a higher degree of protection from federal actions

---

135. See 36 C.F.R. § 65.7 (1981). Prior to adoption of the new NHL program regulations in February 1983, NHL owners were encouraged to enter into voluntary management agreements with the NPS to maintain their sites. The new regulations do not mention such management agreements although nothing therein would seem to prevent their use in the future.

than do other properties listed in, or eligible for listing in, the National Register.[136] Section 110(f) contains three basic requirements. First, if a federal agency affects an NHL, the agency (or its legal delegatee) must also determine whether the effect is both "direct" and "adverse." If it is both, the agency must, to the maximum extent possible, undertake special planning or other actions to minimize harm to the property. This planning requirement is stronger than the protection of the Section 106 process. In addition, the agency must afford the ACHP "a reasonable opportunity to comment," as under Section 106. Because of the required "determination of effect" and special planning, Section 110(f) review is an addition to the 106 requirement, not a substitute for it. Where Sections 106 and 110(f) are both applicable, they can be merged. But where Section 110(f) is not applicable because the effect is not "direct" and "adverse," Section 106 continues to apply.

In the NHPA 1980 amendments, Congress also redesignated all existing NHL properties to prevent future constitutional challenges to the Interior Department's prior designations. This was in response to a federal district court's ruling in Virginia that invalidated the Interior Department's NHL designation because of the lack of procedural rules and substantive standards for national historic significance.[137] The court subsequently confirmed the congressional action on July 20, 1981, but noted that only existing landmarks were sheltered.[138] Future designations must comply with established criteria.[139]

The Historic Sites Act of 1935

The Historic Sites Act of 1935 (HSA)[140] established for the first time a "national policy to preserve for public use historic sites, buildings and objects of national significance for the inspiration and benefit of the people of the United States."[141] Although the policy statement was new, it maintained the traditional emphasis on preservation of properties of national significance, preservation for public use, and preservation for

---

136. 16 U.S.C. § 470h-2(f) (Supp. IV 1980).
137. *Historic Green Springs, Inc. v. Bergland*, 497 F. Supp. 839 (E.D. Va. 1980).
138. *Historic Green Springs, Inc. v. Block, final order vacated*, No. 77-0230-R, slip op. at 1 (E.D. Va. July 20, 1981).
139. 36 C.F.R. § 665.9 (1981).
140. 16 U.S.C. §§ 461-69 (1976).
141. *Id.* at § 461.

patriotic reasons. The setting of criteria to determine national significance was left to the Department of the Interior.

The act gave the Interior Department authority to conduct a range of preservation activities, including:

- making and recording drawings, photographs, and other records of historic and archaeological sites, buildings, and properties;[142]

- surveying historic and archaeological sites to help determine which possess exceptional national values;

- acquiring property;[143]

- entering into cooperative agreements with individuals and other political entities to protect and preserve historic resources;[144]

- commemorating and marking, restoring and maintaining, and operating and managing historic properties;[145]

- providing technical and educational services in preservation;[146] and

- chartering a corporation to protect and administer historic properties.[147]

These authorities provided the legal basis for the creation of three major federal programs still in operation: (1) the Historic American Engineering Record, which documents and maintains records of engineering accomplishments; (2) the Historic American Building Survey, which began prior to the 1935 act but was given added stimulus by the new law; and (3) the National Survey of Historic Sites and Buildings, which began in 1937, using a classification system developed by the NPS in

---

142. *Id.* at § 462(b).
143. *Id.* at § 462(d).
144. *Id.* at § 462(e).
145. *Id.* at § 462(g).
146. *Id.* at § 462(j).
147. *Id.* at § 463.

1933.[148] The National Survey of Historic Sites and Buildings was suspended during World War II, but in 1957 funds were made available to start the survey again. In 1960, as discussed in the preceding section, a program of designating NHLs from the list of properties in the survey was begun and was called the National Register of Historic Landmarks.

The condemnation authority of the HSA was upheld in 1939,[149] but only if federal funds had been appropriated prior to the condemnation. Federal acquisition under the act was rarely used. As Secretary Ickes noted in testimony on bills that became the HSA:

> It would certainly not be desirable for the Federal government to attempt to take over all the historic sites in the country. In fact, by far the greater number of such sites are of local rather than of national significance, and should therefore be cared for by State or local government, or private organizations.[150]

However, the HSA did authorize the Interior Department to enter into cooperative agreements with state and local governments and individuals to protect and preserve properties and to operate historic sites.[151] Financial aid, technical assistance, and other cooperation were available to those cooperating with the Interior Department. Despite the emphasis in the act on nationally significant properties, cooperative agreements often helped preserve properties of less than national

---

148. This classification scheme is still used today. It allows the National Park Service to take a systematic approach to preserving history. Properties constituting the nation's heritage are grouped together and divided into themes, e.g., Commerce and Industry, Arts and Sciences, the Civil War. Nationally significant properties would include the universe of properties used to flesh out the themes, although the initial survey of properties must necessarily include both nationally and regionally significant properties until a comparative evaluation of the properties can be made. As the theme studies become fleshed out, properties are referred from the National Park Service to an advisory board created in the 1935 act (*id.*) which, after review, transmits its recommendations to the secretary for a determination of national significance. The nationally significant properties are designated as landmarks, and those that are threatened are usually proposed for federal acquisition as elements of the National Park System. The documentation of the properties not of national significance is maintained by the National Park Service.

149. The secretary of the interior is empowered to acquire historic properties by eminent domain under the act. *Barnidge v. United States*, 101 F.2d 295 (8th Cir. 1939).

150. *Preservation of Historic American Sites, Buildings, Objects, and Antiquities of National Significance: Hearings on H.R. 6670 and H.R. 6734 Before the Subcommittee on Public Lands of the House Committee on Interior and Insular Affairs*, 74th Cong., 1st Sess. 4-8 (1975).

151. 16 U.S.C. § 462(e) (1976).

significance until a Department of the Interior solicitor's ruling in 1964 limited the use of such agreements to nationally significant sites.

The HSA formed the basis for today's federal preservation program. However, while the declaration of a national policy and the authorization of a survey of historic sites were important developments, the act still was deeply tied to the past. Cooperative work to protect nonfederal properties, for example, was balanced by the act's emphasis on nationally significant properties. The search for a balance between federal concern with nationally significant resources and those of lesser significance continues today.[152]

Archaeology

Archaeological resources are particularly difficult to manage for two reasons. First, many of them are located partly or entirely underground; unlike historic buildings, they may be literally invisible, or at least undetectable, to the untrained eye. Second, their value lies wholly or in part in the information they contain, not usually in their aesthetic qualities, their association with particular historic events or persons, or their capacity for adaptive reuse. Although particular archaeological resources may have other values (significance to an Indian tribe, for example, or potential use in public interpretation), they are primarily valuable to scholarship only, and scientific study is required to realize this value. Because of these factors, archaeological resources are, more than most other historic properties, the province of the specialist professional. At the same time, archaeological resources raise special management problems because of their ubiquity. There are thousands of historic and prehistoric archaeological sites in the United States, most of them not yet identified through field survey or described. Not all sites contain significant information, but deciding which do and which do not can be an exacting and controversial process.

Even where a site is demonstrably significant, deciding on how it should best be treated may be difficult. Both the ACHP[153] and the

---

152. Recent budget proposals to cut federal preservation funds are justified by the fact that most of the resources on the list of nationally significant properties are not of significance to the entire nation. See U.S. Budget, FY 1982, (Washington, D.C.: Government Printing Office, 1981).

153. Advisory Council on Historic Preservation, *Treatment of Archeological Properties: A Handbook* (Washington, D.C.: GPO, Nov. 1980), pp. 10-11.

Department of the Interior,[154] concurring with the generally expressed opinion of the archaeological profession,[155] recommend leaving archaeological sites undisturbed where feasible rather than excavating them. This is justified by the premise that, over time, archaeological research questions change and become more refined while the techniques that can be applied to study of the archaeological record improve; accordingly, it is appropriate to "bank" archaeological sites wherever this can be done. Where a site cannot be preserved in place, the usual alternative is to conduct salvage research projects—in short, to excavate the site using appropriate scientific techniques and to address appropriate research questions before it is destroyed. In this instance, the question becomes, How much salvage is enough? It is seldom efficient to excavate an archaeological site in its entirety, but the extent to which it should be excavated, and the methods to be employed, can be the subject of considerable argument. Different approaches to this problem naturally have fiscal ramifications; one archaeologist's approach may cost $450,000 while another's may cost a million dollars.

A related problem, when confronted with a number of sites subject to damage by a project, is which ones to excavate and which to let go. Both the ACHP[156] and the Department of the Interior[157] emphasize that these decisions should be made on the basis of solid, professionally developed research designs. In other words, scientifically or humanistically important research questions should be formulated, and then enough study should be done, at enough sites, to address these questions effectively. Study beyond what is needed to address such questions is generally regarded as redundant and unnecessary, though both agencies stress the need for flexibility in archaeological planning to allow for unforeseen circumstances and discoveries.[158]

Archaeological resources are given the same consideration provided to other types of historic properties under the various provisions of the

---

154. U.S. Department of the Interior, *Secretary of the Interior's Standards and Guidelines for the Preservation of Archeological Properties* (Washington, D.C.: GPO), pp. 1-5 (review draft circulated July 19, 1982).

155. C. McGimsey and H. Davis, eds., *The Management of Archaeological Resources: The Airlie House Report* (Society for American Archaeology, 1977), p. 28.

156. Advisory Council on Historic Preservation, *Treatment of Archaeological Properties*, pp. 5-14, 24-26.

157. U.S. Department of the Interior, *Secretary of the Interior's Standards and Guidelines*, pp. 1-9.

158. *Id.* at 5-9. Advisory Council on Historic Preservation, *Treatment of Archeological Properties*, p. 31.

NHPA and NEPA. In addition, several statutes refer explicitly and exclusively to archaeological resources.

The Antiquities Act of 1906

The Antiquities Act[159] authorized the president to designate as National Monuments those areas of the public domain containing "historic landmarks, historic and prehistoric structures, and objects of historic or scientific interest."[160] It also created an enforcement program by authorizing fines and imprisonment for those "who shall appropriate, excavate, injure, or destroy any historic or prehistoric ruin or monument, or any object of antiquity situated on lands owned or controlled" by the federal government.[161] To satisfy the interests of the scientific and archaeological community, a permit system was also authorized to be administered by the agency with jurisdiction over ruins, archaeological sites, and objects of antiquity.

The National Monuments have to be on lands owned or controlled by the federal government and are limited to the smallest land areas compatible with the protection of the resource.[162] Condemnation authority was not granted, although the secretary of the interior was authorized to accept gifts of land. This law gave the executive branch discretion to designate areas, in contrast to the previous practice of requiring specific authorizing legislation for each designation. Historic places, structures, and objects of scientific interest, as well as prehistoric sites, could be preserved. Although the sites designated were to be small, their size could be determined based on the need to protect the resource, as opposed to the approach used in the earlier laws to protect historic places, which involved setting an acreage limitation. The law also established an administrative pattern of management: designated areas were to be

---

159. Pub. L. No. 59-209, 34 Stat. 225 (codified as amended at 16 U.S.C. §§ 431-33 (1976)).

160. 16 U.S.C. § 431 (1976). The U.S. Supreme Court held that, pursuant to the Antiquities Act, the withdrawal from the public domain of Devil's Hole as part of Death Valley National Monument implicitly included reservation of the adjacent ground and surface water necessary to the survival of a rare fish. *Cappaert v. United States*, 426 U.S. 128 (1976 & Supp. V 1981).

161. 16 U.S.C. § 433 (1976).

162. The Antiquities Act was found inapplicable to a shipwreck located on the outer continental shelf, outside of U.S. territorial waters. *Treasure Salvors, Inc. v. Unidentified Wrecked and Abandoned Sailing Vessel*, 408 F. Supp 907 (S.D. Fla. 1976), aff'd, 569 F.2d 330 (5th Cir. 1978).

administered by the agency that already held the land, and donated areas were in the Department of the Interior's domain.

Both natural and historic values can lead to the designation of National Monuments. Over 92 National Monuments have been designated,[163] and many have formed the basis for the subsequent creation of parks in the National Park System; both the Grand Canyon and the Grand Teton national parks were originally withdrawn from public land as National Monuments because of "historic landmarks, prehistoric structures and other objects of historic or scientific interest."[164]

The Antiquities Act is still used to create monuments, including vast areas of Alaska in 1978. However, the act's authority to regulate the taking of archaeological relics has been replaced by the Archaeological Resource and Protection Act of 1979 as a result of conflicting federal circuit court decisions as to the validity of the Antiquities Act's provisions.[165]

The National Park Service and the Reservoir Salvage Act

The NPS provides archaeological services and expertise to other federal agencies. In 1960, it received congressional approval for its program advising the water resource development agencies on how to salvage archaeological resources. The Reservoir Salvage Act[166] requires that, "before any agency of the United States shall undertake the construction of a

---

163. U.S. Department of the Interior, *Index of the National Park System and Related Areas* (Washington, D.C.: GPO, 1979).

164. Proclamation No. 2578, 3 C.F.R. § 327 (Compilation 1938-1943), reprinted in 57 Stat. 731 (1943) and in 16 U.S.C.A. § 431 n.2 (1974).

165. 16 U.S.C. § 464. Under Section 433 of the Antiquities Act, anyone excavating, taking, or harming any such remains without permission is subject to civil and criminal penalties. The effectiveness of Section 433 is unclear at present. One court has held the broad and undefined terminology to be unconstitutionally vague in violation of due process requirements. *United States v. Diaz*, 499 F.2d 113 (9th Cir. 1974). The Ninth Circuit Court found fatal "the use of undefined terms of uncommon usage," such as "antiquity," which can refer indiscriminately to the new, the ancient, and even particular uses. *Id.* at 115. On the other hand, the Tenth Circuit Court disagrees with the *Diaz* opinion and has upheld the constitutionality of Section 433. *United States v. Smyer*, 596 F.2d 939 (10th Cir. 1979). The court reasoned that "antiquity," for example, means "times long past" and "conveys a sufficiently definite warning." *Id.* at 941.

166. Pub. L. No. 86-523, 74 Stat. 220 (codified as amended at 16 U.S.C. § 469 (1976 & Supp. V 1981)).

dam, or issue a license for the construction of a dam,"[167] it shall notify the secretary of the interior, who shall act to survey the area. If archaeological resources are found, the NPS can recover them or contract with others to salvage them.

This law was amended in 1974 to apply to any federal agency whenever it received information that its direct, federally licensed, or federally assisted activities may cause the "irreparable loss or destruction of significant scientific, prehistorical, historical, or archaeological data...."[168] The law was also amended because the NPS had little money appropriated to salvage resources under this program. The 1974 amendments authorized agencies to transfer "not more than 1 percent of the total amount authorized to be appropriated for such project"[169] to the NPS to pay for the salvage work. This arbitrary 1 percent figure has proven troublesome as agencies may hit the 1 percent ceiling before all appropriate salvage work is done. While there is no prohibition against the water resources agency transferring other funds to the NPS, the civil works agencies sometimes are willing to spend no more than 1 percent.

The 1980 amendments to the 1966 NHPA clearly authorized federal agencies to spend funds for this purpose, but there is still some agency reluctance to do so.[170] Without budgetary resources of its own to spend, the NPS cannot rescue all of the archaeological data. On the other side of the coin, some agencies suspect that when archaeologists budget salvage projects they "target" 1 percent of project costs whether this amount is needed or not. The ACHP[171] recommends that data recovery plans be developed without consideration of the 1 percent figure either as a "ceiling" or as a "floor," and that the 1 percent limitation be applied only after an adequate program of data recovery has been designed, so that officials can then determine whether sufficient funds are available to carry out the plans. If adjustments are then needed, they should be worked out through the consultation process prescribed by the council's regulations.

---

167. 16 U.S.C. § 469a (1976).
168. *Id.* at § 469a-1(a), (b).
169. *Id.* at § 469(c).
170. 16 U.S.C. § 470g (1976 & Supp. IV 1980).
171. Advisory Council on Historic Preservation, *Treatment of Archeological Properties*, p. 30.

Archaeological Resource Protection Act of 1979

Archeological resources are also protected by the 1979 Archaeological Resource Protection Act.[172] This legislation responded to the 1974 ruling in *United States v. Diaz*[173] that the penalties section of the 1906 Antiquities Act was unconstitutionally broad. This 1979 act supplements and replaces the basic authorities of the 1906 act to regulate the taking of archaeological resources on federal lands by setting a broad policy that archaeological resources are important for the nation and that they should be protected.[174] The 1979 act also authorizes the major federal land-managing agencies to establish permit systems for parties excavating or removing archaeological resources.[175] Penalties for violations of the law, including the sale, purchase, transport, or entry into interstate commerce of items taken in violation of the act, include fines and imprisonment.[176]

Current federal efforts to protect archaeological resources on federal lands are now based on this law. However, the law reflects the general legislative uncertainty in how to deal with these resources. Thus, archaeological resources are arbitrarily defined as being over 100 years of age,[177] and a general exception to the permit process is allowed for those finding arrowheads on the ground.[178] Provisions of the Archaeological Resource Protection Act also regulate takings on Indian lands and the rights of Indians to use religious sites.

Regulations to implement the Archaeological Resource and Protection Act have not yet been issued.

Native American Religious Freedom Act

A 1978 Senate joint resolution set forth a policy of protecting and preserving the rights of native Americans to freedom of religion, including access to sites.[179] However, other than codifying the First Amendment

---

172. 16 U.S.C. § 470aa-11 (1976 & Supp. IV 1980). For an excellent discussion of the act and the shortcomings of earlier laws, see Lorrie D. Northey, *The Archaeological Resources Protection Act of 1979: Protecting Prehistory for the Future*, 6 Harv. Environmental L. Rev. 1982.

173. 499 F.2d 113 (9th Cir. 1974).

174. 16 U.S.C. § 470aa (1976 and Supp. IV 1980).

175. *Id.* at § 470cc.

176. *Id.* at § 70ee-gg.

177. *Id.* at § 470bb(1).

178. *Id.* at § 470ee(g).

179. 42 U.S.C. § 1996 (Supp. IV 1980).

for native Americans and requiring a report to be sent to the Congress on native American religions, the act contains no other mandates or requirements.

General Considerations

Although the various legal authorities relevant to archaeology crosscut and overlap one another in ways that may be complex and confusing, the agencies charged with regulating their implementation (the ACHP and Department of the Interior) generally recommend that they be combined and viewed as follows:
(1) Archaeological sites should be identified, evaluated, and protected in connection with general land-use planning in response to the general requirements of Sections 110(a) and 110(b) of the act and to the specific requirements of Section 106 of NHPA and the council's regulations (36 C.F.R. parts 800 and 801).
(2) Decision making about project and program impacts on archaeological sites should be done with reference to Section 106 and the council's regulations, with consideration of the requirements of the Native American Religious Freedom Act.
(3) Carrying out archaeological data recovery programs, once decided upon pursuant to Section 106, would occur in a manner consistent with the requirements of the Reservoir Salvage Act, as amended.
(4) Archaeological fieldwork should be carried out on federal and Indian lands by persons who hold valid permits under the Archaeological Resource Protection Act, and the requirements of this act should also be a guide to general management of archaeological sites to avoid damage to them by private artifact collectors.

Department of Transportation Act and Other Transportation Legislation

Department of Transportation Act

Of the laws dealing with transportation, the Department of Transportation Act of 1966 (DOTA)[180] is most significant for historic preservation. Section 1653(f), [commonly referred to as Section 4(f)], declares that, as a matter of national policy, a "special effort" should be made

---

180. 49 U.S.C. §§ 1651-59 (1976).

to preserve and enhance the natural beauty of lands traversed by transportation lines. Historic sites are specifically included in this protection. To implement this policy, the secretary of transportation is prohibited from approving any program or project, including federal funding thereof, requiring the use of

> any land from an historic site of national, State, or local significance as so determined by such officials unless (1) there is no feasible and prudent alternative to the use of such land, and (2) such program includes all possible planning to minimize harm to such . . . historic site resulting from such use.[181]

The protective scope of Section 4(f) is much broader than that of NHPA Section 106. Only properties listed on or eligible for listing on the National Register trigger the Section 106 review process. DOTA, on the other hand, protects any property determined to be historically significant by a federal, state, or local official having jurisdiction over the property. Implementing regulations state that the 4(f) determination applies to historic sites "on or eligible for the National Register"[182] but add that any federal, state, or local historic site is assumed to be significant in order to raise 4(f), unless the official jurisdiction in which the property is located determines it not to be of significance.[183]

The "use" of the historic site that triggers Section 1653(f) [Section 4(f)] is as broad as the ACHP's definition of undertaking, i.e., no physical intrusion is required. "Use" can result from the potential of heavy traffic on a proposed road[184] and mere proximity of a project to a site without actual physical intrusion.[185] Once a use is established, however, any degree of use invokes Section 4(f).[186]

The "no feasible and prudent alternative" standard is far more stringent than the requirement imposed by NHPA Section 106. Once NHPA is triggered, Section 106 requires only ACHP "comment"; once DOTA is triggered, Section 4(f) allows a harmful "use" only if: (1)

---

181. *Id.* at § 1653(f).
182. 23 C.F.R. § 771.135(d), (f) (1981).
183. *Id.* at (c).
184. See *Monroe County Conservation Council v. Adams*, 566 F .2d 419, 424 (2d Cir. 1977), *cert. denied*, 435 U.S. 1006 (1978).
185. See *Stop H-3 Association v. Coleman*, 533 F.2d 434, 445 (9th Cir. 1976); *Conservation Society of Southern Vermont, Inc. v. Secretary of Transportation*, 443 F. Supp. 1320 (D. Vt. 1978).
186. *Louisiana Environmental Society, Inc. v. Coleman*, 537 F.2d 79, 84 (5th Cir. 1976).

"no feasible and prudent alternative" exists[187] and (2) "all possible planning to minimize harm" is done.[188] The courts have upheld this high standard and enforced it as a two-part burden.[189]

In *Citizens to Preserve Overton Park v. Volpe*,[190] the U.S. Supreme Court specifically refused to allow a balancing away of preservation values under the two-part standard. Instead, the Court found parkland protection of "paramount importance" under the act in a case involving federal highway construction through a park. Moreover, in the secretary of transportation's determinations of "no feasible or prudent alternative," factors of cost, route, and community disruption are not to be balanced against preservation values absent "truly unusual factors" of "extraordinary magnitudes." The Court clearly perceived that preservation values are not comparably quantifiable and that to hold otherwise would destroy the legislative protection afforded by Section 4(f).[191]

Other Transportation Laws

In addition to the DOTA of 1966, acts dealing with specific modes of transportation also require protection of historic, cultural, and environmental resources. The acts include similar declarations of a national preservation policy and the stringent two-part standard prohibiting a harmful action unless: (1) there is no feasible and prudent alternative and (2) all possible minimization of the harm is planned.[192]

Preservation has also been made a concern of the railroad transportation agencies. The Railroad Revitalization and Regulatory Reform Act of 1976[193] and the Amtrak Improvement Act of 1973[194] both provide grants and directives to reuse old railroad stations.

---

187. 23 C.F.R. § 771.135(a)(1)(i) (1981).
188. *Id.* at (ii).
189. *Coalition for Responsible Regional Development v. Coleman*, 555 F.2d 398, 402 (4th Cir. 1977); *Louisiana Environmental Society, Inc. v. Coleman*, 537 F.2d 79, 85, 86 (5th Cir. 1976).
190. 401 U.S. 402, 412-13 (1971).
191. See also *Louisiana Environmental Society, Inc. v. Coleman*, 524 F.2d 930, 933 (5th Cir. 1975).
192. Airport and Airway Development Act of 1970, 49 U.S.C. § 1716 (c)(4) (Supp. IV 1980); Federal-Aid Highway Act of 1968, 23 U.S.C. § 138 (1976); Urban Mass Transit Act, 49 U.S.C. § 1610 (1976).
193. 45 U.S.C. § 801 (1976 & Supp. IV 1980).
194. *Id.* at § 501 (Supp. IV 1980).

242   A HANDBOOK ON HISTORIC PRESERVATION LAW

Executive Order 11593

The 1966 NHPA was supplemented by a 1971 executive order. Executive Order 11593 required that federal agencies "locate, inventory and nominate all sites, buildings, districts and objects" on their lands no later than July 1, 1973, and take other measures to protect historic resources.[195] Properties appearing to be eligible to meet the criteria for inclusion in the National Register must be brought to the secretary of the interior's attention for a determination of eligibility.[196] Proposed federal impacts on properties determined eligible for listing must be reviewed by the ACHP when agency actions would affect them.[197] This advisory council review of agency actions that affect "eligible" properties was added to the 1966 act in a 1976 amendment.[198] Most of the requirements of the executive order were codified by the 1980 amendments to the NHPA, discussed earlier.

Federal Property Management

The Public Buildings Cooperative Use Act of 1976[199] had authorized the General Services Administration (GSA) to "acquire and utilize space in suitable buildings of historical, architectural or cultural significance unless such space would not prove feasible and prudent."[200] However, GSA made only desultory efforts to identify such space and usually found any space so identified not to be prudent and feasible to use. The 1980 NHPA amendments substantially increased efforts to use space in older buildings by directing such use and applying this directive to all federal agencies, not just to GSA.

Section 110(a)(1) of the 1980 NHPA amendments directs that each federal agency, prior to acquiring, constructing, or leasing buildings, "use, to the maximum extent feasible, historic properties available to the agency." Section 110(e) requires the secretary of the interior's approval of transfers of surplus historic properties to ensure their continued preservation or enhancement. Neither provision of NHPA has yet been implemented or enforced in court.

---

195. Executive Order No. 11593, § 82a, 36 Fed. Reg. 8,921 (1971), reprinted in 16 U.S.C. § 470h-2 (Supp. IV 1980).
196. *Id.*
197. *Id.*
198. 16 U.S.C. § 470(f) (1976).
199. 40 U.S.C. § 601 (1976).
200. *Id.* at § 601(a).

Other laws governing federal property management and development also specify special treatment for historic or architecturally significant properties.[201]

Land-Use Planning Laws

Many federal land-use laws express an affirmative national policy to preserve, protect, manage, develop, restore, and enhance areas of scenic, cultural, aesthetic, historic, or archaeological value. These laws identify the historic and archaeological as nonrenewable environmental resources similar to the nation's minerals, pure waters, and unique land formations. All are perceived to be part of the national heritage. Several laws prohibit actions that harm particularly fragile or critical areas.

The Surface Mining Control and Reclamation Act of 1977,[202] like the NHPA's Section 106, extends federal concern for the preservation of historic properties through indirect channels to private properties. The law requires that permits to mine under the act cannot be issued by the Interior Department's Office of Surface Mining, Reclamation and Enforcement unless the applicant has identified all properties on the lands eligible for listing in the National Register.[203] No permit may be issued if such a property would be adversely affected. Further, any person may petition the permit-issuing agency to declare historic lands unsuitable for mining.[204]

In a related area, Congress directed the secretary of the interior to notify the ACHP whenever he finds evidence that "Historic Landmarks may be irreparably lost or destroyed" by surface mining activity.[205] The advisory council is to devise alternative steps the federal government could take to mitigate or abate such adverse effects.[206] While this law extends a concern for preservation to private lands, there are no re-

---

201. Federal Property and Administrative Services Act of 1949, 40 U.S.C. § 304a-2 (1976); Executive Order No. 12072, § 1-105(1) (1976); 43 Fed. Reg. 36,869; 40 U.S.C. §§ 490n, 601; Intergovernmental Cooperation Act, 42 U.S.C. § 4231 (1976); Surplus Real Property Act, 40 U.S.C. §§ 484(k)(3)(A), (B) (1976).
202. 30 U.S.C. §§ 1201-1328 (Supp. IV 1980); 30 C.F.R. § § 700-950.20 (1981).
203. 30 C.F.R. § 779.12(b) (1982).
204. *Id.* at § 764.1 *et seq.* (1982).
205. 16 U.S.C. § 1908(a) (1976).
206. *Id.* at §1908(a)(b).

quirements that the adverse effects cease, nor are tools made available to stop such adverse activities.[207] (See appendix 1.)

Most of the recent land-use planning laws of the federal government provide that cultural and historic resources should be planned for, identified, and preserved. The Coastal Zone Management Act provides grants to states, not only to plan for such resources, but also to act to protect them.[208] The Federal Land Policy and Management Act[209] requires the Bureau of Land Management to consider and to protect cultural resources on its lands, and the National Forest Management Act of 1976[210] requires similar planning on U.S. Forest Service lands. The Wild and Scenic Rivers Act allows rivers to be protected if they have outstanding national significance, including historic features, but no rivers have yet been protected solely for historic qualities.[211] However, components of the Wild and Scenic Rivers System that have been designated for other qualities may be managed to protect cultural resources.

International Activities

The United States has also signed international conventions relating to the preservation of the world's cultural heritage.[212] The conventions authorize cooperation between nations in cultural resource protection. The World Heritage Convention also provides for the designation of world heritage properties (Mesa Verde National Park is one such area),

---

207. Mining Activities in the National Park System Act, 16 U.S.C. §§ 1901-12 (1976).

208. 16 U.S.C. §§ 1451-64 (1976). See Council on Environmental Quality, *Environmental Quality 1979: The Tenth Annual Report* (Washington, D.C.: GPO, 1979), pp. 505-7, for a list of states using this law to protect cultural resources.

209. 43 U.S.C. §§ 1701-82 (1976).

210. Pub. L. No. 94-588, 90 Stat. 2949-63 (1976) (codified in various sections of 16 U.S.C. (1976 & Supp. 1981)).

211. Wild and Scenic Rivers Act, 16 U.S.C. §§ 1271-87 (1976).

212. Multilateral Convention on Importation of Educational, Scientific and Cultural Materials, November 2, 1950, 17 U.S.T. 1837, T.I.A.S. No. 6129. This convention has been signed by the United States but not put into force, lacking congressional ratification; Multilateral Convention on the Protection of World Cultural and Natural Heritage, December 17, 1975, 27 U.S.T. 37, T.I.A.S. No. 8226; The Hague Convention for the Protection of Cultural Property in the Event of Armed Conflict, May 14, 1954, 249 U.N.T.S. 215. This treaty has not been formally signed by the United States, but the State Department has at various times asserted that its policies be followed. See Stanislaw E. Nahlick, *International Law and the Protection of Cultural Property in Armed Conflict*, 27 Hastings L.J. 1069, 1077 (1976).

although no legal protection ensues. The 1980 NHPA amendments authorize the secretary of the interior to provide technical assistance pursuant to the convention.[213] The NHPA also authorizes the participation of the United States in activities of the International Center for the Study of the Preservation and Restoration of Cultural Property, in Rome.[214]

ASSESSMENT OF FEDERAL PRESERVATION PROGRAMS

Many of the criticisms contained in the Advisory Council on Historic Preservation's 1976 assessment of national preservation programs remain valid today. Despite an ever-broadening concern for historic preservation by some government agencies, despite the special advisory council review process and its expansive definition of historic resources, and despite a funding apparatus and a number of useful tools that pull together state and local efforts in preservation, there is no guaranteed federal protection for historic resources, short of acquisition.

While there have been many important accomplishments, such as the creation of preservation offices in each of the states, there have been significant failures, particularly in the national effort to identify, survey, and inventory cultural resources. There are organizational problems in housing the main historic preservation and cultural resources protection program within an agency (the National Park Service) that is primarily concerned with parks and nationally significant properties. Moreover, the other federal agencies often view preservation as a low priority mission. Another major difficulty is that most of the strong federal mandates in the 1980 amendments to the National Historic Preservation Act have not been implemented, and discretionary preservation activities of the federal government suffer if the annual implementing appropriations are not large enough.

There is also a basic uncertainty about what resources to preserve and how. Should properties, for example, be authentically restored, or should building stock be adapted to new uses that may require changes that are not historically correct? Why the emphasis on buildings and the general neglect of other cultural resources? Archaeology, especially, remains a difficult resource to define and manage.

In sum, although the federal preservation programs have increased and expanded over time, there is no guaranteed federal protection for

---

213. 16 U.S.C. § 470 (1976 & Supp. IV 1980).
214. *Id.* at § 470n.

cultural resources that are not on public lands other than through acquisition. Preservationists who seek substantive protection for cultural resources are not likely to find judicial support based on federal law. While the unimplemented provisions of the 1980 NHPA amendments offer opportunities for legal activism, to date, little use has been made of these provisions in court.

Finally, the entire process remains heavily political. The state historic preservation officers (SHPOs) are creatures of the state, and if the state government wants a federal or federally supported project to go forward, it can pressure the SHPO to forego making a determination that properties in the project's path are worthy of protection. Such a determination is hard to challenge because nowhere are precise findings required as to how properties meet the federal evaluation criteria. With regard to federal agencies, their obligations in the preservation area are secondary to their primary missions and thus preservation may lose out when it is at cross-purposes with other goals. Nonetheless, there is an important role for preservation attorneys in compelling implementation of the various federal preservation laws, particularly to ensure that the requisite procedural steps are followed.

A Legal Analysis of NHPA and NEPA Project Impact Review Requirements

The most frequently litigated federal preservation law provisions involve the project impact review procedures contained in the National Historic Preservation Act's Section 106 and in the National Environmental Policy Act. This section presents a detailed analysis of the regulations and court cases interpreting and implementing these procedures, followed by a discussion of how the review processes under these two laws can be coordinated.

THE SECTION 106 PROCESS[215]

Section 106 of NHPA requires that:

> The head of any Federal agency having direct or indirect jurisdiction over a proposed Federal or federally assisted undertaking in any State and the head of any Federal department or independent agency having authority to license

---

215. For aid in understanding the Section 106 process, see figure on page 249

any undertaking shall prior to the approval of the expenditure of any Federal funds on the undertaking or prior to the issuance of any license, as the case may be, take into account the effect of the undertaking on any district, site, building, structure, or object that is included in or eligible for inclusion in the National Register. The head of any such Federal agency shall afford the Advisory Council on Historic Preservation established under Title II of this Act a reasonable opportunity to comment with regard to such undertaking.[216]

Courts have compelled agencies to comply with this review requirement. Although there are no strong substantive legal requirements in NHPA to protect historic properties, and despite the weaknesses of the Advisory Council on Historic Preservation, the regulations of the council that implement Section 106 establish a number of procedural steps agencies must meet. Thus, on one hand, the ACHP can be said to have constructed an entire process based on a limited mandate, thereby expanding the effectiveness of the NHPA. On the other hand, the process that has been established is only *process* and thus provides only limited legal protection. While it generally works to preserve cultural resources, it can fail under pressure.

ACHP review, as discussed earlier and outlined below, is triggered when federal undertakings may somehow affect properties listed in or eligible for listing in the National Register.[217] To ensure that determinations of eligiblity are made in a timely fashion, the regulations of the ACHP require that the head of an agency first identify eligible properties[218] and evaluate the effect of the proposed action on those properties before taking irreversible actions. As discussed above, the Section 106 review process functions independently of the owner consent provision, applying regardless of consent.

Federal Actions Subject to Section 106

The ACHP has defined federal "undertakings" subject to its review to include any kind of federal involvement or action over which a federal

---

216. 16 U.S.C. § 470(f) (Supp. IV 1980).
217. As enacted in 1966, Section 106 applied only to listed properties, but its coverage was extended to "eligible properties" first by Executive Order 11593, 36 Fed. Reg. 8,921 (1971), reprinted in 16 U.S.C. § 470h-2 (Supp. IV 1980), issued in 1971, and subsequently by amendments to the Land and Water Conservation Fund Act of 1965, 16 U.S.C. §§ 460d, 4601-4 to 1-11 (1976), which amended Section 106.
218. The identification procedures pursuant to Section 106 are discussed earlier in this chapter.

agency has discretionary authority and not just actions occurring on federally owned or controlled lands.[219]

> "Undertaking" means any Federal, federally assisted or federally licensed action, activity, or program or the approval, sanction, assistance, or support of any nonfederal action, activity, or program. Undertakings include new and continuing projects and program activities (or elements of such activities not previously considered under Section 106 or Executive Order 11593) that are: (1) directly undertaken by Federal agencies; (2) supported in whole or in part through Federal contracts, grants, subsidies, loans, loan guarantees, or other forms of direct and indirect funding assistance; (3) carried out pursuant to a Federal lease, permit, license, certificate, approval, or other form of entitlement or permission; or, (4) proposed by a Federal agency for Congressional authorization or appropriation.[220]

Federal agencies and the courts have adopted the ACHP's broad definition of "undertaking." Examples include the following:
- Federal grant money for commercial development of a business district listed in the National Register.[221]
- Military training operations planned for an island containing sites eligible for listing in the National Register.[222]
- Bridge construction project planned in the vicinity of a historic house and requiring federal permit.[223]
- Congressionally authorized dam construction project in an area of archaeological remains.[224]
- Federal construction of a refugee camp at Fort Allen.[225]

---

219. According to the advisory council's regulations, this is a lower threshold than must be met for the preparation of an environmental impact statement under the National Environmental Policy Act (NEPA); that is, NHPA's "federal, federally assisted or federally licensed undertaking" requirement is broader than NEPA's requirement that there be a "major federal action significantly affecting the quality of the human environment." 1980 NHPA amendment, 16 U.S.C. § 470h-2(i) (Supp. IV 1980), states that NHPA alone neither requires preparation of an EIS nor exempts such a requirement under NEPA.

220. 36 C.F.R. § 800.2(c) (1981). This definition, under review as this book went to press, may have changed.

221. *National Center for Preservation Law v. Landrieu*, 496 F. Supp. 716 (D.S.C. 1980), aff'd, 635 F.2d 324 (4th Cir. 1980).

222. *Romero-Barcelo v. Brown*, 643 F.2d 835 (1st Cir. 1981), *cert. denied*, 102 S. Ct. 619 (1981).

223. *Coalition for Responsible Regional Development v. Coleman*, 555 F.2d 398 (4th Cir. 1977).

224. *Environmental Defense Fund, Inc. v. Tennessee Valley Authority*, 371 F. Supp. 1004 (E.D. Tenn. 1973), aff'd, 492 F.2d 466 (6th Cir. 1974).

225. *Commonwealth of Puerto Rico v. Muskie*, 507 F. Supp. 1035 (D.P.R. 1981).

FEDERAL LAW 249

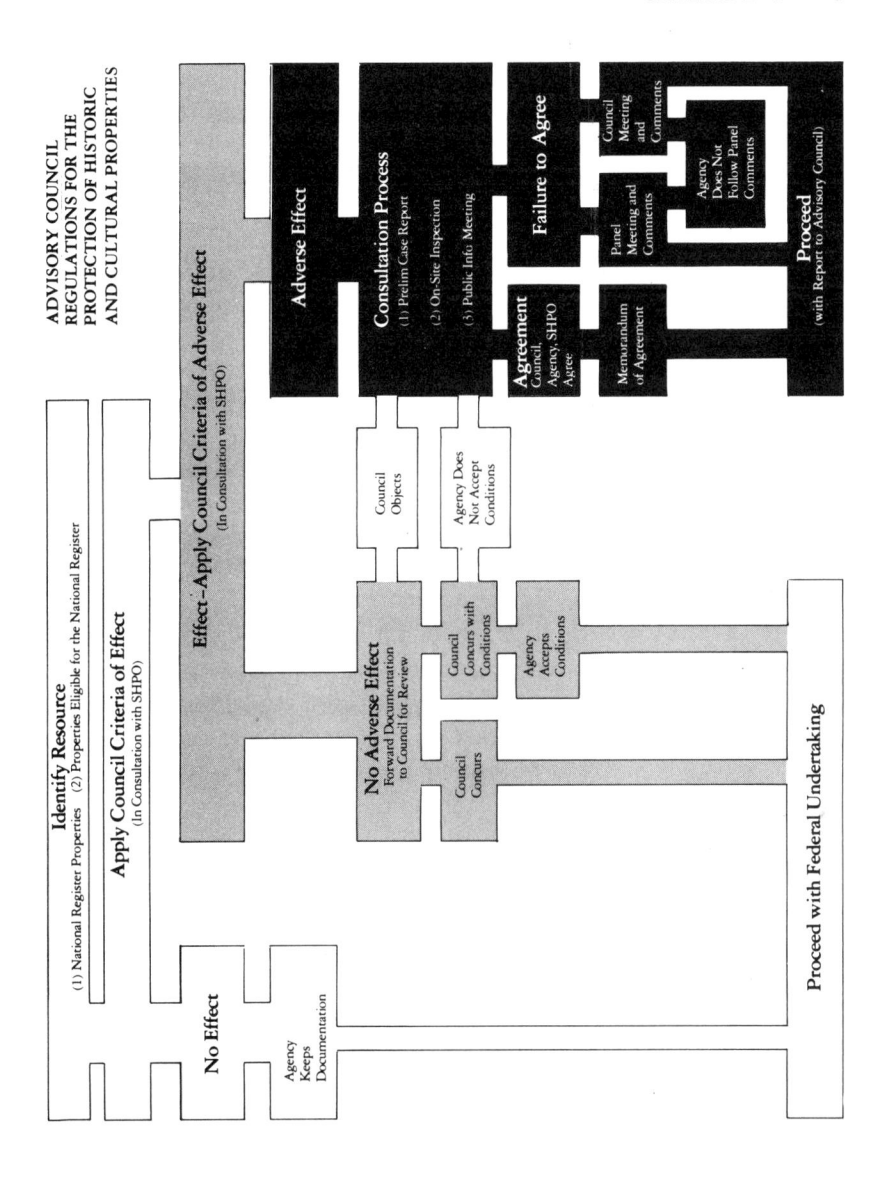

SECTION 106 REVIEW DIAGRAMMED

ADVISORY COUNCIL REGULATIONS FOR THE PROTECTION OF HISTORIC AND CULTURAL PROPERTIES

Identify Resource
(1) National Register Properties (2) Properties Eligible for the National Register

Apply Council Criteria of Effect
(In Consultation with SHPO)

Effect—Apply Council Criteria of Adverse Effect
(In Consultation with SHPO)

No Effect → Agency Keeps Documentation

No Adverse Effect — Forward Documentation to Council for Review
- Council Concurs
- Council Concurs with Conditions → Agency Accepts Conditions
- Agency Does Not Accept Conditions
- Council Objects

Adverse Effect

Consultation Process
(1) Prelim Case Report
(2) On-Site Inspection
(3) Public Info Meeting

Agreement — Council, Agency, SHPO Agree → Memorandum of Agreement

Failure to Agree — Panel Meeting and Comments → Council Meeting and Comments → Agency Does Not Follow Panel Comments

Proceed (with Report to Advisory Council)

Proceed with Federal Undertaking

- Surface mining project pursuant to federally approved lease to take place on Navajo reservation in an area of archaeological remains.[226]
- Renegotiation of an urban renewal program.[227]

Federal undertakings found by the ACHP to trigger Section 106 review include:[228]
- grants for highways and urban development projects;
- approval of acquisition or disposition of property in urban renewal areas;
- transfer of surplus federal buildings;
- federal permitting and licensing;
- construction, alteration, or demolition of a building by a federal agency;
- preparation of land-use plans;
- approval of Federal Housing Authority loan guarantees; and
- construction of dams, pipelines, veterans hospitals, and bridges.

Section 214 of the 1980 amendments to the NHPA authorizes the ACHP to exempt entire federal programs, as well as specific repetitive undertakings, from its review requirement, if the exemption is consistent with the act. In addition, advisory council regulations permit programmatic memorandums of agreement between the council and the action agency concerning how programs or repetitive undertakings will affect Register property. Such memorandums can be written for entire programs, such as the Veterans Administration mortgage insurance program, for repetitive undertakings occurring nationwide, and for individual specific undertakings.[229] Thus, many routine federal actions may fall under an exemption or be covered by a programmatic memorandum of agreement, even though they can produce adverse effects on National Register properties. Regulations to implement Section 214 have not yet been issued by the ACHP.

---

226. *National Indian Youth Council v. Andrus*, 501 F. Supp. 649 (D.N.M. 1980).

227. *WATCH (Waterbury Action to Conserve our Heritage, Inc.) v. Harris*, 603 F.2d 310 (2d Cir. 1979), *cert. denied*, 444 U.S. 995 (1979).

228. See generally Advisory Council on Historic Preservation, *Digest of Cases 1967-1973* (Washington, D.C.: GPO, 1973). Guidance regarding whether a particular federal action is an undertaking subject to NHPA may be obtained from the advisory council or state historic preservation office.

229. 36 C.F.R. § 800 (1981). Examples of such programmatic MOAs are emergency drought relief work, deployment of the MX missile system, the Bureau of Land Management's livestock grazing program and its program to transfer public lands to private parties, and National Park Service preservation grants.

Federal licensing is one form of undertaking covered by the regulations. However, what constitutes federal licensing is not always clear. One court, in *Edwards v. First Bank of Dundee*,[230] held that demolition of a National Register structure by a Federal Deposit Insurance Corporation-regulated bank (FDIC) to permit construction of a new bank building was not a federally licensed undertaking, although the FDIC is authorized to approve relocation of the banks it regulates. The court found that the comptroller of the currency had no licensing authority over the planned demolition sufficient to cause NHPA to apply.

But Section 106 was found applicable in a similar situation in *Weintraub v. Provident National Bank*,[231] in which a historic bank building was to be demolished upon construction of a new bank facility. The court distinguished *Edwards* in several ways: (1) the *Weintraub* case was brought under the National Banking Act, 12 U.S.C. § 36(e), which states that "no branch of any national banking association shall be . . . moved from one location to another without the . . . approval of the Comptroller of the Currency," giving the comptroller discretionary authority over the action; (2) the comptroller was a defendant in the suit; and (3) the building was individually listed in the National Register whereas in *Edwards* it was part of a district.[232]

Federal funding is another form of federal undertaking.[233] Examples include federally funded bridge replacements, dam construction and consequent land flooding, and obsolete property rehabilitation. In one case, *Ely v. Velde*, the Law Enforcement Assistance Administration's (LEAA) approval of state block grants required agency compliance with Section 106.[234] The same court later refused to allow the state to return

---

230. 534 F.2d 1242 (7th Cir. 1976).
231. No. 78-1577 (E.D. Pa. 1978).
232. The court was incorrect in making this last distinction.
233. But see *Weintraub v. Rural Electrification Administration*, 457 F. Supp. 78 (M.D. Pa. 1978), where the court held NHPA inapplicable. The court stated that although federal funds enabled a federation of Rural Electrification Administration borrowers to construct a building that created a need for parking, leading to a proposal for demolition of a National Register building, the demolition was not subject to NHPA. Congress, the court said, intended to control only direct federal spending that would destroy National Register buildings, not every effect of federal spending.
This case appears, however, to have been wrongly decided. The court's reasoning contradicts 36 C.F.R. § 800.3 (1981), which states, "An effect may be direct or indirect."
234. 451 F.2d 1130 (4th Cir. 1971). See also, in the following section on NEPA project review, the discussion of federal actions triggering NEPA.

or reallocate the federal funds to avoid compliance with NHPA. In a related case of the same name,[235] plaintiffs appealed the denial of their application for an injunction blocking construction of a federally funded prison facility and medical center in their neighborhood pending federal compliance with NHPA and NEPA. The lower court had dismissed the complaint, ruling that the state had permissibly transferred federal LEAA funds from the project to other state projects, removing any federal involvement in the undertaking. The Fourth Circuit Court reversed, holding that while the project was not irrevocably federal because federal funds had been accepted for it, if it were to be constructed without compliance with NHPA and other environmental laws the state must reimburse the federal government for funds allocated to the center and not merely divert them to another project.

The courts have refused to allow "segmentation" of a federally funded project to focus NHPA's federal involvement trigger on a harmless portion of the project. In *Thompson v. Fugate*,[236] the plaintiffs sought to enjoin construction through a National Historic Landmark of the final 8.3 miles of a 75-mile circumferential urban highway pending compliance with NHPA. The injunction was granted and the defendants were required to comply with NHPA. The court reasoned that although federal funds had not been sought for the portion of the highway project at issue, the remainder of the project was to be federally assisted.

> The meeting of federal requirements for 21 miles of a 29.2-mile highway project in order to partake of the federal financial allotments for that 21-mile segment, and at the same time circumvent the need to protect the national environment to the fullest extent possible in the remaining 8.3-mile segment by labeling it as a separate project, is to engage in a bureaucratic exercise which, if it is to succeed, must do so without the imprimatur of this court—a task which is doomed to failure unless and until a superior court deems otherwise.[237]

Continuing Federal Actions

A federal undertaking can sometimes continue over an extended period, and one complete project may in fact consist of several development stages and appropriations, approvals, licenses, or other federal actions. Highway construction and urban development projects are prime examples. As with the segmentation issue discussed earlier, courts refuse

---

235. *Ely v. Velde*, 497 F.2d 252 (4th Cir. 1974).
236. 347 F. Supp. 120 (E.D. Va. 1972).
237. *Id*. at 124.

to find that Section 106 compliance at an early stage necessarily constitutes compliance for later stages of an undertaking.[238]

The leading case, *WATCH v. Harris*,[239] holds that federal agency duty to comply with the Section 106 requirements continues as long as the agency retains discretionary authority over an undertaking.[240] The case involved the proposed demolition of historic commercial buildings as part of a HUD-funded urban renewal project. Emphasizing that the contract required the work to be done in phases, each of which required HUD's permission, the court found that only continuing compliance with NHPA provided the "meaningful review" intended by Congress.[241] Moreover, the court distinguished between preliminary and final expenditure approvals, concluding that "these provisions [of NHPA] should apply until the agency has finally approved the expenditure of funds at each stage of the undertaking."[242]

The ACHP interprets Section 106 as allowing comment on a site-specific basis throughout the phases of a continuing federal undertaking. This also allows challenge to a federal approval or license despite compliance with Section 106 at the time of a prior approval or license pertaining to the same project. Council regulation 36 C.F.R. § 800.6(d)(8) specifically provides for "continuing review jurisdiction."

---

238. In the past, some courts have found that any approval, even the first of a series, constituted a "cut-off" of Section 106's application. See *South Hill Neighborhood Association v. Romney*, 421 F.2d 454 (6th Cir. 1969), *cert. denied*, 397 U.S. 1025 (1970); *Save the Courthouse Committee v. Lynn*, 408 F. Supp. 1323 (S.D.N.Y. 1975); *Kent County Council for Historic Preservation v. Romney*, 304 F. Supp. 885 (W.D. Mich. 1969).

239. *WATCH v. Harris*, 603 F.2d 310 (2d Cir. 1979), *cert. denied*, 444 U.S. 995 (1979).

240. At least one court has misinterpreted the term "eligible" and found Section 106 inapplicable where final agency approval occurred prior to a formal determination of eligibility. See, e.g., *Birmingham Realty Co. v. General Services Administration*, 497 F. Supp. 1377 (N.D. Ala. 1980); *Committee to Save the Fox Building v. Birmingham Branch of the Federal Reserve Bank of Atlanta*, 497 F. Supp. 504 (N.D. Ala. 1980). The Alabama district court ignored the express obligation of all federal agencies to identify and nominate eligible properties within a project's scope of possible impact. Executive Order 11593 and the advisory council regulations impose such a duty regarding actions occurring after 1971 and 1974, respectively. See *Romero-Barcelo v. Brown*, 643 F.2d 835 (1st Cir. 1981)(dictum), *cert. denied*, 102 S. Ct. 619 (1981); *Save the Courthouse Committee v. Lynn*, 408 F. Supp. 1323 (S.D.N.Y. 1975).

241. *WATCH v. Harris*, 603 F.2d 310, 324 (2d Cir. 1979).

242. See also *National Indian Youth Council v. Andrus*, 501 F. Supp. 649 (D.N.M. 1980), *cert. denied*, 444 U.S. 995 (1979).

However, where such projects are begun today, the council encourages an early and comprehensive review of resources possibly affected and a memorandum of agreement (MOA) to protect the identified resources throughout the project's stages.[243] Such an MOA does not extinguish an agency's duty to protect resources discovered during project construction.[244] Some federal agencies, however, believe that if historic resources are adequately addressed in the environmental impact statement (EIS) process, the agencies should not have to protect historic properties discovered after the final statement is filed despite the mandates in Section 110 of the NHPA.[245]

A corollary issue to that of a continuing federal action arises in regard to projects begun before 1976. Prior to the 1976 amendments, Section 106 review applied to only those properties "included in" the National Register. However, Executive Order 11593, issued in 1971, made the Section 106 review apply to eligible properties. Courts have held that Section 106 applies to projects begun before 1976 if the federal agency retains discretionary authority over the project.[246]

For example, in *WATCH v. Harris*, discussed above, the project had commenced before 1976, and HUD retained approval authority after enactment of the 1976 amendment extending Section 106 to eligible properties. The court found that HUD should have complied with Section 106 when a carriage house its funds would have helped demolish was found eligible for listing in 1978. Since HUD failed to do so, the court enjoined further demolition pending agency compliance.

The number of continuing federal projects begun before 1976 is fast decreasing. Some may be open to challenge on the grounds outlined above, but few are coming before the ACHP.

---

243. See 36 C.F.R. § 800.8 (1981).

244. In such an event, 36 C.F.R. § 800.7 (1981) requires agency compliance with the data recovery provisions of the Archaeological and Historic Preservation Act of 1974, 16 U.S.C. § 469(a) (1976). The secretary of the interior may require the advisory council to comment. *Id.* at § 800.7(a).

245. See, for example, 23 C.F.R. § 771.135(g), which allows the Department of Transportation to exclude historic sites designated late in the development process from the "no feasible and prudent alternative" determination, if land has already been purchased and if adequate efforts to identify historic resources were made prior to project approval.

246. *WATCH v. Harris*, 603 F.2d 310 (2d Cir. 1979), *cert. denied*, 444 U.S. 995 (1979).

Determination of Effect[247]

For any registered or eligible property in the area of potential impact, the federal agency official, in consultation with the state historic preservation officer (SHPO), must determine whether the undertaking will have any "effect"—beneficial or adverse—on the characteristics of the property that qualify it for the Register.[248] This evaluation focuses on the property's historic, architectural, archaeological, or cultural significance. "Effect" includes changes in location, design, setting, materials, workmanship, feeling, and association but need not be "significant" as it must be under the NEPA.[249]

In addition, "an effect may be direct or indirect."[250] Both direct and indirect effects are caused by the undertaking in question, but direct effects occur at the same time and place, while indirect effects include those reasonably foreseeable in the future or removed in distance. Examples of indirect effects are changes in land-use patterns, population density, or growth rate.[251]

If the federal agency official determines that there will be no effect for Section 106 purposes, he documents the finding and the undertaking may proceed.[252] The SHPO or any other party, however, may object to this finding by notifying the executive director of the ACHP, who then reviews the determination.

Determination of Adverse Effect[253]

If the federal agency official or the executive director of ACHP determines that the undertaking will have an effect, the federal official, in consultation with the SHPO, determines whether the effect will be "adverse" according to the criteria found at 36 C.F.R. § 800.3(b). This is narrower than the actual language of Section 106 requiring that all effects—beneficial as well as adverse—be referred to the ACHP. Adverse effects include:

---

247. See generally 36 C.F.R. § 800.4(b) (1981).
248. See 36 C.F.R. § 800.3(a) (1981) for the advisory council's "Criteria of Effect."
249. See the following section on NEPA project review. 36 C.F.R. § 800.9 (1981).
250. But see *Cobble Hill Association v. Adams*, 470 F. Supp. 1077 (E.D.N.Y. 1979), where the court refused to find indirect effect sufficient to require compliance with NHPA.
251. See generally 36 C.F.R. § 800.3(a) (1981).
252. *Id.* at § 800.4(b).
253. See generally *id.* at § 800.4(b)(2), 800.4(d).

- demolition or alteration of all or part of a property, such as replacement of a historic bridge;
- isolation of a property from its surrounding environment or alteration of that environment, such as highway construction across a corner of a historic district;
- introduction of visual, audible, or atmospheric elements that are out of character with a property or alter its setting, such as construction of a telecommunications tower adjacent to a historic property;
- neglect of a property that results in its deterioration or destruction, such as allowing a historic lighthouse to gradually fall into the sea;
- transfer or sale of a property without adequate restrictions to ensure its preservation or maintenance, such as the conveyance—without easements to protect the element that qualified the property for the Register—of an obsolete historic office.[254]

If the federal agency official finds that the effect will not be adverse,[255] documentation of this finding is forwarded to the executive director of the ACHP for review. If the official finds that the effect will be adverse or if the ACHP executive director rejects the finding of no adverse effect, the official must: (1) prepare and submit a preliminary case report on the undertaking and request the ACHP's comments; (2) notify the SHPO of this requst for comments; and (3) proceed with the consultation process described in 36 C.F.R. § 800.6.[256] Until the advisory council has commented, the agency may not take any action that could result in an adverse effect on historic resources or foreclose alternatives that might minimize adverse effects.[257]

Opportunity to Comment—Consultation Process

Normally the executive director of ACHP will concur in a determination of no adverse effect, and the undertaking may proceed. The executive director may, if he objects to the determination, concur on condition that specified steps be taken by the agency to ameliorate the

---

254. *Id.* at. § 800.3(b) "Criteria of Adverse Effect."
255. *Id.* at § 800.4(c).
256. The report must discuss the points detailed at 36 C.F.R. 800.13(b) (1981). The report may be prepared to serve as the draft environmental impact statement (DEIS) required by NEPA, but it is important to remember that the statutory obligations under NEPA and NHPA are independent of each other.
257. *Id.* at § 800.6(d)(6).

objectionable elements of the undertaking.[258] However, if the executive director objects to the determination or the agency will not agree to the proposed conditions, the executive director initiates the consultation process.

Through the consultation process described at 36 C.F.R. § 800.6(b), the federal agency official, the SHPO, and the executive director of ACHP ("the consulting parties") consider alternatives to the proposed undertaking that might avoid, minimize, or mitigate its adverse effects on historic properties. Other parties, including representatives of local government and public and private organizations, may also be invited to participate, but this is left entirely to the discretion of the consulting parties. At no point in the Section 106 review process does the public have the right to participate uninvited. Any invitations to appear or notifications of information are on a case-by-case basis. Nonetheless, this process presents an opportunity for the public to present its views to the council and its staff and to persuade them to intervene with federal agencies taking actions affecting cultural resources.

To begin the consultation process, the federal agency provides the preliminary case report to the consulting parties. An on-site inspection and a public information meeting on the undertaking and the Section 106 process may be held. The consulting parties then explore alternatives to the undertaking that might alleviate its adverse effects. If such an alternative can be agreed to, the parties execute an MOA to specify how the undertaking may proceed.[259]

Memorandum of Agreement

The MOA is usually prepared by the staff of the ACHP's executive director. It can consist of a proposal written by the federal agency detailing the actions agreed to and the SHPO's concurrence with the proposal, or it may be drafted entirely by the ACHP's staff. Other parties in interest may be permitted to indicate their agreement with or become signatories to the MOA. Once the executive director determines that the MOA accurately represents the agreement of the parties, and all of the parties have signed the document, the director forwards the executed agreement to the chairman of the ACHP for council ratification.[260] Unless the chairman places the matter on the agenda for full council

---

258. *Id.* at § 800.6(a)(2).
259. *Id.* at § 800.6(c).
260. *Id.* at § 880.6(c)(2).

review, the MOA takes effect on chair approval or after 30 days, whichever comes first. The ACHP regulations specify that the MOA constitutes the advisory council comments required by Section 106. This procedure was upheld in *National Center for Preservation Law v. Landrieu*[261] despite the fact that not all members of the council are given an opportunity to approve of or to review the MOA.

Within 90 days of carrying out the terms of the MOA, the federal agency must report to the other signatories on the actions it has taken. If an agency fails to carry out the terms of the MOA, ACHP regulations require it to again seek council comments and to halt the undertaking until comments have been received. The regulations make no reference to the MOA as a binding contractual agreement; however, at least one court has given it this interpretation.[262] If one of the signatories to the MOA finds that its terms cannot be met or wishes to modify a stipulation, an amendment to the MOA must be executed with the agreement of all the consulting parties.

Generally the MOA will specify what measures will be taken to avoid or minimize the adverse effects of the undertaking. However, if the consulting parties can find no feasible and prudent alternative that will avoid or minimize these effects, the parties execute an MOA so accepting the adverse effect and any recording, salvage, or other measures to be taken.[263] It is important to remember that the council is not required to seek protection of historic resources in each case. Rather, the consultation process attempts to develop "feasible and prudent alternatives" that could avoid, mitigate, or minimize the adverse effects of agency undertakings.[264] "If there are no feasible and prudent alternatives that could avoid or satisfactorily mitigate the adverse effects," the project can nevertheless proceed.[265] No court has yet been asked to interpret this "no feasible and prudent alternatives" langauge as rigorously as Section 4(f) of the previously discussed Department of Transportation Act (DOTA).

If the parties cannot agree to terms of an MOA, the executive director notifies the chairman and recommends whether the matter should be scheduled for consideration at a council meeting. Full council con-

---

261. 496 F. Supp. 716 (D.S.C. 1980), *aff'd*, 635 F.2d 324 (4th Cir. 1980).
262. *Don't Tear It Down, Inc. v. Pennsylvania Avenue Development Corp.*, 642 F.2d 527 (D.C. Cir. 1980).
263. 36 C.F.R. § 800.6(b)(6) (1981).
264. *Id.* at § 800.6(b).
265. *Id.* at § 800.6(b)(6).

sideration is quite unusual; of the approximately 1,500 to 2,000 undertakings that go through the Section 106 process each year, only 3 or 4 are actually considered by the full council or a council panel. If the chairman decides against full council consideration, a written summary of the undertaking is sent to each council member. If objections are received from three council members, the matter is heard by the council. Otherwise, the chairman notifies the agency, SHPO, and any other parties in interest that the undertaking may proceed.

If the chairman decides that the undertaking should be considered by the council, then either the matter is scheduled for full council consideration or a five-member panel is designated to review the matter on the council's behalf. Before the council or panel meets, the (federal) agency and the SHPO must submit reports on the proposed undertaking to the executive director.[266] Reports for the meeting are also prepared by the executive director and the secretary of the interior. The council will also consider statements submitted by any other party. Interested parties may also make oral remarks at the council meeting.

Within 15 days of the meeting, the council issues written comments on the undertaking. The comments are first forwarded to the federal agency and to the president and Congress. After receipt of the agency's response, the council comments become available to the SHPO and the public. They are to be included in any EIS for the project prepared pursuant to the NEPA.[267]

The head of the federal agency must take the council's or panel's comments "into account" when reaching a final decision regarding the proposed undertaking. The regulation calls for a written report to be submitted to the ACHP describing the actions to be taken, including whether the federal agency will follow the panel's comments and the potential effect of the planned actions. Few such reports are actually received by the council, however.

Courts interpret NHPA's "take into account" provision to impose a procedural obligation on an agency's exercise of discretionary authority. Specifically:

> Discretion to decide does not include a right to act perfunctorily or arbitrarily . . . the agency must not only observe the prescribed procedural requirements and actually take account of the factors specified but it must also make a sufficiently detailed disclosure so that in the event of a later challenge to the agen-

---

266. *Id.* at § 800.13(c).
267. *Id.* at § 800.9(f).

cy's procedure, the courts will not be left to guess whether the requirements of NHPA . . . have been obeyed.[268]

Theoretically, the agency's final written report should discuss not just the decision reached but also the reasoning behind it. Logically, a court of review would not otherwise be able to determine that a federal agency, in fact, had considered ACHP's comments.[269]

The regulations state that receipt of the written report by the council chairman shall be evidence that the agency has satisfied its Section 106 responsibilities for the particular undertaking. In practice, without notification of agency noncompliance by the SHPO or other signatories, the council will act no further. The council may then issue a final report to the president and Congress describing the agency's response to council comments.

NHPA Section 205(b) authorizes the council's executive director to appoint attorneys to "represent the Council in courts of law whenever appropriate, including enforcement of agreements with Federal agencies to which the Council is a party." However, the council has not yet chosen to enforce an MOA through court action. Enforcement of an agency's Section 106 responsibilities has been largely by citizen suit.

Parties Subject to Section 106

Compliance with Section 106 is legally the responsibility of the federal agency proposing the undertaking.[270] The only exception to this general rule is the delegation of NHPA and other environmental compliance responsibilities to recipients of grants under Title I of the Housing and Community Development Act of 1974.[271] For example, a city seeking a community development block grant (CDBG) whose use may affect properties eligible for Register listing must itself request the council's comments and comply with Section 106.

The reason advanced for delegating environmental responsibilities under the CDBG is that only the local grant recipient has the necessary

---

268. *Ely v. Velde*, 451 F.2d 1130, 1138 (4th Cir. 1971). See also *Philadelphia Council of Neighborhood Organizations v. Coleman*, 437 F. Supp. 1341, 1361 (E.D. Pa. 1977), *motion denied*, 451 F. Supp. 114 (E.D. Pa. 1978), *aff'd*, 578 F.2d 1375 (3d Cir. 1978); *Committee to Save the Fox Building v. Birmingham Branch of the Federal Reserve Bank of Atlanta*, 497 F. Supp. 504, 513 (N.D. Ala. 1980)(dictum); *Wisconsin Heritages, Inc. v. Harris*, 490 F. Supp 1334 (E.D. Wisc. 1980)(dictum).
269. *Ely v. Velde*, 451 F.2d 1130, 1138 (4th Cir. 1971).
270. 36 C.F.R. § 800.4 (1981).
271. 42 U.S.C. § 5304h (1976).

information to analyze the environmental effects of its own decisions about how the grant—an entitlement program over which the recipient has discretion about how it will be allocated—will be spent.[272] This is in contrast to grants that are approved by the federal government for a specific project.

One legal issue, therefore, has been the degree to which HUD must scrutinize the environmental compliance work of the grant recipient. Since the recipient is acting as the agent for HUD and would not be conducting the action without HUD's financial support, preservationists have argued that HUD has a residual responsibility to closely examine the work of the grantee.[273] In a challenge to the adequacy of the EIS prepared by the city of Charleston, South Carolina, for an urban development action grant (UDAG) project, it was held "that the actual review by HUD is limited to a determination that the applicant has followed all of the procedural requirements of the Council on Environmental Quality Guidelines and the regulations. . . ."[274] The court cited dictum in *Colony Federal Savings and Loan Association v. Harris*[275] for the proposition that HUD did not have a duty to critically evaluate the substance of the environmental analysis but only had a duty to see that the procedural requirements were met.[276]

In 1979, the Housing and Community Development Act was amended to allow the delegation not just of NEPA compliance but also of "other provisions of law which further the purposes of [NEPA]."[277] The conference committee report noted that the section made "clear that delegation can also be made with regard to the National Historic Preservation Act of 1966. . . ."[278] While this answered the issue of what environmental laws other than NEPA could be delegated, it was left to the courts to determine whether delegation of environmental respon-

---

272. Letter from Foster C. Knight, CEQ general counsel, to Robert C. Embry, assistant secretary of HUD (October 27, 1980).
273. A lengthy discussion between HUD and the Council on Environmental Quality on this issue can be found in Nicholas Robinson, ed., *Historic Preservation Law* (New York: Practicing Law Institute, 1980), p. 485.
274. *National Center for Preservation Law v. Landrieu*, 496 F. Supp. 716, 731 (D.S.C. 1980), *aff'd*, 635 F.2d 324 (4th Cir. 1980).
275. 482 F. Supp. 296 (W.D. Pa. 1980).
276. *Id.* at 302.
277. 42 U.S.C. § 5304(f)(1) (1976 & Supp. IV 1980).
278. Conference Rep. No. 96-706, 96th Cong., 1st Sess. 7-8 (1979). See also H.R. Rep. No. 96-154, 96th Cong., 1st Sess. 7-8 (1979).

sibilities under Title I applied only to the CDBG or to programs subsequently added to Title I. The plaintiffs in *National Center for Preservation Law v. Landrieu*[279] argued that delegation applied only to the block grant program, the basic program authorized in Title I, and not to the UDAG program, which was authorized by amendment to Title I in 1977.[280] Unlike CDBGs, over which local grant recipients had discretionary spending control, UDAGs are site-specifically approved by HUD for a known purpose. Nevertheless, the court found that delegation applied to all programs authorized by Title I.[281]

Because UDAGs were designed to provide cities with a quick source of funds to help solve urban problems, Congress responded to the complaints of some mayors that an unreasonable amount of time was being taken by the SHPO and the ACHP to review the proposed grant expenditure under Section 106. The 1980 Housing and Community Development Act amendments[282] required that the grant recipient obtain the views of the SHPO within a 45-day period. Another 45 days—but no more—were left for review of the project by the ACHP and the Department of the Interior.[283]

Congress continued to ease the reporting requirements of CDBG and UDAG grant recipients in the 1981 Housing and Community Development Act amendments.[284] Small cities that receive CDBG funds under the competitive (i.e., nonentitlement) portion of the grant program, and all UDAG recipients, need only certify to the satisfaction of the secretary of HUD that all environmental review requirements have been met. Thus, the trend is toward a decreasing role for HUD in reviewing the environmental compliance efforts of its grant recipients.

Public Participation in the Section 106 Process

The Section 106 process is a consultation process involving the federal agency official, the SHPO, and usually—but not necessarily—the ACHP. The advisory council regulations encourage, but do not require, public

---

279. 496 F. Supp. 716, 731 (D.S.C. 1980).
280. Housing and Community Development Act, 42 U.S.C. § 5318 (Supp. IV 1980).
281. *National Center for Preservation Law v. Landrieu*, 496 F. Supp. 716, 731 (D.S.C. 1980).
282. 42 U.S.C. § 5320(c) (1976 & Supp. IV 1980).
283. 46 Fed. Reg. 42,428 (1981) (to be codified at 36 C.F.R. § 801). The advisory council review can be extended beyond 45 days if necessary.
284. Pub. L. No. 97-35, §§ 302(b)(2), 308, 95 Stat. 385, 393 (1981).

involvement in the process. The consulting parties are urged to involve the public in the review process by soliciting information from the public, providing information and documents to the public, holding public information meetings, and informing the public of opportunities for participation.[285] However, the ultimate decision as to whether and to what extent the public will be involved is left to case-by-case determinations by the consulting parties. Private citizens cannot actually participate (aside from letters and telephone calls) without invitations, although they may request opportunities to speak or comment.

Other provisions of the regulations encourage public involvement in the council's implementation of its preservation responsibilities. Section 800.6 provides for public participation through the holding of public information meetings, notice of council meetings in the *Federal Register*, the opportunity for the public to make oral and written statements to the council, and the availability of council comments to the public. Again, however, public participation or provision of information is at the parties' discretion unless a full council meeting is held. Private citizens can help initiate council review by notifying the council of threats to a property listed in or eligible for listing in the National Register when such threats appear to involve a federal agency.[286]

Section 211 of the 1980 amendments to NHPA does require the council to promulgate regulations "to provide for participation by local governments in proceedings and other actions taken by the council with respect to undertakings referred to in Section 106 which affect such local governments." This mandate has not yet been implemented.

Citizen Enforcement of Section 106

As noted previously, Section 106 enforcement in the courts has been exclusively by citizen suit, not litigation by the ACHP. The following subsections examine critical issues in citizen enforcement of Section 106.

Standing

Standing to bring a citizen suit to enforce Section 106 usually requires an "injury in fact," but this can be met if the plaintiff alleges that

---

285. 36 C.F.R. § 800.15 (1981). One court has held that public participation in the Section 106 process is urged by 36 C.F.R. § 800.15 but is not mandatory. *Aertsen v. Landrieu*, 488 F. Supp. 314 (D. Mass. 1980), *aff'd*, 637 F.2d 12 (1st Cir. 1980).
286. 36 C.F.R. § 800.12 (1981).

he uses the property in some way. Although recent decisions have defined "use" as residence in the community or visual enjoyment of the property, prior to the U.S. Supreme Court's decision in *Association of Data Processing Service Organizations, Inc. v. Camp*,[287] courts held that only the owners of historic properties had standing under the NHPA.[288] Since the *Data Processing* decision, courts have held that residents and owners of property in the vicinity of threatened historic properties could have standing under Section 106.[289] This proximity test for standing paralleled the development of the law of standing in natural area protection cases under NEPA.[290]

Courts have also held that harm may occur to people who do not live in the immediate vicinity of a historic property, if they allege that they "use" the threatened buildings. *Neighborhood Development Corp. v. Advisory Council on Historic Preservation*[291] held that:

> We do not believe that injury-in-fact is suffered only by residents of the neighborhood in which the historically and architecturally significant buildings are located . . . . [T]he Act created an interest in the preservation of architecturally and historically significant buildings to be protected by *users* of such buildings. [292]

This form of "use" was interpreted even more broadly in *Edwards v. First Bank of Dundee*,[293] in which the court held that, as residents of the village, the plaintiffs were users of the environment of the village and had a legal interest in its preservation, environmentally, aesthetically, and historically.[294] This argument, however, would be difficult to make in attempts to enforce national preservation policies and programs, for

---

287. 397 U.S. 150 (1970).
288. For cases prior to *Association of Data Processing Service Organizations, Inc. v. Camp*, 397 U.S. 150 (1970), see *Kent County Council for Historic Preservation v. Romney*, 304 F. Supp. 885 (W.D. Mich. 1969); *South Hill Neighborhood Association v. Romney*, 421 F.2d 454 (6th Cir. 1969), *cert. denied*, 397 U.S. 1025 (1970).
289. See, e.g., *Weintraub v. Rural Electrification Administration*, 457 F. Supp. 78 (M.D. Pa. 1978); *Ely v. Velde*, 321 F. Supp. 1088 (E.D. Va. 1971), *rev'd on other grounds*, 451 F.2d 1130 (4th Cir. 1971).
290. See, e.g., *Hawthorn Environmental Preservation Association v. Coleman*, 417 F. Supp. 1091 (N.D. Ga. 1976), *aff'd*, 551 F.2d 1055 (5th Cir. 1977); *Sierra Club v. Morton*, 405 U.S 727 (1972).
291. 632 F.2d 21 (6th Cir. 1980).
292. *Id.* at 24 (emphasis in original).
293. 393 F. Supp. 680 (N.D. Ill. 1975), *rev'd on other grounds*, 534 F.2d 1242 (7th Cir. 1976).
294. *Id.* at 682.

example, by challenging the Interior Department's failure to implement the NHPA's directive to establish a loan guarantee program[295] to protect any nationally significant historic property. Such a claim would most likely be defeated as a generalized grievance shared by all citizens. A valid claim would probably have to refer to specific pieces of property.

While the 1980 NHPA amendments do not directly expand standing, Section 305 authorizes the award of attorneys' fees to "any interested person" who prevails under the act. Although there is no legislative history to indicate that Congress intended to ease the standing requirement, statutes that have granted to "any interested person" the right to seek judicial review have generally been held to follow the standing test of *Sierra Club v. Morton*,[296] that is, that plaintiff suffer injury in fact. *Aluli v. Brown*,[297] however, held the NHPA authorizes standing because it would be necessary to fulfill the purpose of the act.

Jurisdiction

The U.S. district courts have jurisdiction over law suits filed against federal agencies to enforce the provisions of the NHPA.[298]

Proper Compliance

To satisfy Section 106, the agency must:[299]
1. apply the council's "criteria of effect" to proposed federal actions that could have an effect on National Register or Register- eligible properties;
2. if there is such an effect, apply the council's criteria of "adverse" effect to determine the precise nature of the effect;
3. if the effect is found to be adverse, request the comments of the council;
4. obtain the comments of the council, which must be taken into account in the agency's decision-making processes—the comments may be obtained either by (i) an MOA entered into by the council, the federal agency (or its legal delegatee), and the SHPO or

---

295. 16 U.S.C. § 470d (1976 & Supp. IV 1980).
296. 405 U.S. 727 (1972).
297. 437 F. Supp. 602 (D. Hawaii 1977), *rev'd on other grounds*, 602 F.2d 876 (9th Cir. 1979).
298. 16 U.S.C. § 470w-4 (Supp. IV 1980).
299. 36 C.F.R. § 800.4-9 (1981).

(ii) written comments from the full council or a panel of its members;
5. if the comments are in an MOA, the agency must carry out the terms of the agreement. Failure to do so effectively voids the agreement; and
6. if the agency received only the comments of the council, it must demonstrate that it took the comments into account in reaching a final decision on the project and that its behavior falls within the purview of the Administrative Procedures Act, but it is not required to follow the council's advice.

Enforcement of sections other than 106 is difficult if the agencies make some effort to comply with the act. For example, Section 110 directs agencies to institute a program to survey resources, but it does not require that an outstanding level of work be performed. Issues that could be litigated, however, include the adequacy of the survey effort, the professionalism of the survey staff, and the failure to consider all cultural resources. It is not enough to look for historic sites and ignore other cultural and spiritual resources.

Parties

Sections 106 and 110(f) apply directly to federal agencies that are undertaking, funding, or approving projects affecting cultural resources. Such agencies are necessary parties to any judicial action. For CDBGs and UDAGs, HUD may delegate responsibilities for compliance to nonfederal entities. If responsibilities are delegated, the authority to make the delegation and the delegation's validity should be closely examined, and the delegatee might be made a party to the suit.

Others acting under contract as part of the compliance action should also be considered as parties, for example, archaeologists who are conducting data recovery operations under an MOA. The SHPO and the ACHP itself may be included either as defendants or coplaintiffs. Any grant recipient or license applicant under the compliance actions should also be included as a party.

Enforcement Actions

Assuming that standing exists, any person can initiate a lawsuit against a federal agency or its legal delegatees to enforce compliance with the provisions of Sections 106 and 110(f). In such cases, the federal courts have discretionary authority to award a plaintiff who "substantially prevails'' attorneys' fees and related costs.[300]

The ACHP itself has the authority to go into court to enforce compliance, either directly or through the Department of Justice. However, the latter option is unlikely to be taken, as the Justice Department would then be in the position of representing one federal agency against another in court. Enforcement of the terms of the MOA may also occur, but the council has not initiated such legal action to date.

The federal agency involved in the project is responsible for complying with Section 106; the ACHP cannot initiate compliance, although it does frequently issue letters of investigation. Arguably, because the council has authority to enforce compliance with Section 106 by filing a suit, if it refuses to do so, an action could be filed against the council, based on the Administrative Procedures Act, for arbitrary and capricious agency inaction.

The nature of the relief sought in an enforcement action about an MOA will depend on the basis on which the plaintiffs argue standing. If the plaintiff could not obtain standing under the *Sierra Club v. Morton* "use" rule, discussed above, standing could be claimed as a third-party beneficiary to the contract (i.e., the MOA). If the plaintiff is not a contractual party, a "user," or a third-party beneficiary, he may still have standing under the Administrative Procedures Act,[301] although relief will be limited.[302]

Two reported cases deal with the enforcement of MOAs. Standing was denied a plaintiff in *Citizen's Committee for Environmental Protection v. United States Coast Guard*,[303] although the court did imply that a third-party beneficiary could sue. Without such an allegation, though, standing would only be granted to the parties to the MOA (those in privity with the contract). In *Don't Tear It Down, Inc. v. Pennsylvania Avenue Development Corp.*,[304] standing was granted to "a nonprofit organization devoted to protection of the built environment, with a specific interest in preservation of buildings of architectural and historical value in the District of Columbia."[305] It was not made clear

---

300. 16 U.S.C. § 470w-4 (Supp. IV 1980).

301. 5 U.S.C. §§ 701-06 (1976 & Supp. IV 1980).

302. This paragraph and the remaining discussion in this subsection are drawn from a legal memorandum prepared for the National Center for Preservation Law by Kenneth G. Lore of the Washington, D.C., law firm of Brownstein, Zeidman and Schomer.

303. 456 F. Supp. 101 (D.N.J. 1978).

304. 642 F.2d 527 (D.C. Cir. 1980).

305. *Id.* at 531.

whether standing was granted under the *Sierra Club* standard or as third-party beneficiaries. Contract theory, however, was used to resolve the issues of the case, as the court gave credence to the interpretation of the contract by the parties to it.

The Administrative Procedures Act may provide another enforcement opportunity, but the only relief available under it is to set aside the agency's decision if it acts in an arbitrary or capricious manner or *ultra vires*.[306]

The substantive enforcement issue under Section 106 is for agencies to show that they have taken the council's comments into account. Under 36 C.F.R. § 800.6(d)(7), however, the federal agency is merely required to report to the council the actions taken and the effect of the actions on the affected properties. Receipt of this report is deemed to satisfy the agency's responsibilities. No court has yet been asked to hold that an agency has failed to take the council's comments into account.

Remedies

Injunctive relief in the form of a temporary restraining order or permanent or preliminary injunction is the usual remedy for violation of the provisions of Section 106 by a federal agency. When there has been initial compliance with Section 106—i.e., the federal agency has afforded the council an opportunity to comment, and there is an MOA—specific performance of the agreement may be an appropriate remedy, provided that the plaintiff can meet standing requirements under contract theory. It is also possible that a declaratory judgment or order of *mandamus* may be appropriate to compel federal officials to comply with the MOA, although this has not been done to date. Similarly, there is no record of damages being awarded for violations of Section 106.[307]

---

306. 5 U.S.C. § 706(2) (1976). See *Carson v. Alvord*, 487 F. Supp. 1049 (N.D. Ga. 1980), *Save the Courthouse Committee v. Lynn*, 408 F. Supp. 1323 (S.D.N.Y. 1975).

307. Kenneth Tapman, *Protecting National Register and Register-Eligible Properties Affected by Federal Actions* (Washington, D.C.: National Center for Preservation Law, 1981). Under the ruling in *Middlesex County Sewerage Authority v. National Sea Clammers Association*, 453 U.S. 1 (1981), use of the Civil Rights Act (42 U.S.C. § 1983 (1976 & Supp. IV 1980)) remedy for damages is permitted only where

Recovery of Attorneys' Fees[308]

Normally, the prevailing litigant in an American court is not entitled to recover attorneys' fees[309] unless Congress authorizes an exception to this rule. Such an exception was made in the 1980 amendments to the NHPA. Section 305 provides that:

> In any civil action brought in any United States District Court to enforce the provisions of this Act, if such person substantially prevails in such action, the court may award attorney's fees, and other costs of participating in such action, as the court deems reasonable.[310]

There is little legislative history of this section other than a note that the intent of the section is to ensure that those who otherwise lack the means for court action be awarded reasonable costs for actions under the act.[311]

The plaintiff must substantially prevail on issues under the act in federal district court; however, partly prevailing plaintiffs may also receive compensation or a reduced sum, as may plaintiffs who prevail through out-of-court settlements.[312]

Although the awarding of costs is discretionary, awards in nonpreservation cases have set some guidelines that indicate when the awards generally will be made. In cases under the Civil Rights Act, the plain-

---

federal laws do not provide for express remedy and enforcement schemes. Thus, it is questionable that a civil rights action could be brought to enforce the NHPA insofar as it is not clear whether the MOA process is an enforcement scheme or whether the act clearly grants standing. See also chapter 5 for a discussion of the Civil Rights Act damage remedy.

308. This section is drawn from a legal memorandum prepared by Steven J. Hoffman of the Washington, D.C., law firm of Arnold and Porter.

309. *Alyeska Pipeline Service Co. v. Wilderness Society*, 421 U.S. 240 (1975).

310. 16 U.S.C. § 470w-4.

311. See the restatement of the section in H.R. Rep. No. 1457, 96th Cong., 2nd Sess., reprinted in 1980 U.S. Code Cong. and Ad. News 6378.

312. *Maher v. Gagne*, 448 U.S. 122 (1980). See *Oldham v. Ehrlich*, 617 F.2d 163 (8th Cir. 1980). Some courts have held that the recovery of attorneys' fees is not appropriate unless the authorizing statute specifically waives sovereign immunity to allow the United States to be sued. See, e.g., *NAACP v. Civiletti*, 609 F.2d 514 (D.C. Cir. 1979), *cert. denied*, 447 U.S. 992 (1980). In 1981, however, Congress waived its sovereign immunity in all statutorily authorized awards of attorneys' fees in the Equal Access to Justice Act, Pub. L. No. 96-481, § 204, 94 Stat. 2327 (1981) (to be codified at 28 U.S.C. §§ 2401, 2412). In the first claim to recover attorneys' fees under the act, the United States raised sovereign immunity, and the court ruled for the plaintiff. *WATCH v. Harris*, 603 F.2d 310 (2d Cir. 1979), *cert. denied*, 444 U.S. 995 (1979).

tiff "should ordinarily receive an attorney's fee unless special circumstances would render such an award unjust."[313] In non-civil rights cases, judicial discretion seems to rely on a number of factors, such as the degree of culpability or bad faith of the opposing parties and the relative merits of the parties' positions.[314] Freedom of Information Act cases seem to rely primarily on whether the awarding of attorneys' fees is necessary to effectuate the goals of the act.[315] The chief factor in such cases under the Clean Air Act is "whether the suit was of the type that Congress intended to encourage."[316] Thus, plaintiffs under NHPA should argue for an award using the factors delineated in the cases above and, particularly, because such awards would effectuate the goals of NHPA.

PROJECT REVIEW UNDER NEPA

Procedural Requirements

In assessing whether an agency has complied with the National Environmental Policy Act, the first thing to determine is whether an environmental impact statement (EIS) is required. That is, is there a proposal for "a major federal action" "significantly affecting" the quality of the human environment? While both terms reinforce each other and are related, most courts view this as a two-part test, asking first whether there is a proposal for a major federal action, and second, if so, whether that action significantly affects the quality of the human environment.[317]

Major Federal Action

Although a definition of "major federal action" has developed through case law, the Council on Environmental Quality (CEQ) regulations now define "major federal action" as "actions with effects that may be ma-

---

313. *Newman v. Piggie Park Enterprise, Inc.*, 390 U.S. 400, 402 (1968).
314. See *Iron Workers Local No. 272 v. Bowen*, 624 F.2d 1255 (5th Cir. 1980); *Eaves v. Penn*, 587 F.2d 453 (10th Cir. 1978).
315. See *Nationwide Building Maintenance, Inc. v. Sampson*, 559 F.2d 704 (D.C. Cir. 1977).
316. See *Metropolitan Washington Coalition for Clean Air v. District of Columbia*, 639 F.2d 802 (D.C. Cir. 1981).
317. It should be noted, however, that, in defining a major federal action, the CEQ regulations state, " 'Major' reinforces but does not have a meaning independent of significantly." 40 C.F.R. § 1508.18 (1981).

jor"—a higher standard than the National Historic Preservation Act's definition of effects[318]—"and which are potentially subject to federal control and responsibility."[319] Actions include new or continuing activities of federal agencies—adoption of policies, plans, and programs and the approval of federal and federally funded, licensed, or permitted projects. Federal inaction that may potentially have major effects may also be subject to the EIS requirement.[320]

Precise formulas as to the kind and amount of federal involvement that make an action federal are hard to derive; the CEQ regulation only sets forth categories of federal actions, and case law is not clear. Generally there must be federal authority to exercise discretion over the outcome of an action,[321] or there must be federal action that enables the project to go forward. The courts have found the following projects or undertakings that had an impact on the built environment to be major federal actions.

- Changing an urban renewal project from an industrial park project to a neighborhood development program. *San Francisco Tomorrow v. Romney.*[322]
- Department of Housing and Urban Development (HUD) approval of the sale of a National Register property by the Denver Urban Renewal Authority under an urban renewal loan and capital grant contract. *Hart v. Denver Urban Renewal Authority.*[323]
- Issuance of an Army Corps of Engineers permit for construction of a marina by a private developer. *Conservation Council of North Carolina v. Constanzo.*[324]
- Lease of a building by the General Services Administration. *S.W. Neighborhood Assembly v. Eckard.*[325]
- Relocation of several thousand Air Force personnel where the relocation would directly and substantially affect the physical and

---

318. 36 C.F.R. § 800 (1981).
319. 40 C.F.R. § 1508.18 (1981).
320. But see *State of Alaska v. Andrus*, 429 F. Supp. 958 (D. Alaska 1977), *aff'd*, 591 F.2d 537 (9th Cir. 1979), in which nonexercise of power by executive branch official did not require compliance with NEPA.
321. William H. Rodgers, Jr., *Handbook on Environmental Law* (St. Paul: West Publishing, 1977), p. 763, citing *Ely v. Velde*, 451 F.2d 1130, 1137 (4th Cir. 1971).
322. 472 F.2d 1021 (9th Cir. 1973).
323. 551 F.2d 1178 (10th Cir. 1977).
324. 398 F. Supp. 653 (E.D.N.C. 1975), *aff'd*, 528 F.2d 250 (4th Cir. 1975).
325. 445 F. Supp. 1195 (D.D.C. 1978).

economic environments of two major urban centers. *Jackson County, Missouri v. Jones.*[326]
- HUD approval of an urban renewal project with knowledge that a private developer would construct a shopping mall, plus HUD funding of demolition of area buildings. *Dalsis v. Hills.*[327]
- Construction and use of ordnance storage facilities at a Hawaiian naval base. *Catholic Action of Hawaii/Peace Education Project v. Brown.*[328]
- HUD mortgage insurance and interest payment guarantee for an urban renewal project. *Wilson v. Lynn.*[329]
- Construction of a state prison medical center with Law Enforcement Assistance Administration (LEAA) block grant funds. *Ely v. Velde.*[330]
- Construction by the U.S. Postal Service of a new surburban postal facility and abandonment of an older urban facility. *City of Rochester v. United States Postal Service.*[331]
- The granting of a Federal Power Commission license to construct a power line. *Greene County Planning Board v. Federal Power Commission.*[332]
- Federal Highway Administration approval of construction of a section of a federal aid expressway. *Named Individual Members of San Antonio Conservation Society v. Texas Highway Department.*[333]

On the other hand, the following cases were found not to be major federal actions.
- Demolition of a National Register structure by a federally regulated bank to permit private construction of a new bank building. *Edwards v. First Bank of Dundee.*[334]
- Preparation of a regional land-use plan where federal assistance has been received for the planning process and where individual pro-

---

326. 571 F.2d 1004 (8th Cir. 1978).
327. 424 F. Supp. 784 (W.D.N.Y. 1976).
328. 468 F. Supp. 190 (D. Hawaii 1979), *rev'd on other grounds*, 643 F.2d 569 (9th Cir. 1980).
329. 372 F. Supp. 934 (D. Mass. 1974).
330. 451 F.2d 1130 (4th Cir. 1971).
331. 541 F.2d 967 (2d Cir. 1976).
332. 455 F.2d 412 (2d Cir. 1972), *cert. denied*, 409 U.S. 849 (1972).
333. 446 F.2d 1013 (5th Cir. 1971), *cert. denied*, 406 U.S. 933 (1972).
334. 534 F.2d 1242 (7th Cir. 1976).

posed projects would have been federally funded. *Arlington Coalition on Transportation v. Volpe.*[335]
- Granting of an outfall pipeline permit for a privately constructed manufacturing plant. *Save the Bay, Inc. v. Corps of Engineers.*[336]
- Federally funded repair of an existing roadway adjacent to a National Register historic district resulting in no long-term changes in land use or traffic flow. *Cobble Hill Association v. Adams.*[337]
- Nonexercise of power by an executive branch official. *State of Alaska v. Andrus.*[338]
- Actions undertaken by AMTRAK. *Miltenberger v. Chesapeake and Ohio Railway Company.*[339]

A recurring issue in defining a "major federal action" is whether the project can be separated into federal and nonfederal portions of the project for NEPA purposes. When such segmenting is clearly done to avoid preparing an EIS for the nonfederal portion, the courts have overruled it.[340] Often, however, the scope of the federal action is difficult to define.

Another issue is determining when a project in which there is federal involvement becomes "federal" for NEPA purposes. This is a much more complex issue than under NHPA. The Advisory Council on Historic Preservation review of federal "undertakings" includes any "federal, federally assisted, or federally licensed action, activity, or program or the approval, sanction, assistance, or support of any nonfederal action, activity, or program."[341] In NEPA cases, there is no universal rule. The courts try to balance the right of private parties to develop, without federal interference, projects that may or may not become federal against the need to prevent project momentum from rendering EIS review useless. One formulation is that actions, such as federal aid highway

---

335. 458 F.2d 1323 (4th Cir. 1972), *cert. denied*, 409 U.S. 1000 (1972).
336. 610 F.2d 322 (5th Cir. 1980), *cert. denied*, 449 U.S. 900 (1980).
337. 470 F. Supp. 1077 (E.D.N.Y. 1979).
338. 429 F. Supp. 958 (D. Alaska 1977), *aff'd*, 591 F.2d 537 (9th Cir. 1979).
339. 450 F.2d 971 (4th Cir. 1971).
340. *Named Individual Members of San Antonio Conservation Society v. Texas Highway Department*, 446 F.2d 1013 (5th Cir. 1971), *cert. denied*, 406 U.S. 933 (1972).
341. 36 C.F.R. § 800.2(c) (1981).

construction, are federal actions once a distinct federal go-ahead has been given.[342]

In *Indian Lookout Alliance v. Volpe*,[343] the court said that the EIS requirement becomes applicable at least at the stage of location approval by the Federal Highway Administration. In *Scottsdale Mall v. State of Indiana*,[344] the court found that federal participation in preconstruction work on a partially completed highway made the entire project a major federal action requiring an EIS for the remaining segments, even though the project was withdrawn from federal funding consideration.

And in *Ely v. Velde*,[345] the state was not permitted to evade the requirement of NEPA by diverting the federal grant funds allocated for construction of a prison to other projects and building the prison with state funds. (The court did say, however, that, if the federal funds were returned, NEPA compliance would not be required.)

Another complex issue is whether the need for a federal permit (as opposed to funding) "federalizes," and thus requires EIS evaluation of, an otherwise nonfederal project. This question can be an important one in preservation and related fields, such as rural conservation and urban revitalization. It might arise, for example, where an Army Corps of Engineers permit is required for discharge of fill material into navigable waters as landfill on which a shopping mall is to be constructed. Is an EIS required for the permit, and, if so, must the indirect secondary impacts of the mall on buildings in a nearby historic central business district be addressed?

The courts generally adopt an expansive or limited approach to the required scope of the EIS based on whether the federal involvement *enables* the project to proceed, but sometimes decisions are difficult to reconcile. Demonstrating the expansive approach are *Conservation Council of North Carolina v. Constanzo*[346] and *Sierra Club v. Hodel*.[347] In *Conservation Council*, the court stated that in determining whether

---

342. Rodgers, *Handbook on Environmental Law*, p. 775, citing *La Raza Unida of Southern Alameda County v. Volpe*, 488 F.2d 559 (9th Cir. 1973); *Lathan v. Volpe* (I), 455 F.2d 1111 (9th Cir. 1971); *Steubing v. Brinegar*, 511 F.2d 489, 492 (2d Cir. 1975).
343. 484 F.2d 11 (8th Cir. 1973).
344. 549 F.2d 484 (7th Cir. 1977), *cert. denied*, 434 U.S. 1008 (1978).
345. 497 F.2d 252 (4th Cir. 1974).
346. 398 F. Supp. 653 (E.D.N.C. 1975), *aff'd*, 528 F.2d 250 (4th Cir. 1975).
347. 544 F.2d 1036 (9th Cir. 1976).

an EIS is needed, cumulative and secondary effects of the action must be considered in determining the significance of the impact. In *Sierra Club v. Hodel*, the court held that an EIS prepared by the federal Bonneville Power Authority when it entered into a contract to supply power to a private magnesium plant should have considered the impact of the plant as well as of the power transmission line and the contract itself. "By entering into a contract to supply power to the project and to construct the transmission line to the plant," the court held, "the agency has so federalized the entire project that it has become a major Federal action requiring a[n] . . . environmental impact statement."[348]

On the other hand, two recent cases have taken a more restricted view of the scope of the action, and thus of the EIS, in this context. *Save the Bay, Inc. v. Corps of Engineers*[349] held that the granting of a federal discharge pipeline construction permit for a manufacturing plant did not require preparation of an EIS since the pipeline was not necessary for the plant's operation. The court held that a private project does not become a major federal action merely through some incidental federal involvement. The second case, *Winnebago Tribe of Nebraska v. Ray*,[350] involved construction of a 67-mile-long powerline requiring a permit from the Army Corps of Engineers for a short portion. The court upheld the Army Corps of Engineers' determination that the permit issuance was not a major federal action requiring an EIS. Plaintiffs claimed first that the corps exercised sufficient control and responsibility over the entire project to require it to consider the environmental impact of the entire line, and second, assuming limited federal involvement, that the corps must nevertheless consider the impact of nonfederal segments as secondary effects of its grant of the permit. In response to the first claim, the court distinguished factual or veto control from legal control and found that the requirement of securing a permit "cannot be construed as a grant of legal control over the entire project." The court also rejected the plaintiff's second contention, saying that completion of nonfederal aspects of a single project does not constitute a secondary or indirect effect of the federal action.

While these cases indicate the recent tendencies of courts to circumscribe the application of NEPA, care should be taken to consider how each agency treats permits in its own NEPA regulations.

---

348. *Id.* at 1044.
349. 610 F.2d 322 (5th Cir. 1980), *cert. denied*, 449 U.S. 900 (1980).
350. 621 F.2d 269 (8th Cir. 1980), *cert. denied*, 449 U.S. 836 (1980).

"Significantly Affecting the Quality of the Human Environment"

Once a major federal action is found, there must be a determination that the action will have a significant effect on the quality of the human environment. According to the CEQ regulations, "significantly" must be defined by the intensity of the action's environmental impact and the context in which the action is to occur.[351] In assessing intensity, the agency must consider "unique characteristics of the geographic area such as proximity to historical or cultural resources"[352] and the degree to which the action may adversely affect properties listed in or eligible for listing in the National Register "or may cause loss or destruction of significant scientific, cultural, or historical resources.[353] These latter resources are not limited to National Register or Register-eligible properties.

The requirement that resources be included in, or found eligible for inclusion in, the National Register in order for NHPA to apply would appear to make NHPA's scope of coverage narrower than that of the NEPA, which contains no such requirement. Yet, NHPA's definition of "undertaking" is broader than NEPA's "major federal action" requirement, and NHPA's definition of "effect" is broader than NEPA's "significant effect" language. In *Boston Waterfront Residents Association, Inc. v. Romney*,[354] for instance, the court found NEPA applicable where buildings had not been listed in or determined eligible for the Register. In practice, however, most historic resources to which NEPA will be found applicable will be eligible for listing in the Register.

The regulations define "effects" to include both direct effects (such as demolition of a historic structure located in a highway right-of-way) and foreseeable indirect effects (such as change in land-use or growth patterns and aesthetic, historic, cultural, economic, and social impacts). Positive as well as negative effects must be considered.[355] The cumulative impact of actions that individually may not produce significant effects must also be addressed.[356]

Case law has not provided a precise definition of an action "significantly affecting the quality of the human environment." *Natural Resources*

---

351. 40 C.F.R. § 1508.27 (1981).
352. *Id.* at § 1508.27(b)(3).
353. *Id.* at § 1508.27(b)(8).
354. 343 F. Supp. 89 (D. Mass. 1972).
355. 40 C.F.R. § 1508.8b (1981).
356. *City of Rochester v. United States Postal Service*, 541 F.2d 967 (2d Cir. 1976).

Defense Council v. Grant[357] did define "significantly affecting the quality of the human environment" as "having an important or meaningful effect, direct or indirect, upon a broad range of aspects of the human environment."[358] Later, the court in *Hanly v. Kleindienst*[359] listed two factors that have since formed a much-cited test for determining significance: first, the extent to which the action will cause adverse environmental effects in excess of those created by existing uses in the area affected by it, and second, the absolute quantitative adverse environmental effects of the action itself, including the cumulative harm that results from its contribution to existing adverse conditions or uses in the affected area.[360] Generally though, the courts have looked to a variety of factors to evaluate significance of effect.

In the historic preservation and built environment context, the following factors may indicate significance of impact:
- change in the physical character of a neighborhood;[361]
- concentration of population in a neighborhood;[362]
- loss of views from nearby properties;[363]
- impacts extending beyond the area of control of one local or regional government;[364]
- aesthetic considerations;[365]
- increased noise or traffic;[366]
- displacement of businesses;[367]
- impact on air quality;[368]

---

357. 341 F. Supp. 356 (E.D.N.C. 1972).
358. *Id.* at 367.
359. 471 F.2d 823 (2d Cir. 1972), *cert. denied*, 412 U.S. 908 (1973).
360. Although the *Hanly* test is still used, according to the CEQ regulations, "[e]ffects may also include those resulting from actions which may have both beneficial and detrimental effects, even if on balance the agency believes that the effect will be beneficial." 40 C.F.R. § 1508.8(b) (1981).
361. *Goose Hollow Foothills League v. Romney*, 334 F. Supp. 877 (D. Or. 1971).
362. *Id.*
363. *Id.*
364. *Maryland/National Capital Park & Planning Commission v. United States Postal Service*, 487 F.2d 1029 (D.C. Cir. 1973).
365. *Id.*
366. *Sansom Committee v. Lynn*, 382 F. Supp. 1245 (E.D. Pa. 1974); *City of Rochester v. United States Postal Service*, 541 F.2d 967 (2d Cir. 1976).
367. *Sansom Committee v. Lynn*, 382 F. Supp. 1245 (E.D. Pa. 1974).
368. *S.W. Neighborhood Assembly v. Eckard*, 445 F. Supp. 1195 (D.D.C. 1978).

- loss of job opportunities in the area;[369] and
- increasing economic and physical deterioration of the area.[370]

In *WATCH v. Harris*,[371] the court implied that, because properties eligible for the National Register would be affected by an urban renewal project, HUD's granting of approval for their demolition was an action significantly affecting the quality of the human environment.

The courts tend not to find a significant effect when new construction will be compatible with other neighborhood uses[372] or will conform to local zoning regulations[373] or when the project involves mostly interior rehabilitation of existing buildings and no change in use.[374] Some courts find the impact less significant when the location is a particularly good one for a new use[375] or when the project will enhance the neighborhood. Courts also do not regard social impacts such as a feared influx of low-income persons into a neighborhood as properly within NEPA's purview.[376]

The human environment is defined by the CEQ regulations to include "the natural and physical environment and the relationship of people to that environment." Social or economic impacts alone do not trigger the requirement to prepare an EIS, but when an EIS is required and socioeconomic effects and effects on the natural or physical environment are interrelated, all of these effects must be discussed.[377]

Almost across the board, major federal actions adversely affecting historic resources are seen to have a significant effect on the quality of the human environment. Sometimes the courts specifically address the applicability of NEPA to historic preservation or the built or urban en-

---

369. *City of Rochester v. United States Postal Service*, 541 F.2d 967 (2d Cir. 1976).
370. *Id*.
371. 603 F.2d 310 (2d Cir. 1979), *cert. denied*, 444 U.S. 995 (1979).
372. *Hanly v. Kleindienst*, 471 F.2d 823 (2d Cir. 1972), *cert. denied*, 412 U.S. 908 (1973); *First National Bank of Chicago v. Richardson*, 484 F.2d 1369 (7th Cir. 1973).
373. *Maryland/National Capital Park & Planning Commission v. United States Postal Service*, 487 F.2d 1029 (D.C. Cir. 1973).
374. *Wilson v. Lynn*, 372 F. Supp. 934 (D. Mass. 1974).
375. *First National Bank of Chicago v. Richardson*, 484 F.2d 1369 (7th Cir. 1973).
376. *Trinity Episcopal School Corp. v. Romney*, 523 F.2d 88 (2d Cir. 1975), *rev'd on other grounds sub nom.*; *Stryker's Bay Neighborhood Council, Inc. v. Karlen*, 444 U.S. 223 (1980).
377. 40 C.F.R. § 1508.4 (1981).

vironment, but often it is just assumed.[378]

Two lower court decisions, however, hold that NEPA does not apply to the built environment.[379] Although both can be characterized as aberrant trial court decisions, whose reasoning may be easily countered through reference to NEPA, its regulations and legislative history, and the case law, these two rulings have caused some concern in the preservation community.

St. Joseph Historical Society v. Land Clearance for Redevelopment Authority of St. Joseph, Missouri[380] held NEPA to be inapplicable to HUD-funded demolition of buildings in the Market Square historic district because NEPA "was clearly intended to apply to the overall environmental problems facing the Nation and . . . not . . . to situations as exist in the case before us." The court distinguished *Ely v. Velde*,[381] on which the plaintiffs relied, because *Ely* was concerned with construction of a prison facility on 10,000 acres in a historic rural area of Virginia, whereas this case dealt with an urban renewal plan for a limited local area.

In the *Committee to Save the Fox Building v. Birmingham Branch of the Federal Reserve Bank of Atlanta*[382] case, the court refused to enjoin demolition by the Federal Reserve Bank of a 19th-century commercial building listed in the National Register pending preparation of an EIS. The court stated that the plaintiff "has shown an impact on an architecturally and historically significant building—surely a social concern." Both cases used an unnecessarily narrow definition of historic preservation to include only architectural preservation.

---

378. *Hanly v. Mitchell*, 460 F.2d 640 (2d Cir. 1982), *cert. denied*, 409 U.S. 990 (1972); *WATCH v. Harris*, 603 F.2d 310 (2d Cir. 1979); *Aluli v. Brown*, 437 F. Supp. 602 (D. Hawaii 1977), *rev'd on other grounds*, 602 F.2d 876 (9th Cir. 1979); *Ely v. Velde*, 451 F.2d 1130 (4th Cir. 1971); *Save the Courthouse Committee v. Lynn*, 408 F. Supp. 1323 (S.D.N.Y. 1975); *City of Rochester v. United States Postal Service*, 541 F.2d 967 (2d Cir. 1976), do specifically apply NEPA to historic buildings. The following cases assumed that NEPA applied to historic resources. *Chelsea Neighborhood Associations v. United States Postal Service*, 516 F.2d 378 (2d Cir. 1975); *Hart v. Denver Urban Renewal Authority*, 551 F.2d 1178 (10th Cir. 1977); *Wisconsin Heritages, Inc. v. Harris*, 490 F. Supp. 1334 (E.D. Wis. 1980).

379. *St. Joseph Historical Society v. Land Clearance for Redevelopment Authority of St. Joseph, Missouri*, 366 F. Supp. 605 (W.D. Mo. 1973), and *Committee to Save the Fox Building v. Birmingham Branch of the Federal Reserve Bank of Alabama*, 497 F. Supp. 504 (N.D. Ala. 1980).

380. 366 F. Supp. 605 (W.D. Mo. 1973).

381. 321 F. Supp. 1088 (E.D. Va. 1971), *rev'd on other grounds*, 451 F.2d 1130 (4th Cir. 1971).

382. 497 F. Supp. 504 (N.D. Ala. 1980).

However, references to NEPA, the CEQ regulations, legislative history, and case law clearly show NEPA's applicability to the built environment. First, Section 101(b) of NEPA expresses among the act's aims an intent to "assure for all Americans . . . aesthetically and culturally pleasing surroundings" and to "preserve important historic [and] cultural . . . aspects of our national heritage." This language counters both the *St. Joseph* court's finding that NEPA was intended to apply to "the overall environmental problems facing the nation"[383] and not to the destruction of historic and cultural resources, and the *Fox* court's conclusion that destruction of a historically significant building is not within NEPA's purview.

The CEQ regulations also provide guidance. They list as indicators of whether an action is significant for purposes of filing an EIS, the degree to which the action may adversely affect properties listed in or eligible for listing in the National Register or may cause the loss or destruction of significant historic or cultural resources. Courts have found that such an effect alone is enough to require preparation of an EIS for a HUD-funded demolition of historic properties as part of an urban renewal project.[384]

The *Fox* court's finding that demolition is not an impact on the human environment may be countered by reference to the definition of "human environment" in the CEQ regulations. Although demolition of a historic property may have economic or social impacts, its primary effect is certainly a physical one, that of knocking down an existing building. Clearly, destruction of a valuable historic building has an impact on the human environment within the meaning of NEPA. NEPA was enacted to protect valuable historic buildings as well as valuable natural resources. In addition, demolition and new construction (or other federal actions affecting historic structures) frequently have effects such as increased population density and traffic congestion and change in land-use or growth patterns, all of which the courts have found cognizable under NEPA.

The *Fox* court also erroneously relied on *Image of Greater San Antonio, Texas v. Brown*,[385] one of a line of cases dealing with the socioeconomic impacts of the closing of federal installations or the transfer

---

383. 366 F. Supp. 605, 612 (W.D. Mo. 1973).
384. *WATCH v. Harris*, 603 F.2d 310 (2d Cir. 1979), *cert. denied*, 444 U.S. 995 (1979).
385. 570 F.2d 517 (5th Cir. 1978).

of federal employees. Courts in these cases required no EIS because the cases were concerned with the impact on people themselves and not on their environment. In contrast, the *Fox* case plaintiffs hoped to halt demolition of a historic building, an action that clearly would have primarily physical environmental impacts. Thus, the situation in *Fox* is more similar to that in the cases cited above, which found NEPA applicable to the built environment, than it is to *Image*.[386]

St. Joseph's distinguishing of *Ely* as concerning a rural area may be countered by reference to any of numerous cases that found NEPA applicable to an urban setting.[387] *First National Bank of Chicago v. Richardson* held that "NEPA must be construed to include the protection of the quality of life for city residents."[388] *Jones v. HUD* specifically attacked the view that NEPA does not enhance protection of the urban environment and cultural resources by holding that the environment is more than rocks, trees, streams, or air pollution; it also encompasses quality of life factors such as crowding, squalor, and crime.[389] A statement made by Senator Henry M. Jackson (D-Washington), on submitting the conference committee report to the Senate on the bill which became NEPA, is also helpful. Jackson declared that the act would be an important step toward improving the institutional policy and legal framework for dealing with problems such as haphazard urban growth, crowding, congestion, inconsistent and incoherent rural and urban land-use policies, and poor architectural design and ugliness in public and private structures.[390]

NEPA Procedures

If an EIS is required, the next step is to determine whether procedures for EIS preparation and review and for agency decision making have been satisfied. Since most challenges to agency compliance are procedural, a thorough understanding of NEPA procedures is essential. (See chart.)

---

386. *Id.*
387. *WATCH v. Harris*, 603 F.2d 310 (2d Cir. 1979), *cert. denied*, 444 U.S. 995 (1979); *Hart v. Denver Urban Renewal Authority*, 551 F.2d 1178 (10th Cir. 1975); *City of Rochester v. United States Postal Service*, 541 F.2d 967 (2d Cir. 1976); *First National Bank of Chicago v. Richardson*, 484 F.2d 1369 (7th Cir. 1973).
388. 484 F.2d 1369, 1377 (7th Cir. 1973).
389. 390 F. Supp. 579 (E.D. La. 1974).
390. 115 Cong. Rec. 40,417 (1969).

NEPA COORDINATION/INTEGRATION OF HISTORIC PRESERVATION PLANS INTO THE ENVIRONMENTAL PLANNING PROCESS

CEQ NEPA REGULATIONS FLOWCHART (40 C.F.R. 1500-1508)

PHASE I: Must Agency prepare NEPA Implementing Procedures?

Is entity an "agency"? 1508.12. ► No ► Entity may act without regard to NEPA regulations.

▼

Yes ─────────────────► Agency must adopt NEPA implementing procedures. 1507.3.

PHASE II: Whether to prepare EA or EIS.

Is agency the "lead agency"? 1501.5, 1501.6, 1508.16. ► No ► Agency must cooperate with lead agency. 1501.6, 1508.5.

▼

Yes

▼

Is proposed action categorically excluded from NEPA compliance under agency NEPA procedures? 1508.4, 1501.4(a)(2). ► Yes ► Agency may act without preparing environmental documents under NEPA regulations.

▼

No

▼

Is proposed action one that normally requires an EIS under the agency's implementing procedures? ► No ► Prepare EA. 1508.9.

▼

Yes

▼

Is an EIS required in this situation? ► Not clearly so ► Prepare EA. 1508.9.

▼

Yes ─────────────────► Begin EIS process.

PHASE III: What to do with the EA.

Does EA indicate that EIS required? ► No ► Prepare FONSI. 1501.4(e), 1508.13.*

▼

Yes ─────────────────► Begin EIS process.

PHASE IV: EIS process.**

1. Institute scoping. 1501.7.
2. Produce and circulate Draft EIS. Part 1502, 1502.9, 1502.19.
3. Obtain comments. Part 1503, 1506.6.
4. Prepare Final EIS. Part 1502, 1502.9.***
5. Prepare Record of Decision. 1505.2.
6. Take action. See 1505.3, 1506.1, 1506.7, 1506.10.

---

* If proposed action is one that normally requires an EIS or is without precedent, CEQ's regulations require that the FONSI be made available to the public for a period of 30 days before a determination whether to prepare an EIS is made. See 1501.4(e)(2).
** Part 1502 describes the EIS requirements in detail.
*** Prepare supplements to either Draft or Final EIS if necessary. 1502.9(c).

Environmental Assessment. Unless the decision has already been made to prepare an EIS, or the action is one determined under agency procedures to normally require an EIS, an agency usually begins the NEPA process by preparing an environmental assessment as required by the CEQ regulations.[391] The assessment is a public document and is used by the agency to help it determine whether to prepare an EIS, to facilitate preparation of the EIS if one is needed, and to aid in NEPA compliance if an EIS is not required. It must discuss the need for the proposed action, alternatives to the action, and the environmental impacts of the action and alternatives. Agencies and persons consulted must be listed; environmental agencies, project applicants, and the public are to be involved, to the extent practicable, in preparing the assessment. Assessment procedures vary among agencies. The Federal Highway Administration[392] and HUD,[393] for example, have specified and detailed procedural steps to meet, including when reassessments must be prepared. The U.S. Forest Service regulations, in contrast, merely require that an assessment be prepared; additional procedural steps are lacking.[394]

The Determination Not to Prepare an EIS. If on the basis of the environmental assessment, the federal agency decides that an EIS is not necessary, it must prepare a Finding of No Significant Impact[395] that must be made available to the affected public. If an EIS is not required, however, this finding must be prepared as early as possible in the agency's planning process in order to accompany the project proposal through the agency's review process before alternatives are foreclosed by decisions made.

Citing NEPA's "to the fullest extent possible" and "continuing responsibility" language, courts have generally held that compliance with the act is required for projects begun before NEPA's effective date, January 1, 1970, if the agency is still in a position to exercise control

---

391. 40 C.F.R. § 1501.4 (1981). "Environmental assessment" is defined at 40 C.F.R. § 1508.9.
392. 23 C.F.R. § 771.119 (1981).
393. 24 C.F.R. § 50.30 (1982).
394. 7 C.F.R. § 3100.30(b) (1982).
395. 40 C.F.R. § 1508.13 (1981).

over the outcome of the project.[396] (This issue is of declining relevance since few projects begun prior to 1970 are still under construction or consideration.) The rule of law should not be forgotten: so long as the agency can influence whether the project continues or not, it should prepare an EIS to support its decision.

Updating the Analysis of Impacts. One of the key issues stemming from the directive to comply with NEPA "to the fullest extent possible" concerns the agency's responsibilities when historic resources are discovered or agency plans are changed to affect historic resources during or after compliance with NEPA. This issue often arises in the preservation context because historic resources inventories are not complete in many areas and resources are often discovered or brought to the agency's attention after completion of an environmental assessment or EIS. Often, too, the officials responsible for NEPA compliance may not recognize the existence or value of the resources affected.

Section 1502.9(c) of the CEQ regulations offers some guidance in these situations. It states that the "[a]gencies (1) shall prepare supplements to either draft or final environmental impact statements if: (1) the agency makes substantial changes in the proposed action that are relevant to environmental concerns; or (2) there are significant new

---

396. In *Arlington Coalition on Transportation v. Volpe*, 458 F.2d 1323 (4th Cir. 1972), *cert. denied*, 409 U.S. 1000 (1972), plaintiffs sought an injunction barring planning and construction of a section of interstate highway pending compliance with NEPA and other statutes, although the project was begun before NEPA's effective date. The court held that NEPA did apply since the project had not reached the stage of completion where "the costs of altering or abandoning the project . . . so definitely outweigh whatever benefits that might accrue therefrom that it might no longer be possible to change the project in accordance with Section 102 of NEPA."

Similarly, in vacating the trial court's ruling that an EIS was not required for a Boston urban renewal project since the "major federal action" terminated with the signing of a Loan and Grant Contract in 1967, the court found that the lower court should have made detailed findings as to the control of the project HUD might have exercised under the contract and the nature of any future federal project aid and should have supported its conclusion that two amendments to the contract made after NEPA's effective date were not "major federal actions."

The court stated, "We would be reluctant not to find a continuing major federal involvement so long as it was established that HUD retained any significant discretionary powers as might permit it to effect an alteration of building or design plans to enhance the urban living environment." *Jones v. Lynn*, 477 F.2d 885, 890 (1st Cir. 1973). See also *Hart v. Denver Urban Renewal Authority*, 551 F.2d 1178 (10th Cir. 1975); *Boston Waterfront Residents Association v. Romney*, 343 F. Supp. 89 (D. Mass. 1972); *Aertsen v. Harris*, 467 F. Supp. 117 (D. Mass. 1979).

circumstances or information relevant to environmental concerns and bearing on the proposed action or its impacts." Thus the regulations lend support to the contention that a supplemental EIS is required in both of the above situations. The case law, however, is split.

In *Warm Springs Dam Task Force v. Gribble*,[397] the court stated that a federal agency has a continuing duty to gather and evaluate new information related to the environmental impact of its actions even after preparation of a satisfactory EIS. However, the court found that this did not mean supplementation of the EIS was required whenever new information becomes available. Instead, the agency must consider such information and determine whether it is significant enough to require a reexamination of impacts. The agency's decision not to supplement the EIS will be upheld if it is reasonable in light of such factors as the environmental significance of the new information, the care with which the information and its impact were evaluated, and the adequacy of the agency's documentation of its decision not to prepare a supplement.

WATCH v. Harris[398] involved an urban renewal project in Waterbury, Connecticut. HUD had determined that no EIS was required and a local preservation group sued HUD and the Waterbury urban renewal agency to compel compliance with NEPA and the NHPA after historically significant properties were found in the project area. The Second Circuit Court affirmed the lower court decision that, since HUD was required to approve acquisition and demolition of properties in the project area and since that approval was a major federal action, the agency retained significant control over the project. Therefore, once HUD received new information about potential National Register eligibility of properties in the area, it should have conducted a new "threshold determination," and if the determination revealed that eligible properties would be affected, an EIS would be required.

In contrast, in two other preservation suits, *Inman Park Restoration, Inc. v. Urban Mass Transit Administration*[399] and *Central Oklahoma Preservation Alliance, Inc. v. Oklahoma City Urban Renewal Authority*,[400] supplementary environmental review was not required after initial NEPA compliance. In *Inman Park*, the court refused to order preparation of a supplemental EIS evaluating alternatives to individual

---

397. 621 F.2d 1017 (9th Cir. 1980).
398. 603 F.2d 310 (2d Cir. 1979), *cert. denied*, 444 U.S. 995 (1979).
399. 414 F. Supp. 99 (N.D. Ga. 1976), *aff'd*, 576 F. 2d 573 (5th Cir. 1978).
400. 471 F. Supp. 68 (W.D. Okla. 1979).

components of the MARTA mass transit system where an adequate systemwide EIS had already been prepared.

In *Central Oklahoma*, the plaintiff sought to enjoin the demolition of the Hales Building in Oklahoma City as part of an urban renewal project. The court held that the unilateral determination by the Keeper of the National Register that the building was eligible for listing did not require HUD to undertake further environmental assessment of the project when the agency retained no discretionary authority in connection with the site and had fulfilled its responsibilities under NHPA and NEPA before the building was declared eligible for listing on the Register. The court explained its reasoning by saying that, if no assessment has ever been performed, it must be performed, at least where significant action remains to be taken by the federal agency, but that NEPA and its implementing regulations do not require reassessment of that which has been properly assessed.[401] This decision seems to conflict with the *WATCH* decision, and as an appeals court case, *WATCH* carries more weight. *WATCH* may be a more limited holding, however, since there was some question as to the adequacy of the consideration of historic resources. However, the entire *WATCH* decision is characterized by an expansive, liberal view of the applicability of NEPA and NHPA to continuing projects. This view was not adopted in *Central Oklahoma*, a case decided before the NEPA regulations clarified this issue in 1979.

The EIS Process

The EIS is usually prepared by the federal agency undertaking the action in question. If more than one federal agency is involved, one is designated the lead agency and the others serve as cooperating agencies for EIS purposes.

The agencies involved generally decide among themselves which will be the lead agency. If they disagree, factors including magnitude of each agency's involvement, project approval authority, expertise concerning the action's environmental effects, and duration and sequence of each agency's involvement are considered in making the choice. If they are unable to agree, the CEQ may be asked to designate a lead agency.[402]

---

401. The implementing regulations to which the court refers, *id*. at 83-84, are those found in 38 Fed. Reg. 19,181-95 (1973) (to be reprinted in HUD Handbook, 1390.1)
402. 40 C.F.R. § 1501.5 (1981).

Several provisions of NEPA and the CEQ regulations call for participation in the EIS process by various federal agencies and other parties. First, Section 102(2)(A) of NEPA requires federal agencies to "utilize a systematic, interdisciplinary approach which will insure the integrated use of the natural and social sciences and environmental design arts in planning and in decision making which may have an impact on man's environment." The EIS must include a list of its major preparers and their qualifications, and the disciplines of the preparers must be appropriate to the scope of the EIS.[403]

Second, on request of the lead agency, any federal agency which has jurisdiction by law shall be a cooperating agency, and any federal agency with "special expertise" regarding an issue to be addressed in the EIS may be made a cooperating agency for NEPA purposes.[404] State or local agencies with such expertise may also be made cooperating agencies. The cooperating agency may assume responsibility for developing information and preparing environmental analyses, including parts of the EIS, in its area of expertise. The lead agency then uses these analyses in preparing the EIS.

Finally, the lead agency must obtain comments on the draft EIS from any other federal agency with jurisdiction by law or special expertise with respect to any environmental impact involved.[405] The Interior Department and the ACHP are deemed to have "special expertise" on preservation matters.[406] Comments must also be requested from the applicant, appropriate state and federal agencies, involved Indian tribes, any agency that has asked to receive statements on the kind of action involved, and the public, in particular interested or affected persons or organizations. Federal agencies with jurisdiction regarding the impact must comment on the EIS or reply, "No comment." Comments from other parties are optional. Copies of all substantive comments received must be attached to the EIS. The agency preparing the EIS must assess and consider all comments and respond to each in the final EIS,[407] but there is no legal obligation to heed the comments or to avoid identified adverse effects.

---

403. *Id.* at § 1502.17.
404. *Id.* at § 1501.6.
405. *Id.*
406. See Council on Environmental Quality, *Environmental Quality—1978: The Ninth Annual Report* (Washington, D.C.: GPO, 1978), p. 521.
407. 40 C.F.R. § 1503 (1981).

Probably the most difficult issue that arises in determining who should prepare the EIS is that of delegation to a consultant or to a state or local agency. Generally, consultants may be used provided that they are chosen by the agency (rather than by the project developer, for example) and have no interest in the project's outcome and provided that the agency evaluates and retains responsibility for the EIS.[408]

The issue of delegation to a state or local agency arises primarily in two contexts. The first, delegation to a state agency of preparation of the EIS for a project funded through a program of grants to the states, is authorized and limited by Section 102(2)(D) of NEPA, added to the act in 1975. Such delegation commonly occurs in interstate highway projects receiving Federal Highway Administration funding.[409] Section 102(2)(D) states that the federal agency official must furnish guidance and participate in preparing the EIS and must independently evaluate it before approval and adoption. Thus, the federal agency remains responsible for preparation of an adequate EIS, regardless of delegation of much of the actual preparation to the state agency.[410]

The other context, and the one that is currently the more controversial, is HUD's delegation of NEPA responsibilities to local applicants for projects funded under Title I of the Housing and Community Development Act (HCDA) of 1974,[411] especially through the UDAG program. What is at stake in delegation is timing of the review and objectivity: Can an EIS prepared by a local applicant, after HUD has screened project proposals and preliminarily awarded UDAG funds for the undertaking, be expected to objectively evaluate the project's environmental impacts? And should not HUD, in its initial screening of project applications, be required to consider environmental factors through the NEPA process? The basis of the controversy is interpretation of the language of HCDA, as amended in 1977, and NEPA.

Section 104(h)(i) of the HCDA, creating the CDBG program, clearly authorized delegation of environmental review responsibilities for CDBG projects and other programs created by Title I of the 1974 act.

---

408. Some courts have found an EIS to be adequate even when prepared by a financially interested consultant, *Essex County Preservation Association v. Campbell*, 536 F.2d 956 (1st Cir. 1976), or with the involvement of the project's developer, *Sierra Club v. Lynn*, 502 F.2d 43 (5th Cir. 1974), *cert. denied*, 421 U.S. 994 (1975).

409. See, for example, *Conservation Society of Southern Vermont, Inc. v. Secretary of Transportation*, 531 F.2d 637 (2d Cir. 1976).

410. *Farmland Preservation Association v. Goldschmidt*, 611 F.2d 233 (8th Cir. 1979).

411. 42 U.S.C. §§ 5301-17 (1976).

The section is implemented by regulations found at 24 C.F.R. § 58.[412] When a 1977 amendment to the HCDA added the UDAG program to Title I, Section 104(h) was not amended to specifically include or exclude UDAG. The legislative history is not clear as to whether Congress intended to permit delegation of NEPA responsibilities in UDAG projects.

The language of NEPA and the CEQ regulations clearly make NEPA compliance the duty of the *federal* agencies. However, the CEQ regulations[413] do define federal agencies to include units of state and local government assuming NEPA responsibilities under Section 104(h) of the HCDA. On the other hand, Section 102(2)(C) of NEPA requires that *federal* agencies prepare EISs on proposals for major federal actions significantly affecting the quality of the human environment and that those statements *accompany proposals through the agency review process.* Further, Section 102 requires that "to the fullest extent possible . . . the policies, regulations, and public laws of the United States shall be interpreted and administered in accordance with the policies set forth in [NEPA]."

The CEQ has maintained that Section 104(h) may not authorize delegation in UDAG projects, since Title I was adopted before the UDAG program was created and was never amended to explicitly apply to UDAG.[414] The CEQ argues that when two statutes may be read as compatible that both (HCDA and NEPA) apply, and CEQ finds this interpretation is supported by the language of Section 102 of NEPA, quoted above. CEQ finds delegation of actual preparation of the EIS acceptable as long as the EIS is prepared before the local applicant applies for funds so that the EIS can accompany the application through HUD's decision-making process. Otherwise, HUD should prepare its own EIS in determining which UDAG proposals it will fund. These arguments are also advanced by plaintiffs challenging delegation.

---

412. The section requires that implementing regulations be issued only after consultation by the secretary of HUD with the CEQ. The CEQ never agreed to HUD's proposed regulations because they did not require UDAG applicants' documentation prepared pursuant to NEPA to accompany their proposals through HUD's application process. However, CEQ subsequently placed a notice in the *Federal Register* approving HUD's proposed regulations. 47 Fed. Reg. 9,270 (1982).

413. 40 C.F.R. § 1508.12 (1981).

414. An exchange of letters between CEQ and HUD on this issue can be found in Robinson, *Historic Preservation Law*. As noted above, CEQ subsequently put a notice in the *Federal Register* approving HUD's proposed regulations. 47 Fed. Reg. 9,270 (1982).

HUD, on the other hand, follows *Kirchner v. Kansas Turnpike Authority*,[415] which states that, in the absence of legislative history to the contrary, an amendment should be read with the provisions of the original statute as if they were enacted together. Since Section 110 of the HCDA of 1977 created the UDAG program as a new Section 119 of Title I of the 1974 HCDA, HUD maintains an expenditure under UDAG is an expenditure under Title I. HUD argues, therefore, that the clear language of the act and the HUD regulations require delegation of HUD's NEPA responsibilities to the project applicant for all programs for which funds are authorized by Title I, including UDAG. The agency claims that any other interpretation would abrogate delegation to the applicant and would lead to needless delay and wasted resources, since many projects for which applications are submitted are not funded.

To date, the courts have come out on HUD's side of the argument. For instance, in *National Center for Preservation Law v. Landrieu*,[416] the plaintiff preservation and community organizations sought to enjoin the city from beginning construction of a controversial convention center complex in a historic area of Charleston, South Carolina, and to enjoin the release of federal UDAG funds for the project based on allegations of improper delegation of NEPA responsibilities. Citing Section 104(h), especially the provision referring to "expenditure of funds *under this [chapter]*" (i.e., Title I), the legislative history of the HCDA and its amendments, and the *Kirchner* case cited above, the court concluded that "the delegation provision of Section 5304(h) [i.e., Section 104(h)] of the HCDA applies to all funds under Title I of the HCDA, including UDAG grants."[417] Then, citing *Colony Federal Savings and Loan Association v. Harris*,[418] the court continued:

> The scheme of this statutory provision allows an applicant to assume the responsibilities of the Secretary of HUD for the purposes of preparing an EIS, conducting all relevant studies, considering all reasonable alternatives, and in general preparing an EIS which adequately discusses the environmental effects and alternatives of the proposed project. Furthermore, once the applicant certifies that it has, in fact, carried out all of the necessary responsibilities in compliance with NEPA, the Secretary of HUD is also deemed to have satisfied all of his responsibilities under that Act. Accordingly, the actual review by HUD is limited

---

415. 336 F.2d 222, 230 (10th Cir. 1964).
416. 496 F. Supp. 716 (D.S.C. 1980), *aff'd*, 635 F.2d 324 (4th Cir. 1980).
417. *Id.* at 731.
418. 482 F. Supp. 296 (W.D. Pa. 1980).

to a determination that the applicant has followed all of the procedural requirements of the CEQ guidelines and the regulations found at 24 C.F.R. Part 58, in conducting its environmental review.[419]

Courts in other cases in which the timing of the EIS prepared by a delegate has been challenged have decided similarly.[420] *New Yorkers to Preserve the Theater District v. Landrieu* [421] stated that "release of funds, not preliminary approval [by HUD of an applicant's proposal,] [is] the critical event which requires environmental review as a prerequisite."

Preservation attorneys challenging delegation still maintain they have the better argument under Section 104(h) and NEPA. They argue that that the EIS should be prepared by the local applicant before submission of the grant application and should accompany the application through HUD's decision-making process. Where the locality is competent to prepare the EIS, it should do so. Delegation, according to preservationists, does not make sense if the locality is incompetent or prepares the EIS after decisions have been made. But, to date, courts disagree. UDAG litigation, therefore, will have to pursue other arguments to ensure that NEPA's requirements are fulfilled. Possible lines of argument include challenges under state environmental statutes, where they exist (see chapter 3); challenges to the applicant's procedural compliance; and challenges to the adequacy of the EIS. Challenges to the substantive exercise of discretion, however, are unlikely to prevail in view of the mood of the courts as evidenced by *Vermont Yankee* and *Strycker's Bay*.

Contents of the EIS

CEQ regulations divide the EIS into three sections: first, alternatives including the proposed action;[422] second, description of the affected

---

419. 496 F. Supp. 716, 731 (D.S.C. 1980).
420. See, e.g., *Colony Federal Savings & Loan Association v. Harris*, 482 F. Supp. 296 (W.D. Pa. 1980); *Crosby v. Young*, 512 F. Supp. 1363 (E.D. Mich. 1981), also involving a HUD Section 108 loan guarantee; *New Yorkers to Preserve the Theater District v. Landrieu*, 661 F.2d 910 (2d Cir. 1981). See also, *Natural Resources Defense Council, Inc. v. New York City*, 528 F.2d 1245 (S.D.N.Y. 1981); 672 F.2d 292 (2d Cir. 1982).
421. 661 F.2d 910 (2d Cir. 1981).
422. 40 C.F.R. § 1502.14 (1981).

environment;[423] and third, environmental consequences.[424]

Discussion of alternatives to the proposed action is the linchpin of the EIS.[425] CEQ regulations state that the agency must rigorously explore and evaluate all reasonable alternatives to the proposed action. The discussion must be sufficiently detailed to allow reviewers to evaluate the merits of the alternatives presented. Reasonable alternatives not within the agency's jurisdiction and the alternative of no action must be considered. Remote and speculative alternatives need not be discussed,[426] but the agency must give reasons for having eliminated alternatives from detailed study. Alternatives that would require legislative implementation or offer only a partial solution to the problem are not exempt from consideration.[427]

The agency's preferred alternative must be identified, and appropriate mitigation measures must be discussed. The EIS should present the impacts of the proposed action and its alternatives in comparative form so that the EIS defines issues and provides a clear basis for choosing among them. Both environmental impacts and secondary social and economic impacts must be addressed.[428]

Overall, the discussion of alternatives is subject to a rule of reason.[429] Perfection is not required of the agency, but it must take a "hard look" at the action's environmental consequences with good faith objectivity.[430] What is required is information sufficient to permit a reasoned choice of alternatives.[431]

Generally, courts determine whether discussion of alternatives is adequate by looking at the nature and scale of the proposed project. For instance, the plaintiffs in *Wisconsin Heritages, Inc. v. Harris*[432] sued to enjoin demolition, as part of an urban renewal project, of an 1888 Richardsonian Romanesque mansion, listed in the National Register,

---

423. *Id.* at § 1502.15.

424. *Id.* at § 1502.16.

425. *Monroe County Conservation Council, Inc. v. Volpe*, 472 F.2d 693, 697-98 (2d Cir. 1972).

426. *Natural Resources Defense Council, Inc. v. Morton*, 458 F.2d 827, 838 (D.C. Cir. 1972).

427. *Id.* at 836, 837.

428. *Image of Greater San Antonio, Texas v. Brown*, 570 F.2d 517 (5th Cir. 1978).

429. 458 F.2d 827, 834 (D.C. Cir. 1972).

430. *Environmental Defense Fund, Inc. v. Corps of Engineers*, 470 F.2d 289, 296 (8th Cir. 1972), *cert. denied*, 412 U.S. 931 (1973).

431. 458 F.2d 827, 836 (D.C. Cir. 1972).

432. 460 F. Supp. 1120 (E.D. Wis. 1978).

pending preparation of an EIS regarding the demolition. The court required that the EIS consider alternatives only to demolition, not to the larger project. The court did, however, require that relocation of the building be explored.[433]

In *Keith v. Volpe*,[434] the court enjoined construction of a freeway pending preparation of an EIS for the project. It directed the Federal Highway Administration to "consider all possible alternatives to the proposed freeway, including changes in design, changes in the route, different systems of transportation and even abandonment of the project entirely." And in *Inman Park*, the court, in finding that the EIS prepared for the entire MARTA mass transit system adequately discussed alternatives, stated that "[to] a large extent the reasonableness and sufficiency of discussion of alternatives in the EIS is governed by the scope of the EIS. . . . [A]lternatives should be geared to alternatives to the entire project and not necessarily to individual components within the project."[435]

Environmental Consequences

The EIS section on environmental consequences provides the basis for comparing alternatives. The discussion must focus on environmental impacts and unavoidable adverse effects of the proposed action, the action vis-a-vis the relationship between short-term uses of the environment and long-term productivity, and on any irretrievable commitments of resources demanded by the action. It must address direct and indirect impacts of the action and alternatives, cumulative impacts, possible conflicts between the action and other land-use plans for the area

---

433. In subsequent litigation, after an EIS was prepared, *Wisconsin Heritages, Inc. v. Harris*, 490 F. Supp. 1334 (E.D. Wis. 1980), the court found HUD's consideration of alternatives adequate where alternatives considered included no federal action, approval of federal financing of the demolition without modification of project plans, approval of federal financing only after documentation and removal of significant artifacts, on-site adaptive use of the mansion, and relocation and adaptive use of the mansion. Citing *Vermont Yankee Nuclear Power Corp. v. Natural Resources Defense Council, Inc.*, 435 U.S . 519, 553, 555 (1978), the court noted that the adequacy of the EIS must be judged in light of the information available to the agency at the time it was prepared.

434. 352 F. Supp. 1324 (C.D. Cal. 1972).

435. 414 F. Supp. 99, 115 (N.D. Ga. 1976), *aff'd*, 576 F.2d 573 (5th Cir. 1978).

(arguably including preservation plans, where they exist), and possible mitigation measures.[436]

Adequacy

Inadequacy of the EIS is not a favored claim by courts, but the EIS should be scrutinized for conceptual errors, failure to identify or assess alternatives, failure to compare post project with preproject conditions, and failure to assess cultural resources. To evaluate the adequacy of the discussion of environmental consequences and alternatives, one must first determine the scope of the action for the purposes of the EIS. The CEQ regulations[437] direct agencies to consider three kinds of actions in determining the proper scope. *Connected* actions, including those that trigger or are dependent on other actions or are interdependent parts of a larger action, should be discussed in one EIS. *Cumulative* actions should also be discussed in one EIS. *Similar* actions may be analyzed in one EIS. This should be done if it will best facilitate consideration of impacts or alternatives.

The question of the proper scope of the EIS has often arisen in cases involving federally assisted highway projects. Concern developed in the early 1970s over a phenomenon called "segmenting," in which it appeared that, for NEPA purposes, federal agencies were breaking planned highway projects into short segments, the environmental impacts of which did not adequately reflect the impact of the entire project. In other cases, portions of Federal Aid Highways were being funded with state funds to avoid NEPA compliance. The courts have rejected both of these practices.[438]

Several highway suits have generated criteria for determining the proper scope of the action. *River v. Richmond Metropolitan Authority*[439] stated that "[i]n order to determine . . . when a group of segments should be classified as a single project for purposes of federal law, a court must look to a multitude of factors, including the manner in which the roads were planned, their geographic locations, and the utility of each in the absence of the other." More recently, the court in *Lange*

---

436. 40 C.F.R. § 1502.16 (1981).
437. *Id.* at § 1508.25.
438. *Indian Lookout Alliance v. Volpe*, 484 F.2d 11 (8th Cir. 1973); *Named Individual Members of San Antonio Conservation Society v. Texas Highway Department*, 446 F.2d 1013 (5th Cir. 1971), *cert. denied*, 406 U.S. 933 (1972).
439. 359 F. Supp. 611 (E.D. Va. 1973), *aff'd*, 481 F.2d 1280 (4th Cir. 1973).

v. Brinegar[440] adopted the four-part test set forth in *Daly v. Volpe*[441] for determining when segmentation is appropriate: the segment must first be a substantial length of highway connecting "logical termini," such as major population centers or crossroads; second, have "independent utility"; third, make possible adequate consideration of alternatives; and fourth, fulfill important state and local needs.

The proper scope of the EIS is an issue in other situations as well. Although reviewing the case law gives one some sense of proper scope in various situations, generalizing is difficult. In two urban renewal cases, *Hart v. Denver Urban Renewal Authority*[442] and *Wisconsin Heritages, Inc. v. Harris*,[443] the courts ruled that the EIS needed to evaluate only the proposed effect of the federal action on individual historic structures and not on the entire project. In both cases no EIS had been prepared and the project work was well underway when the suit was brought; hence, the object of the suits was to compel preparation of an EIS for the individual structures. These factors weighed heavily in the courts' decisions.

In several other cases, however, courts have recommended or required a comprehensive approach to the EIS. For instance, in *Jones v. Lynn*,[444] the plaintiffs sought to enjoin a continuing urban renewal project in Boston, Massachusetts, for which no EIS had been prepared. The court stated in dictum that, since HUD would be evaluating mortgage insurance applications for virtually every new building in the area, it appeared that one comprehensive study of the uncompleted aspects of the project would be most consistent with NEPA's objective of evaluating the cumulative impacts of federal actions. The court also noted that a comprehensive approach would conserve bureaucratic resources and prevent a multiplicity of litigation. The case was remanded to the district court for further proceedings.

In *City of Rochester v. United States Postal Service*,[445] the issue of scope arose in the context of whether the city had standing to sue the U.S. Postal Service for failing to prepare an EIS for construction of a suburban postal facility and abandonment of the old urban facility and

---

440. 625 F.2d 812 (9th Cir. 1980).
441. 514 F.2d 1106 (9th Cir. 1975).
442. 551 F.2d 1178 (10th Cir. 1977).
443. 460 F. Supp. 1120 (E.D. Wis. 1978).
444. 477 F.2d 885 (1st Cir. 1973).
445. 541 F.2d 967 (2d Cir. 1976).

transfer of employees, which, the city alleged, would result in increased urban blight and decay in downtown Rochester. The court rejected the U.S. Postal Service's contention that construction of the new facility and abandonment of the old were "entirely separate and apart," stating that NEPA does not "permit noncomprehensive consideration of a project divisible into smaller parts, each of which taken alone does not have a significant impact but which taken as a whole has cumulative significant impact."

Kleppe v. Sierra Club[446] offers further guidance regarding whether a comprehensive EIS is required. In *Kleppe*, plaintiffs sought to compel preparation of an EIS for coal development in the entire Great Plains region. The court held that a regional EIS was not required because there had been no proposal for a major federal action of regional scope, and that, although a comprehensive EIS must be prepared if several related proposals pending concurrently before an agency will have cumulative or synergistic environmental effects on a region, plaintiffs in that case did not demonstrate that failure to prepare a regional EIS was arbitrary.

Other Compliance Provisions of NEPA

Although the EIS process forms the heart of NEPA, Section 102(2) places additional duties on federal agencies. Thus, agencies must use a systematic, interdisciplinary approach to planning and decision making;[447] develop methods to ensure that environmental values are appropriately considered in decision making;[448] and study, develop, and describe alternatives to proposals involving unresolved conflicts over resource use,[449] even if the threshold requirements for preparation of an EIS are not met.[450] Since one of NEPA's goals is disclosure to the public of environmental impacts of proposed federal actions, public involvement in the EIS process is essential. The CEQ regulations require agencies to involve the public in preparing the environmental assessment, invite comments from the public on the draft EIS, and respond to those comments in the final EIS; solicit information from the public;

---

446. 427 U.S. 390 (1976).
447. 42 U.S.C. § 4332(2)(A) (1976).
448. *Id.* at § 4332(2)(B).
449. *Id.* at § 4332(2)(E).
450. *Hanly v. Kleindienst*, 471 F.2d 823 (2d Cir. 1972), *cert. denied*, 412 U.S. 408 (1973).

hold hearings where and when appropriate; provide public notice of hearings and make the EIS and related documents available to the public.[451]

Agency Decision Making

Agency decision making is the final part of the EIS process. The CEQ regulations require agencies to adopt procedures to ensure that their decisions are made in accordance with policies of NEPA.[452] The EIS comments and responses must accompany the proposal through the agency's decision-making process to ensure that they are actually used. The agency must consider the alternatives discussed in arriving at a decision. As noted earlier, however, courts have been reluctant to support substantive NEPA claims. Further, the language of NEPA requires decisions to be environmentally sound only if "consistent with other essential considerations of national policy."[453]

To ensure that an agency decision reflects the environmental considerations discussed in the EIS, the agency must prepare a public record of decision, including the alternatives that were considered, which alternatives were environmentally preferable, the nonenvironmental factors that were balanced in making the decision, whether all practicable means to minimize environmental harm had been adopted, and if they were not, why not.[454] Agencies may provide for monitoring and must attach conditions to grants, permits, funding, and other actions, if necessary, to be sure their decisions are carried out.

If an EIS has been prepared and an agency has decided to take action that would destroy a historic or archaeologically significant resource, the agency's record of decision is of vital importance to groups opposed to the action because it may help establish that the action was arbitrary or capricious and hence subject to reversal by a court.[455]

---

451. 40 C.F.R. §§ 1501.4(b), 1506.6 (1981). See also cases including *Save the Courthouse Committee v. Lynn*, 408 F. Supp. 1323, 1342 (S.D.N.Y. 1975); *Lathan v. Volpe*, 350 F. Supp. 262, 265 (W.D. Wash. 1972); *Colony Federal Savings & Loan Association v. Harris*, 482 F. Supp. 296 (W.D. Pa. 1980).
452. 40 C.F.R. § 1505.1 (1981).
453. 42 U.S.C. § 4331(b) (1976).
454. 40 C.F.R. § 1505.2 (1981).
455. 5 U.S.C. § 706(2)(A) (1976).

Mitigation

NEPA may also help to avoid adverse environmental impacts through its provisions regarding mitigation.[456] In both its discussion of alternatives and its evaluation of environmental consequences of the proposed action, the EIS must discuss appropriate means to mitigate adverse impacts.[457] In its record of decision, prepared pursuant to 40 C.F.R. § 1505.2, the agency must "state whether all practicable means to avoid or minimize environmental harm from the alternative selected have been adopted, and if not, why they were not."[458] However, at no point do the regulations require agencies to adopt measures under consideration.[459] In a series of cases, the U.S. Supreme Court has held that NEPA requires the consideration of environmental consequences and less damaging alternatives, but the statute does not require the actual adoption of actions posing less adverse consequences.[460] In short, while agencies must closely adhere to NEPA's procedural mandate to effect a better decision-making process, this mandate does not obligate agencies to actually produce more environmentally sensitive decisions.[461]

On the other hand, CEQ regulation Section 1505.3 requires that agencies shall implement mitigation steps committed to as part of their decisions.

To date, no court has had the opportunity to interpret Section 1505.3. As of this writing, no court has held mitigation commitments to be enforceable. Thus, CEQ's provision is the only support for enforcement. While this area may be a promising avenue of law for the preservation attorney, it should be noted that a few courts have held nonmitigation

---

456. "Mitigation" is defined at 40 C.F.R. § 1508.20 (1981).

457. *Id.* at §§ 1502.14(f), 1502.16(h).

458. See also *id.* at §§ 1502.14(f), 1502.16(h), 1503.3(d), 1502.2(i).

459. The regulations do require agencies to state in the public record of its decision mitigation measures adopted or reasons for nonadoption. *Id.* at §§ 1502.14(f), 1502.16(h).

460. *Stryker's Bay Neighborhood Council, Inc. v. Karlen*, 444 U.S. 223, 227-28 (1980); *Vermont Yankee Nuclear Power Corp. v. Natural Resources Defense Council, Inc.*, 435 U.S. 519 (1978); *Kleppe v. Sierra Club*, 427 U.S. 390 (1976).

461. Of course, agencies are still subject to the "arbitrary, capricious, an abuse of discretion or otherwise not in accordance with law" standard of the Administrative Procedures Act, 5 U.S.C. § 706(2)(A) (1976).

commitments in the EIS to be unenforceable.[462]

Before seeking judicial support for Section 1505.3, environmental public interest litigants should consider the anomalous consequences of success. Agencies might be less likely to include mitigation measures as part of their formal decision if the measures can be judicially enforced. The result may be fewer mitigation commitments in the EIS. Yet, public participation during the comment process and during final stages of preparing the draft EIS can be very influential in forcing an agency to make commitments to undertake certain mitigation measures. Thus, if interest groups stay involved during the comment process and earlier, they can help ensure that agencies will not back off on mitigation.

Judicial Review under NEPA

Since NEPA's inception, judicial review of agency actions has played an essential role in ensuring compliance with the act. Generally the courts employ a conventional standard of judicial review of administrative agency decisions, that is, full review of procedural compliance, with review of substantive compliance limited to the "arbitrary and capricious" standard of Section 706(2)(A) of the Administrative Procedure Act.[463]

The duty of federal agencies to comply with NEPA's procedural requirements "to the fullest extent possible," set forth in Section 102 of the act, is clear. As stated by Judge Skelly Wright in his often-cited opinion in *Calvert Cliffs' Coordinating Committee, Inc. v. United States Atomic Energy Commission*,[464] in discussion of procedural compliance with NEPA:

> Thus the general substantive policy of the Act is a flexible one. It leaves room for a responsible exercise of discretion and may not require particular substantive results in particular problematic instances. However, the Act also contains very important "procedural" provisions—provisions which are designed to see

---

462. See Comment, *Enforcing the Commitments Made in Impact Statements: A Proposed Passage through a Thicket of Case Law*, 10 Envtl. L. Rep. (Envtl. L. Inst.) 10,153 (1980); *Noe v. Metropolitan Atlanta Rapid Transit Authority*, 485 F. Supp. 501 (N.D. Ga. 1980), *aff'd on other grounds*, 644 F.2d 434 (5th Cir. 1981); *City of Blue Ash v. McClucas*, 596 F.2d 709 (6th Cir. 1979); *Ogunquit Village Corp. v. Davis*, 553 F.2d 243 (1st Cir. 1977). For a comparison of mitigation provisions in NEPA and the Fish and Wildlife Coordination Act, see Michael Veiluva, *The Fish and Wildlife Coordination Act in Environmental Litigation*, 9 Ecology L.Q. 489, 506-7 (1981).
463. 5 U.S.C. § 706(2)(A) (1976).
464. 449 F.2d 1109 (D.C. Cir. 1971).

that all federal agencies do in fact exercise the substantive discretion given them. These provisions are not highly flexible. Indeed, they establish a strict standard of compliance.[465]

And according to one NEPA expert, "the procedural provisions of Section 102 of NEPA are enforced with a vengeance."[466]

Substantive review by courts of agency decisions under NEPA is much more limited, but such reviews do exist. The current standards for substantive review of agency actions under NEPA are set forth in the U.S. Supreme Court's decision in *Strycker's Bay Neighborhood Council, Inc. v. Karlen*.[467] In a *per curiam* opinion with Justice Marshall dissenting, the U.S. Supreme Court cited its decision in *Vermont Yankee Nuclear Power Corp. v. Natural Resources Defense Council, Inc.*[468] that:

> NEPA, while establishing "significant substantive goals for the Nation," imposes upon agencies duties that are "essentially procedural." As we stressed in . . . [*Vermont Yankee*], NEPA was designed "to insure a fully-informed and well-considered decision," but not necessarily "a decision the judges of the Court of Appeals or of this court would have reached had they been members of the decisionmaking unit of the agency. *Vermont Yankee* cuts sharply against the Court of Appeals' conclusion that an agency, in selecting a course of action, must elevate environmental concerns over other appropriate considerations. On the contrary, once an agency has made a decision subject to NEPA's procedural requirements, the only role for a court is to insure that the agency has considered the environmental consequences; it cannot "interject itself within the area of discretion of the executive as to the choice of the action to be taken."[469]

This does not imply, however, that substantive judicial review is nonexistent. Indeed, "[t]he Supreme Court reiterated principles that it laid down in previous cases involving NEPA review of agency action."[470]

In defining the scope of substantive review, the court cited its 1976 decision in *Kleppe v. Sierra Club*,[471] which emphasized that, although decisions as to actions to be taken will be left to the discretion of the

---

465. *Id.* at 1112.
466. Rodgers, *Handbook on Environmental Law*, p. 717.
467. 444 U.S. 223 (1980).
468. 435 U.S. 519 (1978).
469. 444 U.S. 223, 227-28 (1980), quoting *Kleppe V. Sierra Club*, 427 U.S. 390, 410 n.21 (1976).
470. Council on Environmental Quality, *1980 Annual Report*, p. 374.
471. 427 U.S. 390, 411 n.21 (1976).

agency, judicial review is to "insure that the agency has taken a 'hard look' at environmental consequences."[472]

In addition, the courts may set aside agency actions where there is substantial evidence in the record that the decision is arbitrary and capricious as tested by the Administrative Procedure Act. In determining whether an agency decision is arbitrary and capricious, the court is to consider "whether the decision was based on a consideration of relevant factors and whether there has been a clear error in judgment."[473] Regarding NEPA decisions, CEQ has written that:

> *Strycker's Bay* does not change the reviewing court's duty to make a "searching and careful" judicial inquiry to determine agency compliance with NEPA; to ensure that the agency has taken a "hard look" at the environmental effect of its proposal; or, in appropriate cases, to set aside or modify agency action that is arbitrary, capricious, or an abuse of discretion; or to set aside or modify agency action in cases in which there are "substantial procedural or substantive reasons as mandated by statute."[474]

In the area of historic preservation, as in other areas, NEPA does not require that a federal agency take or refrain from taking any particular action; its provisions do not forbid demolition of significant buildings or neighborhoods. However, review under NEPA can ensure that federal projects do not proceed until their impact on historic resources has been fully considered.

Remedies

Remedies for NEPA violations include stipulated settlements, consent decrees, and, most commonly, injunctions.[475] No one standard is followed by all courts in issuing preliminary injunctions. One theory provides environmental interests related to health with special judicial

---

472. But several cases have upheld substantive rights under NEPA. See, e.g., *Environmental Defense Fund, Inc. v. Corps of Engineers*, 470 F .2d 289, 297-301 (8th Cir. 1972), *cert. denied*, 421 U.S. 931 (1973); *Inman Park Restoration, Inc. v. Urban Mass Transit Administration*, 414 F. Supp. 99, 112 (N.D. Ga. 1976), *aff'd*, 576 F.2d 573 (5th Cir. 1978).
473. *Citizens to Preserve Overton Park v. Volpe*, 401 U.S. 402, 416 (1971).
474. Rodgers, *Handbook on Environmental Law*, p. 744.
475. For a fuller discussion of appropriate remedies in environmental law cases, see *id.* at 798-809.

302   A HANDBOOK ON HISTORIC PRESERVATION LAW

protection.[476] Indeed, some federal courts have held that any NEPA violation justifies issuing a preliminary injunction.[477] Most courts, however, balance the equities[478] and focus on three requirements[479]

---

476. *Environmental Defense Fund, Inc. v. Ruckelshaus*, 439 F .2d 584, 597-98 (D.C. Cir. 1971), clearly calls for special judicial protection: "[C]ourts are increasingly asked to review administrative action that touches on fundamental personal interests in life, health, and liberty. These interests have always had a special claim to judicial protection in comparison with the economic interests at stake in a ratemaking or licensing proceeding." Accord, *Ethyl Corp. v. Environmental Protection Agency*, 541 F.2d 1, 24 (D.C. Cir. 1976), special judicial interest in health and welfare. The validity of a special judicial interest in environmental issues is debatable after *Vermont Yankee Nuclear Power Corp. v. Natural Resources Defense Council, Inc.*, 435 U.S. 519 (1978) and *Stryker's Bay Neighborhood Council v. Karlen*, 444 U.S. 223 (1980).
477. *Warm Springs Dam Task Force v. Gribble*, 565 F.2d 549, 551 (9th Cir. 1977), standards for granting injunctive relief more liberal than other litigation; *Alpine Lakes Protection Society v. Schlapfer*, 518 F.2d 1089 (9th Cir. 1975), absent unusual circumstances, equities will not be balanced in NEPA cases, since NEPA's policy favors suspending all action until the act's requirements are met; *Environmental Defense Fund, Inc. v. Froehlke*, 477 F.2d 1033 (8th Cir. 1973)(dictum); *Lathan v. Volpe*, 455 F.2d 1111, 1116 (9th Cir. 1971), traditional equity principles do not apply when effecting a declared congressional policy; *State of California v. Bergland*, 483 F. Supp. 465, 498 (E.D. Cal. 1980), "Normally, once a substantial NEPA violation has been shown, an injunction should issue without detailed consideration of traditional equity principles"; *Brooks v. Volpe*, 350 F. Supp. 269, 282 (W.D. Wash. 1972), *aff'd*, 487 F.2d 1344 (9th Cir. 1973). Contra *Citizens for Responsible Area Growth v. Adams*, 477 F. Supp. 994, 1005 (D.N.H. 1979), "I do not believe that there should be an ironclad rule that whenever there has been any kind of violation of NEPA, an injunction must issue," quoting *Essex County Preservation Association v. Campbell*, 399 F. Supp. 208, 218 (D. Mass. 1975) (Bownes, J., by designation), *aff'd*, 536 F.2d 956 (1st Cir. 1976); *City of Romulus v. County of Wayne*, 392 F. Supp. 578, 594 (E.D. Mich. 1975); *Kleppe v. Sierra Club*, 427 U.S. 390, 407-8 (1976) (dictum), equities must be weighed to justify injunction.
478. *Conservation Society of Southern Vermont, Inc. v. Secretary of Transportation*, 508 F.2d 927, 933-34 (2d Cir. 1974), through equitable principles courts can deny injunctions even if deviations from prescribed NEPA procedures have occurred; *City of Romulus v. County of Wayne*, 392 F. Supp. 578, 594-95 (E.D. Mich. 1975), general principles of equity will control court's discretion in issuing injunction for NEPA violations; *Environmental Defense Fund, Inc. v. Armstrong*, 352 F. Supp. 50, 60 (N.D. Cal. 1972).
479. *National Wildlife Federation v. Adams,* 629 F.2d 587, 590 (9th Cir. 1980); *Sierra Club v. Hathaway*, 579 F.2d 1162 (9th Cir. 1978); *Warm Springs Task Force v. Gribble*, 565 F.2d 549, 551 (9th Cir. 1977). Other courts require the same elements but phrase them as four criteria by requiring plaintiffs first to prove irreparable injury and then to prove that injury in absence of an injunction outweighs the foreseeable harm of the injunction to the defendant. *Piedmont Heights Civic Club, Inc. v.*

before issuing a preliminary injunction: (1) the petitioner's likelihood of success on the merits;[480] (2) the balance of irreparable harm;[481] and (3) the injunction's effect on the public interest.[482] Courts have also granted injunctions under an alternative test that directs movants to prove "either a combination of probable success and the possibility of irreparable injury or that serious questions are raised and the balance of hardship tips sharply in their favor."[483]

Moreland, 637 F.2d 430, 435 (5th Cir. 1981); *Mason County Medical Association v. Knebel*, 563 F.2d 256, 261 (6th Cir. 1977); *Canal Authority of the State of Florida v. Callaway*, 489 F.2d 567 (5th Cir. 1974); *Highland Cooperative v. City of Lansing*, 492 F. Supp. 1372, 1381 (W.D. Mich. 1980).

480. *Friends of the Earth, Inc. v. Coleman*, 518 F.2d 323, 330 (9th Cir. 1975).

481. *Minnesota Public Interest Research Group v. Butz*, 498 F.2d 1314, 1323 (8th Cir. 1974), if timber cutting continued while the EIS was being prepared, court would be engaging in an "exercise of futility"; *Canal Authority of the State of Florida v. Callaway*, 489 F.2d 567, 574 (5th Cir. 1974); *Lathan v. Volpe*, 455 F.2d 1111, 1117 (9th Cir. 1971), "[u]nless the plaintiffs receive *now* whatever relief they are entitled to, there is danger that it will be of little or no value to them or to anyone else when finally obtained"; *Texas Committee on Natural Resources v. Bergland*, 433 F. Supp. 1235, 1254 (E.D. Tex. 1977), *rev'd on other grounds*, 573 F.2d 201 (5th Cir. 1978), *cert. denied*, 439 U.S. 966 (1978), clear cutting activity posing irreparable injury warrants injunctive relief; *Save the Courthouse Committee v. Lynn*, 408 F. Supp. 1323, 1343 (S.D.N.Y. 1975), demolishing courthouse is irreparable injury justifying injunctive relief; *Sierra Club v. Morton*, 421 F. Supp. 638 (D.D.C. 1974), injunction denied because no showing of irreparable injury; *Boston Waterfront Residents Association v. Romney*, 343 F. Supp. 89, 91 (D. Mass. 1972); *Sierra Club v. Mason*, 351 F. Supp. 419, 427 (D. Conn. 1972).

482. *Warm Springs Dam Task Force v. Gribble*, 565 F.2d 549, 551 (9th Cir. 1977); *Steubing v. Brinegar*, 511 F.2d 489, 492 (2d Cir. 1975), public interest considerations may support issuance of a preliminary injunction; *Action for Rational Transit v. West Side Highway Project*, 517 F. Supp. 1342, 1344 (S.D.N.Y. 1981), financial injury to city caused by injunction outweighs plaintiff's interest in obtaining injunction; *Society for the Protection of New Hampshire Forests v. Brinegar*, 381 F. Supp. 282 (D.N.H. 1974), key issue for preliminary injunction in any environmental law case is the long-range public interest.

483. *Sierra Club v. Hathaway*, 579 F.2d 1162, 1167 n.7 (9th Cir. 1978), quoting *Wm. Inglis & Sons Baking Co. v. ITT Continental Baking Co.*, 526 F.2d 86, 88 (9th Cir. 1975). The *Hathaway* court only assumed, for the purpose of the case before it, that the alternative test applied to environmental cases and was careful not to decide the issue. See also *Aleknagik Natives Limited v. Andrus*, 648 F.2d 496, 502 (9th Cir. 1980). In an Alaska Native Claims Settlement Act action, the court applied an alternative test, writing that the plaintiff need not show "as robust a likelihood of success on the merits, although the plaintiff must at a minimum have a fair chance of success on the merits"; *Action for Rational Transit v. West Side Highway Project*, 517 F. Supp. 1342, 1343-44, (S.D.N.Y. 1981).

In addition to balancing equities, courts will examine specific circumstances of a case. Relevant to the court's injunction inquiry are the availability of feasible alternatives,[484] the project's stage of completion,[485] the threat of irreparable or serious harm,[486] and an agency's recalcitrance or good faith in complying with the law.[487] Preservation cases generally present the threat of irreparable injury through demolition activities; therefore, plaintiffs should ordinarily receive injunctions so long as their action has any likelihood of success on the merits.

Moreover, courts can enjoin federal as well as nonfederal parties in partnership with the federal government from working on projects that might violate NEPA.[488] Although courts can enjoin all work on a project (not just those with adverse environmental impacts),[489] they have allowed planning and design activities,[490] construction on cleared land,[491] voluntary property acquisition,[492] and the completion of work on ex-

---

484. *Sierra Club v. Mason*, 351 F. Supp. 419, 427 (D. Conn. 1972), "reasonable possibility that adequate consideration of alternatives might disclose some realistic course of action with less risk of damage."

485. *Ogunquit Village Corp. v. Davis*, 553 F.2d 243, 245 (1st Cir. 1977), because there is no NEPA application to projects, an advanced effect on future federal decision making is foreclosed; *City of Rochester v. United States Postal Service*, 541 F.2d 967 (2d Cir. 1976), for a project 18 percent completed, the remaining work poses few environmental problems; *Steubing v. Brinegar*, 511 F.2d 489, 496 (2d Cir. 1975); *Sierra Club v. Alexander*, 484 F. Supp. 455, 473 (N.D.N.Y. 1980), *aff'd*, 633 F.2d 206 (2d Cir. 1980), work was so far along that an injunction would be more harmful than letting the work continue.

486. *Atchison, Topeka & Santa Fe Railway v. Calloway*, 382 F. Supp 610, 624 (D.D.C. 1974); *Steubing v. Brinegar*, 511 F.2d 489 (2d Cir. 1975).

487. *Brooks v. Volpe*, 350 F. Supp. 269, 283 (W.D. Wash. 1972).

488. *Friends of the Earth, Inc. v. Coleman*, 518 F.2d 323 (9th Cir. 1975); *Biderman v. Morton*, 497 F.2d 1141 (2d Cir. 1974); *Silva v. Romney*, 473 F.2d 287, 289-92 (1st Cir. 1973), one in partnership with federal government can be prohibited from acting in a certain manner; *Save the Courthouse Committee v. Lynn*, 408 F. Supp. 1323, 1346 (S.D.N.Y. 1975), even though NHPA and NEPA do not apply to a local agency, the court can enjoin an agency from demolishing a historic courthouse.

489. *Sansom Committee v. Lynn*, 382 F. Supp. 1242, 1245 (E.D. Pa. 1974), the trial court's discretion to halt all or partial work; *Natural Resources Defense Council, Inc. v. Grant*, 341 F. Supp. 356 (E.D.N.C. 1972).

490. *Environmental Defense Fund, Inc. v. Froehlke*, 477 F.2d 1033, 1036 (8th Cir. 1973).

491. *Conservation Council of North Carolina v. Froehlke*, 473 F.2d 664 (4th Cir. 1973); *Brooks v. Volpe*, 350 F. Supp. 287, 290 (W.D. Wash. 1972).

492. 477 F.2d 1033, 1036 (8th Cir. 1973).

isting contracts[493] to proceed.

Summary

NEPA provides procedural protections for historic and cultural resources but shares some of NHPA's weaknesses and limitations. While NEPA applies to a broader range of historic and cultural resources than does NHPA, NHPA applies to a broader range of federal actions and effects than does NEPA. Together, the two laws appear to apply to all historic and cultural resources affected by any federal action. However, neither law requires that agencies make decisions that always protect cultural resources.

The two laws reinforce each other and can be used effectively in tandem: if NHPA does not apply to a historic resource, NEPA might. While some courts may hold that agencies need not continue to comply with NHPA after a federal project has commenced, courts have generally agreed that NEPA does apply in such situations. If NHPA is weakened through funding cuts and revisions to the federal regulations of the ACHP, NEPA can still be used to compel agencies to consider historic properties.

Perhaps the major strength of the two laws is that both can temporarily postpone commencement of a harmful project while compliance takes place. Further, both laws fit easily into a framework of state and local statutes and ordinances to encourage comprehensive planning. NEPA ties neatly to state "little" NEPAs, and the federal preservation program of NHPA dovetails nicely with operations of state historic preservation offices and local survey, designation, and regulatory efforts.

NHPA/NEPA COORDINATION

Because reviews pursuant to the National Historic Preservation Act (NHPA) and the National Environmental Policy Act (NEPA) may overlap, to the extent possible, such reviews should be coordinated. The regulations of the Council on Environmental Quality (CEQ) implementing NEPA and the regulations of the Advisory Council on Historic Preservation (ACHP) implementing NHPA, as well as counterpart NEPA regulations adopted by each agency, require coordinated compliance with NEPA, NHPA, and Executive Order 11593. The CEQ regulations state that "[t]o the fullest extent possible, agencies shall prepare draft

---

493. *Brooks v. Volpe*, 350 F. Supp. 287, 290 (W.D. Wash. 1972).

environmental impact statements concurrently with and integrated with environmental impact analyses and related surveys and studies required by . . . the National Historic Preservation Act of 1966 . . . and other environmental review laws and executive orders."[494]

The ACHP's regulations[495] state that NEPA compliance is to be coordinated with compliance with Section 106 of NHPA and Executive Order 11593 to ensure that historic and cultural resources are given proper consideration in the preparation of the environmental assessment and the environmental impact statement (EIS). The regulations outline how the substance and timing of reviews under NEPA, NHPA, and Executive Order 11593 should be coordinated to produce one document that meets the requirements of both statutes and of the order. Compliance with NHPA should generally be initiated during the initial environmental assessments under NEPA and in any event should begin no later than during preparation of the draft EIS (DEIS).

The NHPA/Executive Order 11593 commenting period should run concurrently with the NEPA review process. The status of compliance with NHPA, Executive Order 11593, and the ACHP regulations should be reflected in all documents prepared under NEPA to provide the public with full information on the effects of federal actions on historic resources and on alternatives available to minimize adverse effects. The environmental assessment and DEIS should fully describe any National Register or Register-eligible properties within the area of the undertaking's potential impact and the nature of the undertaking's effect on them; the DEIS should then suffice as the preliminary case report that must be submitted by the federal agency to the ACHP under 36 C.F.R. § 800.13. If the Section 106/Executive Order 11593 commenting process is completed before the DEIS is issued, ACHP comments should be included in the DEIS. Completion of NHPA commenting should generally precede issuance of the final EIS, and the resulting memorandum of agreement (MOA) or other council comments should be incorporated into the EIS.[496] According to the council's regulations, the ACHP prescribes that certain reports be made available to it to aid it in evaluating the significance of affected properties, understanding the objectives of federal undertakings, assessing the effects of the undertakings and evaluating alternatives. Such reports include those written by

---

494. 40 C.F.R. § 1502.25 (1981).
495. 36 C.F.R. § 800.9 (1981).
496. *Id.* at § 800.9(f).

the agency in making determinations of no adverse effect, preliminary case reports accompanying requests for council comments, and reports submitted by various parties for council meetings. They should address physical, aesthetic, environmental, economic, social, and other effects of the proposed undertaking. 36 C.F.R. § 800.13 states that "[a]gencies should consider these reports in the context of their compliance with NEPA and incorporate their contents into environmental assessments, and draft and final environmental impact statements as specified in 36 C.F.R. § 800.9."

NEPA itself may also be construed to require ACHP and National Register staff involvement in the environmental review process. First, Section 102(2)(c) of NEPA requires that before preparing an EIS the federal agency official must consult with and obtain comments from federal agencies with jurisdiction by law or *special expertise* with regard to *any* environmental impact involved. These comments must then accompany the EIS and the project proposal through the agency's decision-making process. This language lends weight to an argument that the agency must seek a determination of eligibility[497] for affected properties from the Keeper of the National Register and request the comments of the the ACHP on the project even when NHPA's applicability is uncertain. It also supports requiring careful consideration in the EIS process of advisory council comments made pursuant to Section 106 of NHPA.

The staff of the ACHP does review EISs prepared for undertakings affecting National Register or Register-eligible properties for evidence of compliance with NHPA, Executive Order 11593, and the ACHP regulations, pursuant to Section 102(2)(C) of NEPA. The council is to include its views on the agency's compliance with NHPA, Executive Order 11593, and the ACHP regulations in its comments.[498]

A comparison of NEPA and NHPA clarifies the importance of each. A major difference is one of focus. NHPA's purpose is to foster the preservation of historic resources, whereas NEPA is concerned with protection of the entire human environment. Because of NEPA's broader perspective, historic resources tend to be de-emphasized in the EIS process

---

497. *Id.* at § 63.
498. *Id.* at § 800.9(f).

and impacts on them can seem insignificant in the context of a large, complex project. This, of course, is not a problem in Section 106 review.

Second, the threshold for compliance with NHPA and Executive Order 11593 is lower than that for EIS preparation under NEPA; that is, an "undertaking" under NHPA encompasses more than a "major federal action." Similarly, the ACHP's definition of "effect" is broader than the required "significant" effects under NEPA.[499] Agency responsibilities under NHPA and Executive Order 11593 are independent of those under NEPA and must be met even when an EIS is not required.[500] On the other hand, NEPA applies to all historic resources, not just those eligible for inclusion in, or included in, the National Register.

As a practical matter, the Section 106 process tends to require less agency research and paperwork and fewer work hours than does NEPA review, possibly making compliance more palatable to both agencies and developers. Also the NEPA process forces an assessment of the project and the consideration of possible alternatives.

One final difference between NEPA and NHPA, the degree of public participation required by each, cuts against the effectiveness of NHPA. The Section 106 process is essentially a consultation and negotiation process between the federal agency, the state historic preservation officer (SHPO), and the ACHP, the aim of which is to identify and evaluate federal undertakings and to minimize their adverse effects on historic, architectural, archaeological, and cultural resources. The process requires and often involves less public participation than does NEPA review.

However, the Section 106 process is quite simple and straightforward and does provide potential access points for interested persons and organizations. Local citizens can work to get their community's historic properties listed in the National Register.[501] Interested persons can also

---

499. The Second Circuit's decision in *WATCH v. Harris* implies, however, that, at least in the case of HUD projects, a major federal action involving acquisition or demolition of (and possibly other effects on) a National Register or Register-eligible property by definition significantly affects the quality of the human environment and thus requires preparation of an EIS. 603 F.2d 310, 317-18 (2d Cir. 1979), *cert. denied*, 444 U.S. 995 (1979).

500. On the other hand, Section 106 applies only where affected properties are eligible for or listed in the National Register. Under NEPA, the requirement of Register eligibility may not be absolute. See *Boston Waterfront Residents Association v. Romney*, 343 F. Supp. 89, 91 (D. Mass. 1972).

501. Although Section 106 applies to both eligible and listed properties, conducting a survey and inventory and nominating properties make it possible to systematically identify in advance which properties will activate Section 106 review if affected by

monitor the planning and development of federal undertakings that concern them to ensure that Section 106 is being complied with. The staff of the National Register of Historic Places can provide information on whether a determination of eligibility has been sought and, if so, with what result. The SHPO and ACHP will know the status of other aspects of Section 106 review.

Moreover, public involvement is important if the Section 106 process is to succeed in protecting historic resources. Since both the SHPO and the ACHP have limited resources, concerned parties can help draw potentially harmful projects to their attention and help monitor those projects to be sure that the federal agency adequately identifies historic resources and evaluates effects of the project on them.

Since federal projects may be controversial and politically sensitive, the SHPO and ACHP may be willing to take a tougher stand in favor of preservation if it is clear that local government, organizations, or citizens care about the threatened historic resources and that political support for a tough stand exists. Finally, if the controversy reaches litigation, generally because the agency has not complied with Section 106, plaintiffs are more likely to secure an injunction pending compliance if it is clear to the court that there is strong local support for preservation of the affected resources and that the preservation issue is not (as sometimes is the case) just a makeweight pressed by plaintiffs intent on stopping a project in any way possible.

The major similarity between the two laws, however, is that neither requires that agencies avoid or minimize adverse effects on cultural and historic resources.

Housing and Community Development Programs: A Neglected Resource

Preservationists have generally overlooked or ignored federal programs that influence the supply, demand, use, allocation, and ownership of buildings and the enhancement of the economy and quality of life of communities. The programs that have the greatest impact, such as community development block grants (CDBG) and Federal Housing Ad-

---

federal projects. National Register listing also has other benefits. See chapter 7 for a discussion of federal tax benefits.

ministration insurance programs, are found in the Department of Housing and Urban Development (HUD). Other programs are located in the Economic Development Administration of the Department of Commerce, the Farmers Home Administration of the Department of Agriculture, and the Veterans Administration. (See appendix 2.)

These programs can stimulate the reuse of buildings, rehabilitation, lending, and new construction, and can support community development and neighborhood revitalization. They can operate both directly through grants and indirectly by insuring certain mortgage loans from banks to encourage the lenders to extend credit directly to target populations or for certain purposes.

The lion's share of HUD's direct expenditures supports the goal of providing low-income and other targeted groups with decent housing ($28 billion in 1980). The second major expenditure is for community development programs, particularly the CDBG ($4.9 billion in 1980), and the third use ($3 billion in 1980) is to govern the mortgage credit market. The largest visible components of these expenditures have been monitored by preservation attorneys concerned with major change the programs can produce in the built environment. An urban development action grant (UDAG) project, for example, can be as large as $90 million and can leverage over eight dollars more for each federal dollar invested. But the major effects of HUD's actions are felt through the sums of money its direct expenditures regulate or stimulate. The $3 billion direct cost of federal administration of the mortgage credit market, for example, results in regulating over $100 billion in credit from private lenders.[502] Knowledge of the use of these programs is

---

502. U.S. Office of Management and Budget, *Housing Overview—1981 Spring Planning Review* (Washington, D.C.: GPO, 1981). This estimate is larger than many others as it includes off-budget and tax expenditures for housing and community development programs, not just direct expenditures. The components of this estimate are:

1980 Estimates of
Budget Authority
($ in millions)

Direct expenditures	$ 31,982
Tax expenditures	19,935
Off-budget credit activities	104,538
Guarantees and insurance	177,448
Total	$333,903

All data from HUD 1982 Budget Justifications.

necessary for preservationists to obtain funding for preservation projects and neighborhood conservation.

There is no planned or uniform approach of the housing and community development programs toward the built environment as a cultural resource to be managed. Generally, however, the older federal programs encouraged the construction of new housing while more recent programs have encouraged the reuse of buildings. But the wide variety of federal programs seeks varying and sometimes conflicting objectives, as shown in appendix 3.[303]

The federal insurance programs and community development grants can specifically be used to restore historic buildings. The leverage points in other programs are the underwriting criteria for obtaining credit and the participation standards of the secondary mortgage market. Federal minimum housing standards can be applied to public housing projects and to federal mortgage and credit insurance programs, and national protective legislation, such as the National Environmental Policy Act, can be used to control programs harmful to preservation. Federal housing subsidies and policies can be used to support preservation and rehabilitation as well as to support new construction. However, they will not be used for preservation unless local groups ensure that the programs conserve buildings and neighborhoods. Preservationists must monitor the steps lending institutions and local governments are taking in spending the federal funds.

The remainder of this chapter explores the housing and community development programs of HUD. Literature on the uses of these programs by preservationists and their attorneys is scant. This exploratory section describes the programs and focuses on some leverage points in them that can make them benefit preservation, but much more work needs to be done to make these programs into useful preservation tools.

---

303. Henry J. Aaron, *Shelter and Subsidies: Who Benefits from Federal Housing Policies?* 1-22 (Washington, D.C.: Brookings, 1972). Congressional Budget Office, Pub. No. 052-070-04576-1, *Federal Housing Policy: Current Programs and Recurring Issues* (Washington, D.C.: GPO, June 1978), p. 3; U.S. General Accounting Office, Pub. No. CED-81-98, *More Can Be Done to Measure HUD's Success in Using Millions of Dollars for Rehabilitating Housing* (Washington, D.C.: GPO, July 1981).

TYPES OF PROGRAMS

There are a large number of federal housing and community development programs, each with numerous detailed requirements.[504] However, the programs are variations on five basic approaches: (1) federal insurance or guarantees of loans from conventional lending institutions; (2) federal regulation of the national credit market and banking industry; (3) federal grants for community development; (4) federal assistance to localities to operate public housing; and (5) federal payments to assist people with low incomes in securing housing.

Not all of the authorized programs receive annual implementing appropriations.[505] Further, at the time of the writing of this chapter, the federal government was contemplating a variety of changes to the existing federal programs. However, the basic techniques of federal involvement in housing and community development have changed only marginally over time.[506]

Mortgage Insurance and Loan Guarantees

Because buildings are expensive to build and to acquire, credit is the central economic factor affecting the preservation of the built environment. The federal government helps regulate the national credit market through two basic techniques. The first is by insuring mortgages or guaranteeing loans issued by private lending institutions for specified purposes or to target populations. Such programs encourage lenders to issue mortgages for rehabilitation, for example, or to the poor or other

---

504. U.S. Department of Housing and Urban Development, Pub. No. 396-A, *Aids to Understanding the U.S. Department of Housing and Urban Development* (Washington, D.C.: GPO, August 1980). For additional information, see U.S. Office of Management and Budget, *Assistance Programs* (Washington, D.C.: GPO, 1982). For an excellent concise history, see [Background Papers] 7 Housing and Development Reporter (BNA).

505. U.S. Department of Housing and Urban Development, *Congressional Budget Justifications for Fiscal Year 1982* (Washington, D.C.: GPO, 1981).

506. Although they exclude community development programs, useful guides to the history of these programs and long-standing policy issues are: John C. Weicher, *Housing: Federal Policies and Programs* (Washington, D.C.: Am. Enterprise Inst., 1980); Patric H. Hendershott and Kevin H. Villani, *Regulation and Reform of the Housing Finance System* (Washington, D.C.: Am. Enterprise Inst., 1977); Aaron, *Shelter and Subsidies*; and President's Committee on Urban Housing, *A Decent Home* (Washington, D.C.: GPO, 1968).

groups that otherwise may not qualify to obtain loans to buy or build houses. The second is through acquisition of certain mortgages in the so-called "secondary" mortgage market, thus providing funds to private lenders with which they can issue new loans.

Each program has its own requirements, and the administering agency and participating private lender set standards for the types of buildings that qualify for each program and for determining the eligibility of individual credit seekers. These standards are enforced by the lending institutions and are known as underwriting criteria. Among the factors considered in underwriting criteria are eligibility factors for each program, construction cost specifications, credit analyses, loan-to-value ratios, and whether the applicant represents an acceptable credit risk.[507]

The use of insurance and guarantees to stimulate direct lending for rehabilitation makes such programs an important tool to benefit preservation of the built environment. Some cities, including Dallas, New York, and Indianapolis, have issued mortgage insurance by depositing funds locally in private lending institutions that agree to make rehabilitation loans by lending leveraged amounts for each dollar invested (in Dallas, for example, seven dollars for each public dollar invested).

Federal default insurance and its underwriting criteria made mortgage lending, and thus homeownership, more accessible to the public. It also stimulated the demand for housing. Federal underwriting criteria have therefore been key factors in determining the amount of lending and investment in the built environment.

Over 45 insurance and guarantee programs are available for home improvement loans, single-family and multifamily mortgages, mortgages for lower income groups, co-op mortgages, multifamily rental housing mortgages, condominium mortgages, mortgages for the elderly and the handicapped, group practice medical facilities and hospitals, housing in declining areas, historic preservation, and other purposes.[508] One type of mortgage insurance specifically supports historic preservation. This is HUD's Historic Preservation Loan Program, a variety of Title I prop-

---

507. See 24 C.F.R. § 200.98 (1982).

508. Sources of information on these programs and others are: U.S. Department of Housing and Urban Development, *Departmental Programs, Department of Housing and Urban Development* (Washington, D.C.: GPO, issued annually); U.S. Department of Housing and Urban Development, Pub. No. NVACP-320(4), *A Guide to Housing Rehabilitation Programs* (Washington, D.C.: GPO, April 1979); and U.S. Office of Management and Budget, *The Catalogue of Federal Domestic Assistance Programs* (Washington, D.C.: GPO, 1982).

erty insurance that stimulates lending in depressed areas by insuring rehabilitation loans.[509] The Historic Preservation Loan Program[510] insures the rehabilitation of National Register and Register-eligible properties. The preservation loans are slightly more favorable for use in preservation than the Title I loan insurance. These loans can be used for restoration of a project, subject to approval of the state historic preservation officer (SHPO), or can be used by cities as leverage in more sophisticated lending programs. In Hoboken, New Jersey, and Westchester County, New York, Title I loans and community development block grants are used in tandem; the CDBG money is used to lower the 12 percent interest rate on the Title I-insured loans private lenders make to homeowners in a targeted neighborhood down to a rate of 3 percent. The Minnesota Housing Finance Agency issued bonds for rehabilitation that were secured against default by Title I insurance.

All of the loan guarantee or insurance programs protect lenders against default by those obtaining the loans. The programs are chiefly located within the Federal Housing Administration (FHA), although the Veterans Administration and the Farmers Home Administration have similar programs to reduce mortgage interest for veterans and rural dwellers.[511]

All projects funded under any of the FHA insurance programs must meet the minimum property standards or minimum design standards for rehabilitation issued by HUD.[512] These are a unified set of technical and environmental standards that define the minimum level of acceptability of design and construction standards for low-rent public housing and housing approved for mortgage insurance purposes. These standards are both hortatory and specific, ranging from specifying the size and number of rooms per housing unit to directing that land-use planning shall relate to the site and to existing development on adjoining properties.[513] The standards are applied at the level of the area and

---

509. 12 U.S.C. § 1703 (1976).
510. *Id.*
511. For sources of information on these programs, see note 508.
512. U.S. Department of Housing and Urban Development, Handbook No. 4900.1, *Minimum Property Standards for One- and Two-Family Dwellings* (Washington, D.C.: GPO, 1979; updated periodically); U.S. Department of Housing and Urban Development, Handbook No. 4940.4, *Minimum Design Standards for Rehabilitation of Residential Properties* (Washington, D.C.: GPO, 1978).
513. U.S. Department of Housing and Urban Development, *Minimum Property Standards*, pp. 303-62.

regional HUD offices. The local HUD office is likely to be responsive to criticism of its projects or approved housing units that fail to meet these standards.

The impact of insurance programs on the reuse of the built environment has not yet been thoroughly analyzed. Preservationists also need to scrutinize the underwriting criteria applied by mortgage lenders and the use of the programs for renovation versus new construction.[514] Preservationists, for example, should negotiate with local lenders over their underwriting criteria based on information obtained through the Home Mortgage Disclosure Act. (See below for a discussion of that act.)

Federal Credit Institutions

Four federal institutions regulate and support the vital flow of credit for housing:
- the Federal National Mortgage Association (FNMA), a federally chartered, independent, privately owned stock corporation that operates on a profit basis, and the Government National Mortgage Association (GNMA), a private corporation within and regulated by HUD, both of which buy and sell mortgages;
- the Federal Home Loan Mortgage Corporation, which buys mortgages from savings and loan institutions; and
- the Federal Home Loan Bank, which advances funds to savings and loan institutions and other lenders that invest in mortgages.

FNMA was originally established to buy and sell federally insured mortgages of the FHA as a way of encouraging private lenders to issue them. Most of FNMA's original functions were transferred to GNMA in 1968.

In addition to the goal of providing funds to lenders by buying mortgages they have issued, GNMA purchases specific types of mortgages to make them available to targeted populations and to achieve national housing goals.[515] For example, to encourage lending institutions to issue mortgages to private developers of low-income rental housing, the FHA first insured the loans by guaranteeing to buy them or back them up

---

514. Preservationists have successfully used specific HUD programs to reuse older buildings. See, e.g., Center for Community Development and Preservation, *Innovations in Housing Renovations* (October 1979). A comprehensive analysis of available programs and an identification of leverage points that preservationists could use to make programs responsive to preservation concerns have not been undertaken, however.

515. Government National Mortgage Association, *1980 Annual Report* (June 1980).

if default occurred. Because the goal of the program is to make loans available to low-income people, FHA requires that the loans carry a below-market interest rate. To encourage the lenders to part with their money at the low-interest rate, GNMA buys the mortgages at the current market interest rate. This provides lenders with funds with which to issue new mortgages. GNMA, which then receives the lower percentage interest payments from the person to whom the mortgage was issued, sells the mortgage to private investors at a current market interest rate or adds the mortgage to a pool of such mortgages, which are then used to back government-issued securities at the higher competitive market rate. The difference between the low interest received by GNMA and the market rate GNMA pays either to those who buy the mortgages or to the holders of the bonds issued against the mortgages is absorbed by the federal government through annual appropriations.[516]

The Federal Home Loan Bank Board regulates the activities of its member savings and loan institutions. It can control the amount of mortgage credit available by requiring its members to hold certain cash reserves that they may not lend, by setting maximum interest rates on deposits (which determines the liquid assets the lender will have to lend, and hence, the level of mortgages issued), and by providing advances to its members.

The Federal Home Loan Mortgage Corporation, under the control of the Federal Home Loan Bank Board, operates a secondary market in conventional and government-insured mortgages from savings and loan institutions. It combines the mortgages into pools and issues securities, secured by the purchased mortgages, to investors. The Federal Reserve Board backs the Federal Home Loan Bank Board system.

GNMA, FNMA, and the Federal Home Loan Mortgage Corporation are federally backed mortgage credit agencies that can issue bonds and reloan the funds they get. The Federal Deposit Insurance Corporation and the Federal Savings and Loan Insurance Corporation, in contrast, provide insurance and liquidity to lending institutions.

Buying and selling private mortgages and mortgage-backed securities affects the supply, cost, and distribution of credit for construction, renovation, and home purchase. This secondary mortgage market increases mortgage availability, reduces the severity of cyclical decline in the home-building industry, and encourages mortgage lending in credit-

---

516. Weicher, *Housing*, p. 126.

short areas. It can also stimulate the amount of rehabilitation that occurs by making credit available for the renovation of older buildings. Preservationists seeking to finance the rehabilitation of historic buildings will have to become familiar with these federal programs in order to obtain low-interest credit and to secure loans for properties in run-down areas. All of the loan guarantee and insurance programs are available through local lending institutions.

Recently there have been efforts to regulate the credit market, lending practices, and underwriting criteria to end red-lining of areas that would not usually meet the lender's standards. The purpose of the Home Mortgage Disclosure Act "is to disclose to the public information about whether depository institutions are filling their obligations to serve the housing needs of the areas in which they are located. . . ."[517] The law requires that information about loans made be disclosed to the public.[518]

The Community Reinvestment Act states that regulated financial institutions have continuing and affirmative obligations to help meet the credit needs of the communities in which they are chartered.[519] Evidence of the record of investment in the community to meet "the credit needs of its entire community, including low- and moderate-income neighborhoods, consistent with the safe and sound operation of such institution" is to be considered in the examination of financial institutions by federal financial supervisory agencies such as the Comptroller of the Currency, the Federal Reserve Board, the Federal Deposit Insurance Corporation, and the Federal Home Loan Bank Board.[520] Consideration of community investment practices is required whenever a lending institution applies for a charter, renewal of a license, establishment of a branch facility, relocation of the home office or a branch, the merger or consolidation of banks, or the acquisition of shares in another institution. Because of the lack of standards as to what constitutes meeting local credit needs, however, the law has not been used effectively by preservationists to compel lending to older areas of historic interest or

---

517. 12 U.S.C. § 2801(b) (1976).
518. U.S. Department of Housing and Urban Development, Pub. No. PDR 452(a), *Home Mortgage Disclosure Act and Reinvestment Strategies* (Washington, D.C.: GPO, January 1979).
519. 12 U.S.C. § 2901(a)(3) (1976 & Supp. IV 1980).
520. *Id*. at § 2903(l)(2).

distinctive architecture.[521]

Low-Rent Public Housing

The federal government provides low-interest loans to local community housing authorities for the construction, development, rehabilitation and operation of low-rent public housing owned and managed by state or local government. The assistance takes a number of forms, including:
- direct loans to develop, acquire, and administer public housing;
- annual contributions to permit local housing agencies to lease housing for low-income families;
- operating and maintenance subsidies to public housing agencies to assist them in operating public housing;
- annual contributions to local housing agencies to help pay off bonds issued to finance public housing; and
- exemptions from taxation of the income on bonds issued by local or state public housing agencies to finance low- and moderate-income housing.

A wide variety of mechanisms can be used to develop public housing, including private development and operations based on plans approved by the local housing authority. The active preservation attorney will have to work with local government to ensure that public housing programs reuse buildings rather than merely constructing new ones. Should new facilities be constructed, however, they must meet the minimum property standards of HUD.

Housing Assistance Programs

A number of programs exist specifically to help low- or middle-income families buy or rent adequate housing. HUD's basic rental subsidy program, Section 8 (housing assistance payments), subsidizes the difference between the market rent of units and from 15 to 25 percent of an eligible tenant's income. Families determined eligible by a local housing authority may rent in adequate, moderate-cost housing of their own

---

521. U.S. Department of Housing and Urban Development, Pub. No. NVACP-407-1, *Neighborhood Based Reinvestment Strategies* (Washington, D.C.: GPO, October 1980); U.S. Department of Housing and Urban Development, Pub. No. NVACP-485-1, *Assessing Community Credit Needs* (Washington, D.C.: GPO, October 1980).

choosing in the private market. HUD provides funds to the local housing agencies to pay the owner of the rental housing. HUD can also enter into contracts with sponsors of new or rehabilitated rental units for low- and moderate-income persons to pay the difference between rents allowed by HUD and rents paid by tenants.

These programs support rehabilitation while helping to keep rents low, thus avoiding displacement. They can be used specifically to restore historic properties. In Newark, New Jersey, for example, Section 8 funding supported the overall financing for the rehabilitation of the historic Ballantyne Home project as a home for the elderly.

Other programs enable eligible low-income families to buy new or rehabilitated homes that meet HUD standards through FHA insurance programs and monthly payments to lenders to reduce interest payments.[522] HUD can also provide mortgage interest subsidies to developers of rental projects in which some of the units are made available to low-income families at reduced rates.[523]

Other programs for the purchase, rehabilitation, or construction of new or existing housing are operated by the Veterans Administration and the Farmers Home Administration.[524] The Farmers Home Administration provides low-interest loans and grants to low- and moderate-income households in rural areas, to those in rural areas without sufficient housing credit, and to the elderly and other groups to help construct, purchase, improve, or repair housing or to put rental rates within the reach of low-income families. Credit assistance to reduce mortgage interest and to provide rental assistance based on low-interest loans to developers is also provided.

Community Development Programs

Several small categorical grants for local efforts in code enforcement, historic preservation, open-space acquisition, land purchases, and urban beautification were consolidated in 1974 into a block grant to local, state, and metropolitan governments.[525] The grant is allocated as an entitlement payment based on a formula to communities over 50,000

---

522. 12 U.S.C. § 1715 K (1976 & Supp. IV 1980).
523. *Id.* at § 1715 Z-l.
524. Veterans are targeted as a special population to benefit from federal housing programs.
525. 42 U.S.C. §§ 5301-17 (1976).

people and on a competitive basis for other communities.[526] The purpose of the CDBG is community development through the provision of decent housing, a suitable living environment, and the expansion of economic opportunities for low- and moderate-income people.[527] As long as these general objectives are met, localities have great discretion in determining the purposes of the expenditure as well as the method of allocating it. The sums available in the grant are very large and can have a major impact on the preservation of historic properties.[528]

The grant can be used to:
- eliminate slums, blight, and blighting influences;
- eliminate conditions detrimental to health, safety, and the public welfare;
- conserve and expand the nation's housing stock and develop a suitable living environment;
- expand and improve neighborhood services; and
- restore and preserve properties of special value for historic, architectural, or aesthetic reasons.[529]

The grant can also be used to refinance for rehabilitation, rehabilitate to improve energy efficiency, eliminate adverse safety and health conditions, and renovate through alterations, additions, or enhancement of structures.[530] Code enforcement, rehabilitation counseling and related services, relocation assistance, and historic preservation can also be assisted. Preservation projects can include properties listed in or eligible for listing in the National Register, listed in state or local inventories, or designated by other local laws.[531]

Finally, the grant can be used to support certain economic development goals as well as efforts by nonprofit groups to help revitalize neighborhoods and local economic problems.[532] While some eligible activities are listed in general terms in applicable regulations (24 C.F.R. Parts 200 through 207), each proposed use of the grant is subject to review to determine how the program's objectives are being met.

---

526. 24 C.F.R. § 570.101 (1981). For information on this or any of the programs discussed in this chapter, see U.S. Office of Management and Budget, *Catalogue of Federal Domestic Assistance Programs*.
527. 24 C.F.R. § 570.2 (1982).
528. *Id*.
529. *Id*.
530. *Id*. at § 570.202.
531. *Id*. at § 570.202(f).
532. *Id*. at § 570.203.

Most important for preservation is the variety of flexible and creative uses to which the CDBG funds can be put to support rehabilitation. City development officials should consider these alternative financial uses of the grant. Preservationists with projects that the public can reasonably be expected to support should also be aware of the different financial uses of the grant. Among these are the following.

1. *Direct grants*: The locality uses CDBG funds to make direct loans to property owners to pay for rehabilitation and the owners are not required to make repayment.
2. *Direct loans*: The locality uses the grant to make direct loans to property owners to cover rehabilitation costs. The loans carry a lower interest rate and longer repayment term than conventional lending. Loan repayment may be used to issue new loans.
3. *Conditional grants-forgivable loans*: A conditional grant must be repaid if certain conditions are not met. A forgivable loan need not be repaid if the conditions are met.
4. *Partial loans*: A partial loan is made at below-market interest rates by the local public agency to pay for part of the rehabilitation costs. The remainder of the costs might be covered by other sources as determined by the property owner. The effect of this loan is to reduce the total costs of rehabilitation.
5. *Rebate-partial grants*: The local public agency uses the grant to make direct grants to property owners to cover part of the rehabilitation costs. The remainder of the costs are financed from other sources, but the public agency gives a rebate to the property owner.
6. *Interest subsidized loans*: A private lender makes a rehabilitation loan to cover the full rehabilitation costs. The CDBG is used to pay a portion of the monthly payment to the lender, thus creating a lower interest rate for the private party.
7. *Principal subsidized loans*: Rehabilitation is financed partly by a private home improvement loan and partly by a CDBG grant. The owner must repay the loan at a monthly rate.
8. *Guaranteed loans*: CDBG funds are placed in the account of a private lender and are used to guarantee loans made by the lender at below-market interest rates.
9. *Compensating balance loans*: CDBG funds are deposited in a private lending institution, and the institution makes rehabilitation loans at below-market rates. The difference between the market interest rate and the lower rate charged is made up by

withdrawals from the deposit account.
10. *Tax-exempt credit agreements*: Since interest paid to private lenders by public agencies is exempt from federal taxes, the city can borrow money from private lenders at low (below-market) interest rates and thus subsidize homeowners. The agency assures loan repayment to the lender through either the establishment of a loan guarantee fund or by using one of the other FHA insurance programs.[533]

The flexibility of the CDBG for preservation allows it to support preservation in a variety of ways. Springfield, Massachusetts, for example, uses the CDBG to survey historic properties as well as to support housing rehabilitation programs in eligible areas. Hoboken, New Jersey, and Westchester County, New York, use the CDBG to lower the interest rate on rehabilitation loans secured by Title I mortgage insurance. Pittsburgh, Pennsylvania, uses the CDBG to make loans for rehabilitation as well as to issue bonds secured by the CDBG money.

Eligible CDBG activities must be coordinated with other planning efforts and with federal programs in neighborhood strategy areas. Thus, the grant is frequently used with other programs, such as those for public housing or improving code conditions in target neighborhoods.[534]

A number of planning coordination requirements exist in the CDBG application. Opportunities for influencing these plans are ample.[535] For example, housing assistance plans that coordinate housing and community development activities must be submitted to HUD. These plans survey housing stock, identify deteriorated areas, determine what low-income housing needs are, and set a goal for the number of units to be assisted.

The plan offers an opportunity for the recipient community to conserve and expand its housing stock in order to provide a decent home for all persons but principally for those with lower incomes.[536] The plan

---

533. U.S. Department of Housing and Urban Development, *Guide to Housing Rehabilitation Programs*.

534. See also 24 C.F.R. § 570 (1982).

535. See generally 42 U.S.C. § 5304 (1976), as amended by the Housing and Community Development Act Amendments of 1981, Pub. L. No. 97-35, 95 Stat. 384 (1981). Also refer to U.S. Department of Housing and Urban Development, Pub. No. PDR-389, *Citizen Participation in the CDBG Program: A Guidebook* (Washington, D.C.: GPO, December 1978).

536. 24 C.F.R. § 570.306(a)(2) (1982).

must contain a description of existing housing conditions, housing assistance needs of specific populations in the area, and a three-year housing program with stated housing goals.

The applicant must also submit a three-year community development plan indicating community development and housing needs, plans for dilapidated housing, and a program to eliminate or prevent slum or blight conditions. Regulations prescribe the components of the plans, including:[537]

- a community profile providing specified characteristics of the community;
- a narrative summary of the community's housing and development needs;
- a comprehensive strategy for meeting the needs;
- a strategy for revitalizing and preserving neighborhoods;
- an identification of neighborhood strategy areas;
- a discussion of the role of neighborhood organizations, other available resources, and their proposed uses; and
- a description of how the housing assistance plan supports the applicant's neighborhood revitalization strategy.

There must also be a specific housing element of the plan submitted, including the communitywide strategy to improve housing conditions, available rehabilitation financing, proposed regulatory steps, and possible displacement the plan might cause.

Finally, the application materials must include an economic development strategy assessing the needs of identifiable populations within the area, steps to be taken to attract private investment, the number of new jobs expected to result, and the coordination of the use of the grant with other funds that may be available.[538]

The applicant must also certify its compliance with numerous other requirements such as executive orders on floodplains and wetlands, federal environmental laws, laws granting access to the handicapped, and the civil rights, fair housing, and equal opportunity laws.[539] The National Environmental Policy Act and the National Historic Preservation Act must also be complied with, including the provisions relating to public participation.[540]

---

537. *Id.* at § 570.304.
538. *Id.*
539. *Id.* at § 570.307.
540. *Id.* at §§ 58, 570.603, 570.604.

The impact of this grant can greatly affect older buildings.[541] Its large size, relative permanence, the plans required in the application process, and other eligibility requirements all afford opportunities for local community groups and preservationists to help shape its use.[542]

There is little information about the use of CDBG projects for preservation since HUD's accounting systems do not report preservation as a project purpose. However, as long as the other project purposes are met, preservation can qualify as a purpose of the expenditure.[543]

Urban Development Action Grants

The UDAG categorical grant to cities and urban counties is specifically designed to alleviate physical and economic deterioration of distressed cities and pockets of poverty in otherwise healthy locales through stimulation of private investment. Cities compete for funding, and a private economic commitment to a commercial, industrial, or neighborhood project is required before the grant can be made. Distress is based on the percentage of the housing stock built before 1940, poverty levels, population growth, degree of physical and economic deterioration, and other factors.[544]

The grant is designed to make up the difference between what a private investor could expect to make in return for his investment in a profitable location and what he would make from investment in a run-down area. The grant can be used for any activity that is also eligible for CDBG funding (except planning and construction of public facilities), though the UDAG can also be used to underwrite new housing construction, an activity for which the CDBG may not be used. The UDAG also can be used in conjunction with other federal housing and community and economic development programs.

Eligibility criteria include data on the age of housing, per capita income, population decline, unemployment, job decline, and poverty.[545] The cities must demonstrate results in providing low- and moderate-

---

541. U.S. Department of Housing and Urban Development, Pub. No. HUD-401, *CDBG Execution: Problems and Prospects* (Washington, D.C.: GPO, March 1979).

542. Phyllis Myers and Gordon Binder, *Neighborhood Conservation: Lessons from Three Cities* (Washington, D.C.: The Conservation Foundation, 1977).

543. Phone conversation between Donald Dworsky and HUD environmental officer Richard Broun (July 13, 1981).

544. 42 U.S.C. § 5318 (Supp. IV 1980).

545. U.S. Department of Housing and Urban Development, Pub. No. 488-1-CPD, *The Action Grant Information Book* (Washington, D.C.: GPO, 1978).

income housing since 1974 and in meeting their HUD-approved housing assistance plans. Results in providing equal opportunity housing will also be evaluated.[546] In addition, there must be compliance with environmental review requirements, and a citizen participation plan, a community development plan, and a housing assistance plan must also be submitted. The project must provide unique opportunities to attract private investment, stimulate investment in restoration of deteriorated or abandoned housing stock, or solve problems resulting from out-migration or a stagnating tax base. Evidence of a commitment of public and private resources that will be available must be presented.

The secretary of HUD must also find that the project would not result in relocating industry or economic opportunities from one location to another, that the grant would not substitute for other nonfederal funds that are otherwise available, and that there are no private lenders willing to support the project.

The variety of application requirements necessary to obtain a UDAG provide legal handles for the preservation attorney to use even though environmental compliance responsibilities are delegated from HUD to the grantee.[547] These requirements include a secretarial finding that there are no other private sector funds available for the project. The project must contain a housing assistance plan and a community development plan. The public is required to be involved in the planning, and an impact statement must be prepared to analyze the effects of the project on the residents of the area and of the neighborhood. These requirements are in addition to the need to comply with NEPA and NHPA.[548] Unfortunately, these requirements are not substantially reviewed by HUD if the grantee asserts that all procedural steps have been complied with.

Even though UDAGs have been responsible for significant losses of cultural resources,[549] they have been used to renovate large areas of older properties in Hartford, Connecticut, and to rehabilitate Greek Revival houses in a historic district of New London, Connecticut. UDAGs supported the restoration of the Victorian historic district in Savannah,

---

546. 24 C.F.R. § 570.456 (1982).
547. See generally 42 U.S.C. § 5318 (Supp. IV 1980).
548. 24 C.F.R. §§ 58, 570.603, 570.604 (1982).
549. Phyllis Myers, *Urban Conservation and Federally-Assisted Economic Development in Cities: Putting It Together* (Washington, D.C.: The Conservation Foundation, 1980).

Georgia, and restored a historic bank building in Birmingham, Alabama. UDAG also has been used for adaptive reuse of buildings, such as the creation of a hotel from an old grain silo in Akron, Ohio.[550]

Although UDAG has funded a number of historic preservation and adaptive reuse projects, studies by The Conservation Foundation and the National Trust for Historic Preservation have found that the nature of the program—creating a mixed public-private partnership—has often precluded preservation interests from getting involved in designing the project.[551] This is because the private developers who work with the cities to encourage partnerships by using UDAGs are conducting business transactions out of the public light. Over a third of the projects had no extensive environmental review prior to the actual purchase of land or initiation of construction.[552]

Even though UDAG has provided a large investment in adaptive reuse and historic preservation projects, a 1980 amendment to the Housing and Community Development Act limited the review of UDAG proposals by SHPOs and the Advisory Council on Historic Preservation to only 45 days based on complaints by mayors that such reviews were too time-consuming.[553] Given the number of application and eligibility requirements that the recipient cities must perform, preservationists' attorneys should carefully monitor and attempt to influence the manner in which local communities use UDAGs.

Comprehensive Planning Grants[554]

State, areawide, and local planning agencies can receive federal funds (up to two-thirds federal) for the preparation of plans to conserve and improve existing neighborhoods, modify and correct conditions of blight or distress, increase housing, and promote orderly growth and land use while preventing future conditions of distress and conserving existing communities. There are opportunities for citizens to influence these

---

550. U.S. Department of Housing and Urban Development, *Action Grants—Revitalizing and Conserving Cities* (Washington, D.C.: GPO, April 1980), p. 6. This study estimated that 55 UDAG projects specifically for historic preservation cost the program $206 million while leveraging another $1 billion in those projects.

551. Myers, *Urban Conservation and Federally-Assisted Economic Development in Cities.*

552. *Id.*

553. Pub. L. No. 96-399, § 110, 94 Stat. 1619 (1980) (to be codified at 42 U.S.C. §§ 5318, 5320). See also 36 C.F.R. § 801 (1981).

554. 40 U.S.C. § 461 (Supp. IV 1980).

plans. While the program is often criticized for not having produced noticeable results, the plans can serve as guides to the location of distressed areas, housing needs, and planned community development activities.[555]

Rehabilitation Loans[556]

Rehabilitation loans are low-interest (3 percent, as of this writing) funds issued by private lenders to rehabilitate buildings to local building code standards and to refinance the existing debt on multifamily units. Loans can be issued for a long term and can be for as much as 97 percent of the prerehabilitation value of a house. The loans must be used in conjunction with a CDBG program or in a code enforcement or urban renewal area designated by the local government or in an urban homesteading area. There are no income limitations, but priority is given to projects in low- and moderate-income areas. Exceptions are made when the rehabilitation is essential to the revitalization of an entire area and other lending sources cannot be found.[557] By using this program in conjunction with housing subsidy programs, rehabilitation does not necessarily result in displacement of low-income tenants. This program was used to bring a turn-of-the-century residential area in Los Angeles, California, up to minimum property standards and has helped to keep the area ethnically mixed.

Neighborhood Self-Help Development Grants

Grants and other financial assistance can be provided to local nonprofit community groups to prepare and implement neighborhood housing and economic and community development projects for neighborhood revitalization, provided that they are consistent with the goals of local governments.[558]

Urban Homesteading

Under the urban homesteading program,[559] government-owned properties, generally obtained through the foreclosure of Veterans Administra-

---

555. 24 C.F.R. § 600 (1982).
556. 42 U.S.C. § 1452b (Supp. IV 1980).
557. 24 C.F.R. § 510 (1981).
558. 24 C.F.R. § 3610 (1982).
559. 12 U.S.C. § 1706e (1976).

tion, FHA, and Farmers Home Administration mortgages, are transferred to local governments that request them as part of a local neighborhood improvement program. The properties are transferred, without substantial consideration, to owners who must agree to bring them up to code standards within a certain period and to live in them.[560] Urban homesteading programs must be part of a coordinated approach to neighborhood improvement, including upgrading community services and facilities. St. Louis, Missouri, Baltimore, Maryland, and Trenton, New Jersey, have all used this program in conjunction with low-interest loans supported by municipal bonds. New York City has used the program in conjunction with tax abatement for the homestead properties.

Other Programs[561]

There are many other federal housing and community development programs that can be tapped for preservation. The Small Business Administration makes loans to stimulate the flow of equity capital to modernize small businesses. It also administers a loan guarantee program to provide below-market interest rates to small businesses. The Economic Development Administration (EDA) makes direct grants to planning organizations of economic development districts designated by EDA and state agencies. Grants, loans, loan guarantees, and technical assistance can be made to neighborhood-based organizations for facility construction. Many other federal activities also affect the built environment and the factors leading to its maintenance or deterioration. Some are indirect, such as support for transportation, schools, and the infrastructure for development. Others affect the use of housing through enforcement of equal housing laws. Some support the development of new communities; others affect existing communities by directing investment into other areas.

CONCLUSION

All of the federal housing and community development programs can be used to benefit designated historic properties, and many can be used to rehabilitate older buildings or conserve neighborhoods. Some of the programs are specifically targeted to benefit the built environment, while

---

560. 24 C.F.R. § 590 (1982).
561. U.S. Office of Management and Budget, *Catalogue of Domestic Federal Assistance Programs.*

others rely on local government decisions to benefit preservation. A few of the programs are important because they provide funds that can be used in a number of creative ways to advance preservation at the local level.

Most of the programs, however, have not been analyzed by preservationists and their attorneys to understand how they work to support or defeat the goals of preservation. Underwriting criteria used by lenders and by insurance companies are one area of research that needs addressing. The requirements of the secondary mortgage market may determine which properties receive mortgage money. Decisions in the administration of the public housing programs have often supported new construction rather than renovation of older buildings. The most potent legal preservation tools, however, are in the vast array of eligibility and application requirements for the CDBG and the UDAG. The paperwork required to obtain such grants must consider impacts on the built environment, but too few preservationists have worked to ensure that preservation is included in the analyses required by HUD.

FURTHER READINGS

The leading article on federal preservation law prior to the passage of the 1980 Historic Preservation Act amendments is John Fowler's 1974 article entitled "Protection of the Cultural Environment in Federal Law" in *Federal Environmental Law*, ed. Dolgin and Guilbert (St. Paul, Minn.: West Publishing Co., 1974). A fascinating report on progress and developments under the 1966 act can be found in *The National Historic Preservation Program Today* (Committee Print of the Senate Committee on Interior and Insular Affairs, 94th Cong., 2d Sess., Jan. 1976). The best articles on the National Historic Preservation Act, as amended in 1980, are those by Kenneth Tapman that were prepared for the National Center for Preservation Law: "The National Historic Preservation Program: An Overview," "Listing a Property on the National Register," and "Protecting National Register and Eligible Properties Affected by Federal Actions." These are still available from the National Center for Preservation Law. The National Center for Preservation Law also produced a series of interesting legal guides to the federal act, e.g., *Recovery of Attorney's Fees Under the National Historic Preservation Act Amendements of 1980*; *1980 Modification of Historic Preservation Law* and *Standing to Sue Under the*

National Historic Preservation Act.

Several useful articles also have been written about archaeology. Two representative articles are *Protection of American Antiquities 1906-1981* in 21 Nat. Resources J. 935 (Oct. 1981) and *The Archeological Resources Protection Act of 1979: Protecting Prehistory for the Future* in 6 Harv. Envtl. L. Rev. 1 (1982).

Technical and program assistance is provided by both the National Park Service and the Advisory Council on Historic Preservation. The Park Service periodically issues bulletins in its "How To" series on such subjects as "How to Complete Multiple Resources Nominations," "How to Complete National Register Forms," and "How to Apply National Register Criteria." The advisory council periodically publishes reports such as *An Outline of the Process Established by Section 106 of the National Historic Preservation Act* (1980). The council also prepares reports on Section 106 compliance, as well as interesting unpublished reports such as a digest of Section 106 cases.

The best sources of data on the activities of the Park Service and the advisory council are the annual budget justifications for both agencies, found in the first volume of the Annual Budget Hearings by the Interior Appropriations Subcommittee of the House of Representatives' Interior and Insular Affairs Committee.

The best summary of the National Environmental Policy Act can be found in chapter 8 of William H. Rodgers, Jr., *Handbook on Environmental Law* (St. Paul, Minn.: West Publishing Co., 1977).

Information on federal housing programs is scattered and diverse, and sources rarely discuss the use of such programs for historic preservation (in contrast, for example, to general rehabilitation). The best overall explanation of housing programs is Henry J. Aaron's *Shelter and Subsidies: Who Benefits from Federal Housing Policies* (Washington, D.C.: Brookings Institution, 1977). Other short guides to the Department of Housing and Community Development and its programs are cited in the notes for chapter 4.

Appendix 1

PROGRAMMATIC MEMORANDUM OF AGREEMENT
BETWEEN
THE ADVISORY COUNCIL ON HISTORIC PRESERVATION,
THE NATIONAL CONFERENCE OF STATE HISTORIC
PRESERVATION OFFICERS,
AND THE
OFFICE OF SURFACE MINING RECLAMATION AND
ENFORCEMENT,
DEPARTMENT OF THE INTERIOR

I. Background

    A. Section 522(e) of the Surface Mining Control and Reclamation Act of 1977 (SMCRA), 30 U.S.C. 1272, and the permanent program regulations for compliance with SMCRA, 30 CFR Chapter VII, provide protection to publicly owned properties listed on the National Register of Historic Places from the adverse effects of surface coal mining operations and of coal exploration activities of 250 tons or more. SMCRA and the regulatory program specifically prohibit, subject to valid existing rights, new surface coal mining operations and coal exploration activities of 250 tons or more that would have an adverse effect on any publicly owned park or publicly owned place included in the National Register of Historic Places, unless jointly approved by the regulatory authority and the Federal, State, or local agency with jurisdiction over the properties.

    Also, Section 503 of SMCRA provides for States to obtain the approval of the Secretary of the Interior to regulate surface coal mining operations and coal exploration operations on non-Federal and non-Indian lands. Under 30 CFR Chapter VII the States will assume the responsibility for assuring that those properties protected under the National Historic Preservation Act of 1966, as amended (NHPA),

SOURCE: ADVISORY COUNCIL ON HISTORIC PRESERVATION, WASHINGTON, D.C.

16 U.S.C. 470f, are considered by State regulatory authorities (SRA) before making decisions to approve surface coal mining or exploration operations.

B. Section 106 of NHPA requires that the head of any Federal agency having direct or indirect jurisdiction over a proposed Federal or federally assisted or licensed undertaking affecting properties included in or eligible for the National Register of Historic Places shall afford the Advisory Council on Historic Preservation (ACHP) a reasonable opportunity for comment pursuant to its regulations at 36 CFR Part 800.

II. Purpose

A. This Programmatic Memorandum of Agreement (PMOA) sets forth the process for consultation with ACHP in connection with the Secretary of the Interior's approval of State permanent regulatory program submissions received by OSM before or after the date of the execution of this agreement.

B. This PMOA contains OSM's agreement to propose amendments to certain of its permanent program regulations related to historic resources.

III. Effect of Programmatic Memorandum of Agreement

Implementation of this agreement shall constitute fulfillment of ACHP's and OSM's responsibilities under Section 106 of the National Historic Preservation Act and 36 CFR Part 800 with respect to the Secretary's approval or disapproval of the permanent regulatory programs of the following States which submitted programs prior to March 3, 1980, and any states which submit programs hereafter, including: Alabama, Arkansas, Colorado, Illinois, Indiana, Iowa, Kentucky, Kansas, Louisiana, Maryland, Mississippi, Missouri, Montana, New Mexico, North Dakota, Ohio, Oklahoma, Pennsylvania, Tennessee, Texas, Utah, Virginia, West Virginia, and Wyoming.

Pursuant to 36 CFR 800.8, implementation of this agreement shall constitute fulfillment of the Secretary's responsibilities under Section 106 of the NHPA for the proposed undertaking that would otherwise require numerous individual requests for comments under 36 CFR Part 800.

IV. OSM's Proposed Modification of Permanent Regulatory Procedure Regulations

A. Within 120 days after the effective date of this agreement, OSM will propose a modification to the permanent regulatory program as proposed rules in the Federal Register to require the following procedures under State programs:

The applicant for State approval to conduct coal exploration of 250 tons or more or surface coal mining operations shall be required to identify and describe any properties, whether publicly or privately owned, that are listed in the National Register of Historic Places and all properties determined eligible by the Secretary of the Interior for the National Register which may be adversely affected by the proposed activity. An applicant shall also identify and describe properties based on lists which the SRA maintains. These lists shall be based in turn on information provided to the SRA by the State Historic Preservation Officer (SHPO). Such lists shall include lists of National Register properties and those properties determined to be eligible for the National Register by the Secretary of the Interior, locations of public records listing historic properties and locations of lists maintained by organizations or officials that have expertise about cultural and historic properties in the area.

If the SHPO advises that information on historic properties in the permit area is incomplete and a field inspection is necessary to identify any such properties, the applicant shall consult with the SRA, which shall make the final determination of whether a field inspection must be conducted based upon all the information before it, including the SHPO's recommendation, as to the likelihood of harm or risk of destruction to historic properties. OSM will encourage SRAs to require field inspections in areas not previously adequately inspected and require archeological/historical data recovery or avoidance.

The provisions of the following regulations shall not be proposed to be substantively changed at this time:

1. 30 CFR 770.12(c), which requires that the review and issuance of permits be coordinated with the applicable provisions of NHPA, thus protecting all properties listed in, determined to be eligible for, or potentially eligible for the National Register of Historic Places.

2. 30 CFR 786.11(c)(1), which requires that written notification of permit applications be sent to Federal, State, and local government agencies including historic preservation agencies with jurisdiction over or an interest in the area of the proposed operations. This includes the SHPOs.

3. 30 CFR 780.31 and 30 CFR 784.17, which require that a permit applicant describe the measures to be used to prevent or minimize adverse effects on historic places. This will provide information of concern to SHPOs during review of the permit application.

4. 30 CFR 786.23, which requires that the regulatory authority consider public comments, including those of the SHPOs, in deciding to approve, require modification of, or deny applications for permits.

B. Pursuant to 30 CFR 732.17(c)(1), States with approved programs will be required to amend their programs to meet the requirements of the final permanent program regulations as outlined in this PMOA.

C. OSM shall consult with ACHP in the preparation of the proposed regulations to ensure that the intent of this PMOA is carried out.

V. Review of State Programs by ACHP

ACHP will review proposed State programs or amendments to State programs that are submitted to OSM after the effective date of the

PMOA. OSM will provide ACHP with the opportunity to comment on the proposed State programs pursuant to Section 503(b) of SMCRA prior to OSM's recommendations to the Secretary of the Interior on the approval or disapproval of the proposed programs.

VI. Effective Date, Revision and Termination

This agreement is effective on the date of the last signature. It may be revised or amended by mutual agreement of the signers. The agreement may be terminated by any of the signers, provided that the party initiating such termination provides 90 days notice and reasons therefore to the other party.

[SIGNED]

Appendix 2

DESCRIPTION OF PRINCIPAL FEDERAL HOUSING AND COMMUNITY DEVELOPMENT PROGRAMS

Housing Assistance Programs

Low-Rent Public Housing. Pays development costs and annual operating subsidies for rental projects owned and managed by local public agencies and rented to lower-income tenants at reduced charges.

Section 8 New Construction/Substantial Rehabilitation. Subsidizes rents of lower-income households occupying public and privately developed projects. Federal payment per unit equals the difference between government-established fair market rent and one-fourth of tenant income.

Section 8 Existing Housing. Provides assistance on behalf of households occupying physically adequate, moderate-cost rental housing of their own choosing in the private market. Federal payment per unit similar to Section 8 new construction/substantial rehabilitation.

Section 235 Homeownership Assistance. Provides mortgage interest subsidies to lower- and middle-income households purchasing new or substantially rehabilitated homes.

Section 236 Rental Assistance and Rent Supplements. Section 236 subsidizes mortgages for rental housing projects. Rent supplements make subsidy payments to the owners of private rental housing on behalf of lower-income tenants; generally used in conjunction with mortgage subsidy projects.

Section 202 Housing for Elderly and Handicapped. Provides direct loans for the development of rental housing for the elderly and handicapped. Projects also receive Section 8 subsidies.

SOURCE: CONGRESSIONAL BUDGET OFFICE, "FEDERAL HOUSING POLICY: CURRENT PROGRAMS AND RECURRING ISSUES" (JUNE, 1978).

Housing-Related Community Development Programs

Community Development Block Grants. Provides grants to local governments, allocated by needs-based formulae. About one-fourth of all CDBG funds go towards housing rehabilitation, building code enforcement, and relocation assistance.

Urban Development Action Grants. Funds development projects involving both private and public investment. Available to distressed cities only.

Section 312 Rehabilitation Loans. Provides 3-percent interest loans for the rehabilitation of privately owned housing for occupancy by limited-income households.

Urban Homesteading. Makes federally held homes available at nominal expense to limited-income persons willing to rehabilitate and occupy units.

Mortgage Credit Activities

Direct Loan Programs. Farmers Home Administration provides market-rate and subsidized home loans in credit-deficient rural areas. Veterans Administration provides market-rate mortgages to qualifying servicemen and veterans.

Mortgage Insurance Programs. Federal Housing Administration insures market-rate single-family and multi-family mortgages and subsidized mortgages on assisted housing projects. Farmers Home Administration and Veterans Administration guarantee privately written mortgages on credit-deficient areas.

Credit-Market Interventions. Federal National Mortgage Association, Federal Home Loan Mortgage Corporation, and the Government National Mortgage Association purchase and resell mortgages to encourage use of capital for housing and provide limited financing subsidies. Federal Home Loan Banks provide advances to financial institutions to make up temporary credit shortages and stimulate additional lending.

Housing-Related Tax Expenditures

Homeownership Incentives. Permit deduction of mortgage interest and property tax payments for owner-occupied housing; allow deferral of capital gains on the sale of homes under certain circumstances; and exclude capital gains taxation on the sale of residences by elderly homeowners.

Promoting Rental Housing Development. Accelerated depreciation allowances for rental housing and the favorable treatment of construction-period interest and property tax payments for developers.

Tax Benefits for Financial Institutions. Preferential bad-debt deduction allowances for financial institutions that serve as primary sources of residential mortgage credit.

Housing and Credit Market Regulations

Guaranteeing Equal Housing Opportunities. Prohibitions against discrimination in the sale and rental of most housing and in mortgage lending.

Controlling Supply and Cost of Mortgage Credit. Regulations govern maximum interest rates paid on deposits of financial institutions and dictate minimum shares of assets applied to home loans.

Appendix 3
Primary and Secondary Objectives of Current Federal Housing Programs and Housing-Related Activities*

Federal Housing Programs and Activities	Providing Adequate and Affordable Housing	Increasing or Stabilizing Residential Construction Activity	Expanding Access to Mortgage Credit	Encouraging Homeownership	Ensuring Equal Housing Opportunity	Providing Housing for Special Users	Encouraging Community Development and Neighborhood Preservation and Revitalization
Housing Assistance Programs							
Low-rent public housing	XX	XX			X	X	X
Section 8 new construction/substantial rehabilitation	XX	XX			X	X	X
Section 8 existing housing	XX				XX		
Section 235 homeownership assistance	XX	XX	XX	XX	X		X
Section 236 rental assistance and rent supplements	XX	XX				X	
Section 202 elderly/handicapped housing	XX	XX	X			XX	
Community Development Program							
Community development block grants	X						XX
Urban development action grants		X	X				XX
Section 312 rehabilitation loans	XX						XX
Urban homesteading	X			XX			XX
Mortgage Credit Activities							
FmHA direct loans	XX	XX	XX	XX			

VA insured loans	X		XX	
FMHA, GNMA, FHLB and FHLMC secondary mortgage market activities	XX		XX	
Tax Expenditures				
Deduction of mortgage interest and property tax payments		X		XX
Deferrals and exclusions of capital gains on sales of homes		X		XX
Favorable depreciation for rental housing	X	XX		
Favorable treatment of construction-period development costs	X	XX		
Preferential treatment of real estate tax shelter	X	XX		
Tax benefits for financial institutions	X	XX	X	
Housing and Credit-Market Regulations				
Prohibitions against discrimination in sale/rental of housing and mortgage lending			XX	XX
Regulation of financial institutions and mortgage credit markets		XX	XX	

Note: XX—Primary Objectives
      X—Secondary Objectives

* The classification scheme presented here is based on similar typologies developed by several housing analysts. It is meant to depict the key relationships between programs and policy objectives; it is not intended to be exhaustive of possible program effects.

SOURCE: CONGRESSIONAL BUDGET OFFICE, "FEDERAL HOUSING POLICY: CURRENT PROGRAMS AND RECURRING ISSUES" (JUNE 1978)

Chapter 5
Federal Constitutional Issues

DAVID BONDERMAN

A number of federal constitutional issues have been raised in preservation law cases over the past few years. These include, for example, whether regulation of individual landmarks is legally permissible; how far landmark or historic district restrictions can limit owners' rights to develop property as they see fit; and what procedural protections must be afforded in designating landmarks and districts and in controlling demolitions and alterations.

Some of these questions have been set to rest by the Supreme Court's decision in *Penn Central Transportation Co. v. New York City*.[1] For instance, there is no longer any doubt that the state's police powers legitimately may be used for "aesthetic" regulation, including historic district and landmark legislation.[2] Similarly, it is now clear that the designation of individual landmarks is not by itself impermissible discrimination against the property owner involved.[3] Other arguments, particularly claims that the decisions involved in preservation cases are "legislative" in nature and cannot properly be left to a landmark commission or other body, live on in occasional state court decisions (see, for example, *Askew v. Cross Key Waterways*[4]) but have been long put to rest in the federal courts and in most state courts.

There remain, however, a number of significant federal constitutional issues that regularly confront lawyers interested in preservation law. The

---

1. 438 U.S. 104 (1978).

2. *Id.* at 129, "this Court has recognized, in a number of settings, that States and cities may enact land-use restrictions or controls to enhance the quality of life by preserving the character and desirable aesthetic features of a city. . . ." See also *Agins v. City of Tiburon*, 447 U.S. 255 (1980); *City of New Orleans v. Dukes*, 427 U.S. 297 (1976); *Village of Belle Terre v. Boraas*, 416 U.S. 1, 9-10 (1974).

3. *Penn Central Transportation Co. v. New York City*, supra note 1, at 132.

4. 372 So.2d 913 (Fla. 1978).

most important relate to procedures for designating and subsequently controlling demolitions and alterations of historic properties; the extent of legally permissible economic impact of historic preservation legislation on property owners; and the remedies available to owners who claim that the impact is unreasonable. Less common federal constitutional issues relate to designation of church property and to sign-control ordinances and involve the relationship between historic preservation laws and First Amendment rights to freedom of religion and freedom of expression.

This chapter addresses these major federal constitutional law issues and is designed to provide a general background for lawyers and laypersons alike. The chapter first discusses the minimum federal constitutional requirements. It then suggests practical methods to avoid constitutional problems through adequate planning, careful procedures, and the like. State constitutional issues are generally beyond the scope of this chapter, although legal issues arising under many state constitutions are similar to those discussed here and are mentioned in a few instances.[5]

PROCEDURAL DUE PROCESS ISSUES

In the old days, when designation as a landmark or a historic district meant little more than a brass plaque on the wall, there was relatively little concern about procedures. If designation standards were uncertain or if designations were made without notifying the property owner, generally no dispute resulted. Since the impact of designation was largely honorific, it mattered little from a legal standpoint. However, with the advent of much tougher local preservation laws and the federal Tax Reform Act of 1976, designation may substantially affect a property owner, as might the denial of a permit (for example, to demolish or alter a landmark building).

As a result, "procedural due process," the lawyer's shorthand term for the requirements of the Fifth and Fourteenth Amendments to the Constitution that no person be deprived of "life, liberty or property"

---

5. It is worth noting that state constitutions as interpreted by state courts may be more demanding than the federal Constitution, and, accordingly, any preservation litigation should be examined under state law as well. It is also worth noting that, although this chapter outlines minimum federal constitutional requirements, in many instances, good policy, smart politics, or both will suggest additional procedures to be followed. A number of suggestions along this line are contained in the chapter on local law.

without appropriate procedural protections, is now an important consideration in many preservation law decisions. These considerations relate not only to the designation process,[6] but also to the treatment of designated properties in subsequent permit applications.

Right to a Hearing

The Supreme Court has considered, in a number of cases, the right to a hearing. None of these cases dealt directly with historic preservation, but the Supreme Court's decisions and rationale are nonetheless instructive. In *Board of Regents v. Roth*,[7] the Court summarized its position on the right to a hearing.

> Before a person is deprived of a protected interest, he must be afforded opportunity for some kind of hearing. . . . [I]t is fundamental that except in emergency situations . . . due process requires that when a State seeks [to deprive a person of his protected interest] it must afford "notice and opportunity for hearing appropriate to the nature of the case" before the [deprivation] becomes effective.[8]

Among the interests that the Supreme Court has held to be "protected" and thus to require a hearing are revocation of a driver's license,[9] repossession of the family refrigerator,[10] and a three-day suspension from school.[11] There is, therefore, little doubt that designation of a landmark or subsequent denial of a permit (for example, to demolish) is in most cases a sufficient interference with the owner's control over his property to qualify as a protected interest that requires a hearing.[12]

---

6. Since the 1980 amendments to the National Historic Preservation Act, 16 U.S.C. § 470a (a)(6), an owner's objection precludes listing a building or structure on the National Register as a landmark. Accordingly, new landmark Register listings may no longer involve many of these issues, since owner consent would, in most if not all cases, obviate the constitutional questions discussed here. However, even under the 1980 amendments, a building or structure may be incorporated in a historic district without owner consent so long as a majority of the owners in a proposed district do not object, § 470a(a)(6). Moreover, many localities have their own listing or register of landmarks and districts and do not require owner consent. As a result, hearing issues are still of importance for designation. In addition, owner consent to designation does not waive the owner's hearing rights to subsequent permit applications and the like.

7. 408 U.S. 564 (1972).

8. *Id.* at 570 n.7, quoting *Bell v. Burson*, 402 U.S. 535, 542 (1971).

9. *Bell v. Burson*, 402 U.S. 535 (1971).

10. *Sniadach v. Family Finance Corporation*, 395 U.S. 337 (1969).

11. *Goss v. Lopez*, 419 U.S. 565 (1975).

12. See *Historic Green Springs, Inc. v. Bergland*, 497 F. Supp. 839 (E.D. Va. 1980).

346 A HANDBOOK ON HISTORIC PRESERVATION LAW

The two most important questions concerning hearings are: At what point in the process must a hearing be held? What must the nature of the hearing be?[13]

Notice. It is implicit in the hearing requirement that the affected persons will be given timely notice in advance of the hearing so that they may appear and contest the issues. Failure to provide appropriate notice will void the entire process.[14] In many instances, notice by publication is constitutionally sufficient, but if only a small number of property owners are affected, personal notice (for example, by certified mail) is a much better practice and one often required by local ordinances or by federal or state constitutional decisions. In any case, notice should be in plain language "reasonably calculated, under all the circumstances, to apprise the interested parties of the pendancy of the action and afford them an opportunity to present their objections."[15]

Timing. A hearing should be held prior to the ultimate designation of a landmark or a historic district and prior to the final denial of a permit to demolish, alter, or subdivide a historic property. It is permissible, however, for a statute or ordinance to limit an owner's right to alter or demolish a structure prior to the hearing. For example, Section 5-821 of the District of Columbia landmark law (reprinted in appendix A) prohibits demolitions and alterations of landmarks and of structures that contribute to the character of a historic district unless approved on certain narrow grounds by the appropriate administrative agency. The law also applies to any structure for which a landmark designation application has been filed, subject to a requirement that a hearing on the proposed designation be held within 90 days of the application for any alteration or demolition permit.

The leading case in this area is *New Motor Vehicle Board v. Orrin W. Fox Co.*[16] The Court in this case allowed restrictions on property

---

13. In many cities and towns, local ordinances allow landmarks commissions and similar agencies to designate buildings as landmarks based solely on the fact that the buildings are listed on the National Register. This should not pose a problem in those instances in which a hearing was held prior to the Register listing if the local designation procedure was in place at the time of the Register listing *and* the local ordinance in effect at that time placed potentially significant restrictions on designated properties. In the first instance, the owner's rights were protected by a hearing and, in the second, the owner had notice of the potential restrictions and waived his or her rights. However, in other instances, a hearing on the local designation should be held.
14. See *Mullane v. Central Hanover Bank & Trust Co.*, 339 U.S. 306 (1950).
15. *Id.* at 314. See also *Schroeder v. City of New York*, 371 U.S. 208 (1962).
16. 439 U.S. 96 (1978).

pending a hearing to be held within 60 days. This is consistent with prior Supreme Court rulings, which, particularly in the context of business regulation, uniformly hold that a prompt hearing after the regulation is applied suffices to satisfy due process.[17]

The lesson of these cases is that a statute or ordinance that attaches the protection of historic preservation legislation to property for a reasonable length of time prior to a hearing will be sustained. Such protection may well prove necessary when, pending a hearing on landmark designation, an owner applies for a demolition permit. Indeed, without a mechanism for protecting buildings until their status is determined, a notice of intention to designate a building may actually encourage its demolition if an owner plans to demolish the structure and knows that designation will make the demolition more difficult.

Nature of Hearing. The Supreme Court repeatedly has indicated that a trial-type hearing (with witnesses under oath, cross-examination, and so forth) is not always necessary to satisfy the due process hearing requirements. Instead, the Court has indicated that the proper constitutional test of the nature of the hearing required entails a balancing of the importance of the private interests against the government's interest in prompt and efficient decision making.[18] Of course, if the agency does provide a full trial-type hearing, the nature of the hearing will not be at issue. It appears, however, from the foregoing Supreme Court cases that, as a constitutional matter, all that is necessary is that a hearing be provided, that all interested persons be given sufficient notice of the hearing, and that each side have an opportunity to present its case fairly.

In a context of preservation law, this principle means that a landmark commission could adopt any reasonable procedure that safeguards the right to be heard. For example, a commission appropriately could require the submission of direct testimony in writing; could limit the

---

17. See also *Hodel v. Virginia Surface Mining and Reclamation Ass'n*, 452 U.S. 264, 298-304 (1981), hearing may be held after secretary of the interior issues order to require temporary cessation of mining; *Mitchell v. W. T. Grant Co.*, 416 U.S. 600, 611 (1974), hearing may be held after sequestration when the purpose of the statute is to protect assets against destruction or diminution before hearing; *Mathews v. Eldridge*, 424 U.S. 319 (1976), hearing may be held after termination of Social Security benefits; *Goss v. Lopez*, *supra* note 11, hearing may be held after school suspension.

18. See *Mathews v. Eldridge*, *supra* note 17, at 334-35, full hearing not required for Social Security termination; *Goss v. Lopez*, *supra* note 11, at 571-72, 579, full hearing not required for suspension from school; *Bell v. Burson*, *supra* note 8, at 542, hearing for driver's license revocation must be "appropriate to the nature of the case."

time for oral testimony to some reasonable length in view of the issues (whether this is five minutes or five hours or five days will depend on the complexity of the particular case, the number of parties, and so on); and need not always allow cross-examination, as long as each side has a fair opportunity to comment on the testimony of the other. A number of state court decisions, however, do require that cross-examination be allowed whenever a substantive decision is to be made based on the hearing record (this is what is known as a quasi-judicial decision). Thus, it would seem better to allow cross-examination in all such instances when there is any question about the required scope of a hearing.

Decision. Also embraced in the right to a hearing is a right to a responsive decision. This simply means that the deciding judge or body must render a decision that articulates what is being done and why. A number of state court constitutional decisions and occasional state statutes and local ordinances require a variety of additional formal procedures (for example, findings of fact), but the federal Constitution has never been interpreted to require any such particular procedures. Accordingly, as a procedural matter, any reasonable decision supported by some defensible reasons will pass federal constitutional muster.[19] As a matter of good practice, however, a commission usually will find it valuable to make findings of fact and state reasons for its decision. Such an exercise can help articulate a sound decisional basis that will stand up in court if challenged.

Criteria and Standards

Equally important as the right to a hearing are the criteria and standards to be applied by the agency in reaching a decision. Chapter 2 discusses at some length the substantive details of designation criteria, but, for the purposes of this discussion, the nature of the criteria may be less important than their clarity and uniform application. There are a number of federal circuit court decisions requiring administrative agencies to articulate, in advance, standards on which their decisions are to be based. Although the courts, both federal and state, generally strain to uphold local criteria for decision making if at all possible, a few cases have held that if an administrative agency fails to establish, in advance, coherent written standards and regulations to be applied in all cases, this amounts to a denial of a fair hearing and, therefore, a violation

---

19. Contrast *Citizens to Preserve Overton Park v. Volpe*, 401 U.S. 402 (1971), and *Historic Green Springs, Inc. v. Bergland, supra* note 12.

of due process.[20] This principle applies both to designation proceedings and to subsequent attempts by property owners to obtain permits to demolish, alter, or subdivide historic properties.

The Department of the Interior has established a set of criteria for the designation of National Register properties, and it is probable that those criteria are specific enough to satisfy federal constitutional requirements. Many, but not all, state and local statutes and ordinances either contain their own standards or explicitly refer to the Register standards. When there is no such explicit statutory reference to standards, landowners may possibly challenge at least some landmark designations on the ground that they were made without adherence to proper ascertainable standards. Such problems can be avoided if, in the absence of statutory standards, the commission, *in advance*, adopts its own.

The problems ensuing from the absence of articulated standards are demonstrated by a suit brought against the Department of the Interior's National Historic Landmark Program: *Historic Green Springs, Inc. v. Bergland*.[21] In this case, a property owner claimed that the designation by the Secretary of the Interior of a district comprising portions of Louisa County, Virginia, as a national historic landmark and the district's subsequent listing in the National Register were unconstitutional because there were no established written standards for the Interior Department's decision. The court pointed out that the process used in determining national historic landmarks was essentially ad hoc. There were no written standards for designation, and the information relied upon by the Department of the Interior was not contained in the administrative record. As a result, the judge held that the designation of the Green Springs Historic District was unconstitutional and ordered the Secretary of the Interior to strike the district from the National Register. (The decision applied only to the National Historic Landmark Program, not to any other aspect of the National Register Program, for which there are different and more definite standards; moreover, the specific designation set aside by the decision has been reaffirmed by an act of Congress.)

Of course, preservation questions are often to some degree subjective and may escape exact quantification. But sufficient review standards and designation criteria nonetheless can be articulated. (For example, standards for reviewing new construction, such as "compatible with the character of an historic district," while not mathematically

---

20. E. g., *White v. Roughton*, 530 F.2d 750 (7th Cir. 1976); *Holmes v. New York City Housing Authority*, 398 F.2d 262 (2d Cir. 1968).
21. *Historic Green Springs, Inc. v. Bergland, supra* note 12.

precise, have been upheld.) Chapter 2 discusses specific standards in greater detail.

Finally, although this section has discussed the standards issue in relation to designation questions, it must be remembered that the same kinds of issues exist with respect to standards for granting of permits affecting designated properties.

THE "TAKING" ISSUE

Over the years, there have been thousands of cases challenging various land-use regulations on the ground that those regulations are so burdensome as to amount to a "taking" of the landowner's property without just compensation in violation of the Fifth Amendment to the U.S. Constitution. It is frequently argued, for example, that prohibiting demolition of a historic structure amounts to a "taking" because it deprives owners of their "right" to construct a shiny new building. Today, "taking" questions are perhaps the most frequently litigated constitutional issue for land-use regulations in general and preservation ordinances in particular.

What Is a "Taking"?

In a "taking" case, the owner of property contends that the regulation involved is unreasonably burdensome in its restrictions. Such restrictions can be of several general types. First, a preservation ordinance can directly restrict demolition, alteration, or new construction so as to limit the owner's future options for development. Second, a landmark designation can involve tax implications under the Tax Reform Act of 1976 and under other state and local laws and ordinances and thus may make development less financially attractive. Third, an ordinance can affect a property owner's present plans or actual projects (so-called "vested rights")[22] in such a way as to require the owner to change them. Final-

---

22. The term "vested right" is commonly used in zoning and land-use law to refer to a situation in which an owner is grandfathered against a change in the law. In federal constitutional law, however, there is no such thing as a "vested right." As long ago as *Mugler v. Kansas*, 123 U.S. 623 (1887), in rejecting a "taking" claim when an amendment to the Kansas Constitution prohibiting breweries precluded the long-standing use of appellant's property, the Supreme Court observed:

It is true, that, when the defendants in these cases purchased or erected their breweries [their use was lawful]. But the State did not thereby give any assurance, or come under an obligation, that its legislation upon that subject would remain unchanged. 123 U.S. at 669.

ly, an ordinance can place an affirmative duty on an owner, such as maintaining a structure, which requires expenditures. Although these four types of restrictions are obviously quite different in a factual sense, the "taking" analysis is identical.

When does a regulation become a "taking"? The standard constitutional analysis of the regulatory "taking" issue stems from Justice Holmes's comments in *Pennsylvania Coal Co. v. Mahon*,[23] to the effect that: "The general rule at least is, that while property may be regulated to a certain extent, if regulation goes too far it will be recognized as a taking."[24]

The principles discussed in this section apply to cases of regulatory mechanisms that do not involve a physical invasion of property. The Supreme Court has noted that "an actual physical invasion" is different

---

See to the same effect *Goldblatt v. Town of Hempstead*, 369 U.S. 590 (1962), property owner had no "vested right" in continuing long-standing use of the property as a quarry; *Louisville Bridge Co. v. United States*, 242 U.S. 409 (1917), law authorizing private bridge across Ohio River did not create a "vested right" requiring payment of compensation under Fifth Amendment when Congress later amended statute to require rebuilding of bridge; *Hadacheck v. Sebastian*, 239 U.S. 394, 410 (1915), brickyard owner had no "vested right" in continued use of property as brickyard.

Indeed, the very nature of zoning and other land-use planning is such that it can always be expected that such regulations will not be permanent but rather will change from time to time. The Supreme Court long ago recognized as much in *Village of Euclid v. Ambler Realty Co.*, 272 U.S. 365, 386-87 (1926), when it observed that the changing nature of urban life "will continue to require . . . additional restrictions in respect of the use and occupation of private lands in urban communities."

See generally Arden H. Rathkopf, *The Law of Zoning & Planning*, 4th ed. (New York: Boardman, 1975), vol. 2, chap. 57; Norman Williams, ed., *American Land Planning Law* (Chicago: Callaghan, 1974), vol. 4, chap. 111.

As stated in *A Model Land Development Code*, the accepted rule is that an "expectation that a development permit could be obtained does not create any rights that prevent change of a development ordinance." American Law Institute, *A Model Land Development Code: Complete Text & Reporter's Commentary* (Washington, D.C.: American Law Institute, 1976), §2-309(2). A number of state courts, however, have created a "vested rights" doctrine under state constitutions.

23. 260 U.S. 393 (1922).

24. *Id.* at 415. See also *Agins v. City of Tiburon*, *supra* note 2, at 260-61; *Penn Central Transportation Co. v. New York City*, *supra* note 1, at 127-28; *United States v. Central Eureka Mining Co.*, 357 U.S. 155, 168 (1958). Although *Pennsylvania Coal* itself was a due process, not a "taking," case, this line of cases deriving from *Pennsylvania Coal* analyzes the "taking" issue as though a regulation which goes "too far" becomes a "taking" in the terms of the just compensation clause of the Fifth Amendment.

There is, however, another line of cases stemming from *Mugler v. Kansas,* 123 U.S.

for constitutional purposes than a regulatory "devaluation" of property.[25] Thus, the cases uniformly find a "taking" when there is an actual invasion of property along the lines of a trespass, without regard to the remaining use.[26] While of significance, these cases generally are not of direct importance to preservation law issues because preservation statutes and ordinances do not often involve any kind of actual physical invasion of property.

The real question, then, is, When does a regulatory scheme "go too far"? In recent cases, the Supreme Court has noted that it has had "considerable difficulty" developing any "set formula" to determine when a "taking" occurs.[27] Thus, while the Court has developed general tests

---

623 (1887), and *Miller v. Schoene*, 276 U.S. 272 (1928), which indicates that a valid police power regulation can never be a "taking." These cases suggest that the proper analysis of a regulatory scheme, including a land-use regulation, requires a determination of whether the regulation is reasonably related to the health, morals, or safety of the community and, if so, whether it is arbitrary and oppressive and hence in violation of the due process clause of the Fifth Amendment.

A number of courts recently have noted, perhaps correctly, that the traditional "taking" analysis makes little sense in the context of land-use regulations:

[C]onfusion about this issue has been sown by loose language about excessive land use regulations effectuating a "taking." A zoning regulation that exceeds the permissible bounds of the police power does not in reality confiscate the property, but regulates with oppressive or arbitrary severity. "Absent factors of government displacement of private ownership, occupation or management, there [is] no 'taking' within the meaning of the constitutional limitations." A court does not declare that an offensive zoning regulation has taken the property, but that the government cannot impose the restriction without formally paying for it. *Pamel Corporation v. Puerto Rico Highway Authority*, 621 F.2d 33, 35-36 (1st Cir. 1980) (citations omitted).

See to the same effect *Fred F. French Investing Co. v. City of New York*, 39 N.Y.2d 587, 594, 385 N.Y.S.2d 5, 8-9, 350 N.E.2d 381, 385, *appeal dismissed*, 429 U.S. 990 (1976), "[t]rue, many cases have equated an invalid exercise of the regulating zoning power, perhaps only metaphorically, with a 'taking' or a 'confiscation' of property, terminology appropriate to the eminent domain power and the concomitant right to compensation when it is exercised. . . . The metaphor should not be confused with the reality."

However, in the recent decision of the Supreme Court in *San Diego Gas & Electric Co. v. City of San Diego*, 450 U.S. 621, 646-53 (1981), four dissenting justices explicitly rejected the due process analysis in favor of the *Pennsylvania Coal* "taking" analysis.

25. *Kaiser Aetna v. United States*, 444 U.S. 164, 180 (1979); see also *Andrus v. Allard*, 444 U.S. 51, 65 (1979).

26. E. g., *Kaiser Aetna v. United States*, *supra* note 25; *Griggs v. Allegheny County*, 369 U.S. 84 (1962).

27. See *Penn Central Transportation Co. v. New York City*, *supra* note 1, at 123-24; see also *Kaiser Aetna v. United States*, *supra* note 25, at 175.

for determining whether a "taking" has occurred—nature of economic impact, whether the regulation reasonably promotes valid police power objectives, the character of the regulatory action—the analysis really has been on an ad hoc basis.[28] The question of "taking" brings to mind Justice Stewart's famous comment regarding obscenity: a court may not be able to define a "taking," but the court (supposedly) knows it when it sees it.

Accordingly, the only practical method of discerning general rules on when a regulation goes "too far" is to examine the decided cases in some detail. Such an examination leads to the conclusion that the federal courts have more or less uniformly recognized that land-use regulations may severely restrict property as long as there is *some* reasonable remaining use.[29] This is true with respect to all forms of land-use regulation, including, but not limited to, preservation laws.

For example, neither a prohibition of the most beneficial use of a property (the so-called "highest and best use") nor a diminution in a property's tax value as a result of a regulation amounts to a "taking." Thus, in *Village of Euclid v. Ambler Realty Co.*,[30] the Court sustained, as a reasonable exercise of police power not requiring compensation, a zoning ordinance that reduced the plaintiff's property value by 75 percent. In *Hadacheck v. Sebastian*,[31] the Supreme Court approved a regulation that, without compensation, banned brickyards from a portion of Los Angeles, thus closing down the plaintiff's long-existing brick factory and reducing his property's value by over 90 percent. And, in *Goldblatt v. Town of Hempstead*,[32] the Court approved an ordinance that totally prohibited, without compensation, the most beneficial use of a property. All of these cases were cited with approval in *Penn Central Transportation Co. v. New York City*,[33] in which the Court held that precluding development of an office tower that would have net-

---

28. See *Penn Central Transportation Co. v. New York City*, supra note 1, at 124-25, 128.

29. See generally *Penn Central Transportation Co. v. New York City*, supra note 1; *Village of Euclid v. Ambler Realty Co.*, supra note 22; *Hudson County Water Co. v. McCarter*, 209 U.S. 349 (1908); *Welch v. Swasey*, 214 U.S. 91 (1909); *Maher v. City of New Orleans*, 516 F.2d 1051 (5th Cir.), *rehearing denied*, 521 F.2d 815 (1975), *cert. denied*, 426 U.S. 905 (1976); *Steel Hill Development, Inc. v. Town of Sanbornton*, 469 F.2d 956 (1st Cir. 1972).

30. See *Village of Euclid v. Ambler Realty Co.*, supra note 22.
31. 239 U.S. 394 (1915).
32. 369 U.S. 590 (1962).
33. 438 U.S. 104, 131 (1978).

ted Penn Central $150 million over a 50-year period was not a "taking."

The following four lower court cases amply illustrate how difficult it is for a property owner to establish a "taking," at least in the federal courts, and that even a substantial diminution in the value of a property does not amount to a "taking."

1. *Maher v. City of New Orleans.*[34] A property owner claimed that the New Orleans Vieux Carre ordinance, which prohibited him from demolishing a small bungalow and replacing it with an apartment building, was a "taking." The Fifth Circuit held otherwise:

> Nor did Maher demonstrate to the satisfaction of the district court that . . . the ordinance so diminished the property value as to leave Maher, in effect, nothing. In particular, Maher did not show that the sale of the property was impracticable, that commercial rental could not provide a reasonable rate of return, or that other potential use of the property was foreclosed.[35]

2. *William C. Haas & Co. v. City and County of San Francisco.*[36] The court held that a 95 percent reduction in value was not a "taking." A purchaser of a site in the Russian Hill area of San Francisco had intended to construct a high-rise development, but a change in zoning regulations after his purchase precluded the intended use and reduced the value of the property from $2,000,000 to about $100,000. The court noted that the fact that

> . . . the zoning restrictions prevent Haas from recovering its investment does not mean . . . they are constitutionally defective. Of course, Haas would not have paid as much for the property as it did if it had known that it would not be able to build high-rises on it. But its disappointed expectations in that regard cannot be turned into a taking, nor can Haas transform a regulation into a taking by recharacterizing the diminution of the value of its property as an inability to obtain a favorable return on its investment.[37]

3. *South Terminal Corp. v. Environmental Protection Agency.*[38] In this case, the EPA adopted a rule under the Clean Air Act that required the abandonment of some 1,100 parking places at Logan Airport and a permanent 40 percent vacancy rate in parking lots in downtown Boston. The court held that the impact of the regulations was not a "taking," even though some parking lot operators might consequently operate

---

34. 516 F.2d 1051 (5th Cir.), *rehearing denied*, 521 F.2d 815 (1975), *cert. denied*, 426 U.S. 905 (1976).
35. 516 F.2d at 1066.
36. 605 F.2d 1117 (9th Cir. 1979), *cert. denied*, 445 U.S. 928 (1980).
37. 605 F.2d at 1121.
38. 504 F.2d 646 (1st Cir. 1974).

at a loss.[39]

4. *Steel Hill Development, Inc. v. Town of Sanbornton*.[40] A developer had acquired 510 acres of vacant land with the intention to build some 500 houses on the site, as permitted by the then-existing zoning. The town then rezoned the area so that the density for 30 percent of the property was set at 3 acres per house and the density for the remaining 70 percent of the property was set at 6 acres per house. The court rejected the developer's contention that there had been a taking:

> Lastly, we find little merit to appellant's contentions that the zoning ordinance has resulted in a taking of appellant's property without just compensation. . . . As the district court found, appellant still has the land and buildings for which it paid $290,000. The estimated worth, had Steel Hill's original plans been approved, is irrelevant. Though the value of the tract has been decreased considerably, it is not worthless or useless so as to constitute a taking.

Thus, in the federal courts, a land-use regulation literally must deny a property owner all "economically viable use of his land"[41] before a taking will be found.[42] Most state courts follow the same principles,[43]

---

39. 504 F.2d at 678-79.
40. 469 F.2d 956 (1st Cir. 1972).
41. 469 F.2d at 963. See also *Construction Industry Ass'n of Sonoma County v. City of Petaluma*, 522 F.2d 897 (9th Cir. 1975), *cert. denied*, 424 U.S. 934 (1976); *State v. Erickson*, 285 N.W.2d 84, 90 (Minn. 1979); and *Candlestick Properties, Inc. v. San Francisco Bay Conservation and Development Commission*, 11 Cal. App. 3d 557, 89 Cal. Rptr. 897 (1970).
42. In fact, two Court of Claims decisions are the only cases in the past 50 years in which any federal court has found that any regulation not involving a physical invasion of property constituted a "taking." *Benenson v. United States*, 212 Ct. Cl. 375, 548 F.2d 939 (1977); *Bydlon v. United States*, 146 Ct. Cl. 764, 175 F. Supp. 891 (1959). In *Benenson*, the Pennsylvania Avenue Development Corporation Act prohibited demolition of Washington, D.C.'s Willard Hotel, which had been gutted preparatory to demolition prior to passage of the act. In *Bydlon*, the Forest Service prohibited airplane landings at the only air strip within miles of an otherwise totally isolated forest resort. In both cases, the Court of Claims found that the regulations at issue left the property owner with no practical use of its property. There have been strong suggestions from other courts that these cases were wrongly decided. For example, in *Pamel Corporation v. Puerto Rico Highway Authority*, 621 F.2d 33, 35 n.4 (1st Cir. 1980), the court referred to *Bydlon* as "a sport." More recently, the Court of Claims seems to have receded from its stricter views and has begun to follow the principles described in the text. See *Deltona Corporation v. United States*, 657 F.2d 1184 (Ct. Cl. 1981), and *Jentgen v. United States*, 657 F.2d 1210 (1981).
43. See generally *900 G Street Associates v. Department of Housing and Community Development*, 430 A.2d 1387 (D.C. App. 1981); *Broadview Apartments Co. v. Commission for Historical and Architectural Preservation*, 290 Md. 538, 433 A 1214 (Md. App. 1981).

although a few states tend to find a regulatory "taking" under the state constitution if there is substantial interference with the property owner's ability to deal the property, even if there is some remaining use. Accordingly, before litigating a "taking" case, it is imperative that the state authorities be examined. Finally, it cannot be emphasized too strongly that "taking" cases turn on the facts, and it is of crucial importance that those trying to preserve a building develop facts to show that preservation does allow for some economically viable use.

What Is Taken?

Property owners typically recognize that in order to show a "taking" under the traditional analysis discussed above, they must show that the property in question has been left with no reasonable use. As a result, owners often attempt to characterize their loss in a way that suggests that some portion of their property has been rendered worthless. This tack, however, has not always been successful for property owners.

For example, in *Penn Central Transportation Co. v. New York City*,[44] Penn Central contended that the denial of a permit to construct an office tower totally deprived it of the use of the "air rights" over the property. The Supreme Court had little difficulty in concluding that the air rights were merely a portion of the ownership rights to the parcel of land on which the Grand Central Station stood and that the proper analysis was to examine the effect on the property as a whole:

> "Taking" jurisprudence does not divide a single parcel into discrete segments and attempt to determine whether rights in a particular segment have been entirely abrogated. In deciding whether a particular governmental action has effected a taking, this Court focuses rather both on the character of the action and on the nature and extent of the interference with rights in the parcel as a whole. . . .[45]

Indeed, as long ago as *Gorieb v. Fox*,[46] which sustained a mandatory setback law against a claim that the effect of the law was to "take" the portion of the property from the street line to the setback, the Court noted that a property must be considered as a whole in an analysis of whether a regulation goes "too far."

More recently, however, courts have been grappling, without particular success, with ordinances that have differing effects on different portions of large parcels. For example, in *American Savings & Loan Ass'n.*

---

44. *Penn Central Transportation Co. v. New York City, supra* note 1.
45. *Id.* at 130-31.
46. 274 U.S. 603 (1927).

v. County of Marin,⁴⁷ the plaintiff owned 68 acres of land. The county adopted a rezoning that allowed four residences per acre on 20 of the acres and one residence per 5 acres on the remainder. In a suit alleging that the county had "taken" the portion of the property zoned for one residence per 5 acres, the county contended that the impact should be measured over the entire parcel, not merely the portion of the parcel with more onerous zoning. The district court agreed and explained its ruling as follows.

> The problem is that the constitution doesn't protect parcels of land. The constitution protects the owner of land from an uncompensated taking and the owner is a single person. When you look at what is claimed to be the taking, you must look at the entire area of his affected ownership and we are dealing here with what to all of the senses appears to be a single parcel of undeveloped land and the county or community plan for permitting development of it.⁴⁸

In its initial and now withdrawn opinion, the Ninth Circuit concluded that having determined to treat the two portions of the parcel differently in the zoning ordinances, the county could not argue that the entire parcel must be considered as a unit for a "taking" analysis. In support of this result, the court cited *Fifth Avenue Corp. v. Washington County*,⁴⁹ which had reached a somewhat similar conclusion. On rehearing, however, the Ninth Circuit changed its position. The two-judge majority concluded that, since the ordinance treated the two portions of the parcel differently, "this tends to require" that the effect on them be examined separately, but that until a development plan is submitted and then reacted to by the county, it would be impossible to determine whether the parcel should be treated as a unit or not.⁵⁰ The dissenting judge thought the inquiry was not entirely dependent on the statutory treatment but rather that "if it is just and fair under the circumstances" to take into account the economic effect on the entire parcel, then the court should do so and if it is not "just and fair" the court should not.⁵¹

The same type of argument was made by the plaintiff in *San Diego Gas & Electric Co. [SDG&E] v. City of San Diego*.⁵² There, the company had acquired 412 acres of property, approximately 213 of which were later made subject to the city's "open space" plan. The company

---

47. 637 F.2d 601 (advance sheets only) (1980) (opinion withdrawn), *opinion on rehearing*, 653 F.2d 364 (9th Cir. 1981).
48. 653 F.2d at 368.
49. 282 Or. 591, 581 P.2d 50 (1978).
50. 653 F.2d at 371.
51. *Id.* at 372.
52. 450 U.S. 621 (1981).

brought suit claiming that the open space plan amounted to a "taking" of the 213 acres; neither the plaintiff nor the defendant pointed out to the court that the company owned an additional contiguous 199 acres or argued that the impact of the city's actions on the parcel as a whole had to be considered. When the case reached the Supreme Court, the issue was not decided, but remanded for further proceedings. However, both the majority and dissent referred to SDG&E's holdings as a "412 acre parcel," and the majority referred to the original cost of the entire parcel. This tends to suggest that both the majority and the dissent considered that it is the impact on the property as a whole, rather than on some portion of the property, that must be considered in determining whether a regulatory burden amounts to a "taking." The issue in *SDG&E* remains to be resolved.[53]

Who Can Claim a "Taking"?

Although any property owner can claim a "taking," the courts have developed different legal tests for property acquired with notice of restrictions.

When a property owner challenges a land-use regulation that he could not have foreseen and that affects a property after it was acquired, the courts look in some detail at the owner's particular circumstances in evaluating whether a "taking" has occurred.[54] Different criteria are applied to situations in which the regulation is in place *before* the property is acquired or in which the owner acquires the property *with notice* of the impact of the regulation that will take effect thereafter.[55]

When an owner purchases a piece of property knowing that it is subject to restrictions, the price paid presumably reflects these restrictions. Allowing the owner to *circumvent* these restrictions would give the owner

---

53. Questions also can arise as to whether a "taking," if found, is permanent or temporary. For example, assume that a municipality's denial of a demolition permit is held to be a "taking" (which is not very likely). Does that mean that the municipality has permanently "taken" the property and must pay the owner the full value, or can the city change its mind without compensation liability or with liability for only a temporary "taking"? As discussed in some detail in the section on remedies, one of the latter two possibilities is virtually certain to be the case.

54. See *Penn Central Transportation Co. v. New York City*, supra note 1, at 104, 124.

55. See *Salsbery v. District of Columbia Board of Zoning Adjustment*, 357 A.2d 402 (D.C. App. 1976).

a windfall. Thus, it is fair to say that when an owner, in this case a company,

> ... bought land which [it] knew might be subjected to restrictions ... the price paid should have been discounted by the possibility that restrictions would be imposed. Since [it] got exactly what [it] meant to buy, it can perhaps be said that society has effected no redistribution [that is, reduction in value] so far as [it is] concerned. . . .[56]

Furthermore, the courts repeatedly have held that "[a] landowner cannot create his own hardship and then require that zoning [or similar] regulations be changed to meet that hardship . . . [b]ecause [his] own voluntary acts caused the hardship. . . ."[57] Indeed, the result could hardly be otherwise or else any land-use restriction would be inapplicable to anyone who overpaid or acquired a property with the expectation of doing something not permitted by the regulations in place at the time of purchase.

For example, assume that an owner's property, presently zoned as residential, would be worth twice as much with commercial zoning. Assume further that the owner sells to a buyer who pays the commercial-use value for the property. If the buyer is denied commercial zoning, is there a "taking"? Of course not, because the buyer purchased with notice, and the loss is the buyer's own making. In fact, the buyer is in no better position to challenge the regulation than the seller would have been. See *HFH, Ltd. v. Superior Court of Los Angeles County*.[58] The same principle holds for preservation ordinances.

For this reason many courts have adopted the rule that a "volunteer" claiming a "taking" can sustain its case only " . . . if a prior owner would be entitled to such relief."[59] Thus, the "volunteer" may simply inherit the legal position of the previous owner, whatever the particular facts of the "volunteer's" circumstance. And other courts have suggested that a buyer with notice may have no "taking" claim under any circumstances, for the reasons described in the *HFH* case.

---

56. *HFH, Ltd. v. Superior Court of Los Angeles County*, 15 Cal. 3d 508, 521, 542 P.2d 237, 246, 125 Cal. Rptr. 365, 374 (1975), *cert. denied*, 425 U.S. 904 (1976), quoting F. Michelman, *Property, Utility, and Fairness: Comments on the Ethical Foundations of "Just Compensation" Law*, 80 Harv. L. Rev. 1165, 1238 (1967).
57. *C.F. Lytle Co. v. Clark*, 491 F.2d 834, 838 (10th Cir. 1974).
58. See *HFH, Ltd. v. Superior Court of Los Angeles County*, *supra* note 56.
59. *Wilson v. Borough of Mountainside*, 42 N.J. 426, 452, 201 A.2d 540, 554 (1964).

When Can a "Taking" Be Claimed?

Ripeness. While it is, of course, possible in theory to attack a preservation or other ordinance or statute as a "taking" on its face, there are no cases, at least in the federal courts, in which such a claim has been sustained. Indeed, in a recent case, the Supreme Court strongly implied that a regulatory statute could virtually never be found, on its face, to be a "taking."[60] Instead, in the federal courts, the few successful claims appear to be limited to circumstances in which the actual impact of a regulatory scheme on a particular property was judged to be too severe.

In assessing such claims, virtually all courts, in one guise or another, have imposed "an exhaustion of administrative remedies" or "ripeness" requirement. This means that a property owner must complete the administrative appeals process before a court will consider the merits of the case. For example, the California courts have held that when the impact of a regulatory scheme is alleged to be a "taking," before challenging the scheme in the courts, a property owner must apply for the use or uses to which he contends entitlement and must pursue administrative remedies prior to suit.[61]

Many other states have similar rules, and the Supreme Court, in its recent decision in *Agins v. City of Tiburon*,[62] reached essentially the same conclusion. Thus, in *Agins*, the city had enacted a zoning ordinance that reduced the "as of right" number of units—those allowed automatically by statute—for a five-acre parcel from five to one but left the city the option to allow as many as five units, depending on the owner's specific plans. When the property owner claimed the rezoning constituted a "taking," the Supreme Court noted that the owner had not submitted any plans for development and that, until this process was completed, he could not make a "taking" claim. As a result, it will be quite difficult for a property owner to succeed in an attack on a preservation ordinance unless he applies for a permit and is rejected.

Moreover, when the "taking" claim is one which arises out of the application of a general land-use ordinance to a particular person's prop-

---

60. *Hodel v. Virginia Surface Mining & Reclamation Ass'n*, 452 U.S. 264, 293-97 (1981).

61. *Metcalf v. Los Angeles County*, 24 Cal. 2d 267, 269, 148 P.2d 645, 646 (1944); *Pan Pacific Properties, Inc. v. County of Santa Cruz*, 81 Cal. App. 3d 244, 249-51, 146 Cal. Rptr. 428, 431-33 (1978).

62. 447 U.S. 255 (1980).

erty, at least one federal circuit court has held that a "taking" cannot occur until the body responsible for the legislation "is given a realistic opportunity and reasonable time within which to review its . . . legislation vis-a-vis the particular property and to correct the inequity."[63]

Moratorium. A limited moratorium designed to protect the status quo while planning or preservation actions are considered—even if it prevents all use of the property for a temporary period—is almost never found to be a "taking."[64]

For example, the court in *Toms River Affiliates v. Department of Environmental Protection*[65] held that the New Jersey Commissioner of Environmental Protection had the power to deny a building permit for a high-rise residential structure in a coastal area in order to preserve the status quo pending implementation of regulations under the state's Coastal Area Facility Review Act and that such a freeze of the builder's development was not a "taking." The court's rationale is apt here.

> The ultimate test of the validity of the administrative action which freezes the applicant's development until it can be considered in the light of the comprehensive plan to be adopted in the near future is whether it is reasonable. With the adoption of a new statute which requires extensive studies and preparation of a comprehensive plan for development of the coastal area involved it is inevitable that implementation will require a considerable period of time. Does this mean that the agency is powerless to prevent the potential frustration of a consistent and comprehensive plan by uncontrolled helter skelter construction in the interim?
>
> Public welfare sought to be advanced by the police power underlying the jurisdiction of the regulatory agency demands the availability of some interim measures to preserve the status quo pending the adoption of a final plan. "Freeze" regulations have thus been approved as reasonable in the analogous area of planning and zoning. Such "stop gap" legislation is a reasonable exercise of power to prevent changes in the character of the area or a community before officialdom has an opportunity to complete a proper study and final plan which will operate on a permanent basis.[66]

---

63. *Hernandez v. City of Lafayette*, 643 F.2d 1188 (5th Cir. 1981).
64. See, e. g., *Donohue Construction Co. v. Montgomery County Council*, 567 F.2d 603, 606 n.5 (4th Cir. 1977); *Wincamp Partnership v. Anne Arundel County*, 458 F. Supp. 1009, 1015, 1024-25 (D. Md. 1978); *Smoke Rise, Inc. v. Washington Suburban Sanitary Commission* 400 F. Supp. 1369, 1381-90 (D. Md. 1975); *State v. Superior Court of Orange County*, 12 Cal. 3d 237, 252-55, 115 Cal. Rptr. 497, 507-9, 524 P.2d 1281, 1290-93 (1974).
65. 140 N.J. Super. 135, 355 A.2d 679 (1976).
66. 355 A.2d at 688-89 (citation omitted).

The same rationale applies in the historic preservation field, for example, when a locality imposes a ban on demolition permits in a proposed historic district until a plan to deal with the district can be adopted. Of course, a locality's power to adopt such a moratorium as a statutory matter will depend on state law.[67]

What Is the Remedy for a "Taking"?

Constitutional Remedies. In recent years, the nature of the remedy for a "taking" available to an owner under the U.S. Constitution has been litigated frequently. Property owners generally have contended that, if a regulation is so burdensome as to amount to a "taking," compensation must be paid and must be the full market value of the property. According to this argument, an overly burdensome regulation amounts to an "inverse condemnation," and the effect is that the government agency involved has purchased the property. In contrast, government agencies and others have argued that the only relief required for a "taking" is to strike down the offending regulation. To award compensation, they say, and particularly to award compensation equaling the total value of the property, would put the government in the position of purchasing property when it did not intend to and would needlessly chill proper regulation.

The majority view on this issue in the states, as exemplified by the California Supreme Court's decision in *Agins v. City of Tiburon*,[68] which the Supreme Court affirmed in 1980 without considering the damage issue, has been that striking down the offending regulation is normally full relief.

While most of the litigation on this subject has been in state courts, the Supreme Court's comments in *San Diego Gas & Electric Co.*

---

67. A number of state moratorium decisions are discussed in chapter 2.
68. 24 Cal. 3d 266, 157 Cal. Rptr. 372, 598 P.2d 25 (1979), *aff'd*, 447 U.S. 255 (1980). See also the following cases: *Eck v. City of Bismarck*, 283 N.W.2d 193, 201 (N.D. 1979); *Gary D. Reihart, Inc. v. Township of Carroll*, 409 A.2d 1167 (Pa. 1979); *Holaway v. City of Pipestone*, 269 N.W.2d 28, 30-31 (Minn. 1978); *Davis v. Pima County*, 121 Ariz. 343, 590 P.2d 459 (Ariz. App. 1978), *cert. denied*, 442 U.S. 942 (1979); *Fred F. French Investing Co. v. City of New York*, 39 N.Y.2d 587, 385 N.Y.S.2d 5, 350 N.E.2d 381, *appeal dismissed*, 429 U.S. 990 (1976); *Gold Run, Ltd. v. Board of County Commissioners*, 554 P.2d 317, 318-19 (Colo. App. 1976); *Mailman Development Corporation v. City of Hollywood*, 286 So. 2d 614, 615 (Fla. App. 1973), *cert. denied*, 419 U.S. 844 (1974); and *Visidor Corporation v. Borough of Cliffside Park*, 48 N.J. 214, 225 A.2d 105 (1966), *cert. denied*, 386 U.S. 972 (1967).

[SDG&E] v. City of San Diego[69] are of substantial interest here. In this case, SDG&E contended that the land-use regulations of the city of San Diego amounted to a "taking" and sued for the full value of the property on the theory that the city had, in effect, condemned the property. The California appellate court held that, under the rule described above, even if a "taking" had occurred, the only relief to which SDG&E would be entitled was to have the regulation struck down.

The Supreme Court agreed to review the case but ultimately dismissed it on a technicality. However, four dissenting justices (joined in part by one of the justices from the majority) explicitly rejected the argument that, if there is a regulatory "taking," the city has in effect bought the property involved.

> [C]ontrary to appellant's claim that San Diego must formally condemn its property and pay full fair market value, nothing in the Just Compensation Clause empowers a court to order a government entity to condemn the property and pay its full fair market value, where the "taking" already effected is temporary and reversible and the government wants to halt the "taking." Just as the government may cancel condemnation before passage of title, or abandon property it has temporarily occupied or invaded, it must have the same power to rescind a regulatory "taking."[70]

Nevertheless, according to Justice Brennan's dissenting opinion, when a regulatory "taking" occurs, some "compensation *must* be awarded" if there are damages. The opinion makes it very clear, however, that, if the regulation is struck down, compensation need only be awarded to the plaintiff "for any economic loss suffered during the time his property was taken." In other words, the award would cover only interim damages, if any. Perhaps because no one had briefed or argued the issue, the dissenting justices did not attempt to explain in detail what measure of damages they viewed as appropriate if the landowner could prove injury. They did specifically say, however, that there is no particular procedure or form of remedy that the states must adopt and that the states "should be free to experiment in the implementation of this rule. . . ."

Based on the comments of the four dissenters and the fifth justice who more or less agreed with them, it seems likely that, if and when the issue is finally resolved, the Supreme Court will hold that compensation is required for regulatory "takings," but that such damages are limited to interim losses, if any, that occur before the regulation is aban-

---

69. *San Diego Gas & Electric Co. [SDG&E] v. City of San Diego*, *supra* note 24.
70. 450 U.S. 621, 658 (1981) (citations omitted).

doned or struck down. This means, of course, that there is some possible monetary liability for governmental units. But the major contention of the "inverse condemnation" bar—that a regulatory "taking" means that the government has bought the property—is not likely to be accepted by the Supreme Court.

It also appears from the dissent that states and municipalities may limit their liability by procedural measures. One such measure would be to adopt statutes (and ordinances, when authorized) providing that, if "inverse condemnation" compensation was awarded for a regulatory "taking," neither attorneys' fees nor interest may be added to the compensation. This would distinguish regulatory "takings" from true condemnation actions in which land actually is appropriated by the government and would substantially lessen potential exposure. The United States already has such a statute limiting its own liability in this regard. States and municipalities also might consider adopting damage tests, akin to those for breach of contract, that would require a property owner to show that it has in fact been injured by any temporary "taking." Whether any such statute or ordinance would be upheld is not clear, because this is a different test than is normally used in "taking" cases.[71] But in view of the dissent's invitation to states to experiment with different procedural rules on the subject, the idea seems worth trying since in most instances a property owner who is allowed to proceed after winning a "taking" case could probably not show actual damages.

Section 1983. In addition to the remedies available directly under the Constitution, a property owner who claims that land-use regulations are so burdensome as to be unconstitutional may have a statutory remedy under the Civil Rights Act of 1871, 42 U.S.C. § 1983. In brief, Section 1983 provides for injunctive relief and damages against "persons" who, acting under color of state or local law, deprive another of his constitutional rights.[72] The term "under color" of state or local

---

71. In "taking" cases, the traditional measure of compensation has been the value of whatever was "taken" as opposed to the damages suffered by the property owner involved. For example, in a typical situation in which a permit is denied under an ordinance struck down as a "taking," the property may well have appreciated in the interim so that the property owner suffered no actual damages from the delay. On the other hand, if the rental value for the interim period of the delay was considered the measure of compensation, then compensation might be awarded.

72. The statute provides that

[e]very person who, under color of any statute, ordinance, regulation, custom, or usage, of any State or Territory or the District of Columbia, subjects, or causes to be subjected,

law simply means persons acting in an official capacity, even if they exceed their authority.[73] A claim that officials of state or local government adopted or enforced a land-use regulation that amounts to an unconstitutional "taking" or acted in a way that violates due process is thus literally within the terms of the statute.

Until 1978, however, the Supreme Court consistently had held that governments were not "persons" under Section 1983. Accordingly, municipal and state agencies, and their agents acting in their official capacities, could not be sued under the statute. In *Monell v. Department of Social Services*,[74] the Supreme Court overturned its earlier decisions and reversed itself insofar as municipalities are concerned:

> Local governing bodies, therefore, can be sued directly under Section 1983 for monetary, declaratory, and injunctive relief where, as here, the action that is alleged to be unconstitutional implements or executes a policy statement, ordinance, regulation, or decision officially adopted and promulgated by that body's officers.[75]

Moreover, in *Owen v. City of Independence*,[76] the Supreme Court held that municipalities are not entitled to a qualified good faith defense under Section 1983.[77]

It is worth noting that there is still an immunity under Section 1983 for legislative activity. That is, Section 1983 does not cover actions by the legislative branch. This immunity certainly applies to states and probably still applies to municipalities. Thus, for example, in *Lake Country Estates, Inc. v. Tahoe Regional Planning Agency*,[78] which involved regulations adopted by a bistate planning agency, the Supreme Court found that the adoption of zoning-like regulations was essentially legislative in nature and was therefore immune from challenge under

---

any citizen of the United States or other person within the jurisdiction thereof to the deprivation of any rights, privileges, or immunities secured by the Constitution and laws, shall be liable to the party injured in an action at law, suit in equity, or other proper proceeding for redress.

73. *Monroe v. Pape*, 365 U.S. 167, 183-85 (1961).
74. 436 U.S. 658 (1978).
75. *Id.* at 690.
76. 445 U.S. 622 (1980).
77. A qualified good faith defense allows an individual defendant to escape liability under the statute, even if he or she acted unconstitutionally, if the actions were reasonable under the circumstances and the defendant was not aware that the behavior involved was unlawful or unconstitutional.
78. 440 U.S. 391 (1979).

Section 1983. Similarly, in *Gorman Towers, Inc. v. Bogoslavsky*,[79] a developer challenged a city council's rezoning of a site as a "taking," but the court found that no lawsuit could be brought under Section 1983.[80]

These decisions make it clear that local governments are subject to suit under Section 1983 for unconstitutional land-use decisions that are not solely the product of legislative activity. Thus, while there is probably no Section 1983 remedy if a city council creates a historic district, there is a remedy against the local government if a city official refuses to allow a development in such a district (assuming that the official's action is found to amount to a "taking," which is highly unlikely). Moreover, unlike remedies implied directly under the Constitution, there is no doubt that the proper remedy under Section 1983 includes both injunctive relief and damages.

Because the right of action against municipalities under Section 1983 is only three years old, there are few decided cases. It can be expected, however, that Section 1983 suits will become much more frequent.

Practical Suggestions for Avoiding "Takings"[81]

There is no sure-fire method to avoid the "taking" issue—unless a community simply abdicates its responsibility to regulate land in the public interest—since the courts will continue to scrutinize land-use regulations on a case-by-case basis. But there are a number of precautions that can reduce the likelihood that local preservation regulations or decisions will be found to be "takings."

---

79. 626 F.2d 607 (8th Cir. 1980).

80. One recent decision has concluded that the immunity extends to the individuals involved but not to the city government itself. *Hernandez v. City of Lafayette*, 643 F.2d 1188 (5th Cir. 1981). It remains to be seen whether this decision will be followed by other courts. But in any case, as described previously, a "taking" suit would still lie under the Constitution, for legislative activity has no exemption from the Constitution. The significance, then, of the absence of a Section 1983 remedy lies solely in the fact that Section 1983 authorizes damage awards while, as also previously discussed, the availability of damages directly under the Constitution is not so clear. Section 1983 does not authorize punitive damages against municipalities. *City of Newport v. Fact Concerts, Inc.*, 453 U.S. 247, 271 (1981).

81. Some of the material in this subsection originally appeared in Christopher J. Duerksen, "Constitutional Issues in Land-Use Law: The 'Taking Issues,' " in *Land Use Law: Issues for the Eighties*, ed. by Edith Netter (Chicago: American Planning Association, 1981), pp.195-214.

Evidence of Study and Forethought. Courts are usually favorably impressed when a local government can demonstrate that it has conducted studies and surveys prior to enacting land-use regulations. Such studies and surveys support the type of independent legislative judgment that courts are reluctant to overturn and also support general notions of fairness. For example, in *Penn Central Transportation Co. v. New York City*,[82] the Supreme Court pointed out the importance of studying and identifying landmark properties before subjecting them to controls. The Maryland Supreme Court, in *Potomac Sand & Gravel Co. v. Governor of Maryland*,[83] upheld restrictions on gravel mining in tidal lands, emphasizing the extensive evidence the state had compiled on the biological importance of the wetlands. In contrast are cases like *Sturdy Homes, Inc. v. Township of Redford*,[84] in which the court struck down a floodplain zoning ordinance because the township did not produce evidence that the plaintiff's land was subject to flooding. Courts also view with a jaundiced eye last-minute efforts to stop development because of public pressure rather than careful planning. When regulations conform to a local plan, courts are more likely to sustain them as further evidence of forethought.[85]

Spreading Benefits and Burdens. In recent land-use cases, the Supreme Court has attached importance to the fact that the challenged regulations did not single out the plaintiff's property for unduly harsh treatment. For example, in the *Penn Central* case, the Court noted that the challenged landmark restrictions applied to hundreds of properties and districts throughout New York and thus produced a fair and equitable distribution of the benefits and burdens of governmental action.[86] Thus, to the extent possible, preservation regulations should be applied to the entire area or similarly situated individual structures identified by available studies, surveys, and evidence.

Multiple Public Goals. A number of public purposes, such as protection of economic and environmental values, are sufficiently important that the courts tend to sustain regulations based on these considera-

---

82. *Penn Central Transportation Co. v. New York City, supra* note 1.
83. 266 Md. 358, 293 A.2d 241, *cert. denied*, 409 U.S. 1040 (1972).
84. 30 Mich. App. 53, 186 N.W.2d 43 (1971).
85. See, e. g., *Golden v. Planning Board of Town of Ramapo*, 30 N.Y.2d 359, 334 N.Y.S.2d 138, 285 N.E.2d 291 (1971), *appeal dismissed*, 409 U.S. 1003 (1972), and *A-S-P Associates v. City of Raleigh*, 298 N.C. 207, 258 S.E.2d 444 (1979).
86. See also *Agins v. City of Tiburon, supra* note 2.

tions, despite serious economic impacts. At the other end of the spectrum are land-use regulations that serve the public convenience (for example, controlling the color of houses in a new subdivision) but are obviously not crucial to the public welfare. When the evidence so justifies, preservation regulations should invoke a wide range of important public goals (for example, protecting the economy and encouraging tourism, and so forth). This tack proved successful in many cases in the early years of historic preservation controls, before the Supreme Court placed its imprimatur on landmark preservation.[87]

Formal Administrative Review Process. The Supreme Court served notice in *Agins* and *San Diego Gas & Electric* that it will be difficult for a property owner to prove that a land-use regulation constitutes a "taking" unless the owner has applied for development permission and given the local government a fair opportunity to review a specific proposal. This is the so-called exhaustion of administrative remedies doctrine described earlier.

A detailed administrative review process can be used to evaluate the merits of a proposed development, to defuse potential disputes, to elicit economic evidence that will be valuable should a case go to court, and perhaps to preclude the possibility of damages ever being awarded. For example, Washington, D.C., has established an administrative process whereby any owner who claims that denying a demolition permit for a protected historic structure would amount to a "taking" must apply for a permit on that ground and provide the relevant evidence to prove a "taking" before a hearing officer. If the permit is denied, the applicant may appeal the administrative decision in court and, if he prevails, will obtain the permit. Since the permit would be granted whenever a denial would be a "taking," the city runs no risk of having to pay damages. Failure to appeal or unsuccessfully appealing the administrative decision would make the "no taking" finding final and would preclude a separate suit for damages. Either way, the city has protected itself against damage awards.

---

87. E. g., *Opinion of the Justices*, 128 N.E.2d 557 (Mass. 1955), approving landmark restrictions enacted to protect historic Nantucket on economic as well as cultural grounds.

FIRST AMENDMENT ISSUES

The First Amendment to the U.S. Constitution provides, among other things, for freedom of speech and religion. While the relevance of these provisions to historic preservation law may not be immediately apparent, there recently have been several cases in which First Amendment rights have intersected with preservation concerns. For example, a number of communities have adopted antibillboard and other sign ordinances that have an effect on freedom of speech. A number of communities also have regulated church property in a way that churches have maintained interferes with their ability to use their property to promote religious beliefs.

Sign Ordinances

A number of states, cities, and towns have imposed restrictions on billboards and signs. Some of these restrictions are for highway and urban areas; others are particularly designed for historic districts. These regulations vary from design-control standards to limitations on size and shape to outright bans of billboards. Often the ostensible purpose for the regulations is the improvement of highway safety through the removal of distracting signs, but most sign ordinances are based at least in part on aesthetic considerations.

The adoption of sign ordinances has led to a significant amount of litigation, culminating in the recent decision in the United States Supreme Court in *Metromedia, Inc. v. City of San Diego*.[88] Although that case produced five separate opinions from the justices, it does approve of sign controls based on aesthetic considerations and provides relatively clear guidelines for sign control ordinances in most instances.

In *Metromedia*, the city of San Diego had enacted a nearly total ban on billboards within the city limits. The ordinance allowed exceptions for on-site commercial signs; political campaign signs; historic and religious markers; time, temperature, and news signs; and a few others. The Supreme Court of California sustained the measure, but the United States Supreme Court reversed the decision, holding that the San Diego ordinance was in several respects an unconstitutional interference of First Amendment freedom of expression.

Justice White, writing for four members of the Court, concluded that the city's purposes—highway safety and attempts to beautify the city—

---

88. 453 U.S. 490 (1981).

were substantial and provided valid grounds for some limitations on signs. Specifically, Justice White found that the city could validly prohibit off-premises commercial signs.[89] (By commercial, the Court means containing only business-related material, including advertisements and the like, material which previous court decisions have held is entitled to less constitutional protection than noncommercial material.) Justice White also concluded that the city's purposes would allow "time and place restrictions" even on noncommercial signs. Thus, the tenor of Justice White's opinion suggests that it would have been permissible had the ordinance prohibited noncommercial billboards in only a portion of the city (for example, a historic district). However, Justice White's opinion did not decide whether San Diego could have prohibited all off-site noncommercial signs. Instead, the opinion holds that San Diego cannot regulate the content of signs by allowing some exceptions and not allowing others. Accordingly, Justice White concluded that the regulation was unconstitutional in that respect.

Three justices, in three separate opinions, indicated that they agreed with the portion of Justice White's opinion that found the San Diego ordinance permissible for commercial signs, but they dissented from the plurality ruling on noncommercial signs. These three justices concluded that the purposes of highway safety and urban beautification were substantial enough to empower the city of San Diego to ban all, or less than all, billboards regardless of their content, since there remained open many other avenues to convey similar messages.

Two other justices concurred with the part of Justice White's opinion that struck down the restrictions on noncommercial signs but dissented from the portion of the opinion that upheld the restraint on commercial signs. These justices believed that the ordinance should be held invalid in its entirety because the city had not met its burden of showing that the ban was really necessary. (But even the dissenting justices thought that signs could be banned in scenic places like Yellowstone Park.)

Sorting out the various opinions indicates that *Metromedia* has set forth the following constitutional rules of decision for sign ordinances:

---

89. The specific test utilized is that restrictions of truthful speech (including signs) regarding lawful commercial activity are proper only where the restriction (1) seeks to implement a substantial government interest, (2) directly advances that interest, and (3) goes no further than necessary to accomplish the objective. *Id.* at 507. See also *Central Hudson v. Public Service Commission*, 447 U.S. 557, 563-66 (1980).

- A prohibition of all off-premises commercial signs is constitutional.
- A prohibition of all signs, both commercial and noncommercial, is permissible if confined to a relatively limited area of special interest such as a historic district.
- A broad-scale prohibition of all signs is probably not possible unless a total ban supports a "sufficiently substantial government interest."

Thus, the impact of the decision on preservation concerns is relatively clear. An ordinance controlling sign size, shape, color, and so on, and even an ordinance prohibiting all off-premises signs, will be upheld as applied to landmark buildings and historic districts against a First Amendment challenge. Moreover, insofar as the ordinance is limited to landmark structures and historic districts, no exceptions need be made for noncommercial signs.

Church Properties

In a few recent cases, churches have claimed that landmark statutes could not be applied to church-owned property because they would violate the church's First Amendment guarantee of freedom of religion. Such claims have been made in California, New York, and Indiana, and there may be more such claims with the spread of stronger landmark laws.

The U.S. Supreme Court has recognized that the First Amendment does not exempt religious organizations from governmental regulation. For example, in *Braunfeld v. Brown*,[90] the U.S. Supreme Court adopted a balancing test that has become the hallmark of analysis under the free exercise of religion clause of the First Amendment. Under this test,

> . . . if the State regulates conduct by enacting a general law within its power, the purpose and effect of which is to advance the State's secular goals, the statute is valid despite its indirect burden on religious observance unless the State may accomplish its purpose by means which do not impose such a burden.[91]

Applying this test, the Court in *Braunfeld* upheld a "Sunday closing" law that indirectly interfered with the religious practices of Jewish merchants whose beliefs required them to abstain from business on Saturday. The Court said: "To strike down, without the most critical scrutiny, legislation which imposes only an indirect burden on the exercise of religion, i.e., legislation which does not make unlawful the religious

---

90. 366 U.S. 599 (1961).
91. *Id.* at 607. See also *Sherbert v. Verner*, 374 U.S. 398, 406 (1963).

practice itself, would radically restrict the operating latitude of the legislature."[92]

The rule indicates that the First Amendment does not prohibit the application of preservation statutes to church property except, perhaps, in those cases in which the church would be entirely prevented from using its property in a way necessary for religious exercise and in which less restrictive alternatives exist.

A leading case directly in point is *Society for Ethical Culture v. Spatt*.[93] The *Spatt* case involved the landmark designation of a Meeting House of the Society for Ethical Culture, a religious, educational, and charitable organization. The Society planned to demolish the meeting house and to erect an apartment building for investment purposes. Contending that landmark designation precluded this action and thereby foreclosed a source of revenue to be used for charitable purposes, the Society claimed that its right to free exercise of religion under the First Amendment was violated. In support of this contention, the Society relied on *Westchester Reform Temple v. Brown*,[94] in which the New York Court of Appeals held unconstitutional, as applied, a zoning statute that would have prohibited the construction of a synagogue with adjacent parking space virtually anywhere in the town.

Finding that the "Society's dominant purpose was not so much to effect improvement of inadequate or outmoded buildings as it was to exploit the development potential of the site for financial gain, albeit for charitable purposes," the court held that landmark designation did not interfere with the Society's freedom of religion.[95] The court pointed out that church property may be subject to a certain degree of regulation and that

> . . . the Society does not seek simply to replace a religious facility with a new larger facility. Instead, using the need to replace as justification, it seeks the unbridled right to develop its property as it sees fit. This is impermissible, and the restriction here involved cannot be deemed an abridgement of any First Amendment freedom, particularly when the contemplated use, or a large part of it, is wholly unrelated to the exercise of religion, except for the tangential benefit of raising revenue through development. . . . If, at some point in the

---

92. 366 U.S. at 606.
93. 68 A.D.2d 112, 416 N.Y.S.2d 246 (1979), *aff'd*, 51 N.Y.2d 449, 434 N.Y.S.2d 932, 415 N.E.2d 922 (1980).
94. 22 N.Y.2d 488, 293 N.Y.S.2d 297, 239 N.E.2d 891 (1968).
95. 416 N.Y.S.2d 246, 252 (1979).

future, [the Society] decides to seek permission to replace the present Meeting House with a larger one designed to meet the needs which a clearly outmoded building could not provide, and is denied permission, then perhaps a claim of . . . First Amendment impairment might lie.[96]

Similarly, the Indiana Supreme Court has upheld zoning statutes that place reasonable conditions on, rather than prohibit or otherwise make unlawful, church use of property. In *Board of Zoning Appeals of Decatur v. Decatur, Indiana, Company of Jehovah's Witnesses*,[97] the court upheld the application of certain setback restrictions to a church, explaining that "the building of churches is subject to such reasonable regulations as may be necessary to promote the public health, safety or general welfare."[98] And the Pennsylvania supreme court has held that church property is subject to the same land-use regulations as any other property and that a church can avoid land-use regulations only by making the same showing (for example, a "taking") as any other landowner.[99]

Thus, it appears that a church generally cannot raise the First Amendment to prevent landmark designation or application of adequate maintenance and antidemolition provisions. There may be instances, however, in which a church will claim that a particular remodeling or perhaps demolition is necessary for the use of the property for church purposes, and no other solution is feasible. In such a case, the First Amendment issues will receive careful consideration based on the balancing test described above.

FURTHER READINGS

There is no shortage of books, treatises, and articles on constitutional law. A good recent overview, though somewhat lean on Fifth Amendment "taking issue" analysis, is Laurence Tribe's *American Constitutional Law* (Mineola, N.Y.: The Foundation Press, Inc., 1978).

There are fortunately a number of good sources that focus more specifically on constitutional issues involved in land-use regulation. One of the best general surveys, although now somewhat dated, is David

---

96. *Id.* at 253.
97. 233 Ind. 83, 117 N.E.2d 115 (1954).
98. 233 Ind. at 88, 117 N.E.2d at 118.
99. *First Presbyterian Church v. City Council*, 25 Pa. Comwlth. 49, 360 A.2d 257 (1976).

Godschalk et al., *Constitutional Issues of Growth Management*, 2d ed. (Chicago: APA Planners Press, 1979). The American Planning Association has recently issued another publication that supplements Godschalk's work, Edith Netter, ed., *Land-Use Law: Issues for the Eighties* (Chicago: APA Planners Press, 1981). Fred Bosselman, David Callies, and John Banta, *The Taking Issue* (Washington, D.C.: GPO, 1973), remains a key source on the development of the all-important "taking issue." Other excellent general sources include Frank Schnidman and Jane Silverman, eds., *Management and Control of Growth: Updating the Law* (Washington, D.C.: The Urban Land Institute, 1980); Daniel Mandelker, *Land Use Law* (Charlottesville, Va.: Michie Co., 1982); and Norman Williams, *American Land Planning Law* (Chicago: Callaghan, 1974).

The best sources of current developments in this area are the National Trust for Historic Preservation's *Preservation Law Reporter* and the American Planning Association's *Land Use Law and Zoning Digest*.

Mandatory reading for anyone concerned with constitutional law as it applies to historic preservation is a series of recent U.S. Supreme Court decisions including *Penn Central Transportation Co. v. New York City*, 438 U.S. 104 (1978); *San Diego Gas & Electric Co. (SDG&E) v. City of San Diego*, 450 U.S. 261 (1981); and *Metromedia, Inc. v. City of San Diego*, 453 U.S. 490 (1981).

Chapter 6
Administrative and Judicial Litigation

ANTONIO ROSSMANN

In contrast to even two or three decades ago, historic preservation today involves public debates in the halls of government. Preservationists, therefore, must either initiate or respond to formal public processes: to administrative hearings before governmental agencies and to trial and appeal before the courts. Litigation in the administrative and judicial arenas is simply a fact of the modern political process.

This chapter is aimed at helping attorneys who do not specialize in preservation law to prepare for, and participate in, administrative and judicial proceedings involving historic preservation. It also seeks to help the interested layman—landmarks commissioners, preservationists, and the like—understand and participate in the litigation process.

The chapter outlines the essential elements of the preservationist's case—either as petitioner or respondent—in both administrative and judicial tribunals. It does not include specific forms to be applied; the different American jurisdictions and their variety of administrative and judicial institutions preclude such an effort.

The occasional need for litigation should not yield a false sense of its significance. Preservationists must recognize that the best results usually are not produced in the courtroom but rather in the political forums of preservation commissions, city councils, or state legislatures. Even the *Penn Central Transportation Co. v. New York City* decision,[1] often cited as the fount of a contemporary preservation "mandate," resulted only because preservationists first secured the *political judgment* that New York City would favor preservation of its notable landmarks rather than promote maximum-density development.

---

1. *Penn Central Transportation Co. v. City of New York*, 438 U.S. 104 (1978).

This chapter does not espouse a strategy of aggressive litigation. During the 1980s, within the general area of resource and environmental litigation, we are returning to the traditional mode of American decision making. The courts are shying away from the innovative claims of petitioners who seek to challenge the substance of administrative decisions.[2] At the same time, the courts continue to spurn constitutional challenges to consistent and well-documented preservation programs.[3] A new generation of judges appears to lack the "interventionist" ethic of its immediate predecessors. For these reasons, the favored status today in court is that of the defendant or respondent, not plaintiff or petitioner.

Preservationists, therefore, generally should concentrate their efforts in the administrative, rather than the judicial, process. Whether attempting to advance a regulatory program or defeat a demolition permit, preservationists usually can win their battles by securing a favorable government decision. Today, more than ever, the importance of a political victory cannot be underestimated.

Nonetheless, governmental agencies still produce decisions defective in substance or procedure. Moreover, private interests sometimes ignore the law or challenge governmental preservation actions as unconstitutional. When it becomes evident that preservation interests will suffer in the city council chamber, before the preservation board or planning commission, or at the hands of private developers, preservationists must be prepared to enlist the courts for relief.

Preservationists generally will face one or more of the following tasks in administrative and judicial proceedings:

- Delaying demolition until either a preservation ordinance or landmark designation becomes effective;
- Defeating an application for government approval—such as a demolition permit or public funding of a new project resulting in demolition—that threatens the integrity or existence of a historic or cultural site;

---

2. *Strycker's Bay Neighborhood Council, Inc. v. Karlen*, 444 U.S. 223 (1980); *Vermont Yankee Nuclear Power Corp. v. National Resources Defense Council*, 435 U.S. 519 (1978); *Foundation for San Francisco's Architectural Heritage v. City and County of San Francisco*, 106 Cal. App. 3d 893, 165 Cal. Rptr. 401 (1980) [hereinafter cited as *Foundation*]; *Laurel Hills Homeowners Association v. City Council*, 83 Cal. App. 3d 515, 147 Cal. Rptr. 843 (1978).

3. *Penn Central Transportation Co. v. City of New York*, supra note 1; *Society for Ethical Culture v. Spatt*, 416 N.Y.S.2d 246 (1979), aff'd, 415 N.E.2d 922, (N.Y. 1980); see also *City of New Orleans v. Impastato* 198 La. 206, 3 So. 2d 559 (1941); *Maher v. City of New Orleans*, 516 F.2d 1051 (5th Cir. 1975).

- Refuting a claim that preservation of a threatened property will produce an unconstitutional governmental "taking" of private property;
- Enjoining execution of a demolition permit issued in violation of the law.

For some of these tasks, preservationists may have to begin their efforts in court—for example, to enjoin the public agency that issues a demolition permit with no advance hearing. Usually, however, the preservation effort will begin before a governmental body, such as the city council or board of supervisors, preservation or planning commission, or local department for economic development.

While the substantive issues in the tasks listed above may vary greatly, the mechanics of constructing and presenting a good argument do not. This chapter focuses on the mechanics—for example, how to build a good case before going to court; how to frame a legal claim; and what evidence to present, when, and how. The substantive aspects of the preservationist's case are explored elsewhere in this book. This chapter is designed to help preservationists present substantive claims in an effective manner.

LITIGATION STRATEGY: THE FIRST STEPS

Identifying Relevant Agencies

Almost as soon as a preservation "issue" emerges, preservationists will be able to identify the legislative or administrative arena in which the issue will receive its initial public review and decision. For example, the creation or modification of a local historic preservation ordinance generally will be heard and determined in the local legislative body—a city council or county governing board. Landmark designation will likely be determined by a local preservation commission or, if there is no such commission, by a planning commission or the governing body itself. A demolition permit probably will be heard and determined in a planning commission or governing body, although a local preservation commission, if one exists, will have the authority to comment on and perhaps to delay or deny a permit application. In federal projects, administrative review may amount only to an opportunity to comment informally and object to a sponsoring agency, or may involve formal administrative proceedings before a licensing tribunal. In many federal projects that incorporate local sponsorship and delegate federal environmental review responsibilities—such as the Community Development Block Grant (CDBG) and Urban Development Action Grant (UDAG) programs—preservationists will be faced with administrative actions at both the local and federal levels.

Ascertaining Appropriate Standards of Judicial Review

Once the relevant agency has been identified, preservationists should pinpoint the standards that will guide that agency in reviewing the request or action before it. For example, if an application to demolish has been filed, preservationists should determine what standards govern the agency's discretion in ruling on that application. The review standards will frame the preservationists' substantive case.

Virtually all federal legislation and many local planning or zoning ordinances endow an administrative agency with the authority to render discretionary decisions affecting historical and cultural sites. In both federal jurisprudence and that of most states (for example, California and New York), judicial review examines only procedural matters or abuse of discretion in legislative and administrative matters and the support or lack of rational evidence and findings leading to administrative decisions.[4] The court does not reweigh the evidence but accepts the agency's evaluation of factual conflicts. Even if a petitioner successfully challenges an administrative agency, only occasionally will the court order the substantive result that the petitioner seeks (such as preservation or destruction of a building or district); generally, the court remands the matter back to the administrative agency for further proceedings that take account of the law declared in the court's decision.

In some jurisdictions, however, by virtue of local or state law, the ultimate discretion to preserve or destroy a building or neighborhood may be determined by a trial *de novo* in the reviewing court. In these cases, the court will hear anew all the evidence on both sides and render its own judgment on that evidence. For example, a local preservation ordinance may require that, in any actions challenging a commission's action, the person seeking to demolish a landmark must establish in court (as well as in the landmarks commission itself) that there is no economically feasible alternative to demolition.[5] Under another stan-

---

4. Cal. Civ. Proc. Code §§ 1085, 1094.5 (West Supp. 1982); Cal. Pub. Res. Code §§ 21168, 21168.5 (West Supp. 1982); N.Y. Civ. Prac. Law. R. 7801 (McKinney 1981).

5. For example, New York City Landmarks Law, N.Y.C. Charter § 2004; N.Y.C. Admin. Code. ch. 8-A, §205-1.0 *et seq.* (1976); enforced in *Penn Central Transportation Co. v. City of New York, supra* note 1.

dard of review, a state environmental statute may require that the person adversely affecting important resources, whether plaintiff or defendant, prove the economic necessity for doing so.[6] Under still another standard, a landowner challenging a regulation as an unconstitutional "taking" of property without compensation probably will secure an independent judicial review of the "taking" claim, even though the landowner generally will bear the burden of proof and may be confined to the evidence in the administrative record.

Several recent cases illustrate these various standards of review. California courts, following the traditional "substantial evidence" standard of review, have validated a local agency determination to demolish a nationally significant landmark because "substantial evidence" in the planning commission's testimony supported the developer's contention that it could not preserve the building. The trial court did not hear anew the petitioners' witnesses, who asserted that they could purchase and rehabilitate the structure. Most importantly, the trial court did not attempt to resolve the apparent conflict between the developer's and the preservationists' testimonies before the commission.[7]

In a Minnesota court case, by contrast, in which the plaintiff not only challenged a demolisher's action that threatened a protectable site but also established that the buildings were both threatened and protectable, the defendant was forced to prove that no feasible and prudent alternatives existed. The Minnesota Supreme Court remanded the case to the trial court with instructions to evaluate that evidence *de novo*, and to do so giving "paramount consideration" to the protection of cultural resources.[8]

Assessing the Chances of Success

Preservationists usually must make their initial presentation their best case. This action is necessary, first, to persuade the administrative decision maker of the case's merits and, second, to build a solid record for use in any subsequent judicial review. Unfortunately, presentation usually improves with time; it can take weeks or months to ascertain the weakest point in a demolisher's case and still more time to identify experts or

---

6. For example, Minnesota Environmental Rights Act, Minn. Stat. Ann. § 116B.01-.13 (1980), enforced in *State by Powderly v. Erickson*, 285 N.W.2d 84 (Minn. 1979).

7. *Foundation*, *supra* note 2, interpreting Cal. Pub. Res. Code § 21168.5.

8. *State by Powderly v. Erickson*, *supra* note 6.

developers whose testimony will support the preservation of a resource, challenge the demolisher's plan, and prove that the demolisher can act otherwise. Only rarely, however, will circumstances permit the luxury of this gradual learning process.

There is only one case in which preservationists might benefit by withholding their best testimony or evidence in administrative proceedings. If, and only if, the laws of the jurisdiction make clear that preservationists would not bear the burden of proof in a judicial trial *de novo*—regardless of the outcome at the administrative level—placing a best foot forward in the administrative process actually could prove counterproductive. Presenting the best cases and witnesses in the administrative proceedings would give opponents a better opportunity to prepare for rebutting those witnesses in a judicial trial. The success of such a "sophisticated" strategy can never be assured, however, and it is not recommended unless preservationists know that the local agency will not be moved to favorable action by a vigorous presentation.

Thus, even in an unfavorable forum, preservationists should be very wary of withholding any evidence. A compelling evidentiary case before the administrative agency might force the reviewing court, even under the loosest standard of review, to conclude that a decision authorizing demolition proved arbitrary and capricious because of the overwhelming evidence in favor of restoration. With respect to issues of law or legal analysis, however, preservationists may not always be well advised to lay out their full case before an unfavorable administrative body. For example, in the *Foundation for San Francisco's Architectural Heritage v. City and County of San Francisco* (City of Paris Building) dispute, even though preservationists attempted to state their claims in the vaguest way possible, the developer was able to "learn" from them the technical findings needed to support its demolition permit. The findings the developer presented to the final administrative agency were relied on by the court in affirming the destruction of this landmark.[9]

THE ADMINISTRATIVE PROCESS

Building the Preservation Case

The crafting of a case before an administrative agency generally will include three elements: establishing the agency's and the participant's qualifications, presenting an evidentiary or factual case in favor of preser-

---

9. *Foundation, supra* note 2.

vation, and providing a legal argument in support of preservation.

In proceedings before an agency composed of lay citizens serving part time, the question of agency or participant qualifications is usually not raised or discussed. This fact reflects a fortunate tendency of the courts not to require in lay proceedings that doctrines such as "jurisdiction" and "standing" be raised and determined.[10] Preservationists, however, should be aware of these doctrines and should decide carefully whether or not to address them in an administrative proceeding.

If an agency, for example, is about to act beyond its jurisdiction— for example, to issue a permit not authorized by the relevant local ordinances or to rescind, without authorization, a prior landmark designation—preservationists should object to, and thus avoid, the possibility that opponents would later claim in a judicial proceeding that preservationists waived these claims by not raising them before the agency. Of course, challenging an agency's "competency" to render a particular determination is a sensitive task; decision makers do not appreciate being advised that they lack the legal authority to render a particular decision. Preservationists must, nonetheless, meet that burden with grace and humor. There is no point in avoiding it in order not to stir the agency's anger.

Similarly, preservationists should address the question of their "standing" or qualifications early in the administrative process. Although this issue may be pleaded and litigated only in subsequent judicial actions, both common sense and legal prudence argue for preservationists to assert to the administrative agency their interest in the matter. The greater the qualifications and interest that they can establish at this stage, the more weight the agency is likely to give to their presentation. And if the matter ends up in court, the administrative record will support a sufficient interest in the outcome by preservationists to establish their standing.[11]

Preservationists will then prepare their factual and legal case. As mentioned above, the intensity with which this task is approached will depend on the likelihood of success in the administrative process.

Typically, preservationists will first establish the historical, architec-

---

10. See, for example, *State of California v. Superior Court (Veta Corp.)*, 12 Cal. 3d 237, 115 Cal. Rptr. 497 (1974).

11. The requirements for judicial standing will be discussed later in this chapter. Fortunately, a recent federal appellate decision establishes that standing lies with persons who allege deprivation of an aesthetic resource, even though they are not residents in the neighborhood of the structure proposed for demolition. *Neighborhood Development Corp. v. Advisory Council on Historic Preservation*, 632 F.2d 21 (6th Cir. 1980).

tural, and cultural values at stake. This task emerges foremost in the landmark or district designation process,[12] whether before a landmarks commission or in court.[13] This evidence also will be required, however, when a demolition permit is opposed. Even if a structure has been designated on the national, state, or local register, preservationists must (without reopening the designation issue) reaffirm its cultural significance. This need especially applies when designation has occurred at one level (for example, national) and the demolition decision is to be made by another level of government (for example, local). In the City of Paris case, the building appeared on the National Register as a structure of national significance but never had been designated as a local landmark. In the end, both the local administrative agency and the local reviewing court paid little deference to the National Register listing in assessing the historical and architectural values at stake.[14]

The next step in a preservation case usually involves establishing a substantive position by presenting evidence and expert testimony. If the issue at hand, for example, is whether denial of a demolition permit will work an economic hardship, evidence regarding a feasible alternative to demolition is usually persuasive. In some cases, preservationists may be fortunate enough not to face the initial burden of establishing the availability of alternatives; that task may fall to the developer. This task should not be overlooked, however, for, as discussed in chapter 3, state environmental quality control laws may provide an independent justification for adopting an environmentally favorable alternative that is economically unfavorable to the owner. Furthermore, once the

---

12. A good example of successful record building to protect a landmark protection program is *Figarsky v. Historic District of the City of Norwich*, 368 A.2d 163 (Conn. 1976).

13. See, for example, *Society for Ethical Culture v. Spatt*, supra note 3.

14. See *Foundation*, supra note 2. The preservationists were more articulate in describing the aesthetic and environmental loss that would flow from the City of Paris's demolition and from the replacement structure's construction. In that permit proceeding, the planning commission was authorized and indeed required to look at environmental and aesthetic factors. In other proceedings affecting landmarks, however, such as designation under the New York City Landmarks Law, the landmarks commission *cannot* rely on environmental or general planning practices in determining the significance of a building or district; the proponent who presents such "environmental" or aesthetic data in error only invites the risk that the commission will subsequently and successfully be accused of having relied on improper factors in its designation. As an unfortunate example of such false reliance, see *Gumley v. Board of Selectmen of Nantucket*, 358 N.E.2d 1011 (Mass. 1977). This point is developed more fully in chapter 2.

developer makes a *prima facie* case for demolition, preservationists will need to produce at least some evidence that demolition is not economically compelled.

As part of the record, preservationists should ensure that an *independent* economic assessment compares the proposed project with its alternatives. Any firm engaged by preservationists, regardless of its purported independence, *can* be accused of partiality and bias. Often, local preservation or environmental quality laws[15] will require the reviewing agency to perform this comparison. Whether required or not, such an economic assessment should be produced lest preservationists leave a gap between the evidence they first present and the ultimate decision they seek.

In addition to laying out their own record and submitting the conclusions that flow from that record, preservationists must challenge all evidentiary weaknesses in opponents' positions. If the opponents' factual case can be attacked sufficiently, the agency might be persuaded that there can be only one lawful result—the one favorable to preservation. If the agency acts on such a record to approve demolition, a reviewing court might find that the agency lacked sufficient evidence or acted arbitrarily, thus ruling that the agency erred in granting the permit. More likely, of course, some evidence favorable to each position will emerge in the process. Under these circumstances and under the traditional "substantial evidence" standard of review, the agency's decision yea or nay would enjoy sufficient support on evidentiary grounds. Preservationists must, nonetheless, resolutely pursue all evidentiary issues, including the relevance of the opponents' evidence to the issue at hand.

Typically, preservationists will not expect their opponents' position to be insupportable but rather will rely on legal doctrines that constrain the agency's exercise of discretion on the evidence before it. For example, a developer may propose demolition of a locally registered landmark without establishing the economic hardship that must be found under local law to justify demolition. Similarly, notwithstanding the evidence in the record, a developer may propose an action that is inconsistent with the local land-use master plan or that calls for public funding of a project that does not meet the statutory criteria for such assistance.

---

15. For example, California Environmental Quality Act, Cal. Pub. Res. Code § 21000 *et seq.* (West Supp. 1982).

Getting Help from Other Agencies and Institutions

In proceedings before a governmental decision-making body, preservationists should recognize that the most cogent testimony and compelling arguments often come not from the parties to the proceedings but from other governmental agencies and institutions. Any fact or argument, however well presented by an interested party, will inevitably prove more effective if it comes from a governmental agency with expertise and responsibility in historic preservation issues.

For example, in attempting to protect a property listed on the National Register, preservationists should turn to the staffs of the Department of the Interior's (DOI) National Register offices and to the Advisory Council on Historic Preservation for guidance, assistance, and ultimately a letter or statement of support. Similarly, when trying to influence federal, state, or local authorities, the state historic preservation officer should be consulted.

Preservationists must be considerate of the competing concerns and agendas of these agencies. Their aid should be enlisted at the outset of an emerging dispute so that the agencies can formulate their positions and offer support before the decision-making body reaches a decision. Ideally, facts and analyses produced by the agencies will elicit favorable administrative action. Even if the ultimate decision is not favorable, support from outside expert agencies shown in the record will lend substantial credence to any subsequent claim for judicial review.

In federal and state projects that trigger the provisions of environmental quality laws, other agencies have not only the responsibility but the duty to comment on a proposed project that might harm historical or cultural sites. When preparing an environmental impact statement (EIS), preservationists should solicit the positions of the relevant expert agencies. If no environmental assessment is being prepared or if it appears to be proceeding off course, preservationists should enlist the aid of the federal Council on Environmental Quality (CEQ) or a state environmental quality office. (See chapter 3 for a discussion of state environmental quality acts.)

Two salient examples of agency involvement have emerged in recent federal experience. In the first case, in response to citizen complaints about a proposed shopping mall that would have destroyed part of the historic Main Street of Pittsfield, Massachusetts, CEQ officially advised both the Department of Housing and Urban Development (HUD) and the city of Pittsfield that an EIS should be prepared. In the second, involving the question of HUD's compliance with the National Environmental Policy Act (NEPA) in the UDAG program, CEQ not only directly communicated its displeasure to HUD but formally published a notice of disapproval of the HUD regulations.[16]

Indeed, the environmental review process is designed specifically to build a record of other agency positions. In theory, one department of government should not act without giving other interested segments of the government an opportunity to study the proposed action and to comment on it. Preservationists can play a crucial role in making this system work.

In seeking allies from within the government, preservationists should not overlook those whose top duty is to represent community opinion: elected officials. These people should be approached with precision and sensitivity. Only those elected officials whose opinions will count and who are or ought to be interested in the project should be approached; collecting as many "endorsements" as possible is not effective. For example, in a local project that has no federal funding or federal significance, soliciting a congressional member's opinion probably would be an unwise use of resources unless the member has some prior identification with the controversy and is well-respected in the community. On the other hand, in addressing a project that requires federal approval—even if the project is of local origin—preservationists should solicit the support of appropriate senators and representatives.

Preservationists should recognize that elected officials are respected for what they are: representatives of the community at large. Their opinion, transmitted in a dignified and noncoercive manner, should influence the decision-making authority. Preservationists, however, should not expect that, merely because elected officials are on their side, the result will always be beneficial; relying on "political pressure" may produce short-term benefit but long-range resentment by the reviewing body.

Finally, in presenting their position, preservationists should recognize another resource: the media. Generally, local reporters show great interest in significant preservation issues reflecting the community's interest in its heritage. Thus, the written and electronic media can prove crucial in amassing a broader base of support. Regardless of the burdens and inconvenience, preservationists always should find the time and

---

16. 45 Fed. Reg. 77,109 (November 21, 1980). The efficacy of this disapproval must be questioned in light of recent decisions that authorize HUD, and not CEQ, to define environmental review responsibilities in CDBG and UDAG cases. See *New Yorkers to Preserve the Theater District v. Landrieu*, No. 80 Civ. 6893 (S.D.N.Y., Dec. 17, 1980), *aff'd*, 661 F.2d 910 (2d. Cir. 1981); *Crosby v. Young*, 512 F. Supp. 1363 (C.D. Mich. 1981).

courtesy to respond to press inquiries and should offer to keep members of the press informed as the case develops. Credibility with the public at large, as well as with government officers, cannot be sacrificed.

Acting Early

Unfortunately, citizens generally become aware of, and concerned about, the loss of a historic building or cultural site on the eve of its demolition. Even when a preservation controversy is slow to develop, human nature and the press of other business tend to postpone preservation action so long as the building or district remains. But since historic preservation has become a more established segment of federal, state, and local government, the process now requires earlier participation. Because of the mechanisms constructed to encourage early governmental recognition of preservation values, withholding challenges to demolition until the last minute will result in fighting a case that cannot be won.

In the City of Paris litigation,[17] for example, a substantial legal challenge to the project's environmental review and demolition permit was ultimately lost because San Francisco failed to enact a meaningful historic preservation ordinance.[18] This fact was reaffirmed when the city failed to accord the building a landmark designation. To maximize effectiveness, therefore, preservationists must focus their efforts not so much at the "back end" of the cycle (specific project and environmental review in response to a demolition permit application) but rather at the "front end" of the process: the adoption of a historic preservation ordinance and implementation of that ordinance through designation of historic structures.

Buying Time

Occasionally in the administrative process, participants will be accused of stalling. Regardless of how efficiently and fairly preservationists participate in public decisions, they must become accustomed to hearing this charge. Preservationists must give no ground to those who would discredit their efforts by this specious allegation.

In response to those who criticize the public process for creating delay,

---

17. *Foundation*, *supra* note 2.
18. The San Francisco ordinance merely authorized a demolition delay of up to one year but did not prohibit demolition even if a qualified purchaser came forward to preserve the building. San Francisco, Cal., Planning Code art. 10 (1967).

preservationists should keep in mind three factors. First, a competent public review process requires time, thus enabling the reviewing agency to uncover more than superficial details about a proposed project and its implications. Second, time is a commodity or resource that preservationists can use to their advantage. For example, while a project's proponent and perhaps its most focused opposition may know a project from its inception, public awareness generally lags far behind. The inherent delays in an environmental review and approval process should be used by preservationists to educate the public and secure its support. Third, the time consumed in litigating a matter before governmental officials can sometimes produce a serendipity. In the well-known Pittsfield mall case from Massachusetts, while both local citizens and the CEQ raised objections to HUD (which was helping fund a downtown shopping center), thereby necessitating the Pittsfield sponsors to respond, the citizenry turned out of office the mayor who had supported the new shopping center.

Building a Rational Decision

A favorable ruling ideally flows from a logical presentation of facts in the record, coupled with a logical argument that transforms those facts into the reasons for decision. To protect the favorable decision on judicial review and to secure a precedent for future administrative decisions, preservationists should, before the agency's ruling becomes final, present a list of proposed findings built carefully from the evidence presented. They should also explain how those findings support the final decision. Although an agency probably will direct its staff to prepare its own findings and decision, in smaller communities the decision makers may lack the experience or expertise to build their own record of decision; in these cases, preservationists must assist the agency in articulating and recording its grounds for action. Even in more established boards and commissions, careful preservationists should be armed with a set of proposed findings and offer some or all of them to supplement or replace those proposed by the agency's staff.[19]

If the decision appears to be unfavorable, preservationists do not have an obligation to propose findings and have them rejected. If uncontroverted evidence of a crucial fact favoring the preservation position has appeared in the record, preservationists might consider requesting

---

19. See chapter 2 for a discussion of the need for basing a decision on the record before the agency.

the decision makers to adopt a finding to that effect; should the decision not be supported by that finding, preservationists would then secure a ground for judicial reversal independent of the "substantial evidence" test.

Preparing for Judicial Relief

If an administrative action that would result in destruction of a landmark structure appears imminent, preservationists will need to guarantee that the demolition does not take place before judicial relief can be invoked. Preservationists should contact directly those in authority who license demolition or destruction and request immediate written and telephonic notification of both the application for and issuance of any such permits. At the same time, they should contact directly the project proponent and request that it withhold demolition until judicial review is completed. If no response is received from the project proponent, a second communication must follow stating that the preservationists will assume that demolition is intended to proceed if no response is received within a given period. These steps are necessary for two reasons: to ensure that no adverse action will be taken without adequate warning and to build a written record to demonstrate that, once a judicial action is filed and an injunction applied for, the court will be satisfied that such relief is necessary to preserve the status quo.

In submitting such requests to project proponents, preservationists should by no means assume that the answer will be negative. Often the pendency or filing of significant litigation will stay the application of a permit because financial institutions will not commit funds if a substantial legal challenge remains. Without a funding commitment, a developer may be unable to meet all the conditions necessary for a demolition permit, or, at the least, he may be unable to execute its project design. In these circumstances, a project proponent may, to demonstrate good faith to the community, willingly accede to "voluntary" restraint.

Until the outcome of legislative or administrative proceedings is clear, preservationists must maintain a "clean" copy of the record that they and other parties have submitted, as well as of all staff reports and decisions issued by the agency. This clean copy of the record should include the statements of all project proponents or opponents and the relevant reports of all governmental agencies.

The assembled record obviously will assist the preservationists' attorney in preparing the legal contentions to be raised in court. A clean copy of the record will also enable preservationists to lay a proper foundation in court for their statement of the case and to demonstrate whatever legal errors have been committed. Although in many jurisdictions a reviewing court ultimately would rely on the record as produced by the agency whose action is challenged, the agency's preparation of such a record can take weeks or even months. Injunctive relief, however, may be required within days. With their own copy of the essential record, preservationists can present their case in court without being at the mercy of the agency, which may or may not have completed its record.

THE JUDICIAL PROCESS: PETITIONERS FOR JUDICIAL RELIEF

The burdens of litigation are such that most sensible people avoid it if at all possible. In a typical civil case, however, a party need not fully commit its resources at the outset of litigation; often a case commences with the filing of an initial complaint. The lion's share of the work follows, in discovery, depositions, and—should the litigation still prove promising—preparation of witnesses and papers for trial. For preservationists, the burdens of litigation are more extreme. Much of the lawyer's work in a preservation case must be done before that lawyer reaches the county clerk to file a lawsuit; concomitantly, the ideological and financial commitment to the case must be made well in advance. Because "preservation litigation" often involves an action against government for failure to perform a duty required by law, the petitioner must prepare the record of the proceedings below (that is, the prior proceedings), prepare pleadings in great detail (often including legal briefs in final form), and prepare even more detailed and precise information if injunctive relief is sought.

The following discussion assumes that, in a dispute, preservationists as petitioners will require injunctive relief to prevent demolition while awaiting a trial and a decision in the underlying case. In general, the desirability of avoiding the need for injunctive relief cannot be overstated; preservationists should strive either to win at the administrative level, or (once judicial action becomes necessary) they should prosecute such an action early and effectively enough so that an injunction does not have to be requested. Judges will grant injunctions against governmental or private actions only if shown that an injunction is absolutely necessary—that is, that a landmark is in danger of *immediate* destruction. Preservationists in this position are entrusting the building's preservation to a single judge's reaction to preservationists' claims. Not only must preservationists produce a strong and perfectly pleaded legal claim at that point, but they must be fortunate enough to secure a sympathetic, or at least neutral, judge. For all these reasons, therefore, under no circumstances should preservationists—realizing that litigation will be necessary—sit back and wait for the demolisher to take the first step.

The following guidance also assumes that some form of administrative proceeding has occurred and that judicial review will be sought in a trial court of general jurisdiction. Not every case will fit this form, however. Some situations will require judicial relief because there has been *no* administrative review (for example, when the adoption of legislation or landmark designation is pending, or a permit has been issued without a hearing). In other cases, the petitioner will seek review in an appellate court. Notwithstanding these variables, the following principles and observations will apply generally to all forms of judicial review.

Pleadings on the Merits

Verified Petition for Relief

The verified petition for relief, which will be analyzed in greater detail later, must state facts sufficient to establish the court's jurisdiction, the appropriate court or authority of action, the petitioners' standing, the status of the defendant and that of any real or directly affected party or parties in interest, a statement of the proceedings, allegations of unlawfulness flowing from those proceedings, and a prayer, or request, for relief. In most jurisdictions, moreover, the petition must be verified—that is, sworn or declared to under penalty of perjury—by a principal of one of the petitioners so that the petition may be considered on its face as evidence of both the facts asserted and of the petitioners' good faith.

Memorandum of Law in Support of the Petition

The memorandum of law is often as important as the petition itself. Although the petition must carefully state the essential facts of the case, under the rule of liberal pleading that applies in most American jurisdictions, a technical flaw in the petition can be corrected later in the proceedings and generally is not fatal to the relief sought. The memorandum of law, in contrast, requires precise and well-presented legal arguments to establish that an injustice has been done and that petitioners are entitled to legal relief. The petition states the case; the memorandum of law wins or loses it.

In any case in which immediate injunctive relief is requested, the memorandum of law typically must be filed concurrently with the petition. Without the memorandum of law, the court cannot make the requisite determination to justify an injunction: the determination that preservationists are likely to succeed on the merits or at least that they have raised significant and substantial legal issues.

Proposed Order to Show Cause or Notice of Motion for Hearing on the Merits

Aside from filing and serving the petition, preservationists must take some action formally to bring the responding parties before the court. In usual civil practice, a summons is issued after the filing of a complaint and then is served personally, along with the complaint, on the defendant. In some jurisdictions, petitions against governmental decisions are not accompanied by a summons but by an order to show cause (OSC) why the relief prayed for should not be granted; the OSC serves the purpose of a summons. In actions against government—especially if injunctive relief is required—personal service of an OSC or summons will be required to secure the court's jurisdiction over the defendants.

Pleadings to Obtain Injunctive Relief

The pleadings just described commence an action, bring the responding parties into court, and secure against them a ruling on the merits. To secure injunctive relief, however, preservationists will need to engage a separate process, which can prove as demanding and exhausting as the ultimate trial on the merits or can even replace such a final trial.[20]

The Record for Injunctive Relief

Building the record for injunctive relief—that is, documenting that all administrative remedies have been exhausted and that demolition actually will take place unless immediately enjoined—serves two purposes. First, this process disciplines preservationists to explore every avenue short

---

20. Indeed, the leading federal case interpreting the National Historic Preservation Act resulted from the appellate court's decision—at the request of the parties—to treat the hearing for a preliminary injunction as the final hearing on the merits. *WATCH (Waterbury Action to Conserve Our Heritage, Inc.) v. Harris*, 603 F.2d 310 (2d Cir. 1979), *cert. denied sub nom. Waterbury Urban Renewal Agency v. WATCH*, 444 U.S. 995 (1979), *attorneys' fees awarded*, 535 F. Supp. 9 (D. Conn. 1981) [hereinafter cited as *WATCH*].

of placing a landmark's survival in the hands of a single judge. Second, this process enables preservationists to submit to a judge the requisite proof that the court must issue an order to protect the resource pending trial on the merits. In preservation litigation, at least one burden—proving irreparable injury—should be straightforward: demolition of a historic site is generally irreparable.

As a precautionary measure, preservationists must ensure that no destruction is threatened or possible while legislative or administrative actions remain pending before the appropriate authorities. If administrative remedies remain to be exhausted, preservationists should seek from the licensing authorities assurance that no permits will be issued prior to final administrative action. Assurances to the same effect also should be sought from the building's owner. In all instances, although contact might be made informally, a record of any transaction should be maintained in writing. In submitting any request for injunctive relief, preservationists must guard against an owner's failure to respond by demanding that no demolition will take place unless they are notified; such a demand, with proof of actual service on the licensing authorities and on the developer, will either induce a response when action is threatened or else place the demolisher at extreme prejudice should preservationists nonetheless learn of threatened demolition and then go to court.

Situations do arise in which an owner might legally be entitled to commence demolition during the pendency of legislative or administrative action. In these cases, preservationists face three alternatives, in order of desirability: (1) request the owner to withhold action until administrative or legislative matters are completed; (2) request the local jurisdiction to adopt an emergency moratorium measure forbidding demolition until legislative or administrative actions are exhausted;[21] (3) commence immediate action for injunctive relief. The last tactic might prove ineffective if, under existing law, the owner could nonetheless go forward with demolition. If a vital resource is at stake, however, and municipal authorities are investing the time to examine the mechanisms

---

21. Moratoriums against demolition generally will be upheld if of definite duration. See *Candlestick Properties, Inc. v. San Francisco Bay Conservation and Development Commission*, 11 Cal. App. 3d 557, 89 Cal. Rptr. 897 (1970), authorizing a 6-month study; *City of Dallas v. Crownrich*, 506 S.W.2d 654 (Tex. Civ. App. 1974), authorizing a 60-day delay. Indefinite moratoriums, however, have been invalidated. See *Southern National Bank v. City of Austin*, 582 S.W.2d 229 (Tex. Civ. App. 1979). Local authority to enact a moratorium, either by way of state enabling legislation or home rule power, must be confirmed. See discussion in chapter 2.

for its preservation, preservationists might find, in state environmental control statutes, a mandate to prevent demolition. They may be able to transform this mandate into a cause of action that halts demolition until the completion of proceedings that might preserve the structure.[22]

In the City of Paris litigation, preservationists built an adequate record *before trial* of the project proponent's intentions to demolish. When proceeding on appeal and requesting a stay, however, they relied on the trial court record. Even though the project proponent did not object to a stay pending appeal, under conditions that the appeal be expedited, the court of appeal refused to issue the stay. Suspecting that the appellate court had not been convinced of the proponent's intentions to proceed in the absence of injunction, preservationists then placed the question anew to the project proponent before petitioning the California Supreme Court for injunctive relief. The developer "voluntarily" consented to withhold demolition pending appeal. The lesson learned: build the record *at each judicial level* at which an injunction is sought.[23]

Preservationists should attempt in good faith to give the developer an opportunity to show the same good faith; if the voluntary restraint will not prejudice the developer's position, the developer may accede to it in order to benefit from the good will this will engender in the community. If the developer will not "voluntarily" accede, then preservationists have established the requisite to qualify for injunctive relief.

The Pleadings Generally

The documents submitted with a request for injunction are often prepared in haste; even if preservationists know of a project proponent's success in the administrative process and intentions to proceed, they may likely delay their own efforts until an injunction appears absolutely essential. This tendency to wait can prove disastrous, since the successful securing of injunctive relief requires fastidious adherence to jurisdictional and evidentiary points. Too often such precision can be lost under duress. Accordingly, if at all possible, preservationists and their attorney should prepare these papers at the first, and not the last,

---

22. See *Arcata Redwood Co. v. State Board of Forestry*, 7 Envtl. L. Rep. (Envtl. L. Inst.) 20755 (Cal. Super. Ct. 1977), in which—under duty to prevent environmental damage if feasible—state board's moratorium on redwood logging was both authorized and required, if congressional action to include the redwoods within a proposed national park was found likely to be imminent.

23. See *Foundation, supra* note 2.

opportunity.

All pleadings, both for relief on the merits and for an injunction, must be served on the responding parties (both governmental defendants and any real parties in interest) before the court's injunctive order can take effect. If demolition is not expected to take place overnight, ordinary personal service, with sufficient advance notice of a hearing on the preliminary injunction motion, will fulfill this jurisdictional requirement.

On the other hand, a situation may emerge in which a temporary restraining order is necessary; this order is issued *immediately* by the court, restraining any action until the opposing parties have time to respond and enabling the court to review subsequently the need for an injunction. An application for a temporary restraining order (TRO) is generally considered *ex parte*, that is, it is made without notice and without an opportunity for the opposing position to be heard. In actuality, a judge will prove extremely reluctant to issue a TRO against parties who have no actual notice of the application and who have not technically been brought within the jurisdiction of the court. In applying for a temporary restraining order, therefore, preservationists should attempt to effectuate personal service at least four hours before the application to the court—enough time to ensure the judge that the other side has had an opportunity to review the papers and make an appearance but not enough time to permit the opposition to turn a TRO hearing into a full-blown preliminary injunction hearing.

If the timing becomes so compressed as to preclude personal service before application to the court, then preservationists should at least telephone notice to the responding parties, informing them of the time and court of application. In addition, preservationists should bring to the court a written declaration or affidavit outlining their efforts to inform the responding parties as well as copies of papers to be served on the responding parties; petitioners should deliver these papers in court to the responding parties before appearing in front of the judge.

Consequently, the first indispensable pleading in an application for injunctive relief will be the proof of service describing that service has been accomplished or (if not successful) a statement outlining efforts made to advise the responding parties of the application.

Application for Injunctive Relief

Aside from the verified petition necessary to start the action, a separate application for injunctive relief must accompany preservationists' request to the court for an injunction. Such an application must in itself establish with proper evidentiary basis the *facts* warranting relief. Accordingly, the application must consist of declarations or affidavits, made under penalty of perjury, as to a statement of the proceedings below and the probability of demolition if not restrained.

In theory, the verified petition can be relied on to establish its factual allegations. In practice, however, judges often will ask for separate declarations or affidavits, under penalty of perjury, that incorporate the facts alleged in the petition or separately state those facts in sufficient detail as recited by those who witnessed them.

Memorandum of Law

In addition to the legal memorandum in support of the petition itself, an applicant for injunction must separately state the statutory or equitable basis for injunctive relief and relate the facts of the case to those criteria. In this pleading, preservationists must establish that their case meets the general criteria for injunctions in the jurisdiction in which the claim is brought. These criteria generally include the likelihood of success on the merits of the litigation (or the presentation of significant and difficult legal issues), the fact of irreparable injury that would result from failure to grant the injunction, and the willingness and ability to abide by whatever conditions the court imposes. The petitioners' memo must, therefore, address the issue of bonding; substantial federal and state authorities support the proposition that, in citizen-petitioners' lawsuits brought not for economic gain but to enforce the public interest and preserve public values, citizens meeting the other criteria for injunction should not be subjected to a substantial bond.[24] These points must be presented to the court in advance.

Proposed Temporary Stay or Restraining Order

Preservationists as petitioners must know and define the relief for which they will pray at the injunctive stage. Even if the court to which application is made draws its own order rather than using those submit-

---

24. *Scherr v. Volpe*, 466 F.2d 1027, 1036 (7th Cir. 1972); *West Virginia Highlands Conservancy v. Island Creek Coal Co.*, 441 F.2d 232, 236 (4th Cir. 1971); *Natural Resources Defense Council v. Morton*, 337 F. Supp. 167 (D.D.C. 1971); *Wilderness Society v. Hickel*, 325 F. Supp. 422 (D.D.C. 1970); *Powelton Civic Home Owners Association v. Department of HUD*, 284 F. Supp. 809 (E.D. Pa. 1963); *Laurel Hill Homeowners Association v. City Council*, Cal. Adv. Sheets No. 4, at 8 (January 19, 1978).

ted by counsel (especially true of appellate courts), preservationists would be well advised to present to the court a proposed version of the ultimate relief sought.

Proposed Order to Show Cause

A temporary restraining order generally will remain effective for only 10 or 20 days, requiring that a hearing take place on a preliminary injunction within that time if the injunction is to remain effective for the pendency of the lawsuit. Accordingly, the petitioner should have available for the court's adoption and issuance an order to show cause on the preliminary injunction. This preliminary injunction functions as the summons to bring the responding parties before the court and authorizes the court at the conclusion of the hearing (whether or not the respondents appear) to convert the temporary restraining order into an injunction for the duration of the lawsuit.

Framing the Petition for Relief: The Essential Elements of the Case

Court: State or Federal

The choice of state or federal court will depend primarily on two factors: (1) the substance of preservationists' legal claims and (2) the status of the defendants against whom relief is sought. In general, if a cause of action is brought under federal law against federal defendants, relief normally would be sought in the federal courts—although, as a strictly legal matter, the state courts hold concurrent jurisdiction to review such claims. Federal defendants, such as HUD, however, usually will seek to remove to federal court those cases brought against them in state courts. If preservationists' claims are grounded in federal law, such removal cannot be defeated.

Preservationists must determine whether their claim essentially is grounded in federal or state law and (absent other considerations) select the tribunal accordingly. If the claim arises totally under state law, then the state court is the logical forum unless the extraordinary situation arises in which the plaintiffs all reside outside the defendants' state(s) of residence, in which case there is federal diversity jurisdiction.

Practical factors also should be influential. For example, due to geography, filing fees, and other procedural requirements, the state trial and appellate courts might prove far more accessible, particularly in remote areas, than the parallel federal courts. Another legitimate factor is the reputation of the state and federal courts in a given jurisdiction; if one court might show greater sensitivity to environmental, procedural, or preservation factors, while another court might be less receptive to citizen-initiated litigation, preservationists would violate common sense by bringing the litigation in the second court.

A final matter to consider in selecting a court is the availability of attorneys' fees under either state or federal jurisprudence. In a state such as California, which clearly allows for an award of attorneys' fees in litigations conferring a broad public benefit by enforcing important rights in behalf of a needy plaintiff,[25] the state forum generally will prove more favorable. On the other hand, in federal court, attorneys' fees are authorized in litigation to enforce the National Historic Preservation Act[26] and in any federal claim against *nonfederal* defendants for depriving preservationists of rights secured by federal law.[27]

In circumstances in which preservationists are prosecuting both federal and state claims, there is not only a choice between federal or state court, but also the choice of whether to prosecute two separate actions. A mixture of state and federal claims can be prosecuted in a state court alone. If the state claims are truly pendent to the federal claims—that is, if the federal claims constitute the meat of the case and the state claims are subsidiary—then both federal and state claims can be prosecuted in the federal court. When federal and state claims are both claims of substance, however, preservationists might find it to their advantage to prosecute two separate actions; generally it is the petitioner or plaintiff, and not the defendant or respondent, who benefits from "two bites of the apple."[28] A disadvantage of the "two bites" approach is the greater expense. In addition, if innovative claims are brought under state law, the federal court would likely abstain in favor of a state court adjudication; in any event, normally the state court will prove more receptive to such claims.

---

25. Cal. Civ. Proc. Code § 1021.5; see *Woodland Hills Residents Association v. City Council (II)*, 23 Cal. 3d 917, 154 Cal. Rptr. 503 (1979).

26. Pub. L. No. 96-515, § 501, 94 Stat. 2987, adding § 305 to the National Historic Preservation Act, 16 U.S.C. § 470 *et seq.* (Supp. 1981).

27. Civil Rights Attorneys Fees Awards Act of 1976, 42 U.S.C. § 1988, authorizing the award of attorneys' fees in any action to enforce federal rights deprived under color of state action. See *Maine v. Thiboutot*, 448 U.S. 1, 100 S. Ct. 2502 (1980).

28. In the second round of litigation against the Portman Times Square Hotel project, the federal district court first issued but then vacated the ruling allowing the defendants to consolidate in federal court both the federal and the state court complaints; the court remanded the state actions to the state court. *Natural Resources Defense Council v. City of New York*, 528 F. Supp. 1245 (S.D.N.Y. 1981), *aff'd*, 672 F.2d 292 (2d Cir. 1982).

Venue

In general, an action must be commenced in a place—venue—that enables the court to provide the protection that preservationists seek. Since an action generally aims to protect a tangible historical or cultural site (usually real estate), the proper venue generally lies in the county or federal judicial district embracing the threatened structure. If the court's injunction issues during or at the conclusion of the action, that injunction will at least prove enforceable in the county or district in which the court sits. While the injunction also may be valid in other venues, preservationists should not complicate matters by seeking enforcement or introducing the likelihood of nonenforcement of one court's decree in a distant place.

By selecting the venue in which the resource under issue is located, preservationists select the venue in which the respondents are located—at least for jurisdictional purposes. Even if the governmental authority whose action is challenged or the private developer or both maintain their principal offices elsewhere, their actions affecting an asset will suffice to establish that they conduct business within that venue.

One salient exception to the selection of the asset's location as venue: if federal action is being challenged and the receptiveness of the local federal district or appeals court to preservation claims appears questionable, preservationists will want to consider selecting as venue the national capital. In general, both the federal district and appellate courts in Washington, D.C., are as receptive to challenges against the government as are any courts in the nation; moreover, these courts' familiarity with such challenges generally produces quicker and more definitive resolution of the issues.[29] If preservationists select this alternative, they will need to engage Washington counsel to handle the day-to-day tasks of litigation—even if local counsel prepares the written case. Fortunately,

---

29. An exception to the exception can always be found; the U.S. District Court in Butte, Montana, alone among the federal judiciary, sustained a claim that federal preservation responsibilities could not be delegated by HUD to local officials. *Citizens Defense Fund v. Gallager*, No. Cv.-78-63-Bu (D. Mont. 1979), unpublished and reported in 1979 H.P.L. 655. While most district courts considering preservation claims against the federal government have not been so sensitive—for example, *National Center for Preservation Law v. Landrieu*, 496 F. Supp. 716 (D.S.C. 1980), *aff'd per curiam*, 635 F. 2d 324 (4th Cir. 1980)—a local judge may prove more appreciative of the local cultural significance of a threatened building or neighborhood than would a judge in the Washington court. The unfortunate fact remains that politically sensitive projects likely receive less critical scrutiny from a local judge whose career was built in that political environment.

the Washington bar has demonstrated extraordinary generosity in supporting needy preservationists at little or no cost—but *only* when preservationists present a case of truly national legal significance.

Party Petitioner: Establishing Standing

To establish their right to prosecute a legal challenge ("standing"), preservationist-petitioners must assert the facts of their interest in and their objections to the proposed action. The courts do not permit just any person—referred to here as the "officious intermeddler"—to file a lawsuit against proposed destruction of a cultural resource. This rule of standing provides protection both ways: (1) it relieves a governmental agency or private developer from facing a challenger who did not make its views known previously; (2) it protects preservationists by eliminating the claims of those whose interests are casual or belated. The "standing" doctrine ensures that any legal action will be vigorously prosecuted. Eliminating "officious intermeddlers" assures established preservationists that their case will not be preempted by another party who may lose and thereby foreclose the established preservationists from their rightful day in court.

Thus, the rule of "standing" requires establishing a significant stake in the outcome to assure that the case will be vigorously and meritoriously litigated.[30] The courts have further refined this rule to require that the petitioner, usually a preservation organization or its membership, allege and establish that it or they will suffer particular injury arising from the respondents' actions.[31]

Accordingly, preservationists will allege the particular facts of their personal history and involvement with the threatened resource. At the outset, they should describe their history and involvement in other preservation activities to convince the court that they stand as a substantial and representative entity on whom the court can rely to prosecute the case vigorously. Most importantly, preservationists must allege that they will suffer injury from the loss of the threatened structure or district; obviously the strongest claim will arise if an individual preservationist or the membership of a preservation group can establish that they have regularly used the building or district. Actual use, however, is not a prerequisite; a recent federal appellate decision has explained that requisite standing will be attributed to an established preservation organiza-

30. *Warth v. Seldin*, 422 U.S. 490 (1975); *Association of Data Processing Service Organizations v. Camp*, 397 U.S. 150 (1970).
31. *Sierra Club v. Morton*, 405 U.S. 727 (1972).

tion objecting to the community's loss of a part of its heritage—even though the membership did not reside in the neighborhood of the threatened building and did not use the building prior to threatened demolition.[32]

The most probative testimony of preservationists' standing flows from the record of participation in the administrative proceedings leading up to the threatened action. Accordingly, after generally describing their involvement in the administrative process under challenge, preservationists also must allege each specific substantive objection that they raised there. Indeed, while such allegations of "exhaustion of administrative remedies" will in any case serve to establish standing, in some jurisdictions such allegations become absolutely necessary to establish the reviewing court's jurisdiction over the final administrative action.[33]

The paragraphs above anticipate that preservationist-petitioners normally will appear as a membership organization. Most jurisdictions, including the federal system, recognize that a corporate organization may prosecute an action on behalf of its members' interests—without denoting the lawsuit as a "class" or "representative" action.[34] In such a case, the court will look to the individual members' injury to ascertain the organization's standing. If preservationists bring a suit in a jurisdiction where this rule is not well established, then, as a safety measure, one or two individuals should be added as petitioners in addition to the organization.[35]

The courts do look with suspicion on one potential petitioner organization: the public interest law firm. If such a firm is itself a membership organization and capable of alleging particularized injury to its members,

---

32. *Neighborhood Development Corp. v. Advisory Council on Historic Preservation*, *supra* note 11.

33. For example, *Abelliera v. District Court of Appeal*, 17 Cal. 2d 280, 109 P.2d 942 (1941).

34. For example, *Sierra Club v. Morton*, *supra* note 31; *Residents of Beverly Glen v. City of Los Angeles*, 34 Cal. App. 3d 117, 109 Cal. Rptr. 724 (1973).

35. The organization should name itself first, not only to secure its own recognition in the case title, but also to establish within its jurisdiction the right of such an organization to prosecute alone. Naming the individuals only serves as a backup if the organization's standing is disallowed. Naming individuals has the drawback of creating their joint and several liability for costs of court if imposed at the conclusion of an unsuccessful action. (See discussion in this chapter regarding protection from such costs.) If individuals are named, and not with the intent that they be liable for costs if imposed, then at the outset the organization should give the individuals a written indemnity against such liability.

the case may be brought in its name; both the Natural Resources Defense Council and the Environmental Defense Fund have successfully prosecuted claims.[36] If, however, the organization does not maintain a true membership and primarily asserts its desire to secure the faithful and correct interpretation of the law, the courts generally will not recognize such capacity to establish standing.[37] In the preservation arena, no substitute can replace the local historical or cultural society of long standing in the community.

Even better than the "preservation society," however, stands the businessman, landowner, or labor union whose economic well-being will suffer from unwise demolition of a landmark that contributes to the economic vitality of the community. The most successful and legally significant action brought by preservationists—*WATCH v. Harris*[38]—was prosecuted not by a historical society but rather by the small business community of downtown Waterbury. The most convincing (albeit ultimately unsuccessful) opposition to the Portman Hotel project proposed for the New York City theater district came not from a preservation league but from the Actors' Equity Association—the union whose members would lose economic and artistic opportunity if the existing legitimate theaters were destroyed. Indeed, courts readily sustain preservation-engendered restrictions that promote the local economy[39] but on occasion will reject an effort to protect solely on aesthetic values.[40]

Party Defendant or Respondent

To challenge a decision authorizing destruction of a cultural landmark, preservationists will need to bring into court as defendants or respondents all agencies or individuals whose authority is being challenged. The necessary defendants include all those persons or agencies that either directly decide or indispensably assist in deciding to authorize the demolition. It is better to overestimate, rather than underestimate, the number of defendants necessary to secure effective relief.

For example, in challenging the Portman Hotel project and its threatened demolition of the core of the New York theater district, the

---

36. For example, *Natural Resources Defense Council v. Morton*, 458 F.2d 827 (D.C. Cir. 1972); *Environmental Defense Fund v. Ruckelshaus*, 439 F.2d 584 (D.D.C. 1971).
37. For example, *National Center for Preservation Law v. Landrieu*, supra note 29.
38. *WATCH*, supra note 20.
39. *City of New Orleans v. Impastato*, supra note 3; *Opinion of the Justices*, 128 N.E.2d 557 (Mass. 1955).
40. *Board of Supervisors v. Rowe*, 216 Va. 128, 216 S.E.2d 199 (1975).

plaintiffs in the two major lawsuits named as defendants the mayor and Board of Estimate of the City of New York, which sponsored and approved the city's UDAG application; the federal officials who approved the UDAG application; and also the New York state agencies that proposed either to finance or underwrite tax abatements for the proposed project.[41]

In naming defendants, preservationists must remember that causes of action will only lie against those parties who hold a duty imposed by law or who hold the authority to exercise discretion confined by law. In the Portman case, for instance, preservationists did *not* name the private banks contributing financial support; the private banks' exercise of discretion to lend did not appear to be confined by any legally defined duty. The public lenders, in contrast, assertedly held a legal duty to precede their financing commitments by conducting the environmental assessments described in the New York State Environmental Quality Review Act.

Real Party in Interest

Although preservationists' complaints will often lie against a governmental agency for failure to carry out legal duties, their claims ultimately may affect a party outside of the government, such as a private permittee or landowner who is seeking demolition. Because such a private owner holds the ultimate interest in the outcome, the law designates such an affected owner as the "real party in interest."

When bringing action against the defendant governmental authority, preservationists generally also should name and serve the real party or parties in interest. First, as a matter of due process, a permittee or owner affected by the preservationists' claim does hold a constitutional (and, in many jurisdictions, a statutory) right to participate in the litigation affecting its interests.[42] Second, and of great pragmatic concern to preservationists, the permittee or owner must be named in the litigation if the court's injunction is to be effective against the owner's activities. Since demolition usually is carried out by the private owner rather than by a governmental body, preservationists have no choice but to name the real party or parties in interest at the outset of any litigation in which an immediate injunction against demolition is required. Finally,

---

41. *New Yorkers to Preserve the Theater District v. Landrieu*, *supra* note 16; *Natural Resources Defense Council v. City of New York*, *supra* note 28.

42. For example, *California C.C. Corp. v. Superior Court*, 122 Cal. App. 404, 408, 10 P.2d 176 (1922); Cal. Civ. Proc. Code § 1107 (West Supp. 1982).

by naming the known real party or parties in interest, preservationists present to the opposing litigants and to the court an appearance of fairness; that is, they demonstrate their assumption of the burden to bring all the proper parties before the court and to face, without fear of the consequences, the opposition of all affected parties.[43]

Statement of Proceedings Below

Having named the requisite parties, the preservationists' complaint will then include a statement of the proceedings below. This statement describes procedural steps taken, the substance of the claims raised, and their resolutions by administrative agencies. With such a statement in proper form, preservationists then can assert that they have either exhausted administrative remedies or that further resort to remedies before administrative agencies would prove futile. In a nutshell, the statement of proceedings below must present sufficient facts to invoke the court's jurisdiction to review the matter.

The record below can be established by either of two means: attaching selected exhibits (crucial documents from the administrative record) to the petition or incorporating the entire record by reference in the complaint.

The choice of presenting only selected exhibits versus incorporating the entire record usually boils down to expense and time. If fairly immediate injunctive relief is required, preservationists simply may not have time to compile or secure the entire record below. Under these circumstances, the petition will need to be accompanied by sufficient

---

43. One circumstance, however, might justify a decision not to name the real parties in interest and instead bring action only against the governmental authority, thereby forcing the affected property owner to take the initiative to enter the litigation. This circumstance arises when preservationists reasonably fear the real party or real parties in interest might counterclaim for damages arising out of the preservationists' opposition to a particular project. If a permittee or property owner has raised this threat, preservationists might feel more secure by not naming any real parties in interest so that preservationists cannot be accused of bringing a frivolous or malicious action against them; according to this theory, if the developer assumes the initiative to enter the litigation, then the developer cannot complain against the preservationists for bringing it. Although this practice was followed in the two recent litigations over the Portman Hotel project (see note 41), on closer examination it would appear to afford little additional protection. As a practical matter, a preservationist's claim challenging a governmental decision to grant a demolition permit does threaten the permit holder's interests, whether or not preservationists name the real party in interest; that party can (and should) secure redress for actions taken maliciously or without foundation, including the initiation of any unfounded litigation affecting the real party's property.

selected exhibits to demonstrate the legal error of which the petitioners complain. If legal error can be demonstrated from selected exhibits, then financial and tactical factors favor presenting only those selected exhibits; this presentation forces the court to focus on the relevant documents and not become distracted or worn down by a voluminous record.

Incorporation of the entire record, however, guards against two pitfalls. First, when substantial evidence is at issue, incorporating the entire record will prevent the responding parties from claiming that the missing portions of the record contain the substantial evidence to support their position. Moreover, incorporating the entire record will enable preservationists to develop new theories or causes of action during litigation. Often, in response to the pleadings of other parties or in subsequent rethinking of the case, preservationists will discern a more effective claim than those originally perceived. Without a full record, preservationists may be foreclosed from presenting material not part of their evidentiary submission.

In any event, the statement of proceedings should contain a complete factual record of all the *relevant* matters: the nature of the building or district at issue, its cultural value, the application for demolition that gave rise to the present complaint, the course of that application through the administrative process (including participation by the preservationist-petitioners and by other interested parties in support of the petitioners), the reactions of governmental bodies to the petitioners' claims, and the ultimate administrative decision. The statement of proceedings should not contain a verbatim recount of the proceedings below except for extraordinarily probative or prejudicial statements; these should be quoted in their full, original form. Factual allegations in the statement of proceedings should be cited either to the attached exhibits or to page numbers in the incorporated record; this practice acts as a check to ensure that the allegations are supportable and enables the judge to ascertain the factual basis for the allegations.

Causes of Action

Once the administrative proceedings have been set forth, including a final statement that the petitioners have exhausted their available remedies or else would find such exhaustion futile, the petitioners should then list their causes of action. Generally, each case of action should be stated in the following manner: (1) an assertion of a legal criterion or requirement, such as ''section . . . . of the . . . . .

...... Code requires that the city not approve a demolition permit unless ...."; (2) an assertion that "notwithstanding the legal duty cited, defendants in fact carried out the following actions contrary to that legal duty: ...."; (3) an assertion that "defendants .... thereby failed to perform in the manner required by law or abused the discretion vested in them by law"; and (4) the claim that the petitioners were prejudiced by defendants' action.

Prayer for Relief

The petition will conclude with a prayer for specific relief. The first element of this prayer should ask for the ultimate result desired: either vacation of the administrative decision authorizing demolition, or else (if supported by the legal theories raised) an affirmative direction to the defendants to take a particular pro-preservation action. As mentioned above, the preservationist-petitioner usually is not able to secure an affirmative mandate but must be content with vacating the prior decision, leaving the agency to take whatever further action is consistent with the court's decision. Nonetheless, as part of the substantive prayer, preservationists should attempt to place specific constraints on the agency's future action (for example, an order that "defendants shall not authorize demolition until and unless the owners have met their burden of establishing the lack of a feasible alternative"). In any event, preservationists should pray for "permanent" relief enjoining demolition based on the challenged permit.

The prayer also should contain a request for a stay pending determination of the petition if preservationists know they will need such relief or suspect that an injunction will be required prior to the end of trial court litigation. If a stay pending determination is not required at the time of filing the petition, the proper prayer would request "upon subsequent application to the court, if necessary, an order staying physical alteration or demolition pending the determination of this petition."

Finally, the prayer should request costs of suit, and, if brought in a jurisdiction or under a theory that authorizes attorneys' fees, the prayer also should include a request for such fees. As noted above, a properly pleaded complaint under federal law will include a prayer for fees; in some state jurisdictions, such as California, a fee award would be appropriate in "public interest" litigation.

Verification

In most American jurisdictions, a petition for injunctive relief against a governmental agency generally requires verification, that is, an attached statement under oath that the facts alleged in the petition are known to be true and those matters not personally known are believed to be true. The verification, necessarily being an evidentiary statement, must be in the form of a sworn affidavit or, where permitted, a declaration under penalty of perjury. Preferably, the verification should be executed by the officer of one of the petitioners who has the greatest factual knowledge of the history of the dispute. As indicated above, a competently verified petition should itself be considered as evidence of the facts recited in it for purposes of proving the need for injunction.

Discovery: A Strategic Decision

"Discovery" refers to the legal process whereby litigants can ascertain the factual background of their opponents' case prior to trial of the dispute. In most civil litigation, discovery makes eminent sense; it conserves court time by enabling parties to define the contested factual issues and eliminate those issues on which either no conflict exists or the opportunity for proof of either position appears slight. Moreover, in complex civil matters such as antitrust litigation, discovery enables the parties to secure the "raw data" necessary to perfect and prove the allegations made in their complaints.

In governmental and administrative litigation generally and preservation litigation in particular, discovery is not as vital. When a case is being tried on the public record of proceedings, often there is little to "discover" that is not, or should not have been, part of that public record. Moreover, discovery does require both time and expense; whether drafting or responding to written interrogatories, or conducting oral depositions, these matters could prove more expensive than conducting the trial on the merits. For these reasons, the decision to engage in, or resist, discovery in preservation litigation is one of discretion and significance.

Reasons for Securing Discovery

Notwithstanding the premise that in preservation litigation the relevant "facts" should be in the official governmental record, crucial facts often do not appear in that record, and preservationists will need or want to uncover such evidence by discovery. For example, a developer may persuade the governmental authority of the economic infeasibility of preservation without presenting any supporting evidence. Discovery of such economic data and of opportunities to sell the property to others helps establish in a trial *de novo* that demolition would be unlawful. Under a more restrained judicial review, discovery helps to create sufficient doubt about the agency's determination that preservation was infeasible, thus requiring the agency to conduct further research on that question and reconsider it. Similarly, discovery could help nail down the alternatives that a developer truly considered but did not present to the governmental agency.

Discovery also may be necessary when unlawful collateral behavior is at issue—conduct such as *ex parte* contacts between the project applicant and the decision-making body, undue political contributions or gifts, or other elements of assertedly unlawful conduct that do not relate strictly to the merits of the project. For example, in a Maryland trial court decision, *Annapolis Emergency Hospital Association v. Annapolis Historic District*,[44] discovery was used successfully against preservationists to establish that a member of the historic preservation commission had voided the commission's proceedings because of her prior membership in the Annapolis Preservation Society; even though this evidence of dual membership was not presented or raised in the proceedings below, it was received by the trial court as new evidence and, on its basis, the objection to the member's participation in the commission was sustained. In states where such potential conflicts are not required to be identified in advance of the proceedings, preservationists could use discovery to establish the disqualification of decision makers with an institutional bias against preservation.

Finally, discovery allows preservationists to learn in advance the witnesses and other evidence that the opponents intend to produce at trial.

Reasons for Not Pursuing Discovery

Expense is the single most compelling reason for not introducing discovery into a preservation case. Because the preservation case usually involves a government agency and its official record, discovery is not always necessary to secure access to the information and records sufficient to construct a case. Under these circumstances, undertaking

---

44. Anne Arundel Cir. Ct. No. 962 (April 14, 1977). The issue of a commissioner's bias or conflict of interest is discussed in chapter 2.

discovery might prove a great disadvantage; regardless of the amount of discovery that preservationists can undertake, their opposition (either the government or a developer) can generally afford to take much more, thereby using discovery to increase the net cost of the preservationists' securing relief on the merits. By refraining from discovery, preservationists can resist extreme discovery by the responding parties.[45]

Indeed, in jurisdictions where the local law restricts the scope of review to that evidence appearing in the administrative record, discovery generally *cannot* be undertaken to expand that record—at least concerning items on the merits of the project application. Even under the so-called substantial evidence rule, however, discovery may be authorized to ascertain such collateral issues as procedural fairness.[46]

A final disadvantage to initiating discovery is the opportunity it affords the opposing parties to complete their record with evidence that they withheld or failed to provide in the administrative proceedings. Thus, if an agency improperly concluded that preservation of a landmark was economically infeasible, even though no evidence of infeasibility was produced, a clever developer would respond to the discovery by producing such evidence and thereby arguing that the agency's error was harmless. Here preservationists would do better to seek a remand for the *agency* to secure such evidence and render a new decision on it.

Evidence and Experts

As described above, the trial of a preservation lawsuit can range from a simple review by the judge of the written record in prior administrative proceedings to a trial *de novo*, or full-blown rehearing in court of all the evidence and witnesses that the contesting parties can make available. Preservationists, in planning the evidence and experts to be produced at trial, should first ascertain the type and scope of judicial review.

In the most restrained form of court trial—mere review of the administrative record—preservationists generally are confined to the record below and have neither the opportunity nor the burden of presenting additional witnesses and documents. Their first task will be to present a *complete* record, a task facilitated by having maintained a clean copy of all written materials submitted or produced in administrative hear-

---

45. For example, in the *Foundation* litigation, *supra* note 2, preservationists successfully resisted Neiman-Marcus's discovery on the grounds that the matters sought to be discovered would emerge in the administrative proceedings that remained to be completed.

46. *City of Fairfield v. Superior Court*, 14 Cal. 3d 758, 122 Cal. Rptr. 543 (1975).

ings. Although, as mentioned above, expense frequently can be spared by presenting less than a complete record (for example, when an error of law can be established by a few brief passages of an extended debate among the commissioners), prudent preservationists will transcribe the entire proceedings to guard against presumptions that the missing record exonerates the agency and to convince the court that nothing is being withheld deliberately.

In this simplest form of judicial review, the parties to the proceedings, either before or at the beginning of litigation, should stipulate—formally agree to—the contents of the administrative record. Such a stipulation can save time and expense, since proceedings to review administrative action can bog down in unnecessary or insubstantial argument about the contents of the record below. If the opposing parties are including items that should not be included, or vice versa, then preservationists should not stipulate just to prevent dispute; such disputed items may prove vital to the outcome of the case. As much agreement as possible should be reached, and the disputed items submitted separately for resolution by the court.

Several exceptions arise in which new evidence can be produced to review administrative action. For example, newly discovered evidence, which could not with diligence have been presented to the agency, can be presented initially in court. Additionally, evidence outside the formal record may be necessary or appropriate to establish or refute claims of procedural irregularity such as lack of notice or conflicts of interest in decision makers.

In addition, preservationists should consider presenting a few select expert witnesses at trial. Such witnesses would not be used to establish the validity of certain facts but to explain technical, historical, or economic data in, or absent from, the administrative record. For example, if the adequacy of an EIS is at issue, a planner from a different jurisdiction might testify that the statement would not provide an adequate basis for approval of the challenged project. Similarly, if a project proponent is relying on a particular economic or historical analysis, preservationists may present a witness who can establish the professional incompetence or inconclusiveness of such an analysis.

Although technically a proceeding to review administrative action should be confined to the record before the landmarks commission or city council, some judges will welcome—or at least not reject—expert explanation of that record. To be well prepared, preservationists should assemble such expert witnesses for trial. To test the court's amenability to their testimony, their written opinions should be submitted (in the form of affidavits or declarations) as exhibits to the initial complaint or as part of the supporting papers for a preliminary injunction; if neither the opponents nor the court objects, or if the opponents' objection is overruled, then the preservationists have strengthened their case. But, preservationists must also calculate the potential benefits to the opposition of supplementing what may have been an inadequate record to justify the challenged administrative decision.

In a trial *de novo*, preservationists must produce all the evidence—including that of experts—and be prepared to present it by direct oral examination. At the risk of repetition: only witnesses whose testimony is *relevant* to the issue in court should be presented. For example, evidence of feasible alternatives to proposed demolition is not relevant and ought to be excluded from a case involving landmark status. Similarly, if the issue in court concerns alternatives to demolition of a designated landmark, preservationists should not permit relitigation of the structure's architectural or historic significance. If the court overrules their objections to such testimony, preservationists, while stating a nonwaiver of their objection, should counter such testimony by cross-examination and by their own witnesses.

Situations Requiring Experts

Experts generally will be required to establish evidence in the following situations.

Designating Landmarks. When defending a successful designation or challenging a failure to designate, cultural or historical values must be established. Preservationists can rely on architects, historians, archaeologists, anthropologists, and (rarely) personal witnesses to a historic event or people associated with a building or district.

Establishing Alternatives. Under preservation ordinances or environmental quality laws, demolition may not be authorized if a preservation alternative can be established. In this situation, preservationists need developers, potential users of a landmark, construction managers and money lenders, and architects to present the preservation alternative.

The importance of securing *independent* economic assessments cannot be overstated. When a developer is open to preservation, he should be prevailed on to agree to, and possibly fund, such a comparative assessment by an independent firm.[47] When developers are not agreeable,

---

47. This process successfully produced preservation of the threatened Willard Hotel in Washington, D.C. When the same process was applied to the Blenheim Hotel

preservationists should seek assistance from governmental sources, such as the state historic preservation officer, the federal Advisory Council on Historic Preservation, or the Department of the Interior's National Register Programs.

Defeating a "Takings" Claim. In claiming that a preservation law produces an unconstitutional "taking" of property without just compensation, a project proponent must generally establish that no reasonable use of the property exists. Proof of a feasible preservation alternative generally will vitiate any claim of "taking."[48] "Takings" claims can be defeated by the prior economic history of the parcel at issue, testimony regarding market value, evidence of the feasible use of similar properties, and the economic return realized or realizable on similar properties. To defeat a "taking" claim, preservationists can use land-use planners, economists, appraisers, and real estate experts to describe prior transactions involving the threatened property and other comparable properties.

Applying Standards to a Threatened Structure. In challenging a commission's failure to apply ordinance standards or criteria to preserve a threatened structure, preservationists must establish that these criteria were ignored or misinterpreted. Preservationists might rely on architects or staff and members of another jurisdiction's commission with similar criteria in its preservation law. They also might call staff of the local commission if the standards have been applied differently in the past. Occasionally, preservationists might use the author(s) of the specific criteria; courts, however, often will disregard statements of legislative intent by the authors or proponents of a bill.

Crucial Nonpreservation Issues. If a challenged permit will cause local or regional land-use problems (such as increased density, traffic, or secondary growth impacts or decreased property values or general plan violations), preservationists should highlight those impacts. They should rely on the same kinds of witnesses used in normal zoning cases—traffic engineers, land-use planners, appraisers, and the like.

---

in Atlantic City, the assessment proved that preservation could not be achieved—but this conclusion was then *accepted* by the preservation community.

48. See *Agins v. City of Tiburon*, 447 U.S. 255 (1980); *Penn Central Transportation Co. v. City of New York, supra* note 1. For a discussion of the "taking" issue, see chapter 5.

Guidelines For Selecting and Using Experts

In selecting and preparing expert witnesses, the following general guidelines should prove helpful.[49]

Choosing Experts with Care and Caution. The appropriate choice of experts is the most important phase of the process. The "professional" or activist witness should be avoided as vigorously as the nonexpert. Witnesses with favorable institutional affiliations are most helpful. Although this rule may sound elitist or discriminatory, it is practical. Since credibility is the witness's most important trait, the witness must not appear biased. On matters such as historical significance, for example, the best witnesses come from either an academic institution or a government preservation staff—dispassionately intellectual judgment is the trait to be established. On matters such as economic feasibility, however, academicians generally would prove to be the worst choice; instead, to establish bread-and-butter reality, a construction manager or lender, an appraiser, or developer of other restored buildings should be used to prove that the threatened structure can be adapted to contemporary use.

Selecting and Using Experts at the Very Beginning of the Preservation Effort. Even before the first *administrative* hearing, preservationists should assemble and consult their experts. From the beginning, the case must be framed according to the *facts*, and only the experts can identify and qualify these facts. Preservationists who wait until the opposition presents its case before securing expert assistance create their own disadvantage.

Using Experts to Identify Gaps in the Opponents' Case. Experts are not merely purveyors of a preservationist's affirmative case. They can save the attorney time and painful self-education by reviewing the opponents' case and advising the preservation attorney how to overcome that case.

Using Experts as a Source of Information. Experts serve to inform and advise preservationists, their attorney, and the court, not vice versa. While experts must be guided by the preservationists' ultimate objective, they should not be told what evidence or opinion to produce—be wary of "experts" who ask what they should deliver! Rather, once the general objective is stated and the experts are satisfied that the objective is worthy of support, they should produce their own statement of

---

49. See also W. Anthony Wiles, *The Use of Expert Witnesses in Litigation*, 33 Land Use Law and Zoning Digest 7 (1981).

the facts and opinions. Preservationists and their attorney should carefully review the experts' statements to ensure from the outset that their case is well grounded.

Hearings

Temporary Stay Order

If demolition is contemplated within two weeks of filing the complaint, preservationists' first judicial hearing will be for a temporary stay order. As pointed out earlier, opposing parties should be notified, with service of the written pleading if at all possible, at least four hours before a request is made for a temporary stay.

This hearing generally will be informal. Many judges conduct such hearings in their chambers rather than in open court since the judge's task calls for becoming at least sufficiently familiar with the case to justify restraint. At this point, the *only* question presented to the court is that of the need for immediate relief to preserve the status quo pending the hearing on a preliminary injunction; the hearing should not substantiate the merits of the case.

Preservationists should, however, establish at least the appearance of a substantial case to justify a restraint on publicly authorized activities. If preservationists have prepared their case adequately and can demonstrate the imminency of demolition, they should obtain the temporary stay. Ten days or two weeks delay in carrying out a project should not prove sufficiently prejudicial to the owner to overcome the compelling claim that an otherwise intact landmark should remain that way—at least until the court can obtain more than a casual review of the pleadings.

Preservationists must nonetheless be alert to the claims owners can assert to defeat even a temporary stay. Generally, developers make these claims because of their dislike for any judicial restraint, regardless of how temporary, that can frustrate financing arrangements. Indeed, the developer's desire to avoid a judicial injunction can be so strong that it might consent to a voluntary restraint pending adjudication of the matter. If such an offer is made, preservationists should ensure that sufficient procedural safeguards surround such an offer.

For example, the offer should be in writing and on its face exhibit sufficient authority to bind the developer. If a developer is unwilling to offer an indefinite stay—such as until the termination of litigation—then the stay should remain effective until rescinded on sufficient notice (two weeks). This will enable preservationists to move for an injunctive order from the court.

Preliminary Stay, or Injunction, Pending Determination of the Merits

A hearing on a preliminary stay (or injunction) generally requires both sides to present written or oral evidence in support of their principal contentions. Usually this hearing is held on at least 10 days notice to give the opposing parties an opportunity to respond to the legal arguments in the petition. Frequently, however, the respondents will request less than 10 days notice to hasten the injunction decision.

The preliminary hearing requires the court to inquire into the merits of the case since the issuance of a preliminary injunction requires the likelihood of the petitioners' prevailing on appeal or at least the presence of a substantial question of law. Indeed, as pointed out above, occasionally a hearing for preliminary injunction can (if the court is convinced that oral testimony and a further evidentiary showing are not necessary) become the hearing that actually disposes of the case on the merits.

If preservationists win the hearing, then litigation will proceed without threatened demolition of the building. If preservationists lose the hearing, despite their showing that injunctive relief is necessary to prevent imminent demolition, the judge clearly has signaled a lack of belief in the merits of the preservationists' substantive case. Fortunately for preservationists, the denial of an injunction generally forms an appealable order, thereby serving two goals: providing an immediate ear at the appellate level and, more importantly, offering another chance to secure the injunction.

When denied an injunction, preservationists must file a notice of appeal in the trial court. Once that notice of appeal is filed, they can file a petition in the appellate court for a stay pending appeal (sometimes called a writ of supersedeas) or other relief that would set aside the lower court's order refusing to enjoin demolition. Such an application must be accompanied by a memorandum of law in support and also by an appendix consisting of a copy of all documents in the original (trial) court's file.

As noted in reference to the *WATCH v. Harris* case,[50] the appellate court can treat an appeal from a denial of preliminary injunction as

---

50. *WATCH, supra* note 20.

an appeal on the merits, especially if the parties stipulate to that effect. For this tactic to work and give preservationists the least expensive result on the merits, they must prepare an absolutely impeccable record for the trial court, continue to preserve that impeccable record during the preliminary injunction hearing, and be blessed with an enlightened appellate panel unafraid to consider the merits on such short notice.

Hearing on the Merits

The nature of the final hearing on the merits will depend on the scope of judicial review. In traditional judicial review of administrative action under the substantial evidence test, the hearing on the merits will resemble appellate oral advocacy in which the attorneys argue points of law from the fixed written record—in this case, the administrative record of proceedings below. Such an argument would, in even the most complex cases, generally be completed in one day.

If the trial court conducts *de novo* review, the hearing could duplicate the hearings that took place before the administrative agencies. The process offers the opportunity, and threat, of calling witnesses for direct examination and cross-examining witnesses called by other parties. For example, in matters such as architectural and economic assessments, witnesses may be used to render professional opinions on the values at stake, the economic feasibility of preservation, or their willingness to purchase from the developer. The *de novo* hearing thus gives each side a second chance to make its case afresh. The process, however, will be expensive. Whereas administrative proceedings are conducted informally and generally do not require an attorney's full-time attention, in the judicial process, a well-prepared attorney may have to devote several days or weeks to presenting or defeating claims of architectural significance, economic feasibility, and adequacy of environmental assessment.

Obviously, therefore, the *de novo* hearing on the merits presents a mixed blessing. The opportunity to start from scratch may be more than outweighed by the expense of presenting and defending the argument. Accordingly, when the issue before the court is primarily one of law—and preservationists can argue on issues of law even if there is no dispute as to the facts—preservationists may wish to forego a full-blown trial *de novo*. Success in preservation litigation for plaintiffs sometimes depends not so much on undertaking elaborate discovery, presenting many witnesses, and conducting an extensive trial as on the ability to identify a precise *legal* error in the proceedings below.

Post-Trial Findings and Judgment

After the hearing on the merits, the trial court will inform the parties of its intended decision. Rarely will the court do so on the same day the trial concludes; more likely this decision will be made in writing a few weeks after the hearing. The court then either will enter its own judgment or direct one of the parties (usually the prevailing party) to prepare the papers necessary to effectuate a formal judgment.

If preservationists prevail at trial, they should, whether or not requested by the judge or the opposing parties, submit proposed findings of fact and conclusions of law that state the facts as favorably as possible in keeping with the court's decision and prepare an order that grants relief on all alternative causes of action on which the court appears willing to do so. Especially at the trial-court level, judges do not have the substantial time needed to carefully prepare opinions. Thus, the prevailing preservationists should draft such an opinion in the form of findings and conclusions so that the law will be declared for subsequent actions in the dispute and so that the trial court's reasoning will be clearly available to the appellate court; the appellate court will then not reverse on grounds that the trial court failed to explain itself.

In drafting findings and conclusions, preservationists must remember that they are serving not as litigant but as a surrogate of the court itself. Whenever possible, the court's own words explaining its result should be followed. Above all, preservationists should make sure all facts crucial to the judgment are properly set out in the decision.

If preservationists do not prevail at trial, they still must request the entry of findings and conclusions; without such a request, the appellate court may presume that the trial court rendered all findings necessary to support the judgment. In hammering out the ultimate findings and conclusions, preservationists must secure findings that demonstrate least favorably the court position and that do not embellish the issues narrowly decided. Preservationists may contest the findings and conclusions of the opposing parties or propose their own. These findings, of course, become crucial, for they frame the analysis for the appeal and, to the extent that they demonstrate logical inconsistencies in the trial court's reasoning, they eliminate any appellate presumptions of regularity in that reasoning.

These observations also apply to costs and fees. If successful, preservationists should propose an award of costs and attorneys' fees, again reciting reasons in favor of the award. If they lose, preservationists should request the trial court to authorize each party to bear its own costs; this request should be grounded in the preservationists' status as a nonprofit, community-oriented organization, which prosecuted the case not for monetary gain but in the public interest.

If preservationists include a substantial claim for attorneys' fees, they should be prepared to expect further litigation on that matter—but not without having vigorously exhausted the possibility of a settled fee.[51] If the parties cannot agree on fees and if the governmental agency or developer is within reason in pressing for a judgment and remand on the merits, then the parties might agree to a judgment that disposes of all of the issues except the fee question and reserves trial court jurisdiction to resolve fees in a subsequent hearing.

Post-Trial Injunctive Relief

If preservationists lose at trial, they may lack injunctive power between notice of intended decision and the formal entry of judgment—a period that could prove lengthy as findings and conclusions are debated by the parties and approved by the court. The notice of intended decision is not appealable; formal judgment is required before an appeal can be made. A problem will exist if injunctive relief was not granted before trial but now (with the developer holding a pending decision in its favor) demolition appears imminent. During the hiatus before judgment, preservationists may find the appellate court inaccessible for securing an injunctive order.

This problem can be overcome. If at the conclusion of trial or on notice of intended decision some form of injunctive relief appears necessary pending formal judgment, preservationists should move (orally, if necessary) for an injunction pending the entry of formal judgment. Even though the court has indicated its intention to rule against the preservation position, the court might enter an injunctive order to preserve the appellate court's opportunity to grant injunctive relief after the entry of formal judgment. In the more likely event that the trial court denies such an injunctive order, preservationists should ensure that

---

51. If categorical qualification for fees appears well established in the jurisdiction, then the amount of fee should be settled rather than litigated. Few things appear as unseemly as a squabble over the number of hours worked or the value of the services, and often a protracted dispute on fees may consume as much revenue as is being sought in a fee application. Settlement of fees is encouraged by the rule that the time required to litigate fee awards is generally itself compensable. See *Serrano v. Unruh (IV)*, 32 Cal. 3d 621, 186 Cal. Rptr. 754 (1982); *Prandini v. National Tea Co.*, 585 F.2d 47 (3d Cir. 1978).

such a denial is entered in the court minutes. That denial in minute order form *does* constitute an appealable order and thereby permits preservationists to seek supersedeas in the appellate court.[52] Unfortunately, that appeal addresses only the denial of an injunction and subsequently must be consolidated with the appeal on the merits that will follow the entry of formal judgment.

The situation might arise in which the trial court's calendar or defendants' agility will prevent preservationists from appealing before the entry of final judgment. For example, the court may not be in session when preservationists learn of impending demolition, and a hearing on an injunction might not be possible for a week or two; the developer might successfully demand that this much notice be given to defend against an injunction. Under these conditions, preservationists have yet another option: to file an original mandate petition in the appellate court, naming the trial court as respondent and the trial-court defendants as real parties in interest; such a petition would seek an immediate stay from the appellate court, followed by a mandate directing the trial court to enter an injunction pending trial, based on the lack of a normal appellate remedy. As part of such a petition to the appellate court, preservationists must present an appendix containing the pleadings filed in the trial court.

The expense and potential confusion from appellate court proceedings other than appeal on the merits—whether by another appeal, injunction, or mandate—amplify the importance of devoting principal efforts to securing *from the trial court* an injunctive order, as outlined earlier, that will preserve the status quo until formal judgment is entered.

Appeal on the Merits

Once formal judgment is entered, the party or parties dissatisfied with the trial court's decision can file notice of appeal to the appellate court; the filing of such a notice *in the trial court* immediately divests that court of jurisdiction and reposes in the appellate body all authority over the case.

Often, injunctive relief by way of supersedeas forms the first order of business in the appellate court. If such a court denies the writ of supersedeas, preservationists should immediately seek whatever form of review is available from the highest appellate court—even though

---

52. See description in this chapter of the writ of supersedeas to secure an injunction from the appellate court.

the merits trail far behind.[53]

Whether acting as appellant or respondent, preservationists must not look on the appeal as just another judicial review under the substantial evidence test. Rather, they must rethink, restructure, and rewrite their case to respond to lessons learned and contentions raised after the briefing in the trial court. Because of the extensive trial court briefing, however, the appellate process should not prove unduly burdensome. The briefs of the parties on appeal will largely resemble those at trial. If, as a condition of securing appellate injunctive relief, preservationists must proceed on an accelerated briefing schedule, that requirement should be met easily.

In challenging a trial court's decision on appeal, preservationists should keep one stylistic principle in mind: while clearly advising the appellate court of the trial court's error, the appellant will not want its brief to consist entirely of an attack on the trial court's result or reasoning. Rather, the brief should be organized to state the appellant's case—to set forth the facts and law so that they support the appellants' hoped-for resolution of the case. After stating its case, the appellant then should demonstrate how the trial court's decision violated applicable legal principles. This manner of presentation not only enables preservationists to keep command of their case but creates the impression that the appellant, rather than the trial court, correctly comprehended the law.

The details of the appellate process do not require elaboration: the appellant will file an opening brief, the respondent will file a brief in opposition, and the appellant generally will be given an opportunity to reply. The same order will prevail at oral argument, in which the appellant generally proceeds first and has the opportunity for rebuttal.

The appellate court's decision will be announced generally by a formal written opinion, which (unlike the notice of intended decision at trial) will on its own constitute the judgment of the appellate court. Prior to that written decision becoming final—usually 30 days after in-

---

53. Thus, in *Westwood Hills Property Owners Association v. Regents of the University of California*, L.A. Superior Court No. C180760, (May 5, 1977), after the trial court denied a preliminary injunction, the homeowners petitioned for supersedeas (stay) in the intermediate court of appeal, which court denied that petition, Cal. App. 2 Civ. No. 51109, May 12, 1977. The homeowners immediately petitioned for hearing in the California Supreme Court, which first granted a temporary stay and then granted the petition for hearing, ordered the court of appeal to issue its writ of supersedeas to the trial court, and transferred the matter back to the court of appeal to carry out that result, Cal. No. 30789, May 26, 1977. The matter came to trial several months later, with petitioners prevailing on the merits.

itial filing of the opinion—unsuccessful preservationists will want to seek a rehearing (if such a procedure is authorized under local law) to correct errors of fact and law. If the opinion requires them to reimburse their opponents for filing fees, brief printing, and other allowable costs, preservationists should seek to have the opinion modified.

If preservationists are successful on appeal, then (if authorized under the rules of the jurisdiction and prior to finality of the appellate court's decision) they should seek an authorization of attorneys' fees or at least attempt to secure a direction from the appellate court that the trial court consider such a fee on appeal—unless the rules of the jurisdiction plainly do not require such a request from the appellate court.[54]

This entire appellate process will be available for a second time in those jurisdictions with two levels of appellate courts. Two significant differences will generally apply in the court of highest jurisdiction: the briefing schedule will be much more compressed (often with no opportunity for the appellant to reply), and the exercise of the appellate court's jurisdiction will be discretionary, not mandatory. The highest courts of the larger states, like the U.S. Supreme Court, serve not to resolve every dispute and correct every inequity but rather to administer and declare the law of their jurisdictions. Accordingly, to secure a hearing in the highest court, preservationists must establish that their case presents a significant legal issue in need of resolution.

PRESERVATIONISTS AS RESPONDENTS IN COURT

The Government Agency

Government agencies usually enjoy the presumption of validity when their actions are challenged. As respondents, they never have the burden of proof. But a government agency that has promoted preservation can-

---

54. In California, for example, the general rule requires that for a party to recover fees on appeal, the appellate court, prior to the finality of its judgment, had to authorize the trial court to consider such an award. *American City Bank v. Zetlen*, 272 Cal. App. 2d 65, 76 Cal. Rptr. 898 (1969). In public interest cases, in which fees are authorized by statute—Cal. Civ. Proc. Code § 1021.5 (West Supp. 1982)—the courts have now ruled that such a request of the appellate court is not necessary; the trial court on remand should determine the propriety and amount of fees for both trial and appeal. See *Marini v. Municipal Court*, 99 Cal. App. 3d 829, 160 Cal. Rptr. 465 (1979); *T.E. Bearing Co. v. Walter E. Heller & Co.*, 38 Cal. App. 3d 59, 65, 112 Cal. Rptr. 910, 915 (1974).

not, however, become complacent in court. For example, in the celebrated *Lutheran Church*[55] litigation, the New York Court of Appeals overturned the New York City Landmark Commission's decision prohibiting the church from demolishing the J.P. Morgan House in Murray Hill because the city failed to establish cultural values that would justify the hardship of requiring the church to maintain the mansion.[56] The government must not only build an adequate record in the administrative process but must effectively present that record in court. In a more successful effort at preserving church-owned property, New York effectively refuted an owner's allegation that a proposed landmark did not possess sufficient architectural or historic character by introducing evidence on the history of the structure and its architectural significance.[57]

The Private Preservation Society or Citizen

When a governmental authority has acted to preserve preservation values by designating a landmark or denying a demolition permit, a private preservation society or group of citizens need not go to court. They should consider, however, the practical benefits of judicial participation. The two ways in which citizens or private preservationists can participate—intervention or *amicus curiae*—are described below.

Acting as an Intervenor

Formal intervention gives preservationists the right independently to raise contentions of their own and the right to appeal an unfavorable decision in the event that the government decides to fold after losing at trial.

To become a formal intervenor in judicial proceedings brought by a developer against government, preservationists must establish that the governmental respondents will not adequately represent the preservationist viewpoint. Such a circumstance might arise if the government agency admits to having insufficient funding to present a vigorous defense. More likely, the need to intervene will exist if the strongest defense of the governmental action is one that the government, for in-

---

55. *Lutheran Church in America v. City of New York*, 35 N.Y.2d 121, 359 N.Y.S.2d 7 (1974).

56. See also *South of Second Associates v. Town of Georgetown*, 580 P.2d 807 (Colo. 1978).

57. *Society for Ethical Culture v. Spatt*, *supra* note 3.

stitutional reasons, does not wish to present—for example, preservationists might believe local law creates a mandatory duty to preserve, whereas the governmental agency would prefer to characterize its action as discretionary. Under such circumstances, a private preservation organization or group of citizens would not only be entitled, but wisely advised, to intervene.

Intervention requires a formal order of the court and, therefore, an application by preservationists; occasionally, the other parties will eliminate the need for a contested hearing by consenting to the intervention. To justify the court's order, the intervenor ought to prepare and file a formal statement of qualifications and interest. The intervenor has the authority to participate fully in the trial and to appeal the developer's claim. The intervenor may present its own witnesses (in writing or, where permitted, in person) and advance legal arguments in concert with, or independent of, the case presented by the governmental agency. Intervenors, moreover, enjoy the right to appeal issues that the governmental agency may choose not to appeal or to argue points that the government might concede.[58]

Intervention usually is granted, however, on the condition that the intervenor's presentation be coordinated as much as possible with that of the governmental defendant. This is to prevent the intervenor from delaying the litigation, causing duplication, or creating disjointed proceedings.

Acting as Amicus Curiae

A less formal and demanding appearance can be made as an *amicus curiae*—literally, "friend of the court." The *amicus curiae* is permitted to present a written case—that is, a legal brief in support of the governmental agency—and also may be permitted, at oral argument, to present points of law briefly; the *amicus curiae* does not present its own witnesses or participate in other witnesses' examination. Participation as *amicus curiae* requires permission of the court, as does intervention, but at a much lower qualification threshold. Generally, if a preservation society or group of citizens can establish its credentials to speak on preservation issues, can show its past participation in the case (par-

---

58. A handful of jurisdictions allow a person to intervene by filing a notice of appeal, even though that person did not intervene at trial; the notice of appeal must justify the need for intervention. See *Nott v. Wolff*, 18 Ill. 2d 362, 16 N.E.2d 809 (1960). Because this rule is a minority view, reliance upon it is not recommended.

ticularly in the administrative proceedings), and can outline succinctly its legal case, the court will permit its appearance.

Participation as *amicus curiae* affords citizens the opportunity at relatively low cost (that is, the cost of preparing a single brief and appearing at one oral argument) to supplement and complement the government's case. Thus, preservationists can engage the services of a private attorney who is extremely qualified in preservation law—perhaps more qualified than the city attorney—to benefit both the governmental respondent and the court itself. Moreover, participation as *amicus curiae* can demonstrate to the court the breadth of community concern.

Unless the government absolutely cannot be trusted to present an effective trial and appeal, preservationists should usually follow the *amicus curiae* course. Such a route not only finds greater favor with the courts but also conserves resources for the fights preservationists must conduct alone.

Defending Claims for Injunctive Relief

A proponent of landmark destruction may request the court, pending trial, to enjoin operation of a preservation ordinance or, in an extreme situation, to require the issuance of a demolition permit. In these admittedly unusual circumstances, the preservationist-respondent's strongest defense lies in establishing that the project proponent is not likely to prevail at trial.

Mere enactment of an ordinance should not be enjoined, preservationists must argue, because the applicant will be unable to show immediate harm flowing from the ordinance itself. *Application* of the ordinance may present a different case. The project proponent may try to show the economic harm it will suffer from having to run the regulatory gauntlet of preparing an application and supporting data. But the courts have typically rejected arguments of this type; in the *Agins* case, the U.S. Supreme Court expressly refused to credit as potentially "compensable" a developer's cost of processing its application.[59]

If a project proponent nonetheless appears likely to obtain some form of injunctive relief from the court, preservationists should insist on conditions that might undercut the effect of any injunction that issues. For example, even assuming that the application of an ordinance may be enjoined, preservationists should insist on a condition that, pending determination of the ordinance's legality, the project proponent will

---

59. *Agins v. City of Tiburon, supra* note 48.

not irreparably alter a threatened landmark. Such a condition will not prevent the project proponent from securing financing or taking other preliminary steps, such as submitting applications that do not conform to the challenged ordinance. Since these measures do not actually harm a particular structure—even though they may prejudice the orderly administration of government—preservationists must tolerate them.

Above all, any prayer for a mandatory permit issuance can and should be resisted on the ground that the issuance threatens the status quo *pendente lite*—the very purpose for which the injunctive power exists—and effectively grants the developer relief on the merits before adjudication of the case.

Defending on the Merits

With respect to defending on the merits, one point deserves special attention: the need to present a full record to the court. A developer-petitioner may cleverly or foolishly present only selected elements of the record. While, under the substantial evidence test, the court may infer that the record *not* presented contains evidence sufficient to support the governmental decision, the respondents may improve their position by placing the entire record into evidence; this tactic demonstrates not only their thoroughness and their confidence in their position but also their fairness.

Private preservationists must be sensitive to the quality of record keeping in the governmental agency. If the agency is not experienced in preservation litigation or litigation generally and is known for keeping sloppy or inaccurate files, then preservationists should maintain a separate set of files. Often, the interested citizen maintains more complete files, historical materials, and the like, than does a small governmental agency. The court, however, will rely only on *official* records. Therefore, while maintaining a duplicate set of records, preservationists should ensure that their records are officially annotated to show the date of receipt into the official record.

Expanding the Record

As respondents, preservationists will face a crucial decision: whether or not to expand the record beyond that contained in the agency's administrative file. This decision is not one that should be made categorically in advance but rather in response to the petitioner's case. Thus, as respondents, preservationists might take the initiative in discovery to uncover acts or failures to act that might weaken the petitioner's case.

If, for example, the project proponent asserts the economic infeasibility of preservation, and the record below does not reveal whether or not the developer received offers to purchase the property, such evidence can be extracted on discovery. Discovery, moreover, forces the developer-petitioner to disclose and limit its own case. Finally, of course, discovery can impose burdens on the petitioner and thereby end an otherwise unworthy case.

In presenting evidence at trial, preservationists must be prepared to act both under the scope of review that they deem proper and the scope of review that the project proponent asserts. Generally, of course, a project proponent will assert an independent right of review in the trial court, since that gives the proponent a second bite at the "substantive" apple. Thus, while preparing to defend the case under the "substantial evidence" procedure, preservationists also must assemble their own witnesses and be prepared to present at trial the same case that was presented before adoption of an ordinance, designation of a landmark, or denial of a permit.

If the project proponent's case depends on a crucial assertion of fact that can be categorically rebutted, evidence of such rebuttal should be submitted as early in the proceedings as possible. Even if preservationists are technically premature in presenting such evidentiary rebuttals, a firm factual assertion will likely impress the court. Moreover, by presenting such evidence early, preservationists can do so by written, rather than oral, testimony—a procedure that finds judicial favor and deprives the project proponent of cross-examination.

On the other hand, if preservationists believe they can win the case only on a point of law, it does not make sense to pollute the case with factual disputes. Rather, legal objections, such as a demurrer, motion to dismiss, or motion for summary judgment, should be made early; unnecessary expense can harm government as well as private interests. If the preservationists' case in law fails, they can present their factual case at a trial on the merits.

CONCLUSIONS: LITIGATION CANNOT BECOME A WAY OF LIFE

Once the court's decision is final, preservationists must live with it. Even if the victory is decisive, preservationists cannot afford haughtiness, pride, or indifference. In many instances the result may be only transitory with no clear winner, and thus the other parties to the proceedings, whether governmental or private, should be consulted to ascertain, if possible, a mutually agreeable future for the contested historical or cultural site. If the judicial victory is (as usual) not decisive but anticipates further proceedings either in trial court or in local governmental agencies, preservationists should assess the possibility of all sides using the court's directions to produce a stipulated settlement. Not only does this course create good public relations, it is practical. At some point a project proponent may secure a valid approval, and goading the proponent into perpetual opposition will prove to be a losing game—except in those few instances in which the owner or governmental agency is genuinely obstreperous.

If preservationists have lost in court, they have not necessarily lost altogether. Often a building must be demolished or sacrificed before a government recognizes the weakness of its preservation program or before the general citizenry will support efforts to enact new preservation ordinances and statutes. Truly effective preservationists will not dwell on a momentary loss but will go on to improve their own performance in the next dispute and to redefine the framework within which preservation decisions are made in the community.[60]

FURTHER READINGS

While there is not much available in the literature for litigation, local practicing lawyers will find most useful the manuals published by each state's continuing legal education program. Also, the continuing education handbooks published by the American Law Institute and the Practicing Law Institute will be of interest.

---

60. Thus, in the wake of the demolition of the City of Paris Building, San Francisco preservationists are causing a citywide assessment of both their preservation ordinance and downtown development generally. Moreover, because the community took offense at a state legislator's representation of the private developer in the city's administrative proceedings, the City of Paris case led to several bills and California State Bar proposals to outlaw such private representation by assembly and senate members.

Chapter 7
Preservation Law and Economics

RICHARD J. RODDEWIG

In the last two decades, there has been a well-publicized rebirth of many historic residential neighborhoods around the country. Preservationists have a fairly good understanding of the market forces that have prompted a strong new interest in 19th and early 20th century architectural styles and caused "renovation fever" in so many places. As the members of the baby boom generation have come of age, they have created a demand for relatively inexpensive housing close to downtown areas, partly in reaction against the housing patterns and styles of the suburbs where they were raised. Few preservationists, however, understand the economic forces that dictate the success or failure of renovating income-producing structures (e.g., apartment buildings, commercial office buildings, hotels, and industrial buildings converted to retail uses).

Few know the answers to questions such as: Why do some long-time owners of income-producing historic buildings refuse to renovate, preferring to demolish rather than sell to a new owner who might renovate? Why are some income-producing historic buildings ardently sought by investors while others are not? How can government programs most efficiently encourage more renovation and less demolition?

In the past, preservationists and their allies in Congress, state legislatures, and city councils have failed to address these questions in their legislative programs. The result has been a mishmash of incentives, some well designed to do the job, but most ill-conceived, poorly designed, or accompanied by red tape that makes them unattractive to most developers. An honest analysis of existing property tax, income tax, and financing incentives will reveal the shortcomings of current programs designed to foster preservation and renovation of historic landmarks. It also will reveal a "bare bones" outline of the types of incentives that will more effectively and efficiently promote renovation. The necessity of government incentives in making feasible the renovation

GLOSSARY

Accelerated Cost Recovery System (ACRS)—The new term for depreciation now used in the Internal Revenue Code. This system allows an investor in an income-producing building to deduct a portion of his investment each year over a 15-, 35-, or 45-year period.

Accelerated Depreciation—Any form of cost recovery that allows an investor in an income-producing building to take high annual deductions in the early years of his investment that gradually taper down in later years. The annual allowable amount is determined by multiplying a standard rate against the remaining undepreciated basis in the property. After 1981, a 175 percent rate is allowed on residential or commercial income-producing property, and a 200 percent rate is allowed on some forms of residential property.

Amortizable Loan—Repaid by equal periodic installments composed of principal and interest over a specified term. The interest component of each periodic payment declines over the life of the loan, and the principal component increases correspondingly.

Capital Asset—Investments such as real estate specified in the Internal Revenue Code that, when held for at least 12 months, qualify for the exclusion from income tax of 60 percent of any gain at sale.

Capital Gain—The gain from a sale of the capital asset that qualifies for the 60 percent exclusion before taxes are calculated.

Cash-on-Cash Return—The first year's net operating income less the cost of financing divided by initial cash investment.

Debt/Coverage Ratio—The numerical result when annual net operating income is divided by total annual debt service.

Debt/Equity Ratio—The numerical result when investor equity is divided by total mortgage principal.

Depreciable Basis—The portion of the real estate investment against which the investor may take either straight-line or declining balance depreciation. It is most commonly purchase price of an income-producing property less value of the underlying land plus the cost of any subsequent improvements since purchase less previously taken depreciation deductions.

Depreciation—An annual allowable deduction of taxable basis in an income-producing building over a period of time authorized by the Internal Revenue Code. *Straight-line depreciation* is a deduction of the same amount each year over the period authorized by the tax code. *Declining balance depreciation*, or *accelerated depreciation* as it is sometimes called, is the deduction of a portion of taxable basis higher than what would be allowed by the straight-line method in the early years of an investment, but the annual deduction gradually diminishes during the authorized period.

Discounted Cash Flow Analysis—A technique to determine the present value of expected future income by applying an annual rate of discount to future cash flows.

Discount Rate—The rate used to discount future cash flows to present value. Selection of a rate reflects the "time value of money" and the opportunity cost of capital for a particular investor.

Easement—A less than full ownership interest in a piece of real property that allows a neighboring property owner or a third party to use the affected property in a limited way or to control some decisions of the full legal title holder. An *easement appurtenant* gives a neighboring property owner the limited use or control. An *easement in gross* gives a third party the limited use or control.

Equity—An investor's cash investment in real property. It does not include the financing contributed to the project by a lender. Equity can grow as the value of the property increases and the mortgage principal is gradually reduced by periodic repayment.

Income Approach to Value—An appraisal technique to determine market value based on capitalization of net operating income after an analysis of current income and expenses and likely future projections.

Internal Rate of Return (IRR)—An investment analysis technique that searches for the rate that will reduce future cash flows from a real estate investment to the initial cash investment. This is sometimes called the *yield on the investment*.

Land Price Write-down—A subsidy provided to a developer by a government entity that acquires a piece of property for its full market value and then resells to a developer or investor for less than the acquisition price.

Leverage—The use of borrowed funds to finance an investment in real property.

Market Data Approach to Value—An appraisal technique that determines market value of a piece of real property based upon sales of property comparable in size, age, condition, quality, or location.

Minimum Tax—A special surtax in the Internal Revenue Code on items of income called preference items. The tax is generally 15 percent of the total preference items after an allowable exclusion is made. Tax preference items include accelerated depreciation deductions.

Net Operating Income—Total annual income from rent and miscellaneous other charges less all operating expenses (excluding debt service and income taxes).

Operating Ratio—The numerical relationship between total annual operating expenses and total annual gross income from all sources.

Recapture of Depreciation—An Internal Revenue Code requirement that all accelerated depreciation deductions be later included in income when the real estate investment is sold. On some forms of real estate, all accelerated depreciation deductions must be included in total as ordinary income at sale. On some real estate investments—most notably, residential rental properties—only the difference between accelerated depreciation deduction actually taken and the depreciation that would have been allowed if a straight-line method had been used is required to be included as ordinary income at sale.

Reproduction Cost Approach to Value—An appraisal technique that determines market value based on the cost of recreating improvements of a comparable size, configuration, and construction, then deducting for the actual physical, functional, and economic obsolescence of the building being valued and adding in the value of the underlying land.

Tax Bracket—In a progressive system of income taxation such as the Internal Revenue Code, the highest percentage of taxation on any portion of a taxpayer's income. After the Economic Recovery Tax Act of 1981, the maximum tax bracket on individual taxpayers is 50 percent. For married individuals filing joint returns for 1982 income, there are 12 brackets, ranging from 12 percent on taxable income between $3,400 and $5,500 to 50 percent on all income over $85,600.

Tax Deferral—The opportunity to take a deduction against ordinary income today with a requirement that the deducted amount later be included in income.

Tax Shelter—The opportunity to protect current income from taxation by taking current deductions against income that defer taxes until later, and convert the income deferred from an item subject to the ordinary income tax to one qualifying for the 60 percent capital gain exclusion before taxation. Ordinary income this year can thus be converted to a capital gain in a later year.

of many landmarks will become apparent.

Why not let the marketplace decide which buildings should and should not be saved? Because today's marketplace never operates independently of government action and policy. Banking laws, the Internal Revenue Code, real property taxes, building codes, zoning regulations—all of these aspects of government regulation profoundly affect the real estate development process, and all of them fundamentally affect the cost, character, and amount of real estate investment. Government policy must be scrutinized continually for its effect on preservation. The danger in the current determination to foster private sector investment is that some types of economic enterprises will be given unfair "most favored investment" status. Preservationists must make sure that investment in the renovation and continued use of historic buildings is not slighted.

Preservationists and their legislative allies, if alert to the realities of the real estate investment process, will be able to craft incentives that conserve limited government resources and direct incentives to help the preservation projects most in need of them at the least public cost. This chapter, in exploring the developing relationship between preservation, economics, and the law, analyzes the types of government incentives most likely to be helpful to preservation, examines the results of current incentive programs, and recommends changes to make these incentives more effective.

DETERMINING THE FEASIBILITY OF RENOVATION

To design effective incentives for preservation and renovation, preservationists and lawmakers must understand the process for analyzing the income-producing possibilities for older buildings. Every income-producing historic building is analyzed as a real estate investment in light of three considerations: its before-tax income and expense characteristics; its financing possibilities; and its after-tax income potential. To determine the prospects for a neglected unrenovated landmark, these characteristics must be analyzed twice: once based on the structure's current unrenovated state to determine present profit or loss and therefore the likelihood of demolition, and again based on a set of assumptions about renovation expenditures to determine if a profit can be made from the building after renovation. See table 1.

The points in the income/expense analysis in which the government may enter are quite limited; the property tax is the most significant.

TABLE 1
ELEMENTS OF REAL ESTATE INVESTMENT FEASIBILITY

Income/Expense Analysis

    Revenue Forecast
        Rental Income
        Miscellaneous Income
            Total Operating Income
    Operating Expense Forecast
        Net Operating Income

Debt-Financing Considerations

    Market Value of Property
        Income Approach
        Market Data Approach
        Reproduction Cost Approach
    Debt/Equity Ratio
    Debt/Coverage Ratio
    Annual Mortgage Payment
        Total Mortgage Payment
        Interest Rate
        Amortization Term
        Monthly Payments

After-Tax Income Considerations

    Selection of Ownership Arrangement
    Income Tax Brackets: Present and Future
    Comparison of Allowable Depreciation Methods
        Length of Holding Period
        Recapture
        Type of Sale

In contrast, there is substantial room for government involvement in debt financing (e.g., altering the availability and rate of financing) and after-tax income considerations (e.g., manipulating the Internal Revenue Code to encourage maintenance and renovation and discourage demolition). However, financing and tax incentives for preservation are limited by the cost of the programs to the public treasuries. A clear understanding of the three elements of real estate investment will help structure preservation incentives to best use limited government resources.

The three elements are not equally important to every owner or investor. Pension funds or large publicly held corporations may be interested only in the income and expense characteristics because they purchase and hold properties as cash investments without lender financing and cannot utilize the income tax deductions that accompany ownership of income-producing properties. Other types of owners, such as Real Estate Investment Trusts (the so-called REITS) and many types of limited partnerships, may put great emphasis on the after-tax income consequences of ownership and much less on the income and expense characteristics.

The Income and Expense Analysis

An old building may be torn down because it loses money or makes so little money that an owner would prefer tearing it down or selling it to someone who places a high value on the site for a new development project. Table 2 compares the income and expenses on newer and older buildings based on a 1980 survey of downtown office buildings in the United States and Canada, 158 of which were constructed in the last 10 years, and 229 of which were constructed 50 years or more ago.[1] The comparison makes two points clear: gross income per square foot on older buildings is substantially less than on new buildings, and expenses—except for taxes, insurance, and energy—are substantially higher on older buildings. Total income on older buildings is a little more than 70 percent of new building income. On the average, it costs more to operate the same amount of space in an older structure than it does in a new building. The difference in operating costs in some expense categories is quite dramatic. For example, in older buildings, the costs of electrical service, cleaning, and tenant improvements are

---

1. Building Owners and Managers Association International, *1980 Downtown and Suburban Office Building Exchange Report* (Washington, D.C., 1980).

50 percent higher. The costs of heating, ventilating, and air conditioning are about 30 percent higher.

The most important comparison to make in analyzing the economics of renovation is the disparity between the operating ratios (operating expenses as a percentage of total operating income) for new versus old buildings. Expenses consumed only 55 percent of income on newer buildings but 76 percent of income on buildings 50 years of age or older. That means that only 24 percent of total operating income was available to owners of older buildings to pay off mortgage principal and interest and provide a return on the cash equity invested in the building.[2]

How could government intervene to improve the operating cost ratio for older buildings? Perhaps it could directly subsidize some item or items of expense such as electrical, heating, or air conditioning costs. This, however, would be prohibitively expensive if such a program were widespread enough to save significant numbers of historic buildings. It also would conflict with other government programs, for example, those to encourage energy conservation and promote more efficient heating and cooling systems for office buildings.

Or perhaps the government could intervene to boost total operating income for older buildings. Section 8 of the Housing and Community Development Act of 1974 rental assistance program[3] aims to make rental housing for low- and moderate-income households more affordable, while assuring developers of this housing that they will receive full market rents for their units. A similar subsidy program could be constructed to make historic commercial buildings more competitive with new buildings. Again, the problem is the cost of such a program. There is also a question of fairness. Why should the owner of a run-down, older

---

2. Many historic buildings with older mortgages at low interest rates may have quite low annual debt service payments. This may have the effect of making the cash flow after debt service quite attractive as a return on owner equity. "If they won't sell," preservationists ask, "why won't they renovate?" There are numerous answers. First, contrary to academic economic teaching, most owners of any product, especially real estate, are profit maximizers. They are happy to muddle along obtaining what they consider to be a satisfactory return. To an outsider, there may be obvious ways they could maximize their profits from the real estate investment. To the insider, all those alternatives may seem too risky. Someone who has owned an older building for a long period may have little cash invested and may receive a quite good annual return as a percentage of equity. He will be very reluctant to invest more cash or secure refinancing.

3. 42 U.S.C. § 5301, Pub. L. No. 93-383 (1974). This program is discussed in greater detail in chapter 4.

building receive a windfall subsidy merely because the building happens to be historic?

One answer for improving the operating cost ratio for older buildings is, of course, renovation. Many preservationists are convinced that any historic building, after renovation, can compete economically with newer buildings of the same type or use. Current market rents on new commercial office buildings nationwide average $15 per square foot annually. Landmark office buildings before renovation average only $7 per square foot. After total refurbishing and renovation of a landmark, most preservationists believe rents in the landmark will be comparable to rents in new buildings, and expenses as a percentage of total operating income will decrease.

While preservationists often may be right that total renovation of a landmark building can boost income per square foot to the market level for newer buildings, renovation also may increase some expense items. For example, full-scale renovation that upgrades all mechanical and utility systems is most likely to decrease heating, cooling, electricity, and maintenance and repair expenses. Labor costs, however, may increase because of the need to hire additional or more skilled personnel to maintain the new, more complicated equipment. Management, maintenance, and cleaning costs will also increase if management is to provide a level of service commensurate with the new higher rents.

The two expense items likely to increase most dramatically are insurance and real estate taxes, since the costs of both items are pegged to the value of the building. While substantial renovation may improve the fire and safety rating of the building for insurance purposes, that benefit is likely to be more than offset by the increased value of the structure that must now be insured against casualty loss. On the typical renovated landmark office building, real estate taxes will be the expense item that increases the most. They are likely to increase both as a percentage of total operating income and as an expense per square foot of building area. Since real estate taxes are among the largest expense items in renovated buildings, they are probably one of the most effective areas for government intervention.

Developers who specialize in renovation pick and choose among available buildings partly on the basis of the comparative ease with which renovation costs and after-rehabilitation income and expenses can be predicted. Estimating likely renovation costs and forecasting income and expenses is much like soothsaying. Every developer knows the current asking price for new and renovated first-class office space in a particular market area. But no developer can accurately predict a completion date for a renovation project, the amount of space in a renovated building that can be preleased during renovation, the length of time it will take to achieve full rental, and the exact rental price per square foot at time of completion. That uncertainty makes an income forecast for the first few years after completion of renovation a "guesstimate."

Some after-rehabilitation expense items can be predicted with great accuracy before renovation begins. For example, management fees, general administrative costs, insurance, cleaning, and total payroll can be forecast and budgeted quite accurately based on industry norms and the performance of other buildings. The costs of heating and cooling a renovated building can be forecast but with somewhat less accuracy. Quite unpredictable are the costs of maintenance and repairs, tenant improvements, and even real estate taxes.

One way to decrease this uncertainty and, as mentioned before, lower the operating ratio is to provide developers with a property tax incentive. A predictable and dramatic decrease in the property tax expense—even if only for a few years following renovation—can help lower the operating ratio and provide an expense cushion against the uncertainty of the renovation process. A sizable, workable, and easily obtainable property tax incentive available to anyone who renovates an income-producing historic building will attract developers.

Financing Considerations

Every preservationist who has been involved in saving a historic landmark from demolition has first-hand knowledge of the importance of mortgage financing in the acquisition, development, or renovation of old buildings. The principal purpose of financing a real estate acquisition or renovation is to decrease the amount of cash necessary to acquire the benefits that accompany the ownership of a piece of real estate. Real estate is a very expensive commodity; it has "large economic size,"[4] as some economists express it.

For the typical single-family home buyer to purchase a home with cash, he would have to save for many years. In addition, the buyer could not use that cash for any other type of investment or expenditure. Most

---

4. Gaylon Greer, *The Real Estate Investment Decision* (Lexington, Mass.: D.C. Heath and Co., 1979), p. 63. For a detailed discussion of financing as it affects preservation projects, see Shlaes & Co., *Financing Preservation in the Private Market* (Washington, D.C.: National Trust for Historic Preservation, 1981).

home buyers would rather pay more for a home over time—the net effect of borrowing a substantial portion of the purchase price—than use all cash. Through a smaller cash payment at the date of acquisition, the buyer is able to live in a home and enjoy the purchase to the same extent as an all-cash buyer.

The same principle operates in the market for income-producing pieces of real estate, including historic buildings. Most investors in these real estate projects "leverage" their cash investment through the use of someone else's money, the loan provided by a mortgage lender. In fact, lenders are key partners in any historic renovation project.

The loan-to-value ratio, that is, the percentage of total investment in a real estate project provided by a mortgage lender, varies considerably depending upon the type of real estate investment, its location, and its income and expense characteristics. The lender is in reality an investor in the project. But the lender's investment is at a previously agreed upon rate of return. He may be willing to put up anywhere from 60 percent to 90 percent of the value of a project in exchange for a "guarantee" that the return on his investment will equal the mortgage interest rate. The lender will not agree to make such a loan and will not decide what percentage of the value of the project to finance until he has examined the developer's income and expense forecasts in relation to the real estate marketplace and the expected rate of return on the type of project being considered.

The lender insists that there be a comfortable cushion between net operating income from the building and the annual cost of his debt service. Net operating income is the amount left to a developer after deducting total annual operating expenses from total gross operating income. For example, in table 2, for buildings less than 10 years old, net operating income is approximately $4.30 per square foot of building area. For buildings more than 50 years old, it is only $1.68 per square foot. The annual debt service is the total annual cost of a mortgage loan, including both the principal and the interest components of the 12 monthly payments.

The lender will compare the annual debt service to the net operating income he believes is reasonable to expect the project to generate. Of course, no lender will make a loan if the net operating income is less than, or equal to, the debt service costs. The lender wants a cushion between net operating income and debt service so that if something unforeseen happens—revenues from the building decrease unexpectedly or expenses are greater than forecast—there will still be enough cash

TABLE 2
INCOME/EXPENSE COMPARISON OF DOWNTOWN OFFICE BUILDINGS

Income/Expense Item	I. Buildings Less Than 10 Years Old $/S.F.*	I. % Income	II. Buildings More Than 50 Years Old $/S.F.	II. % Income	Ratio between II and I (%)
Revenue					
Rental Income	$9.18	95.7	$6.56	93.6	71.5
Total Operating Income	$9.59	100.0	$7.01	100.0	73.1
Expenses					
Electrical	$0.12	1.3	$0.18	2.6	150.0
Heating, Vent and Air Cond.	0.26	2.7	0.34	4.9	130.8
Energy	1.24	12.9	1.24	17.7	100.0
Cleaning	0.78	8.1	1.13	16.1	144.9
Gen. Bldg.	0.53	5.5	0.59	8.4	111.3
Alterations & Decorating (Tenant areas)	0.24	2.5	0.36	5.1	150.0
Elevators	0.19	2.0	0.26	3.7	136.8
Admin. Costs	0.33	3.4	0.38	5.4	115.2
Insurance	0.11	1.2	0.10	1.4	90.9
Real Estate Taxes	1.44	15.0	0.99	14.1	68.8
Total Operating Expenses	$5.29	55.2	$5.33	76.0	100.8

Source: Building Owners and Managers Association International, *1980 Downtown and Suburban Office Building Experience Exchange Report*.

Note: Columns do not add precisely because each line item is based on a slightly different set of buildings and reporting methods.

* Price per square foot.

generated annually to meet the mortgage loan payments.

This debt coverage ratio, as the relationship between net operating income and total annual debt service is called, varies from one type of building and project to another. It is higher on projects considered by lenders to be riskier. For example, an analysis of mortgage loan commitments over $100,000 made by 20 life insurance companies in 1980 found that the debt coverage ratio was 1.25 on proposed new nonelevator apartment buildings, 1.27 on proposed new office buildings, and 1.57 on new motels.[5]

Accurate income and expense forecasts are essential to arrange financing. Developers must be optimists by nature. They forecast rents based on the high end of the range for a particular location. Lenders are more cautious by nature. Even if an area or market is improving, they know that there is a sizable range of rents in the area and may doubt that the demand is strong enough to warrant the rents so optimistically forecast by the developer. The lender also may be much more hardheaded than the developer about the likely costs of operating the building. The lender will know that expenses may consume much more than 50 percent or 60 percent of gross operating income.

Lenders tend to be much more comfortable with a new construction project than with a renovation project. Construction costs for a new building can be calculated easily. Even the uncertainties of inflation, labor disputes, and material shortages can be projected with some accuracy and added to the formula for estimating the total project cost. In renovation, however, anything can happen. Assumptions made about the structural integrity of the building to be renovated may be proved totally inaccurate once renovation work begins, walls are opened up, and mechanical and structural systems are revealed for the first time. This may cause serious cost overruns that make the projected income from the project less than adequate to carry the additional financing needed to complete it. There are, however, many lenders who have become accustomed to the uncertainty and unique problems of financing renovation projects.

Any developer engaged in large-scale renovation of income-producing historic buildings needs two types of financing. The developer must secure both a short-term construction loan, to carry the project through the renovation period, and a long-term "end" loan. Construction

---

5. American Council of Life Insurance, *Investment Bulletin No. 820* (Washington, D.C., April 24, 1981).

lenders, typically commercial banks or insurance companies, usually will not make a construction loan until the developer has secured a commitment for permanent financing following the renovation period. To secure a permanent loan commitment, the developer must forecast total renovation costs and predict gross rents, expenses, and net income.

Because so many real estate ventures are financed with someone else's money, and because small changes in such items as the loan-to-value ratio and the rate of interest can make a substantial difference in the rate of return to equity investors, government intervention can significantly induce real estate activity. Banking, including mortgage lending, is a highly regulated industry, and changes in, for example, the discount rate, stipulated reserve requirements, and general banking laws can affect the availability and cost of money to the real estate industry. Most government programs designed to assist in financing real estate projects fit into one of the following categories: (1) programs to increase the amount of money available to real estate lenders; (2) programs to make some loans less risky for real estate lenders; and (3) programs to make the cost of the loan to some or all borrowers—the interest rate—lower than market conditions dictate.

The amount of money available for real estate lending can be affected by many types of government actions. For example, on some types of real estate loans, government regulations prohibit the lender from exceeding a specified loan-to-value ratio on any particular loan. Changing government regulations to increase those loan-to-value ratios increases the amount of financing available on some types of real estate projects. Federal government activity to create a secondary mortgage market also may have the same effect. Lenders stuck with a portfolio of long-term, relatively low-interest mortgage loans can sell those mortgages to other investors in the secondary mortgage market and use the proceeds to make new construction or mortgage loans at current interest rates.

Government programs to guarantee repayment of lenders' real estate loans generally do not lower interest rates. Instead, they encourage lenders to make loans to developers they might otherwise consider less-than-perfect credit risks.

In recent years, there has been a great deal of new interest in programs to reduce the interest rate on real estate loans by direct government involvement in money markets. Because interest to investors in many types of government financial instruments is exempt from state and federal income taxes, governmental units can issue notes and bonds at a rate of interest less than that on comparable types of private issues. If the revenues from the government bond issue are used to make real estate loans, the interest cost savings can be passed on to the final real estate borrower. The effect can be to reduce the interest rate on a mortgage loan by two to five percentage points. It also can make money available for real estate loans that would not otherwise be available.

While many of these devices have been used to encourage rehabilitation, few of them have been designed with the specific intention of encouraging the renovation or restoration of historic buildings. The National Historic Preservation Act Amendments of 1980 authorized a federal loan guarantee program for designated National Register properties. Under the proposed program—which does not yet have an appropriation—the federal government would guarantee up to 90 percent of the principal on loans made by private lenders to finance "any project for the preservation of a property included on the National Register."[6]

Until the new preservation loan guarantee program is launched—and even after that, if the program appropriation is small—owners of landmark buildings must try to fit into other federal, state, and local financial incentive programs.

Rather than try to survey the wide assortment of available financial incentives and assess their effectiveness, the concluding portion of this chapter will demonstrate the significant difference that the most important financial incentive—a decrease in the construction loan or permanent mortgage rate—*can* make in improving the appeal, performance, and profitability of a preservation project. This type of financial incentive will be scrutinized as an essential part of the proper "package" of incentives that can be designed and should be available to encourage more renovation of historic buildings.

After-Tax Income Considerations

While the mysteries of an income and expense statement can be explained and the strange incantations in the daily rites of mortgage lenders can be interpreted, the income tax code will always be an enigma to most Americans. Rightly so. No piece of American statutory law is as complex, confusing, and inconsistent as the Internal Revenue Code.

With each attempt at reform and simplification,[7] the tax code grows

---

6. 16 U.S.C. § 470d (Supp. V, 1981).

7. In recent years there have been five attempts at tax reform: The Tax Reform

thicker and more complicated. The reason is simple: social policy goals are given equal billing with the collection of revenues. The code tries to encourage some types of income and investment while discouraging others. Much of the complexity in the Internal Revenue Code is caused by the fine American art of political compromise; a clear-sighted tax policy proposed by one interest group usually can only be enacted after numerous compromises and amendments, which, more often than not, confuse the original purpose. In many cases, congressional intention is quite different from the real effect of a tax provision. Many so-called income tax "incentives" can become income tax "disincentives" if the complex interlocking relationship of many provisions in the Internal Revenue Code is not understood properly.

The special provisions of the Internal Revenue Code governing investment in income-producing real estate are no exception. While the public generally has long believed that real estate investment creates tremendous "tax shelter" opportunities, the 20 years prior to 1981 saw a fairly consistent effort by Congress to eliminate—or at least narrow—the tax shelter opportunities of real estate investments.[8] Although the Economic Recovery Tax Act (ERTA) of 1981[9] radically changed the direc-

---

Act of 1976, Pub. L. No. 94-455, 90 Stat. 1520 (1976); the Revenue Act of 1978, Pub. L. No. 95-600, 92 Stat. 2763 (1978); the Energy Tax Act of 1978, Pub. L. No. 95-618, 92 Stat. 3174 (1978); the Economic Recovery Tax Act of 1981, Pub. L. No. 97-34, 95 Stat. 172 (1981); and the Tax Equity and Fiscal Responsibility Act of 1982, Pub. L. No. 97-248, 96 Stat. 324 (1982).

8. In 1962, I.R.C. § 1245 was enacted to treat depreciation taken on tangible personal property as ordinary income upon sale. In 1964, I.R.C. § 1250 was added to recapture the difference between accelerated depreciation and allowable straight-line depreciation on real property at ordinary income tax rates. As originally enacted, Section 1250 permitted a gradual phase-out of recapture over ten years. The phase-out for most real estate investments was eliminated by the Tax Reform Act of 1976 and the Revenue Act of 1978. The Tax Reform Act of 1976 also added I.R.C. § 461(g) which disallows any immediate deduction of prepaid interest including "points" charged by lenders for originating a loan and also modified I.R.C. § 189 to require that interest on construction loans be amortized over ten years rather than over the construction period. I.R.C. § 709, added in 1976, prohibits a deduction for partnership syndication fees. The Tax Reform Act of 1976 also substantially toughened the rules governing the minimum tax on preference items (which included the difference between accelerated and straight-line depreciation as well as the capital gain exclusion). I.R.C. § 56 was amended so that the minimum tax rate was increased from 10 percent to 15 percent while the allowable exemptions from the bite of the minimum tax were reduced.

9. Pub. L. No. 97-34, 97th Cong., 1st Sess. (1981).

tion of the tax code, there still are many provisions of the code that contradict the intent of the new legislation.

To understand the prospects and pitfalls in the tax code, preservationists must have a clear understanding of three particular elements of the tax treatment of real estate: (1) the deductibility of mortgage interest payments; (2) the depreciation of income-producing real estate; and (3) the opportunity to defer income taxes and to convert ordinary income into capital gain. It is the second and third items that create the most significant tax shelter in the real estate game.

The opportunity to deduct interest payments means that the effective after-tax rate of interest on borrowed money is substantially less than the stated mortgage interest rate. To the real estate investor in a 49 percent federal income tax bracket (in 1981, an income greater than $45,800 per year for a married taxpayer filing a joint return), every dollar of mortgage interest deducted saves 49 cents in income taxes. The effective after-tax mortgage interest rate is therefore slightly over one-half the actual rate. All other factors being equal, this creates some inducement to leverage a real estate investment by means of a mortgage.

Because of the way in which amortization works, the amount of mortgage interest that can be deducted decreases over the term of the mortgage loan. In a fully amortized mortgage, total monthly payments remain constant throughout the term of the loan. However, the portion of the monthly installment that is an interest payment is quite high in the early years of the mortgage term and gradually decreases through the length of the term. The tax benefit from the mortgage interest deduction therefore decreases over the term of the loan. This can be an inducement to early sale or refinancing of a real estate investment.

The opportunity to deduct mortgage interest payments is not a particularly effective or large tax shelter. First, since the Internal Revenue Code allows interest on all types of loans to be deducted, real estate loans are no more advantageous than other types of loans. And second, the interest payment is an actual expense to the real estate investor that must be paid before a deduction can be taken.

In contrast, depreciation deductions do not correspond to actual out-of-pocket expenditures. They, instead, correspond to the useful life of buildings. Buildings wear out: plumbing, heating systems, elevators, electrical wiring all deteriorate and eventually may need to be replaced. Buildings also may suffer from functional obsolescence: for example, multi-story industrial complexes with low ceilings become ill-suited for modern manufacturing and warehousing purposes. Buildings, therefore, have a limited useful life, and investors in income-producing buildings are allowed to write-off—depreciate—their investment over the expected useful life of the property.

Until 1981, the Internal Revenue Service established acceptable useful life periods for a wide variety of income-producing buildings. A taxpayer could select a shorter useful life period only if it could be justified by the particular characteristics of the property involved.

ERTA simplified the useful life rules in an effort to provide consistency and eliminate the sometimes bitter wrangles between the Internal Revenue Service and real estate investors. "Accelerated cost recovery," as depreciation is now called, may be taken over a 15-year useful life on all kinds of investment real estate. At the taxpayer's option, a longer 35-year or 45-year useful life period may be selected.

The rate of depreciation also varies from one type of real estate investment to another. Until 1981, owners of income-producing buildings could choose between straight-line depreciation, component depreciation, sum-of-the-years-digits depreciation, and declining balance depreciation. Straight-line and declining balance have been the favored depreciations among real estate investors. As a result of the 1981 ERTA changes, they are now the only allowable forms. The straight-line method allows the owner to deduct an equal portion of the taxable basis of the property for each year of its useful life. In the declining balance method, the annual allowable depreciation decreases over time. It is higher than straight-line depreciation in the early years and gradually decreases over the useful life. This method is based upon a stable rate of depreciation, but the rate is applied against a declining basis each year.

Depreciation deductions "shelter" current income from taxation. Tax on the amount depreciated is deferred until the real estate investment is sold. This is what causes many to mistakenly label depreciation a form of "tax-free loan" from the federal government to the real estate investor. It is not tax free: taxes are eventually paid, but they may be paid at a much lower tax rate.

The third element of real estate taxes is the opportunity to convert ordinary income into capital gain. Most real estate is treated as a "capital asset," and only 40 percent of its gain at sale is included as income and taxed. Every dollar in depreciation deductions that might otherwise be taxed today is converted to 40 cents in income and taxed later. Note that the investor's higher tax bracket in the year of sale, the recapture of accelerated depreciation, and the minimum tax on preference items can work together to offset most or all of the advantage in deferring taxes and converting ordinary income to capital gain.

A simple example will help clarify. An investor in a 50 percent tax bracket buys an office building for $100,000. The land under the building is worth $25,000, and the building itself has a value of $75,000. He depreciates it on a straight-line basis over 15 years and may, therefore, deduct $5,000 per year from his income. This saves him $2,500 in income taxes every year: without the $5,000 deduction, he would have an additional $5,000 of income of which he would pay $2,500 (50 percent) in taxes.

He does eventually pay taxes on each of these annual deductions of $5,000. The accumulated depreciation must be deducted from his original purchase price to determine the gain at sale that is taxed. If the property is sold after five years for $100,000, the taxable gain will be $25,000—the total amount of the depreciation deductions already taken. The tax on this gain, however, is not 50 percent. Instead, the investor has held this real estate long enough for it to be a capital asset and to qualify for "capital gains treatment." A full 60 percent of this gain, or $15,000, is not taxed at all. Taxes are paid on the remaining $10,000 of the gain only, and his tax liability at sale (if he is still in the 50 percent bracket) is only $5,000. He has, therefore, deferred taxes in each of the five previous years and converted what would have been a total annual accumulated ordinary income tax obligation of $12,500 into capital gains tax of only $5,000. He has saved $7,500 in taxes and had the use of the other $5,000 for five extra years.

All of this means that a very complicated set of calculations must be made in advance to determine the tax consequences of selling a real estate asset. One thing is clear: those tax consequences vary significantly depending upon the method of depreciation selected. They also will vary depending upon the year in which the sale or other "taxable event" (such as a mortgage foreclosure) takes place and the tax bracket of the taxpayer in the year of sale. That tax bracket can be increased significantly by the size of the gain being realized from the sale of the real estate asset.

REAL PROPERTY TAXES

The Importance of Property Taxes

The property tax is one of the largest single expense items for owners of new and old buildings alike. Thus it is a logical place for the government to intervene to create incentives for preservation and renovation.

Although property tax incentives alone would probably not make many old buildings competitive with new buildings, reducing real estate taxes could spur current owners of historic buildings to maintain them or make them attractive for renovation by new owners. A property tax incentive can help save many historic buildings. Owners of older landmark buildings may devote substantially more than 14 percent of their total operating income (see table 2) to real estate taxes. In some cities, older landmarks may pay substantially more on a per-square-foot-of-building-area basis as well as on a percentage-of-total-operating-income basis than new office buildings.

Without a doubt, the American system of assessing the value of, and levying the property tax on, historic structures is a significant threat to the continued use of many income-producing landmark buildings across the country.[10] Few preservationists understand why parking lots are so often more profitable than the older buildings they replace. If they would investigate the differences in assessed valuation of and property taxes on the historic building and on the subsequent parking lot, they would quickly understand.

The American real property tax system assesses the value of the underlying land as well as the value of the improvements on a piece of property. In the case of small, older landmarks on downtown parcels, the value of the underlying land may be substantially greater than the value of the improvements. Although many jurisdictions allow property owners to appeal high property tax assessments by showing that the net operating income from the improvements is quite low, property taxes may continue high even after the assessor lowers the taxes to reflect the low net operating income.

---

10. The interrelationship between market demand, zoning, and the property tax assessment system may provide another incentive for demolition. Historic office buildings, the largest structures in many historic areas, were often built prior to the advent of zoning laws. Their size may have been dictated more by popular fashion and the limits of engineering technology of the day than by zoning or height restrictions. The area later was zoned, and successively rezoned, to meet the demand for office or residential space and to fit new construction technology. As has been explained in the chapter on local law, a zoning ordinance can either undermine or complement preservation efforts. The land under a historic building in an area zoned for high-rise construction may be more valuable than the building itself. That may cause increased market pressure for purchase and demolition of the building for new construction. It may also make it difficult for prospective purchasers interested in renovation to secure financing and keep total renovation costs (including the cost of acquisition) low enough to realize a profit.

Some municipalities assess vacant land at a lower percentage of market value than improved property. That means the property tax burden, as a percentage of market value, is less for vacant land in older areas than it is for existing commercial or residential buildings. The owner of a deteriorating, older residential or office building may have an incentive to demolish the building and be taxed at the lower rate for vacant land.

A predictable and dramatic decrease in the property tax expense—even if only for a few years following renovation—can help lower the operating ratio and provide an expense cushion against the uncertainty inherent in the renovation process. A sizable, workable, and easily obtainable property tax incentive available to anyone who renovates an income-producing historic building will attract developers who know how to renovate but may have steered clear of designated historic buildings.

A Survey of Existing Property Tax Incentives

There are a variety of ways that the real property tax system can provide an incentive to the continued use of landmark structures. For example, it can: (1) remove the typical property tax incentive to demolish deteriorated landmarks and replace them with lower-taxed uses such as parking lots; (2) provide reduced property taxes to designated landmarks to reflect the effect of historic designation on the value of property; and (3) provide an incentive to renovate and reuse landmark structures by taxing landmarks after renovation at less than their real cost or value.

At least 14 states have legislation ostensibly designed to promote one or more of those purposes. With only three exceptions—the states of Oregon, Texas, and North Carolina—all the enabling legislation has been little used and generally ineffective.

In at least 6 states, the legislation is ineffective because it is enabling authority only; that is, it can only be implemented by local ordinance. For example, the property tax relief schemes in Maryland and Tennessee can only be implemented by enactment of a county ordinance. In Alaska, Texas, Connecticut, and Virginia, a municipality must enact an ordinance or pass a resolution if the state property tax relief scheme for landmark structures is to be initiated. Only in Texas has any city passed the required ordinance. Property tax relief for landmark structures in Alaska, Maryland, Tennessee, Connecticut, and Virginia exists on paper only.

The rest of the property tax relief schemes suffer from one or more of the following problems: (1) unclear statutory language that makes it difficult or impossible for local assessors and qualifying property owners to understand the tax relief provided or take advantage of it; (2) limitations on the number of landmark buildings and landmark property owners who qualify for the tax relief; (3) burdensome compliance and application procedures that cause the tax relief program to be viewed by qualifying property owners as more trouble than it is worth. In many cases, local governments and their assessors fear that any tax relief scheme for landmark structures will adversely affect the local property tax base.

State programs fall into one or more of the following four categories: (1) total or partial property tax abatements, exemptions, or assessment freezes for landmark building owners, regardless of whether they renovate or not; (2) exemptions or abatements from property tax assessments for the value of renovation, restoration, or improvement projects to qualifying landmarks; (3) property tax credits based on a percentage of renovation or restoration costs in qualifying projects; and (4) assessed valuations of landmark buildings based on current use or on a recognition of the effect on property values of preservation easements, landmark designations, and the like.[11] Any of these property tax incentives, if properly conceived and enacted, could be an attractive and valuable incentive to the owner of a historic building. Not one of the current state programs, however, is well designed to fit the needs of the typical owner of a landmark building or the typical developer interested in purchasing and sensitively renovating a landmark.

Property Tax Exemptions, Abatements, and Assessment Freezes

Several states provide an exemption from property taxes on some landmarks. For example, Alaska gives authority to municipalities to "classify and exempt from taxation . . . historic sites, buildings and monuments. . . ."[12] This is enabling legislation only, however, and yet to be implemented at the local level.

---

11. The best summary and analysis of the various tax incentives is in Lonnie A. Powers, *Tax Incentives for Historic Preservation: A Survey, Case Studies and Analysis*, 12 Urban Lawyer 103 (1980). See also Robert E. Stipe, "State and Local Tax Incentives for Historic Preservation," in *Tax Incentives for Historic Preservation*, ed. Gregory E. Andrews (Washington, D.C.: The National Trust for Historic Preservation, 1980), p. 91.

12. Alaska Stat. § 29.53.025 (1972).

Texas also has enabling legislation allowing any unit of local government to exempt from property taxes part or all of a landmark designated by both a state and local unit of government, or designated locally as a landmark that needs tax relief to encourage its preservation.[13] The Texas statute has been adopted only by Austin, San Antonio, Houston, Dallas, and two smaller cities. In Austin about 80 properties have applied under the city's program, which offers a property tax exemption equal to 50 percent of the assessed value of the structure and 25 percent of the value of the underlying land. No restoration or rehabilitation is required to receive the exemption. Residential buildings in San Antonio with fewer than four units that are "substantially rehabilitated" have their assessed value frozen for 10 years at the prerehabilitation level. Commercial buildings (including residential buildings with more than four units) that are substantially rehabilitated pay no City of San Antonio property taxes for 5 years after rehabilitation and, thereafter, are assessed at only 50 percent of market value for another 5 years. Only two properties have applied in San Antonio. Houston's program began in 1981. Qualifying buildings must be either on the National Register of Historic Places or be designated Texas Historical Landmarks. To qualify there must be a restoration and the amount of the exemption may not exceed the lesser of the cost of the restoration or 50 percent of the assessed value.

Although the three states (Arizona, Connecticut, and North Carolina) that offer a partial tax abatement to historic structures have avoided the enabling act problem, the number of historic buildings that qualify in two of the states is so limited that the legislation is equally ineffective. For example, in Arizona, properties listed on the National Register of Historic Places are in the lowest category of assessed valuation (8 percent of market value),[14] but to qualify the building owner cannot conduct any for-profit activities within the building and must open the property to the public at least 12 days per year. These requirements assure that the abatement will be little used and ineffective.

Connecticut and New York City take a somewhat different tack. A Connecticut statute gives local governments the authority to abate property taxes on locally designated historic buildings "if it can be shown to the satisfaction of the municipality that the current level of taxation is a material factor which threatens the continued existence of the

---

13. Tex. Rev. Civ. Stat. Ann. art. 7150(i) (Vernon 1978).
14. Ariz. Rev. Stat. Ann. § 42-136A7 (Supp. 1978).

structure."[15] Although not a bad concept, no municipality in the state has yet enacted such an ordinance. New York City's Historic Landmarks Act authorizes the New York City Board of Estimate to grant a partial or complete tax exemption to any building when, upon the recommendation of the New York City landmarks commission, it is determined that the current income of the property is so low that demolition is necessary.[16] No property in New York City has ever been given this exemption.

North Carolina has developed a quite effective program. Locally designated historic structures have an assessed value equal to only one-half of their market value. All locally designated landmarks qualify, and there is no requirement that the property be open for public visitation or that the building be rehabilitated. There is a retroactive tax penalty if the property loses its historic designation. For example, if the owner alters the structure and in the process destroys key historic features that result in "de-designation," the entire property tax savings for the previous three years must be repaid with interest.[17] About 150 properties now qualify for the 50 percent tax reduction, and in cities where owners may apply for landmark designation, it has been a spur to designation, especially for owners wishing to rehabilitate their properties. Although there now are 24 local preservation commissions in North Carolina, fear of the effect of the property tax reduction on the local tax base has made many communities afraid to adopt a local landmarks ordinance.

Two states, Oregon and Illinois, provide an assessment freeze for some landmark buildings. In Oregon, any owner of a property listed on the National Register may apply for a 15-year freeze on increases in the property's assessed valuation.[18] If the owner agrees to open the building to the public for at least one day a year and maintain it according to a rigorous set of standards, the property tax assessed valuation will be frozen at its level in the year of application. Between 1975 and mid-1982, more than 500 of the estimated 1,200 properties eligible for the tax freeze were participating in the program.[19] This means that more landmarks

---

15. Conn. Gen. Stat. Ann. § 12-127(a)(b) (West 1972).
16. New York City Code § 207-8.0(h)-(e), N.Y. Gen. Mun. Law § 9-a (McKinney 1977).
17. N.C. Gen. Stat. § 105-278(a) (Supp. 1977).
18. Or. Rev. Stat. § 358.475-.565 (Supp. 1977) and 1975 Or. Laws 514, §15.
19. Telephone interview with Dave Powers, Deputy State Historic Preservation Officer, Oregon Historic Preservation Office, Salem, Oregon, July 21, 1982.

in Oregon have received property tax relief than in the rest of the United States combined.

If the Oregon law represents the high point in the use of property tax relief to promote historic preservation, an Illinois law is an example of good intentions gone awry. Illinois legislation passed in 1980 provides a 10-year tax assessment freeze to any owner of a single-family home in any National Register district or any municipal landmark district in the state. The freeze went into effect on January 1, 1981, and expires on December 31, 1989. Homeowners must apply for the freeze.[20]

The most obvious problem with the Illinois legislation is that it applies only to single-family homes and only to homes within districts either on the National Register or designated locally. There is no freeze for single-family homes that have been designated individually. A more serious problem is the incentive the legislation creates for continued neglect of single-family landmarks, or at best, for illegal "midnight renovations." Any property owner who has been granted the assessment freeze automatically loses it by making "substantial non-preservation improvements which would increase the assessed valuation of the property."[21] There is no definition in the legislation of "substantial non-preservation improvements," but in the commonly accepted Illinois interpretation, almost any renovation could lose the 10-year assessment freeze.

As a result, there has been continuing controversy in Illinois over the benefits and burdens imposed by property tax relief for owners of one-family landmarks in historic districts. Because municipalities can opt out of the tax freeze for all National Register or local landmark districts within their boundaries, there has been rancorous debate over the legislation, especially in Chicago, which has the largest number of historic districts and the greatest number of single-family homeowners who qualify for the freeze. By 1982, well over 500 homeowners in Illinois had applied for the freeze,[22] but most of them live in municipalities that subsequently have opted out of the legislation. Because of such shortcomings, the Illinois law has been completely revamped, as outlined in a subsequent section on reform.

---

20. Ill. Rev. Stat. ch. 120, § 525.1 (Supp. 1980).
21. *Id*.
22. Telephone interview with Ken Kaval, Office of the Cook County Assessor, Chicago, Illinois, May 14, 1981.

Exemption or Abatement for Renovation Projects

At least four jurisdictions (Tennessee, Virginia, Puerto Rico, and, most recently, Illinois) link property tax relief for landmarks to renovation or restoration. Puerto Rico has special legislation for the San Juan historic district. A complete restoration of a historic building results in total exemption from property taxes for 10 years. A partial restoration that includes at least the exterior, public entryways, and the main staircase results in a 5-year exemption.[23]

Tennessee's enabling legislation for property tax relief allows a 15-year exemption from taxation for total restoration of landmark structures. Partial restorations qualify for a 10-year exemption, and all renovation projects must be conducted in accordance with specific rehabilitation guidelines. The owner also must agree not to demolish or significantly alter the structure during the period of the exemption.[24] The legislation has been implemented only in Memphis.

Until 1980, Virginia had enabling legislation that allowed counties and municipalities to set a lower rate of taxation on rehabilitated older structures, regardless of their landmark status. Rehabilitation work on commercial or industrial structures at least 45 years old qualified if the rehabilitation increased the assessed value by at least $25,000. Residential structures qualified if they were at least 30 years old and the rehabilitation increased their value by at least $5,000.[25] The law was repealed on January 1, 1980.

The owner of any single-family residence in Illinois on the National Register, on the State of Illinois Register, or designated as a local landmark, qualifies for an eight-year property tax assessment freeze and an additional four-year period of gradual increases in assessment if he rehabilitates the home. He must spend 25 percent of the local assessor's calculation of market value in the rehab program, and it must conform to the (U.S.) secretary of the interior's standards for rehabilitation.

It is startling that more states do not link restoration or renovation of landmark structures to a property tax freeze or abatement. The Tennessee and Virginia programs have not been implemented at the local level, and the Puerto Rico program applies to a limited area. The new Illinois law has a better chance for success since it applies to all one-family national, state, and local landmarks in all communities, unless

---

23. P.R. Laws Ann. tit. 13, § 551 (1978).
24. Tenn. Code Ann. § 67-519 (Supp. 1978).
25. Va. Code § 58-759.1 (Supp. 1978), repealed January 1, 1980.

they opt out by ordinance. Since the property tax is one of the biggest expense items for the owner of a landmark building, both before and after renovation, a program of property tax relief that encourages renovation of more landmark buildings by providing a property tax freeze or abatement could be an effective mechanism for returning more landmarks to productive use. As in the Puerto Rico program, and in the legislation recently passed in Illinois, the renovation should be in keeping with a set of standards, such as the secretary of the interior's standards for rehabilitation.

Property Tax Credits for Renovation

Two states, Maryland and New Mexico, provide a credit against real property taxes due for part or all of the cost of restoration projects. Maryland's program is enabling legislation only. Counties are authorized to allow a credit of up to 10 percent of the cost of restoration on buildings in historic districts.[26] If 10 percent of the restoration costs is greater than the property taxes due, the owner is allowed to carry forward the credit for five years. No county in Maryland has enacted the ordinance necessary to implement the legislation, so property owners in the state have yet to use the credit.[27]

In New Mexico, since 1969, there has been legislation providing a property tax credit for the total cost of some restoration projects. The legislation allows for a 10-year carry forward if the cost of the qualifying restoration exceeds the total property tax payment due in a particular year.[28] But to qualify for the credit, the property must be listed on the New Mexico state register and must be made available for educational purposes on one day every month for at least eight hours. This catch has severely limited the number of properties that qualify. Since 1969, 12 New Mexico property owners have applied for the credit.[29] Trailing Oregon and Illinois, the New Mexico program is the third most utilized program in the nation.

Current-Use Assessment

Both California and the District of Columbia have opted for an approach designed to prevent the needless destruction of sound landmark

---

26. Md. Ann. Code art. 81, § 12G (Supp. 1978).
27. Powers, *Tax Incentives, supra* note 11, at 119.
28. N.M. Stat. Ann. § 18-16-13 (Michie 1978).
29. Stipe, "State and Local Tax Incentives," *supra* note 11, at 95.

buildings when their sites are attractive for new development projects. Through current-use assessment of landmark buildings, California and the District of Columbia hope to reduce the property taxes on the most threatened landmarks by limiting the assessed valuation to the value of the property given its present use for a landmark building. In other words, the property tax assessor looks not at the market value of the land and buildings on it but rather at the income that the landmark building currently generates and determines the assessed value of the building by capitalizing that income.

The California provisions are quite complicated and have not been used often. Local assessors in California do not feel comfortable with the program and have not encouraged its use.[30] To obtain the current-use assessment in California, the property owner must enter into a 20-year maintenance contract with a local government entity.[31]

In the District of Columbia, the property owner also must enter into a 20-year contract with the city to obtain the current-use assessment.[32] Only buildings individually designated by the District's Joint Committee on Landmarks are eligible. Although more than 350 owners are eligible, only a handful of landmark owners have applied. The 20-year maintenance agreement provision and the fact that few of the eligible properties have a "highest and best use" value substantially greater than their "current use" value are generally thought to have kept the number of applicants down.[33]

Statutory requirements that assessors consider the effect on property value of a preservation easement or landmark designation are nothing more than a variant of current-use assessment. To take advantage of the income tax deduction for the donation of a preservation easement, the property owner must show that the easement has reduced the market value of the property. That same reduction in market value should enable the owner to argue with the local property tax assessor that the property's assessed valuation—thus, property taxes—also should be reduced by a corresponding amount.[34]

---

30. Powers, *Tax Incentives, supra* note 11, at 112.
31. Cal. Rev. Tax Code § 439.2 (West Supp. 1979) and Cal. Gov't Code § 50282 (West Supp. 1979).
32. D.C. Code Encycl. § 47-652-654 (West Supp. 1979).
33. Stipe, "State and Local Tax Incentives," *supra* note 11, at 96.
34. Of course, there will be no property tax reduction if the appraisal of the property after donation of the easement shows an "after" value higher than the property tax assessor's determination of market value.

The opportunity to argue that a preservation easement should reduce the assessed valuation of a historic structure exists in every state, even in the absence of enabling legislation specifically requiring assessors to take this into consideration. In any state in which the assessor appraises all real property based on "highest and best use," the owner of a landmark building protected by an easement should be able to argue that the "highest and best use" after the donation of the easement is unquestionably its current or potential use as an income-producing landmark structure. Protective preservation easements give the recipient landmark group the opportunity to review and approve any alteration or demolition proposals. They are not likely to approve a demolition to make way for a new construction. Therefore, the protected building has value only to a buyer interested in its current income or income after renovation.

Despite that opportunity in the absence of specific statutory language, some states have adopted clear language recognizing that landmark designation or the donation of an easement should be considered by property tax assessors. South Dakota, Virginia, West Virginia, Illinois, and Colorado all have such language.[35]

There is, however, considerable disagreement in the language of those statutes as to the effect of designation on property values. Virginia's statutes provide that designation by the Virginia Landmarks Commission "shall be *prima facie* evidence that the value of such property for commercial, residential or other purposes is reduced by reason of its designation."[36] That language covers both individual landmarks and districts and apparently leaves no room for the obvious fact that property values often increase in historic districts after designation. The Colorado statute, by contrast, specifically prohibits assessors from increasing the assessed valuation of properties on the Colorado Register of Historic Places because of the designation. The Colorado statutes are silent concerning possible valuation reductions due to designation, perhaps indicating wide acceptance in Colorado of the idea that landmark designation increases property values.[37]

---

35. S.D. Comp. Laws Ann. § 1-19B-20 (1974); Va. Code §§ 10-139, 10-140, 10-142, and 10-155 (1973); W. Va. Code § 8-26A-1-6 (repealed 1976); Ill. Rev. Stat. ch. 24, § 11-48.2-6 (Supp. 1982-83__; Colo. Rev. Stat. § 39-1-104(5) (Supp. 1978).
36. Va. Code § 10-139 (1973).
37. Colo. Rev. Stat. §. 39-1-104(5) (Supp. 1978).

Directions for Reform

Despite the wide array of incentives on the statute books around the country, experience indicates that current legislation could be improved. The biggest problem seems to be a lack of agreement about the purpose of a property tax incentive. Is it to stimulate more restoration of landmark buildings? Is it to help only the most threatened landmarks by reducing the property tax incentive for their demolition? Is it to appease those politicians and real estate representatives who say landmark designation seriously decreases property values and, therefore, should be accompanied by an assessed valuation reduction? Is it to create an incentive for more landmark designations and more use of preservation easements to protect landmark buildings? Or is it to promote all of these goals?

Whatever the objective, some principles for effective legislation for property tax relief are clear. First, state enabling legislation alone simply does not work. Second, the relief must be clearly worded and simple to implement. Third, the incentive must be clearly aimed at the particular preservation problems that most need attention.

Municipalities and counties are reluctant to enact local ordinances providing property tax relief for landmark owners in their jurisdiction only; they fear the fiscal impact of eliminating revenue sources. Enabling legislation merely allows state legislators to take credit for historic preservation measures while passing the burden of tough political decisions to the local level of government. To be effective, a state legislative program for property tax relief for landmark structures must operate automatically and equitably statewide.

Second, the program should be straightforward enough for both local property tax assessors and the public to understand. Even a statewide program can be ineffective if it gives local tax assessors too much discretion. State legislation providing property tax relief to landmark buildings must be worded clearly, key concepts and terms must be defined carefully, and there must be little room for local property tax assessors to circumvent the intent and purpose of the legislation.

The most important points to define carefully in the legislation are:
- The number and type of historic buildings that qualify for the incentive (National Register, state landmark, locally designated, and so on);
- The uses to which the structures can be put and still qualify for the tax incentive (single-family, multifamily, commercial office, in-

dustrial, condominium conversions, income-producing, and others);
- The date on which the incentive takes effect for a particular building (date of owner's application, approval of owner's application, beginning of renovation project, completion of renovation project, effective date of legislation, beginning of a property tax year) and the date on which it terminates;
- The type of incentive (tax freeze, assessment freeze, tax credit, mitigation of increase in taxes or assessment caused by renovation). When devising incentives for owners who renovate historic structures, it is essential to define how much renovation triggers application of the incentive (either a specified dollar amount or a percentage of building value); and
- If renovation costs must exceed a specified percentage of building value, then the definition of "value" must be clear and unequivocal (e.g., purchase price, market value as determined by a qualified appraiser, assessed value determined by the local assessor).

Confusion and the opportunity to circumvent the intent of the incentive program can be avoided if the incentive is provided as an assessment or tax freeze for a specified period of time. Too often a renovation incentive includes a provision that there be "no increase in assessed valuation because of an increase in market value of the property due to renovation." What does that mean? How can the increase in market value caused by the expenditure on renovation be separated from the increase in market value resulting from inflation, a change in market conditions, new construction or major renovation nearby that increases values throughout an area, or other factors? A cash expenditure of $50,000 to renovate a building may increase the market value of that building by much more than $50,000. If the value of the building increases by $100,000 following renovation, does such language allow the local assessor to freeze the assessed valuation on only one-half of the increase? This is typical of the problems caused by poor legislative drafting.

Third, any good property tax incentive program should focus on the most important preservation problems. Establishing priorities can save money and assure fairness in the incentive scheme. An incentive for all is an incentive for none. In other words, the revenues lost from a property tax break for landmark structures will have to be recouped by an increase in property or other taxes paid by other residents of the community. This issue of fairness can haunt and scuttle an overly broad tax incentive program for landmark structures.

The most equitable preservation incentive and the one most likely to gather widespread political support will be narrowly drawn for owners who renovate historic structures. A property tax break can significantly encourage renovation; it can make the difference in whether some deteriorated landmarks are saved or demolished.

Municipalities will resist any tax relief program that provides a significant property tax break to anyone who lives in a historic district and slaps a coat of paint on a building or strips some woodwork. Preservationists must make some hard choices in drafting property tax legislation. Should there be a small property tax incentive that is widely available? Or is it preferable to have a significant property tax break available only to a limited number of developers or others who renovate historic structures? How much renovation expenditure should be required before an owner qualifies for the tax incentive? A small tax break for a large number of building owners may appeal to politicians trying to maximize the vote-getting effect of a piece of legislation. Such legislation will have very little real effect, however, in saving more landmark buildings.

On the other hand, a very substantial property tax incentive available only to major renovation projects may cause more historic buildings to be saved. As an example, consider the legislation recently enacted in Illinois to replace the tax freeze for owners of single-family homes in landmark districts. When owners of any type of landmark structure substantially renovate their property, they will be given an 8-year assessment freeze and an additional 4-year period during which their assessment will be increased gradually to full market value. Renovation costs must exceed 25 percent of the market value of the building determined by the local assessor. This makes it simple for the owner to match the proposed renovation plan against the market value of the property listed on the assessor's permanent records.[38] While only major renovation projects will benefit, such a substantial tax savings over a 12-year period will assure that some deteriorated landmarks in Illinois will become attractive choices for renovation.

Finally, when an incentive program is drafted, some review standard for evaluating renovation proposals should be included. To qualify for the income tax incentives provided by the Economic Recovery Tax Act of 1981, rehabilitation must be reviewed for compliance with the (U.S.) secretary of the interior's standards for rehabilitation. This review en-

---

38. Illinois H.B. 1244, passed.

sures that the renovation encouraged by the incentive does not destroy significant historic or architectural features of the building. Those standards could accomplish the same purpose in an approval process under property tax incentive schemes. In most states, it makes sense to have the same agency that reviews rehabilitation projects under the Economic Recovery Tax Act of 1981 also review them under any statewide property tax incentive program. This would assure quick, consistent, and efficient review.

FEDERAL INCOME TAXES

In 1976, Congress passed a tax reform act designed to put the renovation of historic buildings on an equal footing with new construction projects. As Senator J. Glenn Beall (R-Md.), the principal Senate sponsor of the measures, stated when the legislation was introduced:

> I feel that our current system of tax incentives works in a very direct and definite way against enlisting private funds in historic restoration projects. We can no longer continue to systematically destroy our Nation's history, weaken the fabric of our communities, and deplete our resources as we have in the past. As our national values readjust to the concept of a finite world it is important for us to update our tax system so as to help redirect and achieve socially desirable goals.[39]

Were these tax incentives sufficient enough to accomplish these goals? No—but they did serve a purpose almost as significant; they set the tone, precedent, and incentive for further preservation-related tax reform. In 1978, Congress further amended the tax code with the Revenue Act of 1978, which created additional incentives for renovation and restoration. And in 1981, Congress scrapped many of the incentives introduced in 1976 and substituted a system of investment tax credits to encourage renovation. Are the new tax credits better than the 1976 incentives? Is a dollar in tax credit better than a dollar in depreciation deduction? Do other changes brought about by the Economic Recovery Tax Act of 1981 make renovation of historic buildings more attractive and more feasible?

To answer these questions (and to facilitate preservation), it is essential to analyze the real effects of preservation income tax incentives. The following summation of past and current incentives answers some of these questions and indicates how effective well-developed incentives can be.

---

39. 121 Cong. Rec. 3004 (1975).

Past Legislation

The Tax Reform Act of 1976

The year 1976 marks a watershed in government encouragement of historic preservation. The Tax Reform Act of 1976, enacted by Congress, contained two significant new provisions intended to encourage the renovation, restoration, and protection of historic buildings either on the National Register of Historic Places or in locally designated historic districts across the country.

The first incentive authorized by this legislation was a new Section 191 to the Internal Revenue Code[40] allowing owners of historic buildings used in a trade or business or for the production of income to "amortize" or write off their rehabilitation expenditures over a period of 60 months. This was quite a change from previous tax laws that allowed the owner to write off rehabilitation expenditures over the life of the improvements, typically from 10 to 20 years or more, depending on the scope of the renovation project.

The second incentive was an alternative to that five-year amortization. The owner of a qualifying historic building who performed "substantial rehabilitation" on that building could choose to use the same form of depreciation available to the owner or developer of a new construction project of a similar type. For example, the developer renovating an apartment building in a qualifying historic district could choose to use a 200 percent declining balance form of depreciation rather than the straight-line or 125 percent declining balance rates otherwise available to owners of used residential buildings. Owners of historic commercial buildings could choose to use the 150 percent declining balance depreciation rate normally available only to developers constructing new commercial buildings.[41]

These incentives authorized by the 1976 act were not without their limitations. First, they applied only to buildings either individually listed on the National Register of Historic Places or within districts on the National Register and certified by the secretary of the interior as contributing to the historic character of the district. Second, renovation of historic buildings in state or locally designated historic districts qualified for either one of the incentives only if the statute or ordinance under

---

40. I.R.C. § 191 (1976), repealed by ERTA, Pub. L. No. 97-34, 95 Stat. 239 (1981).
41. I.R.C. § 167(o) (1976), repealed by ERTA, Pub. L. No. 97-34, 95 Stat. 239 (1981).

which the designation occurred was reviewed and approved by the secretary of the interior as having criteria that satisfactorily protected the building.[42] Buildings individually designated under state or local landmark laws did not qualify for either one of the incentives. Third, the renovation program had to be reviewed and approved to assure that it was in keeping with the secretary of the interior's standards for rehabilitation.[43] Those standards attempted to assure, among other things, that the renovation project would not damage, alter, or destroy key historic features of the building, falsify the real historic character of the detail and architecture in the building, or use construction or renovation techniques that would damage the structural or architectural integrity of the building. A fourth limitation was that only projects involving "substantial rehabilitation" qualified for the Section 167(o) accelerated depreciation incentive. "Substantial" was defined to mean that the amount of renovation expenditure during a two-year period generally had to be equal to or greater than the adjusted basis of the property for tax purposes, usually the portion of the developer's purchase price attributable to the building only (excluding the value of the land upon which the building sits).[44]

The effectiveness of income tax incentives is reduced because they do not spur developers to consider the feasibility of renovation.[45] With few exceptions, the income tax effects of a development project are the last feasibility calculations to be made. Unless a renovation project works on a pretax income and expense basis, income tax incentives are virtually meaningless.

The relatively unimportant role of the federal income tax in shaping developers' decisions was astutely analyzed by the Urban Land Institute in a 1978 survey. The survey was prompted by disagreement in legal literature concerning the effect of the tax code in promoting new construction at the expense of renovation and reuse.[46] Twenty-five of the

---

42. I.R.C. § 191(a)(1)(B) (1976), repealed by ERTA, Pub. L. No. 97-34, 95 Stat. 239 (1981).

43. I.R.C. § 191(a)(4) (1976), repealed by ERTA, Pub. L. No. 97-34, 95 Stat. 239 (1981).

44. I.R.C. § 167(o)(2) (1976), repealed by ERTA, Pub. L. No. 97-34, 95 Stat. 239 (1981).

45. See generally Frank Schnidman and W. David East, "Federal Taxation and Urban Land Development: Does the Tail Wag the Dog?" in *Urban Land* (Washington, D.C.: The Urban Land Institute, 1978), p. 14.

46. *Id.*

most respected professionals in the country's largest real estate operations were asked a series of questions about the Internal Revenue Code and its effect on their development decisions. Two questions in particular are relevant here. The first: "When deciding to build or invest in a building, does the more rapid depreciation of new construction provide enough incentive by itself for you to build or buy a new rather than a used building?" Thirteen of the respondents to this question answered yes, while eleven answered no. The Urban Land Institute found a recurring theme in the answer to this question that it summarized as follows: "The extra depreciation is an important factor in the decision but of itself can't put the shirttail in the pants of a real estate investment because the project first has to make sense on a pure cash basis. In other words, it has to project enough cash flow to pay for itself before being considered."

The second significant question relates to another factor perhaps limiting the effectiveness of the 1976 incentives—the underlying assumption that use of accelerated forms of depreciation is more beneficial to the owner of an income-producing historic building than is straight-line depreciation and increases the after-tax return on the owner's investment. The question reads: "In view of the depreciation recapture provisions and the tax preference income tax on excess depreciation, do you find it preferable now to use straight-line depreciation?" Ten of the respondents to this question answered yes, while only four answered no.[47]

Some of the respondents to these questions proved unfamiliar with the calculations needed to compare straight-line and accelerated forms of depreciation. More than 70 percent of these prestigious and relatively knowledgeable developers shied away from accelerated forms of depreciation because of the adverse tax consequences at sale. Corporations were especially unlikely to use accelerated depreciation because, as one of the respondents put it, "rapid depreciation [is] viewed unfavorably by stockholders who are looking only at a corporation's assets."[48] Depreciation, by reducing the book value of the real estate assets held by a corporation, reduces the value of the stock held by investors in that corporation.

---

47. One respondent answered, "No! Dollars today are worth more than dollars in the future, that is the reason—the time value of money. We do have some recapture problems at times; but recapture problems occur as you sell, and rapid depreciation benefits you now, so at worst, it's an interest free loan." *Id.*, p. 18.

48. *Id.* at p. 19.

Though misunderstood, the preservation incentives created by the Tax Reform Act of 1976 have not necessarily failed. The act's greatest success has been the discussion, debate, and analysis it has generated—the constructive discussion it has stimulated between preservation groups and the development industry. Developers have learned to court the preservation community, to determine their attitude toward a particular building before acquiring it, and to find compromises that may allow development to continue while preserving significant historic buildings. Developers have come to understand that preservationists are not "save it at all costs" types. Similarly, preservation groups have learned to think through a development project from the developer's point of view. This atmosphere of understanding and cooperation has facilitated the development of new and better incentives for preservation. The first such improvement is discussed below.

The Revenue Act of 1978 and the Investment Tax Credit

The Revenue Act of 1978 created some additional incentives for the renovation and restoration of historic buildings. Tax rules governing investment tax credits were modified so that more kinds of real estate rehabilitation projects qualified. Rehabilitation expenditures made after October 31, 1978, on commercial buildings that have been in use for at least 20 years became eligible for a 10 percent investment tax credit.[49] Residential buildings did not qualify, but office buildings, hotels, factories, and other types of commercial properties did.

Costs incurred for exterior, as well as interior, renovation work could be included. There were, however, some limitations. For example, at least 75 percent of the exterior walls of the structure had to be retained, and no new additions or new construction associated with the renovation project could be included among the expenditures that qualified for the 10 percent credit.

There were explicit limitations on combining the investment tax credit with the historic preservation rehabilitation incentives provided by the Tax Reform Act of 1976. The Revenue Act of 1978 specifically prohibited combined use of the five-year amortization and the investment tax credit on qualifying historic structures. It did permit, however, use of accelerated depreciation with the investment tax credit.[50] It also required, like the 1976 act, that the proposed renovation be reviewed

---

49. I.R.C. § 48(g) (1981).
50. I.R.C. § 48(g)(2)(B)(iv) (1981).

for compliance with the secretary of the interior's standards for rehabilitation.

Dollar for dollar, an income tax credit provides much greater benefit to a taxpayer than a depreciation deduction. A dollar of tax credit is a dollar of taxes saved. In contrast, the value of a dollar of depreciation deduction depends upon the tax bracket of the taxpayer and the effect of any subsequent recapture, minimum tax, or other repayment provision that limits the real effect of the deduction. At best, a dollar of depreciation deduction saved only 70 cents in income taxes prior to 1982. There is no minimum tax related to the use of an investment tax credit (other tax shelters are subjected to such a surtax) and only a moderate recapture penalty.[51]

The investment tax credit offered so many advantages over depreciation deductions that preservationists began to urge broader use of investment tax credits for renovation of historic structures. The consequences of a tax credit, both for the individual taxpayer and for the U.S. Treasury, are easy to determine. By comparison, the effect of accelerated forms of depreciation is by no means clear. Depreciation deductions have much greater appeal to high bracket taxpayers and usually very little appeal to corporations. The investment tax credit has appeal to anyone who pays income taxes. Of course, the benefit of the credit is greater for those who pay more taxes, but it has as much appeal for a corporation as it does for a limited partnership or individual investor contemplating the renovation of landmark buildings.

At a series of eight hearings in October, 1980, before the Subcommittee on Select Revenue Measures of the Committee on Ways and Means of the House of Representatives, preservationists were forced to

---

51. The potential recapture penalty decreases over time after completion of the rehabilitation. The schedule is as follows:

Holding Period Following Rehab.	% of I.T.C Recaptured at Sale
less than one year	100
one to two years	80
two to three years	60
three to four years	40
four to five years	20

Recapture of the investment tax credit is avoided completely if the rehabilitation project is held for five years or longer. Most investment real estate projects are established with an intended minimum holding period of five to ten years. See I.R.C. § 47 (a) (5) (1981).

recognize the greater attraction of investment tax credits over depreciation deductions. Legislation proposed in 1980 would have increased the 10 percent investment tax credit for rehabilitation to 25 percent on a wider variety of rehabilitation projects. There would have been no special additional incentive for preservation projects, and the new credit could not have been used in conjunction with the five-year amortization of certified rehabilitations. Witness after witness at the Ways and Means Committee hearings testified that a 25 percent tax credit was a more attractive incentive to the real estate investor than accelerated amortization and depreciation, and some feared investors would be drawn away from historic preservation projects to more favored real estate investments if the tax credit concept was expanded without some additional level of incentive to promote certified rehabilitation of historic structures.[52]

These hearings were another watershed in the history of income tax incentives for historic preservation. They clearly showed the members of the House Ways and Means Committee that the preservation incentives provided by the Tax Reform Act of 1976 should be extended. They also convinced key members of the committee that an investment tax credit for rehabilitation projects could be an even greater catalyst to the renovation of historic buildings than accelerated depreciation deductions.[53] Those hearings led directly to the new investment tax credit provisions created by the Economic Recovery Tax Act of 1981.

---

52. See, for example, the statements of Jerry L. Rogers, Deputy Associate Director for Cultural Programs, Heritage Conservation and Recreation Service (San Francisco, October 17, 1980); Sally Oldham, Architectural Historian, National Register of Historic Places (San Francisco, October 17, 1980); C. Grant Spaeth, Attorney, Palo Alto, Calif. (San Francisco, October 17, 1980); J. Miller Blew, Professor, Harvard Graduate School of Design (Boston, October 21, 1980); Roger P. Lang, AIA, Architect, Boston (Boston, October 21, 1980); Ken Orenstein, Executive Director, Providence (R.I.) Foundation (Boston, October 21, 1980); James Conway, Mayor, St. Louis, Mo. (Chicago, October 24, 1980); Arthur Townsend, Colorado State Historic Preservation Officer (Chicago, October 24, 1980); Richard J. Roddewig, Attorney and Real Estate Consultant, Shlaes & Co., Chicago (Chicago, October 24, 1980); and Neil W. Horstman, Executive Director, Historic Kansas City Foundation (Chicago, October 24, 1980), at Expiring Historic Structure Tax Provisions: Hearings Before the Subcommittee on Select Revenue Measures of the Committee on Ways and Means, House of Representatives, on Legislation to Extend the Expiring Provisions of Federal Tax Law Which are Designed to Encourage the Preservation of Historic Structures, San Francisco, Calif., October 17, 1980; Boston, Mass., October 21, 1980; and Chicago, Ill., October 24, 1980 (Washington, D.C.: U.S. Government Printing Office, 1981).

53. During the Ways and Means Oversight Committee Hearings in Chicago in October of 1980, the Landmarks Preservation Council of Illinois chartered a bus and

The Economic Recovery Tax Act of 1981[54]

The Reagan administration's major tax initiative, the Economic Recovery Tax Act of 1981, changes significantly the income tax treatment of real estate. It is a sudden and dramatic shift from the consistent erosion, over the last 20 years, of the tax shelter provided by real estate investment. The most important change affecting historic preservation is the replacement of the five-year amortization and accelerated depreciation incentives introduced by the Tax Reform Act of 1976 by a new system of investment tax credits for rehabilitation of older buildings, including historic structures.

Certified rehabilitation expenditures made after December 31, 1981, may qualify for a 25 percent investment tax credit,[55] and the 10 percent credit created in 1978 for some preservation projects has been eliminated. Buildings qualify for the new credit under the same procedures that applied to the 1976 tax incentives. A building is automatically a "certified" historic structure if it is listed individually on the National Register of Historic Places. Buildings in National Register districts may be certified by the National Park Service as contributing to the historic significance of the district. Buildings in state or locally designated districts also may qualify if the ordinance creating the district has been approved by the National Park Service as having adequate standards for historic designation and adequate protection for designated buildings.

The rehabilitation costs must be "substantial," however, for buildings to qualify. The cost must exceed $5,000 or the taxable basis of the property, whichever is greater.[56] The taxable basis will be calculated in the same way that it was for the accelerated depreciation option of the 1976 legislation—usually the cost of the building plus any capital im-

---

took Congressman Rostenkowski, other committee members, and their staffs on a tour of National Register districts in the city. All were impressed with the amount of renovation activity going on. Congressman Rostenkowski was particularly impressed to learn about the number of designated areas in his congressional district (and the additional areas in his district that might later be designated). He had not realized before that bus tour how important federal tax incentive legislation was to his own constituents. That bus trip may have had more to do with enactment of the investment tax credit provisions of the Economic Recovery Tax Act of 1981 than the lobbying effort of preservation groups.

54. Pub. L. No. 97-34, 97th Cong., 1st Sess. (1981). 26 U.S.C. § 48 *et seq.* This subsection presents a broad overview of ERTA. Appendix B contains a more detailed discussion of its provisions and relevant IRS regulations.

55. See ERTA §. 212(a); 26 U.S.C. §. 48 (a)(2)(F)(i) (Supp. 1981).

56. ERTA § 212(b); 26 U.S.C. § 48(g)(1)(C) (Supp. 1981).

provements less depreciation previously taken or allowed. Again, the value of the land underneath the building must be excluded in determining the basis. These rehabilitation costs must be incurred within a 24-month period unless a set of architectural plans and specifications for the project are submitted for review by the National Park Service prior to the beginning of rehabilitation and there is a reasonable likelihood that the project will be completed according to the plans. In this exception, qualifying rehabilitation expenditures may be made over a 60-month period.[57]

Preservationists have expressed concern that smaller rehabilitation projects encouraged by the five-year amortization incentive of the Tax Reform Act of 1976 will not be undertaken now. For the five-year amortization incentive, there was no requirement that the rehabilitation expenditure match the taxable basis of the property. That was only true for taxpayers utilizing the accelerated depreciation preservation incentive. Some have estimated that one-third of the projects certified under the 1976 incentives would fail to qualify under the new investment tax credit law.[58]

That may be true. However, it might be possible to allocate a little more of the purchase price basis of a property to land, and therefore decrease the amount of depreciable basis (the cost of the building) which the rehabilitation expenditure must match. It may encourage some renovators to spend a little more money on rehabilitation to match the adjusted basis and obtain the investment tax credit. It may make investors more careful to acquire inexpensive buildings or ones that require substantial rehabilitation in amounts greater than their taxable bases. Buildings in neighborhoods where substantial rehabilitation has already occurred (and acquisition prices for buildings in need of renovation are therefore quite high) may not be able to partake in the new investment tax credit program. But it can be argued that buildings in booming neighborhoods are likely to be renovated even without an investment tax credit incentive. The new "substantial" rehabilitation test may make buildings in run-down historic areas particularly attractive.

The rehabilitation itself must be "certified" just as it was under the 1976 incentives. The secretary of the interior's standards for rehabilitation still apply, as does the process for submitting information about

---

57. *Id.*
58. Don Dworsky, *Historic Preservation in the Economic Recovery Tax Act of 1981* (Washington, D.C.: National Center for Preservation Law, 1981), p. 3, citing the director of the Tax Reform Act Certificate Unit in the Department of the Interior.

proposed or completed rehabilitations through state historic preservation offices and on to Washington. The time limit for review also has not been changed. Lessees (in addition to owners) may apply for investment tax credit certification if, on the date they complete their project, there are at least 15 years remaining on their lease.[59]

The 25 percent investment tax credit for rehabilitation of historic structures is only one of three new credits to foster renovation. Nonhistoric buildings qualify for either a 15 percent or 20 percent tax credit. Substantial rehabilitation of nonresidential buildings at least 30 years old qualifies for an investment tax credit equal to 15 percent of the rehabilitation expenditure. Nonresidential buildings at least 40 years old qualify for an investment tax credit equal to 20 percent of the cost of substantial rehabilitation.[60] While only nonresidential buildings qualify for the 15 percent or 20 percent credit, either residential or nonresidential certified historic structures can qualify for the 25 percent credit on rehabilitation of historic structures.

These other incentives may significantly increase renovations of residential buildings, whether individually listed on the National Register, within National Register districts, or within designated state or local districts. Real estate investors and developers may search out those districts that offer attractive rehabilitation prospects. They may also encourage the creation of new National Register designations or districts.[61]

The 5 percent additional credit for the rehabilitation of a historic structure may be sufficient to attract investors to nonresidential historic buildings. However, in an effort to provide an additional increment of incentive, the Economic Recovery Tax Act of 1981 also allows investors in approved rehabilitation of certified historic structures to depreciate the portion of the rehabilitation expenditure taken as a credit. This is not available to investors and developers utilizing the 15 percent or 20 percent credit. For example, consider the hypothetical investors who acquire a property for $250,000, allocate $50,000 to land, and spend $200,000 on the renovation. Under the 1981 rules for historic structures, they may take a $50,000 tax credit and depreciate the entire $200,000 in rehabilitation expenditure. If their building was only 40

---

59. ERTA § 212(b); 26 U.S.C. § 48(g)(2)(B) (Supp. 1981).
60. ERTA § 212(a); 26 U.S.C. § 46(a)(2)(F)(i) (Supp. 1981).
61. Note, however, that districts may not now be put on the National Register of Historic Places if written protests are received from more than 50 percent of the owners of property in the proposed district. This "owner consent" provision is discussed in chapter 4.

years old and not historic, they could only take a 20 percent credit—they would only have a $40,000 tax credit and would only be able to depreciate $160,000 in rehabilitation expenditure.[62]

Those rules were slightly changed by the Tax Equity and Fiscal Responsibility Act of 1982.[63] Investors in certified rehabilitation of historic structures may still take the 25 percent tax credit, but in any rehab project "placed in service" after January 1, 1983, they must deduct one-half of the amount of the credit taken from their depreciable rehabilitation expenditures. For example, on a $200,000 renovation expenditure a $50,000 tax credit is available, but $25,000, one-half of the credit, must be subtracted from the total renovation expenditure included in the depreciable basis. The investors may now only depreciate $175,000 (87.5 percent) of their total rehab expenditure, but that is $15,000 more depreciation than allowed if only a 20 precent tax credit on a nonhistoric structure had been involved. This may take some of the allure out of historic preservation projects, but their tax treatment is still better than any other type of real estate investment, with the possible exception of low-income housing rehabilitation.

The extra credit and depreciation opportunity are designed to make attractive the process for certification of rehabilitation under the secretary of the interior's standards. Investors who want to rehabilitate older buildings without going through the review must be careful not to acquire buildings individually listed on the National Register, within state or locally designated districts, or within National Register districts and contributing to the character of the district. (There is a presumption that all buildings within registered historic districts do contribute to their character. To determine otherwise, an application must be made to the National Park Service.) Any "substantial" rehabilitation of those types of buildings for purposes of the 15 percent or 20 percent investment tax credit must be certified as conforming to the secretary of the interior's standards.

In addition to making tax credits available for historic buildings, the Economic Recovery Tax Act of 1981 changed many other sections of the income tax code affecting real estate. The most significant changes are to the provisions affecting the appropriate useful life for a real estate investment and provisions governing accelerated depreciation.

---

62. ERTA § 212(b); 26 U.S.C. § 48(g)(5)(A) (Supp. 1981).
63. Tax Equity and Fiscal Responsibility Act of September 3, 1982, Pub. L. No. 97-248 (1982).

All of the former confusion in the tax code concerning appropriate useful life has been eliminated. There are now only three useful life periods that may be selected: 15 years, 35 years, or 45 years.[64] Almost all investment real estate, whether it be residential or commercial, now qualifies for a 15-year useful life. That is a significant change from previous law in which 20 years was usually the absolute minimum useful life, and real estate projects typically used 30 or 35 years. The effect of this change is to increase substantially the annual depreciation deduction (now called "accelerated cost recovery"). There are optional 35-year and 45-year useful life periods for those taxpayers (especially some corporate taxpayers) that prefer to hold annual depreciation deductions to a minimum.

Also changed are the complex rules concerning use of accelerated depreciation. Only two forms of accelerated depreciation are now appropriate for real estate projects: 175 percent declining balance for most real estate investment projects and 200 percent declining balance for low-income housing projects.[65] The only other method of depreciation now allowed is straight-line.

The old rule that the difference between accelerated depreciation and allowable straight-line depreciation must be recaptured at sale remains in effect for residential real estate investments. Taxpayers investing in nonresidential real estate projects and using accelerated depreciation are penalized significantly by the 1981 act. The entire amount of the accelerated depreciation taken over the life of the project (not just the difference between accelerated and straight-line) is recaptured as ordinary income upon sale.[66] This will severely limit use of accelerated depreciation on nonresidential buildings and may induce more investors to place their money in residential real estate projects.

The Act in Practice

A discounted cash-flow analysis can be used to demonstrate the combined effect of all the tax changes on a typical rehabilitation project involving a historic building. It also can be used to compare the options open to a real estate investor. For example, an investment tax credit of 25 percent on a certified historic preservation project can be compared to the investment tax credit of 20 percent available for the

---

64. ERTA § 201(a); 26 U.S.C. § 168(b)(3)(A) (Supp. 1981).
65. ERTA § 201(a); 26 U.S.C. § 168(b)(2)(A)(ii) (Supp. 1981).
66. ERTA § 204(c); 26 U.S.C. § 1245(a)(5) (Supp. 1981).

rehabilitation of nonhistoric buildings older than 40 years. While it seems clear that the opportunity to depreciate 87.5 percent of the rehabilitation cost for which a credit has been taken is a clear incentive to undertaking a certified historic rehabilitation project, discounted cash-flow analysis allows a precise comparison of the 20 percent and 25 percent investment tax credit options. Once the annual tax savings and tax consequences of sale in each of those options have been reduced to net present value, the difference can be compared to the additional cost or delay involved in having a rehabilitation project certified under the U.S. secretary of the interior's standards.

Discounted cash-flow analysis also may be used to compare depreciation possibilities when using the 25 percent credit. The Economic Recovery Tax Act makes it clear that the amount of the rehabilitation expenditure must be depreciated using the straight-line method. However, if preferable, it may be possible to depreciate the taxable basis of the building (purchase price plus previous capital improvements less land value and depreciation taken in the past) using the 175 percent declining balance method.[67]

In addition, discounted cash-flow analysis can be used to compare a rehabilitation involving the 25 percent tax credit with rehabilitation that avoids the tax credit altogether in order to depreciate the entire basis of the building plus rehabilitation expenditure at the 175 percent declining balance rate. Only a discounted cash-flow analysis can determine which of these options is preferable.

Assume the following project: five investors purchase a small historic residential building for $250,000, allocate $50,000 to the value of the land, and spend an additional $200,000 to rehabilitate the building. The project was completed in 1981 when the entire amount of the tax credit could also be depreciated. Some of the investors are in the 37 percent tax bracket in the initial year of the project while others are in the 49 percent tax bracket.

While their incomes will be the same each year, as shown in table 3, their tax brackets will not. Perhaps the most significant change to the Internal Revenue Code wrought by the Economic Recovery Tax Act of 1981 is the indexing of the tax brackets to inflation. The maximum tax rate is lowered from 70 percent to 50 percent beginning in 1982.[68] For 1982, 1983, and 1984, tax tables showing the income level and ap-

---

67. This does not seem to be excluded by the Economic Recovery Tax Act of 1981.
68. ERTA § 101(a); 26 U.S.C. § 1 (Supp. 1981).

propriate tax bracket are set out in the Economic Recovery Tax Act.[69] For taxable years after 1984, tax brackets will be adjusted in tune with changes to the Consumer Price Index.

Assume that the investors bought their historic building and completed the renovation in 1981. Table 3 sets out their incomes and tax brackets for the first 10 years of the project—based on the new tax tables through 1984 and on a 7.5 percent annual increase in the Consumer Price Index thereafter—and compares those to the tax brackets in effect prior to the 1981 tax act.

The results are startling. Indexing the tax code to inflation eliminates the "bracket creep" that would have systematically pushed our investors into higher and higher tax brackets as their income increased. The effect is to soften the tax consequences of sale, since the sale proceeds will not push the taxpayer into as high a tax bracket as it would have previously.

It may, however, diminish some of the attraction of real estate as an investment. The cutback in the maximum tax rate from 70 percent to 50 percent may make relatively risky investments, such as real estate, that provide a high degree of tax shelter less appealing for high income taxpayers. Taxpayers may now be content to pay 50 cents for every dollar in income on relatively secure investments rather than risk investment in real estate. Before the Economic Recovery Tax Act, they may have taken additional risks to keep as much income as possible out of the high 70 percent rate previously imposed.

Table 4 compares the taxable gain at sale for the four investment options considered. Table 5 shows the annual tax savings and the present value of the annual tax savings under each of the four available options. (Note that for both the taxpayer in the 37 percent bracket and the one in the 49 percent bracket, the use of a 25 percent investment tax credit in combination with straight-line depreciation on the rehabilitation expenditure and 175 percent depreciation on the basis in the building produces the greatest total annual tax savings over 10 years.) These tax savings are also substantially higher than the best tax savings available under the 1976 incentives, as shown in table 6.

Table 7 shows the tax consequences of sale in the fifth year. Whether starting out in the 37 percent or 49 percent tax bracket, the combination of a 25 percent investment tax credit, straight-line depreciation on the rehabilitation expenditure, and 175 percent declining balance

---

69. *Id.*

TABLE 3
COMPARISON OF ANNUAL INCOMES AND TAX BRACKETS BEFORE AND AFTER ERTA 1981

Year	Income 7.5% Annual Increase	Pre-ERTA Tax Bracket	Post-ERTA Tax Bracket	Income 7.5% Annual Increase	Pre-ERTA Tax Bracket	Post-ERTA Tax Bracket
1	$35,200	37%	37%	$60,000	49%	49%
2	37,933	43%	39%	64,658	54%	49%
3	40,877	43%	35%	69,678	54%	44%
4	44,051	43%	33%	75,087	54%	42%
5	47,471	49%	33%	80,916	54%	42%
6	51,156	49%	33%	87,198	59%	42%
7	55,127	49%	33%	93,967	59%	42%
8	59,407	49%	33%	101,262	59%	42%
9	64,019	54%	33%	109,123	59%	42%
10	68,989	54%	33%	117,595	64%	42%

Note: Based on initial incomes of $35,200 and $60,000.

TABLE 4
TAXABLE GAIN AT SALE (after ERTA 1981)

YEAR OF SALE: 5TH

	I.T.C. (25%) S.L. (Rehab & Basis)	I.T.C. (25%) S.L. (Rehab) 175% (Basis)	I.T.C. (20%) S.L. (Rehab) 175% (Basis)	175% (Rehab & Basis)
Market Value	$724,730	$724,730	$724,730	$724,730
Net Sales Price	673,999	673,999	673,999	673,999
Less: Adjusted Basis	316,665	290,876	264,206	265,081
Gain Subject to Tax	$357,334	$383,123	$409,793	$408,918
Total Accelerated Depreciation	0	$159,124	$145,794	$184,919
Less: Allowable Straight Line	0	133,330	120,000	133,330
Gain Subject to Ordinary Income	0	$ 25,794	$ 25,794	$ 51,589
Capital Gain	$357,334	$357,329	$383,819	$357,329
Less: Exclusion (60%)	214,400	214,397	230,291	214,397
Gain Subject to Ordinary Income	$142,934	$142,932	$153,528	$142,932
Total Gain Subject to Tax	$142,934	$168,726	$179,322	$194,521

YEAR OF SALE: 10TH

	I.T.C. (25%) S.L. (Rehab & Basis)	I.T.C. (25%) S.L. (Rehab) 175% (Basis)	I.T.C. (20%) S.L. (Rehab) 175% (Basis)	175% (Rehab & Basis)
Market Value	$1,167,184	$1,167,184	$1,167,184	$1,167,184
Net Sales Price	1,085,481	1,085,481	1,085,481	1,085,481
Less: Adjusted Basis	183,330	157,546	144,206	131,746
Gain Subject to Tax	$ 902,151	$ 927,935	$ 941,275	$ 953,735
Total Accelerated Depreciation	0	$ 292,454	$ 265,794	$ 318,254
Less: Allowable Straight Line	0	266,660	240,000	266,660
Gain Subject to Ordinary Income	0	$ 25,794	$ 25,794	$ 51,594
Capital Gain	$ 902,151	$ 902,141	$ 915,481	$ 902,141
Less: Exclusion (60%)	541,291	541,285	549,289	541,285
Gain Subject to Ordinary Income	$ 360,860	$ 360,856	$ 366,192	$ 360,856
Total Gain Subject to Tax	$ 360,860	$ 386,650	$ 391,986	$ 412,450

TABLE 5
ANNUAL TAX SAVINGS (after ERTA 1981)

JOINT RETURN: $35,200 INCOME (37% tax bracket)	Year 1	Year 2	Year 3	Year 4	Year 5	Year 6	Year 7	Year 8	Year 9	Year 10	10-Year Sum
25% Credit & S.L.	$11,973	$2,080	$1,867	$1,760	$1,760	$1,760	$1,760	$1,760	$1,760	$1,760	$28,240
P.V.	10,838	1,704	1,385	1,182	1,070	968	877	793	718	650	20,185
25% Credit & S.L.											
(Rehab) & 175% (Basis)	12,714	2,648	2,208	1,942	1,818	1,760	1,760	1,760	1,760	1,760	30,130
P.V.	11,509	2,170	1,638	1,304	1,105	968	877	793	718	650	21,732
No Cr. & 175% (Rehab & Basis)	3,454	3,216	2,549	2,123	1,875	1,760	1,760	1,760	1,760	1,760	22,017
P.V.	3,127	2,635	1,891	1,425	1,140	968	877	793	718	650	14,224
20% Credit & S.L. (Rehab)											
& 175% (Basis)	10,516	2,440	2,021	1,766	1,642	1,584	1,584	1,584	1,584	1,584	26,305
P.V.	9,519	1,999	1,499	1,186	998	872	789	714	646	585	18,807
JOINT RETURN $60,000 INCOME (49% tax bracket)											
25% Credit & S.L.	$12,613	$2,613	$2,347	$2,240	$2,240	$2,240	$2,240	$2,240	$2,240	$2,240	$33,253
P.V.	11,417	2,141	1,741	1,504	1,361	1,232	1,116	1,010	914	828	23,264
25% Credit & S.L.											
(Rehab) & 175% (Basis)	13,594	3,327	2,776	2,471	2,313	2,240	2,240	2,240	2,240	2,240	35,681
P.V.	12,306	2,726	2,059	1,659	1,406	1,232	1,116	1,010	914	828	25,256
No Cr. & 175% (Rehab & Basis)	4,575	4,041	3,205	2,702	2,387	2,240	2,240	2,240	2,240	2,240	28,110
P.V.	4,141	3,311	2,377	1,814	1,451	1,232	1,116	1,010	914	828	18,194
20% Credit & S.L.											
(Rehab) & 175% (Basis)	11,333	3,066	2,541	2,247	2,090	2,016	2,016	2,016	2,016	2,016	31,357
P.V.	10,259	2,512	1,885	1,509	1,270	1,109	1,004	909	823	745	22,025

TABLE 6
ANNUAL TAX SAVINGS (before ERTA 1981)

INITIAL YEAR: $35,200 INCOME (37% tax bracket)	Year 1	Year 2	Year 3	Year 4	Year 5	Year 6	Year 7	Year 8	Year 9	Year 10	10-Year Sum
Straight Line	$1,184	$1,376	$1,376	$1,376	$1,568	$1,568	$1,568	$1,568	$1,728	$1,728	$15,040
P.V.	1,072	1,128	1,021	924	953	863	781	707	705	638	8,792
125%	1,480	1,634	1,552	1,475	1,596	1,568	1,568	1,568	1,728	1,728	15,897
P.V.	1,340	1,339	1,151	990	970	863	781	707	705	638	9,484
TRA '76 (5-Year Amort.)	3,700	4,257	4,216	4,177	4,718	784	784	784	864	864	25,148
P.V.	3,349	3,488	3,127	2,805	2,868	431	390	353	353	319	17,483
TRA '76 (200%)	2,368	2,532	2,329	2,143	2,247	2,067	1,902	1,749	1,774	1,728	20,839
P.V.	2,142	2,075	1,728	1,439	1,366	1,137	947	789	724	638	12,985
INITIAL YEAR: $60,000 **INCOME (49% tax bracket)**											
Straight Line	$1,568	$1,728	$1,728	$1,728	$1,728	$1,888	$1,888	$1,888	$1,888	$2,048	$18,080
P.V.	1,419	1,416	1,282	1,160	1,050	1,039	940	851	770	757	10,684
125%	1,960	2,052	1,949	1,852	1,759	1,888	1,888	1,888	1,888	2,048	19,172
P.V.	1,774	1,681	1,446	1,244	1,069	1,039	940	851	770	757	11,571
TRA '76 (5-Year Amort.)	4,900	5,346	5,295	5,246	5,200	944	944	944	944	1,024	30,787
P.V.	4,436	4,381	3,928	3,522	3,161	519	470	426	385	378	21,606
TRA '76 (200%)	3,136	3,180	2,925	2,691	2,476	2,489	2,290	2,106	1,938	2,048	25,279
P.V.	2,839	2,606	2,170	1,807	1,505	1,369	1,141	949	791	757	15,934

TABLE 7
TAX CONSEQUENCES OF SALE: 5th Year (after ERTA 1981)

INITIAL YEAR: 37% BRACKET TAXPAYER	I.T.C. (25%) S.L. (Rehab & Basis)	I.T.C. (25%) S.L. (Rehab) 175% (Basis)	I.T.C. (25%) S.L. (Rehab) 175% (Basis)	175% (Rehab & Basis)
Taxes Due on Sale				
Ordinary Income Tax	$ 21,161	$ 23,327	$ 24,233	$ 25,495
Bracket (Base: $47,471)	(42%)	(42%)	(42%)	(42%)
Minimum Tax	0	0	0	0
Total Taxes Payable	$ 21,161	$ 23,327	$ 24,233	$ 25,495
Less: Taxes from Income	9,924	9,924	9,924	9,924
Taxes Due to Sale	$ 11,237	$ 13,403	$ 14,309	$ 15,571
Present Value (10% Discount)				
Annual Tax Savings	$ 16,179	$ 17,726	$ 15,201	$ 10,218
Less: Taxes Due to Sale	6,830	8,146	8,697	9,464
Present Value of				
Total Tax Shelter	$ 9,349	$ 9,580	$ 6,504	$ 754
INITIAL YEAR: **49% BRACKET TAXPAYER**				
Taxes Dues on Sale				
Ordinary Income Tax	$ 35,732	$ 38,053	$ 39,007	$ 40,464
Bracket (Base: $80,916)	(45%)	(45%)	(45%)	(49%)
Minimum Tax	0	0	0	0
Total Taxes Payable	$ 35,732	$ 38,053	$ 39,007	$ 40,464
Less: Taxes from Income	23,202	23,202	23,202	23,202
Taxes Due to Sale	$ 12,530	$ 14,851	$ 15,805	$ 17,262
Present Value (10% Discount)				
Annual Tax Savings	$ 18,164	$ 20,156	$ 17,435	$ 13,094
Less: Taxes Due to Sale	7,616	9,026	9,606	10,492
Present Value of				
Total Tax Shelter	$ 10,548	$ 11,130	$ 7,829	$ 2,602

depreciation on the taxable basis in the building is the best option. Note also that every one of the new choices available to the investor in this project after the Economic Recovery Tax Act is superior to any method available previously, as shown by comparing table 7 with table 8. Every one of the net present value calculations in table 8 resulted in a negative number, indicating that the tax consequences of sale more than offset the annual tax savings from depreciation. This is no longer true. The present value of the annual tax savings is greater than the present value of the taxes due at sale. That means after-tax yields on some real estate investments may now be significantly greater than pretax yields, a dramatic change that may make real estate a quite attractive investment.

Table 9 performs the same analysis assuming a sale in the 10th year. Again, the most preferable option for either a 37 percent or 49 percent bracket taxpayer is a combination of a 25 percent investment tax credit, straight-line depreciation on the rehabilitation expenditure, and accelerated 175 percent declining balance depreciation on the basis in the building.

The conclusion is clear. The new investment tax credit for certified historic preservation projects, when considered in combination with all the other changes to the Internal Revenue Code affecting real estate investment, makes rehabilitation of historic structures much more attractive than before. The dangers from use of accelerated depreciation also seem to be reduced. At least for taxpayers holding on to real estate for 5 or 10 years, assuming this particular project and its characteristics, recapture of the difference between accelerated and straight-line depreciation does not offset the additional tax shelter advantage from use of 175 percent declining balance depreciation. The principal cause seems to be in the indexing of the tax brackets so that sale of the real estate asset does not push the investor into as high a tax bracket in year of sale as it did before the Economic Recovery Tax Act.[70]

The 25 Percent Versus the 20 Percent Investment Tax Credit: Is Certification Worth the Cost?

Is the combination of an additional 5 percent tax credit and the oppor-

---

70. Another reason is the shorter useful life period now permissible for real estate investments. The "crossover point" at which it becomes more attractive to use straight-line rather than accelerated depreciation comes quite soon when the allowable useful life is only 15 years.

TABLE 8
TAX CONSEQUENCES OF SALE: 5th Year (before ERTA 1981)

INITIAL YEAR: 37% BRACKET TAXPAYER	Five-Year Amortization	200% Declining Balance	Straight Line	125% Declining Balance
Taxes Due on Sale				
Ordinary Income Tax	$ 44,854	$ 32,133	$ 26,045	$ 27,178
Bracket (Base: $47,741)	(59%)	(54%)	(54%)	(54%)
Minimum Tax	1,593	0	0	0
Total Taxes Payable	$ 46,447	$ 32,133	$ 26,045	$ 27,178
Less: Taxes from Income	13,539	13,539	13,539	13,539
Taxes Due to Sale	$ 32,908	$ 18,594	$ 12,506	$ 13,639
Present Value (10% Discount)				
Annual Tax Savings	$ 15,637	$ 8,750	$ 5,098	$ 5,790
Less: Taxes Due to Sale	20,000	11,301	7,601	8,290
Present Value of				
Total Tax Shelter	$ −4,365	$ −2,551	$ −2,503	$ −2,500

INITIAL YEAR: 49% BRACKET TAXPAYER				
Taxes Dues on Sale				
Ordinary Income Tax	$ 66,030	$ 52,094	$ 45,087	$ 46,325
Bracket (Base: $80,916)	(64%)	(64%)	(59%)	(59%)
Minimum Tax	68	0	0	0
Total Taxes Payable	$ 66,098	$ 52,094	$ 45,087	$ 46,325
Less: Taxes from Income	30,973	30,973	30,973	30,973
Taxes Due to Sale	$ 35,125	$ 21,121	$ 14,114	$ 15,352
Present Value (10% Discount)				
Annual Tax Savings	$ 19,428	$ 10,927	$ 6,327	$ 7,214
Less: Taxes Due to Sale	21,349	12,837	8,578	9,331
Present Value of				
Total Tax Shelter	$ −1,921	$ −1,910	$ −2,251	$ −2,117

TABLE 9
TAX CONSEQUENCES OF SALE: 10th Year (after ERTA 1981)

INITIAL YEAR: 37% BRACKET TAXPAYER	I.T.C. (25%) S.L. (Rehab & Basis)	I.T.C. (25%) S.L. (Rehab) 175% (Basis)	I.T.C. (20%) S.L. (Rehab) 175% (Basis)	175% (Rehab & Basis)
Taxes Due on Sale				
Ordinary Income Tax	$ 45,782	$ 48,157	$ 48,584	$ 50,425
Bracket (Base: $68,989)	(45%)	(45%)	(45%)	(45%)
Minimum Tax	5,942	4,856	5,095	3,878
Total Taxes Payable	$ 51,724	$ 53,013	$ 53,679	$ 54,303
Less: Taxes from Income	14,522	14,522	14,522	14,522
Taxes Due to Sale	$ 37,202	$ 38,491	$ 39,157	$ 39,781
Present Value (10% Discount)				
Annual Tax Savings	$ 20,185	$ 21,732	$ 18,807	$ 14,224
Less: Taxes Due to Sale	13,743	14,219	14,465	14,696
Present Value of				
Total Tax Shelter	$ 6,442	$ 7,513	$ 4,342	$ −472

INITIAL YEAR: 49% BRACKET TAXPAYER				
Taxes Dues on Sale				
Ordinary Income Tax	$ 66,787	$ 69,315	$ 69,837	$ 71,843
Bracket (Base: $117,595)	(49%)	(49%)	(49%)	(49%)
Minimum Tax	0	0	0	0
Total Taxes Payable	$ 66,787	$ 69,315	$ 69,837	$ 71,843
Less: Taxes from Income	32,648	32,648	32,648	32,648
Taxes Due to Sale	$ 34,139	$ 36,667	$ 37,189	$ 39,195
Present Value (10% Discount)				
Annual Tax Savings	$ 23,264	$ 25,256	$ 22,025	$ 18,194
Less: Taxes Due to Sale	12,612	13,546	13,738	14,479
Present Value of				
Total Tax Shelter	$ 10,652	$ 11,710	$ 8,287	$ 3,715

tunity to depreciate 87.5 percent of the rehabilitation expenditure on which a credit is taken enough to offset the additional costs of entering into a certified rehabilitation of a historic building? These additional costs are, first, the time delay caused by the certification process and, second, any extra cost involved in performing the rehabilitation work in accordance with the secretary of the interior's standards for rehabilitation.

There is an old real estate adage that "time equals money." Project delay can be translated into a corresponding dollar value. In the case of a rehabilitation project, any delay caused by the certification process can be measured by the additional interest that must be paid on the construction loan during the period of the delay. Construction loans work as follows: A bank makes a commitment to loan up to a total specified rehabilitation expenditure and stipulates that the loan must be paid back within a specified period of time. The developer then draws upon the promised construction or rehabilitation loan as necessary to pay off subcontractors, contractors, architects, and other project costs. The interest accrues gradually as the amount of the draws builds up. Therefore, if the agreed upon interest rate on the construction loan is 18 percent annually, total interest payments are not 18 percent of the total amount of the loan. It will amount to 1.5 percent per month on the amount of the loan actually drawn down by the developer to pay off project costs.

Assume it is 1981, and five investors acquired a historic building for $250,000, allocated $50,000 to land, and spent $200,000 in 1981 in a certified rehabilitation project. Before they acquired the building, they secured a loan commitment from a friendly neighborhood banker. The banker agreed to loan them $150,000 to buy the building (the banker required them to put up $100,000 in equity on the front end of the project) and agreed to provide them a construction loan for a maximum amount of $200,000 over a 12-month period. The rate of interest on both the purchase price loan and the construction loan was 18 percent annually. The banker also agreed to combine both loans together at the end of the construction period into one permanent loan at a somewhat lower rate—16 percent rate of interest over a 25-year term.

The investors completed their rehabilitation project within 12 months. Therefore, the total monthly interest charge on both the purchase price loan and the construction loan averaged about $3,750 per month. Of that amount, approximately $2,250 represented the interest on the purchase price (1.5 percent interest monthly on a loan of $150,000).

The remaining $1,500 per month was the cost of their construction loan. They drew down their construction loan gradually during the 12 months. In the first few months, monthly interest costs were quite low, and in the last few months, those costs were quite high. It is safe to say that the average monthly cost of construction loan interest was the same as 1.5 percent monthly on $100,000, or $1,500 per month. In the first 6 months, the monthly interest cost was substantially lower than that, and in the last 6 months, it was substantially higher than that. On average, however, it was about $1,500 per month.

The process for certification of a rehabilitation project involving a historic building takes anywhere from 30 to 60 days, usually 45 days. If the certification actually resulted in a two-month delay in project initiation or completion, total cost of the additional interest charge would be $7,500 to these investors.

This can be compared to the additional present value found when the 25 percent investment tax credit is used instead of the 20 percent investment tax credit. See table 10. The net present value benefit from using the 25 percent credit ranges from $3,076 to $3,432 depending upon the tax bracket of the investor and the year of sale.

The total monthly interest charge of $3,750 must be divided among the five investors. If they are sharing equally in interest charges, each would pay $750 per month. If it takes two months for their project to be certified, the cost per investor would be $1,500 in lost interest. That is less than the total present value to each investor from using the 25 percent tax credit. For the taxpayer in the 37 percent bracket in the initial year who plans to sell at the end of the 5th year, the delay caused by certification of the rehabilitation would have to be four months before it would offset the benefit of the 25 percent tax credit. For the taxpayer in the 49 percent tax bracket in the initial year who plans to sell at the end of the 10th year, the certification process would have to take almost five months before the taxpayer would be worse off.

Of course, with careful planning, certification can be undertaken while other aspects of the rehabilitation proceed. If the certification can be handled so it does not delay the project, then there may be no additional cost involved. One more factor must be considered: added project costs may be incurred in order to comply with the secretary of the interior's standards for rehabilitation.

Generally, those standards should not increase project costs; they really are a mechanism for avoiding more costly mistakes. For example, they prohibit sandblasting of brick and encourage gentle chemical or soap

TABLE 10
COMPARISON OF 25% AND 20% INVESTMENT TAX CREDIT

Tax Bracket	Year of Sale	Present Value of Shelter 25% Credit	Present Value of Shelter 20% Credit	Net Benefits
37%	5	$ 9,580	$ 6,504	$ 3,076
37%	10	7,513	4,342	3,171
49%	5	11,130	7,829	3,301
49%	10	11,710	8,287	3,423

Note: The values of the total tax shelters using the 20 percent and 25 percent credits are figured in conjunction with straight-line depreciation on the rehabilitation and 175 percent depreciation on the purchase price basis (under the 1981 rules allowing the entire credit to be depreciated). Data are given for both 37 percent and 49 percent taxpayers, showing the effects of both a 5th-year and 10th-year sale of the project. This table is a compilation of figures indicated in table 8 and table 9.

and water cleaning. They encourage repair of significant historic features rather than their total replacement. Any additional costs incurred as a result of the standards will vary significantly from project to project. If the project architect estimates that complying with the standards will significantly raise costs, those costs can be compared to the difference in the net present values using the 25 percent credit and the 20 percent credit. If the costs of compliance are greater than the present value benefit of the 25 percent credit, then it may not be economically attractive to undertake the certified rehabilitation project rather than a rehabilitation of a nonhistoric building on which the 20 percent credit is available.

CONSERVATION EASEMENTS[71]

A conservation easement is essentially a formal agreement between the owner of a historic building and a private preservation organization or government agency giving the latter the right to review and approve changes to the building before they are undertaken. Owners of historic buildings give easements in order to assure the future protection of the property. The easement "runs with the land" and binds future property owners to its provisions. An easement often provides much stronger protection than a local landmark ordinance.

The income tax code encourages such donations. If the property owner can prove that the donation of the easement has decreased the market value of his historic building, he may take a charitable contribution deduction in the amount of the decrease. Changes in the Tax Reform Act of 1976 have clarified the easement donation requirements. The new law added a subsection (iii) to Internal Revenue Code Section 170(f)(3)(B) to provide specifically for a charitable contribution for a "lease . . ., option to purchase, or easement" to a qualifying organization "exclusively for conservation purposes."[72] Between June 1976 and June 1977, any donated easement could have been for a minimum of 30 years. Since June 1977, any lease, option, or easement donated must be in perpetuity. The Tax Reform Act of 1976 provisions were made a permanent part of the tax code in 1980.

Since 1976, the public debate and discussion concerning preservation easements and the Internal Revenue Code has concentrated on technical legal issues: the relationship between the real property law

---

71. Appendix C contains a comprehensive listing of publications, regulations, and court cases dealing with various aspects of easements.
72. I.R.C. § 170(f)(3)(B)(iii) (1980).

in the state in which the restricted property is located and the language in the Internal Revenue Code, the problems created by the 1977 requirement that the easement be "in perpetuity," and the Treasury Department's fear that the donation of easements will seriously drain tax revenues from the federal government.[73] Only a few preservation organizations have developed meaningful easement programs.[74] The most serious problem is the lack of a clear method for the easement's valuation that will make the tax benefits of an easement donation clearly understood and easy to calculate. Such a method is desperately needed because in many ways the tax treatment of the donation of a preservation easement is much more favorable than other incentives for preservation created by the 1976 and 1981 tax legislation.

Valuation of Easements: The Crucial Inquiry

An easement can be donated on any building on the National Register, within National Register districts (if the building contributes to the character of the district), or protected by state or local ordinances certified by the secretary of the interior.[75] A charitable contribution for the donation of a preservation easement shelters the ordinary income of an individual or a corporation in the same way that depreciation deductions do, but there is no recapture on any portion of the charitable contribution deduction. More importantly, although a charitable deduction decreases the depreciable basis of a real asset (thus converting ordinary income to capital gain), there is nothing in the Internal Revenue Code that limits the total charitable deduction to the basis of the property. In other words, a taxpayer might be able to reduce his or her basis

---

73. Thomas A. Coughlin, Assistant General Counsel, National Trust for Historic Preservation, at "Conservation Easements: The Urban Setting," a workshop to discuss charitable donations of easements for historic preservation, sponsored by Technical Preservation Services Division of the Heritage Conservation and Recreation Service and the Office of Real Estate and Legal Services of the National Trust for Historic Preservation, Washington, D.C., November 14, 1980.

74. Perhaps the most successful programs are those of the Foundation for San Francisco's Heritage, the San Antonio Conservation Society, Historic Annapolis, Inc., the Historic Georgetown Foundation, Inc., and the Landmarks Preservation Council of Illinois.

75 I.R.C. § 170(h)(4)(B) (1980). Prior to 1980, the tax code allowed a deduction for depreciation on any "historic" structure, regardless of its official designation, and even on property that contributed to the preservation of a historically important structure. This created an opportunity for the creation of charitable contribution deductions on a great many more historic buildings than is now possible.

to zero through a charitable contribution deduction and still be able to take further deductions against ordinary income beyond the value of the basis. This creates the possibility of turning taxable ordinary income into income that escapes taxation altogether—the ultimate tax shelter. The best that can be done through a depreciation deduction is to turn ordinary income into a capital gain and defer the tax to a later date.

Internal Revenue Service regulations and opinions provide little help in constructing a proper valuation method. Revenue Ruling 73-339 states that the proper method for valuation is a "before and after" appraisal that calculates "the difference between the fair market value of the total property before the granting of the easement and the fair market value of the property after the grant." This difference is the "fair market value of the easement given up." Fair market value is defined in typical appraisal gibberish as "the price at which the property would change hands between a willing buyer and a willing seller, neither being under any compulsion to buy or sell and both having reasonable knowledge of relevant facts."[76]

The before-and-after calculation is no simple matter. The "before" calculation must take into account not only the value of the property for its existing use, but the suitability and adaptability of the property for other more profitable and presumably better uses. The "after" calculation must consider any economic benefits to the value of the property from the donation of the easement itself. These calculations depend heavily on the skill and subjective judgment of the appraiser.

Case law on the before-and-after valuation method is even more scanty than the information provided by the Internal Revenue Service. There is no case law as yet explaining the theory as it relates to the value of a historic preservation easement in an urban context. There is some limited case law, however, on the valuation of open-space easements. These cases offer some indirect guidance on the much more tricky process of valuing an easement on historic properties, especially urban historic properties.

The leading case is *Robert H. Thayer and Virginia Thayer v. Commissioner*.[77] At issue was the fair market value of the donation of an open-space or scenic easement over a 59-acre farm in Virginia. The property, which was improved with a significant set of structures in-

---

76. Rev. Rul. 73-339, 1973-2 C.B. 68.
77. T.C. Memo, 1977-370.

cluding a large house, a swimming pool, garden, boathouse and dock, two small dwellings, and other assorted structures, had a fine vista over the Potomac and offered a desirable location for home sites.

The text of the decision is important for a number of reasons. First, it provides an explanation of the actual appraisal process involved in both the before and after calculations. Second, it supports the possibility that the value of property subject to conservation easements may decrease substantially. Third, it recognizes the contrasting viewpoint that some easements may actually increase the value of property. And fourth, it fails to lend any weight to some of the more ridiculous valuation techniques proposed by developers or attorneys seeking to find outlandish tax shelters in preservation easements.

The easement donated by the Thayers prohibited the owners of the property from any industrial or commercial activities, and from any construction of any building (other than farm buildings and a one-family dwelling), signs or outdoor advertising, timber cutting, and subdivision. The effect of the easement was to prohibit any future development except farm-related activities. The taxpayers' appraiser concluded that the value of the farm before the easement ($347,005) was $147,688 greater than the value after ($199,317). The Internal Revenue Service appraiser assigned to the case believed that the value of the easement was only $60,000, determined on the basis of a pre-easement property value of $300,000 and a post-easement value of $240,000. The tax court judge in effect split the difference and assessed the value of the easement at $113,000. The key factual issue in the case was the number of subdivision home sites that could have been carved from the property under the best pre-easement set of conditions.

The high percentage decreases in value estimated by each of the appraisals (42.6 percent by the petitioner, 20 percent by the Internal Revenue Service, and 33 percent by the tax court judge) are noteworthy. The court did not reject such large percentage decreases. It is possible that even greater percentage decreases could be upheld in cases where evidence supports higher appraisals.

The decision could have been even more relevant to the valuation of historic preservation easements if the court had not glossed over the valuation by the Internal Revenue Service appraiser of the improvements on the property. That appraiser concluded that the value of the improvements actually increased after the easement from $50,370 to $94,990. He concluded that to achieve the "highest and best use" development of the entire site before the donation of the easement, the demolition of all structures other than the main house would be necessary. Therefore, he attributed no value to the various accessory structures prior to the donation of the easement. Creation of the easement so restricted new development that the preservation of the accessory buildings was assured, and therefore their value had to be added to the "after" calculation. In contrast, the tax court attributed the same value to the principal improvements both before and after the creation of the easement.

Applying the principles of the *Thayer* decision to a situation involving an urban property reveals the fundamental differences in the valuation of an open-space easement and a facade easement. Consider the most common big-city historic building: a three-story townhouse sharing a party wall (or built to the side yard lot line) on a narrow 25- or 45-foot-wide lot. If the area where the building is located already has attracted much renovation interest, the market may be paying a premium value for older buildings with historic character. The imposition of an easement, therefore, probably will not decrease the building's value. In fact, an easement, by calling attention to the character and prestige of a particular building, might even increase its market value to likely renovators who are purchasing the historic character of a neighborhood and building.

That may be true even when applicable zoning allows high intensity uses and buildings of a much greater density than older historic buildings. An easy test to determine if an easement on a historic building in a neighborhood zoned for high-rise development will result in a significant charitable contribution is to compare the price paid by high-rise developers to assemble parcels and the price paid by urban renovators for deteriorated historic structures suitable for total renovation for the luxury market. If the price paid by the latter is as high or higher than the price paid by developers for land, the before-and-after easement calculations may show little effect on value. When the new development market is strong, when small buildings are easily assembled into larger parcels, and when renovators pay token prices for buildings needing substantial renovation, there may be a significant difference between the before and after easement calculations. Note that in the *Thayer* decision, both appraisers separately valued the land and the improvements on the site before and after donation of the easement; in this scenario, an easement may significantly affect the value of the land while the value of the building remains the same or increases only slightly.

Most easements donated on historic urban structures in the last few years have been in older residential neighborhoods where there is already significant interest in renovation. The two most significant easement programs are those of the Historic Georgetown Foundation in Washington, D.C., and the Foundation for San Francisco's Architectural Heritage in California. In the Washington, D.C., area, the decrease in value as determined by the before and after appraisals is typically 5 percent to 20 percent. Occasionally, an easement results in a decreased property value of 50 percent, particularly when the historic building is on a large parcel of land with some development potential.[78] The Foundation for San Francisco's Architectural Heritage has accepted more than 92 easements, and the typical decrease in value determined by the appraisers performing the valuation ranged from 10 percent to 20 percent.[79]

The most problematical twist in valuing urban easements is determining the effect of historic designation. The protection provided a historic building by a strong local landmarks preservation ordinance is much like that provided by an easement. Instead of a not-for-profit preservation organization reviewing any proposed demolition or alteration of the building (as occurs after the donation of an easement), a public landmarks commission performs the review. If the local landmarks commission or the city council has the absolute authority to deny a petition for demolition of a landmark building, the effect of local landmark designation is quite restrictive. Typically, the only difference between the effect of an easement and that of landmark designation is the possibility that local political support for landmarks protection by ordinance may someday wane, resulting in a weakened ordinance allowing demolition or exceptions to the restrictions. A preservation easement, by contrast, is given in perpetuity, although the ardor of a preservation group for its cause also may change over time. Since preservation easements are voluntary and subsequent owners buy with knowledge of the easement on a building, there can be no charge that an unconstitutional "taking" of a property right has occurred.

When an urban historic building already is protected by a strong local landmarks ordinance, it is difficult to argue that the donation of an easement takes anything from the property owner's "bundle of rights"

---

78. Statement of Judith Reynolds, M.A.I., at conservation easements workshop, *supra* note 73.

79. *Id.* Statement of Ellen R. Ramsey, Executive Director, The Foundation for San Francisco's Architectural Heritage, at conservation easements workshop, *supra* note 73.

not already given up as a result of landmark designation. Any decrease in the value of the property occasioned by demolition or alteration restrictions should already have occurred at the time of landmark designation. The donation of an easement would not affect that value.

The evidence is clear, however, that designation of local landmark districts under strong landmarks ordinances has not decreased property values anywhere in the country. In fact, the effect has been just the opposite. Property values increase as dramatically or more so after designation as they did before it. This is at least partially because local landmark designation usually occurs *after* an area has attracted considerable renovation interest. Designation under a strong landmarks ordinance does not "restrict" property values but instead, by "protecting" the historic character of the neighborhood, stimulates buyer interest in purchase and renovation. The effect of an urban facade easement is usually the same.

For the preservation attorney or appraiser truly interested in protecting historic structures while encouraging their proper renovation and reuse, the complexity and problems inherent in preservation easements should not be troublesome. But the practicing preservation attorney must temper enthusiasm for conservation easements with the need to defend local landmarks ordinances against constitutional challenges. The claim that landmark designation affects property values severely enough to constitute a "taking" for which just compensation must be paid is still the gravest threat to the American system of landmarks protection, despite the support provided by the U.S. Supreme Court's decision in *Penn Central Transportation Co. v. City of New York*,[80] as discussed in the chapter on constitutional law. Attorneys who narrowly focus on the opportunities for tax shelter provided by an easement or who attempt to prove huge diminution in value as a result of the easement may inadvertently undermine the constitutional support for local landmarks designation.

That does not mean that the tax shelter opportunities of easements should be ignored. With the proper valuation methods, and on the right kinds of historic buildings, easements can be substantial charitable contributions, with deductions amounting to as much as 50 percent or more of before appraisal property values and not undermining the constitutional foundation of landmarks designation.

Most of what has been written about easement valuation involves ques-

---

80. 438 U.S. 104, 108 (1978).

tionable appraisal techniques.[81] What is the proper appraisal method? The proper before-and-after valuation should not consider the size, value, or profitability of possible new development on the site of the historic building. The appraisals in the *Thayer* decision are instructive. The taxpayers' appraiser did not attempt to determine the size of potential subdivision sites, their value if sold as raw home sites, or the value or profitability of the new homes that could be built. The value of the easement in the *Thayer* decision was not the difference between the profits or cash that could be generated by new home construction and that available from current farming operations. Nor was there any consideration of the owner's present equity position in the property or future equity positions in the likelihood of new development. The proper valuation calculation must start with the three traditional approaches to value: the market data, cost, and income approaches. Both the before and after calculations must be applied against the landmark property as presently developed, not as it might be if a new building were constructed on the site.

Both the reproduction cost approach and the market data approach are relevant to the valuation of preservation easements. Older buildings are actively traded on the market; they are sought because their sites are valuable for new buildings, precisely the threat that a preservation easement tends to eliminate. While a reproduction cost approach to

---

81. Perhaps the most unorthodox method—and one that has caused questionable efforts to find big charitable contribution deductions in the donation of easements on the wrong buildings—is the method outlined in *Space Adrift: Landmark Preservation and the Marketplace* (John J. Costonis, Chicago, Ill.: University of Illinois Press, 1974). This work outlines the "Chicago Plan," a comprehensive strategy for protecting urban landmarks through the transfer of their unused development potential to other sites.

The most serious problem with the Chicago Plan formula is its focus upon an imaginary replacement building. The formula assumes that the value of the replacement building can be calculated with all the certainty that applies to an existing building. The calculation leaves no room for the substantial uncertainty of the new development process, e.g., changes in market conditions that diminish demand for the space, changes in the cost or availability of construction and permanent financing, construction cost overruns, problems in obtaining project approval by appropriate levels of government, and availability of capable and willing developers.

The method of easement valuation proposed in the Chicago Plan formulation has been discussed widely, especially among owners of small landmark properties in big city neighborhoods zoned for high-rise, high-density development. Some local not-for-profit preservation groups are receiving frequent phone calls from building owners who want to know the value of an easement on their buildings. Often an attorney friend has told them that there are significant tax savings in giving away the air rights

value may be difficult because of the complexities of estimating depreciation, it is a technique constantly relied upon by appraisers of old buildings and is useful in determining the value of easements.

Each of the three approaches to value should be considered on the historic building both before and after the creation of the easement. In some cases—the historic, small, residential building in an area undergoing substantial renovation activity—the before and after values will be nearly the same. In other situations, there will be substantial differences. Consider the historic downtown commercial structure in a growing urban center with a strong demand for office space and much new construction activity. The "before" calculations using the capitalization of income approach or reproduction cost approach may result in a very low value. This is because the deteriorated historic downtown office building is likely to have a very low net operating income due to high expenses and low rents. It will suffer from substantial functional, physical, and economic obsolescence. Its market value, however, may be quite high. If, for instance, there is little vacant land available for the new high-rise office structures needed to fill demand, developers will acquire older buildings, demolish them, clear their sites, and assemble those sites for construction of new megastructures. They may be willing to pay substantially more for the historic downtown building than its capitalized income justifies.

Create a preservation easement on that building—or designate it a landmark under a strong local ordinance—and the market value of the historic structure may decrease severely.[82] But the value reflected in the

---

above their landmarks. Usually the attorney claims the tax savings increase with the allowable size of the hypothetical new structure that no longer can be built after donation of the easement.

Sometimes an appraiser can be found who uses a variation of the *Space Adrift* formula to value the "lost profits" or "lost development potential." The most serious danger is that use of the *Space Adrift* approach will be challenged by the Internal Revenue Service and result in a ruling or Tax Court decision that closes the door on the use of preservation easements in the many cases in which proper valuation techniques can provide good tax shelter opportunities.

82. Preservation attorneys may have to reconcile themselves to the distinction between the effect of designation on commercial office landmark buildings and the effect on residential buildings. The evidence indicating that designation increases the value of landmarks is based almost totally on property value increases in residential neighborhoods. There is, as yet, little prestige or added marketable appeal attached to designation of commercial office buildings as landmarks. If strong protection of a landmark building through creation of a preservation easement carries with it the possibility for a sizable tax deduction, it may be better for preservationists to recognize that designation may adversely affect the value of some commercial office buildings.

income approach and reproduction cost approach may be the same for both the after and before calculations. In the market data approach, however, valuation in the "after" calculation will be substantially lower or impossible to determine. If after the easement, sales of similar older office buildings protected by landmark designations or easement provisions are few or nonexistent, the market data approach may not be relevant.

The value of the preservation easement is, therefore, the difference between the "before" valuation (market value as determined by the price paid by office developers to demolish older buildings) and the "after" valuation (the capitalized income value or reproduction cost). The value of the easement may often be quite high. This valuation technique is supported by the *Thayer* decision and existing Internal Revenue Service rulings.

To appreciate how the donation of an easement creates a tax shelter, consider the tax consequences of the hypothetical donation of an easement on a landmark building such as Chicago's Monadnock Building, a 17-story example of the Chicago school of architecture, designed by Burnham & Root in 1891 with an addition by Holabird & Roche in 1893. A 1978 economic analysis for the Department of the Interior estimated the then-current net operating income on the structure before depreciation and debt service to be approximately $307,000 annually.[83] Assuming a 1978 capitalization rate of 15 percent on that particular building, the indicated value by the income approach prior to donation of the easement might have been approximately $2 million.

Now assume that the land under the Monadnock Building had a market value of approximately $200 per square foot (including the cost of demolition) in 1978 to an office building developer seeking a good downtown Chicago site.[84] Sales of prime Loop development sites at the

---

83. Harry Weese and Associates, *Four Landmark Buildings in Chicago's Loop* (Washington, D.C.: Heritage Conservation and Recreation Service, 1978), p. 106.

84. Ignore, for purposes of this example, the fact that the Monadnock Building has been designated as a Chicago landmark by the Chicago Commission on Historical and Architectural Landmarks. In Chicago, that may or may not affect the value of a designated structure because the Chicago landmarks ordinance is peculiar and rather weak. It provides only limited and uncertain protection to designated landmark structures. If the owner of a designated building applies for permission to demolish the structure, the application must be reviewed by the Commission on Historical and Architectural Landmarks and a public hearing must be held. The commission has the power to recommend to the city council that demolition be denied. The final decision is up to the city council, and it has only a limited set of quite costly options if it decides

time ranged between $200 and $300 per square foot. Total site area is 26,200 square feet. At $200 per square foot, the indicated market value (including cost of demolition) would be approximately $5.24 million.

The indicated value of the easement—the difference between the market data approach and the income approach to value of the Monadnock Building—might have been approximately $3.24 million. This was the potential tax deduction available to the owners.

How is the income tax deduction for the value of the easement taken? Generally, a taxpayer can deduct charitable contributions up to a maximum of 50 percent of his adjusted gross income annually.[85] However, an easement often is treated by the Internal Revenue Code as "capital gain property," and annual contributions of capital gain property cannot exceed 30 percent of the taxpayer's adjusted gross income in the year of the gift.[86] If the value of the easement exceeds the maximum allowable percentage of adjusted gross income in the year of donation, the deduction may be carried forward for five additional years with the annual deduction in each year not to exceed 30 percent of the taxpayer's adjusted gross income for that particular year.[87]

The significance of the easement as an income tax deduction depends in part on the type of ownership of the building to which the easement is donated. The most popular form of office building ownership is the limited partnership. If the owners of the Monadnock Building had a limited partnership, they could have donated a conservation easement and each partner could have taken the deduction on his individual income tax return in proportion to his ownership interest in the building.[88] For a corporate owner, the Internal Revenue Code rules are slightly different. The 30 percent and 50 percent annual limitations of adjusted gross income do not apply. Instead, corporate easement donors are

---

to deny the demolition permit: "If the City Council determines that such application should be denied, it shall . . . [initiate] action to lease or sublease said property; or [execute] a contract for the creation of covenants and restrictions binding the land; or [acquire] by eminent domain or by other contract or conveyance of all or any part of interest in said property; . . . or such other or further action as may be contemplated in . . . the Illinois Municipal Code," 21 Mun. Code of Chicago § 64.1(g). No landmark owner has ever been denied a demolition permit and asked for compensation under this section; the meaning and effect of this language are, therefore, uncertain.

85. I.R.C. § 170(b)(1)(A) (1976).
86. I.R.C. § 170(b)(1)(C) (1976).
87. I.R.C. § 170(b)(1)(C) and § 170(d) (1976).
88. I.R.C. § 702(a)(4) (1954).

limited to an annual deduction of 10 percent of corporate taxable income. They also are entitled to a five-year carryover up to a maximum of 10 percent of corporate taxable income in each year.[89]

The difference in the tax treatment of an easement donated by corporations rather than by individuals creates significant differences in the attractiveness of the easement donation as a tax shelter. One of the most frequent uses of the corporation in real estate development and ownership is as the general partner in a limited partnership arrangement. These corporations typically are capitalized at the minimum amount necessary to assure general partner status; to avoid the corporate double tax problem, they frequently distribute income in the form of salaries and expenses. This leaves little taxable income to report. A limitation of 10 percent of taxable income of such corporations—even with a five-year carry forward—may make it difficult for the corporate partner to take the full deduction available for the value of an easement.

Larger corporations, especially publicly held corporations, also may find that an easement donation and the tax shelter it provides are not particularly attractive. That is because donation of an easement reduces the taxable basis of the property. The basis is reduced to the same extent that the donation of the easement reduces market value. For example, in our Monadnock Building hypothetical, the easement may have reduced the value of the building by approximately 60 percent. A corresponding 60 percent decrease in taxable basis also would occur. Because the value of outstanding shares of corporate stock in large corporations holding real estate is determined by the value of the assets, the donation of an easement might reduce the book value of the corporation's real estate assets and therefore the book value (and market value) of the corporation's outstanding shares of stock. That may not sit well with a corporation's shareholders.

For the limited partnership that owns historic buildings, however, the donation of an easement may provide the ultimate tax shelter. Like any good tax shelter, it converts ordinary income (through the annual charitable contribution deduction) to capital gain (as a result of the easement's effect on the basis of the property). Unlike the typical tax shelter, especially the now-repealed, highly popular, and publicized historic preservation five-year amortization or accelerated depreciation incentives, there is no recapture problem at sale of the real asset, and the

---

89. I.R.C. § 170(b)(2) (1981). For years prior to 1982 the limit is 5 percent.

possibilities of an additional minimum tax payment are slight.[90] One of the most vexing problems associated with the donation of an easement, however, is the special rule for the donation of property subject to recapture of accelerated depreciation.[91] The fair market value of the donation must be reduced by the ordinary income that would have resulted—the difference between accelerated and straight-line depreciation—if this had been an outright sale of the property.

This may be easy to calculate in the typical situation in which an owner donates property outright to a charitable organization. In the case of the donation of an easement, however, the legal problems are substantial. For example, in our hypothetical easement on Chicago's Monadnock Building, it could be argued forcefully that the only value given up is the value of the underlying land, not any value associated with the depreciable building. Therefore, sale of the "donated property" (the easement) would be a sale of nondepreciable property (the land) not subject to recapture.[92] Because so few easements have been donated in recent years, the Internal Revenue Service has not yet been forced to clarify the effect of these provisions on the donation of an easement.

A preservation easement also may be the ultimate tax shelter because there is nothing that prohibits a property owner from taking a charitable contribution deduction greater than the taxable basis in the property. Consider, for example, a landmark building that has had the same owner for a long period of time and has a very low tax basis. The market value of the property may have increased dramatically. Donation of an easement could reduce the low basis to nearly zero and result in additional charitable contribution deductions that shelter ordinary income without creating additional capital gain in the future. The effect would be to convert ordinary income into "nontaxable income" since a property's basis can never be less than zero. Unlike the typical tax shelter that converts ordinary income into capital gain and therefore changes the max-

---

90. For individual taxpayers, however, when total annual itemized deductions (including all charitable contributions) exceed 60 percent of adjusted gross income, the excess is a preference item subject to the minimum tax, I.R.C. § 57(b) as amended. Pub. L. 94-455 § 301(c)(2) (1976).

91. I.R.C. § 170(e)(1)(A) (1976).

92. This may run afoul of the language in *Penn Central Transportation Co. v. City of New York*, 438 U.S. 104 (1978), that frowns on efforts "to divide a single parcel into discrete segments and attempt to determine whether rights in a particular segment have been entirely abrogated." While that decision was in response to a "taking" claim, the policy may apply with equal force here.

imum tax bracket from 50 percent to 20 percent, this tax shelter could convert income subject to the maximum tax bracket to totally tax-free income. That is the dream of every high-income taxpayer.

If preservation easements can create such attractive tax shelters, why have they been used so infrequently; generated so little publicity; and, when they have been used, why have they created typical deductions of no more than 10 percent or 20 percent of value? The reason is simple: lack of understanding and promotion by the preservation community and developers. Most attention has been given to easements on the wrong buildings: small residential buildings in neighborhoods undergoing substantial renovation activity and interest. These are the most difficult easements to appraise and the ones least likely to result in a significant— and legally supportable—decrease in market value. Little publicity has been given to the tax shelter possible in the donation of easements on older commercial buildings in a vibrant downtown.[93] Preservationists have been interested either in protecting these buildings through tough landmark restrictions—a designation that compounds the problem of valuing a facade easement on them—or in promoting the availability of the rehabilitation incentives provided by the Tax Reform Act of 1976 and the Economic Recovery Tax Act of 1981. Developers buying older landmark buildings in vibrant downtowns seldom if ever consider the possible tax shelter of a preservation easement. They jump into a rehabilitation program, apply for certification of the rehabilitation to obtain the five-year amortization or accelerated depreciation incentives, and only after the building has been renovated—if ever—consider the donation of an easement. At that point, the value of an easement may be harder to prove. The renovation has substantially increased the net operating income of the building and therefore its value as determined by the income approach. That value now may surpass the value of the site to a developer interested in demolition and redevelopment. It may be difficult to prove that net operating income of the building will be affected by the donation of an easement, and it may be easy for the Internal Revenue Service to challenge any easement valuation that results in a claim for a substantial charitable contribution on the renovated landmark property. Those developers who donate an easement prior

---

93. Two recent articles in *The Appraisal Journal* have finally focused on easements on historic downtown office buildings. See Richard Roddewig and Jared Shlaes, *Appraising the Best Tax Shelter in History*, Appraisal Journal, January 1982, p. 25; and Sally Oldham, *Historic Properties: Variable Valuations*, Appraisal Journal, July 1982, p. 364.

to engaging in a substantial renovation project may more easily be able to reap the substantial tax shelter benefits now available but so seldom realized.

PACKAGING INCENTIVES

The last 10 years have seen the development of a new type of urban renewal for older downtowns. Under the umbrella of such federal initiatives as the Urban Development Action Grant (UDAG) program, Economic Development Administration funding, and the Community Development Block Grant program, partnerships have been formed among private developers, local or state government, and assorted federal agencies to undertake urban renewal projects. One of the most significant twists to these new urban renewal programs is a willingness on the part of local, state, and federal officials to listen to the needs of private real estate developers, to understand the realities of the real estate game, and to provide a variety of flexible government incentives to make creative urban development possible. This new style of urban renewal will survive even if the UDAG program is curtailed.

The UDAG program of the Department of Housing and Urban Development (HUD) is by far the largest of the new urban initiatives to join public/private partnerships for redevelopment. The program disbursed, between its inception in 1977 and the middle of 1980, approximately $1.3 billion in federal assistance. Almost 700 individual projects were involved, and the private development leveraged during that period has been estimated to be more than $7.5 billion.[94] A study by The Conservation Foundation of the 235 projects in which firm contracts with private developers were signed between 1977 and mid-1980 found that 102 of the projects, approximately 43 percent, involved some rehabilitation activity.[95] These 102 projects were located in small as well as large cities and in all regions of the country. Approximately one-third of the rehabilitation projects were in central business districts; almost one-half of the projects involved retail/commercial activities, one-third industrial renovation or expansion, and only 16 percent housing.[96] One of the most significant discoveries of the study was that about one-third of the rehabilitation projects received other public funds in addition

---

94. Phyllis Myers, *Urban Conservation and Urban Economic Development: Collision and Convergence* (Washington, D.C.: The Conservation Foundation, 1980), p. 1.
95. *Id.* at p. 7.
96. *Id.* at p. 8.

to UDAG allocations. The most typical additional sources of federal funds were through the Community Development Block Grant program and the Economic Development Administration, but a wide array of other city and state programs combined to provide additional incentives to private development.

As an indication of the types of assistance that can be provided to developers under the UDAG program, consider some of the projects given preliminary approval by HUD in January 1981. In Hartford, an action grant of $1 million will be used to provide a second mortgage in the renovation of a large old hotel in the downtown area. Interest on the second mortgage will be only 6 percent for the first 3 years and 10 percent thereafter over the 30-year term of the loan. Hartford also will receive an equity participation in the project in the form of 15 percent of the net cash flow above a stipulated minimum.[97] In St. Louis, $18 million in action grant funds will be combined with local revenue bond financing under urban renewal authority for the renovation of two older downtown office buildings and department stores.[98] In Omaha, a $350,000 action grant will be combined with financing provided by a consortium of Omaha banks and money from the city's community development block grant funds to renovate a vacant, 100-unit condominium project into 50 townhouses.[99] In Pittsburgh, a $4.8 million action grant will be used to finance the construction of an 800-space parking garage and to provide necessary street improvements to enable the renovation of a 7-story warehouse into 300,000 square feet of office space and 40,000 square feet of retail space. Pittsburgh will receive 75 percent of the annual net cash flow generated by the parking garage until $3.3 million has been repaid at an overall interest rate of 3 percent. Thereafter, the city will receive 25 percent of the cash flow generated by the garage and will retain a 10 percent interest in any new building to be constructed on the air rights above the garage.[100]

The Unity Example: A Proper Feasibility Analysis

To understand how a combination of financial incentives can be packaged with property tax and other government incentives to make an uneconomic renovation feasible, consider Chicago's North Loop Urban

---

97. [Current Developments], Hous. & Dev. Rep. (BNA) at p. 708 (Jan. 19, 1981).
98. *Id.* at p. 711.
99. *Id.* at p. 712.
100. *Id.* at p. 714.

Renewal Area, seven square blocks in the heart of Chicago's Loop. The city proposed to acquire the seven blocks and turn them over to private developers for a combination of residential, commercial office, and retail projects that will include a mix of renovation and new construction. Chicago has declared this to be the "largest downtown urban renewal effort in American History" and plans to provide a combination of incentives to private developers including a land price write-down, long-term property tax reductions, and revenue bond financing at less than current market interest rates. UDAG money and other types of federal assistance and city funds are being used for the project.

Since initial plans for the project were announced in the early 1970s, there has been considerable controversy over the number of existing buildings to be retained and renovated. Within the project area, there are 14 buildings listed either on the National Register of Historic Places or as Chicago landmarks. Under one early project proposal, all the buildings in the North Loop, including all 14 landmarks, would have been demolished and replaced by new construction. In a 1980 version of the plan, the Chicago Department of Planning proposed that 7 landmark buildings be retained—if possible—and the facades on 3 other landmark buildings be retained—if possible—with new construction behind them. Since then, the National Trust for Historic Preservation, the Landmarks Preservation Council of Illinois, and others have argued that more landmark buildings should be retained and that the "if possible" language should be deleted. They feel that developers seeking to participate in the project should be required to do some renovation.

The city of Chicago argued that the placement of some of the landmark buildings precluded development of the rest of the block on which they were located. The city resisted "must save" designations out of expressed fear that flexibility must be built into the plan to entice developers to the project area and assure the renovation of those buildings considered most suitable by private developers. Preservationists disagreed and argued that new construction could be combined with renovation of the existing buildings and that renovation of all the landmark buildings was economically feasible.

To support their arguments, preservationists published a report entitled *The Feasibility of Incorporating Landmark Buildings in the Redevelopment of Chicago's North Loop*.[101] The heart of the report

---

101. Landmarks Preservation Council of Illinois, *The Feasibility of Incorporating Landmark Buildings in the Redevelopment of Chicago's North Loop* (Chicago, 1981).

was an in-depth analysis of the costs of renovating five landmark buildings on one of the seven blocks in the project area, and a scheme for incorporating renovation with new construction on the remaining portions of the block.

While the report was valuable in documenting the costs of renovation and indicating schematically how new and old buildings could be combined in a visually appealing and exciting concept, it failed to prove that renovation was economically feasible and failed to explain the types of incentives that might help assure successful renovation. In a quick attempt to affirm the feasibility of the proposed renovations, the report stated that the overall average renovation cost was approximately 80 percent of the current cost of new construction and that current rents in older buildings were approximately 71 percent of rents in new buildings.[102] The report made no attempt to estimate net operating income after renovation, examine the availability or cost of financing, or compare operating expenses and real estate taxes for new versus old buildings.

A proper analysis of the feasibility of renovation would take a much different approach. It would first consider the likely income and expenses after renovation of a building, next consider the maximum mortgage principal that could be supported by that net operating income, and only then consider project feasibility, total amount of cash available for renovation, and the effect of any possible incentives. Feasibility both before and after income taxes must be considered.

As an example, consider the feasibility of renovating the Unity Building, the second largest of the five landmark buildings in Chicago's North Loop. The building is a 16-story-plus-basement office building with a total gross area of approximately 147,350 square feet. The first and second floors are devoted to retail uses and have approximately 9,525 square feet each. Floors 3 through 16 are devoted to office uses and contain 8,485 square feet each. Total gross office area is 118,300 square feet, and total gross retail area is 19,040 square feet. When the basement area and unrentable elevator core, stairwells, and elevator lobbies are subtracted, rentable area is approximately 105,350 square feet for office uses and 16,260 square feet for retail uses.

A proper analysis of the feasibility of renovating this building would first examine the probable income and expenses of the building. Income can be determined by calculating average rents for office and retail

---

102. *Id.* at 57-60.

uses. Prime office space in recently renovated buildings in Chicago's Loop now rents for $12 to $20 per square foot. That is somewhat less than $16 to $30 per square foot, the rent commanded in new office buildings recently completed or now under construction in the heart of Chicago's Loop. It would be reasonable for the owners of the Unity Building to expect after renovation an average rent of $16 per square foot of office area. Some leases might be higher and others lower depending upon term, size of area leased, and location within the building.

Leases on retail space in Chicago's Loop are often structured so that the landlord receives an annual base rent plus a percentage of the gross income generated by the retail business. It would be reasonable for the owners of the Unity Building to expect an annual income of approximately $30.00 per square foot for retail portions of the building. One 1979 public survey of 45 buildings of all ages in downtown Chicago containing a total of over 20 million square feet of space estimated an overall average operating expense (including real estate taxes) of $6.92 per square foot.[103] Another privately sponsored study with a smaller sample of 9 well-maintained office buildings varying in age between 15 years and 60 years found an overall weighted average for operating expenses (including real estate taxes) of $5.51. Adjusting those studies to account for the effects of inflation since 1979 and further adjusting them to reflect the considerable operating efficiencies that a total renovation would bring about (especially in heating, ventilating, air conditioning, and electrical service costs), it would be reasonable to expect that, after renovation, operating expenses would be approximately $6 per square foot of gross building area. The net operating income calculation is shown in table 11. Total net operating income would be approximately $1,105,672.

Once the income/expense forecast is calculated, the next step would be to determine the mortgage principal that could be supported by the net operating income projected for the building after total renovation. The size of the mortgage that could be obtained can be determined once the appropriate debt coverage ratio likely to be applied by the typical lender on long-term mortgages for commercial office buildings is known. The American Council of Life Insurance routinely surveys 20 of the largest life insurance companies in the United States to deter-

---

103. Building Owners and Managers Association International, *1980 Downtown and Suburban Office Building Experience Exchange Report* (Washington, D.C., 1980), p. 29.

TABLE 11
UNITY BUILDING: POST-RENOVATION INCOME/EXPENSE FORECAST

Revenue
Office: 105,350 S.F.* @ $16/S.F.†		$1,685,600
Retail: 16,260 S.F. @ $30/S.F.		487,800
	Total	$2,173,400
Less: Vacancy & Collection Loss:		
Office: 8%		134,848
Retail: 10%		48,780
Effective Gross		$1,989,772

Less Operating Expenses:
147,350 S.F. @ $6/S.F. $ 884,100

Net Operating Income $1,105,672

Annual Return on Equity $ 235,064

* Square feet.
† Price per square foot.

mine various characteristics of their mortgage commitments in excess of $100,000. Its survey of 240 such loans on commercial office building projects committed in 1980 indicates an overall average debt coverage ratio of 1.27.[104] The net operating income on the Unity Building after renovation, therefore, is likely to be approximately 127 percent of the annual mortgage interest and principal payment under the terms of a likely mortgage loan to be created on the building. Total supportable annual debt service, therefore, would be approximately $870,608.

In 1982, with the prime rate hovering between 16 percent and 17 percent, it is unlikely that the developer of this rehabilitation project would be able to find a long-term mortgage from a major institutional lender (e.g., an insurance company or pension fund) at anything less than a 15 percent rate of interest. The term of the loan probably would be no longer than 20 years. At 15 percent interest over a 20-year term, a debt service of $870,608 would support a mortgage principal of $5,449,424. This is the maximum mortgage loan that developers could reasonably expect from the private mortgage market.

Is that amount large enough to make this renovation project possible? That depends upon the type of development entity undertaking this project and its expectations of profitability. In the most prevalent type of office investment, the ownership expects to make a return on equity between 8 percent and 15 percent after debt service but before income tax considerations. Assume that the investors would be happy with a 10 percent return on equity that might possibly grow if rent increases outpace expense increases. The income generated by this renovated office building after debt service would be approximately $235,064. As a 10 percent investment, that would support $2,350,640 in equity. Adding that equity investment to the total amount of the maximum mortgage principal indicates a total value for this project of $7,800,064. That is the total project cost—including costs of renovation—that could be supported by the net operating income after renovation assuming a mortgage of 15 percent over a 20-year term and owners who seek a 10 percent return on equity.

If the total money available for purchase and renovation is about $7.8 million, what portion of that will go to renovation costs? The answer is simple: it is the difference between $7.8 million and the cost of acquiring the property.

---

104. American Council of Life Insurance, *Investment Bulletin No. 820*, April 24, 1981, table L.

Of course, if the renovation is to be undertaken by the current owner of a building who has owned it for some time and therefore has a low acquisition cost, the amount available from that $7.8 million for renovation may be quite large. Long-term owners of older landmark buildings, however, seldom are interested in renovating. As discussed earlier, this is one of the biggest obstacles to the renovation of landmark buildings. Usually the building must change hands before renovation will be possible. And the long-term owner is going to demand the maximum price possible for the run-down, older office building. In a vibrant downtown with a strong office market and much new construction, the value of that old landmark building typically will be its value as a cleared piece of land minus the cost of demolishing the landmark. That value is significantly higher than the value of the building as an income-producing older office building.[105]

In the case of the Unity Building, the value of the underlying land is likely to be $250 to $300 per square foot, given its location on one of the prime office streets in Chicago. Total land area under the Unity Building is approximately 10,000 square feet, thus the indicated value of the land will be approximately $3,000,000. The maximum cost of demolishing the building would be somewhere between $1.50 and $2.00 per square foot. So total value of the building prior to demolition to someone interested in acquiring the parcel to construct a new office building might be approximately $2,750,000. That would leave roughly $5,050,064 available for the renovation program.

Is $5,000,000 sufficient to undertake a renovation that would command an overall average rent of $16 per square foot for office portions of the building and $30 per square foot for retail? No, it would not be sufficient according to a study by the Landmarks Preservation Council of Illinois, which estimated the total costs of renovation to be approximately $7.1 million as of the end of 1980.[106] Not included in this estimate are "soft" costs such as architect's fees, construction supervision, and construction financing. Table 12 lists the "hard" renovation costs estimated by the Landmarks Preservation Council and adds the additional "soft" costs they did not calculate.

If the Landmarks Preservation Council's estimate of hard renovation costs is accurate, there is a shortfall of more than $3.9 million that must

---

105. There may be an exception if the local landmark legislation makes demolition impossible.

106. *Feasibility of Incorporating Landmark Buildings, supra* note 103, at p. 31.

TABLE 12
UNITY BUILDING: PROJECTED RENOVATION COSTS

	Cost	$/S.F.*
Rehabilitation	$7,100,000	$48.18
Architect, Construction Supervision, Contractor's Fees (15% of Rehab Costs)	1,065,000	$ 7.23
Construction Financing (12 mos. @ 20%)	816,500	$ 5.54
	$8,981,500	$60.95
Less: Amount Available for Rehab Based on Feasibility Analysis	$5,000,000	$33.93
Additional Funds Necessary	$3,981,500	$27.02

* Price per square foot.

be met to make this renovation possible. There are a number of ways of making up this shortfall. One option might be to scale back renovation costs by $3.9 million, a 44 percent cut. Such a severe cutback, however, would result in a building that could not command the highest rental income possible in a renovated landmark structure. The net operating income would have to be recalculated to reflect the lower rents of a partly renovated building. The amount of potential mortgage would be reduced correspondingly.

A second option would be to require owners to infuse more equity money into the project. We have assumed that the likely investors would want a 10 percent "cash on cash" return in the first year and therefore would invest no more than $2.35 million. If owners also were to increase the difference between total likely renovation costs and feasibility costs, they would have a total investment in the building of $6,332,640. Since the net operating income from the building after renovation would remain the same ($235,064), the owners' first year return on their initial investment would be only 4 percent.[107]

A third possibility would be to put together a program of local government incentives that would make a first-year return of 10 percent—or close to 10 percent—possible while also increasing the dollars available for renovation. Table 13 lists incentives and the likely effect of each on the feasibility of this project.

Consider the effect of each of these possible incentives on project feasibility. Assume that the investors will ask the city of Chicago for a package of incentives to make renovation possible while assuring them a first-year 10 percent return on an equity of no more than $2,350,640.

These incentives can be combined to make this renovation more feasible under these assumptions. When the effect of the additional income tax incentives provided by the Economic Recovery Tax Act of 1981 are considered, the project becomes quite attractive.

Land Cost Write-Down

One incentive that government could provide is a subsidy for buying the unrenovated landmark building. This is one of the most popular uses of UDAG money and one that has been proposed in Chicago's

---

107. An internal rate of return analysis, as discussed earlier, will show that yields are actually somewhat higher when the consequences of increased income in future years and sale of the building are considered.

TABLE 13
POSSIBLE LOCAL GOVERNMENT INCENTIVES

Incentive	Effect
Land Cost Write-down	—Increase money available for rehab
Reduce Construction Loan Interest Rate	—Increase money available for rehab
Reduce Property Taxes	—Increase net operating income —Increase mortgage principal —Increase money available for rehab or —Increase return on equity
Reduce Permanent Mortgage Interest Rate	—Increase mortgage principal —Increase money available for rehab
Provide Second Mortgage at Reduced Interest Rate	—Increase first mortgage principal —Increase money available for rehab or —Reduce income after debt service —Reduce return to investors

North Loop to help the Hilton Hotel Corporation acquire 1.5 square blocks for the construction of a new luxury hotel. The city has agreed to acquire the land for the hotel through condemnation and then transfer it to the Hilton Corporation for approximately $50 per square foot. Let us assume that the city would not be so generous with the developers and would only acquire and sell the building at $100 per square foot. Total cost of acquisition to the developers would be only $1,000,000 rather than $3,000,000. The acquisition cost savings could be used to make up much of the shortfall in funds available for renovation. In fact, that incentive alone would add approximately 44 percent of the additional funds needed.

Reduced Construction Loan Interest Rate

Another frequently used incentive in UDAG projects is a reduction in the interest rate on the construction loan necessary to complete a project. Construction loans are risky, short-term ventures, and the commercial banks or insurance companies most likely to make them usually demand an interest rate above the prime rate on the date of the loan commitment. A substantial reduction in the interest rate on the construction loan can reduce the shortfall in the funds needed to undertake renovation.

If the city of Chicago agreed to provide a construction loan on the total project cost (including costs of architects' fees, construction supervision, and contractors' fees) at a rate of only 10 percent for the one-year construction period, project feasibility would be provided a big boost. Because of the way in which construction loans are made—the funding is set aside, and draw-downs are made as construction bills are paid—the effective rate of interest over the term of the construction loan is about half the agreed upon interest rate. The result of this incentive would be to reduce the cost of construction financing by one-half, or $408,250. This would make available an additional $408,250 for hard renovation costs.

Reduced Property Taxes

Cook County and the city of Chicago have agreed to a property tax incentive program for the North Loop project area and other designated urban renewal areas. Although the city and the county have not yet agreed on whether all or only some of the projects in the North Loop will qualify for the reduction, they agree that some property tax incentive is necessary. The effect of the incentive is to reduce assessed valuation on commercial office buildings in the North Loop project area by 60 percent for a period of 13 years. The incentive is available for renovation as well as new construction.

If the property tax incentive were available to the Unity Building renovation project, it would increase net operating income and thus the total amount of the mortgage loan that could be made to the developers. Property tax payments are the single biggest expense item for operators of commercial office buildings in downtown Chicago. Real property taxes, however, vary widely as a percentage of total operating expenses. Taxes range from 15 percent to 40 percent of total operating expenses, depending on the building, its location, use, and the aggressiveness with which building ownership has appealed property tax assessments. It would be reasonable to expect that the developers in the Unity Building renovation project will pay approximately 25 percent of total operating expenses, or $1.50 per square foot of building area, in property tax payments after renovation. A 60 percent reduction in taxes would decrease property tax payments to only $0.60 per square foot and increase net operating income by $0.90 per square foot of building area. Total net operating income would increase by $132,615.

With the benefit of such a property tax reduction, total net operating income on the building after renovation would be increased to $1,238,287. This income would now support an annual debt service of $975,029. A total mortgage principal of $6,103,031 could be made available. This would make an additional $653,607 available for renovation (assuming that the investors put in the same equity as before).

Reduced Mortgage Interest Rates

Reduced permanent mortgage interest rates and second mortgages at reduced interest rates are alternative forms of the same benefit. A government agency can use its revenue bond powers to provide a permanent mortgage loan or to make up some of the mortgage principal needed by providing a second mortgage at a lower rate of interest. Given the same amount of net operating income available to pay annual debt service costs, either incentive can increase the total mortgage amount and therefore the total amount available for renovation.

Assume that the city of Chicago would be unwilling to provide both a construction loan and a permanent mortgage for the entire project value. Typically a public agency would share some of the risk either at the construction stage or at the permanent financing stage but would be reluctant to take on all of the risk. This is in part because to do so would tie up public funds available to spur investment, thus enabling fewer projects to be assisted.

Using public funds to provide some second mortgage financing, however, can substantially boost a renovation project. Typically the use of public funds as either a first or second mortgage results in an interest rate no more than two percentage points below the market rate. The reduced interest rate is possible because the public funds emanate from a tax exempt revenue bond issue for which bond buyers are willing to accept a slightly reduced interest rate in exchange for the tax-free interest paid to bond buyers. The key questions now become how large a second mortgage will the city of Chicago provide and at what interest rate and over what term.

Assume that the city provides a $2,000,000 second loan using an Urban Development Block Grant, a Community Development Block Grant, or other source of funds such as revenue bond financing. If the term of the loan was 30 years and the rate of interest 13 percent—two points below the assumed mortgage rate—the annual second mortgage payments necessary to fully amortize the loan would be $266,821. This would leave approximately $708,208 (after a property tax incentive has boosted net operating income) for the annual debt service on the conventional first mortgage loan provided by a private funding source. This remaining debt service would finance $4,432,907 in the form of a conventional mortgage loan at 15 percent over a 20-year term. Total first and second mortgage amounts would now add up to $6,432,907. Such a mortgage principal would make available an additional $329,876 for renovation.

This would still leave the project shy of the $3,981,500 renovation shortfall that must be made up through government incentives. If the source of the second mortgage loan was a UDAG or Community Development Block Grant allocation, the interest rate on the second mortgage could be reduced further since the source of the money is a grant from the federal government rather than a revenue bond loan that must be repaid. If the interest payment could be reduced to 10 percent on the $2 million loan, the total mortgage principal provided by a combination of a conventional first mortgage and a government-financed second mortgage loan would be $6,775,056. That would make available an additional $672,025 for renovation. A second mortgage loan at 5 percent would result in a total first and second mortgage principal of $7,098,500, which would result in a total additional amount available for renovation of $995,469.

If a $2 million second mortgage at a 5 percent interest rate over a 30-year term was added to the property tax, construction loan, and land cost write-down incentives already discussed, the total additional amount of money made available for renovation would be $3,807,326 (see table 14). This leaves an additional shortfall of only $174,174. If the developers kicked in that additional amount as equity in the project, their total investment would now be $2,525,314 and their return on investment ($235,064) 9.3 percent. That is close enough to their goal of 10 percent to make this investment attractive.

The Effect of a 25 Percent Investment Tax Credit

To really understand this hypothetical project and whether it is attractive, it is necessary to look beyond the first year. The investors have indicated that they would like to receive a 10 percent "cash on cash" return on their total equity investment in the first year of operations. Their return should increase in future years. Both rents and expenses will be increasing. But the difference (net operating income) between rents and expenses should increase each year because rents will be increasing from a higher starting point. Office building leases are usually written so that tenants bear the burden of expense increases after the first year of their leases. This allows the investors to pass on the increases directly to the tenants. On a very conservative set of assumptions, net operating income might increase about 3 percent annually.

The consequences of sale in some future year also must be considered. The value of the building in that year of sale will be its value based on a capitalization of its income. In other words, what will a future buyer pay for a building that generates a net operating income equal to that generated by the Unity Building? The "capitalization rate" is the factor used to determine the value of the building in the year of sale. For example, if net operating income (before debt service) from 1982 to 1991 was forecast assuming a 3 percent annual compounded rate of increase, total net operating income in 1991 would be $1,615,683. What would other investors pay to acquire a building generating $1.6 million in 1991? They would seek a rate of return no different from other types of long-term investments, such as corporate bonds or other comparable real estate investments. If they found that the rate of return on those other types of investments was 10 percent, they would pay

TABLE 14
UNITY BUILDING: EFFECT OF INCENTIVES ON MONEY AVAILABLE FOR RENOVATION

Renovation Cost Shortfall	$ 3,981,500
Sources of Additional Renovation Funds	
Land Write-down	$ 1,750,000
Construction Loan Financing	408,250
Property Tax Reduction	653,607
Second Mortgage	995,469
Total Additional Renovation Funds Available	$ 3,807,326

no more than the net operating income of the Unity Building divided by 10 percent, or $16,156,830, in 1991. That might be the value of the Unity Building in 1991 under this set of assumptions by the income approach—generally called the reversion.[108]

The cash outlay made by today's investors is the purchase price plus renovation expenditure less funds contributed by the mortgage lender. In this example, the investment is made in the first year. The annual net operating income has been forecast, and the annual mortgage principal and interest payments are known. The amount of the annual cash flow after mortgage payments may therefore be calculated; this is a return to the investors on their original cost to enter into the project. Finally, the sales price in some future year, in this case 1991, has been forecast, and the remaining mortgage balance that will have to be repaid to the mortgage lender at date of sale can be calculated. The proceeds from sale after repayment of the balance on the mortgage is another return to the investors.

Given the amount of initial cash investment that this building requires, the annual cash flows after debt service to the investors, and the net proceeds of sale after repayment of the mortage balance in 1991, is this an attractive investment compared to other types of projects? Only a discounted cash flow analysis can help make this decision. The investors have indicated that they would like to achieve at least a 10 percent rate of return on their initial investment. They also would like some way of comparing this particular proposed investment to others. An "internal rate of return" analysis can do both.[109]

This analysis, commonly known as IRR, finds what interest rate reduces the annual cash flows after mortgage payments, and the net proceeds of sale in some expected future year of sale, to the original first year cash investment. What discount rate makes the present value of the expected future cash flows equal to the initial cash outlay? In other words, what is the yield on this investment?

---

108. For an explanation of the capitalization of income approach to value, see American Institute of Real Estate Appraisers, *The Appraisal of Real Estate*, 7th ed. (Chicago, 1978), pp. 315-23.
109. An excellent general explanation of internal rate of return analysis and net present value calculations is in Greer, *The Real Estate Investment Decision*, supra note 4, at pp. 153-62. For an explanation in the context of a preservation project, see Real Estate Research Corporation, *Economics of Revitalization: A Decisionmaking Guide for Local Officials* (Washington, D.C.: Heritage Conservation and Recreation Service, 1981), pp. 46-48.

An internal rate of return analysis for the Unity Building hypothetical can be run both before and after considering the tax consequences of the investment tax credit provisions and the opportunity to depreciate the building over 15 years. Table 15 shows annual net operating income, debt service, and cash flows before and after consideration of tax consequences. Table 16 shows the consequences of a sale in 1991. If the investment tax credit provisions of the Economic Recovery Tax Act of 1981 were not included in the calculation, the internal rate of return on the pretax cash flows would be 19.19 percent.[110] An IRR analysis applied to the net spendable cash (an after-tax yield analysis), again ignoring the investment tax credit provisions, would be 18.91 percent. That would be the yield on this real estate investment, and it is indeed an attractive yield. It compares favorably, on either a before-tax or after-tax basis, with any other type of investment including corporate bonds, money market certificates, or even after-tax investments such as tax-exempt municipal bonds or all-savers certificates.

The effect of the new investment tax credit for certified rehabilitations is quite significant. The effect of the 25 percent credit is to return to our investors an additional $2.04 million at the end of the first year. If the internal rate of return analysis is again run with $2.04 million as the first year after-tax cash flow, the yield after taxes is 32.574 percent—an extraordinary return.

This analysis indicates that local government officials must be extremely cautious when approached by developers for a joint public/private partnership in the rehabilitation of a historic building or district. Much more than just an analysis of the first year's income from operations is necessary. Future net operating income must be forecast, the consequences of debt service clearly laid out, and the after-tax consequences determined. Assumptions about a year of sale and the cash and tax consequences of that sale must be made. A yield analysis should be run on both a pretax and after-tax basis to determine the real return to the investors in the project. In the Unity Building example just presented, the 25 percent investment tax credit boosted the yield to an extremely high level. This may cancel the need for some of the other incentives proposed as part of the suggested local government package. Once the income tax consequences are known, a local government

---

110. This calculation was made using computer programs in the Real Estate Analytical Package developed by Shlaes & Young Information Systems, Inc., Chicago, Illinois.

TABLE 15
UNITY BUILDING RENOVATION

	1982	1983	1984	1985	1986
Net Operating Income	1,238,287	1,275,435	1,313,698	1,353,109	1,393,702
Debt Service:					
Amortization	43,902	50,828	58,858	68,136	78,895
Interest	922,049	915,124	907,104	897,815	887,057
Total P & I	965,952	965,952	965,952	965,952	965,952
Pre-tax Cash Flow	272,334	309,483	347,746	387,157	427,750
Plus: Amortization	43,902	50,828	58,858	68,136	78,895
Less: Depreciation	648,766	648,766	648,766	648,766	648,766
Taxable Income	−332,529	−288,455	−242,172	−193,472	−142,121
Pre-tax Cash Flow	272,334	309,483	347,746	387,157	427,750
Less: Income Taxes	−166,264	−144,227	−121,086	−96,736	−71,060
Net Spendable Cash	438,599	453,710	468,832	483,893	498,810

	1987	1988	1989	1990	1991
Net Operating Income	1,435,514	1,478,579	1,522,936	1,568,624	1,615,683
Debt Service:					
Amortization	91,355	105,788	122,507	141,873	164,307
Interest	874,596	860,163	843,445	824,078	801,644
Total P & I	965,952	965,952	965,952	965,952	965,952
Pre-tax Cash Flow	469,561	512,626	556,984	602,672	649,731
Plus: Amortization	91,355	105,788	122,507	141,873	164,307
Less: Depreciation	648,766	648,766	648,766	648,766	648,766
Taxable Income	−87,529	−30,350	30,724	95,779	165,272
Pre-tax Cash Flow	469,561	512,626	556,984	602,672	649,731
Less: Income Taxes	−43,924	−15,175	15,362	47,889	82,636
Net Spendable Cash	513,486	527,802	541,621	554,782	567,094

TABLE 16
UNITY BUILDING: REVERSION IN 1991

Gross Sales Price	16,156,836
Less: Mortgage Balance	5,506,461
Net Proceeds of Sale	10,650,374
Original Cost	9,981,500
Less: Cumulative Depreciation	6,487,666
Adjusted Basis	3,493,833
Total Taxable Gain	12,663,003
Ordinary Gain	0
Capital Gain	12,663,003
Net Proceeds of Sale	10,650,374
Less: Income Taxes	2,532,600
Net Proceeds After Tax	8,117,774

package can be provided that will make the pretax yields attractive enough to lure investors and assure project feasibility. No greater incentives than those absolutely necessary to make a project work should be given. To do otherwise is to transfer sorely needed public funds into the pockets of private developers.

CONCLUSION: THE CASE FOR PROPERTY TAX, FINANCING, AND INCOME TAX INCENTIVES

The Unity Building hypothetical shows some of the ways in which government can join hands with private developers to make renovation feasible. There can be as many types of incentives packages as there are types of developers and investors. For example, some investors undertake projects without any source of financing. They have the cash available to purchase and renovate. To these investors, government incentives that lower the cost of financing are meaningless. Only other incentives, such as property tax reductions and 25 percent investment tax credits, may improve the attractiveness of an investment for them.

For other real estate investors, only the after-tax income considerations are important. They are satisfied with real estate projects that return very little positive cash flow because they believe that the after-tax savings from depreciation deductions, interest payment deductions, and capital gains treatment outweigh the need for a positive return on their cash investment. For these investors, government incentives in the form of low-cost loans, property tax reductions, or land cost write-downs may only be frosting on a cake they would gladly eat plain.

All these investors are important to the continued renovation of historic buildings. Thus a variety of government incentives are necessary to attract the largest possible number of developers and real estate investors to historic preservation projects. Unwillingness to consider all three areas of government incentives—property tax, income tax, and financing—will make the future renovation of many landmark buildings difficult.

It is clear from the current mood in Washington and the states that the 1980s will be a time of fundamental change in the types of incentives available for landmarks. Of the three types of general incentives, the one most in danger now is financing. The Reagan administration has indicated its intention to cut back on federal mortgage guarantee programs. In the past, such a cutback would have had little effect on historic preservation projects. It now would mean, however, that the loan insurance program for historic buildings that was authorized by the National Historic Preservation Act Amendments of 1980 might never get off the ground. Also, the Treasury Department, in recent years, has taken a tough stand on alleged abuses in state and local government industrial revenue bond programs. The Treasury is concerned that there has been a tax drain from the increased private purchase of these tax-exempt obligations, and it, therefore, has proposed limitations on the extent to which tax-exempt bonds can be issued. This may make it difficult for state and local governments to develop their own loan insurance programs.

The fundamental changes in the ways the Internal Revenue Code treats depreciable investments—including investments in income-producing real estate—are generally beneficial to real estate. These are the changes caused by the Economic Recovery Tax Act of 1981. Although reducing the maximum tax rate from 70 percent to 50 percent may have reduced real estate's allure as a tax shelter, expanding the investment tax credit may have more than made up for it. Only the experience of the next few years will show which provision is stronger.

The general drift of the financial community away from long-term, low-interest, fixed-rate mortgage loans has had, and will continue to have, a much more severe impact on investment in real estate, including investment in the renovation of historic buildings, than any change in the tax code can possibly have. The overall tightening of availability of funds for real estate finance, the volatility of interest rates in recent years, and the changeover to variable rate (or renegotiable) mortgages substantially increase the uncertainty and risk in real estate as an investment.

Public financing incentives provide a number of benefits for qualifying projects: first, they provide a source of real estate financing when many other sources have dried up or are temporarily out of the market; second, they provide loans at a rate of interest that can make work some leveraged real estate projects that otherwise could not; and third, they can provide to the participating levels of government the opportunity to assure that the accompanying fiscal and economic benefits to the community occur where and when the community wants them.

Procedures for the taxation of real property and the availability of real estate tax incentives are also in a period of fundamental change. Local governments across the country are faced with taxpayer revolts because of the high proportion of local government revenues generated by the real property tax and the effect of inflation on home prices and assessment levels. On the one hand, therefore, local government officials are being pressured to reduce the overall real estate tax burden, especially as it affects homeowners. This could spill over and reduce the tax burden on income-producing properties as well, or it could shift the tax burden from single-family homeowners to other types of real property owners. On the other hand, older urban areas are searching for effective incentives to stimulate more home and office rehabilitation. Many of these jurisdictions now realize that property tax incentives and creative use of the revenue bond power may be the only ways for local government to encourage rehabilitation in a period of sharply curtailed federal funding. The net result should be to increase local government's willingness to enact creative tax incentives that have a good chance of stimulating renovation of older buildings and increasing the property tax base of the community.

Preservationists are now well positioned and organized to deal with these changing conditions. Since the establishment five years ago of Preservation Action, a Washington-based, not-for-profit lobbying organization, it has become much easier for the preservation perspective to be made known to Washington policymakers whenever new legislation affecting historic preservation is proposed. The National Trust for Historic Preservation, too, has shown new willingness to lobby key policymakers in Washington when necessary to assure that effective incentives for historic preservation continue. And the National Park Service in its Tax Reform Act certification unit is becoming increasingly astute in the after-tax consequences of real estate investment.

At the state and local levels, the number of landmarks commissions and not-for-profit historic preservation groups has increased dramatically in recent years. By grappling with the complicated incentives provided by the Tax Reform Act of 1976, many of these local preservationists now have a better understanding of how the real estate development process works. They now are often well equipped to make a strong case to state and local policymakers concerning the need for effective financing and property tax incentives for historic preservation projects.

And in the real estate industry itself, more developers and investors every year become familiar with the opportunities in the renovation and reuse of historic structures. The experience of these developers can be called upon by preservationists to demonstrate that incentives for the renovation of historic structures are necessary and should continue. The real estate developer—once the archenemy of the historic preservation movement—may become its most important ally in the 1980s.

For many older cities, historic preservation may be the only answer to dwindling populations, the flight of the middle class, and the erosion of commercial shopping bases. Promotion of historic preservation renovation projects can revitalize deteriorated neighborhoods, save downtowns, and make cities more attractive to middle-class families.

It is absolutely essential, however, that federal, state, and local governments—whatever their motives for fostering and encouraging historic preservation—be neither too generous nor too cautious in their promotion of incentives for renovation. Only when the actual operations of the real estate development process and the investment decisions behind it are widely known and well understood by preservationists and by federal, state, and local government officials will the right kinds of flexible incentives be designed and applied to those projects—and only those projects—that need incentives to make them possible.

FURTHER READINGS

No one has yet written a treatise on real estate feasibility specifically as it applies to the rehabilitation of historic buildings, but there are good and readable general treatises on real estate feasibility analysis. One of the best is Gaylon Greer's *The Real Estate Investment Decision* (Lexington, Mass.: D.C. Heath and Co., 1979). An even more current treatment of the same subject area is *Real Estate Investment Decisionmaking* by Austin J. Jaffe and C.F. Sirmans (Englewood Cliffs, N.J.: Prentice-Hall, Inc., 1982). *The Real Estate Handbook* (Homewood, Ill.: Dow Jones-Irwin, 1980), written by Maury Seldin, is an encyclopedic treatment of all aspects of real estate and real estate development. *Real Estate Review* is one of the best general real estate journals, often discusses rehab and historic preservation, and is published quarterly.

Income tax incentives for certified rehabilitation of certified historic structures are well covered in a series of National Trust information sheets. See, for example, *Summary of Preservation Tax Incentives and the Economic Recovery Tax Act of 1981* (Washington, D.C.: National Trust for Historic Preservation, 1981) and *Changes in Federal Tax Incentives for Historic Preservation* (Washington, D.C.: National Trust for Historic Preservation, 1982). Another good source of information on various federal, state, and local incentives for the rehabilitation of historic buildings is *Urban Conservation Report*, published on a subscription basis twice-monthly by

Preservation Reports, Inc. in Washington, D.C. The best general compendium of articles on federal, state, and local tax incentives for historic buildings is contained in *Tax Incentives for Historic Preservation* (Washington, D.C.: National Trust for Historic Preservation, 1980) edited by Gregory E. Andrews. A quite recent treatment of the relationship between property taxes and historic preservation with a special emphasis on New York City is David Listokon's *Landmarks Preservation and the Property Tax* (New Brunswick, N.J.: The Center for Urban Policy Research and the New York Landmarks Conservancy, 1982).

Financing for historic preservation projects is discussed in another National Trust information sheet, *Financing Preservation in the Private Market* (Washington, D.C.: National Trust for Historic Preservation, 1981). It explains in more detail the major lending sources and the concepts of leverage, equity, and interim and permanent financing.

Income tax and appraisal aspects of the donation of preservation easements on historic buildings are finally getting some serious attention in the literature. The only full-length treatment of the appraisal of historic buildings is in Judith Reynold's *Historic Properties: Preservation and the Valuation Process* (Chicago: American Institute of Real Estate Appraisers, 1982). Thomas Coughlin of the National Trust has written a comprehensive summary of the legal issues in easement donations in *Preservation Easements: Statutory and Tax Planning Issues* (Preservation Law Reporter, January 1982). Other sources of information on easements include periodic articles in *The Appraisal Journal*, published by the American Institute of Real Estate Appraisers, and *Real Estate Issues*, published by the American Society of Real Estate Counselors; both organizations are based in Chicago.

Appendix A

RECOMMENDED MODEL PROVISIONS FOR A
PRESERVATION ORDINANCE, WITH ANNOTATIONS

PREPARED BY STEPHEN N. DENNIS,
ASSISTANT GENERAL COUNSEL
NATIONAL TRUST FOR HISTORIC PRESERVATION
WASHINGTON, D.C.

©1983 BY
THE NATIONAL TRUST FOR HISTORIC PRESERVATION

Preparation of this material was made possible through a research contract from the Office of Policy Development and Research of the U.S. Department of Housing and Urban Development.

Contents

Index to Quoted Court Opinions	Avii
Index to Quoted Ordinances	Axi
Introduction	A1
I. Purposes of a Preservation Ordinance	A5
II. Creation of a Preservation Commission	A13
A. Creation of the Commission as a Municipal Entity	A13
B. Commission Members: Number, Appointment, Terms, and Compensation	A16
C. Required Qualifications for Commission Members	A19
D. Selection of the Commission's Officers	A22
E. Statement of the Commission's Powers	A22
F. Commission's Power to Adopt Rules of Procedure	A24
G. Commission's Authority to Employ Staff and Consultants	A26
H. Commission's Authority to Receive Funding from Various Sources	A27
I. Records of Commission Meetings	A28
J. Commission's Authority to Request Information from Other Governmental Agencies	A30
K. Annual Report by Commission	A30
III. Designation of Historic Districts and Landmarks	A33
A. Preliminary Research by Commission	A33
a. Commission's Mandate to Conduct a Survey of Local Historical Resources	A33
b. Commission's Power to Recommend Districts and Buildings to City Council for Designation	A34

	c. Preparation of Report on Proposed Designation	A35
B.	Designation of Historic Districts	A36
	a. Criteria for Selection of Historic Districts	A36
	b. Boundaries of Historic Districts	A38
	c. Evaluation of Properties within Historic Districts	A39
	d. Affirmation of Existing Zoning	A41
C.	Designation of Landmarks	A43
	a. Criteria for Selection of Landmarks	A43
	b. Boundary Description	A45
D.	General Matters Affecting Designation of Both Historic Districts and Landmarks	A46
	a. Commission's Jurisdiction to Designate May Not Cover All Local Structures	A46
	b. Referendum or Consent Requirements	A47
	c. Application for Designation of Historic District or Landmark	A48
	d. Filing Fees for Designation Applications	A50
	e. Commission Required to Notify Property Owners of Proposed Designation	A51
	f. Notice of Hearing of Proposed Designation to Nearby Property Owners	A52
	g. Commission Required to Hold Public Hearings	A53
	h. Commission Required to Make Designation Decision Promptly after Public Hearing	A56
	i. Specific Criteria Adopted at Time of Designation	A56
	j. Commission Required to Notify Property Owners of Designation Decision	A58
	k. Commission Required to Notify Other Agencies of Designation	A59
	l. Recording Requirement for Chain of Title Purposes	A60
	m. Plaques to Be Attached to Buildings Following Designation	A61
	n. Commission's Authority to Amend or Rescind Designation	A62
	o. Moratorium on Applications for Alteration or Demolition While Designation Pending	A62

IV. Application to Preservation Commission for Certificate of Appropriateness — A65
   A. Commission Power to Approve Alterations or New Construction — A65
   B. Definition of Alteration Keyed to City Building Code — A69
   C. Permission for a Variety of Styles in New Construction — A70
   D. Guidelines and Criteria for Commission to Use — A71
   E. Publications to Be Used by Commission to Help Establish Standards — A76
   F. Submission of Plans to Commission — A77
   G. Commission Action on Application for Certificate of Appropriateness — A78
   H. Commission Authorized to Delay, But Not Deny, Proposed Alteration — A79
   I. Commission to Hold Public Hearings on Applications for Certificates of Appropriateness — A80
   J. Permission for Commission to Seek Outside Technical Advice — A82
   K. Economic Hardship Arguments — A84
   L. Form of Decision and Required Findings — A87
   M. Giving Notice of Commission's Decision to Applicant — A89
   N. Explanation of Commission's Disapproval of Proposed Plans — A90
   O. Failure of Commission to Review Plans in Timely Fashion — A91
   P. Work Performed Required to Conform with Certificate of Appropriateness — A92
   Q. Certificate of Appropriateness Void if Construction Not Commenced — A93
   R. Change in Scope after Issuance of Certificate — A94

V. Demolition Applications — A97
   A. Commission's Authority to Comment on Demolition Permit Applications — A97
   B. Acceptable Commission Reactions to Applications for Demolition Permits — A99
   C. Consideration of Post-Demolition Plans — A100
   D. Demolition Criteria — A101
   E. Demolition Delay Period — A104

    F. Commission Activities While Action on Demolition
       Permit Suspended   A106
    G. Owner Required to Make Bona Fide Offer to Sell during
       Delay Period   A107
    H. Additional Demolition Delay Period if Condemnation
       Appears Likely   A108

VI. The Preservation Commission and Governmentally Owned Property   A109
    A. Property Owned by Public Agencies   A109
    B. Commission's Authority to Comment on Proposed
       Municipal Land Acquisitions within Historic District   A114

VII. Maintenance of Historic Properties   A115
    A. Ordinary Maintenance Exclusion   A115
    B. Minimum Maintenance Requirement   A116
    C. Public Safety Exclusion   A118

VIII. Enforcement Provision   **A121**

IX. Penalty Provision   **A123**
    A. Criminal Penalty   A123
    B. Civil Remedy   A124

X. Appeal Provision   **A125**

Index to Quoted Court Opinions

This index indicates the pages at which the fifty-four court opinions that are cited or quoted in the annotations to this document can be found.

Annapolis Emergency Hospital Association, Inc. v. Annapolis Historic District Commission (Law No. D-962, Anne Arundel County Cir. Ct., Md., Apr. 14, 1977), A55, A81

A-S-P Associates v. City of Raleigh, 258 S.E.2d 444 (N.C. 1979), A11, A14, A24, A39, A42, A68, A73-74, A127

Bittenbender v. Tibbetts, 202 A.2d 232 (N.H. 1964), A73

Blackmer v. City of Salisbury (No. 76 CVS 313, Rowan County Sup. Ct., N.C., May 4, 1976), A25-26, A72

Bohannan v. City of San Diego, 106 Cal. Rptr. 333 (Cal. 1973), A9, A39

Broadview Apartments Company v. Commission for Historical and Architectural Preservation (No. 0 104101, Baltimore City Ct., July 15, 1980), *rev'd in part*, 433 A.2d 1214 (Md. App. 1981), A81-82

City of Dayton v. Brewer (No. 80 CRB 1772, Dayton Mun. Ct., Ohio, Dec. 8, 1980), A9, A11, A21

City of Ithaca v. County of Tompkins, 355 N.Y.S.2d 275 (N.Y. 1974), A112

City of Miamisburg v. Hannah (No. 80 8 CRB 12, Miamisburg Municipal Ct., Ohio, Feb. 14, 1981), A9, A20-21, A74

City of New Orleans v. Impastato, 3 So.2d 559 (La. 1941), A67

City of New Orleans v. Levy, 98 So.2d 210 (La. 1957), A69

City of New Orleans v. Pergament, 5 So.2d 129 (La. 1941), A10, A24, A37, A67

City of Santa Fe v. Gamble-Skogmo, Inc., 389 P.2d 13 (N.M. 1964), A11, A14, A73, A123-24

Cleckner v. City of Harrisburg, 10 D. & C. 3d 393 (Pa. 1979), A76, A108

Crownrich v. City of Dallas, 506 S.W.2d 654 (Tex. 1974), A63

Dempsey v. Boys' Club of City of St. Louis, 558 S.W.2d 262 (Mo. Ct. App. 1977), A103

Equitable Funding Corporation v. Spatt (No. 12832/77, Kings County Sup. Ct., Feb. 8, 1978), A29

Faulkner v. Town of Chestertown, 428 A.2d 879 (Md. 1981), A13, A68, A73

Figarsky v. Norwich Historic District Commission, 368 A.2d 163 (Conn. 1976), A8-9, A83, A98

First Presbyterian Church v. City Council of City of York, 360 A.2d 257 (Penn. 1976), A98

Forg v. Jaquith (No. 35391, Middlesex Sup. Ct., Mass., July 22, 1975), A76

Fout v. Frederick Historic District Commission (Misc. No. 4005, Frederick County Cir. Ct., Md., Feb. 5, 1980), A81, A88

Galich v. Catholic Bishop of Chicago, 394 N.E.2d 577 (Ill. App. 1979), cert. denied, 445 U.S. 916 (1980), A64

Gumley v. Nantucket Board of Selectmen, 358 N.E.2d 1011 (Mass. 1977), A88

Hall v. Village of Franklin (No. 69-52580, Oakland County Cir.Ct., Mich., Feb. 10, 1972), A10

Hayes v. Smith, 167 A.2d 546 (R.I. 1961), A29, A71, A126

John Donnelly & Sons, Inc. v. Outdoor Advertising Board, 339 N.E.2d 709 (Mass. 1975), A10

Kravetz v. Plenge, 424 N.Y.S.2d 312 (1979), A42-43

Lafayette Park Baptist Church v. Board of Adjustment of City of St. Louis (No. 782-3445, St. Louis City Cir. Ct., Mo., May 3, 1979), A9-10, A98, A103-104

Maher v. City of New Orleans, 516 F.2d 1051 (5th Cir. 1975), A20, A98, A118

Manhattan Club v. New York City Landmarks Preservation Commission, 273 N.Y.S.2d 848 (1966), A36

Mayor and Aldermen of City of Annapolis v. Anne Arundel County, 316 A.2d 807 (Md. 1974), A42, A98, A112

Aix

M & N Enterprises, Inc. v. City of Springfield, 250 N.E.2d 293 (Ill. 1969), A8, A86-87

New York Yacht Club v. Landmarks Preservation Commission of City of New York (No. 550/80, New York County Sup.Ct., Feb. 13, 1980), A44, A55

900 G Street Associates v. Department of Housing and Community Development, 430 A.2d 1387 (D.C.App. 1981), A7, A104

Opinion of the Justices to the Senate, 128 N.E.2d 557 (Mass. 1955), A9, A10-11

Penn Central Transportation Company v. New York City, 438 U.S. 104 (1978), A1, A2, A7, A8, A20, A34, A45, A54, A80, A86

Phillips v. Board of Zoning Adjustments of City of New Orleans, 197 So.2d 916 (La. 1967), A84-85

St. James United Methodist Church, Inc. v. City of Kingston (No. 76-1239, Ulster County Sup. Ct., N.Y., May 6, 1977), A52, A72

Sears v. Brown (No. 75-3849, Middlesex Sup.Ct., Mass., Sept. 25, 1979), A90-91

Sleeper v. Old King's Highway Regional Historic District Commission, (No. 22799, Barnstable Sec. Dist. Ct., March 6, 1978), *aff'd*, 417 N.E.2d 987 (Mass. App. 1981), A66, A68, A69, A75-76, A85

Society for Ethical Culture in City of New York v. Spatt, 415 N.E.2d 922 (N.Y. 1980), A85-86, A98-99

South of Second Associates v. Town of Georgetown, 580 P.2d 807 (Colo. 1978), A20, A75

Southern National Bank of Houston v. City of Austin, 582 S.W.2d 299 (Tex. App. 1979), A45, A63-64

Springfield Preservation Trust, Inc. v. Springfield Historical Commission, 402 N.E.2d 488 (Mass. 1980), A127

State v. City of Seattle, 615 P 2d 461 (Wash. 1980), A47, A113

State v. Jones, 290 S.E.2d 675 (N.C. 1982), A11

Trustees of Sailors' Snug Harbor v. Platt, 288 N.Y.S.2d 314 (1968), A7, A85

Vieux Carre Property Owners and Associates, Inc. v. City of New Orleans, 167 So.2d 367 (La. 1964), A38

Whitty v. City of New Orleans (No. 6367 Civil Action, E.D.La., Oct. 21, 1959), A100-101

Wolk v. Reisem, 413 N.Y.S.2d 60 (App. Div. 1979), A91, A101, A119

Zartman v. Reisem, 399 N.Y.S.2d 506 (1977), A88, A127

Index to Quoted Ordinances

This index indicates the pages at which the thirty-seven local preservation ordinances or state enabling statutes that have been used in the compilation of this document are quoted.

Alabama Legislation: A47
Alexandria: A16, A118
Berkeley: A22, A33, A49, A50, A53, A62-63, A78, A87, A99, A103, A106, A109, A118
Boston: A13, A26, A27, A35, A44, A49, A56-57, A60, A110, A122
Boulder, Colo.: A28, A49
Charleston: A5, A13, A16, A19, A38, A115, A116, A125
Chicago: A28, A34, A47, A56, A59, A61, A62
Cincinnati: A57, A97
Coral Gables: A105, A116
District of Columbia: A6, A63, A84, A97, A100, A102, A117, A124
Enfield, Conn.: A23, A125
Fort Collins, Colo.: A122
Galena, Ill.: A121
Huntsville, Ala.: A91
Los Angeles: A66, A94, A101-102, A107
Loudoun County, Va.: A70, A104-105, A107
Louisville: A17, A19-20, A22, A23, A25, A27, A30, A33, A59, A92-93, A123
Madison, Wis.: A65-66
Mansfield, Conn.: A40, A70, A89, A93, A94
Natchez: A87
New Haven: A40, A41, A77, A82, A92
New Orleans: A16, A51, A53-54, A60
New York: A5-6, A43, A51, A109-110
Oak Park, Ill.: A16, A114
Paducah, Ky.: A90
Pensacola: A100, A125
Sacramento: A22-23
Salisbury, N.C.: A25

Savannah: A39-40, A65
Seattle: A36-37, A48, A58, A72, A80, A126
Springfield, Mass.: A46
Telluride, Colo.: A93-94, A115
Trenton: A26, A61, A69-70, A79-80, A108
Vicksburg, Miss.: A24-25, A71-72
Vieux Carre: A13, A19, A77-78, A116-117, A121
Wichita, Kan.: A123
Wilmington, Del.: A59, A92, A100

Introduction

Since Charleston's enactment of the first American preservation ordinance in 1931, more then 800 communities have enacted such ordinances.[1] State enabling legislation to permit municipalities to create preservation commissions has been enacted in many, but not all, states.[2] Because these acts differ significantly from state to state, the National Trust considers it inadvisable to produce a single model preservation ordinance. Instead, representative provisions indicating a range of possible approaches to particular issues have been selected.[3] These recommended model provisions for a historic preservation ordinance are arranged as separate entries, each divided into an annotation and one or more quota-

---

1. *See* Dennis, *Directory of American Preservation Commissions* (National Trust for Historic Preservation, 1981). Though New Orleans may have attempted to create a preservation commission in the mid-1920s, Charleston enacted the first effective local preservation ordinance.

2. "Over the past 50 years, all 50 states and over 500 municipalities have enacted laws to encourage or require the preservation of buildings and areas with historic or aesthetic importance." *Penn Central Transportation Company v. New York City*, 438 U.S. 104, 107 (1978). Lists of state statutes for historic preservation may be found in: (1) *A Guide to State Historic Preservation Programs* (National Trust for Historic Preservation, 1976); (2) Beckwith, "Developments in the Law of Historic Preservation and a Reflection on Liberty," 12 *Wake Forest Law Review* 93 (Spring 1976); (3) "Significant State Historic Preservation Statutes," an *Information* publication prepared for the National Trust for Historic Preservation by James P. Beckwith, Jr.; and (4) Beckwith, "Preservation Law 1976-1980: Faction, Property Rights, and Ideology," 11 *North Carolina Central Law Journal* 276 (Spring 1980).

3. During the summer of 1976 the Trust's Office of the General Counsel requested from each known landmark or historic district commission a copy of the ordinance establishing the commission and enumerating its powers and procedures. As these ordinances reached the Trust, a number of representative ordinances were selected for use in compiling these annotated model provisions, based on factors such as geographical location, community size, history of local preservation efforts, and success of an ordinance in preservation litigation. The selected ordinances establish and define both commissions with strong independent powers and commissions with a limited advisory role. These selected ordinances were then reviewed so that representative provisions could be culled from them for use in this compilation. The selection

tions from existing preservation ordinances.[4]

The rapid proliferation of preservation ordinances and amendments has caused a substantial increase in the number of requests for National Trust review of enacted or proposed ordinances and amendments. The U.S. Supreme Court's 1978 opinion in *Penn Central Transportation Company v. New York City*, 438 U.S. 104, should lead to the enactment or revision of preservation ordinances in many communities. The following recommended provisions have been compiled to help communities develop new ordinances or amend existing ones.

Readers of the provisions in these suggested categories will realize that every preservation ordinance is necessarily tailored to fit a local situation, and that provisions suitable to, and workable in, one community may be undesirable for another community. Frequently an ordinance contains provisions necessitated by local political forces.

Because state enabling legislation for preservation ordinances differs widely from state to state and is nonexistent in a few states, no local ordinance should be drafted without the assistance of an attorney thoroughly familiar with state enabling legislation and applicable state court decisions. Provisions developed for an ordinance in one state may be highly inappropriate for an ordinance in another state.

In some states it might eventually be necessary to amend existing state enabling legislation to permit the delegation to preservation commissions of sufficient regulatory authority to administer successful municipal

---

of one or more provisions from an ordinance does not constitute a recommendation of the entire ordinance.

Provisions have been selected from ordinances in the following states and communities: Alabama (Huntsville), California (Berkeley, Los Angeles, Sacramento), Colorado (Boulder, Fort Collins, Telluride), Connecticut (Enfield, Mansfield, New Haven), Delaware (Wilmington), District of Columbia, Florida (Coral Gables, Pensacola), Georgia (Savannah), Illinois (Chicago, Galena, Oak Park), Kansas (Wichita), Kentucky (Louisville, Paducah), Louisiana (New Orleans—both Vieux Carre ordinance and citywide ordinance), Massachusetts (Boston, Springfield), Mississippi (Natchez, Vicksburg), New Jersey (Trenton), New York (New York), North Carolina (Salisbury), South Carolina (Charleston), Virginia (Alexandria, Loudoun County), Washington (Seattle), and Wisconsin (Madison). In addition, a provision from the state enabling legislation for Alabama has been cited.

4. Annotations include references to appropriate court cases and references to pertinent articles that appeared in the *Landmark and Historic District Commissions* newsletter, formerly published by the National Trust's Office of the General Counsel. A complete set of the issues of this newsletter from September 1975 through March 1981 is available from that office for $12.

preservation programs. Existing commissions are likely to seek full authority to exercise the powers sanctioned by the Supreme Court's Penn Central decision. Drafters of proposed amendments to existing legislation might find these recommended model provisions useful and will want to consult also *Guidelines for State Historic Preservation Legislation*, issued by the Advisory Council on Historic Preservation in 1971.

Local preservation commissions should be aware of which local structures and districts have been listed in, or nominated to, the National Register of Historic Places. In states that have established state register programs, preservation commissions should also be aware of local listings on the state register. An active preservation commission will encourage the nomination of additional structures and districts to both the National Register and any state register. For maximum protection, a building should be both locally designated and listed in the National Register and the state register. In 1980, amendments to the National Historic Preservation Act of 1976, 16 U.S.C. § 470 et seq., made it possible for "certified local governments" to participate in the nomination of local properties to the National Register.

In the long run, the effectiveness of a local preservation commission will depend as much on the caliber of appointments to the commission and the care with which commission members discharge their responsibilities as it will on the strength of the preservation ordinance itself. Weak implementation of a good ordinance will necessarily lead to an ineffective municipal preservation program.[5]

                                    Stephen N. Dennis
                                    Assistant General Counsel
                                    National Trust for Historic
                                    Preservation
                                    May 1983

---

5. Both Robert E. Stipe and John Fowler have made helpful comments on earlier drafts of this appendix.

I. Purposes of a Preservation Ordinance

Typical Ordinance Provisions:

CHARLESTON:

In order to promote the economic and general welfare of the people of the city of Charleston and of the public generally, and to insure the harmonious, orderly and efficient growth and development of the municipality, it is deemed essential by the city council of the city of Charleston that the qualities relating to the history of the city of Charleston and a harmonious outward appearance of structures which preserve property values and attract tourists and residents alike be preserved; some of these qualities being the continued existence and preservation of historic areas and buildings; continued construction of buildings in the historic styles and a general harmony as to style, form, color, proportion, texture and material between buildings of historic design and those of more modern design; that such purpose is advanced through the preservation and protection of the old historic or architecturally worthy structures and quaint neighborhoods which impart a distinct aspect to the city of Charleston and which serve as visible reminders of the historical and cultural heritage of the city of Charleston, the State, and the nation. (Charleston, South Carolina, Ordinance, Section 5423)

NEW YORK:

Purpose and declaration of public policy.
  a. The council finds that many improvements, as herein defined, and landscape features, as herein defined, having a special character or a special historical or aesthetic interest or value and many improvements representing the finest architectural products of distinct periods in the history of the city, have been uprooted, notwithstanding the feasibility of preserving and continuing the use of such improvements and landscape features, and without adequate consideration of the irreplaceable loss to the people of the city of the aesthetic, cultural and historic values represented by such improvements and landscape features. In addition distinct areas may be similarly uprooted or may have their distinctiveness destroyed, although the preservation thereof may be both feasible and desirable. It is the sense of the council that the standing of this city as a world-wide tourist center

and world capital of business, culture and government cannot be maintained or enhanced by disregarding the historical and architectural heritage of the city and by countenancing the destruction of such cultural assets.

b. It is hereby declared as a matter of public policy that the protection, enhancement, perpetuation and use of improvements and landscape features of special character or a special historical or aesthetic interest or value is a public necessity and is required in the interest of the health, prosperity, safety and welfare of the people. The purpose of this chapter is to (a) effect and accomplish the protection, enhancement and perpetuation of such improvements and landscape features and of districts which represent or reflect elements of the city's cultural, social, economic, political and architectural history; (b) safeguard the city's historic, aesthetic and cultural heritage, as embodied and reflected in such improvements, landscape features and districts; (c) stabilize and improve property values in such districts; (d) foster civic pride in the beauty and noble accomplishments of the past; (e) protect and enhance the city's attractions to tourists and visitors and the support and stimulus to business and industry thereby provided; (f) strengthen the economy of the city; and (g) promote the use of historic districts, landmarks, interior landmarks and scenic landmarks for the education, pleasure and welfare of the people of the city. (New York, New York, Landmarks Ordinance, Section 205-1.0)

District of Columbia:

(b) It is further declared that the purposes of this act are:
   (1) with respect to the properties in historic districts:
      (A) to retain and enhance those properties which contribute to the character of the historic district and to encourage their adaptation for current use;
      (B) to assure that alterations of existing structures are compatible with the character of the historic district; and
      (C) to assure that new construction and subdivision of lots in an historic district are compatible with the character of the historic district;
   (2) with respect to historic landmarks:
      (A) to retain and enhance historic landmarks in the District of Columbia and to encourage their adaptation for current use; and
      (B) to encourage the restoration of historic landmarks. (District of Columbia Historic Landmark and Historic District Protection Act of 1978, D.C. Law 2-144, Section 2)

Annotation:

Background:

Municipal efforts to preserve architecturally and historically significant structures have been "universally recognized as a legitimate exercise of governmental power."[1] The U.S. Supreme Court has recognized "two concerns" that have led to the enactment of many local preservation ordinances:

> The first is recognition that, in recent years, large numbers of historic structures, landmarks, and areas have been destroyed without adequate consideration of either the values represented therein or the possibility of preserving the destroyed properties for use in economically productive ways. The second is a widely shared belief that structures with special historic, cultural, or architectural significance enhance the quality of life for all. *Penn Central Transportation Company v. New York City*, 438 U.S. 104, 108 (1978).[2]

Need for purpose clause:

Every preservation ordinance should contain a purpose clause stating clearly all of a municipality's reasons for enacting the ordinance. An attempt to invalidate a preservation ordinance as an impermissible use of the police power may succeed if this clause recites improper or inadequate purposes. It should be remembered that although the U. S. Supreme Court has found the New York City Landmarks Preservation Ordinance constitutionally permissible under the U.S. Constitution, a local preservation ordinance must also meet the requirements of an individual state's constitution, which might be in some particulars more stringent than those of the U.S. Constitution. It may be helpful also

---

1. *900 G Street Associates v. Department of Housing and Community Development*, 430 A.2d 1387, 1389 (D.C. App. 1981).
2. In an early but still important preservation decision, a New York State court used similar language to summarize the purposes of the New York City Landmarks Preservation Ordinance:

> This court is well aware of the problem posed by the tendency of property owners in New York City to demolish old and beautiful buildings, which could reasonably be preserved, in order that the owners might harvest a quick profit. Surely the State and City have the power to take reasonable steps to prevent the destruction of the City's heritage and to provide for the preservation of those buildings that may contribute to civic pride, to the education and cultural benefit of the public, and to encouragement of tourism. *Trustees of Sailors' Snug Harbor v. Platt*, 280 N.Y.S.2d 75, 77 (1967).

for a purpose clause to recite briefly the history of a community, as evidence of the need to preserve its surviving heritage.

The purpose clause should be one of the most carefully drafted provisions of the entire preservation ordinance. A well-drafted purpose clause will help to prevent broad attacks on a local preservation ordinance. The Supreme Court stated in *Penn Central* that the validity of New York City's preservation goals was not being challenged:

> Because this Court has recognized, in a number of settings, that States and cities may enact land-use restrictions or controls to enhance the quality of life by preserving the character and desirable aesthetic features of a city . . . appellants do not contest that New York City's objective of preserving structures and areas with special historic, architectural, or cultural significance is an entirely permissible governmental goal. They also do not dispute that the restrictions imposed on its parcel are appropriate means of securing the purposes of the New York City law. 438 U.S. at 129.

The drafter of a purpose clause will quite properly want to look at the clauses of ordinances in municipalities whose preservation programs have been particularly effective and at guidelines in any state enabling legislation, but he must look with equal care and attention to state court decisions involving other preservation or zoning ordinances of communities within his state. If there are no state preservation decisions in his jurisdiction, he will need to draft a purpose clause for a preservation ordinance with even greater care, since he will have no locally approved precedent to follow.

The fewer the state court statements about preservation ordinances that exist, the longer a purpose clause may need to be in order to recite among its list of purposes several that would almost certainly meet with a local court's approval. In states whose courts disapprove of aesthetic zoning, the benefits accruing to the "general welfare" should be highlighted in order to avoid the possible accusation that the purpose clause is solely "aesthetically" motivated.

An Illinois court has held that the enactment of enabling legislation for preservation commissions "essentially created a new concept of public welfare and is a specific declaration by the Legislature that preservation and enhancement of historical areas is within the concept of the exercise of police powers for the public welfare."[3] A Connecticut court has stated that "the preservation of an area or cluster of buildings with exceptional historical and architectural significance may serve the public

---

3. *M & N Enterprises, Inc. v. City of Springfield*, 250 N.E.2d 289, 293 (Ill. 1969).

welfare."[4]

Some courts have found more than one reason for upholding the constitutionality of a challenged local preservation ordinance. In the second of two companion decisions affirming the permissibility of legislative acts similar to preservation ordinances written to permit the creation of historic districts on the island of Nantucket and on Boston's Beacon Hill, the Supreme Judicial Court of Massachusetts noted in 1955 that the proposed act would lead to the educational, cultural, and economic advantage of the public. *Opinion of the Justices to the Senate*, 128 N.E.2d 563 (Mass. 1955). Many local preservation ordinances have since applied this court's language in their purpose clauses by stating that creation of a historic district would have one or all of the three benefits suggested by the court.

A California court similarly upheld a challenged local historic district because of its educational, cultural, and economic benefits. *Bohannan v. City of San Diego*, 106 Cal. Rptr. 333, 336-37 (1973).

A Missouri court articulated the fact that preservation ordinances frequently have more than one valid purpose:

> Historic district ordinances frequently have several bases for enactment. They serve to preserve culturally and historically important aspects of the life of the

---

4. *Figarsky v. Historic District Commission of City of Norwich*, 368 A.2d 163, 170 (Conn. 1976). Despite such strong statements, a trial court in Ohio recently invalidated a local preservation ordinance because evidence presented at trial tended to show that the ordinance was an exercise of police power for aesthetic purposes alone:

> During the hearing on this motion, it was undisputed that the ARO (Architectural Review Ordinance) has done nothing to affect the health and safety of the public. . . . The Planner has no evidence of the enhancement of economic and property values, and she testified on cross-examination that numerous downtown businesses in the Market Square District had left the area. . . . The determination of whether the ordinance is enacted for the principal purpose of aesthetics or for the general welfare of the community depends on the evidence presented at the trial. . . . The ARO does violate the right of the Defendants to hold and protect their property in that the primary purpose of the ordinance is one of aesthetic considerations. *City of Miamisburg v. Hannah* (No. 80 8 CRB 12, Miamisburg Mun. Ct., Feb. 14, 1981), slip op. at 3-4, 6.

But this case, which turned on the city's poor evidentiary record, should be read against an earlier Ohio case, *City of Dayton v. Brewer* (No. 80 CRB 1772, Dayton Mun. Ct., Dec. 8, 1980):

> In requiring maintenance of the historic appearance of the St. Anne's Hill area, the City Commission could quite reasonably have found . . . that preservation of the historic character of the neighborhood would contribute significantly to the general welfare of the City. Slip op. at 1.

locality, state or nation. They sometimes serve to preserve areas which are tourist attractions to the economic benefit of the community. They also can serve an important public function in protecting and preserving definable neighborhoods threatened with urban blight. In so doing, they can provide viability and strength to the urban community as a whole. *Lafayette Park Baptist Church v. Scott*, 553 S.W.2d 856, 861 (Mo. 1977).

At least one court outside Massachusetts has noted that a historic district has educational value, aside from any possible economic benefits. In Michigan, a trial court upheld a local preservation ordinance that had been challenged and did so largely because of the educational value of a historic district:

The history of this State, as found in writing and in display of ancient objects, is essential to a full and adequate education of the people. Education is surely of greatest concern to the community. It follows and this Court finds that the creation and preservation of Historic Districts does contribute to the public welfare and violates no constitutional restraint. *Hall v. Village of Franklin* (No. 69-52580, Oakland County Cir. Ct., Mich., Feb. 10, 1972), slip op. at 3.

Early decisions upholding the constitutionality of local preservation ordinances tended to emphasize nonaesthetic considerations because of the reluctance of most state courts before the 1970s to uphold ordinances solely on aesthetic considerations. Accordingly, a Louisiana court in 1941 upheld the Vieux Carre Ordinance in New Orleans in part because of its likely economic impact:

The preservation of the Vieux Carre as it was originally is a benefit to the inhabitants of New Orleans generally, not only for the sentimental value of this show place but for its commercial value as well, because it attracts tourists and conventions to the city, and is in fact a justification for the slogan, America's most interesting city. *City of New Orleans v. Pergament*, 5 So.2d 129, 131 (La. 1941).

Although the Supreme Judicial Court of Massachusetts held in 1975 in *John Donnelly & Sons, Inc. v. Outdoor Advertising Board*, 339 N.E.2d 709 (Mass. 1975), that "aesthetics alone may justify the exercise of the police power," *id.* at 717, that court had, in 1955, upheld the legislative act that provided for the protection of a historic district on Nantucket on much narrower economic grounds:

We may also take judicial notice . . . that the sedate and quaint appearance of the old island town has to a large extent still remained unspoiled and in all probability constitutes a substantial part of the appeal which has enabled it to build up its summer vacation business to take the place of its former means of livelihood. . . . It is not difficult to imagine how the erection of a few wholly incongruous structures might destroy one of the principal assets of the town.

... *Opinion of the Justices to the Senate*, 128 N.E.2d 557, 562 (Mass. 1955).[5]

At least one court has suggested that cases holding that aesthetic considerations will not support the use of the police power for a preservation ordinance can be distinguished if they did not involve the preservation of a historical area:

> The cases relied upon by defendants deal with purely aesthetic regulations having no connection with preservation of an historical area or an historical style of architecture, and are, accordingly, either distinguishable upon their facts or are not persuasive under the facts of the instant case. *City of Santa Fe v. Gamble-Skogmo, Inc.*, 389 P.2d 13, 17 (N.M. 1964).

The North Carolina Supreme Court held local historic district ordinances to be a valid use of the police power even before holding in *State v. Jones*, 290 S.E.2d 675 (1982), that aesthetics alone may provide a reasonable purpose for exercise of the police power:

> [We] find no difficulty in holding that the police power encompasses the right to control the exterior appearance of private property when the object of such control is the preservation of the State's legacy of historically significant structures. *A-S-P Associates v. City of Raleigh*, 258 S.E.2d 444, 449-50 (N.C. 1979).

The North Carolina court examined at length the ways in which historic preservation activities can promote the general welfare:

> The preservation of historically significant residential and commercial districts protects and promotes the general welfare in distinct yet intricately related ways. It provides a visual, educational medium by which an understanding of our country's historic and cultural heritage may be imparted to present and future generations. That understanding provides in turn a unique and valuable perspective on the social, cultural, and economic mores of past generations of Americans, which remain operative to varying degrees today. . . . Historic preservation moreover serves as a stimulus to protection and promotion of the general welfare in related, more tangible respects. It can stimulate revitalization of deteriorating residential and commercial districts in urban areas, thus contributing to their economic and social stability. . . . It tends to foster architectural creativity by preserving physical examples of outstanding architectural techniques of the past. . . . It also has the potential, documented in numerous instances . . . of generating substantial tourism revenues. *Id.* at 444, 450.

---

5. An Ohio court upheld on economic grounds a local ordinance against a "taking" challenge brought by an owner of property in a local historic district:

> Although the Commission does not advert to it in the relevant R.C.G.O. sections, the historic district designation and maintenance of appearance may also be expected to substantially increase the property values of individual landowners in the area. . . . This is a quite traditional justifying purpose of zoning legislation. *City of Dayton v. Brewer* (No. 80 CRB 1772, Dayton Mun. Ct., Dec. 8, 1980). Slip op. at 2.

II. Creation of a Preservation Commission

A. CREATION OF THE COMMISSION AS A MUNICIPAL ENTITY

Typical Ordinance Provisions:

VIEUX CARRE:

There is hereby created a Commission to be known as the Vieux Carre Commission of the city. (New Orleans, Louisiana, Vieux Carre Ordinance, Section 65-1)

CHARLESTON:

A board of architectural review is hereby established. (Charleston, South Carolina, Ordinance, Section 54-26)

BOSTON:

There shall be in the Boston Redevelopment Authority a Boston Landmarks Commission. . . . (Boston, Massachusetts, Landmarks Ordinance, Section 3)

Annotation:

Normally, preservation commissions are created by municipalities pursuant to state enabling legislation authorizing the creation of such commissions, although some major cities have independent charter or home rule authority. Recently the Maryland Court of Appeals noted at the beginning of an opinion upholding a challenged action of the Chestertown preservation commission that the Chestertown ordinance "is virtually a copy of the State's enabling act." *Faulkner v. Town of Chestertown*, 428 A.2d 879, 880 (Md. 1981).

At least one court in a state without enabling legislation has upheld the authority of municipalities to create preservation commissions under their general zoning authority:

Since the legislature can preserve such historical areas by direct legislation as a measure for the general welfare, it follows that municipal ordinances protecting such areas are authorized under enabling legislation granting power to zone for the public welfare. *City of Santa Fe v. Gamble-Skogmo, Inc.*, 389 P.2d 13, 17 (N.M. 1964).

Near the beginning of a preservation ordinance there should be a sentence creating and naming the preservation commission. Existing preservation commissions are typically called either "historic district commissions" or "landmark commissions" or "boards of architectural review." Local nomenclature should be in conformity with state enabling legislation if any exists.

The North Carolina Supreme Court has held that although a community has discretion to decide whether to create a preservation commission, state enabling legislation establishes the parameters within which a commission may be created:

> The statutory authorization of historic district ordinances is, therefore, a mixture of delegated legislative and administrative power. A municipal governing body has unlimited discretion to determine whether or not to establish a historic district or districts. Once it chooses to do so, however its discretion insofar as the method and the standard by which a historic district ordinance is to be administered is, by contrast, extremely limited. *A-S-P Associates v. City of Raleigh*, 258 S.E.2d 444, 452 (N.C. 1979).

If a community is likely to have more than one historic district, it is preferable to have a single preservation commission rather than a separate preservation commission for each district. Having a single commission will promote uniformity of decisions, even though multiple commissions enable more citizens to become involved in a city's preservation program.

Occasionally, a municipality will wish an existing municipal entity, such as a planning commission, to exercise the functions normally delegated to a separate preservation commission. It is preferable, though, for a preservation commission to have a separate identity within municipal government. Otherwise, its preservation responsibilities may on occasion conflict with its other duties.

A HUD-funded report in Rome, New York, entitled *A Report of Rome's Historical Assets and How to Protect Them,* emphasized the reasons for creating a separate preservation commission:

It is evident that a specially created Board for the sole purpose of administering the Historic and Scenic District would have the time and expertise needed to truly make it work for the Community for the following reasons: Historic Preservation and architectural excellence warrant special and separate attention by the community. Items of this nature should not be merely thrown into multi-caseload agendas; the concern of a Commission would be exclusively the enhancement, perpetuation and preservation of actual landmarks; the Planning Board would retain its caseload of other types of concerns while the Historic and Scenic considerations would receive the complete attention of a separate Board; the Historic Preservation Commission could devise methods such as tax deductions or other incentives to stop demolition of structures which are of historic significance to the Community. (*See* June 1977 *Landmark and Historic District Commissions* newsletter.)

It is highly inadvisable to permit the board of an existing private organization in a community to act ex officio as a preservation commission; the members of a preservation commission should be individually appointed by city officials and not elected by a private organization. Otherwise, difficult conflict-of-interest situations may arise if city goals and the private organization's objectives differ.

Though a few preservation commissions may designate properties as landmarks or historic districts, most preservation commissions have only advisory authority to recommend possible designations to another component of municipal government, frequently a city council.

In a few instances, a preservation commission is established by ordinance within an existing municipal agency, rather than as a totally independent municipal entity. Because it is often difficult for a beginning preservation commission to secure budget authorization for separate staff members, placing the commission within an existing agency will make it possible for existing city staff members to serve as staff for the commission.

Most preservation commissions with a specified position in city government are connected to the city's planning department rather than to a redevelopment agency.

B. COMMISSION MEMBERS: NUMBER, APPOINTMENT, TERMS, AND COMPENSATION

Typical Ordinance Provisions:

Number:

ALEXANDRIA:

[The board is] to be composed of nine members who are residents of the city and have resided in the city or extended limits thereof at least one year next preceding their appointment. . . . (Alexandria, Virginia, Ordinance, Section 42-89)

NEW ORLEANS:

The Commission shall consist initially of nine (9) members, ... For each historic district created by the City Council, not less than one (1) member shall be appointed (whether by appointment or reappointment) who shall be a resident or property owner within said historic district area up to a maximum of fifteen (15) members. (New Orleans, Louisiana, Ordinance, Section II)

OAK PARK, ILLINOIS:

The number of members of such Commission and their terms of office shall be established by the President and Board of Trustees. (Oak Park, Illinois, Ordinance, Section 2)

Appointment:

CHARLESTON:

[There shall be seven members] with five (5) to be appointed by city council and two (2) to be appointed by the Mayor. (Charleston, South Carolina, Ordinance, Section 54-26).

ALEXANDRIA:

[The board is to consist of nine members] eight of whom shall be appointed by the city council. (Alexandria, Virginia, Ordinance, Section 42-89)

LOUISVILLE:

Said Commission shall consist of eleven (11) members, eight (8) of whom shall be appointed by the Mayor subject to the approval of the Board of Aldermen; the remaining members shall be the Director of Building and Housing Inspection of the City of Louisville, the Executive Director of Louisville and Jefferson County Planning Commission, who shall act as Secretary of the Commission, and a member of the Board of Aldermen appointed by the President of the Board. (Louisville, Kentucky, Ordinance, Section 2(a))

Compensation:

LOUISVILLE:

The members shall serve without compensation but shall be reimbursed for expenses necessarily incurred in the performance of their duties. (Louisville, Kentucky, Ordinance, Section 2(c))

Annotation:

Number:

There should be an odd number of members on a preservation commission, in order to minimize the possibility of tie votes. The number of members should not be less than five, and probably should not exceed eleven. Too small a commission will be open to charges of individual bias, and too large a commission may become unwieldy.

Some ordinances require that commission members have resided in the community for a specified number of days or months, while others merely require that commission members be residents of the city. Some ordinances require that commission members either reside within or own property in the historic district created by the ordinance. It is preferable, though, for a preservation commission to be able to benefit from the talents of individuals within the community who might not reside within the district but who have expertise in historic preservation. In smaller communities it may be difficult to require that all commission members be residents.

A few ordinances, in cities with several historic districts, require that there be at least one member on the commission from each designated historic district within the municipality. Accordingly, these ordinances will prescribe both a minimum number of commission members and maximum number. The commission will begin with the minimum number of members, and one member will be added to the commission as each new historic district is designated.

Appointment:

Regardless of what local political decision is made about appointment procedures, such procedures should be detailed carefully in the preservation ordinance. Few provisions in preservation ordinances differ as greatly from ordinance to ordinance as the appointment provision. Some commissions are appointed entirely by a mayor, others entirely by a city council. In certain communities, the mayor appoints some commission members, and the city council appoints others. In a few communities, the mayor and the city council make joint appointments. In others, the mayor appoints commission members subject to the city council's approval.

In many communities, the mayor and the city council are required to appoint commission members from either the memberships of specified organizations or from nominations to be made by such organizations. If appointments are to be made from lists of nominees, each organization should be required to submit the names of at least two nominees for each position under consideration. It is best for commission appointments not to depend on nominations by existing organizations, lest rivalries between such organizations be institutionalized.

Terms:

Commission members tend to serve either three or four-year terms. Ideally, the terms of commission members are staggered to protect the commission from being completely reconstituted by each new municipal administration. If staggered membership is desired, a provision should be included in the ordinance to accomplish this.

Continuity of experience is extremely important if a preservation commission is to be perceived as acting fairly and consistently. Some preservation ordinances prohibit commission members from serving consecutively more than a specified number of years on the commission; others permit commission members to serve indefinitely. In small communities, the replacement of experienced commission members may be undesirable. A decision on this matter should be made as the ordinance is being drafted.

Compensation:

It is unusual for commission members to receive any salary for service to the commission, though commission members are normally reimbursed for expenses they incur while on commission business.

C. REQUIRED QUALIFICATIONS FOR COMMISSION MEMBERS

Typical Ordinance Provisions:

VIEUX CARRE:

The members of the Commission shall be appointed by the Mayor as follows: one from a list of two persons recommended by the Louisiana Historical Society; one from a list of two persons recommended by the Curators of the Louisiana State Museum; one from a list of two persons recommended by the Association of Commerce of the city; three qualified architects from a list of six qualified architects recommended by the New Orleans Chapter of the American Institute of Architects and three at large. (New Orleans, Louisiana, Vieux Carre Ordinance, Section 65-2)

CHARLESTON:

Members appointed by the mayor shall be persons who in the opinion of the mayor have demonstrated outstanding interest and knowledge in historical or architectural development within the city. Members appointed by the city council shall consist of a member of the American Institute of Architects, a member of the Carolina Art Association, a member of the city planning and zoning commission, a member of the American Society of Civil Engineers and a member of the Real Estate Board. In making its appointments, the city council may request and consider recommendations submitted by resident members of such organizations, provided that any persons so recommended shall be residents of the city of Charleston. If any of the organizations requested to make recommendations shall fail to do so within thirty (30) days after a written request therefor by the clerk of council, city council on its own nomination shall appoint the member or members from resident members of such organizations. (Charleston, South Carolina, Ordinance, Section 54-26)

LOUISVILLE:

Of the members to be appointed by the Mayor at least one shall be an architect; at least one shall be an historian qualified in the field of historic preservation; at least one shall be a licensed real estate broker; at least one shall be an attorney; and all members shall have a known interest in historic landmarks and districts preservation. (Louisville, Kentucky, Ordinance, Section 2 (a))

Annotation:

Preservation ordinances typically specify that several members of a preservation commission must have specified professional backgrounds. Such professional requirements are intended to guarantee that the commission will possess, as a body, the knowledge and experience to make informed decisions on the matters that come before it.

In *Penn Central Transportation Company v. New York City*, 438 U.S. 104 (1978), the U. S. Supreme Court characterized with approval the New York City Landmarks Preservation Commission as "broad based" and noted the commission's "prudent tradition" of including attorneys with experience in municipal government. *Id.* at 110. In *Maher v. City of New Orleans*, 516 F.2d 1051 (5th Cir., 1975), the court noted that:

> Another method by which the lawmaking body curbed the possibility for abuse by the Commission was by specifying the composition of that body and its manner of selection. Thus, the City is assured that the Commission includes architects, historians and business persons offering complementary skills, experience and interests. *Id.* at 1062.

Finally, in *South of Second Associates v. Town of Georgetown*, 580 P.2d 807 (Colo. 1978), a court hinted in dicta that membership qualifications should be able to withstand judicial scrutiny:

> Under Ordinance No. 205, the seven-member Commission had to include an architect, the Chairman of the City Planning Commission and the Chairman of the Board of Adjustment. These membership requirements were abolished by Ordinance No. 206 after which Commission members were required only to be residents and property owners within the town of Georgetown. Although the composition of the Commission is a matter exclusively within the municipality's legislative discretion, we note that the membership requirements under Ordinance No. 205 ensured that applications for certificates of appropriateness would be considered by a commission partially composed of persons familiar with architectural styles and zoning provisions in general. Such factors, while not important in the context of the present proceeding, may weigh heavily in a Rule 106 action concerned with an alleged arbitrary enforcement of an otherwise valid ordinance. *Id.* at 808-9, n. 1.

An Ohio trial court recently invalidated a local preservation ordinance in part because of the lack of qualifications for members of the commission:

> In the case of the ARO (Architectural Review Ordinance), the Board is required to have one member appointed from the Community Development Council

and the other four members are to be appointed on the basis of profession or business qualifications and/or by reason of civic interest. . . . In this case, a Board without professional qualifications may or may not grant permission for a proposal upon which it lacks clear standards to either grant or deny that permit. In such a situation, the Board has unregulated authority and may make arbitrary or discriminatory decisions in any instance. *City of Miamisburg v. Hannah* (No. 80 8 CRB 12, Miamisburg Mun. Ct., Ohio, Feb. 14, 1981), slip op. at 8-9.

But this case should be read against an earlier and also unreported Ohio opinion, *City of Dayton v. Brewer* (No. 80 CRB 1772, Dayton Mun. Ct., Ohio, Dec. 8, 1980), in which a property owner had unsuccessfully argued an improper delegation of authority to commission members:

> The Commission has given the Historical Architecture Committee a very plain standard to apply—they do not have to speculate as to legislative purpose or supply a purpose of their own. . . . In reaching [a] decision, this particular committee is gifted with internal expertise, since at least a third of its members must be architects. *Id.*, slip op. at 2.

The most frequently required professionals are (1) an architect, (2) a historian, (3) a real estate expert, (4) an attorney, and (5) an engineer. All commission members should be required to meet the general requirement that they be interested in and knowledgeable about the history of the community.

In addition to possessing certain professional qualifications, commission members may need to meet residence requirements. These are seldom more elaborate than the requirement that the commission's members be residents of the community whose buildings they will be regulating, or that several of the commission's members be residents of any historic district subject to the commission's regulatory authority.

The National Historic Preservation Act of 1966 was amended in 1980 to permit certified local governments to receive federal funding for their historic preservation activities. In order to receive certification, a local government should have a "historic preservation review commission" whose members are chosen from among:

> (A) professionals in the disciplines of architecture, history, architectural history, planning, archeology, or related disciplines, to the extent such professionals are available in the community concerned, and
> (B) such other persons as have demonstrated special interest, experience, or knowledge in history, architecture, or related disciplines and as will provide for an adequate and qualified commission. 16 U.S.C. § 470w(13) (1980).

D. SELECTION OF THE COMMISSION'S OFFICERS

Typical Ordinance Provisions:

LOUISVILLE:

The Mayor shall designate one of the members of the Commission to be Chairman and one to be Vice-Chairman. (Louisville, Kentucky, Ordinance, Section 2(b))

BERKELEY:

The Director of Housing and Development, or his or her representative, shall serve as Secretary of the Commission, without vote. The Department of Housing and Urban Development shall provide staff assistance to the Commission. (Berkeley, California, Ordinance, Section 2(d))

Annotation:

A commission may have the authority to select its own officers from among commission members, or the commission's officers may be designated by a mayor or city council. Occasionally a preservation ordinance will specify that the position of secretary or executive director will be filled ex officio by a specified local official. Regardless of how this local political decision is resolved, a method of selection should be specified in the ordinance creating the preservation commission.

E. STATEMENT OF THE COMMISSION'S POWERS

Typical Ordinance Provisions:

SACRAMENTO:

Unless otherwise specified herein the powers and duties of the board shall be as follows:
a) Adopt criteria for the identification of essential structures, priority structures and preservation areas;
b) Prepare or cause to be prepared a comprehensive inventory of essential structures, priority structures and preservation areas within the Old City;

c) Approve or disapprove applications for permits pursuant to articles VI, VII and VIII of this chapter;
d) Make recommendations to the council concerning the acquisition of development rights, facade easements, and the imposition of other restrictions and the negotiation of historical property contracts for the purposes of historic preservation;
e) Increase public awareness of the value of historic, architectural and cultural preservation by developing and participating in public information programs and by recommending the update of the preservation program;
f) Make recommendations to the council concerning the utilization of grants from federal and state agencies, private groups and individuals and the utilization of budgetary appropriations to promote the preservation of historic or architecturally significant structures in the Old City;
g) Promulgate standards for architectural review;
h) Evaluate and comment upon decisions by other public agencies affecting the physical development and land use patterns in the Old City; and
i) Recommend to the council that the city purchase an essential structure where private preservation is not feasible.
j) Any other functions which may be designated by resolution or motion of the council. (Sacramento, California, City Code, Section 32.208)

ENFIELD, CONNECTICUT:

The Commission shall exercise the powers and responsibilities imposed upon an Historic District Commission by the provisions of the Connecticut General Statutes. (Enfield, Connecticut, Ordinance, Section 7)

LOUISVILLE:

The Commission shall have the power to establish committees as it deems necessary, from both within and without its membership. (Louisville, Kentucky, Ordinance, Section 2(e))

Annotation:

A list of the commission's powers and of required or permitted activities should be included in the preservation ordinance and should indicate clearly that the commission is the municipal agency responsible for developing and coordinating the municipality's historic preservation activities. Some commissions are given the power to acquire property, particularly easements.

Preservation commissions in larger cities will frequently need to establish a number of committees to supervise the preparation of information for consideration by the full commission. Such committees may be set up to study properties for possible designation, to develop guidelines for the commission's use in granting or denying certificates of appropriateness, or to work with property owners whose demolition permit applications are to be delayed or denied.

In *City of New Orleans v. Pergament*, 5 So.2d 129 (La. 1941), a court noted that the city of New Orleans had been empowered by constitutional amendment (rather than by state enabling legislation, the more typical mechanism) to confer upon a local preservation commission "all such powers and duties as the municipal council might deem fit and necessary to carry out the main purpose of preserving the architectural and historical value of the buildings in the Vieux Carre." *Id.* at 131.

In its first case considering the constitutionality of "historic district preservation," the North Carolina Supreme Court was careful to point out the controlling role of state enabling legislation:

> A historic district commission's action is limited by G.S. Sec. 160A-397 to "preventing the construction, reconstruction, alteration, restoration, or moving of buildings, structures, appurtenant fixtures, or outdoor advertising signs in the historic district which would be incongruous with the historic aspects of the district." *A-S-P Associates v. City of Raleigh*, 258 S.E.2d 444, 446 (N.C. 1979).

In some states, local ordinances incorporate by reference those provisions in state enabling legislation that define the power a local preservation commission may exercise. Incorporation by reference may shorten a local ordinance but make it more difficult for interested citizens to learn the powers of a preservation commission. For this reason, incorporation by reference is inadvisable. A local commission's powers should be listed in the local ordinance, even if the ordinance is supplemented in part by rules of procedure.

In general, the longer preservation ordinances are the more carefully drafted. Too brief an ordinance may invite litigation.

F. COMMISSION'S POWER TO ADOPT RULES OF PROCEDURE

Typical Ordinance Provisions:

VICKSBURG, MISSISSIPPI:

> The Board has the authority to promulgate and publish such additional rules and regulations as it deems necessary to discharge its responsibilities including,

but not limited to, the providing of additional procedures for a faster disposition of applications before the Board so long as the legal rights of applicants, this municipality and the general public are fully protected. (Vicksburg, Mississippi, Ordinance, Section 7(D))

LOUISVILLE:

The Commission shall have the authority to adopt all rules and regulations necessary to carry out its functions under the provisions of this Ordinance. Every such rule and regulation shall be submitted to the Board of Aldermen of the City of Louisville for approval or rejection. (Louisville, Kentucky, Ordinance, Section 2(g))

SALISBURY, NORTH CAROLINA:

The Historic District Commission shall develop and adopt rules of procedure which shall govern the conduct of its business in accordance with the provisions of this ordinance. Such rules of procedure shall also include as an appendix an illustrated portfolio including photographs, illustrations, color charts, descriptions, and other similar material interpreting the criteria for determining appropriateness as set out in Section 8.18 of this ordinance. Such appendix shall be placed on file in the Salisbury City Offices and made available to the general public during the regular City Office business hours. (Salisbury, North Carolina, Ordinance, Section 12A. 04)

Annotation:

Because it is easier to amend a preservation commission's rules of procedure than to amend the ordinance creating the commission, permitting the commission to adopt rules of procedure will give the commission necessary operating flexibility.

Even if the state enabling legislation authorizing the creation of a preservation commission is quite detailed and the local ordinance creating a commission duplicates its provisions, the local ordinance should permit a commission to adopt rules of procedure just as a private organization would adopt bylaws.

A commission subject to a requirement to submit its rules to the city council for approval before they become effective must be careful to comply.

It is important that a commission draft and adopt rules of procedure as soon as possible; otherwise the commission may be unable to function at all, or will function less effectively than it might. In *Blackmer v. Salisbury Zoning Board of Adjustment* (No. 76 CVS 313, Rowan County Sup. Ct., May 4, 1976), an unreported 1976 trial court opinion in North Carolina, a court noted the Salisbury ordinance's requirement for the adoption of rules of procedure and held a portion of the ordinance unenforceable until the rules of procedure were adopted.

G. COMMISSION'S AUTHORITY TO EMPLOY STAFF AND CONSULTANTS

Typical Ordinance Provisions:

TRENTON:

Within the limits of funds appropriated generally for the performance of its work, the commission may obtain the services of qualified persons to direct, advise and assist the commission and may obtain the equipment, supplies and other material necessary to its effective operation. (Trenton, New Jersey, Ordinance, Section 2-22.4 (c) (4))

BOSTON:

Without regard to chapter thirty-one of the General Laws, the Boston Redevelopment Authority shall provide the commission with an administrative staff acceptable to the commission and adequate to carry on the functions of the commission as provided for in this act. Such staff shall be employees of the Boston Redevelopment Authority. Notwithstanding the foregoing the commission may contract directly for such professional and expert technical assistance as such business shall require. (Boston, Massachusetts, Landmarks Ordinance, Section 3)

Annotation:

A similar provision about municipal employees should be included whenever a commisson's budget can be expected to be large enough to permit the commission to hire an executive director or secretary. Selection and hiring should be in conformity with local civil service practices. Many commissions operate with staff assigned to them from other municipal agencies, such as the planning department or a community development agency. This is likely to be the case with commissions whose authority is advisory only.

H. COMMISSION'S AUTHORITY TO RECEIVE FUNDING FROM VARIOUS SOURCES

Typical Ordinance Provisions:

LOUISVILLE:

The Commission, in addition to the appropriations made by the City of Louisville, shall have the right to receive, hold, and spend funds which it may legally receive from any and every source both in and out of the Commonwealth of Kentucky for the purpose of carrying out the provisions of this Ordinance subject to the provisions of Subsection b of this section. (Louisville, Kentucky, Ordinance, Section 2(f))

BOSTON:

In the name of the city and in order to effect the purposes of this act, the commission may, with the consent of the mayor and council, apply for any gift or grant of any property and any form of subvention and subject to the consent of the mayor and council, may receive any such gift, grant, or subvention and acquire by gift, purchase, grant, bequest, devise, lease, or otherwise the fee, any lesser interest, development right, easement, including any scenic easement, covenant, or other contractual right, including conveyances on conditions or with limitations or reversions, in any property in the city. The commission may, with the consent of the mayor and council, apply for, receive, or expend any federal, state or private grant, grant-in-aid, gift or bequest, in furtherance of the general purposes of this act, and, with consent of the mayor and council, may, notwithstanding any provision of law or ordinance to the contrary, for the purpose of matching or qualifying for such a grant, grant-in-aid, gift or bequest, obligate the expenditure of funds which the commission may have, or have appropriated to it, whether or not the same is to be spent within the then current municipal or fiscal year. (Boston, Massachusetts, Landmarks Ordinance, Section 11)

Annotation:

Few preservation commissions are able to obtain municipal appropriations as large as they would desire. A preservation commission should have the authority to accept donations from other sources and will want to point out to potential donors that the commission, as a governmental agency, enables donors to enjoy the favorable tax consequences of a contribution to a Section 501(c)(3) organization. (IRS Code, Section 170 (c)(1)) The commission should attempt to ensure that funds raised from private sources can be added to the commission's existing budget and will not displace appropriated governmental funds or be added to a governmental unit's general fund. It may be helpful for a preservation commission to be authorized to maintain a small checking account for petty cash expenditures. In some communities, auxiliary organizations have been created to solicit operating funds for a commission to supplement monies appropriated by the local government. The Friends of the Cleveland Landmarks Commission, Inc., has been formed "to maintain an association of persons who are interested in increasing, improving, and making better known the resources and services of The Cleveland Landmarks Commission." (*See* April 1977 *Landmark and Historic District Commissions* newsletter.)

Preservation commissions will want to stay aware of funding available through state or federal agencies and should determine which local, regional, or national foundations and corporations have an interest in historic preservation and could be encouraged to assist the commission by funding a publication or underwriting the expenses of a survey.

I. RECORDS OF COMMISSION MEETINGS

Typical Ordinance Provisions:

BOULDER:

A record shall be kept of pertinent information presented at all public hearings. A verbatim record may be made by any interested party but shall not be required unless directed by the Board. (Boulder, Colorado, Ordinance, Section 51-202(c))

CHICAGO:

The Commission on Chicago Historical and Architectural Landmarks shall keep minutes of all its proceedings showing the vote of each member upon each question, or if absent or failing to vote, indicating such fact. All records of the Commission shall be kept by the Secretary at the office of the Commission. Public records shall be made available for inspection, but in no instance shall any record be removed from the office unless so directed by court order and accompanied by a representative of the Secretary. Photostatic copies of public records may be obtained upon written request and the cost of such copies shall be borne by the person or persons requesting same. (Chicago, Illinois, Rules of Procedure, Article I (D))

Annotation:

Although relatively few commissions have been involved in litigation, it is essential that a preservation commission keep careful records of its actions. Full commission records are particularly necessary when a commission has denied a certificate of appropriateness.

If possible, commissions should act by resolution, and written resolutions should be prepared in advance of commission meetings for routine matters to which opposition is not expected. When a commission acts after a public hearing in which comments were made by a number of parties on both sides of an issue, it is important that the commission record its reasons for its action. Recorded minutes should state clearly the actions taken by the preservation commission at each of its meetings, and ideally will indicate by reference to the preservation ordinance the authority under which each action was taken, the findings made by the commission, and the criteria met by those findings.

In an early Rhode Island case, a reviewing court noted incidentally the inadequacy of the commission's records:

> The record before us does not disclose the identity of those who spoke in favor of or in opposition to the application of the church, but it does contain a brief summary thereof which was made by the secretary of the commission. . . . The record is silent as to the reasons for the rejection. *Hayes v. Smith*, 167 A.2d 546, 547-48 (R.I. 1961).

In *Equitable Funding Corporation v. Spatt* (No. 12832/77, Kings County Sup. Ct., Feb. 8, 1978), an unreported 1978 New York decision, a trial court held that the New York City Landmarks Preservation Commission had violated its own ordinance by failing to give reasons for the denial of a certificate of appropriateness. The matter was remanded to the commission for reconsideration.

If a commission senses that a property owner may wish to challenge by litigation a commission decision, the commission may need to employ the services of a professional stenographer to prepare a full transcript of the hearing. Some commissions routinely tape all of their meetings.

J. COMMISSION'S AUTHORITY TO REQUEST INFORMATION FROM OTHER GOVERNMENTAL AGENCIES

Typical Ordinance Provision:

LOUISVILLE:

In accordance with the powers, duties and responsibilities imposed on the Commission by this Ordinance, the Commission shall have the power and authority to request and receive any appropriate information, cooperation, assistance or studies from any city departments, boards, agencies or commissions and any joint city-county departments, boards, agencies or commissions. (Louisville, Kentucky, Ordinance, Section 3(b))

Annotation:

It is important that commissions establish good working relationships with other components of city government. This provision, though it should not have to be invoked, will give a preservation commission additional authority. A commission should be careful, though, not to abuse its right to request the cooperation of other city agencies. Assistance from other parts of city government will be essential when a designated building is threatened with destruction and a commission is seeking facts for the development of alternative solutions to the problem.

K. ANNUAL REPORT BY COMMISSION

Typical Ordinance Provision:

LOUISVILLE:

The Commission shall submit an annual report of its activities to the Mayor and submit an annual budget to the Mayor and the Board of Aldermen for approval. (Louisville, Kentucky, Ordinance, Section 2(b))

Annotation:

It is helpful for a commission, particularly one in a large community, to prepare an annual report detailing, in at least brief statistical fashion, the matters that have come before it for decision during the previous year. Particularly controversial matters may merit individual discussion in the report, or decisions may be treated in categories: alterations permitted or denied, new construction permitted or denied, and demolitions permitted or denied. Because a preservation commission is a governmental entity, it is important that a commission develop a history of its activities and policies that can serve as precedents for making future decisions. New commission members will find past annual reports extremely useful, and a community's residents are less likely to resist the actions of a commission whose goals and activities are regularly summarized.

An effective annual report should state the number of designations made by the commission during the previous year. It might also enumerate other activities during the year, such as surveys conducted or programs sponsored, as these are an important aspect of a preservation commission's overall effectiveness. A commission should be encouraged to forecast its projects for the following year.

Annual reports that convey full information about a commission's work may be useful when budget decisions affecting the commission must be made. Informed city officials are more likely to understand a commission's staffing and budgetary needs than are officials only slightly aware of a commission's goals and accomplishments.

III. Designation of Historic Districts and Landmarks

A. PRELIMINARY RESEARCH BY COMMISSION

a. Commission's Mandate to Conduct a Survey of Local Historical Resources

Typical Ordinance Provisions:

LOUISVILLE:

In addition to such other powers . . . the Commission shall (1) Conduct a general study and survey of neighborhoods, areas, places, structures and improvements within the City of Louisville for the purpose of determining those of distinctive character or special historic, aesthetic, architectural, archaeological or cultural interest or value and of compiling appropriate descriptions, facts and lists. In accomplishing such a study and survey, the Commission shall place particular emphasis upon evaluating and incorporating the findings of studies and surveys already completed and upon preserving the oral history of the community by appropriate methods. (Louisville, Kentucky, Ordinance, Section 3(a)(1))

BERKELEY:

The Commission shall (1) After the effective date of this ordinance, undertake to establish and maintain a list of structures, sites and areas having a special historical, architectural or aesthetic interest or value. This list may include single structures or sites, portions of structures, groups of structures, man-made or natural landscape elements, works of art, or integrated combinations thereof. After public hearings, the Commission may designate landmarks and historic districts from said list. In the establishment of the foregoing list, the Commission shall notify and solicit the views of property owners and residents of structures, sites and areas proposed by the Commission to be included in such a list. (Berkeley, California, Ordinance, Section 2(g))

Annotation:

Though not all preservation commissions are required by ordinance to conduct formal surveys of an entire community before beginning to designate properties as landmarks or historic districts, it is well for a preservation commission to have the explicit authority to conduct surveys. If a commission has such authority, no question can be raised about the propriety of its spending a portion of its budget for a survey. The U. S. Supreme Court noted in *Penn Central Transportation Company v. New York City*, 438 U.S. 104 (1978), that the "function . . . of identifying properties and areas" with architectural or historical significance is "critical to any landmark preservation effort." *Id.* at 110.

Preservation surveys are useful for two reasons: they help to ensure that designation decisions made by a preservation commission are made objectively, and they ensure consideration and evaluation of the surviving architectural resources of an entire community.

A preservation commission should be encouraged to build upon the research that may already have been done by other local groups on a community's history and architecture. National Register nominations of local properties and Historic American Buildings Survey (HABS) or Historic American Engineering Record (HAER) records should suggest buildings or districts to be designated. A preservation commission will want to develop a reciprocal working relationship with the state historic preservation officer so that research information is shared for local designation or National Register nomination purposes.

b. **Commission's Power to Recommend Districts and Buildings to City Council for Designation**

Typical Ordinance Provision:

CHICAGO:

The Commission on Chicago Historical and Architectural Landmarks shall have the responsibility of recommending to the City Council the adoption of ordinances designating areas, places, buildings, structures, works of art and other objects having a special historical, community or aesthetic interest or value as "Chicago Landmarks," thereby necessitating their preservation, protection, enhancement, rehabilitation and perpetuation. (Chicago, Illinois, Rules of Procedure, Article II (A))

Annotation:

If a commission does not itself have the power to designate landmarks and historic districts, it can make advisory recommendations to another group, generally a city council, that does have the power. The responsibility of a preservation commission to make such advisory recommendations should be specified in the ordinance creating the commission, so that persons interested in the commission's activities will understand that the commission's recommendations are not binding until ratified by the city council.

c. **Preparation of Report on Proposed Designation**

Typical Ordinance Provision:

BOSTON:

Prior to the designation or amendment of designation of any landmark, landmark district, architectural conservation district or protection area, an investigation and report on the historical and architectural significance of the structures, sites or objects to be designated shall be made. Such report will also attempt to provide an indication of the economic status of the property or properties under consideration for designation by providing such information as assessed value, recent real estate transactions or other appropriate data. The report shall also recommend the boundaries of any proposed landmark, landmark district, architectural conservation district or protection area and recommend standards to be adopted by the commission in carrying out its regulatory functions provided under section five of this act. All recommendations shall be made in consideration of any master plan, zoning requirements, projected public improvements and existing and proposed renewal and development plans applicable to the section of the city to be affected by the designation or amendment of designation. (Boston, Massachusetts, Landmarks Ordinance, Section 4)

Annotation:

Some commissions are required to prepare formal reports on proposed designations in advance of the scheduled hearings. Such reports may be extremely useful to the commission because they can be used to educate both a property owner and an entire community to the significance of the property in question. After designation, an initial report may help a preservation commission monitor changes to the designated district or landmark structure and may eventually help document the beneficial effects of designation.

It is important to prepare material at the time the commission acts so that there will be a permanent record giving the basis for the designation. At a later date, the courts and others will give great weight to a decision in which the commission had evidence in front of it:

> There is no merit to petitioner's contention that the determination is unsupported by substantial evidence. A hearing was held and the issue thoroughly aired. The architectural, historical and aesthetic value of the improvement was fully established, and the court may not substitute its judgment for that of the administrative agency. . . . *Manhattan Club v. New York City Landmarks Preservation Commission*, 273 N.Y.S.2d 848, 851 (1966).

B. DESIGNATION OF HISTORIC DISTRICTS

a. Criteria for Selection of Historic Districts

Typical Ordinance Provision:

SEATTLE:

Standards for Designation of Structures and Districts for Preservation. A structure, group of structures, site or district may be designated for preservation as a landmark or landmark district if it:

Historical, Cultural Importance

(1) has significant character, interest or value, as part of the development, heritage or
(2) is the site of an historic event with a significant effect upon society; or
(3) exemplifies the cultural, political, economic, social or historic heritage of the community; or

Architectural, Engineering Importance

(4) portrays the environment in an era of history characterized by a distinctive architectural style; or
(5) embodies those distinguishing characteristics of an architectural-type or engineering specimen; or
(6) is the work of a designer whose individual work has significantly influenced the development of Seattle; or

(7) contains elements of design, detail, materials or craftsmanship which represent a significant innovation; or

Geographic Importance

(8) by being part of or related to a square, park or other distinctive area, should be developed or preserved according to a plan based on an historic, cultural or architectural motif; or
(9) owing to its unique location or singular physical characteristic, represents an established and familiar visual feature of the neighborhood, community or city; or

Archeological Importance

(10) has yielded, or may be likely to yield, information important in pre-history or history. (Seattle, Washington, Landmarks Ordinance No. 102229, Section 6)

Annotation:

The necessity for such criteria will vary from state to state. Although an ordinance with broad criteria might be challenged in one state as insufficiently specific, the same ordinance might satisfy judicial requirements in another state. The local attorney who drafts the preservation ordinance will want to take a careful look at judicial requirements for specificity of criteria in his state. Once criteria have been developed, a commission should refer to them whenever a district is being designated so that in case of a court challenge the administrative record will show that the criteria were followed.

Increasingly, historic districts are collections of buildings, few of which may be individually of outstanding significance but the group of which have a distinctive ambience that is worth maintaining. The phrase "tout ensemble" has often been used to describe the totality of an architecturally or historically unique neighborhood. The phrase, as applied to historic preservation, comes from a 1941 decision of the Supreme Court of Louisiana, *City of New Orleans v. Pergament*, 5 So.2d 129, which upheld the authority of a preservation commission to regulate all buildings within a designated historic district. Too specific a set of criteria may make it impossible for certain types of interesting older neighborhoods to be protected by historic district designation. Drafters of a preservation ordinance should consider local potential for historic districts and should not create criteria that cannot be met.

b. Boundaries of Historic Districts

Typical Ordinance Provision:

CHARLESTON:

For the purposes of this Article, two types of special districts are established, as follows:
(a) The old city. The boundaries of the old city district shall include the entire peninsular city of the city of Charleston, south of Line Street and south of lines projected from the eastern and western ends of Line Street, in easterly and westerly directions to the Ashley and Cooper Rivers, excluding the old and historic districts.
(b) Old and historic districts. The boundaries of the old and historic districts are as delineated upon the zone map, a part of the zoning ordinance of the city of Charleston. (Charleston, South Carolina, Ordinance, Section 54-24)

Annotation:

An ordinance creating a preservation commission to regulate a historic district should specify the boundaries of the district. An ordinance creating a preservation commission to designate both individual landmark structures and historic districts will not contain district boundaries; such boundaries will be specified in the separate ordinances designating local historic districts. The boundaries of a historic district must be carefully specified. An ordinance may refer to a zoning map on which the boundaries of the historic district are clearly indicated. For some historic districts, it is possible to draw lines which follow existing street patterns, and to list the district's boundaries as running along these streets. For other historic districts, the boundaries must be much more detailed and will approximate the listing of boundary lines in a deed.

One court has noted the importance of carefully drawn boundaries for a historic district:

> The clear purpose of defining the boundaries of the Vieux Carre was to enable the city and commission not only to preserve historically and architecturally significant buildings themselves, but to enable that authority to exercise "reasonable control" over all other buildings within the Vieux Carre in order that their use would not destroy the "quaint and distinctive character" of the Vieux Carre. *Vieux Carre Property Owners and Associates, Inc. v. City of New Orleans*, 167 So.2d 367, 374 (La. 1964).

A thorough discussion of the decisions that must be made in setting the boundaries for a historic district is contained in the National Trust publication *A Guide to Delineating Edges of Historic Districts.* Among the factors to be considered are (1) historic factors, (2) visual factors, (3) physical factors, (4) surveyed lines and lines of convenience, and (5) political, economic, and social factors.

Care should be taken that the boundaries specified in necessary legal notices published in advance of public hearings coincide with the boundaries of a district as designated or are larger than such final boundaries. Otherwise a property owner may later decide to challenge the inclusion of his property within a historic district by alleging that he received no notice or inadequate notice of the proposed creation of a historic district.

A California property owner was unsuccessful in an attempt to argue that the boundaries of a local historic district were too extensive: "The city council is authorized to determine the boundaries of the area subject to control, and the court should not interfere with its determination absent a clear showing of abuse of its authority." *Bohannan v. City of San Diego*, 106 Cal. Rptr. 333, 336 (Cal. 1973).

The North Carolina Supreme Court has upheld inclusion of a vacant lot within a historic district even though the lot is on the district's boundary:

> In drawing the boundaries of the Historic District the City merely decided not to include certain property owned by the Medical Society, while including that owned by Associates and others in the same block. . . . [We] cannot say that the superior court erred in its conclusion of law that a reasonable basis existed for the exclusion of the Medical Society's property while other property in the same block was included in the Historic District. . . . Exclusion from the Historic District of only that property owned by the Medical Society on which its building is located might have been a wiser choice. But it is well settled that legislative bodies may make rational distinctions with substantially less than mathematical exactitude. *A-S-P Associates v. City of Raleigh*, 258 S.E.2d 444, 447 (N.C. 1979).

c. Evaluation of Properties within Historic Districts

Typical Ordinance Provisions:

SAVANNAH:

Classification of buildings and structures: Within the Historic District, all buildings and structures shall be classified and designated on the Historic

A40   A HANDBOOK ON HISTORIC PRESERVATION LAW

Building Map adopted and approved by the Mayor and Aldermen and made a part of the zoning map. Such buildings and structures shall be divided into two (2) classes:

1. Historic: Those buildings classified as Historic shall possess identified historical or architectural merit of a degree warranting their preservation. They shall be further classified as:
    A. Exceptional
    B. Excellent
    C. Notable
    D. Of value as part of the scene
2. Contemporary: Those buildings and structures not classified on the Historic Building Map as Exceptional, Excellent, Notable, or Of value as part of the scene. (Savannah, Georgia, Ordinance, Section 4)

New Haven:

The Commission should have PRIORITY LISTS for all buildings in the historic district(s). *Top priority:* all plaqued structures in those buildings which conform to the criteria set down by the Connecticut Historical Commission's regulations, particularly items 1, 2, and 4. *Middle priority:* buildings not individually of great merit but harmonious and appropriate to the whole restoration. *Low priority:* mutilated buildings beyond reasonable hope for restoration. The latter may be torn down and new structures erected, provided that the new structures, even if in a different architectural style, are harmonious to the whole district and appropriate in such elements as setbacks, massing, height, and scale. (New Haven, Connecticut, Rules of Procedure, Section II(B))

Mansfield, Connecticut:

As soon as practicable, the Historic District Commission shall compile the pertinent data on each property in each Historic District and prepare an evaluation sheet, taking into consideration historical and architectural values and significance, architectural style, general design, texture and materials of the building, and its features, relationship of the building and its features to the immediate neighborhood, and the importance of the building to the neighborhood. The information on these evaluation sheets shall be reviewed periodically. (Mansfield, Connecticut, Rules and Regulations, Section 12)

Annotation:

Several ordinances require a preservation commission to evaluate and rate all properties within a historic district. Such ordinances frequently create categories within which all properties in the district must be ranked. Occasionally demolition delays are keyed to these individual categories, and delay lengths will depend on the different categories.

The disadvantage of categories is that the lowest category may be seen by antagonists to historic preservation as a "hunting license" on the buildings within that category, though occasionally a commission will want to identify nonconforming structures whose removal or demolition it would approve. Once buildings have been listed by a preservation commission as of least importance within a historic district, pressures for their alteration or demolition may begin to mount. Several court cases have established the principle that a historic district commission may regulate changes to or the proposed demolition of architecturally and historically undistinguished properties in order to protect the "tout ensemble" of the entire district. For this reason, the initial official evaluation of all properties within the district may undermine the purposes of a preservation ordinance if by ranking buildings it suggests that buildings in the lowest categories are expendable. The commission should be able to make individual decisions on demolition applications as they come before it after a district has been designated; such decisions should not be made as a survey is conducted.

A professional preservation survey which has identified the architectural style of each structure within a proposed historic district but has not rated the buildings can be useful because it will give information to both the commission and building owners to help them develop acceptable proposals for renovation or rehabilitation.

d. Affirmation of Existing Zoning

Typical Ordinance Provision:

NEW HAVEN:

Nothing contained herein shall supersede the powers of other local legislative or regulatory bodies or relieve any property owner of complying with the requirements of any other state statutes or municipal ordinances or regulations. (New Haven, Connecticut, Ordinance, Section 4)

Annotation:

A provision affirming or recognizing existing zoning may stem from the awareness that a preservation ordinance is a maintenance ordinance, whereas more traditional zoning ordinances are frequently only use ordinances combined with size or setback requirements for new construction:

> First of all, traditional zoning is primarily directed at the use of land, as well as the *density* and the *location* of buildings on the land. Historic area zoning, on the other hand, is not directed at any of these factors, but *only* at the preservation of the *exterior* of *buildings* having *historic or architectural merit. Mayor and Aldermen of City of Annapolis v. Anne Arundel County*, 316 A.2d 807, 821 (Md. 1974)

A provision affirming existing zoning in a community is not approval of existing zoning, nor does it preclude the municipality from later amending the list of permitted uses in a designated historic district. It merely states that previous local zoning laws, insofar as they are not expressly affected by the ordinance creating a preservation commission and designating a historic district, remain in effect until modified.

The North Carolina Supreme Court pointed out, in an introduction to a 1979 opinion, that in North Carolina a local historic district is an overlay zoning district:

> The Historic District thus created is an overlay zoning district. All zoning regulations in the area in effect prior to passage of the Oakwood Ordinance remain in effect.... That the creation of an overlay historic district may impose additional regulations on some property within an underlying use-district and not on all of the property within it, does not destroy the uniformity of the regulations applicable to the underlying use-district.... *A-S-P Associates v. City of Raleigh*, 258 S.E. 2d 444, 447, 458-59 (N.C. 1979).

Once a local historic district has been designated, it may be advisable to review existing zoning ordinances to ensure their compatibility with a community's announced intention to develop an effective historic preservation program for the designated district. In a few communities, designation of a property qualifies it for additional, but conditional uses. Denver has enacted a Use-Exception Ordinance that authorizes the Zoning Board of Adjustment to permit designated structures to be used for office or gallery space. (*Historic Denver News*, October 1977) As of 1977, at least thirteen Denver structures had benefited from such an exception.

A New York trial court has held that an amendment increasing the number of allowable special uses in a historic district can require an environmental impact statement under the New York State Environmental Quality Review Act:

> Additionally, the purpose of the H-4 district is to promote, maintain, and enhance historic medium to high density residential neighborhoods located within a preservation district.... Retail businesses are excluded from the adop-

tive uses permitted in the H-4 district. The amendment to the zoning ordinance would not only permit luxury hotels to be established but would also permit drug stores, beauty shops, newsstands, health clubs, restaurants and bars, subject to a special permit. Consideration was not given to the fact that the amendment, on its face, conflicts with the community's existing plans as officially adopted and what the environmental impact of that conflict may be. *Kravetz v. Plenge*, 424 N.Y.S.2d 312, 317-18 (1979).

C. DESIGNATION OF LANDMARKS

a. Criteria for Selection of Landmarks

Typical Ordinance Provisions:

NEW YORK:

Interior Landmark: An interior, or part thereof, any part of which is thirty years old or older, and which is customarily open or accessible to the public, or to which the public is customarily invited [not including interiors utilized as places of religious worship], and which has a special historical or aesthetic interest or value as part of the development, heritage or cultural characteristics of the city, state or nation and which has been designated as an interior landmark pursuant to the provisions of this chapter.

Landmark. Any improvement, any part of which is thirty years old or older, which has a special character or special historical or aesthetic interest or value as part of the development, heritage or cultural characteristics of the city, state or nation and which has been designated as a landmark pursuant to the provisions of this chapter.

Landmark Site: An improvement parcel or part thereof on which is situated a landmark and any abutting improvement parcel or part thereof used as and constituting part of the premises on which the landmark is situated, and which has been designated as a landmark site pursuant to the provisions of this chapter.

Scenic Landmark: Any landscape feature or aggregate of landscape features, any part of which is thirty years [old] or older [located on property owned by the city], which has or have a special character or special historical or aesthetic interest or value as part of the development, heritage or cultural characteristics of the city, state or nation and which has been designated a scenic landmark pursuant to the provisions of this chapter. (New York, New York, Landmarks Ordinance, Sections 207-1.0(m)-(o) and 207-1.0(w))

BOSTON:

The commission may designate any improvement or physical feature as a landmark, and may designate any area in the city as a landmark district, or architectural conservation district and may amend any such designation as herein provided upon a finding by the commission that the designation or amendment meets any of the following criteria: (a) inclusion in National Register of Historic Places as provided in the National Historic Preservation Act of 1966; (b) structures, sites, objects, man-made or natural, at which events occurred that have made an outstanding contribution to, and are identified prominently with, or which best represent some important aspect of the cultural, political, economic, military, or social history of the city, the commonwealth, the New England region or the nation; (c) structures, sites, objects, man-made or natural, associated significantly with the lives of outstanding historic personages; (d) structures, sites, objects, man-made or natural, representative of elements of architectural or landscape design or craftsmanship which embody distinctive characteristics of a type inherently valuable for study of a period, style or method of construction or development, or a notable work of an architect, landscape architect, designer, or builder whose work influenced the development of the city, the commonwealth, the New England region, or the nation. (Boston, Massachusetts, Landmarks Ordinance, Section 4)

Annotation:

Preservation commissions must follow designation criteria carefully in making their decisions, so that the administrative record before a reviewing court will show clearly that the commission's decision to designate was an objective and professional one. A New York trial court upheld the designation of the New York Yacht Club against a challenge that the New York City Landmarks Preservation Commission had mistakenly found that the structure possessed characteristics warranting landmark status:

The claim by petitioner that there is no rational basis for the designation is self-serving at best. The Commission found that the building, the first New York commission of the noted architectural firm of Warren & Wetmore, is a classic example of Beaux-Arts design and a historic symbol of the nation's oldest yachting organization. There is ample evidence in the report to support the finding of the Commission's architectural and historical expert that the Club possesses value as part of the heritage of this City . . . and accordingly, this Court may not disturb that finding. . . . *New York Yacht Club v. Landmarks Preservation Commission of City of New York* (No. 550/80, New York County Sup. Ct., Feb. 13, 1980), slip op. at 2.

No preservation ordinance that will permit the designation of landmarks should fail to include criteria for the selection of landmarks. A

Texas court invalidated a portion of the Austin preservation ordinance because it did not contain adequate criteria for the selection of potential landmarks:

> Another defect in Section 45-51.1 is its complete lack of standards for guidance of the persons who may place its restrictions on landowners merely by listing their property on the Commission's agenda. *Southern National Bank of Houston v. City of Austin*, 582 S.W.2d 229, 239 (Tex. App. 1979).

In some communities criteria will be quite broadly worded because of the wide range of buildings likely to be considered for designation. The drafter of an ordinance should realize that older commercial buildings can be a community's most distinguished architectural resources.

Some preservation commissions are required to develop predesignation files for buildings whose designation is under consideration. Listed criteria should permit the designation of some landmarks whose significance is primarily local, as well as of others with regional or national significance.

If a preservation commission does not have the power to designate landmarks itself but must recommend designation to another body, the commission should maintain its credibility by recommending only buildings clearly qualified for landmark status.

The United States Supreme Court has noted in *Penn Central Transportation Company v. New York City*, 438 U.S. 104 (1978), that the process of designating landmarks "is a continuing one." *Id.* at 111. A commission should not plan to designate one long list of landmarks at one time and then cease considering possible additional designations.

b. Boundary Description

Typical Provision:

AUSTIN:

Chapter 45 of the Austin City Code of 1967 is hereby amended to change the USE designation from "C-2" Commercial District to "C-2-H" Commercial Historic District on the property described in File C14h-74-018; to wit: The North 12' × 80' and the South 34' × 100' of the east part of Lot 9, the North 22 feet of the East 100 feet, and the South 24 feet, of Lot 10; and all of Lots 11 and 12, Block 69, of the Original City of Austin, as recorded in Volume

4046, at Page 1364, of the Deed Records of Travis County, Texas.

Annotation:

A preservation commission should not inadvertently designate both a landmark structure and a portion of a nearby building, lest the owner of the nearby building join in any attack on the landmark designation. Similarly, a preservation commission must be careful to designate an entire landmark structure, unless the commission intends to designate only selected portions of the structure. Deed descriptions may be misleading if the site of a landmark structure has been assembled or subdivided. A careful reading of recent deed descriptions and a tour of the site of a proposed landmark may indicate any discrepancy between the descriptions and the actual configuration of the building.

D. GENERAL MATTERS AFFECTING DESIGNATION OF BOTH HISTORIC DISTRICTS AND LANDMARKS

a. Commission's Jurisdiction to Designate May Not Cover All Local Structures

Typical Ordinance Provision:

SPRINGFIELD, MASSACHUSETTS:

In accordance with section 8, paragraph b of said Historic Districts Act, so called, the authority of said Commission shall, however be limited so as not to extend to any buildings, structures or properties however owned or controlled by the Springfield Library and Museum Association and Roman Catholic Bishop of the Diocese of Springfield. (Springfield, Massachusetts, Ordinance, Section 27-2)

Annotation:

Only rarely does a local preservation ordinance specify that certain categories of buildings may not be designated. A more typical question is whether a commission may designate properties that are in county, state or federal ownership. As to federal buildings, it must be remembered that structures eligible for listing in the National Register of Historic Places receive some protection under Section 106 of the National Historic Preservation Act. This protection may be even greater in some communities than could be provided by designation under a local ordinance. Thus the question of whether a local commission may designate a property owned by a federal agency has not been litigated.

A recent case in Washington involved an attempt by the city of Seattle to designate a commercial building owned by the University of Washington, a state agency. Though the court ruled that Seattle could not designate the building, the court declined to rule that no state-owned building could be designated by a community in Washington:

> We decline to apply a rule of immunity, and find it unnecessary to express an opinion on the validity of such a rule. . . . The City of Seattle has no power to nominate or designate any buildings as landmarks within the University's Metropolitan Tract. . . . *State v. City of Seattle*, 615 P.2d 461, 463-64 (Wash. 1980).

Increasingly, courts have recognized the ability of local governments to subject property owned by state agencies to regulation under local land-use ordinances. *See* Ross 7 *Land Use Zoning Digest* 6 (1980).

b. Referendum or Consent Requirements

Typical Ordinance Provisions:

CHICAGO:

The Commission on Chicago Historical and Architectural Landmarks shall thereafter contact the owner or owners of such property and outline the reasons and effect of its proposed designation and, whenever possible, shall secure the owner's or owners' written consent for submittal of said proposition for the proposed designation to the City Council. (Chicago, Illinois, Rules of Procedure, Article II (D)(1))

ALABAMA:

However, no ordinance designating an Historic Preservation District, as hereinabove provided, shall become effective unless the establishment of such district is requested in writing to the governing body by not less than 60 per cent of the property owners within the proposed Historic Preservation District. (H 2095, Alabama 1971 Session: cities with populations between 135,000 and 185,000)

Annotation:

In at least two states, Alabama and Connecticut, specified percentages of the property owners within any proposed historic district must agree in advance to the establishment of the district before it may be created. If there is such a requirement, care should be exercised to comply with it to avoid later challenges on the technical ground that an insufficient number of property owners had agreed to the district's establishment. Multiple partial owners of a single property should be required to cast fractional votes; a difficult question will arise if a structure has been subdivided into condominiums and each owner may cast a whole vote. An ordinance should also make clear whether corporate property owners may vote on designation before a district is created.

Though some preservation commissions are prohibited from designating as landmarks buildings whose owners oppose landmark designation, other preservation commissions are encouraged, but not required, to obtain owner consent before designation. The requirement of owner consent is not recommended, because it will enable objecting owners of potential landmarks to thwart community preservation efforts and may make designation of historic districts almost impossible. Some owners of potential local landmarks that have already been listed in the National Register of Historic Places may not be aware of the tax benefits permitted by the Tax Reform Act of 1976 or the Economic Recovery Tax Act of 1981 (ERTA). A commission should explain designation procedures carefully to owners of potential landmarks and may need to meet several times with some owners to be sure that the commission's objectives are understood.

c. **Application for Designation of Historic District or Landmark**

Typical Ordinance Provisions:

SEATTLE:

Designation may be proposed by the Council, the Commission, the Board, or on the application of the owners or authorized agents of the individual property to be designated or of 30% of the property in a proposed district, measured by the assessed valuation of such property. Any such proposal shall be filed with the Director upon forms prescribed by him and shall include all data required by the Board and the Commission. (Seattle, Washington, Ordinance,

No. 102229, Section 7)

BERKELEY:

Initiation of designation shall be by the Commission, or by a resolution of intention of the City Council, or by the Planning Commission, or by the Civic Art Commission, or by the verified application of the owners of the property to be designated or their authorized agents, or by the verified application of at least fifty (50) residents of the City. Any such application shall be filed with the Commission upon forms prescribed by the Commission, and shall be accompanied by all data required by the Commission. Where such application is submitted for designation of an historic district, the application must be subscribed by or on behalf of a majority of the property owners or residents of the proposed district. (Berkeley, California, Ordinance, Section 4)

BOULDER:

Designations may be initiated by resolution of the City Council or Landmarks Board, on the verified application of the owner(s) of the property to be designated or their authorized agents, or on the verified application of any organization with a recognized interest in historic preservation. (Boulder, Colorado, Ordinance, Section 51-302)

BOSTON:

The mayor, any ten registered voters of the city or any commission member may petition to the commission to designate a landmark, landmark district, architectural conservation district or protection area or to amend or rescind such a designation, and the Commission shall within thirty days next following the filing of such petition hold a preliminary hearing on such petition with the petitioners and arrange for the preparation of a report and, if required, request the appointment of a study committee. (Boston, Massachusetts, Landmarks Ordinance, Section 4)

Annotation:

Historic Districts:

A few ordinances permit property owners within a potential historic district or the owners of possible landmarks to apply to have their properties designated. These ordinances usually include, for historic district applications, a percentage requirement that may be measured by either number of owners in the area or total value of property in the area. A provision such as this may be desirable to prevent a preservation commission from ignoring an area whose residents wish to have their properties designated. Some preservation commissions are finding that it is politically easier to designate as a historic district an area where property owners have requested designation than an area where owners have not previously approached the commission.

The drafter of a preservation ordinance should decide how to compute votes of multiple owners of a single structure and whether an owner of a parcel containing more than one structure will be limited to a single vote.

Landmark Structures:

The owner of a significant building may wish the building to be designated as a landmark. A preservation commission should welcome the opportunity to work toward designation with such an owner. In larger cities, preservation commissions will realize that careful survey work to identify all potential landmarks might take years to complete. Thus it is advisable to have a procedure whereby owners whose properties have not yet been surveyed by the preservation commission may nevertheless petition to have their buildings designated as landmarks. Because owner consent is only infrequently required for landmark designations, most preservation commissions are able to initiate procedures to designate significant properties whose owners oppose designation.

d. Filing Fees for Designation Applications

Typical Ordinance Provision:

BERKELEY:

For each application for designation of a landmark, the fee shall be fifty dollars ($50.00).

For each application for designation of an historic district, the fee shall be one hundred dollars ($100.00).

There shall be no fee for each application for designation of a landmark, or for each application for designation of an historic district, if such application for designation is initiated by the Commission, or by resolution of intention of the City Council, or by the Planning Commission, or by the Civic Art Commission. (Berkeley, California, Ordinance, Section 13)

Annotation:

A few ordinances that permit property owners to petition to have a historic district designated require a filing fee from petitioning property owners. This fee should not be set so high that it will discourage property owners from petitioning for designation.

Filing fees will not generate a significant amount of income, and no attempt should be made to set them high enough to cover the preservation commission's time and expenses in considering a designation. High fees will still generate relatively little income and will discourage applications for designation. A waiver of the fee, when a designation is proposed by the commission itself, may be read as an intention to discourage independent applications to the commission.

e. **Commission Required to Notify Property Owners of Proposed Designation**

Typical Ordinance Provisions:

NEW ORLEANS:

Notice of a proposed designation shall be sent by registered mail to the owner of property proposed for landmark designation, describing the property proposed and announcing a public hearing by the Commission to consider said designation. (New Orleans, Louisiana, Ordinance, Section X(A)(2))

NEW YORK:

The owner of any improvement parcel on which a landmark or a proposed landmark is situated or which is a part of a landmark site or proposed landmark site or which contains an interior landmark or proposed interior landmark, or any property which includes a scenic landmark, the amendment to any designation thereof or the proposed rescission of any designation or amendment thereto. Such notice may be served by the commission by registered mail addressed to the owner or owners at his or their last known address or addresses, as the same appear in the records of the office of the city director of finance or if there is no name in such records, such notice may be served by ordinary mail addressed to "Owner" at the street address of the improvement parcel or property in question. Failure by the commission to give such notice shall not invalidate or affect any proceedings pursuant to this chapter relating to such improvement parcel or pursuant to this chapter relating to such improvement parcel or property. (New York, New York, Landmarks Ordinance, Section 207-12.0)

Annotation:

Notifying property owners of the proposed designation of their buildings is procedurally necessary but has the additional useful effect of alerting a preservation commission to possible opposition well in advance of the public hearing that must be held before designation. When a possible landmark designation is under consideration, only one person or a small number of individuals will need to be notified, but if a potential historic district is under consideration, there may be several hundred properties whose owners should be notified. Care must be taken to ensure that the actual owners of properties under consideration for designation are notified, not merely apparent owners. It is inadvisable to take such names from local tax lists without verifying them by searching local deed records, although trusts may conceal the true owners of some properties.

In some communities, careful maps have been prepared indicating which property owners would oppose designation. Such maps indicate which property owners need to be contacted in person so that the advantages of historic district designations can be explained to them.

Failure to notify a property owner of a proposed designation may lead to invalidation of the designation:

> The Landmark Law could have made provision for giving other than personal notice, but it did not. Accordingly, the base statutory requirement that "notice" be given must be accorded its common law meaning and a published notice was not compliance. Furthermore, because the published notice described plaintiff's structure only by setting forth its street address, there is some question as to whether it could pass the . . . adequacy test. . . . The aforesaid letter of November 7, 1974 stated only that the plaintiff's property had been recommended for designation but did not advise that designation was being considered, and while it advised that a public hearing would be held at a specified time and place, it did not identify the subject of the hearing or the body which would conduct it. Furthermore, the said letter came not from any representative of the Common Council or its said hearing committee but from the secretary of the said Landmark Preservation Commission. . . . *St. James United Methodist Church, Inc. v. City of Kingston* (No. 76-1239, Ulster County Sup. Ct., May 6, 1977), slip op. at 4-5.

f. Notice of Hearing on Proposed Designation to Nearby Property Owners

Typical Ordinance Provision:

BERKELEY:

In addition to the posting of notice, a notice of the hearing shall be mailed not less than ten (10) days prior to the date of such hearing to all property owners having property and each residential or other unit within three hundred (300) feet of the property referred to in the application; provided, however, that the failure of any such property owner or resident to receive such notice shall not affect the validity of the proceedings. (Berkeley, California, Ordinance, Section 4.1(a)(2))

Annotation:

At least one ordinance requires notice of a proposed designation to the owners of adjoining properties. Such a provision may be unnecessary, as general notice of a proposed designation should generate community input, but provides an indication to a court that parties other than an owner-applicant are able to appeal a decision by a preservation commission.

g. Commission Required to Hold Public Hearings

Typical Ordinance Provision:

NEW ORLEANS:

The Commission shall also send notice of a proposed designation to all city agencies having previously requested notification of such proceedings; to the landmark area advisory board in whose area the proposed landmark is located, if any exists; and to other parties customarily informed by the Commission of such proceedings.

The Commission shall also cause notice of the proposed designation to be published at least once at least thirty (30) days prior to the public hearing in the official journal of Orleans Parish and shall post notice of the hearing in the place where the Commission meets, and in addition, such notice may be also published in a newspaper having general circulation in Orleans Parish.

The Commission may solicit expert testimony regarding the historic and architectural importance of the building, structure, site, monument, area, or other landmark under consideration for designation.

The Commission may present testimony or documentary evidence of its own to establish a record regarding the historic and architectural importance of the proposed landmark property.

The Commission shall afford to the owner of said property reasonable opportunity to present testimony or documentary evidence regarding the historic and architectural importance of the proposed landmark property.

The owner of property proposed for landmark designation shall be afforded the right of representation by counsel and reasonable opportunity to cross-examine witnesses presented by the Commission.

Any interested party may present testimony or documentary evidence regarding the proposed landmark designation at the public hearing and may submit to the Commission documentary evidence within three days after the hearing. (New Orleans, Louisiana, Ordinance, Section X(A))

Annotation:

In order to comply with due process requirements, a preservation commission ought to conduct a public hearing on each proposed designation of a landmark or historic district. Several proposed designations may be considered in one hearing, though. The date, time, and place of the hearing should be announced in advance through local newspapers and in writing to owners of properties whose designation will be discussed at the hearing. Some preservation commissions are required to notify as well the owners of properties adjoining proposed landmarks. A preservation commission must be careful to meet all notice requirements for holding public hearings that are established by ordinance or rules of procedure, lest an attempt be made at some future date to invalidate a designation on the ground that inadequate notice was given.

The procedures approved by the U.S. Supreme Court in *Penn Central Transportation Company v. New York City* include "giving all interested parties an opportunity to be heard." 438 U.S. 104, 110 (1978). To date, the most elaborate suggested procedures for preservation commissions to follow have been developed in North Carolina in two publications prepared by Robert M. Leary & Associates, Ltd., for Keep North Carolina Beautiful, *A Manual for North Carolina Historic District Commissions* (1979) and *A Manual for North Carolina Historic Properties Commissions* (1980). Both publications contain model rules of procedure. The suggestion is made that North Carolina historic properties commissions should follow procedures outlined by the North Carolina Supreme Court for zoning boards.

Increasingly, courts have begun to focus on due process requirements for local preservation commissions. In certain situations, there may be members of a preservation commission who should plan not to vote on an individual matter before the commission. A Maryland trial court considered at length whether the chairman of the Annapolis Historic District Commission should have declined to vote on a matter that an organization of which she was currently vice-president had vigorously opposed. The court concluded that the chairman should not have voted on the matter:

> It is well-settled that a policy bias is not a ground for disqualification. . . . It is clear that [the chairman] had no direct or indirect financial interest involved in the subject matter of the application or any family relationship to any of the parties in the proceedings. . . . Also, in the usual sense, [the chairman] had no business association with, or employment by, an interested party. . . . However, the element of monetary gain is, fortunately, not always with all persons, the dominant interest. Strong feelings are not confined to pecuniary motives. . . . [H]er participation, as a member of the Commission, in the hearing in question, under the circumstances described must be held to have denied procedural due process to the appellant . . . . For this reason, if no other, the decision and order of the Commission must be reversed and the case remanded for a new hearing. *Annapolis Emergency Hospital Association, Inc. v. Annapolis Historic District Commission* (Law No. D-962, Anne Arundel County Cir. Ct., Md., Apr. 14, 1977), slip op. at 5, 12.

A New York trial court upheld the designation of the New York Yacht Club against a claim that, because the chairman of the New York City Landmarks Preservation Commission was associated with a private organization that had earlier sought the designation of the building, the designation process was tainted by a conflict of interest:

> Finally, the charge of partiality is unsubstantiated. The Chairman of the Commission, whom petitioner charged with a conflict of interest, neither moved to calendar the Yacht Club for reconsideration nor voted on the designation. That he represented an organization which, in 1970, sought approval of the Club's designation is insufficient to establish that the entire decision making process was tainted. *New York Yacht Club v. Landmarks Preservation Commission of City of New York* (No. 550/80, New York County Sup. Ct., Feb. 13, 1980), slip op. at 3.

A beginning preservation commission should seek the advice of the city or county attorney on necessary procedures for a designation hearing. Rules of procedure must meet state statutory or judicial requirements as well as federal constitutional requirements. Although an opportunity to cross-examine may be required in some states or appropriate in some contested situations, it is not an invariable requirement.

h. Commission Required to Make Designation Decision Promptly After Public Hearing

Typical Ordinance Provision:

CHICAGO:

The Commission shall make a determination with respect to the proposed designation in writing within fifteen (15) days after the initial hearing date and shall forthwith send a copy or copies thereof to the owner or owners and all persons having a legal or equitable interest in said property, as well as such other interested parties as may request a copy thereof, setting forth those findings of fact which constitute the basis for its decision. The Commission shall also forthwith transmit such recommendation concerning the proposed designation to the City Council. (Chicago, Illinois, Rules of Procedure, Article II (D)(2))

Annotation:

Because the two primary reasons for designating a property are to give local recognition to its merits and to protect the property against demolition or inadvisable alterations, a preservation commission will want to act promptly on the question of designation once a public hearing has been held. Designations should always be by resolution, and the commission's reasons for designating the property should be given. It is best to pass a separate resolution for each property to be designated, despite the present practice of some commissions of designating a number of properties by a single resolution. Preservation commissions should remember that if designation is challenged by a dissatisfied property owner, a thoughtful and comprehensive explanation of the commission's reasons, prepared at the time of designation, will greatly strengthen the commission's case for designation.

i. Specific Criteria Adopted at Time of Designation

Typical Ordinance Provisions:

BOSTON:

As part of every such designation or amendment of designation, the commission shall adopt regulations which shall specify general standards and other appropriate criteria consistent with the purposes of this act and the provisions of section five which shall be applied by the commission in making any determination under section six with respect to the designated landmark or within the designated landmark district, architectural conservation district or protection area. Such standards and criteria shall be adopted by the commission after it has considered the study report as provided for in this section. Such standards and criteria shall take account of the differences in significance and purpose of designation among a landmark, landmark district, architectural conservation district or protection area; provided, however, that the standards and criteria applicable within any protection area shall relate only to demolition, land coverage, height of structure, landscape or topography. (Boston, Massachusetts, Landmarks Ordinance, Section 4)

CINCINNATI:

At the time of designation the conservation guidelines shall be adopted by council for each historic structure, site, or district. The conservation guidelines shall promote the conservation, development, and use of structures, sites, and districts within the city and shall promote the special historic, architectural, community, or aesthetic interest or value of the structures, sites, and districts. Insofar as practicable, the conservation guidelines shall promote redevelopment of historic structures and compatible new development within historic districts. The guidelines shall not limit new construction within an historic site or district to any one period or architectural style but shall seek to preserve the integrity of existing historic structures. The conservation guidelines shall take into account the impact of the designation of a structure, site, or district on the residents of the affected area, the effect of the designation on the economic and social characteristics of the affected area, the projected impact of the designation on the budget of the city. . . . (Cincinnati, Ohio, Ordinance, Section 741-11)

Annotation:

A few preservation ordinances require that the preservation commission adopt specific criteria for a landmark or historic district at the time of designation. Such criteria would highlight architectural features to be protected or retained. This procedure is likely to be workable only in a community with an established history of preservation efforts; it will require adequate staffing for the preservation commission. Criteria that are too specific may prevent a preservation commission from coping with a proposed but unanticipated alteration, and may make it difficult for the commission to be uniform in its decisions.

j. Commission Required to Notify Owners of Designation Decision

Typical Ordinance Provision:

SEATTLE:

Within ten days after approval of the ordinance designating property as a landmark or landmark district, the Secretary of the Board shall send to the owner of record of each property so designated or each property within the designated district, by registered or certified mail, and to the Superintendent a copy of the ordinance and a letter outlining the basis for such designation and the obligations and restrictions which result from such designation. (Seattle, Washington, Ordinance, No. 102229, Section 7(h))

Annotation:

If an owner's property is designated by the preservation commission, the commission should give prompt notice to the property owner. In some jurisdictions notice by publication will be sufficient, though notice of such a limited type may create political problems for a commission. Actual notice need not be given by registered or certified mail, but such notice may be advisable if a commission anticipates the need for a permanent record of the fact that a property owner was notified of a designation. The New York City Landmarks Preservation Commission sends two letters to property owners, one before a public hearing on designation and another after the commission has voted to designate a historic district or landmark.

A preservation commission should prepare a form letter that may be sent to all property owners whose property is designated; some commissions refer to this as a "designation letter." If a copy of the preservation ordinance is appended to the form letter, all owners of designated properties will be aware of their obligation to contact the preservation commission before undertaking alteration or demolition of their properties. Property owners are less likely to try to argue later that they did not understand their obligations under a preservation ordinance if they have been sent a copy of the ordinance. Because such a procedure will be expensive for a large historic district, a commission should maximize newspaper publicity whenever such a district is being proposed and will benefit if the entire text of a proposed ordinance can be printed several times in local newspapers.

Some commissions will encounter in large districts a number of absentee owners whose local agents may be difficult to identify if one entity is listed for tax purposes but another entity is responsible for daily management of a property. Particular care may need to be used in these situations to send notices both to the actual owners and to their agents. In New York City, the procedure is to send notices to whomever is listed in local tax records, on the assumption that that person or organization will notify the true owner if actual ownership is for some reason not revealed by the tax records.

k. Commission Required to Notify Other Agencies of Designation

Typical Ordinance Provisions:

CHICAGO:

Further, as soon thereafter as is reasonably possible, the Commission shall notify the Building Department of the City of Chicago of the official designation and shall also file with the Recorder of Deeds of Cook County and the Assessor of Cook County a certified copy of the designation ordinance together with a notice briefly stating the fact of said designation and a summary of the effect said designation will have, as well as sending a certified copy of said ordinance and notice to the owner or owners and all persons having a legal or equitable interest in said property by registered mail. (Chicago, Illinois, Rules of Procedure, Article II(E))

LOUISVILLE:

Within five days after making any such designation as provided for in Subsection a . . . the Commission shall file a copy of same with the Clerk of the Board of Aldermen, the Department of Building and Housing Inspection, the Department of Works, the Division of Fire, the Board of Health, the Planning Commission, the Urban Renewal Agency, and the Metropolitan Sewer District. (Louisville, Kentucky, Ordinance, Section 4(d))

WILMINGTON:

For purposes of clarity in the designation of such property, all properties located in a historic district shall be recorded in the offices of the Department of Licenses and Inspections, and of the Department of Public Works, and shall be available for public inspection. (Wilmington, Delaware, Ordinance, Section I(d))

Annotation:

This provision is essential to an effective preservation ordinance. Unless other municipal agencies are aware that a preservation commission has designated a landmark or a historic district, the other agencies cannot work with the preservation commission to protect the designated properties. The preservation commission should be notified of all applications for demolition permits affecting designated properties. The commission also will want to know if city inspectors have found buildings to be so far below code standards that demolition would ordinarily be ordered to protect the public welfare.

In order for other public agencies to give adequate consideration to designated landmarks or historic district properties, it is useful to require that all properties subject to the jurisdiction of a preservation commission be listed in the offices of other agencies that should consider the preservation commission's expertise before making their own decisions.

1. **Recording Requirement for Chain of Title Purposes**

Typical Ordinance Provisions:

NEW ORLEANS:

Within thirty (30) days of the date on which the Commission designates or the City Council ratifies, as the case may be, any building, structure, site, or monument as a landmark worthy of preservation, the Commission shall cause to be filed in the conveyance office of Orleans Parish a certificate of notification that such property is designated a landmark, and said certificate of notification shall be maintained on the public records until such time as the landmark designation may be withdrawn by the Commission or the City Council. (New Orleans, Louisiana, Ordinance, Section X(A)(13))

BOSTON:

No designation of or amendment of such a designation shall be effective as to any person without actual notice thereof or as to any parcel of property until recorded in the Suffolk County registry of deeds and indexed in the grantor index under the name of the record owner or owners thereof and, with respect to registered land, filed in said registry and noted on the certificate of title of the owner or owners. (Boston, Massachusetts, Landmarks Ordinance, Section 4)

Annotation:

It is essential that notice of designation be recorded with other deed records so that subsequent purchasers of designated properties will have clear notice of the fact that properties have been designated. The recording effort should include buildings within a designated historic district. For properties judicially registered under the Torrens System, notice of designation on the judicially issued certificate of title itself will be necessary.

m. **Plaques to Be Attached to Buildings Following Designation**

Typical Ordinance Provisions:

CHICAGO:

The Commission on Chicago Historical and Architectural Landmarks, upon being notified by the City Council of any designation by ordinance of an area, place, building, structure, work of art or other similar object as a "Chicago Landmark," shall create or cause to be created a suitable plaque or plaques appropriately identifying said landmark, setting forth thereon a brief and concise statement of such information as will inform the public of the character of said landmark, which plaque shall be affixed to private property only after the written consent of the owner or owners thereof or to any public property as in the discretion of the Commission shall be deemed appropriate. (Chicago, Illinois, Rules of Procedure, Article II(E))

TRENTON:

Each designated landmark, landmark site and historic district may be marked by an appropriate plaque carrying a brief description and account of the historical significance of the property. (Trenton, New Jersey, Ordinance, p. 7)

Annotation:

An effective preservation commission will be careful to identify designated buildings as part of its public relations efforts. In addition to notification to owners of designated properties, some notification should be given to the general public. Publicity at the time of designation is one form such notification may take, but the attachment of a plaque to each designated building is more permanent and is more likely to inform nonresidents of a building's designation. Since one rationale for the creation of many preservation commissions has been a desire to increase local tourist business, plaques help alert tourists to the importance of designated buildings. Plaques may also help establish local pride in designated buildings and make the effectiveness of the preservation commission's activities generally visible.

n. Commission's Authority to Amend or Rescind Designation

Typical Ordinance Provision:

CHICAGO:

The Commission on Chicago Historical and Architectural Landmarks may effect the amendment or rescission of any designation of an area, place, building, structure, work of art or other similar object as a "Chicago Landmark" in the same manner and procedure as was followed in the original designation. (Chicago, Illinois, Rules of Procedure, Article II (F))

Annotation:

If a preservation commission has the power to modify or withdraw the designation of a landmark or historic district, this power should be specified in the preservation ordinance. The procedures to be followed by the preservation commission when it modifies or withdraws a designation should also be indicated in the ordinance.

Such a procedure seems unlikely to be used, unless a commission has made an error in professional judgment or historical information used by the commission as the basis for a designation turns out to have been inaccurate.

o. Moratorium on Applications for Alteration or Demolition While Designation Pending

Typical Ordinance Provisions:

BERKELEY:

No applications for a permit to construct, alter or demolish any structure or other feature on a landmark site or in an historic district, filed subsequent to the day that an application has been filed or a resolution adopted to initiate designation of the said landmark site or historic district, shall be approved by the Commission while proceedings are pending on such designation; provided, however, that after one hundred eighty (180) days have elapsed from the date of initiation of said designation, unless the application has been suspended pursuant to Section 6.1, if final action on such designation has not been completed, the permit application may be approved.

The provisions of this ordinance shall be inapplicable to the construction, alteration or demolition of any structure or other feature on a landmark site or in an historic district, where a permit for the performance of such work was issued prior to the day that an application has been filed or a resolution adopted to initiate the designation of the said landmark site or historic district, and where such permit has not expired or been cancelled or revoked, provided that construction is started and diligently prosecuted to completion in accordance with the Building Code. (Berkeley, California, Ordinance, Section 15)

DISTRICT OF COLUMBIA:

"[H]istoric landmark" means a building, structure, object or feature, and its site, or a site (1) listed in the National Register of Historic Places as of the effective date of this act; or (2) listed in the District of Columbia's inventory of historic sites, or for which application for such listing is pending with the Historic Preservation Review Board: PROVIDED, That the Review Board will determine within ninety (90) days of receipt of an application pursuant to section 5, 6, 7, 8 or 9 of this act whether to list such property, and any property not so listed will not be considered an historic landmark within the terms of this act. (District of Columbia Historic Landmark and Historic District Protection Act of 1978, D.C. Law 2-144, Section 3(f))

Annotation:

Once a preservation commission has begun to consider the designation of a possible landmark or historic district, the commission will want to "freeze" the status of the involved property or buildings if possible. Two recent cases dealt with ordinance provisions that explicitly extended protections to properties whose designation had been considered, or that had been interpreted to protect structures whose designation was pending.

A Texas case, *Crownrich v. City of Dallas*, 506 S.W.2d 654, held in 1974 that a building permit moratorium is permissible under Texas law while a preservation ordinance is being developed. But *Crownrich* must be read against a later Texas case, *Southern National Bank of Houston v. City of Austin*, 582 S.W.2d 229 (Tex. App. 1979), that found a portion of the Austin preservation ordinance "constitutionally defective" because restrictions could be attached to properties by placing them on the agenda of the Austin Landmark Commission, with no time limit for commission action:

> We hold, therefore, that Section 45-51.1 is constitutionally defective in that it acts to deprive property owners of their property without due process as well as depriving them of the equal protection of the laws, because it fails to provide a reasonable time limit on final City Council action after a parcel of property has been listed on the agenda of the Landmark Commission. *Id.* at 239.

The rationale of *Crownrich* might extend even in Texas to demolition moratoriums. A demolition moratorium would seem to be even more advisable during the period between the enactment of a local preservation ordinance and the designation under that ordinance of a proposed landmark or historic district than during the period preceding enactment of the ordinance. Drafters of future Texas ordinances are likely to avoid the defect found in the Austin ordinance. Moratoriums have been imposed in New Orleans and in other cities while preservation ordinances were drafted or potential areas for designation were being identified. (*See* October 1977 *Landmark and Historic District Commissions* newsletter.)

New Orleans first enacted in April 1974 a demolition moratorium ordinance to control the problem of speculative demolitions in the city's central business district. Building owners could still obtain demolition permits by appealing to the city council and proving hardship or showing definite plans to construct new buildings on the sites to be cleared. Successive moratorium ordinances extended the original moratorium for several years until New Orleans planners could identify potential landmarks and historic districts within the area subject to the moratorium.

The District of Columbia preservation ordinance protects, for up to ninety days, potential landmarks for which a designation application has been filed. An Illinois court has held that a possible landmark designation may be insufficient to justify a temporary restraining order to prevent the demolition of a structure:

> Plaintiffs next contend that the trial court should have issued a temporary restraining order to prevent the demolition of the church pending the determination of its possible landmark status. . . . Defendant argues that plaintiffs may not enjoin him from destroying the building because of its possible landmark status since neither the City of Chicago nor the Landmark Commission has that authority. . . . To restrain defendant from exercising his legal rights concerning the building would amount to a taking or damage for a public use of his property for which he should be compensated. *Galich v. Catholic Bishop of Chicago,* 394 N.E.2d 577-78 (Ill. App. 1979), *cert. denied,* 445 U.S. 916 (1980).

IV. Application to Preservation Commission for Certificate of Appropriateness

A. COMMISSION POWER TO APPROVE ALTERATIONS OR NEW CONSTRUCTION

Typical Ordinance Provisions:

SAVANNAH:

Certificate of Appropriateness required. A certificate of appropriateness issued by the Zoning Administrator after approval by the Board of Review shall be required before a permit is issued for any of the following:

(1) Within all zones of the Historic District:
   A. Demolition of a historic building.
   B. Moving a historic building.
   C. Material change in the exterior appearance of existing buildings classified as Historic by additions, reconstruction, alteration, or maintenance involving exterior color change; and
(2) Within Historic Zone I:
   A. Any new construction of a principal building or accessory building or structure subject to view from a public street.
   B. Change in existing walls and fences, or construction of new walls and fences, if along public street rights-of-way, excluding lanes.
   C. Material change in the exterior appearance of existing contemporary buildings by additions, reconstruction, alteration, or maintenance involving exterior color change, if subject to view from a public street. (Savannah, Georgia, Ordinance, Section 5)

MADISON:

No owner or person in charge of a landmark, landmark site or structure within an Historic District shall reconstruct or alter all or any part of the exterior of such property or construct any improvement upon such designated property or properties within an Historic District or cause or permit any such work to be performed upon such property unless a Certificate of Appropriateness has been granted by the Landmarks Commission. Unless such certificate has been granted by the commission, the Building Inspection Superintendent shall not issue a permit for any such work. (Madison, Wisconsin, Landmarks Ordinance, Section 33.01(5)(b)(2))

Los Angeles:

No person shall change in occupancy, construct, alter, demolish, relocate or remove any structure, natural feature or site within or from a Preservation Zone unless a Certificate of Appropriateness shall have been approved by the Planning Commission for such action pursuant to this Section. No Certificate of Appropriateness shall be approved unless the plans for said changes in occupancy, construction, demolition, alteration, relocation, or removal conform with the provisions of this section. Any approval or denial shall include written findings in support thereof. (Los Angeles, California, Ordinance No. 152-422, Section 1(F)(1))

Annotation:

The essential provision in any preservation ordinance is a requirement that proposed alterations to existing structures within a designated historic district or to designated landmarks be reviewed by a preservation commission and approved by the commission or some other administrative body, such as a planning commission or city council. No other provision in a preservation ordinance is so fundamental. Of almost equal importance is a requirement that all proposed new buildings within a historic district be reviewed in advance by a local preservation commission to ensure their compatibility with the existing structures in the district.

A Massachusetts trial court noted in an unpublished 1978 opinion, *Sleeper v. Old King's Highway Regional Historic District Commission* (No. 22799, Barnstable Div. Dist. Ct., March 6, 1978), the latitude given to a preservation commission to pass upon applications for certificates of appropriateness:

> Substantial discretionary power is given to the commission to determine the appropriateness of exterior architectural features. The commission and the board must keep in mind the statutory purposes and the factors listed in the statute and arrive at its determination in that context. Of course, a decision based solely upon personal tastes would have to be invalidated by the court. However, within the latitude expressed, the commission's judgment will be sustained unless arbitrary or capricious, or unless unsupported by substantial evidence, or is otherwise tainted by an incorrect application of law. Slip op. at 9-10.

The preservation commission should have the authority to review and approve *all* changes affecting the exterior of a landmark or a structure within a historic district. In some communities, specified minor categories of changes may be approved or disapproved by commission staff; such an arrangement is helpful because it can produce a quicker decision for a property owner and can permit a commission to give full consideration to more important matters. Some ordinances will restrict a commission's authority to alterations affecting only those exterior facades that may be viewed from public streets, but a few preservation ordinances give commissions the authority to review changes to all exterior facades. *City of New Orleans v. Impastato,* 3 So.2d 559 (La. 1941), upheld the power of one commission to review proposed alterations to "the sides, rear and roof of any building in the Vieux Carre section." *Id.* at 561.

A few preservation commissions may review and approve or disapprove only those changes for which a building permit is otherwise required. The authority of the preservation commission should not be limited to alterations costing more than the threshold amount that locally triggers the requirement of a building permit. Instead, a preservation commission should review all proposed alterations, regardless of whether they would require a building permit.

In at least one state, Michigan, an attorney general's opinion holds that preservation commissions may review only alterations proposed for "historic" properties within a historic district. (Letter of Attorney General Frank J. Kelley to Max Altekruse, secretary of Franklin Village Historic District Commission, March 6, 1975) A preservation commission's authority should not be so limited. A commission should review alterations to all structures within a historic district in order to protect and aid in the improvement of the distinctive ambience of the district, and to prevent the loss of those qualities for whose protection the preservation commission was originally created. *City of New Orleans v. Pergament,* 5 So.2d 129 (La. 1941), upheld the power of one commission to regulate both historic and nonhistoric buildings within a historic district:

> The purpose of the ordinance is not only to preserve the old buildings themselves, but to preserve the antiquity of the whole French and Spanish quarter, the tout ensemble, so to speak, by defending this relic against iconoclasm or vandalism. Preventing or prohibiting eyesores in such a locality is within the police power and within the scope of this municipal ordinance. *Id.* at 131.

A Massachusetts court has held that nonhistoric sub-areas within a local historic district are not exempt from regulation by a preservation commission:

> The Act does not exempt, from the restrictions it imposes, subareas within the historic district which, taken in isolation, may have little or no historic significance. *Sleeper v. Old King's Highway Regional Historic District Commission*, 417 N.E.2d 987, 989 (Mass. App. 1981).

More recently, the Maryland Court of Appeals noted in *Faulkner v. Town of Chestertown*, 428 A.2d 879 (Md. 1981), that "the whole concept of historic zoning 'would be about as futile as shoveling smoke' if . . . because a building being demolished had no architectural or historical significance a historic district commission was powerless to prevent its demolition and the construction in its stead of a modernistic drive-in restaurant immediately adjacent to the State House in Annapolis." *Id.* at 884. The Maryland court concluded easily that "[s]ince the Faulkner's building was located within one of Chestertown's historic districts, we hold it to have been subject to the jurisdiction of the Commission notwithstanding the fact that it had no architectural or historical significance." *Id.*

A preservation commission should have the authority to review and approve or deny proposed plans for new construction within a historic district. An incompatible new building may do more to alter the character of a historic district than a number of small alterations to existing structures within the district.

The North Carolina Supreme Court has held that a local preservation commission has the authority to review plans for new construction even on a currently vacant lot in a local historic district:

> Associates' contention that the provisions in the Oakwood Ordinance requiring issuance of a certificate of appropriateness for *new construction* is unreasonable, particularly when applied to Associates' plans to construct an office building on its now vacant lot, is without merit. It is widely recognized that preservation of the historic aspects of a district requires more than simply the preservation of those buildings of historical and architectural significance within the district. . . . [The] 'tout ensemble' doctrine, as it is now often termed, is an integral and reasonable part of effective historic district preservation. *A-S-P Associates v. City of Raleigh*, 258 S.E.2d 444, 451 (N.C. 1979).

It is important, though, that members of the preservation commission have some knowledge of, and sensitivity to, contemporary architecture. Increasingly, preservation commissions are coming to realize that the sensitively designed building in a contemporary style may be a more desirable addition to a historic district than a mediocre adaptation of a traditional style.

A preservation commission must review carefully all applications for certificates of appropriateness lest it be accused of a denial of equal protection. In *City of New Orleans v. Levy*, 98 So.2d 210 (La. 1957), a court refused to affirm an injunction requiring the removal of a plastic covering over a courtyard, even though the covering had been installed without the approval of the Vieux Carre Commission, because "the record conclusively discloses that in recent years there have been innumerable non-conforming alterations of buildings throughout the French Quarter against which the city has sought no injunctive relief. . . ." *Id.* at 212-13.

A Massachusetts trial court noted, in an unreported 1978 opinion, *Sleeper v. Old King's Highway Regional Historic District Commission* (No. 22799, Barnstable Div. Dist. Ct., March 6, 1978), *aff'd*, 417 N.E.2d 987 (Mass. App. 1981), that historic preservation ordinances do not necessarily require the "freezing" of an area as of a particular moment in time:

> I do not view this act as requiring that the architectural and cultural motif be frozen at a particular moment in the history of the Cape. It is more general and more flexible than that. Obviously, the legislature must have contemplated that there are several types of architecture and construction that typify the Cape Region from the small cape half-houses of an earlier period to the more substantial structures associated with the 19th and early 20th centuries. The mandate is not that one type be preserved to the exclusion of the other, but that the cultural heritage in its entirety be preserved from encroachments by incongruous structures. Thus, findings as to the specific conditions at some past time are not required. Slip op. at 12-13.

B. DEFINITION OF ALTERATION KEYED TO CITY BUILDING CODE

Typical Ordinance Provision:

TRENTON:

"Alteration" shall mean any act defined as an alteration by the building code of the City of Trenton as set forth in the Standard Building Code of New Jersey. An alteration or construction shall be deemed to be "major" if it is the kind of work which is not normally done without the aid of plans or specifications; an alteration or construction shall be deemed to be "minor" if it is the kind of work which is normally done without the aid of plans, specifications or skilled labor and which would not substantially or radically change the external appearance of the site. (Trenton, New Jersey, Ordinance, p. 2)

Annotation:

The definition of "alteration" should be contained within the preservation ordinance itself and should not be defined by reference to a local building code. Terms used in a preservation ordinance should be self-explanatory or defined within the ordinance itself. Otherwise the full requirements of the ordinance will be difficult for property owners to understand.

C. PERMISSION FOR A VARIETY OF STYLES IN NEW CONSTRUCTION

Typical Ordinance Provisions:

Mansfield, Connecticut:

It is not the intent to limit new construction to any one period or architectural style, but to preserve the integrity of historic buildings and to insure the compatibility of any new work constructed in the vicinity. (Mansfield, Connecticut, Rules and Regulations, Section 7(b))

Loudoun County, Virginia:

The Board of Supervisors shall consider the following in passing upon the appropriateness of architectural features: . . . The extent to which the building or structure would be harmonious with or incongruous to the old and historic aspects of the surroundings. It is not the intent of this consideration to discourage contemporary architectural expression or to encourage the emulation of existing buildings or structures of historic or architectural interest in specific detail. Harmony or incompatibility should be evaluated in terms of the appropriateness of materials, scale, size, height, placement, and use of a new building or structure in relationship to existing buildings and structures and to the setting thereof. (Loudoun County, Virginia, Historic District Zoning, Ordinance, Section 750.15.1(e))

Annotation:

Preservation ordinances may specifically encourage good contemporary architecture within a historic district. Such ordinances assume that contemporary architecture per se is not incompatible with historic buildings, all of which were once new. These ordinances encourage a preservation commission to recognize that some contemporary buildings will be more "compatible" or "harmonious" than others with existing buildings within the historic district. Ordinances may require that commission members consider certain described factors of proposed new buildings, in order to protect commission decisions from charges of arbitrariness or subjectivity.

Though there has been little litigation involving this question, a Rhode Island case may indicate how some courts will approach the issue. In *Hayes v. Smith*, 167 A.2d 546 (R.I. 1961), the court upheld the reversal by a local zoning board of review of a preservation commission's denial of a certificate of appropriateness for new construction within a historic district. The court focused on the phrase "general compatibility" in the local ordinance:

> It seems to us that there is no requirement of rigid adherence in proposed construction or alterations to existing architectural style. It is enough if it can be said that the proposed plans are generally compatible with the architectural character of the district. It is not likely that the legislature intended to require such absolute duplication of existing style as to jeopardize the validity of historic zoning. The decision of the board in the instant cause, when read in its entirety, demonstrates that the board, while agreeing with the finding of the commission that the proposed plans lacked similarity, found nevertheless that they were compatible, even if not so compatible as the commission deemed advisable. *Id.* at 549-50.

D. GUIDELINES AND CRITERIA FOR COMMISSION TO USE

Typical Ordinance Provisions:

VICKSBURG, MISSISSIPPI:

> The Board shall promulgate and publish such standards as are a necessary supplement to the provisions of this Article to inform District residents, property owners and the general public of those criteria by which the applications for

a Certificate of Appropriateness are to be measured. (Vicksburg, Mississippi, Ordinance, Section 7(C))

SEATTLE:

The Board in considering the appropriateness of any alteration, demolition, new construction, reconstruction, restoration, remodeling or other modification of any building shall consider, among other things, the purposes of this ordinance, the historical and architectural value and significance of the landmark or landmark district, the texture, material and color of the building or structure in question or its appurtenant fixtures, including signs and the relationship of such features to similar features of other buildings within a landmark district, and the position of such building or structure in relation to the street or public way and to other buildings and structures. (Seattle, Washington, Landmarks Ordinance, Section 8(c))

Annotation:

Need to develop criteria:

If a preservation ordinance requires a preservation commission to develop and publish guidelines for the commission's use in considering applications for certificates of appropriateness, the commission must develop such guidelines. The effectiveness of the preservation commission in one community was temporarily curtailed by a lawsuit because of that commission's failure to have developed and published required guidelines prior to the commencement of litigation challenging the commission's authority. *Blackmer v. Salisbury Zoning Board of Adjustment* (76 CV 313, Rowan County Sup. Ct., N.C., May 4, 1976).

A New York trial court noted with suspicion the lack of necessary procedures for the guidance of the preservation commission in Kingston, New York:

> Any applicant for such a certificate will find no procedural guidance in the Landmark Law since none is contained therein and that law neither restrains nor guides the manner in which official discretion may be exercised upon any application for such a certificate. *St. James United Methodist Church, Inc., v. City of Kingston* (No. 76-1239, Ulster County Sup. Ct., May 6, 1977), slip op. at 2.

This court invalidated the landmark designation of a local church because the Kingston commission had not met notice requirements before designating the church's property.

The National Endowment for the Arts has published *Design Guidelines, An Annotated Bibliography* (November 1977). This helpful catalog, prepared by Merrill Ware Carrington, has been available without charge from the regional offices of the National Trust.

Required specificity for criteria:
Early preservation litigation tended to focus on the question of whether a particular ordinance contained sufficiently specific standards to prevent the members of a preservation commission from exercising unbridled discretion. One court stated:

> As we have pointed out, the purpose of the ordinance is to preserve the historic style of architecture. To that end the "Old Santa Fe Style" is described in great detail, including such things as roof lines, fire walls, inset and exterior portals, canales, decorative panels, etc. . . . Since the council recognized that it would be impossible to rigidly and literally set forth every detail without impairing the underlying public purpose, it adopted a policy expressed in the ordinance which enables some variances consistent with the public interest and the purpose of the overall zone plan. *City of Santa Fe v. Gamble-Skogmo, Inc.*, 389 P.2d 13, 19 (N.M. 1964).

Another court sustained a determination by a local preservation commission that a proposed structure would be incompatible with the "atmosphere" of a small town, and held that the "standard" of the ordinance was sufficient. *Bittenbender v. Tibbetts*, 202 A.2d 232, 235-36 (N.H. 1964).

The Maryland Court of Appeals recently upheld the Chestertown ordinance against a vagueness challenge:

> In plain language what the ordinance and the Act are saying is that if one proposes to do anything to a building within a historic district which will involve changes to the exterior appearance of the structure visible from a street or alley in the district, then one must obtain a permit. That is so plain we see no reason why people of ordinary intelligence would be unable to comprehend the meaning of the Act and the ordinance. *Faulkner v. Town of Chestertown*, 428 A.2d 879, 885 (Md. 1981).

The North Carolina Supreme Court has upheld the incorporation of guidelines which add specificity to a general standard of "incongruity":

> Although we cannot ignore in our consideration the guidelines and standards incorporated into the Oakwood Ordinance, if the general standard of "incongruity" is legally sufficient to withstand a delegation challenge, the incorporated guidelines and standards, which give varying degrees of specificity to

that general standard, are sufficient *a fortiori*. *A-S-P Associates v. City of Raleigh*, 258 S.E.2d 444, 453 (N.C. 1979).

The North Carolina court found a standard of "incongruity" a permissible "contextual standard":

> The general policy and standard of "incongruity," adopted by both the General Assembly and the Raleigh City Council, in this instance is best denominated as "a contextual standard." A contextual standard is one which derives its meaning from the objectively determinable, interrelated conditions and characteristics of the subject to which the standard is to be applied. . . . In this instance the standard of "incongruity" must derive its meaning, if any, from the total physical environment of the Historic District. . . . Although the neighborhood encompassed by the Historic District is to a considerable extent an architectural melange, that heterogeneity of architectural style is not such as to render the standard of "incongruity" meaningless. . . . It is therefore sufficient that a general, yet meaningful, contextual standard has been set forth to limit the discretion of the Historic District Commission. Strikingly similar standards for administration of historic district ordinances have long been approved by courts of other jurisdictions. *Id*. at 454.

The explicitness of the criteria to which a commission must adhere in making its decisions varies considerably from state to state. The drafter of a preservation ordinance should be familiar with state court decisions in order to be sure that, if needed, appropriate criteria are specified for the commission's use. Criteria that are too explicit and detailed, however, may eventually restrict the building styles within a historic district to plans that copy or adapt traditional forms.

It is important that those criteria stated in an ordinance be applicable to all categories of structures that will fall under the jurisdiction of a preservation commission, or that different criteria be available for the commission to use in judging applications involving buildings in different categories. An Ohio trial court has recently invalidated a local preservation ordinance because its criteria did not deal specifically and separately with signs, though sign regulation was a power given by ordinance to the local commission:

> There is a complete lack of standards relating to signs in these cases and all of the criteria recited in the ARO [Architectural Review Ordinance] concern themselves with spacing, continuities and proportions of openings or windows, etc. Even where the ARO deals with relationships of materials and textures and colors, it speaks of predominant materials, textures and colors, which would not govern a sign which takes up only a small space on a building. *City of Miamisburg v. Hannah* (No. 80 8 CRB 12, Miamisburg Mun. Ct., Feb. 14, 1981), slip op. at 7. (*See* 1 *Preservation Law Reporter* 3017 (1982))

In 1978, the Colorado Supreme Court declared two preservation ordinances for Georgetown void for vagueness because they failed to define the "areas" within Georgetown:

> The record indicates that the Commission members divide Georgetown into two or three distinct areas. Several members testified that Georgetown was divided into northern and southern areas. Still others, while agreeing that the northern and southern areas exist, felt that a transitional or buffer area exists between the two larger areas. The Commisson's unpublished and indefinite delineation of the areas is legally insufficient. *South of Second Associates v. Town of Georgetown*, 580 P.2d 807, 811 (Colo. 1978).

If buildings within a historic district are relatively homogeneous in age and style, guidelines need not be complicated. But if the buildings within the district represent a number of different periods and styles, then a much more complicated set of guidelines may have to be developed for the use of property owners wishing to gain commission approval for alterations to their properties.

No community should copy the guidelines developed for another community without checking to determine whether the two communities are similar enough for the same guidelines to work in both.

Size of area to which criteria apply:

An issue that has begun to attract the attention of courts is whether a preservation commission may consider an application for a certificate of appropriateness in terms of a small area within a historic district or must instead consider it in terms of the entire district. In 1978, a Massachusetts trial court stated in an unreported decision, *Sleeper v. Old King's Highway Regional Historic District Commission* (No. 22799, Barnstable Div. Dist. Ct., March 6, 1978), *aff'd*, 417 N.E.2d 987 (Mass. App. 1981), that:

> [T]he issue of compatibility of a structure must be determined in the context of its immediate surroundings. What may be compatible from an aesthetic or historic viewpoint at the Marconi Site in South Wellfleet is obviously not determinative of compatibility of a similar structure in the Scargo Lake Area of Dennis. As previously suggested, there is no legislative intent requiring uniformity throughout the entire region covered by the Old King's Highway Act. Slip op. at 12.

The appellate court in *Sleeper* did not address this issue but made it clear that nonhistoric sub-areas are not exempt from commission regulation:

> The Act does not exempt, from the restrictions it imposes, subareas within the

historic district which, taken in isolation, may have little or no historic significance. 417 N.E.2d at 989.

Although Massachusetts courts seem to favor commission decisions focusing on compatibility within neighborhoods of a historic district, this approach has not been approved in Pennsylvania. In 1979, a Pennsylvania trial court suggested that the proper area for a preservation commission to consider would be an entire historic district:

> When considering "historic district" matters the emphasis is on linkage among buildings in the entire district, not, as in landmark legislation, on the individual significance of a particular structure. . . . It has been pointed out by appellant that the block of Pine Street on which the buildings are located also contains several modern structures, and it is argued that the buildings referred to are thus out of place. Apart from the fact that there are contiguous historic houses on Pine Street, the suggested frame of reference is too narrow, and the review board properly considered more than simply the impact of a proposed demolition on a single block. . . . On balance, we conclude that the Board of Historical Architectural Review could reasonably find the demolition of appellant's buildings detrimental to the preservation of the fabric of the historic district in which they are situate. *Cleckner v. City of Harrisburg*, 10 D. & C. 3d 393, 397-98 (Pa. 1979).

At least one Massachusetts court has suggested that a preservation commission may apply stricter standards within one portion of a historic district than used elsewhere within the historic district. In an unreported 1975 trial court opinion, *Forg v. Jaquith* (No. 35391, Middlesex Sup. Ct., July 22, 1975), the court affirmed a decision by the Lexington Historic District Commission that stated in part:

> Although the Commission has previously permitted the installation of vinyl siding on buidings in areas of lesser historical importance, it has not done so on any building facing the Battle Green or any other key historical site. In these key historical areas, and particularly around the Battle Green itself, the Commission believes stricter standards should apply, and that the surrounding buildings should appear genuine and authentic so that the site may retain as much as possible of its historical ambience. Supplementary notice of determination at 5.

E. PUBLICATIONS TO BE USED BY COMMISSION TO HELP ESTABLISH STANDARDS

Typical Ordinance Provision:

New Haven:

In deciding upon applications for CERTIFICATES OF APPROPRIATENESS, the Commission shall, in addition to the standards for determining appropriateness set forth in Section 5-5d, take into account the design and architectural considerations expressed in the documents . . . attached as appendix I, when reviewing applications having to do with the importance of the Square itself and its relationship to the surrounding buildings. (New Haven, Connecticut, Guidelines II(A))

Annotation:

A preservation commission should develop its own criteria or guidelines to be used in reviewing applications for certificates of appropriateness or demolition permits. Occasionally such criteria will have been developed in a preservation survey completed before enactment of the ordinance creating the preservation commission and will be viewed as a prerequisite to enactment of the ordinance. Such criteria may be reprinted, though some guidelines may be too lengthy to reprint fully, or incorporated by reference in the ordinance. When guidelines are incorporated by reference, however, it may be unnecessarily difficult to amend these criteria after the commission has been in operation for several years and realizes that the criteria are, for some reason, not workable.

Preservation surveys or recommended architectural guidelines are typically printed in limited quantities and thus cannot be freely distributed to all property owners under a preservation commission's jurisdiction. If such documents have been incorporated by reference into a preservation ordinance, copies should be deposited in several locations, such as local public libraries, that are convenient to the general public.

F. SUBMISSION OF PLANS TO COMMISSION

Typical Ordinance Provision:

Vieux Carre:

Before the commencement of any work in the erection of any new building or in the alteration or addition to, or painting or repainting or demolishing of any existing building, any portion of which is to front on any public street or alley in the Vieux Carre Section, application by the owner for a permit therefor shall be made to the Vieux Carre Commission, accompanied by the full plans and specifications thereof so far as they relate to the proposed appearance, color, texture of materials and architectural design of the exterior, including the front, sides, rear and roof of such building, alteration or addition or of any out building, part wall, courtyard, fence or other dependency thereof. (New Orleans, Vieux Carre Ordinance, Section 65-8)

Annotation:

A preservation ordinance should require that an applicant for a certificate of appropriateness submit his proposed plans to the preservation commission in sufficient detail for the commission to have full knowledge of the requested alteration. It should be clear that the applicant has made firm decisions about colors, materials, textures, shapes, and sizes. For simple projects, a brief description of the proposal with paint chips or samples of materials to be applied to a building may be sufficient. For more complicated projects, full architectural drawings should be attached to the application to permit the commission to visualize the effect of the proposed alteration. The applicant should provide enough information to enable the commission to understand the relationship of his proposed work to adjacent buildings.

G. COMMISSION ACTION ON APPLICATION FOR CERTIFICATE OF APPROPRIATENESS

Typical Ordinance Provision:

BERKELEY:

If the application is for a permit to make exterior alterations or to carry out new construction, the Commission shall approve, modify or disapprove the application in whole or in part, or suspend action on it for a period not to exceed one hundred eighty (180) days. (Berkeley, California, Ordinance, Section 6.1(c)(1))

Annotation:

The possible responses that a preservation commission may take to an application for a certificate of appropriateness should be specified in a preservation ordinance. Normally, a commission may approve, deny, or approve in modified form an application. Or a commission may have the power to approve an application in amended form, subject to the acceptance of the amendment by the applicant. If an applicant were to choose not to accept a proposed amendment, his application would be considered to have been denied.

In a limited number of instances, a commission has the authority to suspend action on an application for a specified period of time. The purpose of such a delay is, of course, to permit the commission to consult with the applicant to see if he cannot be persuaded to amend the application so that the commission will approve it. It is better, though, to provide for a preapplication procedure designed to warn an applicant of probable commission disapproval of an application not yet formally submitted than to suspend action on a formal application. Ordinances giving a commission the power to suspend action on an application must be carefully written so that this provision meshes well with the usual provision requiring a commission to take some action on each application within a specified number of days.

H. COMMISSION AUTHORIZED TO DELAY, BUT NOT DENY, PROPOSED ALTERATION

Typical Ordinance Provision:

TRENTON:

Should the commission conclude that the proposed alteration would have a significant effect detrimental to the importance of the landmark, landmark site or historic district in question, an official notice of postponement shall be submitted to the building inspector which shall operate to bar the issuance of the permit for a period not to exceed six months. Reasons for postponing for a specified time within the six month limit shall be forwarded with the official notice.

If, at the expiration of the period of postponement, no resolution or compromise agreement is reached and no action has been taken by the city or state toward condemnation of the property in question, a permit authorizing the alteration or construction work as originally applied for shall be issued by the building inspector without the need for further commission action. (Trenton, New Jersey, Ordinance, p. 10)

Annotation:

Municipalities unwilling to permit a preservation commission to deny certificates of appropriateness for requested changes may instead restrict the commission's authority to the delay of proposed building alterations. A commission with such a limitation has little real power and will be largely ineffective since it will have influence over only those property owners who might accept suggestions from private preservation organizations. Drafters of preservation ordinances should be aware of the broad commission powers sanctioned by the U.S. Supreme Court in its 1978 decision in *Penn Central Transportation Company v. New York City*, 438 U.S. 104 (1978), though not all states have enabling legislation broad enough to permit communities to create commissions with such full powers.

Though a delay period may be designed to permit a municipality to consider the advisability of using its eminent domain powers to condemn a property and thus prevent an undesirable alteration, few communities are likely to want to condemn property simply because the owner proposes an undesirable alteration. Even those communities willing to condemn an important property may lack the funds to pay for it.

I. COMMISSION TO HOLD PUBLIC HEARINGS ON APPLICATIONS FOR CERTIFICATES OF APPROPRIATENESS

Typical Ordinance Provision:

SEATTLE:

The Board shall hold a public hearing on all applications for Certificate of Approval referred to it after notice given in the same manner as for hearings before the Board of Adjustment in Section 26.34 of the Zoning Ordinance (86300). A report of the action taken or determination made shall be forwarded to the Superintendent not later than 45 days after receipt of the application by the Board. (Seattle, Washington, Landmarks Ordinance, Section 8(b))

Annotation:

Recent court cases have focused increasingly on procedural requirements for local preservation commissions. Several Maryland court opinions have stated standards requiring commissions to permit an applicant to present evidence and cross-examine witnesses:

> The issue before the Commission was a factual one. Its determination was a quasi-judicial function. Therefore, Broadview was entitled to a trial-type hearing which included an adequate opportunity to present evidence and the right to cross-examine opposition witnesses. Broadview argues it was denied both. *Broadview Apartments Company v. Commission for Historical and Architectural Preservation* (No. 0 104101, Baltimore City Ct., July 15, 1980), *rev'd in part*, 433 A.2d 1214 (Md. App. 1981), slip op. at 3-4..

Two Maryland courts have pointed out the need for commission members with professional expertise to base their opinions in a particular matter on evidence presented to them at a public hearing. These cases suggest that commissioners may not base their decisions on personal knowledge of a situation, though they may use their professional knowledge and experience in evaluating testimony presented to them.

> Since there must be another hearing, it may not be amiss to observe that the Commission, in making its findings and arriving at its decision, is required to act solely on the evidence before it. . . . The personal knowledge of the members of the Commission cannot be considered as evidence. *Annapolis Emergency Hospital Association, Inc. v. Annapolis Historic District Commission* (Law No. D-962, Anne Arundel County Cir. Ct., Md., Apr. 14, 1977), slip op. at 12.
>
> Section 8.03 provides that the Commission shall have a membership of three to seven persons, all qualified by public interest, knowledge or training in such fields as history, architectural preservation or urban design. This does not mean, however, that the Commission members may apply their own expertise in granting or refusing exterior structural change. They must base their opinions on the testimony and evidence presented by others. *Fout v. Frederick Historic District Commission* (Misc. No. 4005, Frederick County Cir. Ct., Md., Feb. 5, 1980), slip op. at 4-5.

This does not mean that commission members are not entitled to weigh the credibility of individual witnesses and to consider the reliability of written reports that may be presented to the commission:

> On the question of financial hardship Broadview presented two expert witnesses. All of the opposing evidence was in the form of written reports. As pointed out above, Broadview did not object to the introduction of the reports nor did it demand the right to cross-examine. Thus, the reports were properly before the Commission. The credibility of the witnesses and the reliability of the reports

are matters exclusively for the Commission. *Broadview Apartments Company v. Commission for Historical and Architectural Preservation* (No. 0 104101, Baltimore City Ct., July 15, 1980), *rev'd in part*, 433 A.2d. 1214 (Md. App. 1981), slip op. at 5.

The applicant will, in many instances, be the only party wishing to speak on a particular application. Nevertheless, the commission should conduct its meetings in anticipation of unexpected opposition and must be prepared to offer opponents an opportunity to address the commission. Some preservation commissions choose to leave the record of a public hearing open for a few days after the hearing in order to receive written submissions.

There will be occasions when one or more members of a preservation commission will need to disqualify themselves from voting on a matter in order to avoid the appearance of a conflict of interest or a denial of procedural due process. As discussed earlier on page A55, a Maryland trial court considered at length whether the chairman of a local preservation commission should have declined to vote on a matter that an organization of which she was currently vice-president had vigorously opposed and concluded that the chairman should not have voted on the matter.

A preservation commission must be careful to comply with applicable notice requirements before holding a public hearing lest a property owner dissatisfied with the commission's decision attack that decision as improperly reached.

J. PERMISSION FOR COMMISSION TO SEEK OUTSIDE TECHNICAL ADVICE

Typical Ordinance Provision:

NEW HAVEN:

The Commission may seek technical advice from outside its members on any application. The Clerk of the Commission shall see that the applicant and each Commissioner receives a copy of the consultant's written opinion at least 7 days before the hearing. (New Haven, Connecticut, Guidelines, Section I(B)(6))

Annotation:

The prudent preservation commission will anticipate and attempt to avoid litigation. There will be occasions when a commission will wish to deny a certificate of appropriateness for a requested alteration but will need to consult in advance with persons whose knowledge or experience will enable them to advise the commission on reasons for denying the certificate. Several commissions have built careful records to justify their denials of certificates of appropriateness requested for the application of aluminum or vinyl siding to houses within historic districts.

In Connecticut, the Norwich Historic District Commission realized in 1972 that a pending request for a certificate of appropriateness for the demolition of Lord's Tavern, an 18th century structure fronting on the Norwichtown Green, posed a serious threat to preservation goals in Norwich. Accordingly, the commission requested testimony from the Southeastern Connecticut Regional Planning Agency, the Connecticut Historical Commission, and the Connecticut Society of Architects. This testimony was presented at the public hearing on the certificate of appropriateness. After this hearing, the Norwich commission denied the request for a certificate of appropriateness.

As soon as it was apparent that the owner of the property would appeal in state court, the Norwich commission contacted the National Trust to inform it of the situation and to request legal assistance. Thereafter, the Norwich commission remained in close contact with the Connecticut Historical Commission, the Connecticut Trust for Historic Preservation, and the National Trust. The Connecticut Supreme Court upheld the initial decision of the Norwich commission (*Figarsky v. Norwich Historic District Commission*, 368 A.2d 163 (Conn. 1976)), and ultimately, the Connecticut Trust for Historic Preservation purchased Lord's Tavern for rehabilitation and resale. Without the careful record before the Norwich commission, based in part on testimony from organizations that had been requested to testify, it would have been more difficult to argue that the commission's decision had been correct and should be sustained.

K. ECONOMIC HARDSHIP ARGUMENTS

Typical Ordinance Provision:

DISTRICT OF COLUMBIA:

No permit shall be issued unless the Mayor finds that such issuance is necessary in the public interest or that a failure to issue a permit will result in unreasonable economic hardship to the owner. (District of Columbia Historic Landmark and Historic District Protection Act of 1978, D.C. Law 2-144, Section 6(f))

Annotation:

Though many property owners have made hardship arguments when applying for certificates of appropriateness, few court decisions have yet turned on or involved a hardship issue. Future cases involving preservation commissions are likely to focus increasingly on hardship issues. Some owners will argue that designation forces them to continue or institute expensive maintenance procedures, and others will argue that designation so burdens their property or inhibits its usefulness that a constitutional "taking" has occurred.

A Louisiana court held that the location of property within a historic district would not automatically make a case for hardship:

> And here the hardship referred to, the requirement of conformity to two separate and sometimes conflicting standards of construction, is neither "unusual" nor "particular" to Mercier. It is common to all property owners in the zoning district in which Mercier's lot is located and therefore is not a hardship which justifies the granting of a variance. To hold otherwise would have the effect of destroying the zoning district. *Phillips v. Board of Zoning Adjustments of City of New Orleans,* 197 So.2d 916, 920 (La. 1967).

Property owners making a hardship argument have often ignored alternatives open to them. The court in *Phillips* noted that though the property owner wished to violate a local ordinance prohibiting the construction of a second main building on his lot, alternatives were open to him:

> According to its own architect, Mercier could have accomplished its purpose by construction which did not violate the prohibition against two main buildings on one lot. Therefore, in the absence of a showing that approval of such nonviolative construction could not have been obtained from the Vieux Carre Commission, we cannot hold appellant suffered financial loss in being denied an opportunity to obtain an increased return from its property. Even if financial

loss had been shown, such loss is only a factor to be considered in determining hardship and will not, standing alone, constitute a hardship sufficient to justify a variance. *Id.* at 919.

Courts display an interest in hardship questions, though an insistence that a commission should consider hardship is not an indication of willingness to decide a case on the hardship issue alone. A Massachusetts trial court has stated in *Sleeper v. Old King's Highway Regional Historic District Commission* (No. 22799, Barnstable Div. Dist. Ct., March 6, 1987), *aff'd*, 417 N.E.2d 987 (Mass. App. 1981), that hardship is a factor to be considered by a preservation commission, even though a local ordinance may not require its consideration:

> Although not required to do so by the Act . . . it would be helpful to the court and would facilitate judicial review if, in the future, the commission would include in its decision specific findings of fact on the issue of substantial hardship. . . . The plaintiff is correct in concluding that the issue of hardship ought to be considered by the committee on its own initiative, whether or not the issue is specifically raised by an applicant. Slip op. at 15.

The issue of hardship is, of course, closely related to the issue of reasonable return. In the case of a charitable organization, the question whether designation of a significant structure owned by the charity prevents a reasonable return becomes instead whether the charity can make a reasonable beneficial use of its property. As with other important preservation issues, this question was first litigated in New York State:

> The criterion for commercial property is where the continuance of the landmark prevents the owner from obtaining an adequate return. A comparable test for a charity would be where maintenance of the landmark either physically or financially prevents or seriously interferes with carrying out the charitable purpose. In this instance the answer would depend on the proper resolution of subsidiary questions, namely, whether the preservation of these buildings would seriously interfere with the use of the property, whether the buildings are capable of conversion to a useful purpose without excessive cost, or whether the cost of maintaining them without use would entail serious expenditure— all in the light of the purposes and resources of the petitioner. *Trustees of Sailors' Snug Harbor v. Platt*, 288 N.Y.S.2d 314, 316 (1968).

More recently, the New York Court of Appeals has stated firmly that "charitable organizations are not created for financial return in the same sense as private businesses":

> [F]or them the standard is refined to permit the landmark designation restriction only so long as it does not physically or financially prevent, or seriously

interfere with the carrying out of the charitable purpose. *Society for Ethical Culture in City of New York v. Spatt*, 415 N.E.2d 922, 925 (N.Y. 1980).

The New York Court held that the Society had failed to show "compelling circumstances" that would require a demolition permit for its meetinghouse:

> Particularly significant in the *Lutheran Church* case was the fact that the church had tried unsuccessfully to modify the structure to suit its needs, and that no further accommodation, short of demolition and rebuilding, would have alleviated the serious space problems which had arisen. . . . The Society has shown no such compelling circumstances here. . . . Although the Society does argue that the physical structure of the Meeting House is ill-adapted to its present needs, by no means are we assured that the only feasible solution to this problem would entail the demolition of the now protected building facade. There is no genuine complaint that eleemosynary activities within the landmark are wrongfully disrupted, but rather the complaint is instead that the landmark stands as an effective bar against putting the property to its most lucrative use. But there simply is no constitutional requirement that a landowner always be allowed his property's most beneficial use. . . . *Id.* at 926.

In *Penn Central Transportation Company v. New York City*, 438 U.S. 104 (1978), the U.S. Supreme Court upheld the designation of Grand Central Terminal against arguments that designation was a "taking" and noted that the owners of the structure could still obtain a "reasonable return" from their property:

> On this record, we conclude that the application of New York City's Landmarks Law has not effected a "taking" of appellants' property. The restrictions imposed are substantially related to the promotion of the general welfare and not only permit reasonable beneficial use of the landmark site but also afford appellants opportunities further to enhance not only the Terminal site proper but also other properties. *Id.* at 138.

An Illinois court has recognized the possibility that when the value of property has been enhanced because of its location within a historic district or its proximity to a structure of major historical importance for whose protection a historic district has been created, regulation of the uses and structures permitted on that property is not unreasonable:

> The proximity of the property to the Lincoln Home increases its value, and yet it is clear that use not in conformity with the existing zoning would be detrimental to the Lincoln Home Area and the total concept of the municipality relating to historical preservation. When property has an enhanced value by reason of planning and zoning for historical preservation, the zoning ordinances to implement the planning can hardly be said to be confiscatory or unreasonable or unconstitutional simply because the owners seek to use it for commercial purposes to exploit the visitors and tourists attracted, in part at least, by the

creation of the Historical District. *M & N Enterprises, Inc. v. City of Springfield*, 250 N.E.2d 289, 293 (Ill. 1969).

L. FORM OF DECISION AND REQUIRED FINDINGS

Typical Ordinance Provisions:

NATCHEZ:

The decision of the Commission shall be in the form of a written order to the Municipal Building Inspector. . . . In cases where the Commission has disapproved the plans, the Building Inspector shall furnish the applicant with a copy of the Commission's written order, together with a copy of any recommendations the Commission may have made for changes necessary to be made before the plans will be reconsidered. (Natchez, Mississippi, Ordinance, Sections III(3 and 4))

BERKELEY:

For applications relating to landmark sites, the proposed work shall not adversely affect the exterior architectural features of the landmark and, where specified in the designation for a publicly owned landmark, its major interior architectural features; nor shall the proposed work adversely affect the special character or special historical, architectural or aesthetic interest or value of the landmark and its site, as viewed both in themselves and in their setting.

For applications relating to property in historic districts, the proposed work shall not adversely affect the exterior architectural features of the subject property or the relationship and congruity between the subject structure or feature and its neighboring structures and surroundings, including facade, setback and height; nor shall the proposed work adversely affect the special character or special historical, architectural or aesthetic interest or value of the district. The proposed work shall also conform to such further standards as may be embodied in the designation of the historic district. (Berkeley, California, Ordinance, Sections 6.2 (a)(1) and (2))

Annotation:

The preservation commission's decision to approve or deny a certificate of appropriateness may either take the form of an order to another municipal official to take certain action or a decision to be sent to the applicant. If the decision is in the form of an order to an official, a copy of the order should be furnished to the applicant.

Many decisions that a preservation commission must make will be routine approvals of applications for certificates of appropriateness. In making certain more controversial decisions, the commission will want to be careful to specify its reasons for approving or denying a certificate. If a preservation ordinance contains criteria for the commission to follow in reaching a decision, the commission's decision should recite these criteria and state the findings made in accordance with them. Commission staff should remember that criteria can be stated in the form of work to be avoided or prohibited. The commission's written decision will constitute an important part of the record if the decision is challenged in court by a dissatisfied applicant and must contain enough information to let a court know why the commission reached a particular decision:

> The record must disclose the facts on which the Commission acted and a statement of the reasons for its action. Without such a record the reviewing court cannot perform its duty of determining whether the action of the Commission was arbitrary or capricious. . . . The record in this case is completely void of any reference to the historic or architectural value of the subject property. . . . There must be a finding of fact to that effect and that finding must be spread upon the record and supported by evidence. . . . It is quite proper for the Commission to act informally in arriving at their decision, but once made, the decision of the Commission should be a formal writing setting forth the factors which it considered, the evidence in support thereof and the reasons for its decision. *Fout v. Frederick Historic District Commission* (Misc. No. 4005, Frederick County Cir. Ct., Md., Feb. 5, 1980), slip op. at 4-5.

In *Zartman v. Reisem*, 399 N.Y.S.2d 506 (1977), a New York trial court emphasized the importance of a connection between the stated purposes of a local preservation ordinance and a specific decision by a preservation commission: "If the Board's decision, based upon sufficient evidence, is consistent with the values which the municipality sought to preserve in the special district involved, the Board's action is not arbitrary or capricious." *Id.* at 510.

In *Gumley v. Nantucket Board of Selectmen*, the Supreme Judicial Court of Massachusetts stated in 1977:

> The statute does not give the plaintiffs an absolute right to the certificates they seek. The commission is not compelled to grant the certificates. It has discretionary power in acting thereon. It must act fairly and reasonably on the application presented to it, keeping in mind the purposes of the statute. The decision of the commisson cannot be disturbed either by the board or by the court "unless it is based on a legally untenable ground, or is unreasonable, whimsical, capricious or arbitrary." 358 N.E.2d 1011, 1015 (Mass. 1977).

M. GIVING NOTICE OF COMMISSION'S DECISION TO APPLICANT

Typical Ordinance Provision:

MANSFIELD, CONNECTICUT:

All decisions of the Commission granting or refusing a Certificate of Appropriateness shall be in writing, a copy thereof shall be sent to the applicant by certified mail with a return receipt requested, and a copy filed with the Town Clerk. (Mansfield, Connecticut, Rules and Regulations, Section 6(a))

Annotation:

A preservation commission must notify each applicant for a certificate of appropriateness of its decision. Some form of *written* notification should be sent to the applicant. If an application has been approved, the notification need not be elaborate, though it should refer to the date of the application's submission in case an applicant has submitted more than one application. For the same reason, the notification should identify the property involved in the application.

At times a certificate may have been approved in part and denied in part. If so, a clear explanation of which portions of the application were approved and which denied should be given to the applicant. If an application has been denied, notification should be sent to the applicant and by registered mail if the application has been particularly controversial. There should be a clear record that the commission notified the applicant of the denial of the application within the required time period. Otherwise an applicant may later charge the commission with failure to act on the application and invoke the provision in many preservation ordinances granting constructive approval to any application on which a commission did not act promptly, within a required time period. The commission should keep a copy of each notification sent. Some commissions establish a separate file for *each* designated landmark and for *every* property in the historic districts under their jurisdiction.

N. EXPLANATION OF COMMISSION'S DISAPPROVAL OF PROPOSED PLANS

Typical Ordinance Provision:

PADUCAH, KENTUCKY:

In case of the disapproval of plans by the HARC, the Commission shall state the reasons for such disapproval in writing and transmit the written statement to the applicant. The written statement shall also contain suggestions of the Commission in regard to appropriateness within the zone of the property in question. (Paducah, Kentucky, Zoning Ordinance, Section 62.05)

Annotation:

A preservation commission must provide an adequate explanation of its reasons for disapproving a plan submitted to it and denying a requested certificate of appropriateness. This cannot be overemphasized. Unless a commission can explain and justify its decision, the decision may be challenged as arbitrary and capricious. A commission that has established guidelines for local property owners to follow may be able to refer to such guidelines in its explanation, but a commission that has not established guidelines will need to write a careful exposition of its decision. It should be kept in mind, though, that some commission decisions will set precedents to be followed in the future, and that, accordingly, the written explanations of these decisions should focus on principles the commission will follow in making future decisions.

Because a denial statement issued by a preservation commission may be the prelude to litigation brought by a dissatisfied property owner, the wording of the denial statement is extremely important. All members of the preservation commission should have the opportunity to read a proposed denial statement before it is sent to a property owner. A preservation commission will need to keep in its files copies of all denial statements issued by it.

In an unreported 1979 Massachusetts trial court opinion, *Sears v. Brown* (No. 75-3849, Middlesex Sup. Ct., Sept. 25, 1979), the court noted with approval the careful statement by the Bedford Historic District Commission of its reasons for denying a certificate of appropriateness for the piercing of a stone wall within a local historic district:

The Commission stated seven "reasons" for its decision. In paragraph #1 of its statement of reasons, the Commission states that the proposed change "would cause a significant change in the character to an area of prime historic value and interest. The general area abutting and including the proposed walkway is unique in the Town." The Commission proceeded to discuss in detail the particular character and features of the immediate area and concluded that, "The stone walls themselves are an integral and attractive feature which serve to define and enhance the general historic ambience of the entire contiguous area." Clearly, this is the statement of an adequate reason for the decision denying the permit. It reflects the fact that the Commission considered the factors they were required to consider under § 9 of the Act. It was consistent with the stated purpose of the Act. . . . In its second stated reason, the Commission referred to anticipated use of the walkway by the public with the increased potential for damage and debris. And, in its third stated reason, the Commission referred to the possibility of use by vehicles. Slip op. at 3-4.

Even a careful statement of reasons for denying a requested certificate must rest on evidence in the record. A commission in Rochester, New York, was judicially overruled because its stated reasons for denying a requested certificate were not supported by the record:

> The Board also based its determination upon its finding that "the house seems to be suitable for conversion to income-producing use." That finding is wholly arbitrary and unsupported in the record. The Board has not identified any such use and no proof was submitted in that regard. *Wolk v. Reisem*, 413 N.Y.S.2d 60, 61 (App. Div. 1979).

O. FAILURE OF COMMISSION TO REVIEW PLANS IN TIMELY FASHION

Typical Ordinance Provisions:

HUNTSVILLE:

If no action upon an application for a certificate submitted to the Commission has been taken at the expiration of thirty (30) days from the date of application and submission of plans, such application shall be deemed to have been approved and, if all other requirements of the City have been met, the Building Inspector may issue a permit for the proposed building. (Huntsville, Alabama, Regulations, Section I(E))

Wilmington:

The commission shall act upon each application within forty-five days from the date of filing the application. If action is not taken within forty-five days from the date of filing, the application shall be deemed to be approved, and a certificate showing the filing date and failure by the commission to take action within the stated time shall be issued by the commission, if requested. This time limit may be waived by mutual consent of the applicant and the Design Review Commission. (Wilmington, Delaware, Ordinance, Section 1(f)(2))

New Haven:

Failure of the Commission to act within 120 days shall constitute approval and no other evidence of approval shall be needed. (New Haven, Connecticut, Ordinance, Section 6(b))

Annotation:

Property owners planning a large project will work closely with an architect and may have entered into involved financing arrangements. Preservation commissions occasionally need to be reminded that substantial costs can be added to a project if the commission does not act with reasonable promptness.

Provisions such as those cited above appear increasingly in preservation ordinances. They serve to prevent a preservation commission from "sitting" on an application for a certificate of appropriateness and let a property owner know a period within which he can expect a decision from the commission. Thirty days is probably as short a period and three months as long a period as should be specified, unless the application is particularly complex or the project's impact is very broad.

P. WORK PERFORMED REQUIRED TO CONFORM WITH CERTIFICATE OF APPROPRIATENESS

Typical Ordinance Provision:

Louisville:

All work performed pursuant to the issuance of a certificate of no exterior effect or certificate of appropriateness shall conform to the requirements of such certificate. It shall be the duty of the Department of Building and Housing Inspection to inspect from time to time any work performed pursuant to such certificate to assure such compliance. In the event work is performed not in accordance with such certificate, the Director of the Department of Building and Housing Inspection or his designated representative shall issue a stop work order and all work shall cease. No person, firm or corporation shall undertake any work on such project as long as such stop work order shall continue in effect. (Louisville, Kentucky, Ordinance, Section 9)

Annotation:

Though an effective preservation ordinance will contain both enforcement and penalty provisions, it may be useful to include a provision permitting work not in accordance with an issued certificate of appropriateness to be halted before it is completed. Authorization for this type of immediate action may be the most effective way to get the commission's directions followed. Some communities may wish to consider requiring property owners to post performance bonds to guarantee that a major project will not deviate from the terms of a certificate of appropriateness. Unfortunately, in many communities, small contractors and owners of single properties cause more headaches for commissions than do major projects, because work may be completed before a commission realizes that a certificate of appropriateness has been violated.

Q. CERTIFICATE OF APPROPRIATENESS VOID IF CONSTRUCTION NOT COMMENCED

Typical Ordinance Provisions:

MANSFIELD, CONNECTICUT:

A Certificate of Appropriateness shall become void unless construction is commenced within six months of date of issue. Certificates of Appropriateness shall be issued for a period of eighteen months and are renewable. (Mansfield, Connecticut, Rules, Section 6(c))

TELLURIDE, COLORADO:

A Certificate of Appropriateness shall expire twenty-four (24) months after issuance unless a building permit has been issued. If twenty-four (24) months after expiration of the last building permit issued for the project, the project is not completed as shown on the Certificate of Appropriateness the project shall be deemed in violation of this Ordinance. (Telluride, Colorado, Ordinance 311)

Los Angeles:

Any Certificate of Appropriateness which has been approved under the provisions of this Section shall expire twenty-four (24) months from the date of issuance if the work authorized is not commenced within this time period. Further, such Certificate will expire if the work authorized is not completed within five (5) years of the date of issuance. (Los Angeles, California, Ordinance No. 152-422, Section 1, L)

Annotation:

Such a provision discourages property owners from applying for certificates of appropriateness for alterations they are incapable of financing. Ideally, a property owner should first seek financing for a proposed alteration and then approach the preservation commission for approval of the alteration.

In some communities, it will be necessary to define carefully the event or events that will trigger the running of such time periods. Mere groundbreaking that is not followed by other construction activities should not be sufficient to constitute the undertaking of construction, though under applicable legal precedents it may be "commencement" of a project in some states.

R. CHANGE IN SCOPE AFTER ISSUANCE OF CERTIFICATE

Typical Ordinance Provision:

Mansfield, Connecticut:

Any change in the scope of work subsequent to the issuance of a Certificate of Appropriateness shall require issuance of a new Certificate of Appropriateness for said changes. (Mansfield, Connecticut, Rules, Section 8(b))

Annotation:

After a property owner has obtained a certificate of appropriateness for a desired alteration to his property, he may wish to change the proposed alteration. Any such change should require a new application for a second certificate. Certain types of amendments to projects may be handled expeditiously if a commission has approved, in advance, specified categories of changes. Some preservation commissions, for instance, approve, in advance, lists of acceptable paint colors so that a property owner desiring to use one of the approved colors does not need to apply for a certificate of appropriateness, though a property owner desiring to use a nonlisted color might seek approval through the normal application procedures.

V. Demolition Applications

A. COMMISSION'S AUTHORITY TO COMMENT ON DEMOLITION PERMIT APPLICATIONS

Typical Ordinance Provisions:

CINCINNATI:

In addition to the provisions of Section 741-13, if an application for a certificate of appropriateness seeks approval of demolition, the historic conservation board may delay determination of the application for a period of 180 days upon a finding that the structure is of such importance that alternatives to demolition may be feasible and should be actively pursued by both the applicant and the board. In the event that action on an application is delayed as provided herein, the board may take such steps as it deems necessary to preserve the structure concerned, in accordance with the purposes of this ordinance. Such steps may include but shall not be limited to, consultation with civic groups, public agencies and interested citizens, recommendations for acquisition of property by public or private bodies or agencies, and exploration of the possibility of moving one or more structures or other features. (Cincinnati, Ohio, Ordinance, Section 741-15)

DISTRICT OF COLUMBIA:

Before the Mayor may issue a permit to demolish an historic landmark or a building or structure in an historic district, the Mayor shall review the permit application in accordance with this section and place notice of the application in the *District of Columbia Register*. . . . No permit shall be issued unless the Mayor finds that issuance of the permit is necessary in the public interest, or that failure to issue a permit will result in unreasonable economic hardship to the owner. (District of Columbia Historic Landmark and Historic District Protection Act of 1978, D.C. Law 2-144, Section 5)

Annotation:

A provision requiring the municipal agency responsible for issuing demolition permits to notify the preservation commission whenever a permit is requested for the demolition of a building under the commission's jurisdiction will help alert the commission to impending demolitions.

In San Antonio, all demolition permit applications must be reviewed by the city's Historic Preservation Officer. (*See* August 1977 *Landmark and Historic District Commissions* newsletter.)

A preservation commission should have the authority to comment on any request for a permit to demolish a designated landmark or a structure within a historic district, though not all preservation commissions will have authority to do more than delay a proposed demolition. Occasionally a preservation commission may be able to encourage a property owner not to demolish his building until an attempt can be made to locate either suitable tenants to make the building economically viable again or a purchaser willing to acquire and rehabilitate the structure. The strongest preservation commissions have the power to deny demolition permission. The use of such power by preservation commissions has now been upheld by courts in Maryland, Louisiana, Connecticut, Pennsylvania, and Missouri. *Mayor and Aldermen of City of Annapolis v. Anne Arundel County*, 316 A.2d 807 (Md. 1974); *Maher v. City of New Orleans*, 516 F.2d 1051 (5th Cir. 1975); *Figarsky v. Norwich Historic District Commission*, 368 A.2d 163 (Conn. 1976); *First Presbyterian Church v. City Council of City of York*, 360 A.2d 257 (Penn. 1976); *Lafayette Park Baptist Church v. Board of Adjustment of City of St. Louis* (No. 782-3445, St. Louis City Cir. Ct., May 3, 1979).

In *Maher v. City of New Orleans*, 516 F.2d 1051 (5th Cir. 1975), a court stated:

> An ordinance forbidding the demolition of certain structures if it serves a permissible goal in an otherwise reasonable fashion, does not seem on its face constitutionally distinguishable from ordinances regulating other aspects of land ownership, such as building height, set back or limitations on use. We conclude that the provision requiring a permit before demolition and the fact that in some cases permits may not be obtained does not alone make out a case of taking. *Id.* at 1066.

The New York Court of Apeals noted in *Society for Ethical Culture v. Spatt*, 415 N.E.2d 922 (N.Y. 1980), that "there simply is no constitutional requirement that a landowner always be allowed his property's most beneficial use." *Id.* at 926. The Court went on to suggest that a charitable applicant seeking permission to demolish a designated landmark must establish that remodeling of the landmark's interior would not permit the applicant's charitable work to be continued:

> Although the Society does argue that the physical structure of the Meeting House is ill adapted to its present needs, by no means are we assured that the only feasible solution to this problem would entail the demolition of the now protected building facade. . . . It is noteworthy that the designation we are here

concerned with applies only to the building facade, and it is possible that studies would reveal that without disturbing this protected portion, feasible modifications could be employed to allow the Society to continue its charitable activities in the building, as it has for over sixty years. *Id.*

B. ACCEPTABLE COMMISSION REACTIONS TO APPLICATIONS FOR DEMOLITION PERMITS

Typical Ordinance Provision:

BERKELEY:

If the application is for a permit to demolish, the Commission shall approve or modify the application in whole or in part, or suspend action on it for a period not to exceed one (1) year. (Berkeley, California, Ordinance, Section 6.1 (c) (2))

Annotation:

The possible responses that a preservation commission may make to an application for a demolition permit should be specified in a preservation ordinance. The strongest preservation ordinances permit commissions to deny demolition permit applications. Less strong ordinances permit commissions to impose demolition delays of varying lengths. Still less strong ordinances authorize a commission to comment on a proposed demolition, in hopes that the commission may be able to negotiate with the owner applying for the demolition permit.

Strong preservation commissions, those with the authority to deny demolition permission, are far more effective in maintaining the existing integrity of a community's surviving architectural resources than are those commissions with only the authority to delay demolition for specified periods of time. It is always possible, though, to amend an existing ordinance to give more responsibility and greater authority to a preservation commission after its goals have become widely understood throughout a community.

C. CONSIDERATION OF POST-DEMOLITION PLANS

Typical Ordinance Provisions:

WILMINGTON:

The Design Review Commission shall consider, for buildings to be demolished . . . post-demolition plans for any site in a Historic District and the relation of those plans to the singular quality or public purpose of the unique public improvement in the District. (Wilmington, Delaware, Standards, Section 112)

PENSACOLA:

As used herein, plans shall mean drawings or sketches with sufficient detail to show, as far as they relate to exterior appearance, the architectural design of the building (both before and after the proposed work is done in the cases of altering, renovating, demolishing or razing a building or structure). . . . (Pensacola, Florida, Ordinance, Section Three (a))

DISTRICT OF COLUMBIA:

In those cases in which the Mayor finds that the demolition is necessary to allow the construction of a project of special merit, no demolition permit shall be issued unless a permit for new construction is issued simultaneously under section 8 of this act and the owner demonstrates the ability to complete the project. (District of Columbia Historic Landmark and Historic District Protection Act of 1978, D.C. Law 2-144, Section 5)

Annotation:

A preservation commission should not, if possible, grant demolition permission without reviewing, at the same time, the plans for the building that would replace the structure to be demolished. No preservation commission should participate in site-clearing programs. A Louisiana federal district court upheld, in an unreported opinion, the denial by the Vieux Carre Commission of a demolition permit because the owner/applicant did not present to the commission plans for the construction of a new building on the site that would be compatible with other Vieux Carre buildings:

> The Vieux Carre Commission would be willing to permit the demolition of the present structures if the plaintiff would agree to erect replacement struc-

ture or structures which would be in keeping with the architecture of the Vieux Carre. However, the plaintiff intends to use the space which would be made available by such demolition for a parking lot. . . . [T]he said Commission has a legal and constitutional right to impress reasonable conditions relative to replacement of the demolished structure before granting a demolition permit. *Whitty v. City of New Orleans* (No. 6367 Civil Action, E.D. La., Oct. 21, 1959), slip op. at 2-3, 4.

The City of New Orleans enacted, between April 1974 and December 1976, a series of seven ordinances imposing a demolition moratorium on certain portions of the city's central business district. Owners able to meet specified conditions were still able to obtain demolition permission. One such condition was that a property owner have definite plans to construct a new building on the site of the structure he sought to demolish. (*See* October 1977 *Landmark and Historic District Commissions* newsletter.)

Nevertheless, a New York court has ruled that the Rochester preservation commission may not require an applicant for a demolition permit to submit a request for a certificate of appropriateness for new construction at the same time:

> In our view, the Board erroneously interpreted the ordinance. The only reasonable construction which may be placed upon its language is that demolition and new construction are separate events each of which require[s] the issuance of a certificate of appropriateness before its undertaking. *Wolk v. Reisem*, 413 N.Y.S.2d 60, 61 (App. Div. 1979).

Accordingly, the drafter of a preservation ordinance should decide whether he wishes a local commission to have the power of the Vieux Carre Commission to consider post-demolition plans or would prefer that the commission be prohibited, as in Rochester, from weighing an applicant's post-demolition plans as a factor in deciding whether to approve demolition.

D. DEMOLITION CRITERIA

Typical Ordinance Provisions:

LOS ANGELES:

Upon receipt of an application for a Certificate of Appropriateness for demoli-

tion, the Planning Commission shall as soon as possible make a determination, supported by written findings, whether one or more of the following criteria are met:
(1) The structure is of such interest or quality that it would reasonably meet national, state or local criteria for designation as an historic or architectural landmark.
(2) The structure is of such unusual or uncommon design texture or materials that it could not be reproduced or be reproduced only with great difficulty and expense.
(3) Retention of the structure would aid substantially in preserving and protecting a structure which meets criteria (1) or (2) hereinabove.

Where the Planning Commission determines that one or more of these criteria are met, no Certificate of Appropriateness shall be issued and the application shall be denied. (Los Angeles, California, Ordinance, No. 152-422, Section 1(F)(4)(b))

District of Columbia:

In any instance where there is a claim of unreasonable economic hardship, the owner shall submit, by affidavit, to the Mayor at least twenty (20) days prior to the public hearing, at least the following information:

(A) for all property:

(i) the amount paid for the property, the date of purchase and the party from whom purchased, including a description of the relationship, if any, between the owner and the person from whom the property was purchased;

(ii) the assessed value of the land and improvements thereon according to the two (2) most recent assessments;

(iii) real estate taxes for the previous two (2) years;

(iv) annual debt service, if any, for the previous two (2) years;

(v) all appraisals obtained within the previous two (2) years by the owner or applicant in connection with his purchase, financing or ownership of the property;

(vi) any listing of the property for sale or rent, price asked and offers received, if any; and

(vii) any consideration by the owner as to profitable adaptive uses for the property; and

(B) for income-producing property:

(i) annual gross income from the property for the previous two (2) years;

(ii) itemized operating and maintenance expenses for the previous two (2) years;

(iii) annual cash flow, if any, for the previous two (2) years. (District of Columbia Historic Landmark and Historic District Protection Act of 1978, D.C. Law 2-144, Section 5)

BERKELEY:

The Commission shall find that the designated landmark or portion thereof is in such condition that it is not feasible to preserve or restore it, taking into consideration the economic feasibility of alternatives to the proposal, and balancing the interest of the public in preserving the designated landmark or portion thereof and the interest of the owner of the landmark site in its utilization. (Berkeley, California, Ordinance, Section 6.2(b))

Annotation:

Carefully drafted criteria for a preservation commission to consider when deciding whether to grant or deny a requested demolition permit may help the commission build a strong case for denying a permit request. If criteria are specified in an ordinance, then the preservation commission will be able to collect evidence to uphold several criteria and thus justify its decision, should the owner of the property wish to appeal the preservation commission's denial of his demolition permit application.

Recently a number of court decisions have focused on the question of the economic feasibility of rehabilitation. In *Dempsey v. Boys' Club of City of St. Louis*, 558 S.W.2d 262 (Mo. Ct. App. 1977), a court indicated issues that must be weighed when economic feasibility is considered:

> The term "rehabilitation impracticable" as used in the ordinance implies something more than infeasibility of restoration because of physical condition. It contemplates the broader question whether the property can be turned to use or account profitably. If so, the declared public policy of protecting the historic and cultural heritage of the city saves the property from destruction in the absence of constitutional limitations. There is in this record no substantial evidence that it would be uneconomic to restore and rehabilitate these buildings—no evidence that the cost of restoration and rehabilitation precludes the owner from making any reasonably economic use of the properties. . . . There is no evidence that Boys' Club cannot economically utilize the properties or that it is impracticable to sell or lease them, or that Boys' Club is incapable of obtaining a reasonable return from the properties, or that no market exists for this type of property at a reasonable price. *Id.* at 266-67.

In another recent Missouri decision, *Lafayette Park Baptist Church v. Board of Adjustment of City of St. Louis*, 553 S.W.2d 856 (Mo. Ct. App. 1977), the court stated:

> [I]t is necessary that the standards established governing demolition in an historic district take into account the economic impact upon a given parcel where demoli-

tion is sought. It is not necessary that the standards be unduly rigid or specific, "so long as they are capable of a reasonable application and are sufficient to limit and define the Board's discretionary powers." . . . And these standards may achieve certain of their meaning from the observable character of the district to which they apply. *Id.* at 862.

A recent District of Columbia decision illustrates the difficulty property owners will have in that jurisdiction in the future making successful claims of economic hardship when they are denied demolition permits:

> [T]here was evidence that supported the Mayor's Agent's conclusions that petitioner had not met its burden of proof to show that no reasonable economic alternative use for the Building existed. There was evidence to substantiate the claims that the Building could be rented "as is" or with minimal renovation and that the Building could be fully renovated at a cost of less than that claimed by petitioner and then rented. . . . Since the issue is whether there was an alternative economic use for the Building, without consideration of the cost of its acquisition or the profit petitioner anticipated from its operation, use, or sale, the determination by the Mayor's Agent upon this record that such an alternative existed must be upheld. There may be a case in which the alternative economic use of a property placed under restriction by the Act so diminishes the value of the property as to make it an unreasonable alternative, but this is not that case. *900 G Street Associates v. Department of Housing and Community Development*, 430 A.2d 1387 (D.C.App. 1981).

E. DEMOLITION DELAY PERIOD

Typical Ordinance Provisions:

LOUDOUN COUNTY, VIRGINIA:

The owner of a building or structure, the razing or demolition of which is subject to the provisions of this article, shall, as a matter of right be entitled to raze or demolish such building or structure provided that:
  a. He has applied to the Board for such right.
  b. The owner has for a period of time set forth in the time schedule hereinafter contained, and at a price reasonably related to its fair market value, made a bona fide offer to sell such building or structure, and the land pertaining thereto, to any person, firm, corporation, government or agency thereof, or political subdivision or agency thereof, which gives reasonable assurance that it will preserve and restore the building or structure and the land pertaining thereto.
  c. No bona fide contract, binding upon all parties thereto, shall have been

executed for the sale of any such building or structure, and the land pertaining thereto, prior to the expiration of the applicable time period as set forth in the time schedule hereinafter contained. Any appeal which may be taken to the court from the decision of the Board of Supervisors, shall not affect the right of the owner to make a bona fide offer to sell. Offers to sell as provided in Section 750.19 (b) shall be made within one year of the date of application to the Board of Supervisors. The time schedule for offers to sell shall be as follows:

Property Valued At:	Minimum Offer to Sell Period:
$25,000 or less	2 months
$25,000-$40,000	3 months
$40,000-$55,000	4 months
$55,000-$75,000	5 months
$75,000-$90,000	6 months
$90,000 or more	9 months

(Loudoun County, Virginia, Ordinance, Section 750-19)

CORAL GABLES:

If the appeal is upheld by the City Commission, such building may be demolished, provided, however, that before a demolition permit is issued, notice of proposed demolition shall be given as follows:

(1) For buildings rated Exceptional	180 days notice
(2) For buildings rated Excellent	120 days notice
(3) For buildings rated Notable	90 days notice
(4) For buildings of Value as Part of the Scene	60 days notice

(Coral Gables, Florida, Ordinance, Section 6(2)(b))

Annotation:

If a preservation commission cannot deny a demolition permit, it should have the power to impose a demolition delay, in order to give the commission and other local preservation groups a period of time in which they can negotiate with the building owner. Under some preservation ordinances, the length of the demolition delay will depend upon the market value or architectural significance of the building, with longer delays for more valuable buildings. Such a sliding scale of delay periods recognizes the fact that larger and more valuable buildings will generally require more sophisticated preservation schemes, and that preparation of such schemes can be extremely time-consuming for all parties involved.

In some communities, power to impose a demolition delay will be as much authority as the municipality will be willing to delegate to a preservation commission. If delegation of the power to deny demolition is politically infeasible, it is nonetheless imperative that an effective preservation commission do everything in its power to negotiate with a property owner who wishes to demolish an architecturally significant building.

A preservation ordinance should not contain an unreasonably brief demolition delay period.

F. COMMISSION ACTIVITIES WHILE ACTION ON DEMOLITION PERMIT SUSPENDED

Typical Ordinance Provision:

> BERKELEY:
>
> In the event action on the application is suspended as provided above in this section, the Commission may take such steps as it deems necessary to preserve the structure concerned, in accordance with the purposes of this ordinance. Such steps may include, but shall not be limited to, consultation with civic groups, public agencies and interested citizens, recommendations for acquisition of property by public or private bodies or agencies, and exploration of the possibility of moving one or more structures or other features. (Berkeley, California, Ordinance, Section 6.1 (d))

Annotation:

It is helpful for a preservation ordinance to suggest approaches a preservation commission may take to help save all or part of a designated building during any demolition delay imposed by the commission. Though few municipalities will have the necessary funding to acquire especially significant buildings through condemnation and even fewer communities might find condemnation a politically feasible approach to a building's preservation, condemnation is an alternative that should be considered and recommended by a preservation commission after other alternatives for a building's preservation have proven unsuccessful.

G. OWNER REQUIRED TO MAKE BONA FIDE OFFER TO SELL DURING DELAY PERIOD

Typical Ordinance Provisions:

LOUDOUN COUNTY, VIRGINIA:

NOTICE: Before making a bona fide offer to sell, provided for in section 750.19, an owner shall first file a statement with the Board of Supervisors of Loudoun County. The statement shall identify the property, state the offering price, the date the offer of sale is to begin and name and addresses of listing real estate agent, if any. The statement shall provide assurances that the building or structure shall be preserved and/or restored, as appropriate. No time period set forth in the time schedule contained in Section 750.18 shall begin to run until the statement has been filed. Within five days of receipt of a statement, copies of the statement shall be delivered to the members of the Board of Supervisors, members of the Planning Commission, and subscribers to notice provided in Article 12. (Loudoun County, Virginia, Ordinance, Section 750.19.1)

LOS ANGELES:

No Certificate of Appropriateness for such demolition shall be approved by the Planning Commission unless it finds that the applicant has, for a time period prescribed in the schedule below, made a good faith effort to sell or otherwise dispose of such structure at or below fair market value to any public or private person or agency which gives a reasonable assurance of its willingness to preserve and restore such structure and the land pertaining thereto. The time periods in the schedule below shall commence with the date of the filing of the certification of fair market value to subsection (a) above. (Los Angeles, California, Ordinance No. 152-422, Section 1(F)(4)(d))

Annotation:

Several ordinances require that owners wishing to demolish designated buildings offer the buildings and the land on which they stand for sale for a specified period of time, which will depend on each property's value. The delay period often does not begin to run until the property owner files certain information, so that an owner slow to file the information is effectively subject to a delay period longer than the one specified in the ordinance.

In *Cleckner v. City of Harrisburg*, a Pennsylvania trial court upheld the denial of a demolition permit because an owner did not prove his inability to sell properties at their fair market value:

> It can be fairly said that the appellant did not proceed prudently in offering his properties for sale. He did not offer the properties for sale through a real estate broker, evidently did not advertise them in a local newspaper, and set an inflated asking price of $125,000. All of these factors in our judgment only served to guarantee that a sale would not be consummated based on the fair market value of the properties. 10 D. & C. 3d 393, 401 (Pa. 1979).

H. ADDITIONAL DEMOLITION DELAY PERIOD IF CONDEMNATION APPEARS LIKELY

Typical Ordinance Provision:

TRENTON:

> If, at the expiration of this period of postponement, it appears to the commission that condemnation will be instituted by the city or the state governments within a reasonable time thereafter, the commission shall notify the building inspector in writing of an extension of the period of postponement for any period not to exceed 60 days. (Trenton, New Jersey, Ordinance, p. 10)

Annotation:

At least one preservation ordinance provides for an extension of the initial demolition delay period if it appears likely that the power of eminent domain will be used by either the city or by the state to acquire a threatened property. The necessity for such a provision can be avoided by making the initial delay period sufficiently long for condemnation possibilities to be thoroughly explored before the expiration of that period. The city of Louisville, Kentucky, instituted condemnation procedures to acquire two architecturally significant houses whose owner wished to demolish them, and the city of Alexandria, Virginia, acquired by condemnation a building that had been offered for sale at a price exceeding the condemnation amount.

APPENDIX A: MODEL ORDINANCE   A109

VI. The Preservation Commission and Governmentally Owned Property

A. PROPERTY OWNED BY PUBLIC AGENCIES

Typical Ordinance Provisions:

BERKELEY:

The Commission shall take appropriate steps to notify all public agencies which own or may acquire property in the City of Berkeley about the existence and character of designated landmarks and historic districts, and the Commission shall cause a current record of such landmarks and districts to be maintained in each such public agency. In the case of any publicly owned property on a landmark site or in an historic district which is not subject to the permit review procedures of the City, the agency owning the said property shall seek the advice of the Commission prior to approval or authorization of any construction, alteration or demolition thereon, including the placement of street furniture, lighting and landscaping; and the Commission in consultation with the Design Review Committee of the Civic Art Commission, in appropriate cases, shall render a report to the owner as expeditiously as possible, based on the purposes and standards of this ordinance. If Commission review of a public project involving construction, alteration or demolition on a landmark site or in an historic district is required under any other law or under the Charter, the Commission shall render the report referred to in this section to such public agency without specific request therefor. (Berkeley, California, Ordinance, Section 11)

NEW YORK:

Reports by commission on plans for proposed projects.
   a. Plans for the construction, reconstruction, alteration or demolition of any

improvement or proposed improvement which:
  (1) is owned by the city or is to be constructed upon property owned by the city; and
  (2) is or is to be located on a landmark site or in an historic district or contains an interior landmark; shall, prior to city action approving or otherwise authorizing the use of such plans with respect to securing the performance of such work, be referred by the agency of the city having responsibility for the preparation of such plans to the commission for a report. Such report shall be submitted to the mayor, the city council and to the agency having such responsibility and shall be published in the City Record within 45 days after such referral.

b. (1) No officer or agency of the city whose approval is required by law for the construction or effectuation of a city-aided project shall approve the plans or proposal for, or application for approval of, such project, unless, prior to such approval, such officer or agency has received from the commission a report on such plans, proposal or application for approval.
  (2) All such plans, proposals or applications for approval shall be referred to the commission for a report thereon before consideration of approval thereof is undertaken by any such officer or agency and the commission shall submit its report to each such officer and agency and such report shall be published in the City Record within 45 days after such referral. (New York, New York, Landmarks Ordinance, Section 207-17)

BOSTON:

No construction, reconstruction, exterior erection, replacement or alteration or demolition not requiring such a building permit or sign permit shall be undertaken by any person or by an officer, department, agency, authority or board of the city or commonwealth with respect to any improvement or exterior architectural feature in any landmark district or architectural conservation district or any improvement in any protection area, unless such person, officer, department, agency, authority, or board shall first have applied for and received such a certificate. The regulatory functions of the commission as described in this section shall extend to any property however owned and designated as a landmark or located in or to be constructed in any landmark district, architectural conservation district or protection area and to plans, projects or work to be executed or assisted by any governmental body or its officers, departments, agencies, authorities or boards and affecting any landmark or any improvement or exterior architectural feature located in or to be constructed in any landmark district, architectural conservation district or protection area. (Boston, Massachusetts, Landmarks Ordinance, Sections 5(d) and (e))

Annotation:

If a preservation commission is to be fully effective, it should have the authority to comment on proposed alterations or demolitions of municipally owned buildings, and to comment on proposed new construction on municipal property. In many communities the most architecturally significant buildings are municipally, or otherwise governmentally, owned. A preservation commission will want to assist companion municipal agencies in maintaining these distinctive and valuable structures.

A preservation commission should be careful to maintain a cordial relationship with other municipal agencies, so that when it becomes necessary for the commission to comment on the plans of another agency, the commission's purposes will be understood and the commission will not be thought meddlesome or obstructionist. A few preservation commissions have explicit authority to review proposed alterations to designated properties that are municipally owned.

The Indianapolis Historic Preservation Commission requested a formal opinion from the corporation counsel's office in Indianapolis concerning its powers to review proposed governmental work in locally designated historic districts. The opinion upheld a provision in the Indianapolis preservation ordinance and concluded:

> I would strongly advise that the principally affected Unigov Department and the Indianapolis Historic Preservation Commission cooperate at the planning stage of any proposed developments within an "historic area" so as to facilitate the prompt and efficient functioning of the Indianapolis Historic Preservation Commission and the other Unigov Departments or Agencies. (*See* October 1975 *Landmark and Historic District Commissions* newsletter.)

Ira J. Bach, secretary of the Commission on Chicago Historical and Architectural Landmarks, stated at a workshop for preservation commissions held in Boston in conjunction with the 1975 annual meeting of the National Trust for Historic Preservation that:

> Preservation cannot succeed as an afterthought. The resources are irretrievable. An awareness of the environment must be built into the planning process from the beginning, before momentum takes over to rule out options. . . . Agencies must be concerned first with environmental integrity as part of their responsibility and be receptive to preservation input if liaison is to proceed. . . . Environmental integrity must become first and foremost a local issue of great import, one as topical as the budget. It must have a following that demands understanding and positive action—then liaison can begin. (*See* February 1976 *Landmark and Historic District Commissions* newsletter.)

In Chicago, the preservation commission has taken preliminary steps toward the designation by the Chicago City Council of structures located on land owned by the Chicago Park District, an independent governmental body. Rather than trying to assert city authority to designate park property, the Commission on Chicago Historical and Architectural Landmarks began to negotiate with each involved institution after the Chicago Park District indicated that it might defer to each institution on the issue of designation. Written requests for consent to designation have been sent to each institution. The next step will be for the commission to hold a public hearing on each proposed designation. (*See* February 1977 *Landmark and Historic District Commissions* newsletter.)

In *Mayor and Aldermen of City of Annapolis v. Anne Arundel County*, 316 A.2d 807 (Md. 1974), a court held that a local preservation commission had jurisdiction over a structure owned by a county and could refuse a demolition permit:

> Secondly, to accomplish the primary purposes of historic area zoning, it is necessary that the exterior of the building having historic or architectural value be preserved against destruction or substantial impairment by *every one*, whether a private citizen or a governmental body. In short, the historically or architecturally valuable building is just as much lost by destruction by a public body as it would be by a private owner. The facts in the present case should lay to rest the notion that public bodies—as contrasted with private owners—would not be likely to press for demolition of buildings having established historic or architectural value. The General Assembly could well conclude that, to accomplish historic and architectural preservation, the jurisdiction of the Commission should extend to all owners be they private persons or governmental agencies. Otherwise, the primary purpose of the legislation would be frustated. *Id.* at 821.

A similar result was reached in *City of Ithaca v. County of Tompkins*, 355 N.Y.S.2d 275 (1974), though the court relied heavily on the statutory construction of state enabling legislation for local preservation commissions:

> [L]andmark preservation ordinances are directed at preserving buildings rather than policing the erection and use of buildings on the land. . . . By granting to all political subdivisions this special and additional source of power, the Legislature recognized that each local government has an independent and important interest in the protection of landmarks. As a consequence realty owned by a County which has been designated as an historic landmark or which is within an historic district is subject to the jurisdiction of that historic area's commission. *Id.* at 276-77.

To date, only one case has involved the power of a local preservation commission to designate property owned by a state agency, though commissions in cities such as New York have designated a number of significant buildings in state ownership. In *State v. City of Seattle*, 615 P.2d 461 (Wash. 1980), the court was careful to avoid holding that in all situations state-owned property would be immune from regulation by a local preservation commission:

> The University contends that a blanket rule of immunity applies to exempt state property from municipal regulation unless the legislature specifically provides otherwise. . . . Since the University is a state agency and no statute expressly provides that the Tract is subject to local laws, the University argues that the Tract is immune from the city's landmarks ordinance. . . . We decline to apply a rule of immunity, and find it unnecessary to express an opinion on the validity of such a rule. *Id.* at 463.

The dissenting judge in *City of Seattle* argued strongly that the state legislature's expressed concern for the preservation of architecturally and historically significant buildings was ignored by the majority:

> It is not unreasonable to conclude that the legislature not only did not bar the exercise of the police power of the City of Seattle as it related to the buildings in the Metropolitan Tract but actually gave authorization and encouragement for the kind of action taken by the City. *Id.* at 465.

No cases have yet involved the question whether a local preservation commission may regulate the property of a federal agency. Though technically a local commission may not regulate federal property, the eligibility of those properties that a local commission might choose to regulate for listing in the National Register of Historic Places will often have the effect of subjecting such properties to substantial regulation through the review process conducted by the Advisory Council on Historic Preservation pursuant to Section 106 of the National Historic Preservation Act.

B. COMMISSION'S AUTHORITY TO COMMENT ON PROPOSED MUNICIPAL LAND ACQUISITIONS WITHIN HISTORIC DISTRICT

Typical Ordinance Provision:

OAK PARK, ILLINOIS:

The Director of the Department of Planning and Development shall advise the chairman of the Landmarks Commission of all proposed acquisitions of property in the Historic District for public use, whether by the Village of Oak Park or by any other public agency. The Landmarks Commission shall evaluate the proposed public use and shall, in its discretion, make recommendations to the President and Board of Trustees in connection therewith. (Oak Park, Illinois, Ordinance, Section 4)

Annotation:

It is useful for a preservation commission to have the authority to comment on proposed municipal land acquisitions. The early involvement of a preservation commission in municipal land acquisition decisions is an important element in an overall municipal preservation program and helps assure the adequate consideration of possible alternative sites on which municipal construction would pose a lesser threat to designated landmarks or historic districts.

VII. Maintenance of Historic Properties

A. ORDINARY MAINTENANCE EXCLUSION

Typical Ordinance Provisions:

CHARLESTON:

Nothing in this article shall be construed to prevent the ordinary maintenance or repair of any exterior elements of any building or structure described in Section 54-25. (Charleston, South Carolina, Ordinance, Section 54-33)

TELLURIDE, COLORADO:

Any work, for which a building permit is not required by law, where the purpose and effect of such work is to correct any deterioration or decay of or damage to a structure or any part thereof and to restore the same, as nearly as may be practicable, to its condition prior to the occurrence of such deterioration, decay, or damage. (Telluride, Colorado, Ordinance, Article III (B)(7))

Annotation:

Most preservation ordinances include a provision exempting alterations that can be considered "ordinary maintenance" from the requirement that a certificate of appropriateness be obtained. This exemption is intended to reduce the workload of the preservation commission and to lessen the likelihood that local property owners will perceive the commission as intrusive or burdensome.

A loose definition of ordinary maintenance may remove certain types of alteration from the review powers of the preservation commission. However, a more specific definition of ordinary maintenance that takes into account the types of buildings likely to be designated in a particular community is needed. A replacement that necessitates a change in material, though not a change in appearance, should probably require a certificate of appropriateness. Repainting that involves a change in color may or may not be considered ordinary maintenance.

B. MINIMUM MAINTENANCE REQUIREMENT

Typical Ordinance Provisions:

Coral Gables:

Structures and sites designated as significant shall be maintained to meet requirements of the Minimum Housing code, the South Florida Building Code and any other regulatory codes. (Coral Gables, Florida, Ordinance, Section 8(3))

Charleston:

The board of architectural review, on its own initiative, may file a petition with the public safety and housing officer requesting that said officer proceed under the public safety and housing ordinance to require correction of defects or repairs to any structure covered by this article so that such structure shall be preserved and protected in consonance with the purpose of this article and the public safety and housing ordinance. (Charleston, South Carolina, Ordinance, Section 54-32)

Vieux Carre:

All buildings and structures in that section of the city known as the Vieux Carre Section and so defined generally in section 65-6, section 65-7, under the jurisdiction of the Vieux Carre Commission, as provided by Article 14 of Section 22A of the Louisiana Constitution, shall be preserved against decay and deterioration and free from certain structural defects in the following manner, by the owner thereof or such other person or persons who may have the legal custody and control thereof. The owner or other person having legal custody and control thereof shall repair such building if it is found to have any of the following defects:
(a) Those which have parts thereof which are so attached that they may fall and injure members of the public or property.
(b) Deteriorated or inadequate foundation.
(c) Defective or deteriorated flooring or floor supports or flooring or floor supports of insufficient size to carry imposed loads with safety.
(d) Members of walls, partitions or other vertical supports that split, lean, list

or buckle due to defective material or deterioration.
(e) Members of walls, partitions or other vertical supports that are of insufficient size to carry imposed loads with safety.
(f) Members of ceilings, roofs, ceiling and roof supports or other horizontal members which sag, split or buckle due to defective material or deterioration.
(g) Members of ceilings, roofs, ceiling and roof supports or other horizontal members that are of insufficient size to carry imposed loads with safety.
(h) Fireplaces or chimneys which list, bulge or settle due to defective material or deterioration.
(i) Fireplaces or chimneys which are of insufficient size or strength to carry imposed loads with safety.
(j) Deteriorated, crumbling or loose plaster.
(k) Deteriorated or ineffective waterproofing of exterior walls, roofs, foundations or floors, including broken windows or doors.
(l) Defective or lack of weather protection for exterior wall coverings, including lack of paint, or weathering due to lack of paint or other protective covering.
(m) Any fault or defect in the building which renders the same structurally unsafe or not properly watertight. (New Orleans, Louisiana, Vieux Carre Ordinance, Section 65-36)

DISTRICT OF COLUMBIA:

(a) Nothing in this act shall interfere with the authority of the Board of Condemnation to put a building or structure into sanitary condition or to demolish it pursuant to the provisions of the Act of May 1, 1906 (34 Stat. 157; D.C. Code, secs. 5-616 through 5-6341): EXCEPT, That no permit for the demolition of an historic landmark or building or structure in an historic district shall be issued to the owner except in accordance with the provisions of this act.
(b) Nothing in this act shall affect the authority of the District of Columbia to secure or remove an unsafe building or structure pursuant to the Act of March 1, 1899 (30 Stat. 923; D.C. Code, secs. 5-501 through 5-503). (District of Columbia Historic Landmark and Historic District Protection Act of 1978, D.C. Law 2-144, Section 12)

Annotation:

Increasingly, preservation ordinances contain a provision designed to reduce the incidence of "demolition by neglect." This slow deterioration sometimes occurs when an owner does nothing to maintain a building in hopes that it will eventually be in such poor condition that local health or building inspectors will issue a demolition order for it.

Several preservation ordinances provide that a municipality may repair a building whose owner refuses to repair it and treat the cost of repairs as a lien against the building.

A minimum maintenance provision may require only that local buildings be maintained in conformity with a local building code or may be extremely detailed and specify a number of structural defects that must be prevented or corrected.

The minimum maintenance provision of the Vieux Carre Ordinance in New Orleans was upheld in *Maher v. City of New Orleans*, 516 F.2d 1051 (5th Cir. 1975):

> Once it has been determined that the purpose of the Vieux Carre legislation is a proper one, upkeep of buildings appears reasonably necessary to the accomplishment of the goals of the ordinance. . . . The fact that an owner may incidentally be required to make out-of-pocket expenditures in order to remain in compliance with an ordinance does not per se render that ordinance a taking. In the interest of safety, it would seem that an ordinance might reasonably require buildings to have fire sprinklers or to provide emergency facilities for exits and light. In pursuit of health, provisions for plumbing or sewage disposal might be demanded. Compliance could well require owners to spend money. Yet, if the purpose be legitimate and the means reasonably consistent with the objective, the ordinance can withstand a frontal attack of invalidity. *Id.* at 1066-67.

C. PUBLIC SAFETY EXCLUSION

Typical Ordinance Provisions:

ALEXANDRIA:

Nothing in this article shall apply to or in any way prevent the razing of any building or structure in the city which is in such a dangerous, hazardous or unsafe condition that it has been ordered demolished by the director of construction and inspection or by the board of housing hygiene, pursuant to this Code; provided, however, that before a razing can be ordered by the board, the director of public health of the city shall have first mailed to the subscribers provided for in section 42-98, not less than ten days before the meeting, a notice of the meeting of the board of housing hygiene to be held pursuant to section 18-31; and provided further, that before a razing can be ordered by the director of construction and inspection, the director of construction and inspection shall have first delivered a copy of the proposed order to the city manager and mailed to the subscribers provided for in section 42-98 a copy of the proposed order. (Alexandria, Virginia, Ordinance, Section 42-97)

BERKELEY:

None of the provisions of this ordinance shall be construed to prevent any measures of construction, alteration, or demolition necessary to correct or abate the unsafe or dangerous condition of any structure, other feature or part thereof, where such condition has been declared unsafe or dangerous by the Department of Inspection Services or the Fire Department, and where the proposed measures have been declared necessary, by such department or departments, to correct the said condition; provided, however, that only such work as is reasonably necessary to correct the unsafe or dangerous condition may be performed pursuant to this section. In the event any structure or other feature shall be damaged by fire or other calamity, or by Act of God or by the public enemy, to such an extent that in the opinion of the aforesaid department or departments it cannot reasonably be repaired and restored, it may be removed in conformity with normal permit procedures and applicable laws. (Berkeley, California, Ordinance, Section 7)

Annotation:

Many preservation ordinances contain a provision that would permit a building declared to be a public safety hazard to be demolished without the need for a preservation commission's approval. Though the public safety exclusion in a preservation ordinance is likely to be invoked only in extreme instances, a preservation commission should have both the opportunity and the authority to make recommendations to the property owner and involved municipal agencies in order to avert the necessity for the building's demolition.

Nonetheless, a preservation commission should be prepared for the possibility that an irrefutable case will be made that a structure must be demolished. The commission in Rochester, New York, was judicially overruled on such an issue:

While the Board's purposes and goals are indisputable, laudable and generally deserving of unfettered support, we find its determination in the circumstances of this case to be arbitrary, capricious and an abuse of discretion. In the face of a clear threat to the public health and safety, the governmental duty to its citizens and civil servants to protect such vital interest must take precedence over the aesthetic and historical concerns expressed by the majority of the Preservation Board in denying petitioner's application. *Wolk v. Reisem*, 413 N.Y.S.2d 60, 61 (App. Div. 1979).

In Sacramento, California, a city ordinance permits vacant historic structures to be secured at city expense if they are in danger of being vandalized or have been found to have severe code violations. While a structure is secured, staff from the city's preservation commission can work with the building's owner and other city agencies to achieve a preservation solution. This type of coordination among municipal departments helps to ensure an effective implementation of a city's preservation program. (*See* June 1976 *Landmark and Historic District Commissions* newsletter.)

The public safety exclusion and the minimum maintenance requirement must be written so that they will mesh well. A stiff minimum maintenance requirement, if it is enforced, will reduce the likelihood that the public safety exclusion will be invoked against a damaged building.

A provision to permit the owner of a building damaged by fire or a natural calamity to stabilize and later rehabilitate the building should be included.

Both the National Uniform Building Code and the three regional model building codes now incorporate historic building provisions. A preservation commission should seek to have a suitable historic building provision incorporated into the local building code ordinance.

VIII. Enforcement Provision

Typical Ordinance Provisions:

Vieux Carre:

The Director of the Division of Regulatory Inspections shall promptly stop any work attempted to be done without or contrary to a permit issued under this article and shall promptly prosecute any person responsible for such a violation of this chapter or engaged in such violation. Any officer or authorized agent of the Commission shall exercise concurrent or independent powers with the Director in prosecuting violations of this chapter and stopping any work attempted to be done without or contrary to the permits required by this chapter.

Any sign or exterior illumination of walls, exteriors, roofs or appurtenances of buildings displayed contrary to the provision of this article shall be removed.

Failure of the owner, or the other proper person having legal custody of the structure or building to correct the defects as outlined in section 65-36 after knowledge of the existence of such defects has been brought to their attention, shall constitute a violation of this article and shall be punishable as provided in section 1-6. (New Orleans, Louisiana, Vieux Carre Ordinance, Sections 65-15, 65-33, and 65-37)

Galena, Illinois:

The Galena Planning and Zoning Commission shall give written notification of any violation of this Section of the ordinance to the owner or lessor of or the trustee or other legally responsible party for such property, stating in such notification that they have inspected the property and have found it in violation of this Ordinance. They shall state in the notification in clear precise terms a description or explanation of the violation. The property owner, trustee, lessor, or legally responsible party shall have thirty days in which to correct such violation or to give satisfactory evidence that they have taken steps that will lead to correcting such violation within a stated period of time, which time must be agreeable to the Planning and Zoning Commission as being fair and reasonable. (Galena, Illinois, Ordinance, Section IV)

Fort Collins, Colorado:

In case any building or structure is erected, constructed, externally reconstructed, externally altered, added to or demolished in violation of this ordinance, the City or any proper person may institute an appropriate action or proceeding to prevent such unlawful action. The imposition of any penalty hereunder shall not preclude the City or any proper person from instituting any proper action or proceeding to require compliance with the provisions of this ordinance and with administrative orders and determinations made hereunder. (Fort Collins, Colorado, Ordinance, Section 7(b))

Boston:

Upon petition of the commission, the superior court for Suffolk County may restrain any construction, reconstruction, restoration, erection, replacement, alteration, or demolition in violation of this act and may order the removal in whole or part of any exterior architectural feature permitted to exist in violation of this act and may order such reconstruction or restoration as may be necessary or desirable to redress any alteration or demolition in violation of this act. (Boston, Massachusetts, Landmarks Ordinance, Section 10)

Annotation:

If a preservation ordinance is to be more than advisory, it must contain an enforcement provision. The preservation ordinance's provisions may become part of a larger zoning code and therefore may not need to contain separate enforcement provisions. Even so, it is preferable to draft enforcement provisions intended to cover the particular types of situations likely to arise under the preservation ordinance. The creation of such enforcement provisions will not necessarily negate the applicability of other enforcement provisions.

Care should be taken to grant enforcement powers to the preservation commission, as well as to those municipal officers who customarily enforce zoning or building code provisions.

IX. Penalty Provision

A. CRIMINAL PENALTY

Typical Ordinance Provisions:

LOUISVILLE:

Any person violating any of the provisions of this Ordinance shall be fined not less than fifteen ($15.00) dollars, nor more than one hundred ($100.00) dollars, or imprisoned not more than fifty (50) days, or both such fine and imprisonment, for each offense. Each day's continued violation shall constitute a separate offense. (Louisville, Kentucky, Ordinance, Section 12)

WICHITA:

Any person violating any provision of this ordinance shall be guilty of a separate offense for each day or portion thereof during which any such violation is committed, continued or permitted, and each offense shall be punishable by a fine of not more than Two Hundred Dollars ($200.00). (Wichita, Kansas, Ordinance, Section 2.12.1025(b))

Annotation:

Care should be taken to draft a penalty provision strong enough to deter potential violators of the preservation ordinance, yet not so strong that the ordinance is unlikely to be enforced. If the amount of a penalty is too small, the penalty may come to be looked upon as only an additional cost for a permit to build or demolish.

At least one court has held that a criminal penalty may be imposed in the absence of a penalty clause in a preservation ordinance:

> We find no merit to defendants' first contention that a criminal conviction cannot be supported because the historical zoning ordinance contains no penalty clause. The historical zoning act prescribes the conditions for approval of plans and specifications upon which a building permit is issued under the building code. Defendants were charged and found guilty in city court with violation

of that provision of the Uniform Building Code which requires all construction work to be according to the plans and specifications approved with the building permit. *City of Santa Fe v. Gamble-Skogmo, Inc.*, 389 P.2d 13, 14-15 (N.M. 1964).

B. CIVIL REMEDY

Typical Ordinance Provision:

DISTRICT OF COLUMBIA:

Any person who demolishes, alters or constructs a building or structure in violation of sections 5, 6 or 8 of this act shall be required to restore the building or structure and its site to its appearance prior to the violation. Any action to enforce this subsection shall be brought by the Corporation Counsel. This civil remedy shall be in addition to and not in lieu of any criminal prosecution and penalty. (District of Columbia Historic Landmark and Historic District Protection Act of 1978, D.C. Law 2-144, Section 11(b))

Annotation:

The civil remedy contained in the amended preservation ordinance for the District of Columbia has not yet been invoked.

X. Appeal Provision

Typical Ordinance Provisions:

CHARLESTON:

Any person or persons jointly or severally aggrieved by any final decision of the board of architectural review, any taxpayer, or any officer, department or board of the city of Charleston may present to a court of record a petition duly verified setting forth that the decision of the board of architectural review is illegal, in whole or in part, specifying the grounds of the illegality. Such petition shall be presented to the court within thirty (30) days after the filing of the decision of the board. . . . (Charleston, South Carolina, Ordinance, Section 54-35)

PENSACOLA:

Any person aggrieved by a decision of the Board may, within fifteen (15) days thereafter, apply to the Council of the City of Pensacola for review of the Board's decision. He shall file with the City Manager a written notice requesting the Council to review said decision. (Pensacola, Florida, Ordinance, Section Five)

ENFIELD, CONNECTICUT:

Any person or persons severally or jointly aggrieved by any decision of the Commission or of any officer thereof may, within fifteen (15) days from the date when such decision was rendered, take an appeal to the Court of Common Pleas for Hartford County, which appeal shall be made returnable to such court in the same manner as that prescribed for civil actions brought to such court. Notice of such appeal shall be given by leaving a true and attested copy thereof in the hands of or at the usual place of abode of the chairman or clerk of the Commission within twelve (12) days before the return day to which such appeal has been taken. Procedure upon such appeal shall be the same as that defined in Section 8-8 of the General Statutes of Connecticut (Revision of 1958) as amended. (Enfield, Connecticut, Ordinance, Section 13)

SEATTLE:

[P]rovided, the applicant may appeal to the Council within 20 days of the date of the letter finally denying the application, and the Council may, after a public hearing, reverse or modify the decision of the Board, but only if it finds that:
1. every reasonable effort has been made by the applicant to agree to the requirements of the Board, and;
2. owing to special conditions pertaining to the specific piece of property, denial of the Certificate of Approval will cause undue and unnecessary hardship. (Seattle, Washington, Landmarks Ordinance, Section 8(d))

Annotation:

Every preservation ordinance should contain an appeal provision permitting the property owner whose application for a certificate of appropriateness or a demolition permit has been denied by a preservation commission to appeal the commission's decision. The appeal provision should state clearly the time period within which notice of an appeal must be filed, the court or municipal entity to which appeal may be made, and whether the body to hear the appeal will be permitted to take new evidence or must reach a decision based upon the evidence presented originally to the preservation commission. If this question is left unclear, a reviewing court may permit new evidence to be heard by the body hearing the appeal:

> We are of the opinion that in appeals from decisions of historic zoning commissions, the board does not merely exercise appellate jurisdiction, limited as it were to a review of the record compiled at a hearing held by the commission. Rather it is authorized to consider the question de novo. *Hayes v. Smith*, 167 A.2d 546, 550 (R.I. 1961).

In several cities the initial appeal is to the city council or an administrative body such as a planning commission. Such an arrangement can ensure that a full administrative record will be created on hardship or "taking" issues, but a disadvantage may be the insertion of political considerations into what is supposed to be an objective professional decision. A few preservation ordinances specify the grounds on which a city council may reverse the decision of a preservation commission. The specification of such grounds should not encourage the city council to reverse the commission's decisions and should be so worded that only in truly exceptional cases will the city council be likely to reverse a decision denying a certificate of appropriateness or a demolition permit.

The appeal provision in a preservation ordinance should be broad enough to permit an appeal from a commission's decision by parties other than an owner-applicant. The Supreme Judicial Court of Massachusetts has held that because of the wording of state enabling legislation, only "an applicant" can appeal the decision of a Massachusetts preservation commission. *Springfield Preservation Trust, Inc. v. Springfield Historical Commission*, 402 N.E.2d 488 (Mass. 1980). An adjacent or nearby property owner may wish to appeal if the owner believes that a commission's decision will have an adverse impact on his own property, and in rare instances a local preservation organization may wish to appeal a commission decision that it believes is erroneous. In *Zartman v. Reisem*, 399 N.Y.S.2d 506 (App. Div. 1977), an adjacent property owner appealed a decision of a preservation commission; the *Springfield Preservation Trust* case arose because a local preservation organization wished to appeal a decision by the local commission.

The presence of an appeal provision will also help to satisfy due process requirements, as noted by the North Carolina Supreme Court:

> The procedural safeguards provided will serve as an additional check on potential abuse of the Historic District Commission's discretion. . . . Provisions for appeal to the Board of Adjustment from an adverse decision of the Historic District Commission will afford an affected property owner the opportunity to offer expert evidence, cross-examine witnesses, inspect documents, and offer rebuttal evidence. . . . Similar protection is afforded to a property owner by the right to appeal from a decision of the Board of Adjustment to the Superior Court of Wake County. *A-S-P Associates v. City of Raleigh*, 258 S.E. 2d 444, 455 (N.C. 1979).

Appendix B

OVERVIEW: ECONOMIC RECOVERY TAX ACT OF 1981 ("ERTA") RULES FOR REAL ESTATE DEPRECIATION AND INVESTMENT TAX CREDIT FOR QUALIFIED REHABILITATIONS, AS REVISED BY THE TAX EQUITY AND FISCAL RESPONSIBILITY ACT OF 1982 ("TEFRA") AND THE TECHNICAL CORRECTIONS ACT OF 1982

THOMAS A. COUGHLIN III
ASSISTANT GENERAL COUNSEL
NATIONAL TRUST FOR HISTORIC PRESERVATION
WASHINGTON, D.C.
© 1983 BY
THE NATIONAL TRUST FOR HISTORIC PRESERVATION

I. **Changes in Individual Income Tax Provisions**

   A. *Reduction in Individual Income Tax Rates* (ERTA §101; I.R.C. §1)

   1. By 1984 individual income tax rates will be approximately 23% less than they would have been prior to ERTA. Phased cumulative reductions equal 1.25% in 1981, 10% in 1982, 19% in 1983 and 23% in 1984 and subsequent years. These reductions will be reflected in both witholding reductions and reductions in estimated tax payments.

   2. Effective January 1, 1982, the maximum tax on non-personal service income is reduced from 70% to 50%.

   3. Reductions in the marginal tax rate schedules for a 50% bracket taxpayer filing a joint return are:

1981 (pre-ERTA)	49% bracket at $45,800
1982	50% bracket at $85,600
1983	50% bracket at $109,400
1984	50% bracket at $162,400

   4. Rate reductions are indexed to inflation for taxable years beginning after 1984 (ERTA §104; I.R.C. §1(f)).

   B. *Maximum Long-Term Capital Gains Tax Rate Is Reduced from 28% to 20% Effective June 9, 1981* (ERTA §102; I.R.C. §1202)

   C. *Estate and Gift Tax Changes*

   1. Tax-free interspousal transfers permitted for lifetime and testamentary transfers (ERTA §403; I.R.C. §2523).

   2. Phased increase in Unified Credit will increase the value of estates exempt from Estate and Gift taxation from $175,000 in 1981 to $600,000 in 1987 (ERTA §401; I.R.C. §2010).

   3. Maximum Estate and Gift Tax rate will be reduced from 70% to 50% in phased reductions over 3 years, ending December 31, 1984 (ERTA §402; I.R.C. §2001(c)).

4. Annual Gift Tax Exclusion is increased from $3,000 to $10,000 effective for transfers made after December 31, 1981 (ERTA §441; I.R.C. §2503(b)).

D. *Extension of Carryover Period for Net Operating Losses and Credits* (ERTA §207)

The period for using Net Operating Losses (NOL's) under I.R.C. §172 and unused Investment Tax Credits under I.R.C. §46(b) is increased from 7 to 15 years.

II. **Real Estate Depreciation—The Accelerated Cost Recovery System (the "ACRS") (ERTA §§201-209; I.R.C. §168)**

A. *General*

ERTA substitutes the ACRS, under new I.R.C. §168, for depreciation previously allowable under I.R.C. §167.

1. ACRS permits accelerated cost recovery for both new and used real property over a 15 year audit-proof recovery period. Special rules apply for public utility property and certain other special use real property classes (I.R.C. §168(b)(2)).

2. Accelerated cost recovery is computed according to Treasury Department Tables incorporating depreciation allowable under the 175% declining balance method of depreciation (200% in the case of low income housing) switching to the straight-line method at a point which maximizes the allowable deduction (I.R.C. §168(b)(2)(A)).

3. As an alternative to accelerated cost recovery a taxpayer may elect to use the straight-line method over a 15, 35 or 45 year recovery period (I.R.C. §168(b)(3)).

4. Component Depreciation is repealed (I.R.C. §168(f)(1)).

B. *Applicablility*

ACRS applies to all "Recovery Property" acquired or placed in service after December 31, 1980. Use of ACRS is mandatory for Recovery Property (I.R.C. §167(a)).

1. Recovery Property is property of a character subject to the allowance for depreciation, i.e., used in a trade or business or held for the production of income (I.R.C §168(c)).

2. ACRS does not apply to property or expenditures that are required to be amortized. Examples include low-income housing rehabilitation expenditures under IRC §167(k) or leasehold improvements where the leasehold is for less than 15 years (I.R.C. §167).

C. *Substantial Improvements*

Generally, property placed in service before December 31, 1980, cannot use ACRS. Similarly, because the component method of cost recovery is repealed by ERTA, a taxpayer is generally precluded from using different methods of cost recovery or different recovery periods for discrete components of a building. An exception is provided for a "Substantial Improvement" (ERTA §201(f); I.R.C. §168(f)(1)(C)).

1. A Substantial Improvement is treated as a separate building, entitling it to qualify separately to use ACRS, to be "depreciated" at a different cost recovery rate, or to be depreciated over a different recovery period than the principal building.

2. A Substantial Improvement is defined as "the improvements added to capital account with respect to any building during any 24 month period, but only if the sum of the amounts added to such account during such period equals or exceeds 25 percent of the adjusted basis of the building . . . as of the first day of such period."

3. Generally, at least 3 years must have elapsed between the date the building was placed in service and the date the improvement is made. A special rule is provided for Qualified Rehabilitated Buildings: "In the case of any qualified rehabilitated building (as defined in §48(g)(1), an election . . .

may be made at any time before the date 3 years after the building was placed in service" (I.R.C. §168(f)(4)(B)(ii), as amended by by the Technical Corrections Act, P.L. 97-448, §102(f)(4)).

D. *Disposal and Recapture*

1. Commercial Properties. ACRS treats non-residential real estate that uses accelerated cost recovery as Section 1245 property. Upon disposal of Section 1245 property all accelerated cost recovery deductions are taxed as ordinary income to the extent the amount realized exceeds the taxpayer's adjusted basis in the property (I.R.C. §1245(a)(5)(c)).

2. Residential Rental Properties. ACRS retains the traditional recapture rules under I.R.C. §1250 for disposals of residential rental property. Upon disposal, only the excess of accelerated cost recovery deductions over that which would have been allowable under the straight-line method is treated as ordinary income to the extent the amount realized exceeds the taxpayer's adjusted basis in the property (I.R.C. §§1245(a)(5)(D) and 1250).

3. Exposure to full recapture of accelerated cost recovery deductions for commercial properties renders accelerated recovery for commercial properties uneconomical for most investors. However, it may remain attractive for "owner-users" which have no intention of disposing of the property.

E. *Anti-Churning Rules* (ERTA §201(e)(4)(B))

These rules are designed to prevent taxpayers having used property placed in service before December 31, 1980, from using ACRS. The rules exclude from the definition of "Recovery Property" real property if:

1. It was owned by the taxpayer or by a related person at any time during 1980 (I.R.C. §168(e)(4)(B)(i)); or

2. The taxpayer leases such property to a person (or a person related

to such person) who owned such property at any time during 1980 (I.R.C. §168(e)(4)(B)(ii)); or

3. Such property was acquired in a tax free exchange under I.R.C. §§1031, 1033, 1038 or 1039 to the extent the basis of such property includes an amount representing the adjusted basis of other property owned by a taxpayer or a related person during 1980 (I.R.C. §168(e)(4)(B)(iii)); or

4. Such property was acquired in certain "non-recognition" transactions involving property which was placed in service by the transferor before January 1, 1981, to the extent basis is determined by reference to the basis of the property in the hands of the transferor. The non-recognition transactions are those described in I.R.C. §§332, 351, 361, 371(a), 374(a), 721 or 731 (I.R.C. §168(e)(4)(c)).

5. Related Person Defined. For purposes of paragraphs 1-3 above, a person is related if he bears a relationship described in I.R.C. §§267(b) or 707(b)(1) or if the persons are engaged in trades or businesses under common control under I.R.C. §52(a) and (b). In applying §§267(b) and 707(b)(1) "10 percent" must be substituted for "50 percent." The related person determination is made as of the time the taxpayer acquires the property (I.R.C. §168(e)(4)(D)).

6. Exceptions to the related person rules are provided in connection with certain corporate liquidations (I.R.C. §168(e)(4)(E)).

7. General Anti-Avoidance Rule. The Treasury Department is given broad discretion to promulgate regulations excluding from the definition of Recovery Property property acquired in a transaction one of the principal purposes of which was to avoid the general prohibition against use of ACRS for property placed in service before January 1, 1981 (I.R.C. §168(e)(4)(F)).

III. Investment Tax Credit for Non-Historic Qualified Rehabilitated Buildings (ERTA §212)

A. *General*

ERTA establishes a 3-tier Investment Tax Credit for Qualified Rehabilitation Expenditures incurred in connection with the rehabilitation of Qualified Rehabilitated Buildings (ERTA §211). The credit is equal to 15% of the Qualified Rehabilitation Expenditures for rehabilitation of 30 year old buildings, 20% for 40 year old buildings, and 25% for Certified Historic Structures (I.R.C. §46(a)(2)(F)).

Except for Certified Historic Structures, residential rental properties do not qualify for the tax credit. Also, except for Certified Historic Structures, the basis of property for computing cost recovery allowances must be reduced by the amount of the tax credit. Certified historic structures must reduce basis by one-half the allowable tax credit (I.R.C. §§48(a)(3) and 48(g)(5), as amended by TEFRA, P.L. 97-248, § 205(a)(1)).

B. *Rules for Using ITC*

The tax credit is available only when the building is "placed in service" in its rehabilitated use. To avoid the dollar limitations on the investment tax credit for "used" property, Qualified Rehabilitated Buildings are treated as "new section 38 property" (I.R.C. §48(g)(4)). Thus, the full amount of rehabilitation expenditures qualify for the tax credit.

The tax credit is available the year the building is placed in service. The credit offsets the first $25,000 of tax liability in full and 85% of any excess tax liability in the year the building is placed in service. Any unused tax credit must be carried back 3 years and forward 15 years until fully used (I.R.C. §§46(a)(3) & 46(b), as amended by TEFRA, P.L. 248, § 205(b)(1)).

Although the tax credit is not treated as a "tax preference" item, under the new alternative minimum tax (I.R.C. § 55, enacted by §201(a) of ERTA) taxable income that exceeds a statutory "exemption amount" is subject to a 20% alternative minimum tax. The exemption amount is $30,000 for individuals and $40,000 for taxpayers filing joint returns. The ITC for qualified rehabilitated buildings may not be used to offset alternative minimum tax liability.

C. *Qualified Rehabilitated Building*

A Qualified Rehabilitated Buiding is any building which has been "substantially rehabilitated," which was placed in service before the beginning of the rehabilitation, and "75% or more of the existing external walls of which are retained in place as external walls in the rehabilitation process." Except for a Certified Historic Structure, 30 years must have elapsed between "the date the physical work on the rehabilitation began and the date the building was first placed in service" (I.R.C. §46(g)(1)).

D. *Substantially Rehabilitated*

A building is substantially rehabilitated only if the Qualified Rehabilitation Expenditures "during the 24-month period selected by the taxpayer (at the time and in the manner prescribed by regulations) and ending with or within the taxable year" exceed the greater of $5,000 or the adjusted basis of the building, determined as of the first day of the 24-month period (I.R.C. §48(g)(1)(C) as amended by the Technical Corrections Act of 1982, P.L. 97-448, §102(f)(2)).

1. *Special Rule for Phased Rehabilitation.* "In the case of any rehabilitation which may reasonably be expected to be completed in phases set forth in architectural plans and specifications completed before the rehabilitation begins," the rehabilitation may be accomplished over a 60-month period selected by the taxpayer and "ending with or within the taxable year" (I.R.C. §48(g)(1)(C)(ii)).

E. *Qualified Rehabilitation Expenditures*

Qualified Rehabilitation Expenditures are additions to capital account incurred after December 31, 1981 in connection with (i) the rehabilitation of 15 year Recovery Property and (ii) the rehabilitation of a Qualified Rehabilitated Building, provided:

1. The straight-line method is used with respect to the Qualified Rehabilitation Expenditures. Accelerated cost recovery may be used on the shell of the building provided the Qualified Rehabilitation Expenditures are treated as a Substantial Improve-

ment under ACRS (I.R.C. §§48(g)(2)(B)(i)); 168(f)(1)(C));

2. Costs of acquisition are excluded (I.R.C. §48(g)(2)(B)(ii));

3. The expenditure is not attributable to an enlargement (I.R.C, §48(g)(2)(B)(iii));

4. In the case of a Lessee, the lease term, on the date the rehabilitation is completed, is at least 15 years, excluding renewal periods (I.R.C. §48(g)(2)(B)(v)); and

5. In the case of a Certified Historic Structure or a building in a Registered Historic District, the rehabilitation is a Certified Rehabilitation. The requirement to do a Certified Rehabilitation of a building in a Registered Historic District does not apply if:
   a. The building was not a Certified Historic Structure;
   b. The Secretary of the Interior certified that the building was not of historic significance to the district; and
   c. If the certification occurs after the beginning of the rehabilitation, the taxpayer certifies that, at the beginning of such rehabilitation, he was in good faith not aware of the requirement to get the Secretary of the Interior's certification of nonsignificance (I.R.C. §48(g)(2)(B)(iv)).

6. The regular and energy credits do not apply to expenses attributable to Qualified Rehabilitation Expenditures (I.R.C. §46(2)(2)(F)(ii)).

F. *Recapture of the Investment Tax Credit upon Disposal*

There is no recapture if the rehabilitated property is held for at least five years after the building has been placed in service in its rehabilitated use. If the property is disposed of within the first year after it is placed in service the full tax credit is recaptured as ordinary income upon disposal. Thereafter, the portion of the credit subject to recapture is reduced by 20% per year. Thus, for a disposal in the 2nd year after the building was placed in service, 80% of the credit would be recaptured, while in the 5th year, only 20% would be subject to recapture (I.R.C. §47(a)(5)).

G. *Repeal of Former Tax Incentives and Straight-Line Discentive*

ERTA repealed the 10% tax credit for rehabilitations of 20-year old buildings added by the Revenue Act of 1978 and the 60-month amortization deduction for certified historic structures, accelerated depreciation for substantially rehabilitated historic structures and the straight-line disincentive against demolishing historic structures (added by the Tax Reform Act of 1976) effective December 31, 1981. The demolition disincentive under I.R.C. §280B remains in effect until December 31, 1983. (ERTA §212(d)).

H. *Effective Dates and Transition Rule*

Like the effective dates for repeal of the 10% tax credit and tax incentives for historic preservation, the new credits apply to expenditures incurred after December 31, 1981. A special transition rule provides that the amendments (including the repeals) do not apply with respect to rehabilitations if the physical work on such building began before January 1, 1982, and the building met the requirements of I.R.C. §48(g)(1) prior to amendment but fails to meet the requirements of §48(g)(1) as amended. Such projects may continue to use the 10% tax credit for rehabilitations of 20-year old commercial buildings or the tax incentives for historic preservation (ERTA §212(e)).

I. *Qualified Rehabilitated Buildings leased to tax exempt organizations or Units of Government qualify for the Investment Tax Credit for Qualified Rehabilitation Expenditures, effective July 29, 1980* (ERTA §214; I.R.C. §§48(a)(4) and (5)).

IV. **Investment Tax Credit for Certified Rehabilitations of Historic Structures** (ERTA §212)

A. A *Certified Historic Structure* is any building listed on the National Register of Historic Places or located in a Registered Historic District and certified by the Secretary of the Interior as being of historic significance to the District (I.R.C. §48(g)(3)(a)).

B. A *Registered Historic District* is any district listed in the National Register and any district:

(I) which is designated under a statute of the appropriate State or local government, if such statute is certified by the Secretary of the Interior to the Secretary of the Treasury as containing criteria which will substantially achieve the purpose of preserving and rehabilitating buidings of historic significance to the district, and (II) which is certified by the Secretary of the Interior to the Secretary as meeting substantially all of the requirements for the listing of districts in the National Register (I.R.C. §48(g)(3)(b)).

C. A *Certified Rehabilitation* is any rehabilitation of a certified historic structure which the Secretary of the Interior has certified to the Secretary as being consistent with the historic character of such property or the district in which such property is located (I.R.C. §48(g)(2)(c)).

D. *Program Overview*

The National Register is administered by the Secretary of the Interior, through the National Park Service and, at the state level, through each state's State Historic Preservation Officer. Requests for determinations of eligibility for National Register listing, certifications of historic significance or non-significance to registered historic districts, and certifications that rehabilitation work conforms with the Secretary of the Interior's *Standards for Rehabilitation and Guidelines for Rehabilitating Historic Buildings* are initiated through the State Historic Preservation Officer in the state where the property is located.

Historic Preservation Certification Applications, Applications for Nomination to the National Register and detailed explanatory materials are available from the State Historic Preservation Officers, Regional Offices of the National Park Service or the National Park Service Headquarters in Washington, D.C.

CURRENT REGULATIONS: NATIONAL REGISTER PROGRAM

National Register of Historic Places, Interim Rules 36 CFR Part 60, 46 *Federal Register* 56183, November 16, 1981.

National Register of Historic Places, Proposed Rules 36 CFR Part 60, 46 *Federal Register* 56209, November 16, 1981.

APPENDIX B: OVERVIEW ERTA 1981   B11

REGULATIONS UNDER TAX REFORM ACT OF 1976 AND REVENUE ACT OF 1978

Internal Revenue Service, "Income Tax; Amortization of Certain Rehabilitation Costs for Certified Historic Structures"
26 CFR Parts 1 and 7, 45 *Federal Register* 38050, June 6, 1980.

Internal Revenue Service, Proposed Regulations, "Investment Tax Credit for Qualified Rehabilitated Buildings"
45 *Federal Register* 71367, October 28, 1980.

National Register of Historic Places, Historic Preservation Certifications Pursuant to the Tax Reform Act of 1976 and the Revenue Act of 1978
36 CFR Part 67, 45 *Federal Register* 83488, December 19, 1980.

Appendix C

EASEMENTS: INTRODUCTORY MATERIALS

THOMAS A. COUGHLIN III
ASSISTANT GENERAL COUNSEL
NATIONAL TRUST FOR HISTORIC PRESERVATION
WASHINGTON, D.C.

©1983 BY
THE NATIONAL TRUST FOR HISTORIC PRESERVATION

I. GENERAL BACKGROUND

Saxe, Emma Jane, *How to Qualify Historic Properties under the New Law Affecting Easements,* How to #6, National Park Service, U.S. Department of the Interior, 444 G St. N.W., Washington, D.C. 20240 (202) 272-2506

Coughlin, Thomas A., *Easements and Other Legal Techniques to Protect Historic Houses in Private Ownership,* Historic House Association of America—1600 H Street, N.W., Washington, D.C. 20006 (202) 673-4025

Watson, Elizabeth, *Establishing an Easement Program to Protect Historic, Scenic and Natural Resources* (Information Sheet #25), National Trust for Historic Preservation, 1785 Massachusetts Ave., N.W., Washington, D.C. 20036 (202) 673-4000

Maryland Historical Trust—*Preservation Easements,* 21 State Circle, Annapolis, MD 21401 (301) 269-1576

Maine Coast Heritage Trust—*The Landowner's Options,* 335 Water Street, Augusta, ME 04430 (207) 622-1576

II. LEGAL AND TAX MATERIALS

Report of the Committee on Finance, on H.R. 6975, "The Tax Treatment Extension Act of 1980" (Senate Report 1007) and Section 6, P.L. 96-541 reprinted in *Tax Incentives for Historic Preservation,* National Trust for Historic Preservation (Rev'd., 1981)

Coughlin, Thomas A., Preservation Easements: Statutory and Tax Planning Issues, 1 *Preservation Law Reporter* 2011 (1982)

Kliman, Burton S., The Use of Conservation Restrictions on Historic Properties as Charitable Donations for Federal Income Tax Purposes, 9 *Boston College Environmental Affairs Law Review* 513 (1981-1982)

Shuster, Marla, Charitable Contributions of Real Property for Conservation Purposes, 1981-6 *The Estates, Gifts and Trusts Journal* 25 (Nov.-Dec. 1981)

Hambrick, Kenton W., Charitable Donations of Conservation Easements: Valuation, Enforcement and Public Benefit, 59 *Taxes: The Tax Magazine* 347 (June, 1981)

Coughlin, Fisher, MacRostie, and Sowick, editors, *Conservation Easements: The Urban Setting,* November 14, 1980. Available from National Park Service, Technical Preservation Services Division, 444 G St. N.W., Washington, D.C. 20240

Tax Incentives for Sensible Land Use through Gifts of Conservation Easements, 15 *Real Property, Probate and Trust Journal* 1 (Spring, 1980)

Environmental Conservation and Historic Preservation through Recorded Land-Use Agreements, 14 *Real Property, Probate and Trust Journal* 540 (Fall, 1979)

Small, Stephen, The Tax Benefits of Donating Easements in Scenic and Historic Property, 7 *Real Estate Law Journal* 304 (1979) and 9 *Environmental Law Reporter* 50009 (March, 1979)

Browne, Kingsbury and Van Dorn, Walter, Charitable Gifts of Partial Interests in Real Property for Conservation Purposes, 29 *Tax Lawyer* 69 (Fall, 1975)

Brenneman, Russell, *Private Approaches to the Preservation of Open Land* (Connecticut College Conservation Research Foundation, 1967)

III. CASE LAW RECOGNIZING VALIDITY OF EASEMENTS IN GROSS, EQUITABLE SERVITUDES, PROTECTIVE COVENANTS AND SIMILAR USE RESTRICTIONS

A. *Gifts to Federal Government or Pursuant to Federal Program*

U.S. v. Albrecht 496 F.2d 906 (1974)

Rev. Rul. 64-205

B. *General*

IRS Technical Advice Memorandum 8032013

Tulk v. Moxhay (chancery, 1848) 2 Phillips 774, Reprinted in Chafee and Re, *Equity Cases and Materials* (The Foundation Press Inc., 1967) at 346

Maryland Pennsylvania Railroad Company v. Silver 110 Md. 510, 73 A. 297 (1909)

Neponsit Property Owner's Assoc., Inc. v. Emigrant Industrial Savings Bank 278 N.Y. 245, 15 N.E.2d 793 (1938)

165 Broadway Building v. City Investing Co. 120 F.2d 813 (1941), cert. denied, 314 U.S. 682 (1941)

Reed v. Dent 194 Va. 156, 72 S.E.2d 252 (1952)

City of Richmond v. Richmond Sand Gravel Company 123 Va. 1, 96 S.E. 204 (1918)

Cheatham v. Taylor 148 Va. 26, 138 S.E. 545 (1927)

Hercules Powder Company v. Continental Can Company 196 Va. 935, 86 S.E.2d 128 (1955)

IV. EASEMENTS—FEDERAL TAX CONSEQUENCES

A. *Internal Revenue Code Provisions*

Section 6 of P.L. 96-541, the Tax Treatment Extension Act of 1980, revised, codified and made permanent authority for Federal income, estate and gift tax charitable contribution deductions for gifts of preservation easements as "a Qualified Conservation Contribution" under Internal Revenue Code Sec. 170(f)(3)(B)(iii).

The term "Qualified Conservation Contribution" is defined in subsection 170(h) as a gift of a "Qualified Real Property Interest" given to "a Qualified Organization" "Exclusively for Conservation Purposes." A "Qualified Real Property Interest" includes "a restriction (granted in perpetuity) on the use which may be made of the real property." A Qualified Organization is defined broadly to embrace most publicly supported charities.

The term "Conservation Purpose" is defined as:

> (i) the preservation of land areas for outdoor recreation by, or the education of, the general public,
> (ii) the protection of a relatively natural habitat of fish, wildlife, or plants, or similar ecosystem,
> (iii) the preservation of open space (including farmland and forest land) where such preservaion is
>> (I) for the scenic enjoyment of the general public, or
>> (II) pursuant to a clearly delineated Federal, State, or local governmental conservation policy,
>
> and will yield a significant public benefit,
> or
> (iv) the preservation of an historically important land area or a Certified Historic Structure.

The term "Certified Historic Structure" is defined as "any building, structure, or land area which (i) is listed in the National Register, or (ii) is located in a registered historic district (as defined in section 191(d)(2)) and is certified by the Secretary of the Interior to the Secretary as being of historic significance to the district. A building, structure, or land area satisfies the preceding sentence if it satisfies such sentence either at the time of the transfer or on the due date (including extensions) for filing the transferor's return under this chapter for the taxable year in which the transfer is made."

The Code further requires that the gift be "Exclusively for Conservation Purposes." The Code states, in explanation, "a contribution shall not be treated as exclusively for conservation purposes unless the conservation purpose is protected in perpetuity."

B. *Income Tax Regulations*

Income Tax Regulations are not expected until the late Summer or Fall of 1982. Until proposed Regulations are issued, the statute and accompanying Committee Reports afford the best guidance concerning the types of property intended to qualify under the new "Conservation Purpose" test. Although the Finance Committee Report indicates the "open space easement in gross" Regulations in Section 1.170A-7(b)(1)(ii) are repealed effective December 17, 1980, the Revenue Rulings and case law decided under the old rules may be helpful in understanding the approach IRS will employ in handling questions under the revised Code provisions.

C. *Revenue Rulings and Case Law Interpreting Charitable Gifts of Open Space Easements in Gross—Prior to 1980 Amendments*

Rev. Rul. 64-205

Rev. Rul. 73-339

Rev. Rul. 74-583

Rev. Rul. 75-358

Rev. Rul. 75-373

Rev. Rul. 76-376

Private Letter Ruling 77 34024 (5/24/77)

Thayer v. Commissioner, T.C. Memorandum Decision 1977-370 (10/25/77)

Letter Rul. 8010139

I.R.S. Technical Advice Memorandum 8032013

D. *Valuation of Easements*

Roddewig, Richard and Shlaes, Jared, Appraising the Best Tax Shelter in History, 50 *The Appraisal Journal* 25 (1982)

Reynolds, Judith, Preservation Easements: An Introduction to Mackall Square, 44 *The Appraisal Journal* (July 1976) p. 355

Thayer v. Commissioner, T.C. Memorandum Decision 1977-370 (10/25/77)

Rev. Rul. 73-339

Rev. Rul. 76-376

National Trust Information Sheet, *Factors Affecting The Valuation Of Historic Properties*

V. ADDITION TO TAX IN CASE OF VALUATION OVERSTATEMENTS

Sec. 722 of the Economic Recovery Act of 1981, added Section 6659, "Addition to Tax in the Case of Valuation Overstatements for Purposes of the Income Tax," to the Internal Revenue Code of 1954.

(1) *Applicability*

The Section applies to properties held by the taxpayer for less than 5 years as of the close of the taxable year for which there is a valuation overstatement which results in an underpayment for the taxable year of $1,000 or more. The Section applies to individuals, closely held corporations and personal holding companies that have an underpayment of tax attributable to a Valuation Overstatment.

(2) *Valuation Overstatement Defined*

A Valuation Overstatement occurs "if the value of any property, or the adjusted basis of any property, claimed on any return exceeds 150 percent of the amount determined to be the correct amount of such valuation or adjusted basis (as the case may be)."

(3) *Penalty*

The penalty is 10 percent of the additional tax owed where the claimed valuation is 150 percent but not more than 200 percent of the correct valuation, 20 percent of the additional tax owed where the claimed valuation is 200 percent but not more than 250 percent of the correct valuation, and 30 percent where the claimed valuation is more than 250 percent of the correct valuation.

(4) *Waivers*

Treasury may waive "all or any part of the additions to tax . . . on a showing by the taxpayer that there was a reasonable basis for the valuation or adjusted basis claimed on the return and that such claim was made in good faith. The authority to permit waivers of the overvaluation penalty upon showings of "reasonable basis" and "good faith" underscores the need for taxpayers to obtain and rely on qualified appraisers and legal counsel.

VI. TAX TREATMENT OF CHARITABLE GIFTS OF PROPERTY

A. *General Rules*

(1) *Lifetime Gifts—Internal Revenue Code Sec. 170,* Income Tax Regulations—*Sec. 1.170-A through 1.170A-12*

Generally, the Internal Revenue Code authorizes a charitable contribution deduction for up to 50% of a taxpayer's adjusted gross income for gifts of cash and other "ordinary income" property made to publicly supported charities. Gifts to public charities that exceed 50% of the taxpayer's adjusted gross income in the year of donation may be carried forward for five succeeding tax years or until the full value of the charitable gift is used, whichever occurs first.

Gifts of appreciated property held for more than 12 months (long term capital gain property) are limited to 30% of the taxpayer's adjusted gross income in the year of the gift, with five year carry-forward rights for the balance. Deductibility may be increased to 50% of adjusted gross income if the value of long-term capital gain property is first reduced by 40% of its appreciation prior to claiming the charitable contribution deduction. A gift tax deduction is allowed for the full value of the gift.

(2) *Exceptions to Rules for Lifetime Gifts*

"Dealers" and persons who have not held appreciated real property for more than the 12 month holding period required to qualify the property as long term capital gain property are limited to their basis in the donated property (Internal Revenue Code Sec. 170(e)(1)(A)).

(3) *Testamentary Gifts—Internal Revenue Code Sec. 2055 Estate Tax Regulations—Sec. 20.2055-1 through 20.2055-5*

Unlike charitable gifts made during the donor's lifetime, there is no percentage limitation on the amount of the charitable contribution deduction allowable for estate tax purposes.

(4) *Charitable Gifts by Corporations*

Gifts by corporations are limited to 5 percent of the corporation's adjusted gross income with 5 year carry-forward rights for the balance. (Internal Revenue Code Sec. 170(b)(2)).

B. *Internal Revenue Service Materials on Charitable Gifts*

Internal Revenue Service Publication 526, *Income Tax Deductions for Contributions*

Internal Revenue Service Publication 561, *Valuation of Donated Property*

Table of Cases

A

A-S-P Associates v. City of Raleigh, 40, 44n, 66n, 67n, 71, 81n, 86, 92, 95, 96, 97, 133n, 367n

Abelliera v. District Court of Appeal, 400n

Action for Rational Transit v. West Side Highway Project, 303n

Aertsen v. Harris, 284n

Aertsen v. Landrieu, 263n

Agins v. City of Tiburon, 87n, 133n, 343n, 351n, 360, 362, 367n, 368, 411n, 423,

Aleknagik Natives Limited v. Andrus, 303n

Alpine Lakes Protection Society v. Schlapfer, 302n

Aluli v. Brown, 220, 265, 279n

Alyeska Pipeline Service Co. v. Wilderness Society, 269n

Amdur v. City of Chicago, 48n,

American City Bank v. Zetlen, 420n

American National Bank and Trust Co. v. City of Chicago, 101n

American Savings & Loan Ass'n v. County of Marin, 357

Andrus v. Allard, 352n

Andrus v. Sierra Club, 218

Annapolis Emergency Hosp. Assoc. v. Annapolis Hist. District, 407

Arcata Redwood Co. v. State Board of Forestry, 393n

Arlington Coalition on Transportation v. Volpe, 273, 284

Armstrong v. United States, 33

Askew v. Cross Key Waterways, 82n, 343

Association of Data Processing Service Organizations, Inc. v. Camp, 264, 399n

Atchison, Topeka & Santa Fe Railway v. Calloway, 304n

B

Barnidge v. United States, 232n

Barrie v. Kitsap County, 176n

Battista v. Watt, 202n

Bayou St. John Improvement Association v. Sands, 210n

Bell v. Burson, 345n, 347n

Benenson v. United States, 355n

Berger v. United States, 68n

Berman v. Parker, 7, 13n

Biderman v. Morton, 207n, 304n

Birmingham Realty Co. v. General Services Administration, 253n

Board of Regents v. Roth, 345

Board of Supervisors v. Rowe, 50n, 65n, 133n, 401n

Board of Supervisors of James City County v. Rowe, see **Board of Supervisors v. Rowe.**

Board of Zoning Appeals of Decatur v. Decatur, Indiana Company of Jehovah's Witnesses, 107n, 373

Bohannan v. City of San Diego, 13n, 38, 40n, 81n, 82n, 134n, 136n

Boston Waterfront Residents Association, Inc. v. Romney, 276, 284n, 303n, 308n

Braunfeld v. Brown, 371

Broadview Apartments Co. v. Commission for Historical and Architectural Preservation, 92n, 101n, 355n

Brooks v. Volpe, 302n, 304n, 395n

Brown v. Kansas Forestry, Fish & Game Commission, 115n

Buckley v. Valeo, 211n

Buell v. City of Bremerton, 103n

Burkart Randall v. Marshall, 111n

Bydlon v. United States, 355n

C

C.F. Lytle Co. v. Clark, 99n, 359n

California C.C. Corp. v. Superior Court, 402n

Calvert Cliffs' Coordinating Committee, Inc. v. United States Atomic Energy Commission, 299

Camara v. Municipal Court of the City and County of San Francisco, 110, 111n

Canal Authority of the State of Florida v. Callaway, 303n

Candlestick Properties, Inc. v. San Francisco Bay Conservation and Development Commission, 392n, 355n

Cappaert v. United States, 235n

Carson v. Alvord, 268n

Catholic Action of Hawaii/Peace Education Project v. Brown, 272

Central Hudson v. Public Service Commission, 370n

Central Oklahoma Preservation Alliance, Inc. v. Oklahoma City Urban Renewal Authority, 210n, 285, 286

Chelsea Neighborhood Associations v. United States Postal Service, 279n

Citizen's Committee for Environmental Protection v. United States Coast Guard, 267

Citizens Committee to Save Historic Rhodes Tavern v. District of Columbia Department of Housing and Community Development, 106

Citizens Defense Fund v. Gallager, 398n

Citizens for Responsible Area Growth v. Adams, 302n

Citizens for Saving the Historic Thurston County Courthouse v. Department of General Services Administration (GSA), 181

Citizens to Preserve Overton Park v. Volpe, 12, 241, 301n, 348n

City of Blue Ash v. McClucas, 299n

City of Chicago v. Atwood, 112n

City of Chicago v. Kutil, 110n

City of Dallas v. Crownrich, 41, 120n, 392n

City of Fairfield v. Superior Court, 408n

City of Fargo v. Harwood Township, 115n

City of Ithaca v. County of Tompkins, 114n

City of Miamisburg v. Hannah, 76

City of New Orleans v. Dukes, 13n, 17n, 81n, 343n

City of New Orleans v. Impastato, 7n, 65n, 134n, 376n, 401n

City of New Orleans v. Levy, 126

City of New Orleans v. Pergament, 73, 86n

City of Newport v. Fact Concerts, Inc., 366n

City of Rochester v. United States Postal Service, 58n, 272, 276n, 277n, 278n, 279n, 281n, 295, 304n

City of Romulus v. County of Wayne, 302n

City of Santa Fe v. Armijo, 114n, 166

City of Santa Fe v. Gamble-Skogmo, Inc., 13n, 66n, 93n, 98n, 133n

City of Temple Terrace v. Hillsborough Association for Retarded Citizens, Inc., 115

Coalition for Responsible Regional Development v. Coleman, 241n, 248

Cobble Hill Association v. Adams, 255n, 273

Cochran v. Preston, 3n

Coliseum Square Association v. Board of Zoning Adjustment of City of New Orleans, 49n

Colony Federal Savings & Loan Association v. Harris, 261, 290, 291n, 297n

Commissioner of District of Columbia v. Benenson, 76

Committee to Save the Bishop's House v. Medical Center Hospital of Vermont, Inc., 44n, 142n

Committee to Save the Bishop's House v. Medical Center, Inc., see Committee to Save the Bishop's House v. Medical Center Hospital of Vermont, Inc.

Committee to Save the Fox Building vs. Birmingham Branch of the Federal Reserve Bank of Atlanta, 39, 253n, 260n, 279, 280, 281

Commonwealth v. National Gettysburg Battlefield Tower, Inc., 184n

Commonwealth of Puerto Rico v. Muskie, 209n, 248n

Connally v. General Construction Company, 78

Conservation Council of North Carolina v. Constanzo, 271, 274

Conservation Council of North Carolina v. Froehlke, 304n

Conservation Society of Southern Vermont, Inc. v. Secretary of Transportation, 240n, 288n, 302n

Construction Industry Ass'n of Sonoma County v. City of Petaluma, 355n

Corporation of Presiding Bishop of Church of Jesus Christ of Latter Day Saints v. City of Portersville, 107n

Crall v. Leonminster, 103n

Crosby v. Young, 291n, 385

D

Dalsis v. Hills, 272

Daly v. Volpe, 295

Davis v. Pima County, 362n

De Mendoza v. Town of Palm Beach, 81n

Deltona Corp. v. United States, 355n

Demetriadis v. United States Postal Service, 116n

Dempsey v. Boys' Club of City of St. Louis, 43n, 100n 103

Don't Tear It Down, Inc. v. Washington, 41, 120n

Don't Tear It Down, Inc. v. Pennsylvania Avenue Development Corp., 258n, 267

Donohue Construction Co. v. Montgomery County Council, 361n

E

Eaves v. Penn, 270n

Eck v. City of Bismarck, 362n

Edwards v. First Bank of Dundee, 251, 264, 272

Ely v. Velde, 219, 251, 252n, 260n, 271n, 272, 274, 279, 281

Environmental Defense Fund, Inc. v. Armstrong, 302n

Environmental Defense Fund, Inc. v. Corps of Engineers, 216n, 292n, 301n

Environmental Defense Fund, Inc. v. Froehlke, 302n, 304n

Environmental Defense Fund, Inc. v. Ruckelshaus, 83n, 202n, 302n, 401n

Environmental Defense Fund, Inc. v. Tennessee Valley Authority, 248n

Environmental Law Fund, Inc. v. City of Watsonville, 172n

Essex County Preservation Association v. Campbell, 288n, 302n

Ethyl Corp. v. Environmental Protection Agency, 302n

Euclid v. Ambler, see Village of Euclid v. Ambler Realty Company.

Euclid v. Fitzthum, 50n

Ewing v. Mytinger & Casselberry, Inc., 88n, 118

F

Farmland Preservation Association v. Goldschmidt, 288n

Faulkner v. Town of Chestertown, 86n, 87n, 94n

Fifth Avenue Corp. v. Washington County, 357

Figarsky v. Historic District Commission of City of Norwich, 13n, 86n, 96, 102, 382n

First National Bank of Chicago v. Richardson, 278n, 281

First Presbyterian Church of York v. City Council of York, 100, 101n, 373n

Foundation for San Francisco's Architectural Heritage v. City and County of San Francisco, 174n, 176n, 376n, 379n, 380, 382n, 386n, 393n, 408n

Fred F. French Investing Co. v. City of New York, 56, 352n, 362n

Friends of the Earth, Inc. v. Coleman, 303n, 304n

Fuentes v. Shevin, 79n

G

Gary D. Reihart, Inc. v. Township of Carroll, 362n

Gold Run, Ltd. v. Board of County Commissioners, 362n

Goldblatt v. Town of Hempstead, 351n, 353

Golden v. Planning Board of Town of Ramapo, 367n

Goose Hollow Foothills League v. Romney, 277n

Gorieb v. Fox, 356

Gorman Towers, Inc. v. Bogoslavsky, 366

Goss v. Lopez, 345n, 347n

Greene County Planning Board v. Federal Power Commission, 218n, 272

Griggs v. Allegheny County, 352n

Groch v. City of Berkeley, 67, 93n

Gumley v. Board of Selectmen of Nantucket, 102, 382n

H

HFH, Ltd. v. Superior Court of Los Angeles County, 359

Hadacheck v. Sebastian, 351n, 353

Hanly v. Kleindienst, 58n, 277, 278n, 296n

Hanly v. Mitchell, 279n

Hanna v. Drobnick, 111n

Hart v. Denver Urban Renewal Authority, 271, 279n, 281n, 284n, 295

Hawthorn Environmental Preservation Association v. Coleman, 264n

Hayes v. Smith, 52n, 75

Helvering v. United States Trust Co., 206n

Heritage Hill Association v. City of Grand Rapids, 52n, 74

Hernandez v. City of Lafayette, 361n, 366n

Highland Cooperative v. City of Lansing, 303n

Hiram Clarke Civic Club, Inc. v. Lynn, 218n

Historic Green Springs, Inc. v. Bergland, 84, 87n, 89n, 102, 206n, 209n, 230n, 345n, 349

Historic Green Springs, Inc. v. Block, (see also, Historic Green Springs, Inc. v. Bergland), 230n

Hoboken Environment Committee, Inc. v. German Seaman's Mission of New York, 58n, 163n

Hodel v. Virginia Surface Mining and Reclamation Ass'n., 347n, 360

Holaway v. City of Pipestone, 352n

Holmes v. New York City Housing Authority, 349n

Housing and Development Administration v. Johan Realty Co., 112n

Hudson County Water Co. v. McCarter, 353n

I

Image of Greater San Antonio, Texas v. Brown, 280, 281, 292n

In Re Clinton Ave, 2n

Indian Lookout Alliance v. Volpe, 274, 294n

Inman Park Restoration, Inc. v. Urban Mass Transit Administration, 285m, 293, 301n

Iron Workers Local No. 272 v. Bowen, 270n

J

Jackson County, Missouri v. Jones, 272

Jentgen v. United States, 355n

Jones v. Lynn, 207n, 284n, 295

Jones v. HUD, 281

K

Kaiser Aetna v. United States, 352n

Kaukus v. City of Chicago, 110n

Keith v. Volpe, 293

Kent County Council for Historic Preservation v. Romney, 253n, 264n

Kirchner v. Kansas Turnpike Authority, 290

Kleppe v. Sierra Club, 217n, 296, 298n, 300, 302n

Kurman v. Zoning Board of Adjustment of City of Philadelphia, 107n

L

La Raza Unida of Southern Alameda County v. Volpe, 274n

Lafayette Park Baptist Church v. Scott, 51, 65n, 99n, 100n

Lafayette Park Baptist Church v. Board of Adjustment of City of St. Louis, 101

Laird v. Tatum, 68n

Lake Country Estates, Inc. v. Tahoe Regional Planning Agency, 365

Lange v. Brinegar, 295

Lathan v. Volpe, 274n, 297n, 302n, 303n

Laurel Hill Homeowners Association v. City Council, 178n, 376n, 395

Lead Industries Association v. Environmental Protection Agency, 104n

Life of the Land, Inc. v. City of Honolulu, 39

Lincoln County v. Johnson, 115n

Louisiana Environmental Society, Inc. v. Coleman, 240n, 241n

Louisville Bridge Co. v. United States, 351n

Lutheran Church in America v. New York City, 51n, 421

M

Maher v. City of New Orleans, 18n, 40n, 51n, 65n, 69, 71, 73, 75, 93n, 94, 96, 100n, 101n, 109, 353n, 354, 376n

Maher v. Gagne, 269n

Mailman Development Corporation v. City of Hollywood, 362n

Maine v. Thiboutot, 397n

Manhattan Club v. New York City Landmarks Preservation Commission, 38n, 80

Marini v. Municipal Court, 420n

Marshall v. Barlow's, Inc., 111n

Maryland/National Capital Park & Planning Commission v. United States Postal Service, 277n, 278n

Mason County Medical Ass'n v. Knebel, 303n

Mathews v. Eldridge, 347n

Maun v. United States, 116n

Mayor of Annapolis v. Anne Arundel County, 113

Metcalf v. Los Angeles County, 360n

Metromedia, Inc. v. City of San Diego, 369, 374

Metropolitan Washington Coalition for Clean Air v. District of Columbia, 270n

Middlesex County Sewerage Authority v. National Sea Clammers Association, 268n

Miller v. Schoene, 352n

Miltenberger v. Chesapeake and Ohio Railway Company, 273

Minnesota Public Interest Research Group v. Butz, 303n

Mitchell v. W. T. Grant Co., 347n

Monell v. Department of Social Services, 365

Monroe v. Pape, 365n

Monroe County Conservation Council v. Adams, 240n

Monroe County Conservation Council, Inc. v. Volpe, 292n

Montgomery County v. Woodward & Lothrop, Inc., 134n

Morristown Road Associates v. Bernardsville, 97

Mugler v. Kansas, 350n, 351n

Mullane v. Central Hanover Bank & Trust Co., 346n

N

NAACP v. Civiletti, 269n

NLRB v. Donnelly Garment Co., 68n

Named Individual Members of San Antonio Conservation Society v. Texas Highway Department, 272, 273n, 294n

Natale v. Kennebunkport Board of Zoning Appeals, 49n

National Center for Preservation Law v. Landrieu, 211, 219n, 248n, 258, 261n, 262, 290, 398n, 401n

National Indian Youth Council v. Andrus, 218n, 219n, 250n, 253n

National Wildlife Federation v. Adams, 302n

Nationwide Building Maintenance, Inc., v. Sampson, 270n

Natural Resources Defense Council, Inc., v. Callaway, 218n

Natural Resources Defense Council, Inc., v. Grant, 277, 304n

Natural Resources Defense Council, Inc., v. Morton, 292n, 395n, 401n

Natural Resources Defense Council, Inc., v. City of New York, 218n, 397n, 402n

Nectow v. City of Cambridge, 5n, 31

Neighborhood Development Corp. v. Advisory Council on Historic Preservation, 264, 381n, 400n

New Motor Vehicle Board v. Orrin W. Fox Co., 119n, 346

New Yorkers to Preserve the Theater District v. Landrieu, 291, 385n, 402n

New Orleans v. Dukes, see City of New Orleans v. Dukes.

Newman v. Piggie Park Enterprise, Inc., 270n

900 G Street Associates v. D.C. Department of Housing and Community Development, 18n, 73, 99, 100n, 355n

Noe v. Metropolitan Atlanta Rapid Transit Authority, 299n

Nott v. Wolff, 422n

O

Ogunquit Village Corp. v. Davis, 182n, 299n, 304n

Ohio Bell Telephone Co. v. Public Utilities Commission, 104n

Oldham v. Ehrlich, 269n

Olley Valley Estates, Inc. v. Fussell, 103n

Opinion of the Justices to the Senate, 7n, 65n, 368n, 401n

Owen v. City of Independence, 365

P

Pamel Corp. v. Puerto Rico Highway Authority, 209n, 352n, 355n

Pan Pacific Properties, Inc. v. County of Santa Cruz, 360n

Payne v. Kassab, 184n

Penn Central Transportation Co. v. City of New York, 4, 16n, 17, 18, 30, 33, 34n, 39, 41, 42, 49, 51, 65, 74, 79n, 99, 133, 209n, 343, 351n, 352n, 353, 356, 358n, 367, 374, 375, 376n, 378n, 411n, 491, 497n

Pennsylvania Coal Co. v. Mahon, 4n, 351, 352n

People ex rel. Marbro Corp. v. Ramsey, 60n

Philadelphia Council of Neighborhood Organizations v. Coleman, 260n

Phillips v. Board of Zoning Adjustments of City of New Orleans, 106n

Piedmont Heights Civic Club, Inc. v. Moreland, 303n

Pillman v. Village of Northbrook, 101n

Pitman v. Washington Suburban Sanitary Commission, 178n

Polygon Corp. v. City of Seattle, 175n

Potomac Sand & Gravel Co. v. Governor of Maryland, 367

Powelton Civic Home Owners Ass'n v. Department of HUD, 395n

Prandini v. National Tea Co., 417n

R

Rebman v. City of Springfield, 51n, 134n

Residents of Beverly Glen v. City of Los Angeles, 400n

River v. Richmond Metropolitan Authority, 294

Robert H. Thayer & Virginia Thayer v. Commissioner, 487, 489, 492, 494

Robinson v. Kunach, 172n

Roe v. Kansas ex. rel. Smith, 2n

Romero-Barcelo v. Brown, 248n, 253n

Rose v. Locke, 78n

Russo v. Stevens, 104n

Rutgers v. Piluso, 115n

S

S.W. Neighborhood Assembly v. Eckard, 271, 277n

St. Joseph Historical Society v. Land Clearance for Redevelopment Authority of St. Joseph, Missouri, 279, 280, 281

Salsbery v. District of Columbia Board of Zoning Adjustment, 358n

San Antonio Conservation Society v. City of San Antonio, 168n

San Diego Gas & Electric Co. v. City of San Diego, 209n, 352n, 357, 358n, 363, 368, 374

San Diego Trust & Savings Bank v. Friends of Gill, 172n

San Francisco Tomorrow v. Romney, 271

Sansom Committee v. Lynn, 277n, 304n

Santa Fe v. Gamble-Skogmo, Inc., see City of Santa Fe v. Gamble-Skogmo.

Save the Bay, Inc. v. Corps of Engineers, 273, 275

Save the Courthouse Committee v. Lynn, 207n, 220, 253n, 268n, 279n, 297n, 303n

Scherr v. Volpe, 395n

Schroeder v. City of New York, 346n

Scottsdale Mall v. State of Indiana, 274

See v. City of Seattle, 110, 111

Serrano v. Unrun, 417n

Sherbert v. Verner, 371n

Shoemaker v. U.S., 2n

Sierra Club v. Alexander, 304n

Sierra Club v. Hathaway, 302n, 303n

Sierra Club v. Hodel, 274, 275

Sierra Club v. Lynn, 288n

Sierra Club v. Mason, 303n, 304n

Sierra Club v. Morton, 218n, 264n, 265, 267, 268, 303n, 399n, 400n

Silva v. Romney, 304n

Smoke Rise, Inc. v. Washington Suburban Sanitary Commission 361n

Sniadach v. Family Finance Corporation, 345n

Snowden v. Hughes, 126n

Society for Ethical Culture v. Spatt, 38, 81n, 83n, 85, 89, 107n, 372, 376n, 382n

Society for the Protection of New Hampshire Forests v. Brinegar, 303n

South Hill Neighborhood Association v. Romney, 12, 253n, 264n

South Terminal Corp. v. The Environmental Protection Agency, 354

South of Second Associates v. Georgetown, Colorado, 40, 69, 81, 93, 97

Southern National Bank v. City of Austin, 40n, 120n, 392n

St. Louis, Iron Mountain and Southern Railway Co.v. Williams, 123n

State v. Jones, 65n

State v. Larsen Transfer and Storage, Inc., 110n

State v. Smith, 65n

State v. Superior Court of Orange County, 361n

State by Powderly v. Erickson (see State of Minnesota by Powderly v. Erickson).

State ex rel. Christian v. Miller, 118n

State ex rel. Powderly v. Erickson, (see State of Minnesota by Powderly v. Erickson).

State of Alaska v. Andrus, 271n, 273

State of California v. Bergland, 302n

State of California v. Superior Court (Veta Corp.), 381n

State of Minnesota by Powderly v. Erickson, 110n, 177, 355n, 379n

State of Washington v. City of Seattle, 114, 166

Steel Hill Development, Inc. v. Town of Sanbornton, 353n, 355

Steubing v. Brinegar, 303n, 304n

Stop H-3 v. Brinegar, 220n

Stop H-3 Association v. Coleman, 210n, 240n

Strycker's Bay Neighborhood Council, Inc. v. Karlen, 216, 278n, 291, 298n, 300, 302n, 376n

Sturdy Homes, Inc. v. Township of Redford, 367

T

T.E. Bearing Co. v. Walter E. Heller & Co., 420n

Tanner v. Armco Steel Corp., 216n

Texas Antiquities Commission v. Dallas County Community College District, 38, 82, 83, 84, 114n

Texas Committee on Natural Resources v. Bergland, 303n

Thompson v. Fugate, 252

Toms River Affiliates v. Department of Environmental Protection, 361

Town of Deering v. Tibbetts, 92

Treasure Salvors, Inc. v. Unidentified Wrecked and Abandoned Sailing Vessel, 235n

Trinity Episcopal School Corp. v. Romney, 278n

Tucker v. City Council for the City of New Orleans, 74

Tuxedo Conservation and Taxpayers Association v. Town Board of the Town of Tuxedo, 103n

U

Udell v. Haas, 34n

United States v. Central Eureka Mining Co., 351n

United States v. Diaz, 236n, 238

United States v. Gettysburg Electric Railway Co., 2

United States v. Smyer, 236n

United States Trust Co. of New York v. Commission of Internal Revenue, 206n

V

Vermont Yankee Nuclear Power Corp. v. Natural Resources Defense Council, Inc., 291, 293n, 298n, 300, 302n, 376n

Village of Belle Terre v. Boraas, 343n

Village of Euclid v. Ambler Realty Company, 5, 31, 351n, 353

Virginia Historic Landmarks Commission v. Board of Supervisors of Louisa County, 87

Visidor Corporation v. Borough of Cliffside Park, 362n

W

WATCH (Waterbury Action to Conserve Our Heritage, Inc.) v. Harris, (see also Waterbury Urban Renewal Agency v. WATCH), 214n, 250n, 253, 254, 269n, 278, 279n, 280, 281n, 285, 286, 308n, 391n, 401n, 414

Warm Springs Dam Task Force v. Gribble, 218n, 285, 302n, 303n

Warth v. Seldin, 399n

Washington Mobilization Committee v. Cullinane, 78

Waterbury Urban Renewal Agency v. WATCH, (see also WATCH v. Harris) 391n

Weintraub v. Provident National Bank, 251

Weintraub v. Rural Electrification Administration, 251n, 264n

Welch v. Swasey, 3, 353n

West Virginia Highlands Conservancy v. Island Creek Coal Co., 395n

Westchester Reform Temple v. Brown, 372

Westwood Hills Property Owners Association v. Regents of the University of California, 419n

White v. Roughton, 349n

Wilderness Society v. Hickel, 395n

William C. Haas & Co. v. City and County of San Francisco, 18n, 354

Williams v. Parker, 3n

Wilson v. Borough of Mountainside, 359n

Wilson v. Lynn, 272, 278n

Wincamp Partnership v. Anne Arundel County, 361n

Winnebago Tribe of Nebraska v. Ray, 275

Wisconsin Heritages, Inc. v. Harris, 260n, 279n, 292, 293n, 295

Wm. Inglis & Sons Baking Co. v. ITT Continental Baking Co., 303n

Wolk v. Reisem, 112n

Woodland Hills Residents Association v. City Council (II), 397n

Woodstock v. Gallup, 2n

Y

Young v. American Mini-Theatres, Inc., 13n

Young v. Mellon, 72, 202

Index

A

ACHP
  See Advisory Council on Historic Preservation

Acquisition
  easements, 143-145

Administrative Procedures, 375-389
  Administrative Procedures Act, 267-268
  historic preservation ordinances, 78-106
  National Environmental Policy Act, 281-286
  ripeness, 360-362
  See also Constitutional Law; Federal Agencies; Litigation and Remedies; State Agencies

Administrative Procedures Act, 267-268

Advisory Council on Historic Preservation, 331-335
  archaeology, 233-234
  creation, 193-196
  duties, 210-212
  establishment, 9-10
  membership, 210-211

Section 106, 246-270

Aesthetic Controls
  challenges, 50-51
  constitutional law, 65n
  purpose, 64-65, 66-67
  signs, 369-371

Agencies, Federal
  See Federal Agencies

Agencies, State
  See State Agencies

Amicus Curiae, 421-423

American Bar Association
  preservation law, 19

American Institute of Architects
  building codes, 54

American Law Institute
  Model Land Development Code, 77-78, 89, 124

American Planning Association, 6,8

American Society of Planning Officials

See American Planning
Association

Amtrak Improvement Act, 241

Antiquities Act of 1906, 8,
235-236

Appeals
See Litigation and Remedies

Archaeology
Archaeological Resource
Protection Act, 238
federal programs, 233-235
general considerations, 239
National Park Service, 228

Attorneys
administrative process,
380-389
American Bar Association,
19
case building, 380-383,
387-388, 396-406,
408-413
easement appraisers, 491-493
environmental law, 10
federal preservation law
development, 11, 24
fees, 24-25, 269-270
judicial relief preparation,
388-389
litiginous issues, 375-377
litigation strategy, 377-380
local preservation law, 25-27
respondents, 420-425
state preservation law, 25-26
technical assistance, 384-386

See also Litigation and
Remedies; Pleadings

B

Beautification
See Aesthetic Controls

Building Codes
American Institute of
Architects, 54
Building Officials and Code
Administrators
International, 54-56
coordination with
preservation program,
53-57
National Trust, 54
permits, 55-56
state enabling authority,
142-143
See also Land-Use
Regulations; Zoning

Building Officials and Code
Administrators International
Basic Building Code, 54-56

Building Permits
See Certificates of
Appropriateness

C

Categorical Grants
See Funding

Certificates of Appropriateness
alternative uses, 100-101

disclosure, 102-104
economic hardship, 104-107
economics, 98-101
maintenance, 107-113
owners attempt to sell or rent, 100
review procedures, 101-103
review standards, 90-126
See also Taking

Certification
historic districts, 155-156
National Register properties, 154-155
rehabilitation, 156-157
SHPO, 149-157
See also Appendix B; National Park Service

Challenges
See Litigation and Remedies

Coastal Zone Management Act, 44n, 57-58, 165, 244

Code of Federal Regulations, 199-200

Codes
See Building Codes

Community Development Block Grant, 210-211, 320-324

Comprehensive Landmarks Program
coordination with local master plan, 37, 43-58
economic assistance, 37, 41-43
elements of, 32-58
legal precedents, 32-35
moratoriums, 41
practical justification, 35-37
surveys, 37, 38-41
technical assistance, 37, 41-43
See also Coordination

Constitutional Law, 343-373
administration of ordinances, 124-126
administrative searches, 110-111
aesthetic controls, 65n
comprehensive landmarks program, 32-37
designation procedures, 88-89
first amendment issues, 369-373
hearings, 345-348
listing, 208-209
moratoriums, 117-120
ordinance standards, 78, 80-88
procedural due process, 118, 344-350
review standards, 98
state enabling authority, 139-141
states, 182-185
taking, 4, 16-17, 87n, 208-209, 209n, 350-368
vested rights, 118
See also Historic Preservation Law, Federal; Litigations and Remedies

Controls
  See Historic Preservation
    Ordinances

Coordination
  comprehensive landmarks
    program and local master
    plan, 37, 43-58
  environmental law, 57-58
  historic preservation
    ordinances, 117
  legal reasons, 44-46
  National Historic
    Preservation Act and
    National Environmental
    Policy Act, 305-309
  state agencies, 164-167
  state and national
    environmental policy acts,
    180-181
  zoning, 43, 47-53

Courts
  See Litigation and Remedies

D

Defederalization
  preservation law, 20-22
  Section 106, 21-22
  state preservation role,
    130-131

Demolition
  National Register status, 29
  review body power, 72
  taxation, 18
  urban development action
    grant, 23-24
  See also Appendix A;
    Certificates of
    Appropriateness; Taking

Demolition Moratoriums
  See Moratoriums

Demolition Permits
  See Certificates of
    Appropriateness

Department of Transportation
  Act
  protective scope, 240-241
  See also Highways

Designation
  criteria and standards,
    348-350
  economics, 87-88
  federal government, 20
  historic landmarks, 225
  National Register
    nomination, 82, 88-89
  owner's role, 75-76
  procedures, 88-126
  scope, 85-87
  standards, 80-88
  state enabling acts, 135-138
  surveys, 38-41, 81-82
  taking, 87n
  See also Appendix A;
    Constitutional Law

Development Moratoriums
  See Moratoriums

Donation
  See Easement

Drafting Preservation
   Ordinances
   See Appendix A; Historic
      Preservation Ordinances,
      Drafting

Due Process
   See Constitutional Law

E

Easements
   defined, 143n
   economics, 143-145
   effect of donor, 496-497
   programs, 490
   property tax, 455-456
   Tax Reform Act, 485-486
   tax shelter, 485-499
   valuation, 486-499
   See also Appendix C

Economic Recovery Tax Act
   accelerated depreciation,
      470-471
   property tax reform, 459-460
   renovation incentives,
      467-479
   tax incentives, 19, 21, 154
   tax shelter, 443-444
   See also Appendix B

Economic Assistance
   comprehensive landmarks
      program, 37, 41-43
   transferable development
      rights, 42
   See also Financing; Funding;
      Taxation

Economic Hardship
   certificates of appropriateness
      review, 98-101, 104-107
   current return, 99
   designation, 87-88
   owner's knowledge, 99
   preservation law future,
      25-27
   purpose, 63-64
   reasonable use, 87, 107n
   review body discretion, 72
   safety valve provisions,
      104-107
   state enabling authority, 141
   taking, 4-5, 16-17, 87n,
      139-141, 209n, 350-368
   See also Economic
      Assistance; Financing;
      Funding; Taxation

EIS
   See Enviromental Impact
      Statement

Eligibility
   National Park Service, 225
   owner objection, 209-210

Environmental Impact
   Statement
   adequacy, 294-296
   compliance regulations,
      218-220
   contents, 291-293
   environmental consequences,
      293-294
   mitigation, 298-299

National Environmental
Policy Act process,
216-217, 286-291
state environmental policy
acts process, 173-178

Environmental Law
attorneys, 11
Coastal Zone Management
Act, 44n, 57, 165, 244
coordination, 57-58
National Environmental
Policy Act, 58n, 215-220
state constitutions, 182-185
state environmental policy
acts, 168-178
state historic preservation
laws, 165-167

Environmental Policy
See Environmental Law

ERTA
See Economic Recovery Tax
Act

Exhaustion of Administrative
Remedies
See Ripeness

F

Federal Agencies
Advisory Council on Historic
Preservation, 193-195,
210-212
administrative process,
380-389
Bureau of Land
Management, 244
Council on Environmental
Quality, 217, passim
Department of Agriculture,
219
Department of Commerce, 4
Department of Housing and
Urban Development, 10,
11, 219, passim
Department of the Interior, 8,
9, 19, 20, 59, 71, 72, 84,
196-197, 231-234, passim
Department of
Transportation, 10, 12,
239-241
discretion under National
Historic Preservation Act,
213-214
environmental impact
statement, 297-299
Environmental Protection
Agency, 219
Forest Service, 244
General Services
Administration, 212, 242
National Park Service, 193,
220-239
Office of Surface Mining,
Reclamation and
Enforcement, 243
respondents, 420-421
technical assistance, 227
See also Administrative
Procedures

Federal Land Policy and
Management Act, 244

Federal Preservation Law
See Historic Preservation
Law, Federal

Financing
  community development block grant, 499-500
  glossary of terms, 428-431
  government subsidies, 435-436
  investment tax credit, 513-519
  land cost write down, 508-510
  lenders, 440-441
  mortgage interest rate reductions, 511-513
  National Historic Preservation Act, 442
  property tax reductions, 510-511
  reduced construction loan interest rate, 510
  renovation, 437-442
  packages, 499-519
  urban development action grants, 499-500
  See also Funding; Taxation

Funding
  Advisory Council on Historic Preservation, 21
  community development block grant, 320-324
  community development programs, 319-328, 336-341
  comprehensive planning grants, 326-327
  federal credit institutions, 315-318
  government subsidy, 508-519
  Historic Preservation Loan Program, 313-314
  housing assistance programs, 318-319, 336-431
  listing, 207-209
  low-rent public housing, 318
  mortgage insurance and loan guarantees, 312-315
  National Historic Preservation Fund grants-in-aid, 208, 226
  National Park Service, 226
  National Trust, 21
  neighborhood self-help development grants, 327
  rehabilitation loans, 327
  Section 106, 251-252
  SHPO, 152-153
  urban development action grants, 20, 23-24, 45, 324-326
  urban homesteading, 327-328
  See also Financing; Taxation

G

Governmental Coordination
  See Coordination

Government, Federal
  See Federal Agencies

Government, Local
  See Local Agencies

Government-Owned Property
  historic preservation ordinances, 113-117

management, 242-243
surplus transfer, 226

Government, State
See State Agencies

H

HABS/HAER
surveys, 227
See also Historic American
Buildings Survey

Hearings
decision, 348
on merits, 415
nature, 347-348
notice, 346
rights, 345-346
stay order, 413-414
stay, pending determination
of merits, 414-415
timing, 346-347
See also Administrative
Procedures; Constitutional
Law

Highways
Amtrak Improvement Act,
241
Transportation Act of 1966,
10, 239-241
Railroad Revitalization and
Regulatory Reform Act,
241

Historic American Buildings
Survey, 9, 231

Historic American Building
Survey/Historic American
Engineering Record
See HABS/HAER

Historic American Engineering
Record, 231

Historic Districts
Abe Lincoln, Springfield,
Illinois, 51n
Beacon Hill, 6
Green Springs, Virginia, 87
legal definition, 29n
Oakwood, North Carolina,
92
Old Santa Fe, 91
Old Town Alexandria,
Virginia, 91
Pioneer Square, 48
Vieux Carre, 69, 71-72, 91,
97, 134, passim
See also Historic Preservation
Ordinances

Historic Landmarks
designation, 225
Hasbrouck House, 2
Gettysburg, 2
Grand Central Terminal,
12-13, 14-18, 34-35,
passim
Historic Sites Act, 84-85
J.P. Morgan House, 421
legal definition, 29n
Monadnock Building,
494-495
Mount Vernon, 1
National Historic Landmarks
Program, 8

Norwichtown Green,
  Connecticut, 96
Portman Hotel, 23-24, 401
Rhodes Tavern, District of
  Columbia, 106
Stock Exchange Building, 12
Unity Building, Chicago,
  502-508
Willard Hotel, 76
See also Comprehensive
  Landmarks Program;
  Historic Preservation
  Ordinances

Historic Preservation Act,
  National
  See National Historic
  Preservation Act

Historic Preservation
  Commissions
  See Preservation
  Commissions

Historic Preservation Grant-in-Aid Manual, 200

Historic Preservation Law,
  Federal, 191-328
  Advisory Council on Historic
    Preservation, 210-212,
    passim
  Antiquities Act of 1906, 8,
    235-236
  Archaeological Resource
    Protection Act, 238
  archaeology, 234-235
  Coastal Zone Management
    Act, 44n, 57-58, 165, 244
  community development
    block grant, 260-261
  constitutional issues,
    343-373
  defederalization, 20-22
  development, 1-27, 193-215
  Economic Recovery Tax Act,
    467-479
  economics, 427-522
  executive order 11593, 242
  Federal Land Policy and
    Management Act, 244
  future, 22-25
  Historic Sites Act, 8, 84-85,
    230-233
  Housing and Community
    Development Act,
    261-262, 435
  housing and community
    development programs
    309-328, 336-339
  land-use planning laws,
    243-244
  Model Cities Act, 10
  National Environmental
    Policy Act, 215-220,
    270-304
  National Forest Management
    Act, 244
  National Historic Landmarks
    Program, 228-230
  National Historic
    Preservation Act, 10,
    147-153, 193, 195-215,
    246-270
  Native American Religious
    Freedom Act, 238-239
  program assessment, 245-246
  Public Buildings Cooperative
    Use Act, 212, 242

Reservoir Salvage Act,
  236-237
Revenue Act (1978),
  464-466
state responsibility, 147-157
Surface Mining Control and
  Reclamation Act, 243
Tax Reform Act, 461-464
Transportation Act of 1966,
  10, 239-241
transportation legislation,
  239-242
See also Appendixes B and
  C; Federal Agencies;
  Preservation Law
  Development

Historic Preservation Law,
  Local
  See Historic Preservation
  Ordinances

Historic Preservation Law,
  State, 129-185
  coordination, 164-167
  defederalization, 130-131
  environmental policy,
    168-185
  federal programs, 147-157
  future, 25-27
  National Historic
    Preservation Act
    amendments, 129-131
  registers, 159-164
  state agencies, 164-167
  state constitutions, 182-185
  state enabling acts, 134-143
  similarities among, 158-187
  tax laws, 167-168
  See also State Agencies;
    State Enabling Authority

Historic Preservation Loan
  Program, 313-314

Historic Preservation
  Ordinances, 29-126
  administration, 58-126
  aesthetic controls, 50-51,
    65n, 64-65, 66-67,
    369-371
  building codes, 53-57
  certificate of appropriateness,
    90-126
  certificate of appropriateness
    procedures, 96-124
  certificate of appropriateness
    standards, 91-97
  coordination with
    environmental laws, 57-58
  coordination with local
    master plans, 31, 32-58,
    117
  development, 5-8
  drafting, 58-126
  enabling authority, 60-61
  enforcement, 120-124
  future, 25-27
  government-owned property,
    113-116
  hearings, 89
  Interior Department
    guidelines, 61
  maintenance standards,
    107-113
  National Historic
    Preservation Act
    amendments, 36-37
  National Trust, 59

New York City Landmarks
Law, 13-14
notice, 89
owner's consent, 75-76
precise definitions, 76-78
procedures, 88-126
purpose, 63-67
relationship to building
codes, 53-56
relationship to land-use
regulations, 32
relationship to subdivision
regulations, 56-57
review body, 67-75
state enabling authority,
131-147
standards, 80-88
See also Appendix A;
Comprehensive Landmarks
Program; Environmental
Law; Land-Use
Regulations

Historic Preservation Program
See Comprehensive
Landmarks Program

Historic Sites Act, 8, 84-85,
230-233

History of Preservation Law
See Preservation Law
Development

Home rule charters
See State Enabling
Authority

Housing Codes
See Building Codes

I

Incentives
See Renovation

Interagency Resource
Management Division,
224-225

Internal Revenue Code
See Taxation

Inventories
See Surveys

J

Judicial Review
See Litigation and Remedies

K

Keeper of the National
Register, 202-203

L

Landmarks Commissions
See Preservation
Commissions

Land-Use Regulations
development of preservation
law, 4-8
federal planning laws,
243-244
state enabling authority,
133-134
subdivisions, 56-57
taking, 353-356

zoning, 43, 47-53
zoning enabling act, 4-5
See also Building Codes;
Zoning

Legislation, Federal
See Historic Preservation
Law, Federal

Legislation, State
See Historic Preservation
Law, State

Listing
effects, 207-209
eligibility, 209-210
National Park Service,
224-225
National Register, 197-98
nomination by certified local
governments, 203-204
nomination by federal
agencies, 204-205
nomination by SHPO,
200-203
owner objection/consent,
205-207
Section 106, 207-209
taking, 208-209
See also Designation;
National Register

Litigation and Remedies,
375-426
acting early, 386
appeal on merits, 418-420
challenges, 50-53, 69
compliance orders, 121-122
defending on merit, 424
discovery, 406-408

evidence, 408-413
expanding the record,
424-425
experts, 379-380, 408-413
forced reconstruction,
123-124
government-owned property,
114-117
Grand Central Terminal,
15-18
hearings, 413-415
injunctive relief, 121-122,
417-418, 423-424
judicial review standards,
378-379
judicial review strategies,
389-426
monetary fines, 121,
122-123
National Environmental
Policy Act, 299-305
owner's consent, 75-76
permit review, 75-76
petition for relief, 396-406
pleadings for injunctive
relief, 391-396
pleadings on the merits,
390-391
post-trial, 416-420
procedural standards, 96-98
receiverships, 122
Section 106 enforcement,
266-268
Section 106 process, 246-270
Section 106 remedies, 268
standing, 263-265
state enabling authority,
136-138
state environmental policy
acts, 176, 178-182

taking, 362-368
See also Attorneys;
  Constitutional Law

M

Master Plan
See Comprehensive
  Landmarks Program

Memorandums of Agreement
See Section 106

Model Cities Act of 1966, 10

Model Land Development Code, 77-78, 89, 124

Model Provisions
See Appendix A

Moratoriums
  constitutional issues, 117-120
  demolition, 117-120
  development, 117-120
  program drafting, 41
  review body power, 72
  taking, 361-362

N

National Center for Preservation Law, 19, 24

National Conference of State Historic Preservation Officers, 331-335

National Environmental Policy Act
  application to built environment, 215-220
  archaeology, 234-235
  coordination with National Historic Preservation Act, 305-309
  environmental impact statement, 216-217
  environmental impact statement process, 286-291
  judicial review, 299-301
  preservation law, 58n
  procedural requirements, 270-281
  procedures, 281-286
  remedies, 299-301
  See also State Environmental Policy Acts

National Forest Management Act, 244

National Historic Landmarks Program, 8, 228-230

National Historic Preservation Act
  Advisory Council on Historic Preservation, 210-212
  amendments, 21-22
  archaeology, 234-235
  attorneys fees, 24
  building reuse, 212
  coordination with National Environmental Policy Act, 305-309
  enabling authority, 193-195

federal agency discretion,
  213-214
historic preservation
  ordinances, 36-37
National Register, 195-210
review body, 67-68
Section 106, 21-22, 246-270
SHPOs, 148-153
state preservation role,
  129-130
surveys, 39
See also Section 106

National Historic Preservation
  Fund, 208

National Monuments, 235,
  236

National Park Service
  archaeological programs, 228
  HABS/HAER, 227
  Interagency Resource
    Management Division,
    224
  Keeper of the National
    Register, 197-198
  National Historic Landmarks
    Program, 228-230
  National Historic
    Preservation Act authority,
    193
  National Park System, 236
  National Register eligibility,
    225
  National Register listing,
    224-225
  Preservation Assistance
    Division, 225-227
  preservation programs,
    220-239

Reservoir Salvage Act, 236

National Register
  certification delay, 482
  Code of Federal Regulations,
    199-200
  creation, 9-10, 20, 195
  demolition, 29
  designation, 20
  designation procedures,
    88-89
  eligibility, 209-210
  history, 8
  listing qualifications,
    199-200
  nomination criteria, 82
  nomination procedures,
    200-207
  nomination requirements,
    197-198
  property certification,
    154-155
  property types, 198
  review body nominations,
    70-75
  tax credits, 479-485
  Tax Reform Act of 1976, 18
  See also Registers

National Register of Historic
  Places
  See National Register

National Trust, 17, 19, 21
  building codes, 54
  designation standards, 83
  historic preservation
    ordinances, 59
  program planning, 39, 40

National Trust for Historic
  Preservation
  See National Trust

National Survey of Historic
  Sites and Buildings, 231

New York Landmarks
  Commission
  technical assistance, 43

New York City Landmarks
  Law, 13-14

New York City Landmarks
  Preservation Commission,
  14-16, 17-18

NEPA
  See National Environmental
  Policy Act

NHPA
  See National Historic
  Preservation Act

Nomination
  See National Register
  See also Designation; Listing

Nomination to National
  Register
  See National Register

Noncompliance
  See Litigation and Remedies

Notice
  listing, 201

O

Ordinances
  See Historic Preservation
    Ordinances and Controls
  See also Building Codes;
    Environmental Law; Land-
    Use Regulations; Taxation

Owners
  attempt to sell or rent, 100
  consent, 75-76, 205-207,
    209-210
  economic assistance, 42-43
  economic hardship, 104-107
  eligibility, 209-210
  knowledge, 99
  National Historic Landmarks
    Program, 228-229
  notice, 201
  renovation investment,
    432-434
  rights, 345-346
  taking, 350-357
  technical assistance, 43
  See also Renovation

P

Permits
  See Certificates of
    Appropriateness

Petition for Relief
  causes of action, 404-405
  prayer for relief, 405
  real party in interest,
    402-403
  respondents, 401-402
  standing, 399-401

state or federal, 396-399
statement of proceedings
   below, 403
verification, 406

Planning
   See Comprehensive
      Landmarks Program;
      Coordination

Planning for Preservation, 8

Pleadings
   application for injunctive
      relief, 394-395
   memorandum of law,
      390-391, 395
   order to show cause, 391,
      396
   record for injunctive relief,
      391-394
   restraining order, 395-396
   verified petition for relief,
      390

Preservation Action, 19

Preservation Assistance Division
   designation, 225-227

Preservation Commissions
   composition, 67-70
   disclosure, 102-104
   jurisdictions, 136-137
   membership, 136-137
   New York City Landmarks
      Preservation Commission,
      14-16, 17-18
   powers, 70-75
   veto powers, 53

See also Appendix A;
   Landmarks Commissions;
   Review Body

Preservationists
   See Attorneys

Preservation Law
   See Historic Preservation
      Law, Federal; Historic
      Preservation Law, State;
      Historic Preservation
      Ordinances

Preservation Law Development
   Advisory Council on Historic
      Preservation, 9-10
   American Society of
      Planning Officials, 6, 8
   Antiquities Act of 1906, 8
   attorneys, 11
   defederalization, 20-22
   demolition deterrent, 18
   Department of Housing and
      Urban Development, 11
   Department of
      Transportation, 12
   economics, 22
   expansion of regulatory
      powers, 3-5
   federal preservation policy,
      9-11
   federal role, 193-195
   future policy, 24-25
   Grand Central Terminal,
      14-18
   Historic American Buildings
      Survey, 9
   Historic Sites Act, 8
   Land-use regulations, 4-8

Model Cities Act, 10
National Historic Landmarks
  Program, 8
National Historic
  Preservation Act, 10
National Register, 8, 9-10,
  20
National Trust, 8
New York City landmarks
  law, 13-14
19th century, 1-3
pioneer ordinances, 6-8
Planning for Preservation, 8
state role, 8-11
taking clause, 4-5
tax incentives, 18-20
Tax Reform Act of 1976, 18
20th century, 3-22
With Heritage So Rich, 9,
  10
See also Historic Preservation
  Law, Federal

Private Property
  church-owned, 371-373
  eligibility, 209-210
  National Historic Landmarks
    Program, 8
  taking, 350-357
  transferable development
    rights, 42
  See also Constitutional Law;
    Economic Hardship;
    Owners

Procedural Due Process
  See Constitutional Law

Program Planning
  See Coordination

Property Owners
  See Owners

Property Rights
  See Government-Owned
    Property; Private Property

Property Tax
  abatements, 450-451,
    453-454
  assessment freeze, 451-452
  credits, 454
  current-use assessment,
    454-456
  easements, 455-456
  exemptions, 449-450,
    453-454
  incentives, 448-449
  reform, 457-460
  renovation investment,
    446-448
  state, 145-146
  See also Taxation

Public Buildings Cooperative
  Use Act, 212, 242

Public Property
  See Government-Owned
    Property

Purpose
  aesthetics, 50-51, 64, 66-67
  economic, 63-64
  educational/cultural, 64
  social, 64
  See also Appendix A

R

Rehabilitation
  See Renovation

Railroad Revitalization and
  Regulatory Reform Act, 241

Registers
  state, 159-164
  See also National Register

Renovation
  after-tax income, 442-446
  Economic Recovery Tax Act,
    467-479
  economics, 432-446
  feasibility analysis, 502-508
  financing considerations,
    437-442
  government subsidies,
    435-436, 441-442
  income and expense
    analysis, 434-437
  investment, 432-434
  investment tax credit,
    464-466
  land cost write down,
    508-510
  property tax credits, 454
  property tax relief, 453-454
  Revenue Act (1978),
    464-466
  tax shelter, 443-445
  See also Taxation

Reservoir Salvage Act
  technical assistance, 236-237

Revenue Act (1978)
  renovation, 464-466

Review Body
  composition, 67-70
  final review authority, 73-75
  National Historic Policy Act
    amendments, 67-68
  powers, 70-73
  See also Preservation
    Commissions

Ripeness
  taking, 360-361
  See also Administrative
    Procedures

S

Section 106
  attorneys' fees, 269-270
  citizen enforcement, 263-270
  compliance, 265-266
  consultation process,
    256-257
  determination of adverse
    effect, 255-256
  determination of effect, 255
  enforcement actions,
    266-268
  federal funding, 251-252
  federal "undertakings,"
    247-254
  jurisdictions, 265
  licensing, 251
  listing, 207-209
  local government, 21-22
  memorandums of
    agreement, 250, 252-254,
    257-260
  parties, 266
  programmatic memorandum
    of agreement, 331-335
  public participation, 262-263

remedies, 268
review process, 150-151
SHPO, 150-151
standing, 263-265
subject parties, 260-262
urban renewal programs,
    252-254

SEPA
See State Environmental
    Policy Acts

SHPO
  duties, 148-153
  liaison, 151-152
  National Register
    nomination, 200-203
  state registers, 159-164
  taxation, 153-157

Signs
  See Aesthetic Controls

Standing
  petitions for relief, 399-401

State Agencies
  administrative process,
    380-389
  final environmental impact
    statement decision,
    177-178
  preservation programs,
    164-167
  preservation role, 129-131
  See also Administrative
    Procedures; Historic
    Preservation Law, State

State Enabling Authority
  acquisition, 143-145
  administration process,
    135-138
  building codes, 142-143
  commission specifications,
    137-138
  designation process, 135-138
  government-owned property,
    114
  grants of powers, 138-141
  historic district and
    landmark preservation
    enabling acts, 134-143
  historic preservation
    ordinances, 60-61
  improving regulatory
    enabling laws, 141-143
  land-use regulation, 133-134
  local government power,
    131-147
  local programs, 36n
  objectives, 135
  preservation commission
    membership, 136-137
  taking, 139-141
  taxation, 145-147

State Environmental Policy
    Acts
  defined, 169-171
  determinations, 172-176
  draft environmental impact
    statement, 173-176
  final environmental impact
    statement, 177-178
  policy, 171-172
  process, 172-178
  See also Historic Preservation
    Laws, State; National
    Environmental Policy Act

State Historic Preservation Law
See Historic Preservation
Law, State

State Historic Preservation
Officers
See SHPO

Surface Mining Control and
Reclamation Act, 243,
331-335

Surveys
comprehensive landmarks
program, 37, 38-41
Department of the Interior,
8
HABS/HAER, 227
Historic American Buildings
Survey, 9, 231
methodology, 40n
National Historic
Preservation Act
amendments, 39
National Survey of Historic
Sites and Buildings, 231
surveyor qualifications,
39-41
techniques, 81-82

T

Taking
avoidance, 366-368
claiming, 358-359
constitutional analysis,
350-357
constitutionality, 4, 16-17
constitutional remedies,
362-364

defined, 4, 209n
designation, 87n
listing, 208-209
moratoriums, 361-362
reasonable use, 353-356
ripeness, 360-361
Section 1983, 364-366
See also Constitutional Law;
Demolition; Economic
Hardship

Taxation
certification, 225-226
code changes, 10-11
credits, 21, 467-485
demolition, 18
depreciation deductions,
464-466
developers, 462-464
Economic Recovery Tax Act
of 1981, 19, 21, 154,
443-444, 459-460,
467-485
easements, 455-456, 485-499
federal incentives, 153-157
federal income, 460-485
future reductions, 508-519
incentives, 18-20, 461-464,
467-469, 519-522
incentive packages, 499-519
indexing, 471-479
investment credit, 464-466
National Register
certification, 467-485
property, 446-460
real estate investment,
444-446
rehabilitation incentives, 225
relief, 448-460
review body composition, 71

shelter, 443-445, 485-499
state and local incentives,
  146-147, 167-168
Tax Reform Act of 1976,
  18, 153-154, 350-351
See also Appendixes B and
  C

Tax Reform Act of 1976
  easements, 485-486
  preservation law
    development, 18
  taking, 350-351
  tax incentives, 153-154,
    461-464

Technical Assistance
  case building, 384-386
  comprehensive landmarks
    program, 37, 41-43
  federal, 227
  international, 244-245
  owners, 43
  Reservoir Salvage Act,
    236-237
  See also Economic Assistance

Transferable Development
  Rights
  economic assistance, 42
  See also Taking

Transportation
  See Highways

Transportation Act of 1966, 10

U

Urban Development Action
  Grant, 20, 261, 324-326,
    499-500

Urban Land Institute, 462,
  463
  program planning, 39, 45

U.S. Supreme Court
  See Historic Preservation
    Law, Federal
  See also Table of Cases

V

Vested Rights
  See Constitutional Law

W

With Heritage So Rich, 9, 10

Z

Zoning
  coordination with
    preservation program, 43,
    47-53
  Department of Commerce,
    4-5
  enabling act, 4-5
  rural, 50
  state enabling authority,
    133-134
  urban, 48-49
  See also Land-Use
    Regulations

Zoning Moratoriums
  See Moratoriums

Authors Biographies

David Bonderman is a member of the law firm of Arnold & Porter in Washington, D.C. He has represented the National Trust for Historic Preservation, The Conservation Foundation, the National Center for Preservation Law, and Don't Tear It Down in a number of preservation cases. He filed briefs in the Supreme Court in the *Penn Central*, *Agins*, and *San Diego Gas and Electric* cases, and was a member of the task force that drafted the District of Columbia Historic Landmark and Historic District Protection Act of 1978.

Thomas A. Coughlin, III, is an Assistant General Counsel at the National Trust for Historic Preservation in Washington, D.C. His principal areas of practice are tax, real estate, and historic preservation law. He is admitted to practice in Massachusetts and the District of Columbia and is a member of the American Bar Association's Tax, Real Estate and Local Government Law Sections and of the District of Columbia Bar's Sections on Tax and Real Estate. Prior to coming to the Trust, Mr. Coughlin was employed as an Attorney-Advisor in the Department of Housing and Urban Development's Office of General Counsel. He has authored several articles on easements and federal tax incentives for historic preservation, including the editor's note *Tax Incentives for Historic Preservation*, *Preservation Easements: Statutory and Tax Planning Issues*, and *Easements and Other Legal Techniques to Protect Historic Houses in Private Ownership*. Mr. Coughlin is a graduate of Brandeis University and Boston College Law School.

Stephen N. Dennis is an Assistant General Counsel at the National Trust for Historic Preservation. He is also Litigation Editor of the *Preservation Law Reporter* and was formerly editor of the *Landmark and Historic District Commissions* newsletter of the National Trust. He is the author of *Recommended Model Provisions for a Preservation Ordinance, with Annotations*, which has been published by the National Trust as an independent publication and appears in an updated form in this handbook. For six years he has monitored historic preservation litigation for the National Trust and has written and spoken on trends in preservation litigation. Mr. Dennis is a graduate of the University of North Carolina at Chapel Hill, Cornell University, and Duke Law School.

Christopher J. Duerksen, a Senior Associate with The Conservation Foundation, is codirector of the Foundation's Use of Land Project, principal investigator for its Industrial Siting Project, and a contributor to the National Parks Project. In 1982, the Foundation published Mr. Duerksen's book *Dow vs. California*; his overview book for the Industrial Siting Project will appear in the fall of 1983. Mr. Duerksen has also directed the Foundation's Low-Level Radioactive Waste Management Project. Before joining the Foundation in 1978, he was an attorney with the Chicago law firm of Ross, Hardies, O'Keefe, Babcock & Parsons, where he specialized in land use and environmental law. Prior to that, he was resident staff consultant in England for the Foundation's International Comparative Land Use Project, doing research in environmental and planning law issues. Mr. Duerksen currently serves as vice-chairman of the Land Use Committee of the American Bar Association Section of Urban, State and Local Government Law. He is also active in the historic preservation movement, serving as cochairman for two historic preservation law conferences on "Reusing Old Buildings: Preservation Law and the Development Process," cosponsored by The Conservation Foundation, National Trust for Historic Preservation, and the American Bar Association Section of Urban, State and Local Government Law. He currently is a member of the Historic Fredericksburg Foundation, Inc., board, the board of advisors of the Mary Washington College Center for Historic Preservation, and is a member of the 1983 editorial advisory board for the National Trust's "Preservation Law Reporter." He has also served as commissioner on the Oak Park (Illinois) Landmarks Commission and as a board member of the Chicago Landmarks Preservation Council. Mr. Duerksen is a graduate of the University of Chicago Law School.

Donald Dworsky, Visiting Assistant Professor at Lewis and Clark College, School of Law, in Portland, Oregon, teaches historic preservation, property, and environmental law. He has written about and practiced preservation law and has advised local, state, and federal agencies on preservation law and policy both in his current position and in previous positions at the U.S. Office of Management and Budget and as Director of the National Center for Preservation Law.

Virginia A. McVarish received a B.A. degree from Hampshire College in Amherst, Massachusetts, and a J.D. degree from Harvard Law School in June, 1983. She was formerly project planner with the Connecticut Trust for Historic Preservation and spent the summer of 1981 as a legal intern with The Conservation Foundation.

Michael Mantell is an Associate with The Conservation Foundation, where he works on private and public land-use issues. He is a contributor to the Foundation's Use of Land and National Parks projects, and has been involved in Foundation work on industrial siting, radioactive waste disposal, coastal zone management, and the *State of the Environment 1982* report. He has participated in U.S. Supreme Court land-use cases as well as several forums on state historic preservation and environmental policies. Before joining the Foundation in 1979, Mr. Mantell worked on various environmental issues for the city attorney's office in Los Angeles. He is a graduate of the University of California at Berkeley and Lewis and Clark College School of Law.

Kate M. Perry is an attorney with the Advisory Council on Historic Preservation. Prior to that she was a staff attorney with the National Center for Preservation Law. Ms. Perry has a B.A. degree from Wesleyan University (Connecticut), and a J.D. from Georgetown University Law Center.

Susan Mead Robinson is in private practice in Dallas. She has served at the President's Advisory Council for Historic Preservation and was affiliated with the National Center for Preservation Law. Ms. Robinson received a B.A. degree from Trinity Collge, Hartford, Connecticut, and a J.D. from Southern Methodist University Law School, Dallas, Texas.

Richard J. Roddewig is an attorney in private practice, a real estate consultant associated with Shlaes & Co. in Chicago, and Vice President and General Counsel of Shlaes & Young Information Systems, Inc. Mr. Roddewig has drafted preservation ordinances and counseled communities throughout the Midwest on preservation matters. As a real estate consultant he has worked on rehabilitation feasibility studies and appraisals of more than a dozen landmark buildings in Chicago, Nashville, San Antonio, Pittsburgh, and Cleveland in recent years. He has authored more than a dozen articles in publications such as *Real Estate Review*, *The Appraisal Journal*, *Real Estate Issues*, *Real Estate Today*, and *The Urban Lawyer* and is an adjunct professor in the School of Urban Sciences at the University of Illinois at Chicago Circle. A graduate of the University of Notre Dame, Mr. Roddewig has both a law degree and a masters degree from the University of Chicago.

Antonio Rossmann practices natural resources, environmental, and historic preservation law on a nationwide basis, as part of the San Francisco firm of McCutchen, Doyle, Brown & Enersen. Mr. Rossmann is also a professor at the University of California Hastings College of Law. Mr. Rossmann served as Chair of the California State Bar Committee on the Environment and as the first executive director of the National Center for Preservation Law. Mr. Rossmann is an honors graduate of Harvard Law School, where he edited the *Law Review*, and Harvard College.

Notes

Notes

Notes

Notes

Notes

Notes